LYLE

OFFICIAL

ANTIQUES

REVIEW 2004

LYLE

OFFICIAL

ANTIQUES
REVIEW 2004

A PERIGEE BOOK

A Perigee Book
Published by The Berkley Publishing Group
A division of Penguin Group (USA) Inc.
375 Hudson Street
New York, New York 10014

First Perigee edition: December 2003

ISBN: 0-399-52924-1
ISSN: 1089-1544

Visit our website at
www.penguin.com

Printed in the United States of America

10 9 8 7 6 5 4 3 2 1

INTRODUCTION

This year over 100,000 Antique Dealers and Collectors will make full and profitable use of their Lyle Antiques Price Guide. They know that only in this one volume will they find the widest possible variety of goods – illustrated, described and given a current market value to assist them to BUY RIGHT AND SELL RIGHT throughout the year of issue.

They know, too, that by building a collection of these immensely valuable volumes year by year, they will equip themselves with an unparalleled reference library of facts, figures and illustrations which, properly used, cannot fail to help them keep one step ahead of the market.

In its thirty four years of publication, Lyle has gone from strength to strength and has become without doubt the pre-eminent book of reference for the antique trade throughout the world. Each of its fact filled pages is packed with precisely the kind of profitable information the professional Dealer needs – including descriptions, illustrations and values of thousands and thousands of individual items carefully selected to give a representative picture of the current market in antiques and collectibles – and remember all values are prices actually paid, based on accurate sales records in the twelve months prior to publication from the best established and most highly respected auction houses and retail outlets in Europe and America.

This is THE book for the Professional Antiques Dealer. 'The Lyle Book' - we've even heard it called 'The Dealer's Bible'.

Compiled and published afresh each year, the Lyle Antiques Price Guide is the most comprehensive up-to-date antiques price guide available. THIS COULD BE YOUR WISEST INVESTMENT OF THE YEAR!

Anthony Curtis

The publishers wish to express their sincere thanks to the following for their involvement and assistance in the production of this volume.

ANTHONY CURTIS (Editor)

EELIN McIVOR (Sub Editor)

ANNETTE CURTIS (Editorial)

CATRIONA McKINVEN (Art Production)

ANGIE DEMARCO (Art Production)

NICKY FAIRBURN (Art Production)

PHILIP SPRINGTHORPE (Photography)

CONTENTS

ACKNOWLEDGEMENTS

AB Stockholms Auktionsverk, Box 16256, 103 25 Stockholm, Sweden
Abbotts Auction Rooms, The Auction Rooms, Campsea Ash, Suffolk IP13 OPS
James Adam, 26, St Stephens Green, Dublin 2
Afonwen Antiques, Arts & Crafts Centre, Afonwen, Mold, Flintshire
Henry Aldridge & Son, Devizes Auction Rooms, Wine Street, Devizes
Ambrose, Ambrose House, Old Station Road, Loughton, Essex IG10 4PE
Amersham Auction Rooms, 125 Station Road, Amersham, Bucks.
Jean Claude Anaf, Lyon Brotteaux, 13 bis place Jules Ferry, 69456, Lyon, France
Anderson & Garland, Marlborough Crescent, Newcastle upon Tyne
Antiques on High, 85 High Street, Oxford
The Antiques Warehouse, Badshot Farm, Runfold, Surrey GU9 9HR
Atlantic Antiques, Chenil House, 181–183 Kings Road, London
The Auction Galleries, Mount Rd., Tweedmouth, Berwick on Tweed
Auction Team Köln, Postfach 50 11 19, D-50971 Köln, Germany
Auktionshaus Arnold, Bleichstr. 42, 6000 Frankfurt a/M, Germany
Baddow Antiques Centre, Church Street, Great Baddow, Chelmsford
Banners Collectables & Antiques, Banners Buildings, 620-636 Attercliffe Rd, Sheffield S9 3QS
Barkham Antiques Centre, Barkham Street, Barkham, Berkshire
Barmouth Court Antiques Centre, Barmouth Road, Sheffield S7 2DH
Bartlett St. Antiques Centre, 5/10 Bartlett Street, Bath BA11 3BN
Bearne's, St Edmunds Court, Okehampton Street, Exeter EX4 1DU
Biddle & Webb, Ladywood Middleway, Birmingham B16 0PP
Boardman Fine Art Auctioneers, Station Road Corner, Haverhill, Suffolk
Bonhams & Brooks, Montpelier Street, Knightsbridge, London
Bonhams & Brooks Chelsea, 65–69 Lots Road, London SW10 0RN
Bonhams & Brooks West Country, Dowell Street, Honiton, Devon
Bosleys, The White House, Marlow, Bucks SL7 1AH
Michael J. Bowman, 6 Haccombe House, Newton Abbot, Devon, TQ12 4SJ
Brightwells, Antiques & Fine Art Saleroom, Ryelands Road, Leominster
Bristol Auction Rooms, St John Place, Apsley Road, Clifton, Bristol
British Antique Replicas, School Close, Queen Elizabeth Avenue, Burgess Hill RH15 9RX
Butterfield & Butterfield, 220 San Bruno Av., San Francisco CA 94103, USA
Butterfield & Butterfield, 7601 Sunset Boulevard, Los Angeles CA 90046, USA
Canterbury Auction Galleries, 40 Station Road West, Canterbury
Cavern Antiques & Collectors Centre, Failsworth Mill, Ashton Rd. West, Failsworth, Manchester M35 OED
Central Motor Auctions, Barfield House, Britannia Road, Morley, Leeds
Chapel Antiques Centre, High Street, Barmouth, Gwynedd LL42 1DS
H.C. Chapman & Son, The Auction Mart, North Street, Scarborough.
Chapman Moore & Mugford, 8 High Street, Shaftesbury SP7 8JB
Chappells & The Antiques Centre, King Street, Bakewell, Derbyshire
Cheffins Grain & Comins, 2 Clifton Road, Cambridge
Chipping Norton Antiques Centre, Ivy House, 1 Market Square, Chipping Norton, Oxon.
Christie's (In'tional) SA, 8 place de la Taconnerie, 1204 Genève, Switzerland
Christie's France, 9 avenue Matignon, 75008 Paris
Christie's Monaco, S.A.M, Park Palace 98000 Monte Carlo, Monaco
Christie's South Kensington Ltd., 85 Old Brompton Road, London SW7 3LD
Christie's, 8 King Street, London SW1Y 6QT
Christie's East, 219 East 67th Street, New York, NY 10021, USA
Christie's, Cornelis Schuytstraat 57, 1071 JG Amsterdam, Netherlands
Christie's SA Roma, 114 Piazza Navona, 00186 Rome, Italy
Christie's Swire, 2804–6 Alexandra House, 16–20 Chater Road, Hong Kong
Christie's Australia Pty Ltd.,1 Darling Street, South Yarra, Victoria 3141, Australia
Clarke Gammon, The Guildford Auction Rooms, Bedford Road, Guildford,
Cleethorpes Collectables, 34 Alexandra Road, Cleethorpes, DN35 8LF
Bryan Clisby, Andwells Antiques, Hartley Wintney, North Hants.
The Clock House, 75 Pound Street, Carshalton, Surrey SM5 3PG
Collectors Corner, PO Box 8, Congleton, Cheshire CW12 4GD
Collins Antiques, Wheathampstead, St Albans AL4 8AP
Cooper Hirst Auctions, The Granary Saleroom, Victoria Rd, Chelmsford,
Coppelia Antiques, Holford Lodge, Plumley, Cheshire, WA16 9RS
The Cotswold Auction Co., Chapel Walk Saleroom, Chapel Walk, Cheltenham
Court House Antiques Centre, Town End Road, Ecclesfield, Sheffield
The Crested China Co., Station House, Driffield, E. Yorks YO25 7PY
Cumbrian Antique Centre, St. Martin Hall, Front Street, Brampton, Cumbria CA8 1NT
Dandelion Clock Antiques Centre, Lewes Road, Forest Row, East Sussex
Dargate Auction Galleries, 5607 Baum Blvd., Pittsburgh PA 15206

Dee & Atkinson & Harrison, The Exchange Saleroom, Driffield, Nth Humberside
Diamond Mills & Co., 117 Hamilton Road, Felixstowe, Suffolk
Dorking Desk Shop, 41 West Street, Dorking, Surrey, RH4 1BU
William Doyle Galleries, 175 East 87th Street, New York, NY 10128, USA
Douglas Ross, Charter House, 42 Avebury Boulevard, Central Milton Keynes
Dreweatt Neate, Donnington Priory, Newbury, Berks.
Hy. Duke & Son, 40 South Street, Dorchester, Dorset
Du Mouchelles Art Galleries, 409 E. Jefferson Avenue, Detroit, Michigan 48226, USA
Sala de Artes y Subastas Durán, Serrano 12, 28001 Madrid, Spain
Eldred's, Box 796, E. Dennis, MA 02641, USA
R H Ellis & Sons, 44/46 High Street, Worthing, BN11 1LL
The Emporium, 908 Christchurch Road, Boscombe, Bournemouth BH7 6DL
Ewbanks, Burnt Common Auction Rooms, London Road, Send, Woking
Fellows & Son, Augusta House, 19 Augusta Street, Hockley, Birmingham
Fidler Taylor & Co., Crown Square, Matlock, Derbyshire DE4 3AT
Finan & Co., The Square, Mere, Wiltshire BA12 6DJ
Finarte, 20121 Milano, Piazzetta Bossi 4, Italy
Peter Francis,19 King Street, Carmarthen, Dyfed
Fraser Pinney's, 8290 Devonshire, Montreal, Quebec, Canada H4P 2PZ
Freeman Fine Arts, 1808 Chestnut Street, Philadelphia PA19103, USA
Galerie Koller, Rämistr. 8, CH 8024 Zürich, Switzerland
Galerie Moderne, 3 rue du Parnasse, 1040 Bruxelles, Belgium
GB Antiques Centre, Lancaster Leisure Park, Wynesdale Rd, Lancaster
Gloucester Antiques Centre, 1 Severn Road, Gloucester GL1 2LE
The Goss and Crested China Co., 62 Murray Road, Horndean, Hants
The Grandfather Clock Shop, Little House, Sheep Street, Stow on the Wold GL54 1JS
Graves Son & Pilcher, Hove Auction Rooms, Hove Street, Hove, East Sussex
Green Dragon Antiques Centre, 24 High Street, Wincanton, Somerset BA9 9FJ
Greenslade Hunt, Magdalene House, Church Square, Taunton, Somerset,
Hampton's Fine Art, 93 High Street, Godalming, Surrey
Hanseatisches Auktionshaus für Historica, Neuer Wall 57, 2000 Hamburg 36
William Hardie Ltd., 141 West Regent Street, Glasgow G2 2SG
Andrew Hartley Fine Arts, Victoria Hall, Little Lane, Ilkley
Hastings Antiques Centre, 59–61 Norman Road, St Leonards on Sea
Hauswedell & Nolte, D-2000 Hamburg 13, Pöseldorfer Weg 1, Germany
Halifax Antiques Centre, Queens Road/Gibbet Street, Halifax HX1 4LR
Hobbs Parker, New Ashford Market, Monument Way, Orbital Park, Ashford
Honiton Antiques Centre, Abingdon House, 136 High Street, Honiton
Paul Hopwell Antiques, 30 High Street, West Haddon, Northants NN6 7AP
Ironchurch Antiques Centre, The Ironchurch, Blackburn Road, Bolton BL1 8DR
Hotel de Ventes Horta, 390 Chaussée de Waterloo ,1060 Bruxelles
Jackson's, 2229 Lincoln Street, Cedar Falls, Iowa 50613, USA.
Jacobs & Hunt, Lavant Street, Petersfield, Hants. GU33 3EF
P Herholdt Jensens Auktioner, Rundforbivej 188, 2850 Nerum, Denmark
G A Key, Aylsham Saleroom, Palmers Lane, Aylsham, Norfolk, NR11 6EH
George Kidner, The Old School, The Square, Pennington, Lymington, Hants
Kunsthaus am Museum, Drususgasse 1–5, 5000 Köln 1, Germany
Kunsthaus Lempertz, Neumarkt 3, 5000 Köln 1, Germany
Lambert & Foster, The Auction Sales Room, 102 High Street, Tenterden, Kent
Lawrence Butler Fine Art Salerooms, Marine Walk, Hythe, Kent, CT21 5AJ
Lawrence Fine Art, South Street, Crewkerne, Somerset TA18 8AB
Lawrence's Fine Art Auctioneers, Norfolk House, 80 High Street, Bletchingley
David Lay, The Penzance Auction House, Alverton, Penzance, Cornwall
Lloyd International Auctions, 118 Putney Bridge Road, London SW15 2NQ
Locke & England, 18 Guy Street, Leamington Spa, Warwicks. CV32 4RT
Long Sutton Antiques Centre, 72-74 London Rd., Long Sutton, Spalding, Lincs. PE12 9ED
Longmynd Antiques, Crossways, Church Stretton, Shropshire SY6 6NX
Brian Loomes, Calf Haugh Farm, Pateley Bridge, North Yorkshire
Lots Road Chelsea Auction Galleries, 71 Lots Road, Chelsea, London
Duncan McAlpine, Stateside Comics plc, 125 East Barnet Road, London
Mainstreet Trading, Main Street, St. Boswells TD6 0AT
John Mann, The Clock Showrooms, Canonbie, Dumfries DG14 0RY
Christopher Matthews, 23 Mount Street, Harrogate HG2 8DG
John Maxwell, 133a Woodford Road, Wilmslow, Cheshire, SK7 1QD
May & Son, 18 Bridge Street, Andover, Hants
Morphets, 4–6 Albert Street, Harrogate, North Yorks HG1 1JL

Louis C Morton, Monte Athos 179, Lomas de Chapultepec, CP11000 Mexico
The Mount Antique & Gift Centre, 1 & 2 The Mount, Castle Hill, Carmarthen SA31 1JW
D M Nesbit & Co, 7 Clarendon Road, Southsea, Hants PO5 2ED
Newark Antiques Centre, Regent House, Lombard Street, Newark NG24 1XP
Newark Antiques Warehouse, Old Kelham Rd, Newark, Notts., NG24 1BX
John Nicholson, Longfield, Midhurst Road, Fernhurst GU27 3HA
Norwich Tombland Antique Centre, Augustine Steward House, 14 Tombland, Norwich NR3 1HF
The Old Brigade, 10a Harborough Rd, Kingsthorpe, Northampton NN1 7AZ
Old Mill Antiques Centre, Mill Street, Low Town, Bridgnorth, Shropshire
Onslow's, The Depot, 2 Michael Road, London, SW6 2AD
Outhwaite & Litherland, Kingsley Galleries, Fontenoy Street, Liverpool
Oxford Street Antiques Centre, 16-26 Oxford Street, Leicester LE1 5XU
Packhouse Antique Centre, Hewitts Kiln, Tongham Road, Runford, Farnham, Surrey GU10 1PQ
W & H Peacock, 26 Newnham Street Bedford MK40 3JR
Pendulum of Mayfair, 51 Maddox Street, London W1
Pieces of Time, 26 South Molton Lane, London W1Y 2LP
Pooley & Rogers, Regent Auction Rooms, Abbey Street, Penzance
Preston Antiques Centre, The Mill, Newhall Lane Preston, Lancashire PR1 5UH
The Quay Centre, Topsham Quay, nr Exeter, Devon, EX3 0JA
Peter M Raw, Thornfield, Hurdle Way, Compton Down, Winchester, Hants
Remmey Galleries, 30 Maple Street, Summit, NJ 07901
Ritchie's, 429 Richmond Street East, Toronto, Canada M5A 1R1
Derek Roberts Antiques, 24–25 Shipbourne Road, Tonbridge, Kent
Saltire Antiques, Fenton Barn Leisure & Retail Village, Drem, North Berwick EH39 5BW
Schrager Auction Galleries, PO Box 10390, Milwaukee WI 53210, USA
Scottish Antique & Arts Centre, Abernyte, Perthshire
Scottish Antique & Arts Centre, Doune, Stirlingshire
Selkirk's, 4166 Olive Street, St Louis, Missouri 63108, USA
Sidmouth Antiques Centre, All Saints Road, Sidmouth, Devon EX10 8ES
Skinner Inc., Bolton Gallery, Route 117, Bolton MA, USA
Allan Smith, Amity Cottage, 162 Beechcroft Rd. Upper Stratton, Swindon
Soccer Nostalgia, Albion Chambers, Birchington, Kent CT7 9DN
Sotheby's, 34–35 New Bond Street, London W1A 2AA
Sotheby's, 1334 York Avenue, New York NY 10021
Sotheby's, 112 George Street, Edinburgh EH2 2LH
Sotheby's, Summers Place, Billingshurst, West Sussex RH14 9AD
Sotheby's, Monaco, BP 45, 98001 Monte Carlo
David South, Kings House, 15 High Street, Pateley Bridge HG3 5AP
Don Spencer Antiques, 36a Market Place, Warwick CV34 4SH
Spink & Son Ltd., 5–7 King Street, St James's, London SW1Y 6QS
Michael Stainer Ltd., St Andrews Auction Rooms, Wolverton Rd, Boscombe
David Stanley Auctions, Stordon Grange, Osgathorpe, Leics. LE12 9SR
Michael Stanton, 7 Rowood Drive, Solihull, West Midlands B92 9LT
Station Mill Antiques Centre, Station Road, Chipping Norton, Oxon OX7 5HX
Street Jewellery, 5 Runnymede Road, Ponteland, Northumbria NE20 9HE
G E Sworder & Son, 14 Cambridge Road, Stansted Mountfitchet, Essex
Tennants, Harmby Road, Leyburn, Yorkshire
Thomson Roddick & Medcalf, Coleridge House, Shaddongate, Carlisle
Thomson Roddick & Medcalf, 60 Whitesands, Dumfries
Thomson Roddick & Medcalf, 42 Moray Place, Edinburgh, EH3 6BT
Tool Shop Auctions, 78 High Street, Needham Market, Suffolk IP6 8AW
Venator & Hanstein, Cäcilienstr. 48, 5000 Köln 1, Germany
T Vennett Smith, 11 Nottingham Road, Gotham, Nottingham NG11 0HE
Victorian Village, 93 West Regent Street, Glasgow G2 2BA
Garth Vincent, The Old Manor House, Allington, nr. Grantham, Lincs.
Wallis & Wallis, West Street Auction Galleries, West Street, Lewes, E. Sussex
Wentworth Arts Crafts & Antique Centre, Cortworth Lane, Wentworth, Rotherham S62 7SB
West Street Antiques, 63 West Street, Dorking, Surrey
Whitworths, 32–34 Wood Street, Huddersfield HD1 1DX
A J Williams, 607 Sixth Avenue, Central Business Park, Hengrove, Bristol
Peter Wilson, Victoria Gallery, Market Street, Nantwich, Cheshire CW5 5DG
Wintertons Ltd., Lichfield Auction Centre, Fradley Park, Lichfield, Staffs
Woodbridge Gallery, 23 Market Hill, Woodbridge, Suffolk IP12 4LX
Woolley & Wallis, The Castle Auction Mart, Salisbury, Wilts SP1 3SU
Worthing Auction Galleries, 31 Chatsworth Road, Worthing, W. Sussex
Robert Young Antiques, 68 Battersea Bridge Road, London SW11 3AG

ANTIQUES
REVIEW
2004

The Lyle Antiques Price Guide is compiled and published with completely fresh information annually, enabling you to begin each new year with an up-to-date knowledge of the current trends, together with the verified values of antiques of all descriptions.

We have endeavored to obtain a balance between the more expensive collector's items and those which, although not in their true sense antiques, are handled daily by the antiques trade.

The illustrations and prices in the following sections have been arranged to make it easy for the reader to assess the period and value of all items with speed.

You will find illustrations for almost every category of antique and curio, together with a corresponding price collated during the last twelve months, from the auction rooms and retail outlets of the major trading countries.

When dealing with the more popular trade pieces, in some instances, a calculation of an average price has been estimated from the varying accounts researched.

As regards prices, when 'one of a pair' is given in the description the price quoted is for a pair and so that we can make maximum use of the available space it is generally considered that one illustration is sufficient.

It will be noted that in some descriptions taken directly from sales catalogs originating from many different countries, terms such as bureau, secretary and davenport are used in a broader sense than is customary, but in all cases the term used is self explanatory.

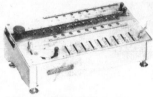

A Peerless Baby miniature step cylinder machine,with 9-place insertion, 8-place conversion and 12-place result, German, 1904.
(Auction Team Köln) $776

A very early Berolina four-function adding machine by Ernst Schuster, Berlin, with sliding crank and turned wooden handle, 1901.
(Auction Team Köln) $541

A Golden Gem seven-place chain adding machine, with carry-ten facility, with leather case and 8-page instructions in English, 1904.
(Auction Team Köln) $141

A Facit Model 1drum wheel calculator, Swedish, 1918.
(Auction Team Köln) $291

A demonstration model Brunsviga Model A four-function calculator, 1899.
(Auction Team Köln) $813

A very rare Adma manual 10-place full-keyboard calculating machine, with long side handle, German, 1919.
(Auction Team Köln) $238

A Burroughs No. 9 calculating machine with 10 row keyboard and printer, circa 1900.
(Auction Team Köln) $129

A black Curta Type II miniature four-function cylinder calculator by Kurt Herzstark, Vienna, 1948.
(Auction Team Köln) $645

A Thales Model MEZ cylinder calculating machine, without carry-ten facility, insertion to six places, result to 10, 1925.
(Auction Team Köln) $103

A rare Chateau miniature step-wheel calculating machine, with 9-place insertion and 13-place result, French, circa 1909.
(Auction Team Köln) $400

A Multifix Norwegian barrel calculator, with original instructions, one of only a few models produced, circa 1950.
(Auction Team Köln) $636

An Archimedes Model B German cylinder adding machine by Reinhold Pöthig, Saxony, with original wooden case, 1906.
(Auction Team Köln) $881

An Adix/Reports demonstration model rapid calculator with nine keys and lever.
(Auction Team Köln) $305

A Russian Original Odhner drum adding machine, with 9-place insertion, 13-place answer, circa 1900.
(Auction Team Köln) $232

A Doppel-Brunsviga 13ZK combination calculator for scientific calculations, 1932.
(Auction Team Köln) $534

A Mercedes Euclid Model 16 manual four-function calculator by Christel Hamann, Berlin, 1927.
(Auction Team Köln) $420

A Double Brunsviga D 13 R-2 calculator for special calculations, circa 1962.
(Auction Team Köln) $524

A tinplate toy calculator for multiplication.
(Auction Team Köln) $65

A rare demonstration model of the Curta Type 1 adding machine, in cross-section form, with central step drum and separate carriage, in original case, circa 1950.
(Auction Team Köln) $4,704

A Comptator 9-place rack adding machine by Schubert & Salzer, Chemnitz, with original case, 1908.
(Auction Team Köln)   £175

Adix three-place adding machine with geared drive and 9 keys, by Pallweber & Bordt, Mannheim, 1903.
(Auction Team Köln) $420

A Demos III Swiss four-function adding machine by Theo Muggli, Zürich, with eight place insertion 14-place result, 1923.
(Auction Team Köln) $338

An Additor eight-row, full-keyboard adding machine with geared drive, by Knudsen & Bommen, Sweden, 1910.
(Auction Team Köln) $441

Skeleton demonstration model of the the Vaucanson AVA four-function adding machine, French.
(Auction Team Köln) $711

A Ben Hur amusement machine by Caille Bros., Detroit, produced from 1908 until the 1930s, 60cm. high. (Auction Team Köln) $1,746

A German Totomat machine by Günter Wulff, Berlin, finger operated machine, wooden case, 61 x 82 x 16cm., 1950. (Auction Team Köln) $1,246

A Bajazzo pinball machine by Jentzsch & Meerz, Leipzig, brass mounted wooden case, post 1904, 63cm. high. (Auction Team Köln) $2,372

An Imo-Looping early electro-mechanical catapult action machine with points/win display with three lamps and an electric bell, wooden case, 51.5 x 78 x 20cm., circa 1930. (Auction Team Köln) $2,296

The game of 'Toupe Royale', a French style table-top game of skittles with a spinning top, the gilt brass gallery with leaf finials enclosing playing surface, 67in. (Canterbury) $2,970

A rare pinball machine, Le Douze, by Bussoz, France. The object is to gain twelve points with just two balls, silver metal mounted wooden case, 1895. (Auction Team Köln)

  $1,742

An Rotomat Juwel gaming machine by Günter Wulff, Berlin, 3-cylinder machine with start button and two stop buttons, wooden case, 55 x 71.5 x 25cm., 1953. (Auction Team Köln) $590

A fine one-cent arcade game, 'Kicker & Catcher' football theme, wood case with reverse painted glass, very fine working condition, 18in. high. (Jacksons) $632

A Mills Silent War Eagle one-arm bandit by the Mills Novelty Co., Chicago, blue, gold and red aluminum and wood case, 65cm. high, 1931. (Auction Team Köln) $1,741

A fragmentary basalt head of Osiris wearing the atef crown, late New Kingdom, circa 12th–11th century B.C. 4in. high.
(Bonhams) $874

A fragmentary terracotta coffin lid, Giza-type, with large ears and added black, red and white paint remaining, circa 1400 B.C., 8in.
(Bonhams) $465

A Graeco-Roman marble torso of the god Dionysos, naked apart from a goat skin slung over his left shoulder, 1st century A.D., 6½in.
(Bonhams) $3,339

A small Etruscan core-formed glass Aryballos, late 6th-early 5th century B.C., of translucent blue glass with thin dolphin handles, the globular body decorated with opaque turquoise and yellow trailed glass tooled into a zig-zag pattern, 1¾in. high.(Bonhams & Brooks) $672

Two similar Canosan terracotta funerary vases both in the form of a female head wearing a radiate diadem, circa 4th century B.C., 16½in. high.
(Bonhams) $1,826

An Attic Red-Figure pelike, decorated on both sides with a draped female figure wearing a saccos headdress, 450-430 B.C., 5½in. (Bonhams) $3,498

A pale blue glass storage vessel with ovoid body, short neck and collar rim, Roman, 3rd-4th century A.D., 4¾in.
(Bonhams) $556

A Roman and a Coptic limestone head, circa 3rd and 4th centuries A.D., the Roman head with pudgy features framed by wavy hair; the Coptic head with a dimpled chin and lidded eyes, 5in. high for the first. (Christie's) $575

A small Roman bronze seated figure of a comic actor wearing a short tunic, his hands clasped on his lap, 2nd century A.D., 2in.
(Bonhams) $1,613

One of a pair of French limestone figures of sphinxes, 19th century, each recumbent figure with female head slightly turned and draped with a tasselled cloth, on a rectangular plinth, 28½in. high. (Christie's) (Two) $5,520

An Egyptian black basalt male head, middle Kingdom, circa 2050-1786, shown wearing a layered wig, 2¼in. (Bonhams & Brooks) $1,120

A sizeable Mesopotamian hanging jar, 3rd Millennium B.C., of squat ovoid form, with a broad disk rim, the sloping shoulder decorated with a broad band in relief, incised with a cross-hatched design, 13.7cm. high. (Bonhams & Brooks) $1,890

A Roman bronze chariot fitting in the form of a Pantheress, circa 3rd-4th century A.D., shown resting her front right paw on the head of a horned animal with curved snout, probably a ram, her jaws agape, 7¾in. diameter.(Bonhams & Brooks) $39,200

A Hellenistic hollow-backed bronze bust of Pan, circa 1st century B.C./A.D., shown in profile, his head turned forward facing, well modelled with thick wavy hair and prominent curled-back horns, 13.3cm. (Bonhams & Brooks) $3,080

A native Apulian pottery bowl, perhaps Messapian, circa late 4th-early 3rd century B.C., the interior with a rosette in the tondo enclosed within a band of alternating lines and dots, 33.3cm. diameter. (Christie's) $575

A Roman terracotta oil lamp, circa 1st century A.D., with a voluted nozzle, the discus molded with a couple in the act of lovemaking, shown embracing on a couch, 12.2cm. long. (Bonhams & Brooks) $3,360

A Cypriot Bichrome ware Iron Age amphora, Cypro-Geometric, circa 1050-750 B.C., of buff pottery, decorated with encircling umber and crimson bands of varying widths, a band of zig-zags around the neck, 12in. (Bonhams & Brooks) $840

A Julio-Claudian marble male head, late 1st century B.C.- 1st century A.D., shown with close-cropped hair, furrowed brow, undrilled eyes and a closed mouth with recesses for insertion of the nose and ears, 9¼in. (Bonhams & Brooks) $6,720

A corroded Roman silver panther, circa 1st-2nd century A.D., naturalistically rendered with its front right leg raised, its neck arched ears back and shown with its jaw apart, 8.6cm. long.
(Bonhams & Brooks) $1,400

A Roman alabaster head of Serapis, circa 2nd-3rd century A.D., with deeply drilled hair and beard, the head originally surmounted by a modius, 5in. high.
(Christie's) $2,300

A Campanian terracotta guttus, circa 4th century B.C., in the form of a high-soled sandalled foot, naturalistically rendered with long toes, the straps molded in relief with a shaped clasp at the apex of the thongs, 5¼in. long.
(Bonhams & Brooks) $2,800

A Roman bronze equestrian figure of an Emperor, probably Alexander the Great, circa 2nd-3rd century A.D. the rearing horse balancing on its hind legs, the neck arching to the right, the bridle, breast and girdle strap shown in relief with some incised details, 13.6cm. diameter. (Bonhams & Brooks) $35,000

A Roman marble architectural fragment, 2nd-3rd century A.D., carved in relief with the head of Dionysos with centrally parted flowing, curly hair, the eyes with incised pupils, 14¼in.
(Bonhams & Brooks) $4,760

A Roman olive green glass cup, Rhineland, circa 4th-5th century A.D., decorated with two groups of three dark blue blobs applied to form a triangle, alternating with two single applied dark blue blobs, 6.7cm.
(Bonhams & Brooks) $1,190

An Attic Black-Figure Nestoris, early mid 6th century B.C., the body carinated and set on a short flared foot, decorated with a band of linked lotus buds on the reserved shoulder, 14.4cm.
(Bonhams & Brooks) $910

A Roman bronze figure of a lion, circa 2nd century A.D., shown walking, with well defined heavy mane and open mouth, the hollowed eyes inlaid with bronze studs, 2¾in. long.
(Bonhams & Brooks) $1,400

A North African Red Slip Ware bowl, circa 3rd-4th century A.D., the interior decorated with three large appliqués, consisting of three running wild boars, a seated leopard and a leafy tree, 17.2cm. diameter.
(Bonhams & Brooks) $2,100

A Roman marble stele depicting the deceased couple in relief within an arched niche, circa 2nd century A.D., 18 x 11¼in.
(Bonhams) $1,590

A marble Janus-head, with the face of a youth on one side and a bearded man on the other, Roman, 10¼in. high.
(Bonhams) $4,770

A Canosan hollow terracotta figure of the winged Cupid wearing a leafy wreath, riding on a swan, 4th–3rd century B.C., 4½in.
(Bonhams) $286

A small Roman marble funerary stele carved with a scene showing a draped reclining man holding out a wreath to a seated draped female, circa 1st-2nd century A.D., 12 x 8⅜in.
(Bonhams)   £913

A Lucanian Red-Figure bell krater decorated on side A with a draped female standing before an altar, 4th century B.C., 11⅝in. high.
(Bonhams) $2,656

A Palmyran limestone commemorative relief, carved with the iconography of the Roman standard, inscription below, 1st-2nd century A.D., 21¼in. x 14¾in.
(Bonhams) $1,272

A Mycenaean piriform bodied single-handled pottery vessel, the body decorated with three snakes, extending from the shoulder to the base, circa 1400 B.C., 9½in. high.
(Bonhams) $2,580

A bronze lamp in the form of sandalled foot, an aperture at the ankle decorated with calyx leaves, Roman, circa 1st–2nd century A.D., 4⅜in. long.
(Bonhams) $1,669

An Egyptian polychrome painted cartonnage mummy mask of a female, with central frontal uraeus, Late Period after 500 B.C., 17in. high.
(Bonhams) $2,988

An Attic Black-Figure kylix, decorated around the exterior with, on one side, Hercules, 5th century B.C., 2¾in. high.
(Bonhams) $3,021

An Egyptian bronze striding Apis bull with sun disc and uraeus between the horns, Late Period, after 500 B.C., 3in. long.
(Bonhams) $645

An Etruscan pottery amphora decorated on both sides of the neck with a grazing stag, circa 6th century B.C., 14¾in. high.
(Bonhams)   £6,773

An unusual Egyptian wooden headrest carved from a single piece of wood curved to form a long base support, New Kingdom, circa 14th–13th century B.C., 7in. high.
(Bonhams) $922

A Lucanian Red-Figure bell krater, showing a naked satyr, looking back towards a maenad, Greek South Italy, circa 380 B.C., 12¾in. high.
(Bonhams) $3,339

An Egyptian granite fragment from a seated royal figure, with a hieroglyphic inscription of one of the Ramesside Kings, New Kingdom, 19th–20th Dynasty, circa 1292–1075 B.C., 12¹/₈in. high.
(Bonhams) $2,067

An Egyptian polychrome wood mummy mask with flared head-dress and remains of pink, white and black paint, Ptolemaic Period, circa 300–30 B.C., 10³/₈in. high.
(Bonhams) $613

A Roman red-slip ware multiple wick oil lamp, the eight wicks surround a sunk discus pierced twice, 2nd-3rd century A.D., 8in. diam.
(Bonhams) $664

A late Roman/early Byzantine bronze steelyard weight in the form of the goddess Athena wearing an aegis, circa 4th–6th centuries A.D., 8¼in.
(Bonhams) $3,339

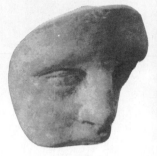

A South Italian terracotta mask, the lower lip and chin left unmodelled, with high bridge to the nose, 4th-3rd century B.C., 4in.
(Bonhams) $322

An attic Red-Figure kylix, the tondo decorated with the figure of a young man reclining against a cushion on a kline, mid-5th century B.C., 16.2cm. diameter.
(Bonhams) $2,576

An Egyptian hollow bronze head of a cat with deep set eyes, incised details and four mouldings for attachments around the base of the neck, Late Period, after 500 B.C., 3¼in. (Bonhams) $1,932

A Roman marble statue of a standing naked young boy with rounded belly and well-modelled buttocks, cradling a rabbit, circa 2nd century A.D., 16in.
(Bonhams) $11,270

A Ptolemaic schist fragmentary statue base of rectangular form, with the feet and part of the throne remaining, inscribed with hieroglyphs, circa 300-30 B.C., 8¼ x 3½in. (Bonhams) $1,570

A 'Tel Halaf' female idol, head missing, with arms looped below the breasts, the decoration in added umber slip of stripes over the body and strokes around the conical breasts, 6th-5th Millennium B.C., 2½in.
(Bonhams) $1,932

A Roman marble head of a youth, with close cropped fringed hair, a slightly dimpled chin and pursed lips, circa 2nd-3rd century A.D., 22.7cm. (Bonhams) $4,830

An Etruscan bronze boar with curled tail and prominent dorsal ridge, the front legs tanged, circa 5th-4th century B.C., 5.3cm. high.
(Bonhams) $1,127

A Daunian buff pottery double askos, with twin spouts, one a strainer, Greek South Italy, circa 300-250 B.C., 9in.
(Bonhams) $644

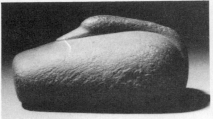

An Etruscan hollow terracotta 'half' head of a female showing the left side of the face, her hair dressed in curls around her face and falling in wavy locks, circa 4th century B.C., 11½in. (Bonhams) $1,155

A large stone trussed duck weight, broad across the wings, with squared-off tail and long slender neck, circa 2nd Millennium B.C., 4¼in. (Bonhams) $9,240

A limestone relief frament carved in raised relief with the profile figure of a naked male in the stance of a boxer, circa 1st century B.C./A.D., 16.2 x 8cm. (Bonhams) $554

A small Apulian red-figure hydria, decorated with a female wearing a finely pleated chiton standing within an Ionic naiskos, Greek South Italy, circa 350-300 B.C., 9¼in. (Bonhams) $3,542

A Hellenistic bronze statuette of Poseidon standing naked with his right foot resting on a rock, leaning forward, circa 2nd-1st century B.C., 11.3cm. high. (Bonhams) $6,468

A sizeable Egyptian wood sarcophagus mask with ochre paint on the face, added black paint for the facial details, Late Period, after 600 B.C., 22½in. (Bonhams) $5,852

A South Arabian alabaster head of a male, the eyes and eyebrows recessed for inlay, with long, narrow nose and small mouth, circa 1st century B.C., 25cm. (Bonhams) $7,222

A Cypriot base ring ware bull askos with strap handle linking the back and upper neck, an aperture in front where it joins the neck and a spout at the snout, Late Cypriot, circa 1650-1050 B.C., 4¼in. (Bonhams) $616

A large stone idol carved from a rectangular block, of an abstract anthropomorphic figure, the arms bent up, 3rd-2nd Millennium B.C. (Bonhams) $6,160

A red-figure Campanian skyphos, Greek South Italy, mid 4th century B.C., the body tapering in towards the ridged base and decorated on either side with a himation clad male profile, 4¾in. high.
(Bonhams & Brooks) $980

A hollow steatite bull's head, circa 1st Millennium B.C., with slightly recessed eyes, well delineated arched eyebrows, wearing a decorative bridle, 4in.
(Bonhams & Brooks) $3,640

A Roman bronze bucket, circa 1st-2nd century B.C., of cylindrical form, the sides slightly concave, with two sets of incised bands around the middle, 8in. diameter.
(Bonhams & Brooks) $1,540

An Egyptian wooden headrest, New Kingdom, circa 14th century B.C., imitating a folding stool, with a deep scooping support, the rounded upturned ends, thickened to take the two cross-over folding legs, 6½in. diameter.
(Bonhams & Brooks) $7,000

A Persian terracotta rhyton, circa 1st Millennium B.C., in buff-colored terracotta, flaring towards the rim, terminating in the foreparts of a bull, its legs neatly folded back under itself to form a stable base, 27.3cm. long.
(Bonhams & Brooks) $3,640

An Egyptian black steatite pectoral, Dynasty XIX-XX, circa 1320-1085 B.C., in the form of a temple pylon, the front carved in raised relief with a heart scarab set in the center of an incised scene with the figures of Horus and Khnum on either side, 3¾in. high.
(Bonhams & Brooks) $7,000

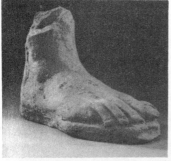

An Etruscan terracotta hollow foot, circa 5th-4th century B.C., with modelled toes, 8¼in. long, broken off above the ankle.
(Bonhams & Brooks) $672

A Greek hollow-backed terracotta head, circa 5th century B.C., of a female with archaic features, her hair dressed in three rows of neat curls, held within a cloth head-dress tucked behind her ears, 8½in.
(Bonhams & Brooks) $1,050

A late Roman facet-cut glass bowl, circa 4th-6th centuries A.D., the walls decorated in three registers, with facets, 4in. diameter.
(Bonhams & Brooks) $12,600

A good early ·22in. BSA 'T' prefix 'Standard' underlever air rifle, 45¼in. overall, barrel 19in., 3 hole trigger block; air chamber etching fairly clear, well figured walnut butt with impressed checkering. (Wallis & Wallis) $382

An unusual early 19th century 180 bore pneumatic air pistol, 9½in. overall, turn off round barrel 3¾in. with brass foresight and engraved fern tip border at breech, conventional boxlock action with cocking lever on right. (Wallis & Wallis) $4,448

A good .22in. Webley Premier series E air pistol, five pin trigger action, stamped E behind trigger, mirror black finish overall, brown plastic grips, with spare .177in. barrel, in its original carton with parts sheet. (Wallis & Wallis) $220

A good ·22in. pre war 'slant grip' Webley Senior air pistol No S13951, 8¼in., barrel 6½in. Frame with patent dates to 1925, 2 piece checkered plastic grips. (Wallis & Wallis) $746

A .177in. Lincoln air pistol No 415, 12in., barrel 9in., octagonal breech stamped The Lincoln Air Pistol, Best English Make, sprung securing catch, top of grip stamped Patt No 18127. (Wallis & Wallis) $589

An early 19th century 80 bore air gun, by Goodwin & Co, 47½in. overall; slender barrel 30in. with ram rod beneath; boxlock action with large side cocking lever, engraved with trophies of flags, and maker's name; iron ball reservoir beneath; walnut butt with checkered wrist. (Wallis & Wallis) $685

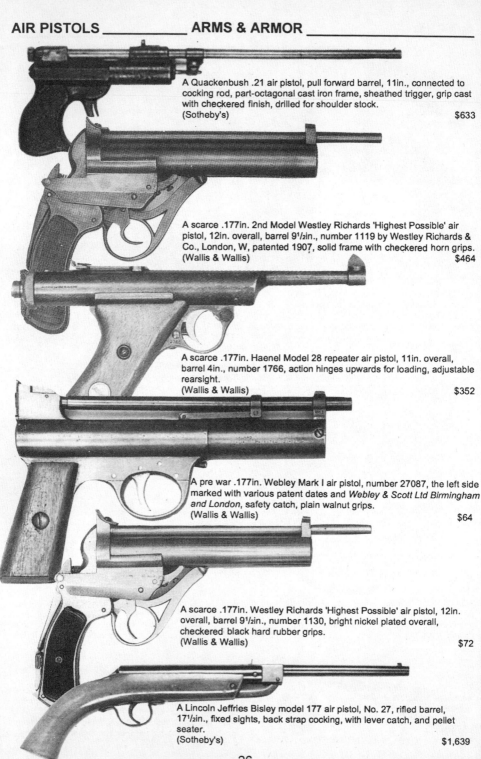

A Quackenbush .21 air pistol, pull forward barrel, 11in., connected to cocking rod, part-octagonal cast iron frame, sheathed trigger, grip cast with checkered finish, drilled for shoulder stock.
(Sotheby's) $633

A scarce .177in. 2nd Model Westley Richards 'Highest Possible' air pistol, 12in. overall, barrel 9½in., number 1119 by Westley Richards & Co., London, W, patented 1907, solid frame with checkered horn grips.
(Wallis & Wallis) $464

A scarce .177in. Haenel Model 28 repeater air pistol, 11in. overall, barrel 4in., number 1766, action hinges upwards for loading, adjustable rearsight.
(Wallis & Wallis) $352

A pre war .177in. Webley Mark I air pistol, number 27087, the left side marked with various patent dates and *Webley & Scott Ltd Birmingham and London*, safety catch, plain walnut grips.
(Wallis & Wallis) $64

A scarce .177in. Westley Richards 'Highest Possible' air pistol, 12in. overall, barrel 9½in., number 1130, bright nickel plated overall, checkered black hard rubber grips.
(Wallis & Wallis) $72

A Lincoln Jeffries Bisley model 177 air pistol, No. 27, rifled barrel, 17½in., fixed sights, back strap cocking, with lever catch, and pellet seater.
(Sotheby's) $1,639

A Persian Bazu-band armguard, steel plate with gold koftgari, probably 18th century. (Stockholms AV) $525

A Japanese Kon-Ito- kebiki No Ni Mai-Gusoku, large close laced kebiki dark blue laced black lacquered Do with Kasazuri. Small sode. Good quality kote with mail and pierced reinforcing plates. Late 17th to mid 18th century. (Wallis & Wallis) $2,079

A Japanese Kon-Ito-Odoshi Nuinobe armor , widely spaced medium blue laced black lacquered Do with close spaced (kebiki) lacing for the apron defence (Kusazuri) and the lined shoulder defences (sode). Mid 18th century. (Wallis & Wallis) $809

Mid-Edo Period (18th century), a fine bold red-lacquered iron mask, the nose detachable with hinges, the hinge pins secured by short chains, the simple mouth without teeth. (Christie's) $5,000

A good copy of an early 16th century armor for foot combat, comprising close helmet, gorget, breast plate and back plate with short skirt, arm and leg defences, 6ft.4in. high. (Andrew Bottomley) $2,573

A Somen, late Muromachi Period (late 14th/early 15th century), the russet-iron mask in three sections, boldly yet simply forged with large eye-holes and a small toothless mouth.(Christie's) $16,226

Royal Horse Guards Officer's cuirass in case, comprising front and back plates of nickel silver complete with gilt brass shoulder scales ornamented with silvered lion's heads. (Bosleys) $1,820

A good heavy 17th century Indian chain mail and lamellar shirt, the mail of alternate rows of thickly forged solid ring and riveted rings, square shaped collar, 3 vertical rows of lamellar backplates. (Wallis & Wallis) $1,080

A mid 17th century English pikeman's breast plate, borders with incised bands, with pronounced central rib and well formed skirt to take the tassets. (Andrew Bottomley) $1,308

An attractive Japanese armor , comprising kabuto, menpo, 3 plate throat guard, do, sode, with shoulder defences, lacquered skirt plates and shin guards.
(Wallis & Wallis) $6,280

Gothic-style suit of armor for foot combat, Germany, 19th century in late 15th century style, possibly Schmidt Workshops, hammered steel plate with fluting.
(Skinner) $5,750

A composite half- armor partly 17th century, a roped comb morion, heavy breast plate, back plate formed en suite, articulated arm and leg defences.
(Christie's) $4,025

A Japanese Okegawa-Do, simple plate cuirass with blue/green lacing and circular gilt dragon motif on front black lacquer.
(Wallis & Wallis) $1,208

Suite of armor for a man, 19th century, in late 15th century style, probably Schmidt Workshops, salade helmet with fluted decoration, poulaine with extreme tips, and star-shaped spurs.
(Skinner) $5,750

A Japanese Shiro-Ito-Odoshi-Do cuirass, closed spaced white laced Do (front and back) on black lacquered plates, probably 18th century.
(Wallis & Wallis) $1,208

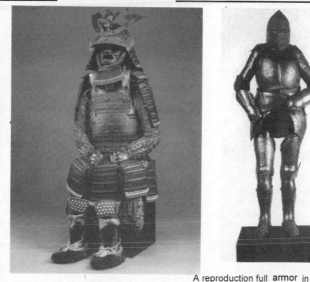

A fluted 'Maximilian' full armor in German early 16th century style, 19th century, of bright steel, including close-helmet, laminated gorget, pauldrons and haute-pieces, full arm defences.
(Bonhams) $25,760

An armor with the cuirass in two sections of horizontal plates, Edo Period (18th century), the thirty-two plate russet lacquered iron bowl with forecrest of gilded metal horns and a gilded wood shishi associated.
(Christie's) $9,027

A reproduction full armor in 15th/16th century style, of pressed steel, comprising pointed two-piece close-helmet, embossed breast-plate and plain back-plate, skirt, tassets, arm defences, mitten gauntlets, leg defences, and with imitation mail shirt.
(Bonhams) $1,771

A good mail and plate Indian 17th century armor, long sleeves and skirt, 4 front plates with pierced trisula shaped ornamental buckle finials.
(Wallis & Wallis) $2,120

An armor with solid horizontal plate cuirass in five sections, helmet bowl Edo Period (17th century), mask, armor Edo Period (18th century).
(Christie's) $54,169

A full armor in German 16th century style, 19th century, including a cuirassier helmet in early 17th century style, with rounded two-piece skull and low file-roped comb.
(Bonhams) $6,440

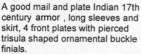

A 17th century Indian mail coif kulah zirah, made from riveted links, triangular shaped face flap, circular steel top with engraved short Indian inscription.
(Wallis & Wallis) $600

A Noga land beaded trefoil breast plate, decorated with a prominent central agate stud along with six other similar agate studs arranged symmetrically on a bed of multi-colored beads, 16½in. long, 19th century. (Christie's) $1,091

A Turkish bazu band, 15th/16th century, steel, shaped to the fore-arm and engraved overall with wrigglework foliage, two wrist-plates engraved en suite, 33.5cm.
(Bonhams) $1,380

An English Civil War breastplate, mid 17th century, steel, with low medial ridge drawn out to a point at the base, deep flange beneath with turned border, 42.5cm. high.
(Bonhams) $559

A breastplate of siege weight, mid 17th century, with low medial ridge, shaped around the arms and narrow flange at the neck and with narrow skirt drawn down to a point, 44cm. high.
(Bonhams) $834

A steel armor breastplate and apron, in the 16th century style, 27in. high.
(Christie's) $3,365

A full size replica of a suit of armor in the 'Gothic' style with enclosed helmet and breastplate with twin pierced heart pattern edging, an chain mail for same, 70in. high, and standing on oak plinth.
(Canterbury) $3,770

A Menpo (Half Mask), Edo Period (mid-18th century), the black lacquered iron mask with a long hair moustache.
(Christie's) $2,062

A Turkish shaffron, 16th century, of steel, shaped at the ears and narrowing sharply below the forehead to form the nose-defence, 52cm. (Bonhams) $2,484

A French cuirass, by Bouchet A Besancon, probably late 17th century, steel, the breast-plate of flattened form with low medial ridge drawn out to a blunt point at the bottom, 46cm. high. (Bonhams & Brooks) $3,102

A rare Turkish bazu band for the left arm, 15th/16th century, of steel, the outer surfaces throughout engraved with symmetrical designs of running foliated arabesques, 39.5cm. (Bonhams) $4,416

Royal Horse Guards cuirass, comprising front and back polished steel plates complete with gilt brass shoulder scales, center with high comb. (Bosleys) $1,136

A pair of gauntlets in Gothic style, 19th century, each with pointed lames over the back of the lower arm, articulated by four lames to a broader metacarpal plate, 35cm. (Bonhams) $556

English Civil War Period breast plate, a heavy example, with raised central comb, with two brass buckles to the shoulder. (Wallis & Wallis) $462

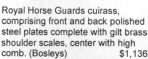

A German breastplate and tassets, 16th century, of bright steel, the first of slightly flattened form with low medial ridge, the later tassets each of five upward lapping lames, 59cm. high. (Bonhams) $1,112

A German backplate, late 16th century, of fluted form, shaped to the back and incised with line decoration, single lame at the base with turned edge, 44cm. high. (Bonhams) $487

A pair of mid 17th century breast and backplates, the breast plate stamped with an L.. (Wallis & Wallis) $1,562

31

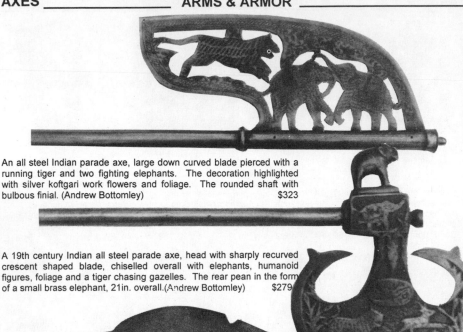

An all steel Indian parade axe, large down curved blade pierced with a running tiger and two fighting elephants. The decoration highlighted with silver koftgari work flowers and foliage. The rounded shaft with bulbous finial. (Andrew Bottomley) $323

A 19th century Indian all steel parade axe, head with sharply recurved crescent shaped blade, chiselled overall with elephants, humanoid figures, foliage and a tiger chasing gazelles. The rear pean in the form of a small brass elephant, 21in. overall.(Andrew Bottomley) $279

An unusual early poleaxe of Lochaber type, 79in. overall, head 13½in. riveted to collars wrought around haft, an iron hook sunk into the haft is secured to the head through an opening; leaf shaped top blade 8in. good age patina. (Wallis & Wallis) $662

An early iron head American Indian tomahawk pipe circa 1800, height 8¾in., cutting edge 3¼in., the wooden haft drilled for pipe, covered partly in red cloth and stitched leather Indian coloured beadwork behind axe head. Probably an English trade axe.
(Wallis & Wallis) $1,544

A very rare African throwing axe, short steel blade projecting from a carved wooden handle, inlaid and decorated with copper bands and brass wire. 17in. overall length.
(Andrew Bottomley) $426

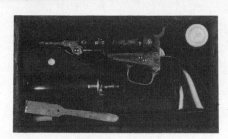

A cased Colt 1849 Model pocket five-shot percussion revolver, No. 2678 for 1854, the blued barrel with London address, cylinder with scroll engraved stagecoach hold-up scene, rammer, case-hardened frame, silvered trigger-guard and grip-strap, 22.5cm. (Bonhams) $4,396

A good Continental 5 shot 120 bore Adams Model 1851 self cocking percussion revolver, made under licence, 9½in. overall, barrel 4¾in., scroll engraved frame, numbered 214; unusually large trigger guard; chequered walnut butt with engraved butt cap. (Wallis & Wallis) $1,610

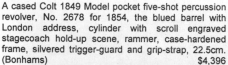

A cased 25-bore double barrelled percussion sporting rifle, by Charles Lancaster, 151 New Bond St., London, No. 1576, mid-19th century, with rebrowned twist sighted barrels, leaf-sighted to 150 yards, and rifled for a belted ball, case-hardened breeches each with slotted platinum plug, 76cm. barrels. (Bonhams) $4,480

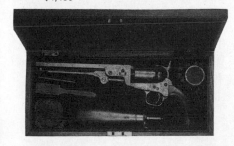

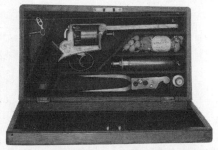

A 6 shot .36in. Colt Model 1851 presentation engraved Navy percussion revolver, 13in. overall, barrel 7½in. with London; the frame, breech, muzzle and rammer engraved with scrollwork, the frame also engraved Colt's Patent in Gothic script; polished dark walnut grips. (Wallis & Wallis) $4,200

A good 5 shot 54 bore Adams Model 1851 self-cocking percussion revolver, 11¼in. overall, barrel 6¼ engraved on top strap Boss, London; London proved; the frame engraved with scrollwork; chequered walnut butt; hinged trap in butt cap. (Wallis & Wallis) $3,080

A cased 18-bore double barrelled percussion sporting gun, by Westley Richards, 170 New Bond St., London, No. 9826 for 1862, with twist sighted barrels signed in full on the rib, breeches each with platinum line, pierced platinum plug and engraved foliage between, scroll engraved tang, signed scroll engraved locks, 76.2cm. barrels. (Bonhams) $1,148

A cased matched pair of double barrelled 16-bore box-lock ejector guns, the barrels signed *Bonehill*, with 28in. sleeved nitro barrels bored 1/ and ½ choke, 2½in. chambers, cross-bolt extensions, gold inlaid figures to breech ends. (Bonhams) $2,940

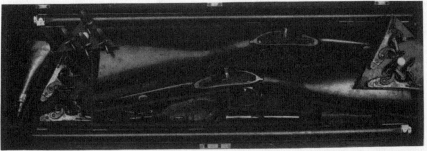

An extremely rare cased pair of 18-bore double barrelled flintlock sporting guns, by John Manton & Son, Dover Street, London, Nos. 7593/4 for 1820, with rebrowned twist barrels each signed in full on the rib, silver fore-sights, starburst engraved case-hardened recessed patent breeches each with platinum line and touch-hole, foliate engraved tangs, V-shaped rainproof pan with raised platinum line, 'French' cocks, 81.3cm. barrels. (Bonhams) $20,300

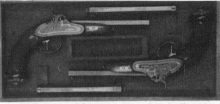

A very fine pair of German percussion duelling pistols by F Ulrich in Stuttgart, 1838, 12½in. overall, octagonal browned twist barrels 7½in. with gold poinçons dated *1838* at breeches, the blued locks engraved with scrollwork and game dogs and with gold inlaid borders and name; walnut halfstocks with chequered panels to butts.
(Wallis & Wallis) $3,780

An extremely rare and fine cased 28-bore over-and-under tubelock pistol by John Manton & Son, Dover Street, London No. 10899 for 1832, with browned twist octagonal scratch-rifled barrels with silver foresight, gold line, case-hardened serial numbered hook breeches, 29cm. (Bonhams) $23,550

A boxed 7.65 Model PPK Walther semi-automatic pistol No. 838424, blued overall, chequered plastic grips, and retaining all its original finish, 15cm. (Bonhams) $812

A fine cased .450 five-shot double-action revolver for The Ulster Bank Ltd., Belfast retailed by J. Braddell & Son, Belfast, No. 20716, late 19th century, with sighted barrel, butt with chequered walnut grip-scales, in original fitted oak case, 16cm.
(Bonhams) $1,491

A fine pair of 42 bore percussion duelling pistols, by C Moore, London, circa 1835, 15in. overall, heavy octagonal twist barrels 10in. with platinum poinçons at breeches , flat locks with safety bolts, the plates engraved with scrollwork, walnut halfstocks with horn fore end caps and rounded chequered butts.
(Wallis & Wallis) $6,440

A cased American Colt 1849 Model pocket percussion revolver, No. 90396 for 1856, engraved with Gustave Yound style scrolling foliage against a stippled ground, the 10.2cm. barrel engraved *Sam 1. Colt* in Old English script, the frame engraved *Colts Patent*, cylinder with roll engraved stagecoach hold-up scene, varnished figured walnut grips, 22cm.
(Bonhams) $2,520

A 5 shot 54 bore Beaumont Adams double action percussion revolver, 12in overall, barrel 5¾in., chequered walnut butt, in its fitted green baize lined oak case. (Wallis & Wallis) $1,480

Mahogany cased Colt Model 1849 pocket revolver, stagecoach holdup cylinder 4in. barrel, case also includes Massachusetts Arms Company brass powder flask, bronze Colt's patent bullet mould and box of caps, box 10 x 5¾in. (Skinner) $9,200

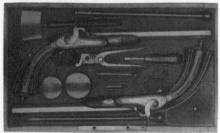

A pair of French percussion target pistols by Devisme À Paris, circa 1850, with octagonal sighted smooth-bored barrels signed in gold, ebony half-stocks with carved fore-ends and fluted butts, engraved butt-caps, and engraved spurred trigger-guards, 41cm. (Sotheby's) $4,416

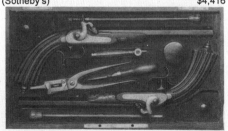

A pair of Belgian percussion target pistols by Th. Bodson Arqᵉʳ a Liège, mid-19th century, with reblued multigroove rifled sighted octagonal barrels numbered 1 and 2, engraved breeches and breech tangs, signed locks engraved with scrolling foliage, figured walnut half stocks, 16½in. (Sotheby's) $4,232

A very unusual cased pair of 50-bore percussion travelling pistols by Joseph Manton, 11 Hanover Square, London, No. 6822 for 1815, converted from flintlock, with browned octagonal sighted barrels, case-hardened breeches, foliate engraved tangs, in original lined and fitted mahogany case, 25cm. (Bonhams) $3,622

A five shot .31in. Colt Pocket single action revolver No 4074, 9¾in., octagonal barrel 5in. London proved, underlever rammer, cylinder roll engraved with stagecoach hold up scene, steel trigger guard and gripstrap (plating removed). (Wallis & Wallis) $2,400

A 5 shot 54 bore Model 1851 Adams Patent self cocking percussion revolver, 11½in. barrel 6¼in. London proved, foliate engraved frame with Adams' Patent No 11643 R. Spring safety to hammer, one piece chequered walnut grip with cap box in buttcap. (Wallis & Wallis) $1,760

A very fine cased 140-bore gold-decorated percussion target rifle by William Moore & Grey, 43 Old Bond Street, London, No. 1932, circa 1873, with browned eccentrically twist octagonal barrel signed in full at the breech, rifled with four grooves and fitted with its original browned twist telescope sight, London proof marks, 81.8cm. barrel. (Bonhams) $13,685

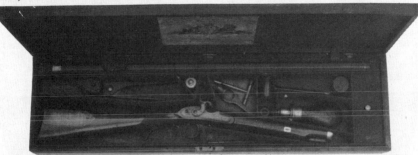

An 18 bore percussion sporting rifle by R Fenton, breech converted from flintlock, 46in., octagonal twist barrel 30in., London proved, later ladder rearsight to 1000 yards. Halfstocked. Nicely engraved steel furniture, pineapple finialled trigger guard. (Wallis & Wallis) $2,320

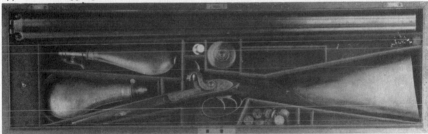

A cased 12-bore double barrelled percussion sporting gun by J. Purdey, 314½ Oxford Street, London, with rebrowned damascus twist sighted barrels signed in full on the rib, engraved case-hardened breeches each with platinum line and engraved pierced platinum plug, case-hardened scroll engraved tang, 76.2cm. (Bonhams) $7,245

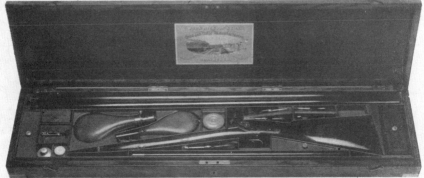

A fine cased 9-bore double barrelled percussion wildfowling gun built for Charles Gordon, by John Dickson & Son, 63 Princes Street, Edinburgh, No. 5613 for 31 December 1903, with very long browned Whitworth steel sighted barrels signed in full on the rib, London proof marks, 115.6cm. barrels. (Bonhams) $16,100

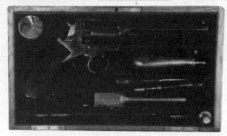

A cased 54-bore early Beaumont-Adams five-shot double-action percussion revolver by Deane, Adams & Deane, circa 1855, with blued octagonal sighted barrel, blued border engraved frame, checkered walnut butt, in later and fitted oak case, 30.5cm. (Bonhams & Brooks) $2,760

A fine cased pair of 40 bore rifled percussion duelling pistols by Charles Lancaster, circa 1850, with browned twist octagonal sighted barrels signed in full on the top flat and rifled for a belted ball, highly figured walnut half-stocks, checkered butts, 40.5cm. (Bonhams) $5,520

An unusual cased combined double barrelled percussion 32 bore rifle and 16 bore shotgun by John Dickson & Son, 63 Princes Street, Edinburgh, circa 1852, with browned twist leaf-sighted barrels, border engraved case-hardened breeches, figured walnut half-stock, in original oak case lined in tooled pigskin, 71cm. barrels. (Bonhams & Brooks) $3,312

Victorian Adams Patent cased six shot percussion revolver, 54 bore solid frame, the strap of the 8.5in. octagonal barrel is engraved Deane Adams & Deane, wooden grip with checkered cut decoration. (Wallis & Wallis) $1,104

A cased pair of 120 bore percussion box-lock pocket pistols by Sykes, Oxford, early 19th century, converted from flintlock, with turn-off barrels each engraved with a band of foliage around the muzzle, rounded checkered figured walnut butts each with engraved lion-mask butt-cap, in contemporary lined and fitted mahogany case, 12.5cm. (Bonhams & Brooks) $1,242

A Caucasian kindjal, dated *1912*, with bright sharply-pointed double-edged blade with off-set fuller on each side, the characteristic hilt and scabbard entirely covered with nielloed silver embossed and chased on the outside, 50.5cm. (Bonhams)   **$897**

An unusual 17th century Indian silver inlaid katar, 16in., finely watered broad blade 8½in. with raised central rib, and armor piercing tip. Hilt of conventional form inlaid with approximately 300 silver flower heads in relief. (Wallis & Wallis)   **$621**

A Japanese bone-mounted tanto, late 19th century, the hilt and saya carved with scenes of Japanese agriculture and peasant life, 36cm. (Bonhams & Brooks)   **$226**

A large 19th century Persian Qjar chiselled steel dagger jambiya, 18in., broad tapered watered blade 11in., with raised central rib, chiselled at the forte with lions attacking deer. Steel hilt and sheath chiselled overall with gold damascened cartouches. (Wallis & Wallis)   **$800**

A good quality late 19th century silver mounted Nepalese kukri, heavy swollen blade 13¼in., with twin fullers. One piece horn grip with silver ferrule. In its black leather covered sheath. (Wallis & Wallis)   **$250**

An aikuchi with guri mounts, unsigned, Edo Period (19th century), the blade honzukuri, iorimune, shallow torii-zori with chukissaki, choji-midare hamon of nioi, chu-maru boshi, o-suriage nakago, the ura chiselled with a dragon, 14¾in., in its finely ribbed black lacquer saya. (Christie's)   **$4,405**

A Third Reich police dagger, with bright fullered Hörster, Solingen blade, nickel-plated hilt, cast eagle-head pommel, and natural staghorn grips applied with an aluminum eagle and swastika badge on one side, in leather scabbard, 47cm. (Bonhams)   **$235**

A rare Swedish 80 bore double barrelled percussion dagger-pistol of Dumonthier type, by C.G. Gramberg of Eskilstuna, circa 1870, with leaf-shaped blade double edged towards the point, 51.5cm. (Bonhams)   **$1,242**

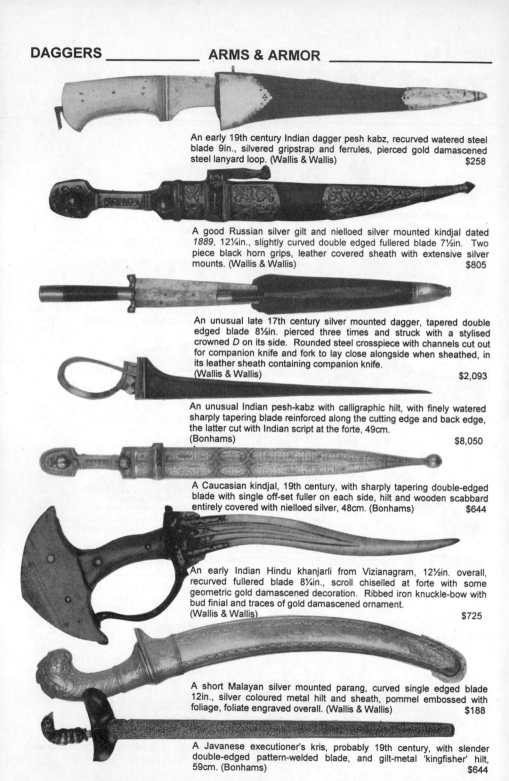

An early 19th century Indian dagger pesh kabz, recurved watered steel blade 9in., silvered gripstrap and ferrules, pierced gold damascened steel lanyard loop. (Wallis & Wallis) $258

A good Russian silver gilt and nielloed silver mounted kindjal dated *1889*, 12¼in., slightly curved double edged fullered blade 7½in. Two piece black horn grips, leather covered sheath with extensive silver mounts. (Wallis & Wallis) $805

An unusual late 17th century silver mounted dagger, tapered double edged blade 8½in. pierced three times and struck with a stylised crowned *D* on its side. Rounded steel crosspiece with channels cut out for companion knife and fork to lay close alongside when sheathed, in its leather sheath containing companion knife.
(Wallis & Wallis) $2,093

An unusual Indian pesh-kabz with calligraphic hilt, with finely watered sharply tapering blade reinforced along the cutting edge and back edge, the latter cut with Indian script at the forte, 49cm.
(Bonhams) $8,050

A Caucasian kindjal, 19th century, with sharply tapering double-edged blade with single off-set fuller on each side, hilt and wooden scabbard entirely covered with nielloed silver, 48cm. (Bonhams) $644

An early Indian Hindu khanjarli from Vizianagram, 12½in. overall, recurved fullered blade 8¼in., scroll chiselled at forte with some geometric gold damascened decoration. Ribbed iron knuckle-bow with bud finial and traces of gold damascened ornament.
(Wallis & Wallis) $725

A short Malayan silver mounted parang, curved single edged blade 12in., silver coloured metal hilt and sheath, pommel embossed with foliage, foliate engraved overall. (Wallis & Wallis) $188

A Javanese executioner's kris, probably 19th century, with slender double-edged pattern-welded blade, and gilt-metal 'kingfisher' hilt, 59cm. (Bonhams) $644

An early 19th century ceremonial dagger, double edged blade, the hilt with three figures carved in bronze, the scabbard well carved in the gothic style, 29cm. long. (Stockholms AV) $297

An early Javanese kris, straight pamor blade 14¾in., one piece ivory hilt with much age patina, (carving not complete), in its wooden sheath. (Wallis & Wallis) $185

A 17th century Italian stiletto with narrow blade, steel cross piece and hide covered grip, 34cm. long. (Stockholms AV) $936

A silver mounted Burmese dagger dha, blade 8in. carved bone hilt in the form of an anthropoid demon astride another, inlaid eyes. Silver covered sheath and ferrule with filigree bands. (Wallis & Wallis) $108

A rare high quality 19th century Nubian dagger, worn on the upper left arm underneath the robes. The grip of carved ebony, set with silver coloured mounts, straight double edge blade with three narrow fullers, blade 6in. (Andrew Bottomley) $426

A very fine quality Georgian Masonic dagger, wavy blade 12¼in. etched and polished with 12 Masonic symbols against a brightly gilt ground, copper gilt hilt with skull pommel, crossed bones quillons, and fluted mother of pearl grips. (Wallis & Wallis) $1,260

Late 19th century Caucasus kindjal, broad double edged blade with four fullers, stamped on both sides with maker's marks, typical form hilt with horn grips held in position by silver dome headed rivets, blade length 14.5in. (Bosleys) $206

A very attractive French decorative dagger, probably Dieppe, carved bone grip decorated with foliage and a horned demon's face, guard with short quillons, double edge blade of diamond section. Bone scabbard decorated with Judith carrying the head of Holofernes, blade 8½in. (Andrew Bottomley) $853

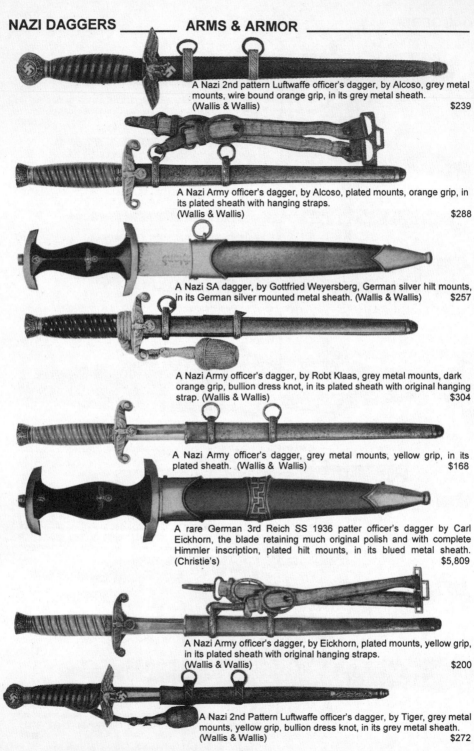

A Nazi 2nd pattern Luftwaffe officer's dagger, by Alcoso, grey metal mounts, wire bound orange grip, in its grey metal sheath. (Wallis & Wallis) $239

A Nazi Army officer's dagger, by Alcoso, plated mounts, orange grip, in its plated sheath with hanging straps. (Wallis & Wallis) $288

A Nazi SA dagger, by Gottfried Weyersberg, German silver hilt mounts, in its German silver mounted metal sheath. (Wallis & Wallis) $257

A Nazi Army officer's dagger, by Robt Klaas, grey metal mounts, dark orange grip, bullion dress knot, in its plated sheath with original hanging strap. (Wallis & Wallis) $304

A Nazi Army officer's dagger, grey metal mounts, yellow grip, in its plated sheath. (Wallis & Wallis) $168

A rare German 3rd Reich SS 1936 patter officer's dagger by Carl Eickhorn, the blade retaining much original polish and with complete Himmler inscription, plated hilt mounts, in its blued metal sheath. (Christie's) $5,809

A Nazi Army officer's dagger, by Eickhorn, plated mounts, yellow grip, in its plated sheath with original hanging straps. (Wallis & Wallis) $200

A Nazi 2nd Pattern Luftwaffe officer's dagger, by Tiger, grey metal mounts, yellow grip, bullion dress knot, in its grey metal sheath. (Wallis & Wallis) $272

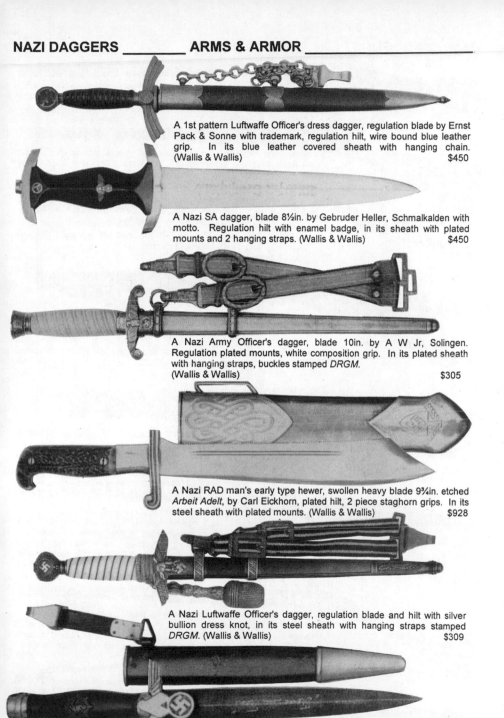

A 1st pattern Luftwaffe Officer's dress dagger, regulation blade by Ernst Pack & Sonne with trademark, regulation hilt, wire bound blue leather grip. In its blue leather covered sheath with hanging chain. (Wallis & Wallis) $450

A Nazi SA dagger, blade 8½in. by Gebruder Heller, Schmalkalden with motto. Regulation hilt with enamel badge, in its sheath with plated mounts and 2 hanging straps. (Wallis & Wallis) $450

A Nazi Army Officer's dagger, blade 10in. by A W Jr, Solingen. Regulation plated mounts, white composition grip. In its plated sheath with hanging straps, buckles stamped *DRGM*. (Wallis & Wallis) $305

A Nazi RAD man's early type hewer, swollen heavy blade 9¾in. etched *Arbeit Adelt*, by Carl Eickhorn, plated hilt, 2 piece staghorn grips. In its steel sheath with plated mounts. (Wallis & Wallis) $928

A Nazi Luftwaffe Officer's dagger, regulation blade and hilt with silver bullion dress knot, in its steel sheath with hanging straps stamped *DRGM*. (Wallis & Wallis) $309

A scarce 2nd Model Third Reich presentation RLB man's dagger, imitation damascus blade 8½in., plated alloy pommel and crosspiece; enamelled swastika on star badge on black wood grips; in its black painted sheath. (Wallis & Wallis) $578

43

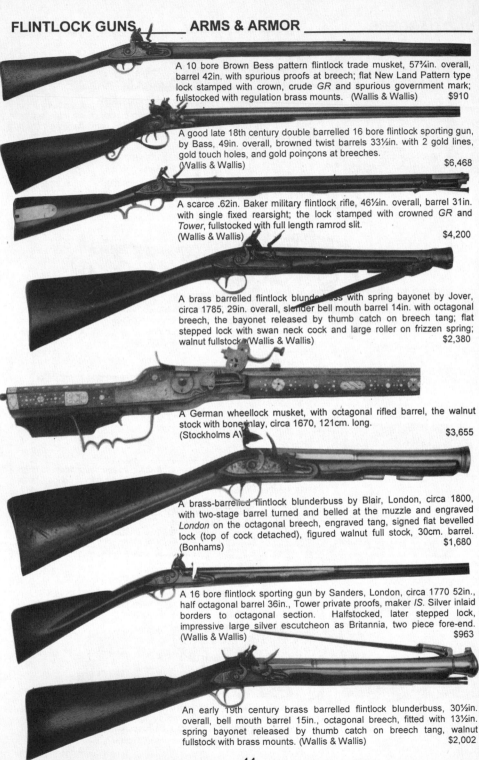

A 10 bore Brown Bess pattern flintlock trade musket, 57¾in. overall, barrel 42in. with spurious proofs at breech; flat New Land Pattern type lock stamped with crown, crude *GR* and spurious government mark; fullstocked with regulation brass mounts. (Wallis & Wallis) $910

A good late 18th century double barrelled 16 bore flintlock sporting gun, by Bass, 49in. overall, browned twist barrels 33½in. with 2 gold lines, gold touch holes, and gold poinçons at breeches. (Wallis & Wallis) $6,468

A scarce .62in. Baker military flintlock rifle, 46½in. overall, barrel 31in. with single fixed rearsight; the lock stamped with crowned *GR* and *Tower*, fullstocked with full length ramrod slit. (Wallis & Wallis) $4,200

A brass barrelled flintlock blunderbuss with spring bayonet by Jover, circa 1785, 29in. overall, slender bell mouth barrel 14in. with octagonal breech, the bayonet released by thumb catch on breech tang; flat stepped lock with swan neck cock and large roller on frizzen spring; walnut fullstock (Wallis & Wallis) $2,380

A German wheellock musket, with octagonal rifled barrel, the walnut stock with bone inlay, circa 1670, 121cm. long. (Stockholms A) $3,655

A brass-barrelled flintlock blunderbuss by Blair, London, circa 1800, with two-stage barrel turned and belled at the muzzle and engraved *London* on the octagonal breech, engraved tang, signed flat bevelled lock (top of cock detached), figured walnut full stock, 30cm. barrel. (Bonhams) $1,680

A 16 bore flintlock sporting gun by Sanders, London, circa 1770 52in., half octagonal barrel 36in., Tower private proofs, maker *IS*. Silver inlaid borders to octagonal section. Halfstocked, later stepped lock, impressive large silver escutcheon as Britannia, two piece fore-end. (Wallis & Wallis) $963

An early 19th century brass barrelled flintlock blunderbuss, 30½in. overall, bell mouth barrel 15in., octagonal breech, fitted with 13½in. spring bayonet released by thumb catch on breech tang, walnut fullstock with brass mounts. (Wallis & Wallis) $2,002

A 22 bore Queen Anne style cannon barrelled flintlock boxlock holster pistol, by Freeman circa 1760, 12in. overall, turn off barrel 5¼in., unusual proofs at breech, swan neck cock, sliding trigger guard safety, rounded butt with silver wire inlay. (Wallis & Wallis) $936

A 65 bore German wheel lock holster pistol, circa 1630, 29½in. overall, slender octagonal barrel 21½in. with fluted breech and raised copper bands, large flat lock with external wheel, slender fullstock with shaped butt, decorated overall with brass wire and mother of pearl inlay. (Wallis & Wallis) $7,560

A .65in. William IV flintlock cavalry pistol, 15in. barrel 9in., Tower military proofs. Fullstocked, regulation brass mounts, swivel ramrod. Stock struck with BO, broad arrow, stock maker Barnett and inspector's marks. (Wallis & Wallis) $1,540

A 20-bore flintlock turn-off pistol, by John 2 Smart. London, circa 1720, with two-stage cannon barrel numbered 3 and engraved with a band of foliage at the breech, action stamped with maker's mark IS, a crown above, moulded swelling walnut butt, 27.5 cm. (Bonhams) $952

A Dutch 16 bore flintlock holster pistol, by G Lasonder, Utrecht, circa 1715, 20in. overall, barrels 13¼in. with chiselled panels and rib, the breech struck with the Utrecht town mark; plain flat banana shaped lock with swan neck cock; fullstocks. (Wallis & Wallis) $2,310

A 28-bore all-steel flintlock belt pistol of Highland type signed Murdock, mid-19th century, with four-stage barrel etched with a martial trophy and a thistle, flared octagonal muzzle, with rainproof pan and roller, stock with ram's horn butt, 29.5cm. (Bonhams) $1,727

A Balkan 18-bore flintlock holster pistol, 19th century, with iron barrel damascened with silver foliage over most of its length and with a gold-damascended Arabic inscription on the top flat, gold-damascened breech struck with three marks, 51cm. (Bonhams) $350

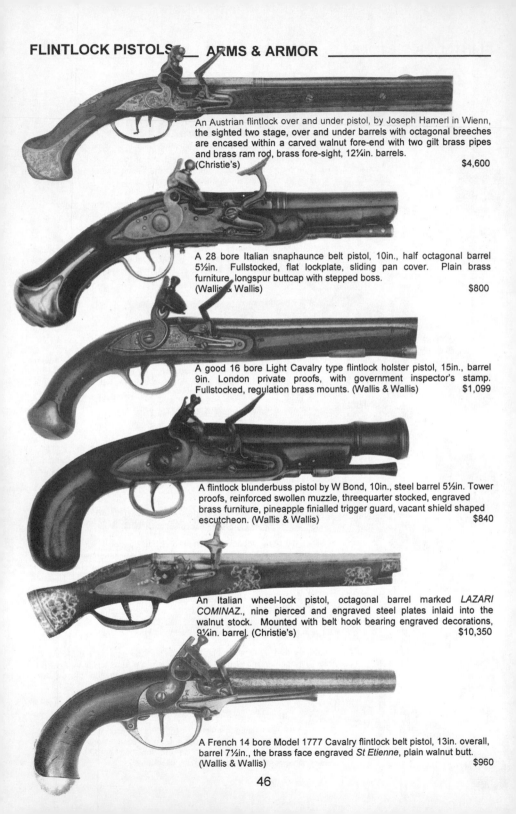

An Austrian flintlock over and under pistol, by Joseph Hamerl in Wienn, the sighted two stage, over and under barrels with octagonal breeches are encased within a carved walnut fore-end with two gilt brass pipes and brass ram rod, brass fore-sight, 12¼in. barrels. (Christie's) $4,600

A 28 bore Italian snaphaunce belt pistol, 10in., half octagonal barrel 5½in. Fullstocked, flat lockplate, sliding pan cover. Plain brass furniture, longspur buttcap with stepped boss. (Wallis & Wallis) $800

A good 16 bore Light Cavalry type flintlock holster pistol, 15in., barrel 9in. London private proofs, with government inspector's stamp. Fullstocked, regulation brass mounts. (Wallis & Wallis) $1,099

A flintlock blunderbuss pistol by W Bond, 10in., steel barrel 5½in. Tower proofs, reinforced swollen muzzle, threequarter stocked, engraved brass furniture, pineapple finialled trigger guard, vacant shield shaped escutcheon. (Wallis & Wallis) $840

An Italian wheel-lock pistol, octagonal barrel marked *LAZARI COMINAZ.*, nine pierced and engraved steel plates inlaid into the walnut stock. Mounted with belt hook bearing engraved decorations, 9¼in. barrel. (Christie's) $10,350

A French 14 bore Model 1777 Cavalry flintlock belt pistol, 13in. overall, barrel 7½in., the brass face engraved *St Etienne*, plain walnut butt. (Wallis & Wallis) $960

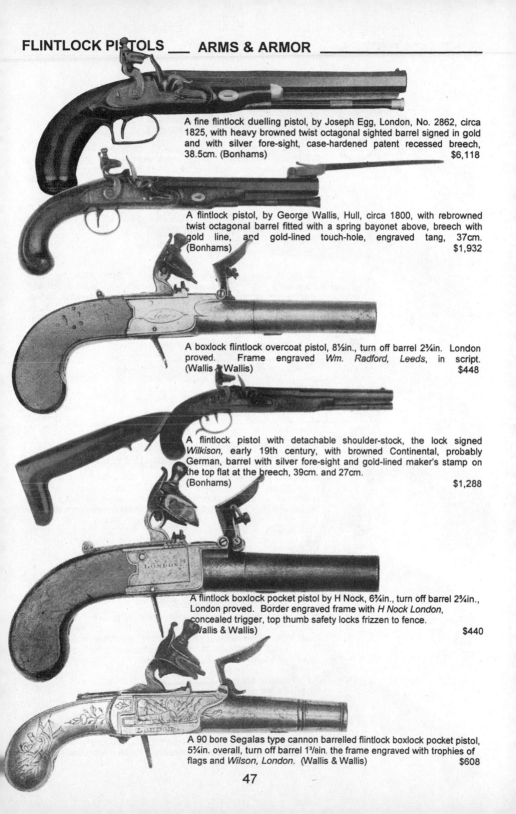

A fine flintlock duelling pistol, by Joseph Egg, London, No. 2862, circa 1825, with heavy browned twist octagonal sighted barrel signed in gold and with silver fore-sight, case-hardened patent recessed breech, 38.5cm. (Bonhams) $6,118

A flintlock pistol, by George Wallis, Hull, circa 1800, with rebrowned twist octagonal barrel fitted with a spring bayonet above, breech with gold line, and gold-lined touch-hole, engraved tang, 37cm. (Bonhams) $1,932

A boxlock flintlock overcoat pistol, 8½in., turn off barrel 2¾in. London proved. Frame engraved *Wm. Radford, Leeds*, in script. (Wallis & Wallis) $448

A flintlock pistol with detachable shoulder-stock, the lock signed *Wilkison*, early 19th century, with browned Continental, probably German, barrel with silver fore-sight and gold-lined maker's stamp on the top flat at the breech, 39cm. and 27cm. (Bonhams) $1,288

A flintlock boxlock pocket pistol by H Nock, 6¾in., turn off barrel 2¾in., London proved. Border engraved frame with *H Nock London*, concealed trigger, top thumb safety locks frizzen to fence. (Wallis & Wallis) $440

A 90 bore Segalas type cannon barrelled flintlock boxlock pocket pistol, 5¾in. overall, turn off barrel 1³⁄₈in. the frame engraved with trophies of flags and *Wilson, London*. (Wallis & Wallis) $608

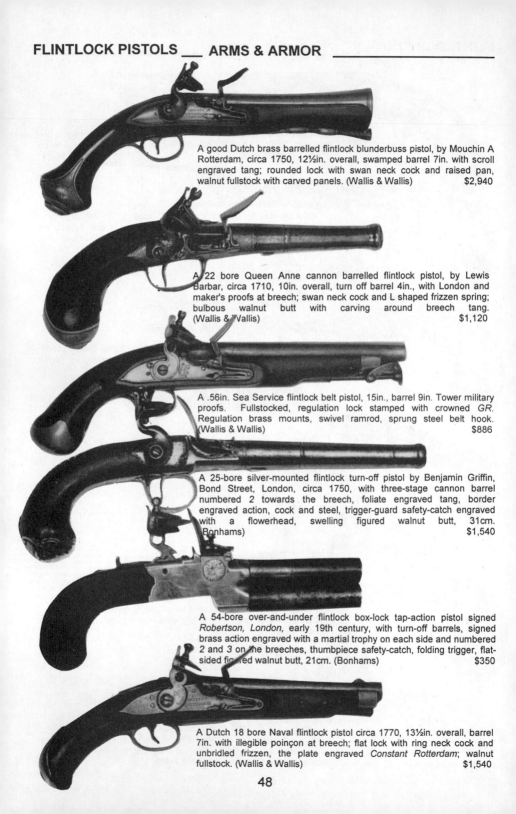

A good Dutch brass barrelled flintlock blunderbuss pistol, by Mouchin A Rotterdam, circa 1750, 12½in. overall, swamped barrel 7in. with scroll engraved tang; rounded lock with swan neck cock and raised pan, walnut fullstock with carved panels. (Wallis & Wallis) $2,940

A 22 bore Queen Anne cannon barrelled flintlock pistol, by Lewis Barbar, circa 1710, 10in. overall, turn off barrel 4in., with London and maker's proofs at breech; swan neck cock and L shaped frizzen spring; bulbous walnut butt with carving around breech tang. (Wallis & Wallis) $1,120

A .56in. Sea Service flintlock belt pistol, 15in., barrel 9in. Tower military proofs. Fullstocked, regulation lock stamped with crowned *GR*. Regulation brass mounts, swivel ramrod, sprung steel belt hook. (Wallis & Wallis) $886

A 25-bore silver-mounted flintlock turn-off pistol by Benjamin Griffin, Bond Street, London, circa 1750, with three-stage cannon barrel numbered 2 towards the breech, foliate engraved tang, border engraved action, cock and steel, trigger-guard safety-catch engraved with a flowerhead, swelling figured walnut butt, 31cm. (Bonhams) $1,540

A 54-bore over-and-under flintlock box-lock tap-action pistol signed *Robertson, London,* early 19th century, with turn-off barrels, signed brass action engraved with a martial trophy on each side and numbered 2 and 3 on the breeches, thumbpiece safety-catch, folding trigger, flat-sided figured walnut butt, 21cm. (Bonhams) $350

A Dutch 18 bore Naval flintlock pistol circa 1770, 13½in. overall, barrel 7in. with illegible poinçon at breech; flat lock with ring neck cock and unbridled frizzen, the plate engraved *Constant Rotterdam*; walnut fullstock. (Wallis & Wallis) $1,540

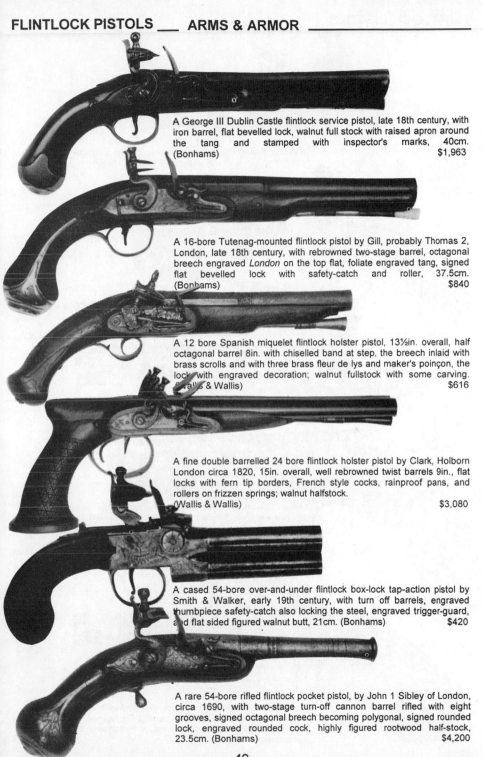

A George III Dublin Castle flintlock service pistol, late 18th century, with iron barrel, flat bevelled lock, walnut full stock with raised apron around the tang and stamped with inspector's marks, 40cm. (Bonhams) $1,963

A 16-bore Tutenag-mounted flintlock pistol by Gill, probably Thomas 2, London, late 18th century, with rebrowned two-stage barrel, octagonal breech engraved *London* on the top flat, foliate engraved tang, signed flat bevelled lock with safety-catch and roller, 37.5cm. (Bonhams) $840

A 12 bore Spanish miquelet flintlock holster pistol, 13½in. overall, half octagonal barrel 8in. with chiselled band at step, the breech inlaid with brass scrolls and with three brass fleur de lys and maker's poinçon, the lock with engraved decoration; walnut fullstock with some carving. (Wallis & Wallis) $616

A fine double barrelled 24 bore flintlock holster pistol by Clark, Holborn London circa 1820, 15in. overall, well rebrowned twist barrels 9in., flat locks with fern tip borders, French style cocks, rainproof pans, and rollers on frizzen springs; walnut halfstock. (Wallis & Wallis) $3,080

A cased 54-bore over-and-under flintlock box-lock tap-action pistol by Smith & Walker, early 19th century, with turn off barrels, engraved thumbpiece safety-catch also locking the steel, engraved trigger-guard, and flat sided figured walnut butt, 21cm. (Bonhams) $420

A rare 54-bore rifled flintlock pocket pistol, by John 1 Sibley of London, circa 1690, with two-stage turn-off cannon barrel rifled with eight grooves, signed octagonal breech becoming polygonal, signed rounded lock, engraved rounded cock, highly figured rootwood half-stock, 23.5cm. (Bonhams) $4,200

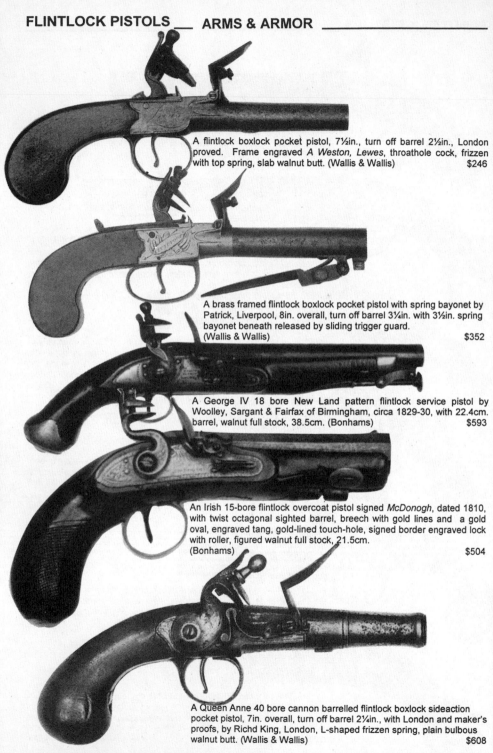

A flintlock boxlock pocket pistol, 7½in., turn off barrel 2½in., London proved. Frame engraved *A Weston, Lewes*, throathole cock, frizzen with top spring, slab walnut butt. (Wallis & Wallis) $246

A brass framed flintlock boxlock pocket pistol with spring bayonet by Patrick, Liverpool, 8in. overall, turn off barrel 3¼in. with 3½in. spring bayonet beneath released by sliding trigger guard. (Wallis & Wallis) $352

A George IV 18 bore New Land pattern flintlock service pistol by Woolley, Sargant & Fairfax of Birmingham, circa 1829-30, with 22.4cm. barrel, walnut full stock, 38.5cm. (Bonhams) $593

An Irish 15-bore flintlock overcoat pistol signed *McDonogh*, dated 1810, with twist octagonal sighted barrel, breech with gold lines and a gold oval, engraved tang, gold-lined touch-hole, signed border engraved lock with roller, figured walnut full stock, 21.5cm. (Bonhams) $504

A Queen Anne 40 bore cannon barrelled flintlock boxlock sideaction pocket pistol, 7in. overall, turn off barrel 2¼in., with London and maker's proofs, by Richd King, London, L-shaped frizzen spring, plain bulbous walnut butt. (Wallis & Wallis) $608

NS Reichskriegerbund Standard Bearer's gorget, pattern introduced 1938, polished aluminum plate with raised edges mounted with gilt oak wreath set on a trophy of flags. (Bosleys) $234

Foot Guards Georgian Officer's gorget, circa 1815 by R.Johnston, 68 St. James's Street, London, gilt gorget mounted with the Royal Arms in silver. (Bosleys) $1,194

SA / SS Standard Bearer's gorget, heart shaped polished steel with raised border. Mounted to the center, a gilt metal eight pointed star. (Bosleys) $497

Irish Volunteer Infantry George III Officer's gorget, rare example attributed to the Mallow Boyne Infantry of Co. Cork. Rich fire gilt on copper crescent with raised edge. (Wallis & Wallis) $1,088

Nazi period German Army Standard Bearer's gorget, the crescent mounted with crossed standards, overlaid with an army eagle clutching the swastika. (Bosleys) $781

George IV Officer's gorget, circa 1820-30, comprising a gilt on copper crescent with raised edge, crowned GR cypher, reversed and entwined, in relief. (Bosleys) $559

Georgian officer's 1796-1830 Universal Pattern gorget, fire gilt on copper crescent with raised edge, the center part engraved with crowned GR. (Bosleys) $329

A Georgian Officer's 1768 pattern brass gorget, engraved Royal arms with G and R above, die struck trophy of arms in each corner, traces of original gilt. (Wallis & Wallis) $1,680

A George III officer's gorget, circa 1800, of brass and of universal pattern, the front finely engraved with the full royal arms and mottos, 13cm. (Bonhams & Brooks) $524

A good French Officer's black cloth shako, gilt plate of the Arms of Paris, red, white and blue roundel above plate, red feather plume. (Wallis & Wallis) $853

Royal Air Force officer's full dress busby, scarce pre war example, skull of black chromed leather trimmed with seal dyed nutria, to the front gold and blue plaited lace cord. (Bosleys) $568

2nd Devonshire Artillery Volunteers officer's 1878 pattern helmet, early rounded peak example of the Home Service 1878 Pattern blue cloth helmet complete with silvered metal cross piece. (Bosleys) $1,193

18th Hussars Officer's busby, brown fur body retaining blue bag with three lines of gold flat braid and bullion gimp pearl button, to the front, an oval bullion gilt cockade. (Bosleys) $973

An English pikeman's pot, first quarter of the 17th century, with two-piece skull rising to a low comb, the base with a single line of rivets and a plume-holder at the rear, 24cm. high. (Bonhams) $966

A post-1902 other ranks lance cap of the 5th Royal Irish Lancers, black patent leather skull, peak and top, red cloth sides, yellow headband, dark green hair plume in brass socket. (Wallis & Wallis) $931

Worcestershire Regiment officer's 1878 pattern helmet, post 1902 Home Service Pattern blue cloth helmet complete with gilt metal cross piece, spike and rose bosses. (Bosleys) $639

A scarce Standard Pattern other ranks blue peaked cap of the Army Pay Corps, yellow piping, patent leather peak and chinstrap, brass badge and buttons, oil cloth liner. (Wallis & Wallis) $411

Scottish Rifles (Cameronians) Other rank's shako, turn of the century example of rifle green. Across the front a plaited mohair cord swag, that terminates with acorn devices.(Bosleys) $323

A good French Republican Guard officer's 1880 pattern shako, black cloth, gilt lace, blue, white and red rosette, red feather plume in socket. (Wallis & Wallis) $566

A Victorian officer's blue peaked forage cap of the 3rd Vol Bn The Lancashire Fusiliers, black lace headband, silver embroidered peak and grenade badge with solid centre. (Wallis & Wallis) $290

A German black and white comb morion, probably for The Guard of The Counts Khevenhüller zu Aichelberg, circa 1580, with two-piece skull and high roped comb. (Bonhams) $1,794

A Victorian other ranks lance cap of the 16th (The Queen's) Lancers, black patent leather skull, peak and top, plate bearing battle honors to Aliwal, black hair plume in brass socket.
(Wallis & Wallis) $1,088

Trial pattern RAF bone dome flying helmet, rare pre 1953 example, in the style of a skull cap with white finish to the exterior and full leather lining to the interior.
(Bosleys) $568

A Hoshibachi kabuto, Edo Period (18th century), the sixty-two plate russet iron bowl of goshozan form with standing rivets on each plate mounted with a simple tehen kanamono and kasa jisukashi no kan.
(Christie's) $6,665

A Victorian other ranks lance cap of The 12th Prince of Wales's Royal Lancers, black patent leather skull, peak and top, red cloth sides, red hair plume in brass socket.
(Wallis & Wallis) $759

An officer's 1869 pattern shako of the 1st Dorset Militia, patent leather peak, silver lace trim, good silver plated crowned star plate bearing *1* within title circle.
(Wallis & Wallis) $649

Lancashire Fusiliers Officer's fur cap, bearing gilt metal flaming grenade to front, the ball mounted with a silvered Sphinx resting on a tablet inscribed *Egypt*.
(Bosleys) $616

A US black cloth kepi of the 8th Cavalry, 2 part brass badge 8/crossed carbines/C, giltcord and buttons, patent leather peak, leather and cotton liner with label.
(Wallis & Wallis) $544

A rare single decal M42 SS combat helmet, with original paint, liner and chinstrap, clean condition.
(Wallis & Wallis) $838

A good mid 17th century "Dutch" lobster tail helmet, one-piece ribbed skull, 4 piece articulated neck guard, adjustable nasal bar.
(Wallis & Wallis) $1,232

A well made 19th century copy of a late 16th century close helmet of Maximilian type, fluted skull with roped comb, pierced sights and radial breaths. Roped borders.
(Wallis & Wallis) $806

A good Victorian copy of a medieval great helm. The skull formed of three plates riveted together, the lower portion of two plates.
(Andrew Bottomley) $706

Second Somerset Militia Officer's 1844-55 "Albert" shako of black felt with black patent leather crown, neck and front peaks. To the front, a gilt metal eight pointed star.
(Bosleys) $1,204

A kawari kabuto, mid-Edo Period (18th century), a six-plate russet-iron bowl of the conical form usually described as kaki-nari, the suji engraved with a rope effect and a row of zaboshi down the centre of each plate.
(Christie's) $16,966

A Scottish Kilmarnock bonnet, post 1904 dark blue wool example with red, white and dark blue diced band, red woollen ball tuft or toorie.
(Bosleys) $188

A good French Light Cavalry trooper's brass helmet, white metal mounts including peak binding, black stand up hair crest, plume holder on left with pale blue feather plume. (Wallis & Wallis) $924

A good bugler's busby of The King's Royal Rifle Corps, rifle green top, cord trim with white cord line introduced to back section, white metal strung bugle on cord boss in front, black over red hair plume. (Wallis & Wallis) $456

38th Foot Attributed Officer's 1844-55 Albert pattern shako, body of black beaver skin with black patent leather crown, neck and front peaks. (Bosleys) $1,884

An Italian or Spanish cabasset circa 1600, tall one-piece skull with pear stalk finial, distinct medial ridge. Brim with turned over re-inforced edge. (Wallis & Wallis) $576

A Prussian 1867 pattern O.R's garde du corps helmet, with white-metal mounted brass skull, peak and neck lames, 31.5cm. high. (Bonhams) $3,697

A Cromwellian lobster tail helmet, 2 piece skull with medial ridge, 1 piece neck guard with simulated lames, pivoted visor with triple bar guard, hinged ear flaps. (Wallis & Wallis) $1,044

An OR's grey cloth spiked helmet of the 20th (Artists) Middlesex Rifle Vols, darkened mounts, leather backed chinchain and ear rosette, Maltese Cross helmet plate, leather liner, in a tin case. (Wallis & Wallis) $1,305

An early very rare 16th century burgonet, two pieces, riveted and forge welded along the join, the lower edge of the skull pierced with holes. (Andrew Bottomley) $7,056

2nd VB Northumberland Fusiliers OR's cap, of short black fur with regimental pattern white metal grenade to the front. The interior with cotton lining. (Bosleys) $168

Leeds Pals foreign service helmet, Wolseley pattern helmet worn by a member of Kitchener's New Army Pals Battalion, of Officer quality with large pagri adorned on both sides with a Brigade Battle patch. (Bosleys) $235

Soviet Army pre War cloth Budenovka cap, period head-dress adopted by the new Soviet Russian Army, green cloth material. (Bosleys) $305

A Japanese twelve-plate iron suji-kabuto, 17th century, formed of overlapping plates, the front and rear plates with stud borders. (Bonhams) $725

A Prussian infantry officer's Pickelhaube, gilt helmet plate, leather backed brass chinscales, brass mounts, with parade brass chimney mount with white horsehair plume. (Wallis & Wallis) $853

A WWI Philip Baker's Patent alloy spike attached to an other rank's khaki peaked cap, a flat plate, 4in. diameter, is mounted on the top of the cap with a 4¼in. blade, in the form of a miniature triangular bayonet, on a swivel. (Wallis & Wallis) $1,248

A scarce Crimean War Period Russian OR's black leather helmet, metal helmet plate in form of Imperial crowned eagle up scroll with numeral 10. (Wallis & Wallis) $1,920

1844-55 Warwickshire Militia officer's 1844-55 Albert pattern shako, the body of black beaver skin with black patent leather crown, neck and front peaks. (Bosleys) $1,046

A scarce Nazi 1943 model Waffen SS steel helmet, retaining much original field green painted finish, and with SS transfer shield to RHS, original leather lining and chinstrap, stamped inside neckguard S62. (Wallis & Wallis) $453

A rare 1768 pattern Grenadier mitre cap, original black japanned plate, black fur, scarlet cloth top with tassel hessian lining. (Wallis & Wallis) $4,025

A Prussian Infantryman's ersatz Pickelhaube (of pressed felt), grey metal helmet plate and spike, leather lining and chinstrap. (Wallis & Wallis) $306

A Persian chiselled and gold-damascened steel kulah khud, 19th century, the skull decorated at the rear with panels of pierced scrolling arabesques within gold-damascened borders. (Bonhams) $885

Crimea War period Russian Pickelhaube, worn by soldiers of line Regiments throughout the war, black polished leather skull. (Bosleys) $1,288

An Imperial German artillery officer's Pickelhaube, gilt helmet plate, leather backed chinscales and mounts, leather and silk lining, in its oilskin covered conical carrying case. (Wallis & Wallis) $589

A Prussian Landwehr shako dated 1871, of black leather, oval helmet plate of pressed tin with rayed pattern and Landwehr cross, painted in state colours, cloth cockade. (Wallis & Wallis) $392

Bedford Imperial Yeomanry officer's lance cap, post 1902 example, skull of black patent leather, with the upper portion of black melton cloth, with patent leather to the crown. (Bosleys) $6,038

A Japanese nomonari kabuto, 19th century, of black lacquered leather, the inside of the mabizashi and each jukigaeshi lacquered red. (Bonhams) $1,046

WW2 Luftwaffe officer's cap, with silver bullion piping to the welt of the crown, mounted with bullion Luftwaffe Eagle and national cockade. (Bosleys) $283

A Victorian officer's gilt helmet of The 6th Dragoon Guards (Carabiniers), gilt ear to ear wreath, top mount and spike, leather backed chinchain and ear rosettes. (Wallis & Wallis) $903

A lobster-tailed pot, probably second quarter of the 17th century, the one-piece hemispherical ribbed skull with ring-shaped finial, pointed fixed peak, 31cm. high.
(Bonhams) $1,046

WWII period M43 Army Mountain Troops ski cap, green wool material, cotton lined example with embroidered one piece Army eagle and cockade.
(Bosleys) $177

A Victorian officer's Albert pattern helmet of the Queens Own Royal Yeomanry (Staffordshire), black painted skull, silver plated copper acanthus ornaments.
(Wallis & Wallis)   · $1,280

Imperial Russian fur 'Papakha' cap, Great War period example, lamb's wool, with light green cloth material, to the front a metal cockade with orange to the centre.
(Bosleys) $195

An interesting composite close helmet assembled as a funerary achievement, comprising two piece skull of a 17th century pikeman's pot, visor from a 16th century close helmet, neck plates, bevor and lower fall of visor all late 17th or early 18th century.
(Wallis & Wallis) $1,208

Royal Navy officer's Boer War Foreign Service helmet, khaki material, with seven-fold pagri, the top fold is with blue silk line denoting Royal Navy.
(Bosleys) $1,224

An Italian Dragoon officer's helmet of the Royal Piedmontese Cavalry, plated skull top to fur covered leather body, large gilt pressed metal comb with oak leaf decoration terminating in a mask.
(Wallis & Wallis) $606

A Prussian Ersatz Pickelhaube, circa 1916, of all-metal construction and painted grey, with pierced and embossed crowned Prussian eagle helmet-plate, central spike, cockades, and leather chin-strap.
(Bonhams) $193

A post-1902 officer's green cloth spiked helmet of The Kings Shropshire Light Infantry, gilt mounts, velvet backed chinchain and ear rosettes, gilt and silver plated helmet plate.
(Wallis & Wallis) $982

1878 Eton Volunteer Rifle Corps Victorian helmet, light grey cloth Home Service Pattern helmet complete with white metal cross piece, spike and rose head bosses. (Bosleys) $837

Prussian General officer's Pickelhaube, the skull of polished black patent leather, mounted to the front with a fire gilt Imperial Eagle. (Bosleys) $2,093

Highland Light Infantry OR's shako, the dark blue body with diced band of red and white, red and green and red and white. (Bosleys) $563

A cased 1871 pattern officer's Home Service helmet, by Hawkes & Co., 14 Piccadilly, London, circa 1910, covered with blue velvet and retaining its original leather and silk linings, and brass mounts. (Bonhams) $837

Royal Fusiliers Volunteer Battalion officer's fur cap, black bearskin; to the front a silvered regimental pattern grenade. (Bosleys) $885

A French mounted gendarmerie trooper's helmet, steel skull with brass embossed comb with black horsehair plume, Medusa head at base of plume holder containing scarlet brush plume. (Wallis & Wallis) $906

A Victorian officer's gilt 1834 pattern helmet of the 6th (Inniskilling) Dragoons, with acanthus foliage decoration, rayed plate bearing Victorian Royal Arms with 'Waterloo' scroll below. (Wallis & Wallis) $7,065

48th (Northamptonshire) Foot officer's 1869-78 shako, a fine fresh example, dark blue melton cloth body and crown, patent leather peak. Garter with pierced number 48, velvet backed chin chain, gilt rose pattern bosses, gilt lion's mask at the rear. (Bosleys) $1,404

An Imperial German other rank's hussar busby of the 17th (Brunswick) Hussars, Death's head badge below brass scroll with battle honours, white hair plume, cloth cockade. (Wallis & Wallis) $1,648

A German combined rim-fire pistol and pocket-knife, circa 1880, with short steel barrel, bar-hammer also cocking the folding trigger, 9cm. (Bonhams) $759

19th century folding Bowie lock knife, single edged blade with clipped point, cutler's details of *W.S.* to the forte. German silver mounts, with embossed foliage decoration. Slab sided horn grips the obverse inlaid with mother of pearl circlets. Locking action remains in fully working order. (Bosleys) $617

A Third Reich 'Teno' hewer, with single-edged Eickhorn, Solingen blade widening towards the clipped-back point and cut with a fuller along the back-edge on each side, silvered hilt, comprising quillon-block with scrolled quillon and eagle and swastika with service badge, 40.2cm. (Bonhams) $1,173

A gold and silver mounted presentation gaucho knife, blade 6in. stamped *Brogua* and *Scholberg Montevideo*, silver hilt and sheath chiselled with foliage and applied bird and floral images in gold. (Wallis & Wallis) $292

A rare US Army knife, with grooved wooden grip, bronze guard marked *US Springfield 734* and broad single edged trowel shaped blade. (Andrew Bottomley) $323

A Nazi War Order of the German Cross in gold, in fitted case. (Wallis & Wallis) $746

An early Dickin medal to the homing pigeon 'Tyke' for the Mediterranean Campaign, 1943, No. 1263 MEPS 43, AFMC No. 530, Bronze medal. (Sotheby's) $5,830

The Dunbar Medal, 3.9.1650, larger size in silver (34 x 29mm), with a 2 ring suspender. (Wallis & Wallis) ₵204

Denmark, Order of the Dannebrog, Christian VI issue, circa 1810, Knight's breast badge, in gold and enamel, in red leather case of issue. (Sotheby's) $922

A fine K.H. and Waterloo pair: Major P. Bishop, 40th Regiment: Royal Guelphic Order Military Division, Knight's breast badge, in gold and enamel, Waterloo medal, 1815. (Sotheby's) $5,962

Germany, Bavaria, Order of the Bavarian Crown, French manufacture, circa 1810, Commander's neck badge, in gold and enamel, with central red translucent enamel. (Sotheby's) $4,033

Russia, Order of St. Alexander Nevsky, by Keibel of St. Petersburg, pre-1898, Non-Christian breast star, 91.2mm. (Sotheby's) $1,555

Civil Grand Army of the Republic commander's medal, with eagle, crossed cannon, ten cannon balls and sword on ribbon top mount. (Wallis & Wallis) $136

Germany, Baden, Order of the Lion of Zahringen, Commander's breast star, in silver, with gold and enamel centre. (Sotheby's) $1,069

Three: DCM Victorian issue, with additional ribbon brooch 'Wreath', Crimea medal 4 bars Alma, Bal, Ink, Seb, Turkish Crimea British issue. (Wallis & Wallis) $1,217

Order of the Rising Sun, breast star in silver and enamels, 90mm., Japanese characters to reverse. (Wallis & Wallis) $438

Three: MGS 1793, 3 bars St Seb., Nivelle, Nive; Waterloo, Army LS & GC Hanoverian issue. (Wallis & Wallis) $4,239

Waterloo 1815 (John Lee 1st Reg Dragoon Guards). John Lee was killed at Waterloo. (Wallis & Wallis) $1,920

M16 Secret Service Group of 10 medals, awarded to Lt Col. Sir Anthony Gerald Roderick Rouse served during the Second World War with the Intelligence Corps. (Bosleys) $2,028

Imperial Russian Order of St. Anne, a fine gilt and enamel 4th Class military breast badge with swords. (Bosleys) $797

King's Medal for Service in the Cause of Freedom, WW2 attributed example to a lady contained in its original cream velvet and silk lined Royal Mint case of issue. (Bosleys) $655

Royal Garrison Artillery group of five medals, 1914/15 Star, British War Medal, Victory Medal, Meritorious Service Medal and Army Long Service and Good Conduct Medal. (Bosleys) $187

An Imperial German 1914 Iron Cross 1st Class with a 'field made' Nazi bar attached to the top arm by means of a back plate. (Wallis & Wallis) $313

France, Order of St. Louis, unmarked, 18th century, Grand Cross sash badge, in gold and enamel, with original sash. (Sotheby's) $5,762

Pair: Egypt 1882, 3 bars Tel-El-Kebir, The Nile 1884–5, Abu Klea; Khedive's star 1882 (1st named 2221 Sadlr J. Kandish 2/Dgn Gds). (Wallis & Wallis) $592

Russia, Order of the White Eagle, by Keibel of St. Petersburg, pre-1896, Non-Christian breast star, in silver-gilt and enamel, 90mm. (Sotheby's) $1,555

Three: South Africa 1877–79, bar 1879 (2073 Pte J. Baggot 1st Dragoon Guards); Egypt 1882, 1 bar Tel-El-Kebir, Khedives Star 1882. (Wallis & Wallis) $576

A Nazi silver medal of Merit of the Order of the German Eagle, (without swords), in its original red leather bound case by Deutsche Verdienstmedaille, gilt Nazi eagle on lid. (Wallis & Wallis) $464

Three: QSA 5 bars CC, OFS, Trans, SA01, SA02 (2541 Far S. Sjt O. Fawkes 2nd Dragoon Guards); Army LS & GC George V Military bust; MSM George V coinage bust. (Wallis & Wallis) $384

Pair: Indian Mutiny, 1 bar Lucknow, Army LS & GC, Vic scroll suspender, (impressed *199 Pte S. Kettle 2nd Dragoon Guards*). (Wallis & Wallis) $416

An excessively rare Great War M.C. and two bars group: Major T. Buckley, Royal Marines. (Sotheby's) $2,981

Pair: South Africa 1877–79, bar 1879 (Lieut N.H. Sadlier 1st Dragoon Guards); QSA 1 bar Cape Colony. (Wallis & Wallis) $1,440

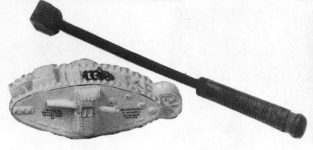

Large Great War crested tank "Tonbridge", with steering boggie to the rear and the color transfer crest to the top, 7in. long.
(Bosleys) $99

Imperial German Great War trench club, spring pattern, end is made from a square piece of iron, mounted onto a coiled spring shaft.
(Bosleys) $208

Woven wool American flag blanket, circa 1836-37, twenty-five stars on a field of blue with seven red and six white stripes, 62½in. wide.
(Skinner) $12,650

Civil War period snare drum, 19th century, hand decorated U.S. Eagle above a shield and flags with scrolls beneath, 17⅝in., diameter.
(Skinner) $1,150

A Wehrmacht direction-finder belt, for tracing enemy agents in the field, by Kapsch, Vienna, with accessories, in original wooden box, 1943. One of only 5 known worldwide. (Auction Team Köln) $23,722

A breech-loading bronze field gun, circa 1860-80, almost certainly Continental, with heavy moulded barrel cast in four stepped stages diminishing towards the flared moulded muzzle, plain trunnions, and previously fitted with an iron fore-sight, 92.5cm. barrel.
(Sotheby's) $3,680

A cartridge display board by Eley, with sporting shotgun cartridge cases of calibers .410 through to a signal cartridge, framed and glazed, 19¾ x 27¾in.
(Bonhams) $1,280

Hermann Goering's wallet, contains a postcard size photograph of Goering with his second wife Emmy and his daughter Edda; it bears ink signatures of all three.
(Bosleys) $1,600

A cartridge display board by Eley & Kynoch, with sporting and military shotgun, rifle and pistol cartridges, percussion caps, wads and numbered shot disks, 64 x 78cm.
(Bonhams) $12,000

Fougasse, And Please Don't Throw Food Away Either, (RAFairmen), double crown.
(Onslows) $118

Great War anti zeppelin aerial dart, large heavy weight dart, with steel tip and brass body supporting feather flights.
(Bosleys) $685

A rare Georgian trooper's combined shoulder belt and carbine sling with cartridge pouch, buff leather belt with brass buckle, tip and slide, black leather pouch.
(Wallis & Wallis) $1,336

A 1942 manufactured 'Mickey Mouse' gas mask, red rubber with blue filter canister, complete with blue elastic straps, contained in original cardboard box.
(Bosleys) $69

Civil War naval battle flag, America, circa 1863, the hand-sewn wool bunting and cotton flag stitched to a canvas heading which bears inscription, _Sumpter April 7 Wagner July 10, 11, 17_, with printed statement, flag size 23¾ x 31½in.
(Skinner) $17,250

A scarce WW1 officer's khaki weatherproof trench cap, designed to fit over a peaked cap, with flap to cover the peak, neck protector and stud fastening under the chin.
(Wallis & Wallis) $139

Graf Zeppelin souvenir glass plate, to the center, the bust of Graf von Zeppelin, above him can be seen one of his great airships in flight with ribbon, _Deutschland's Ruhm_ below. (Bosleys) $260

They've evidently seen me and a darn good job too, inscribed (but not at Neuve Eglise this time), signed, pencil and gray washes heightened with white, 45 x 33cm., page notes on reverse, framed.
(Onslows) $647

Suffolk Regiment Great War patriotic pin cushion, a fine, clean and rare pin cushion in the form of a heart, to the center a printed Regimental device of the Suffolks. To one side a sentimental verse _Remember Me_. (Bosleys) $125

Crimean War Grenadier Guards 'Trotter' knapsack, introduced to the British Army in 1805 and used until 1871, of wood box form construction and covered with black oilskin. (Bosleys) $2,415

British Union of Fascist Party Record, a rare pre war recording of Sir Oswald Mosely speeches. (Bosleys) $120

British campaign brass mounted military travelling case, mid-19th century, the flush mount engraved with monogram and Prince of Wales plume, 14in. long. (Skinner) $1,840

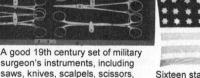

An original autopilot for a V1 rocket as developed by Wernher von Braun, circa 1940. (Auction Team Köln) $14,636

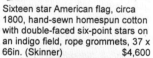

A pair of gilt-bronze stirrups, early 17th century, probably German, of arched form, with tapering straps punched and chased with stylised foliage, oval treads decorated en suite, 15cm. (Sotheby's) $1,195

A good 19th century set of military surgeon's instruments, including saws, knives, scalpels, scissors, clamps, tweezers, catheters and needles; in velvet lined fitted brass bound mahogany case with lift out tray. (Wallis & Wallis) $1,610

Sixteen star American flag, circa 1800, hand-sewn homespun cotton with double-faced six-point stars on an indigo field, rope grommets, 37 x 66in. (Skinner) $4,600

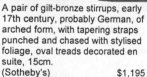

Bengal Engineers pair of 1830 pattern shoulder scales. Blue melton cloth ground, with gold lace and edged with scarlet piping. (Bosleys) $592

Confederate States of America flag, 19th century, some rips and holes, minor fading. Provenance: Descended in the Parker Family of Fayetteville, North Carolina. (Skinner) $2,990

A cartridge display board by Eley, with sporting paper and brass shotgun cartridges, wads and discs surrounding the registered trade mark, framed glazed, 24¾ x 31½in. (Bonhams) $8,000

Nitsche & Gunther Luftwaffe flying goggles, of rare "splinter" pattern. Small tinted lens, Bakelite frames retaining original green elasticated strap. (Bosleys) $910

Earl De Grey's brass-bound oak cartridge magazine, for approximately 1000 cartridges escutcheon engraved with crowned crest above *Earl de Grey*. (Bonhams) $2,826

A rare Turkish Bazu band for the left arm, 15th/16th century, of steel, shaped to the forearm and back of the hand, two narrow side-plates attached by mail, 39.5cm. (Bonhams) $3,640

A pair of all steel flintlock muff pistols with floral and scroll engraving, inscribed *Richards, Strand, London* in original shagreen case. (Brightwells) $6,042

4th VB Black Watch sporran, 1882-1908 example by Wm. Anderson & Sons of Edinburgh & Glasgow, the metal edged black patent leather cantle bearing collar badge size regimental double headed eagle device. (Bosleys) $182

A flintlock box-lock tinderlighter, signed *Bond*, early 19th century, with signed engraved brass action, engraved tinderbox with hinged side-plate, candle-holder, 19.5cm. (Bonhams) $1,492

A mid 17th century cavalry trooper's bridle gauntlet. With long cuff made of two pieces and articulated thumb and fingers. (Andrew Bottomley) $1,570

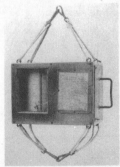

Great War German Airship altigraph (altimeter), a rare example of the issue pattern Hohenschreiber, that records the height of the Zeppelin during its flight, this example with a range up to 8,000 metres. (Bosleys) $3,864

A cased set of commemorative Napoleon medallions, second quarter 19th century, ten relief cast metal plaques, portrait busts and notable events including *Siege de la Bastille, Arrivée du Roi a Paris*, each stamped *Andrieu*, the case 14in. high.(Christie's) $2,194

Household Cavalry officer's jackboots, worn by mounted officers of the Household Cavalry. (Bosleys) $512

An exceptionally rare embroidered silk guidon of The St. Thomas-In-The-Vale Light Horse, presented to the troop by H.R.H. Prince William Henry, Duke of Clarence, later King William IV, dated *March 1783*, 111.8 x 76.2cm.
(Bonhams) $12,600

A very rare pair of Forsyth Patent First Model sliding primer locks for a double barrelled sporting gun, by Forsyth & Co., Patent, Nos. 668/9, circa 1812, each signed and finely engraved, 11.5cm.
(Bonhams) $3,640

A post-1902 scarlet cloth shabraque of the Royal Horse Guards, scrolls with 11 battle honours *Dettingen* to *Paarderberg*, and the Garter Star, across the front another scroll *France and Flanders 1914 1918*.
(Wallis & Wallis) $1,050

Bargains In Bombs – Anarchists at a sale on the Western Front Several good hand-grenades suitable for elections were also sold, unsigned, pencil and grey washes heightened with white, 48 x 36cm. framed.
(Onslows) $493

A steel ball and bullet mould for .64 Colt revolving rifle, 8in., cut off stamped *Colts Patent*, sides stamped *.56S* and *16*, wooden handles.(Wallis & Wallis) $246

Spanish Civil War Condor Legion cigarette case, the niello front decorated with Luftwaffe eagle and swastika with *LC 88* all within elliptical device inscribed *Im Kampf gegen den Bolschewismus Spanien 1936-38*.
(Bosleys) $738

A good early 18th century English brass framed flintlock tinder lighter, 5¾ overall, with folding bipod stand, hinged baluster turned candle holder, spring loaded door to tinder compartment released by thumb catch.(Wallis & Wallis) $1,160

A painted bentwood Revolutionary War drum, The Property of Benjamin Fay II (1744-1824) of Westborough, Massachusetts, painted with a gold spread-winged American eagle grasping a banner, 16¾in. diameter.
(Sotheby's) $25,300

A painted side drum of the 2nd (City of London Regt) The Royal Fusiliers, with city arms, badge, title scroll and 11 battle honours South Africa 1900-02 and WWI.
(Wallis & Wallis) $628

A cartridge display board by Eley, with sporting and military inert rifle, pistol and shotgun ammunition, various wads, top wads, glazed cap tins, set within a glazed oak frame, 64.5 x 80cm.
(Bonhams) $4,396

Winston Churchill 'Victory' ash tray, a good World War II patriotic ash tray, made from cast alloy. To the centre a 'V' for Victory with the head of Sir Winston Churchill with cigar and dicky bow, 7¼in. diameter.
(Bosleys) $118

A framed and glazed cartridge display board by Eley Nobel Industries Limited, with various sporting and military shotgun, rifle and pistol cartridges, percussion caps, shot sizes 5 and 6, 64.5cm. x 79cm. (Bonhams) $4,239

WW2 period German Luftwaffe camera by Robot of the pattern sometimes used in the wing of Luftwaffe aeroplanes; the back of the camera stamped *Luftwaffe-Eigentum*. (Bosleys) $420

Luftwaffe tail fin swastika, a rare example of the black painted swastika, edged with white. Removed from the tail of fighter size aircraft. Size 13 x 13in.
(Bosleys) $2,058

The Highlanders pipe banner, modern, one side blue, the other grey. Both sides heavily embroidered with bullion stag's head and *Cuidich'n Rich* scroll, Thistle and Crown.
(Bosleys) $235

A framed and glazed cartridge board, by Eley, with metallic and paper sporting cartridges from 4 to 360-bore, the cases surrounding the central trademark flanked by four demonstration cartridges, wads and numbered disks, 64 x 79.5.
(Bonhams & Brooks) $2,030

3rd Regiment of Aberdeen Local Militia 1809, "envelope" style canvas knapsack, the flap painted to the centre with crowned George III cypher within a red oval.
(Bosleys) $1,691

A small cartridge display board, by Eley, retailed by Stephen Grant & Joseph Lang, Ltd., with 12,16,20 and 28-bore paper sporting shotgun cartridges surrounding the central Eley trade mark cartouche, 40 x 42.5cm. (Bonhams) $1,400

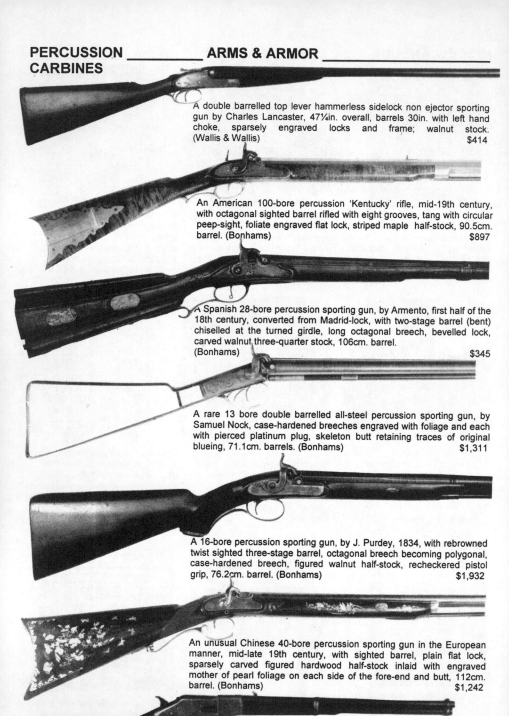

A double barrelled top lever hammerless sidelock non ejector sporting gun by Charles Lancaster, 47¼in. overall, barrels 30in. with left hand choke, sparsely engraved locks and frame; walnut stock. (Wallis & Wallis) $414

An American 100-bore percussion 'Kentucky' rifle, mid-19th century, with octagonal sighted barrel rifled with eight grooves, tang with circular peep-sight, foliate engraved flat lock, striped maple half-stock, 90.5cm. barrel. (Bonhams) $897

A Spanish 28-bore percussion sporting gun, by Armento, first half of the 18th century, converted from Madrid-lock, with two-stage barrel (bent) chiselled at the turned girdle, long octagonal breech, bevelled lock, carved walnut three-quarter stock, 106cm. barrel. (Bonhams) $345

A rare 13 bore double barrelled all-steel percussion sporting gun, by Samuel Nock, case-hardened breeches engraved with foliage and each with pierced platinum plug, skeleton butt retaining traces of original blueing, 71.1cm. barrels. (Bonhams) $1,311

A 16-bore percussion sporting gun, by J. Purdey, 1834, with rebrowned twist sighted three-stage barrel, octagonal breech becoming polygonal, case-hardened breech, figured walnut half-stock, recheckered pistol grip, 76.2cm. barrel. (Bonhams) $1,932

An unusual Chinese 40-bore percussion sporting gun in the European manner, mid-late 19th century, with sighted barrel, plain flat lock, sparsely carved figured hardwood half-stock inlaid with engraved mother of pearl foliage on each side of the fore-end and butt, 112cm. barrel. (Bonhams) $1,242

A scarce ·44 rimfire Winchester Model 1866 third model carbine, 39in. overall, round barrel 20in. with 2 way hinged rearsight, bronze frame with saddle ring on left side, plain walnut fore-end and butt. (Wallis & Wallis) $2,070

70

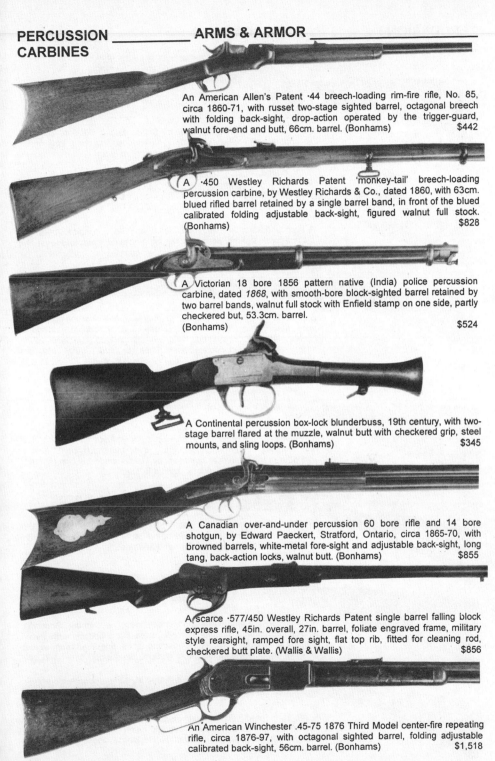

An American Allen's Patent ·44 breech-loading rim-fire rifle, No. 85, circa 1860-71, with russet two-stage sighted barrel, octagonal breech with folding back-sight, drop-action operated by the trigger-guard, walnut fore-end and butt, 66cm. barrel. (Bonhams) $442

A ·450 Westley Richards Patent 'monkey-tail' breech-loading percussion carbine, by Westley Richards & Co., dated 1860, with 63cm. blued rifled barrel retained by a single barrel band, in front of the blued calibrated folding adjustable back-sight, figured walnut full stock. (Bonhams) $828

A Victorian 18 bore 1856 pattern native (India) police percussion carbine, dated *1868*, with smooth-bore block-sighted barrel retained by two barrel bands, walnut full stock with Enfield stamp on one side, partly checkered but, 53.3cm. barrel.
(Bonhams) $524

A Continental percussion box-lock blunderbuss, 19th century, with two-stage barrel flared at the muzzle, walnut butt with checkered grip, steel mounts, and sling loops. (Bonhams) $345

A Canadian over-and-under percussion 60 bore rifle and 14 bore shotgun, by Edward Paeckert, Stratford, Ontario, circa 1865-70, with browned barrels, white-metal fore-sight and adjustable back-sight, long tang, back-action locks, walnut butt. (Bonhams) $855

A scarce ·577/450 Westley Richards Patent single barrel falling block express rifle, 45in. overall, 27in. barrel, foliate engraved frame, military style rearsight, ramped fore sight, flat top rib, fitted for cleaning rod, checkered butt plate. (Wallis & Wallis) $856

An American Winchester .45-75 1876 Third Model center-fire repeating rifle, circa 1876-97, with octagonal sighted barrel, folding adjustable calibrated back-sight, 56cm. barrel. (Bonhams) $1,518

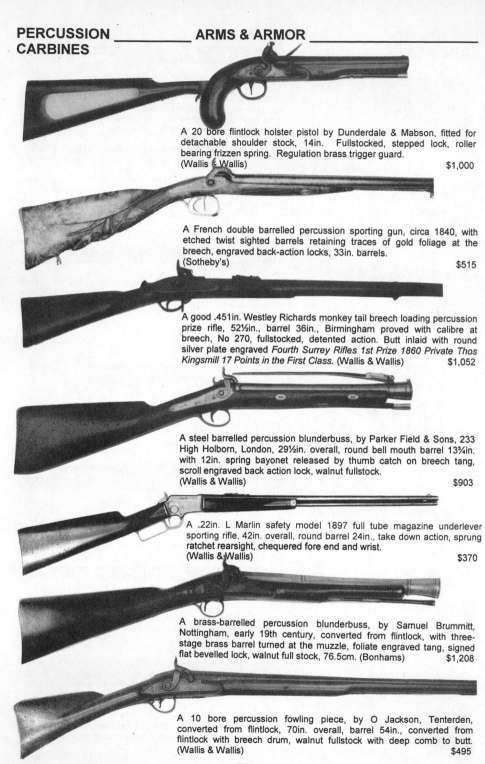

A 20 bore flintlock holster pistol by Dunderdale & Mabson, fitted for detachable shoulder stock, 14in. Fullstocked, stepped lock, roller bearing frizzen spring. Regulation brass trigger guard. (Wallis & Wallis) $1,000

A French double barrelled percussion sporting gun, circa 1840, with etched twist sighted barrels retaining traces of gold foliage at the breech, engraved back-action locks, 33in. barrels. (Sotheby's) $515

A good .451in. Westley Richards monkey tail breech loading percussion prize rifle, 52½in., barrel 36in., Birmingham proved with calibre at breech, No 270, fullstocked, detented action. Butt inlaid with round silver plate engraved *Fourth Surrey Rifles 1st Prize 1860 Private Thos Kingsmill 17 Points in the First Class.* (Wallis & Wallis) $1,052

A steel barrelled percussion blunderbuss, by Parker Field & Sons, 233 High Holborn, London, 29½in. overall, round bell mouth barrel 13¾in. with 12in. spring bayonet released by thumb catch on breech tang, scroll engraved back action lock, walnut fullstock. (Wallis & Wallis) $903

A .22in. L Marlin safety model 1897 full tube magazine underlever sporting rifle, 42in. overall, round barrel 24in., take down action, sprung ratchet rearsight, chequered fore end and wrist. (Wallis & Wallis) $370

A brass-barrelled percussion blunderbuss, by Samuel Brummitt, Nottingham, early 19th century, converted from flintlock, with three-stage brass barrel turned at the muzzle, foliate engraved tang, signed flat bevelled lock, walnut full stock, 76.5cm. (Bonhams) $1,208

A 10 bore percussion fowling piece, by O Jackson, Tenterden, converted from flintlock, 70in. overall, barrel 54in., converted from flintlock with breech drum, walnut fullstock with deep comb to butt. (Wallis & Wallis) $495

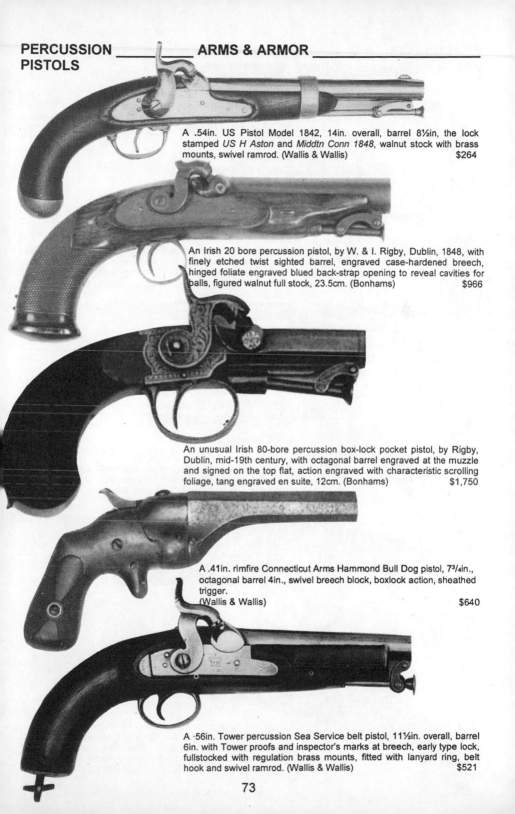

A .54in. US Pistol Model 1842, 14in. overall, barrel 8½in, the lock stamped *US H Aston* and *Middtn Conn 1848*, walnut stock with brass mounts, swivel ramrod. (Wallis & Wallis) $264

An Irish 20 bore percussion pistol, by W. & I. Rigby, Dublin, 1848, with finely etched twist sighted barrel, engraved case-hardened breech, hinged foliate engraved blued back-strap opening to reveal cavities for balls, figured walnut full stock, 23.5cm. (Bonhams) $966

An unusual Irish 80-bore percussion box-lock pocket pistol, by Rigby, Dublin, mid-19th century, with octagonal barrel engraved at the muzzle and signed on the top flat, action engraved with characteristic scrolling foliage, tang engraved en suite, 12cm. (Bonhams) $1,750

A .41in. rimfire Connecticut Arms Hammond Bull Dog pistol, 7³/₄in., octagonal barrel 4in., swivel breech block, boxlock action, sheathed trigger.
(Wallis & Wallis) $640

A ·56in. Tower percussion Sea Service belt pistol, 11½in. overall, barrel 6in. with Tower proofs and inspector's marks at breech, early type lock, fullstocked with regulation brass mounts, fitted with lanyard ring, belt hook and swivel ramrod. (Wallis & Wallis) $521

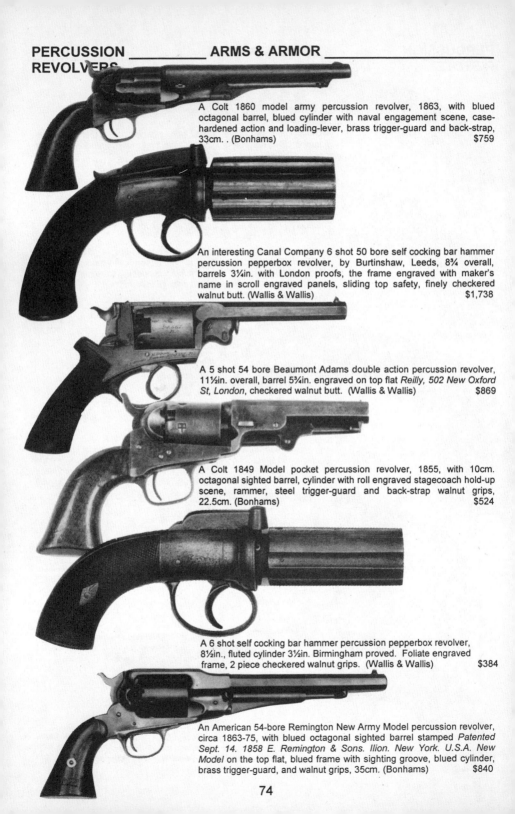

A Colt 1860 model army percussion revolver, 1863, with blued octagonal barrel, blued cylinder with naval engagement scene, case-hardened action and loading-lever, brass trigger-guard and back-strap, 33cm. . (Bonhams) $759

An interesting Canal Company 6 shot 50 bore self cocking bar hammer percussion pepperbox revolver, by Burtinshaw, Leeds, 8¾ overall, barrels 3¼in. with London proofs, the frame engraved with maker's name in scroll engraved panels, sliding top safety, finely checkered walnut butt. (Wallis & Wallis) $1,738

A 5 shot 54 bore Beaumont Adams double action percussion revolver, 11½in. overall, barrel 5¾in. engraved on top flat *Reilly, 502 New Oxford St, London*, checkered walnut butt. (Wallis & Wallis) $869

A Colt 1849 Model pocket percussion revolver, 1855, with 10cm. octagonal sighted barrel, cylinder with roll engraved stagecoach hold-up scene, rammer, steel trigger-guard and back-strap walnut grips, 22.5cm. (Bonhams) $524

A 6 shot self cocking bar hammer percussion pepperbox revolver, 8½in., fluted cylinder 3½in. Birmingham proved. Foliate engraved frame, 2 piece checkered walnut grips. (Wallis & Wallis) $384

An American 54-bore Remington New Army Model percussion revolver, circa 1863-75, with blued octagonal sighted barrel stamped *Patented Sept. 14. 1858 E. Remington & Sons. Ilion. New York. U.S.A. New Model* on the top flat, blued frame with sighting groove, blued cylinder, brass trigger-guard, and walnut grips, 35cm. (Bonhams) $840

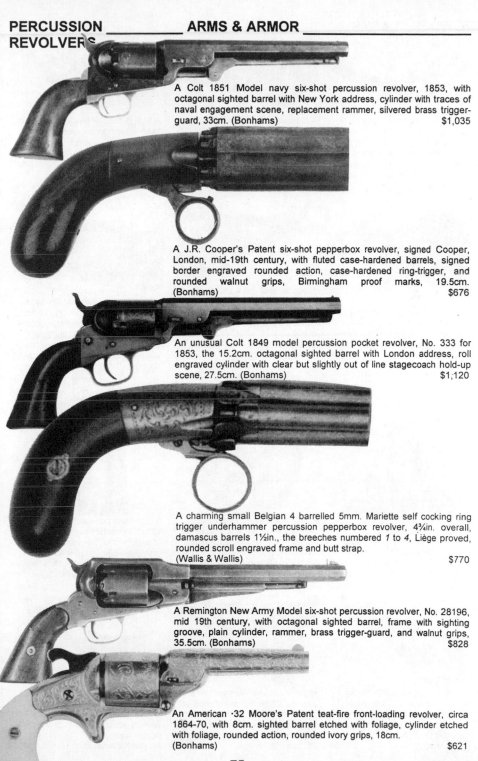

A Colt 1851 Model navy six-shot percussion revolver, 1853, with octagonal sighted barrel with New York address, cylinder with traces of naval engagement scene, replacement rammer, silvered brass trigger-guard, 33cm. (Bonhams) $1,035

A J.R. Cooper's Patent six-shot pepperbox revolver, signed Cooper, London, mid-19th century, with fluted case-hardened barrels, signed border engraved rounded action, case-hardened ring-trigger, and rounded walnut grips, Birmingham proof marks, 19.5cm. (Bonhams) $676

An unusual Colt 1849 model percussion pocket revolver, No. 333 for 1853, the 15.2cm. octagonal sighted barrel with London address, roll engraved cylinder with clear but slightly out of line stagecoach hold-up scene, 27.5cm. (Bonhams) $1;120

A charming small Belgian 4 barrelled 5mm. Mariette self cocking ring trigger underhammer percussion pepperbox revolver, 4¾in. overall, damascus barrels 1½in., the breeches numbered 1 to 4, Liège proved, rounded scroll engraved frame and butt strap. (Wallis & Wallis) $770

A Remington New Army Model six-shot percussion revolver, No. 28196, mid 19th century, with octagonal sighted barrel, frame with sighting groove, plain cylinder, rammer, brass trigger-guard, and walnut grips, 35.5cm. (Bonhams) $828

An American ·32 Moore's Patent teat-fire front-loading revolver, circa 1864-70, with 8cm. sighted barrel etched with foliage, cylinder etched with foliage, rounded action, rounded ivory grips, 18cm. (Bonhams) $621

A Caucasian silver-mounted priming-flask, 19th century, with curved tapering wooden body of oval section covered in black shagreen and with shaped silver mounts decorated with nielloed foliage, 19cm.(Bonhams) $690

A brass-mounted powder-flask, by James Dixon & Sons, Sheffield, 19th century, the bag-shaped copper body with scalloped edge and finely embossed on one side with stylized strapwork, 20.5cm. (Bonhams) $621

A Victorian silver mounted Scottish flattened cowhorn dress powder horn, 12½in., large end cap with foiled pink faceted glass 'end stone' in thistle engraved silver mount, ensuite with nozzle. (Wallis & Wallis) $684

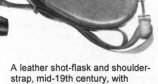

A Saxon 'musketeer's' priming-flask, late 16th century, the wooden body covered with black leather and with steel mounts, stout tapering nozzle, 14cm. (Bonhams) $828

A leather shot-flask and shoulder-strap, mid-19th century, with kidney-shaped leather body for 3lbs of shot, lacquered brass nozzle, complete with adjustable leather shoulder-strap stamped *Sykes*, 21.5cm. (Bonhams) $235

A Spanish cowhorn powder-flask, by Zuluaga (sic), probably Ramón, circa 1800, with curved translucent horn body of tapering triangular form with faceted sides, horn baseplate, 20cm.(Bonhams) $455

A German musketeer's powder-flask, late 16th/early 17th century, wooden body covered in black leather, and blackened iron mounts including tapering muzzle, 21cm. (Bonhams) $524

A circular brass priming-flask, German or Swiss, late 17th century, with turned body decorated with concentric circles on each side and double line borders around the outer edge, 8.5cm. diameter. (Bonhams) $414

A Japanese powder-flask, 18th/19th century, with copper body of slightly tapering oval section covered in blackened leather decorated on the front with a family mon in gold hiramakie, 10.5cm. high. (Bonhams) $442

A brass-mounted powder-flask, by Sykes, 19th century, with bag-shaped copper body embossed on each side with a scallop-shell motif and foliage, 20.5cm. (Bonhams) $304

A brass-mounted copper powder-flask by Dixon & Sons of Sheffield, mid-19th century, with bag-shaped body embossed on one side with a gundog in a wooded landscape, 20.5cm. (Bonhams) $483

An iron mounted leather covered powder flask of flattened horn shape, 11¼in. overall, possibly 17th century, sprung cut off lever and nozzle lever. (Wallis & Wallis) $166

Royal Engineers pre 1901 officer's sabretache, black patent leather mounted with a fire gilt Royal Arms regimental device. (Wallis & Wallis) $408

3rd Punjab Cavalry Victorian officer's sabretache, full dress example circa 1881, dark blue cloth face, edged with padded gold lace. (Bosleys) $1,738

Victorian Yorkshire Hussars sabretache attributed to the Earl of Feversham, scarlet cloth face, edged with silver lace of regimental pattern. (Bosleys) $923

Queen's Own officer's Glasgow Yeomanry Cavalry Victorian sabretache, face of dark blue melton cloth embroidered in gold bullion with entwined initials QOGYC. (Wallis & Wallis) $884

Duke of York's Own Loyal Suffolk Hussars Victorian sabretache, full dress example, the scarlet cloth face, edged with gold lace bearing central silk line, richly embroidered with large padded Crown with bullion *VR* cypher beneath. (Wallis & Wallis) $1,224

A Victorian Officer's uniform and accessories of the North Irish Division, Royal Artillery, circa 1895, comprising a sabretache of dark blue morocco leather; dress and undress back pouches ensuite; two tunics of dark blue cloth; and blue cloth overalls. (Bonhams) $1,413

A Victorian officer's full dress embroidered scarlet sabretache of the Suffolk Yeomanry Cavalry, silver lace border with red central stripe, embroidered crowned VR cypher. (Wallis & Wallis) $644

Middlesex Yeomanry Officer's sabretache, late 19th century example, flap mounted with dark blue velvet ground richly embroidered with a crowned VR cypher. (Bosleys) $359

10th Prince of Wales' Own Hussars Victorian officer's sabretache, circa 1856-81, scarlet cloth face edged with two inch gold lace of regimental pattern, embroidered on the face. (Bosleys) $994

A lightweight T. Horsley 1863 and 1867 Patent 12-bore bar-in-wood hammer gun by T. Horsley, No. 1754, 29in. barrels.
(Christie's) $1,666

A fine 12-bore (2¾in.) /8 x 60mm. (flanged) over-and-under sidelock ejector gun/rifle by Gebrüder Merkel, No. 18697, with a Hensoldt 'Diatal-D' 4 x 32 telescopic-sight, 26¾in. barrels.
(Christie's) $9,258

A matched pair of 12-bore bar-in-wood hammer ejector guns by T. Horsley, No. 2393 (1) and 2945 (2), 1877 & 1885, 30in. barrels.
(Christie's) $8,887

A fine 7mm (Remington Magnum) Heeren system falling-block rifle by Hartmann & Weiss, the patent falling-block action with integral triggerguard-underlever and set-trigger, with telescope, 26½in. barrel.
(Christie's) $28,807

A fine .450/.400 double barrelled hammerless Royal sidelock ejector rifle by Holland and Holland, the treble-grip action body with rounded bar, bolted manual safe and hand-detachable lockplates, 26in. barrels.
(Christie's) $24,966

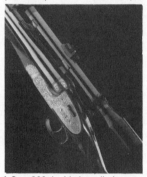

A fine .300 double barrelled hammerless Royal sidelock ejector rifle by Holland & Holland, the treble-grip action body with side-bolsters, hand-detachable lockplates, rolled-edge triggerguard, 24in. barrels.
(Christie's) $30,728

A fine W. & Scott C.1865 Patent 12-bore hammer gun by W. & C. Scott, No. 30236, the rebounding sidelocks with carved hammers, 30in. barrels.
(Christie's) $2,222

A fine pair of 12-bore single-trigger self-opening sidelock ejector guns by Boss, No. 8103/4, finely-figured stocks with recoil-pads, 28in. barrels, 1933.
(Christie's) $40,733

A fine .450 (3¼in. Nitro Express) 'Gold Name' double-barrelled hammerless detachable-boxlock ejector rifle by Westley Richards, No. 8725, 26in. barrels, 1906.
(Christie's) $18,512

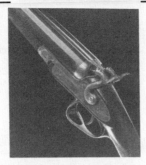

A 12-bore sidelock ejector gun by J. Rigby, No. 16192, dipped-edge lockplates, the fences carved with stylised acanthus-leaves, 30in. barrels, 1892.
(Christie's) $4,073

A fine 10-bore bar-in-wood hammer gun by J. Purdey, No. 8623, the rebounding sidelocks with dolphin hammers, 31in. barrels, 1871.
(Christie's) $13,886

A fine 20-bore (2¾in.) sidelock ejector gun by Ugartechea, No. 29364, the treble-grip action-body with side-clips, articulated front trigger, 28½in. barrels.
(Christie's) $3,703

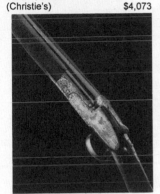

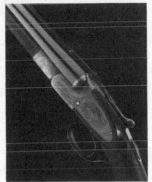

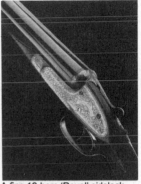

A fine Pedretti-engraved .410 single-trigger over-and-under sidelock ejector gun by Abbiatico & Salvinelli, the non-selective single-trigger with rolled-edge triggerguard, 27in. barrels.
(Christie's) $33,948

A rare 20-bore 'Crown' grade single-trigger sidelock ejector gun by L.C. Smith, the fully-selective 'Hunter One Trigger' single-trigger with barrel-selector switch, 30in. barrels.
(Christie's) $6,035

A fine 12-bore 'Royal' sidelock ejector gun by Holland & Holland, rounded bar, gold-inlaid cocking-indicators, best bold foliate-scroll engraving with some hardening-colour, 30in. barrels.
(Christie's) $9,218

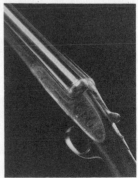

A rare Kell-engraved 12-bore (2¾in.) hammer ejector pigeon-gun by J. Purdey, No. 22182, the treble-grip action-body with side-clips and percussion fences, 32in. barrels, 1922. (Christie's) $29,624

A fine lightweight 12-bore over-and-under sidelock ejector gun by J. Woodward, No. 6604, hold-open toplever, gold-inlaid cocking-indicators, 28in. barrels, 1921.
(Christie's) $29,624

A fine round-body 12-bore single-trigger self-opening sidelock ejector gun by Boss, No. 8616, Boss system full self-opening action, 28in. barrels, 1944.
(Christie's) $25,921

An 1814 pattern Household Cavalry Officer's dress sword, plain straight, double fullered blade 34in., regimental pattern gilt half basket shell guard, wirebound fishskin covered grip, in its brass scabbard. (Wallis & Wallis) $9,548

A Victorian basket hilted Officer's sword of the Royal Lanark Militia, straight bi-fullered blade 31½in. etched with crowned *VR* and *Royal Lanark Militia* within banners upon foliage. Regulation steel basket hilt, wire bound fishskin covered grip. (Wallis & Wallis) $700

A 19th century Indian concealed crutch sword Zafar Takieh, 22½in., diamond section tapered blade 13¾in. Hard wood top carved with bird's head finials, silver ferrule, hilt twists to release silver mounted shaft to release blade. (Wallis & Wallis) $245

A George V Officer's sword of the Royal Horse Guards, straight fullered blade 37in., by Wilkinson, etched with 8 battle honours *Dettingen* to *Paardeberg* within foliate scrolls, nickel plated hilt, wire bound fishskin covered grip. (Wallis & Wallis) $770

A late 17th century North Italian or Venetian Sciavona, hilt with characteristic multi bar basket guard incorporating thumb ring and short quillon. Wooden grip, straight double edged blade with short fuller. Blade 37½in. (Andrew Bottomley) $2,058

An 1805 pattern Georgian naval Officer's sword for the rank of Commander and above, slender blade 27in., etched blued and gilt with military trophies, floral and foliate devices. Brass stirrup hilt with crowned fouled anchor on langets, lion's head pommel, diced wire bound ivory grip. Bullion 1825 pattern dress knot. (Wallis & Wallis) $1,050

A Cromwellian basket hilted broadsword, blade 32in. stamped *Andrea Ferara* with running wolf. Basket hilt chiselled with foliage, 3 hilt bars screwed to foliate chiselled pommel, wooden grip. (Wallis & Wallis) $1,295

An English Civil War period rapier, slender diamond section blade 37in., struck in the short deep fullers *Wundis Ihn Solingen*. Pierced iron guard. Pairs of bust portraits also chiselled on quillon terminals, knucklebow and pommel. (Wallis & Wallis) $2,156

A long North European rapier of Pappenheimer type circa 1630, diamond section blade 46¼in. Geometrically pierced guards, swept hilt with swollen fluted quillon finials en-suite with knucklebow. Swollen faceted pommel, spiral shaped woven steel wire bound grip and Turk's heads. (Wallis & Wallis) $2,772

A 19ᵗʰ century Renaissance-style two handed sword, the blade with foliate etching, 128cm long. (Stockholms AV) $799

A pre-1881 Scottish Officer's sword of The 71st (Highland Light Infantry) Regt, blade 32½in. etched with Royal Cypher, regimental badge and title, and battle honours to the Crimea; steel crosspiece with langets, and tapered pommel; in leather field service scabbard. (Wallis & Wallis) $616

A Georgian Officer's sabre of the Bombay Artillery, curved, pipe back blade 35in., with pronounced double edged point, by *Prosser Manufacturer to the King*, East India Company lion and sprays of laurel and palm within frosted panels, steel hilt of 1821 pattern with large quillon. (Wallis & Wallis) $2,310

A very rare late 15th century Italian sword of similar overall form to a Cinquedea. With six sided pommel, wire bound wooden grip and simple guard comprising down turned quillons and single langet. The blade of broad tapered form, with narrow fuller to the forte. Blade 27in. (Andrew Bottomley) $9,555

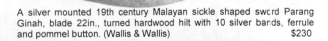

A silver mounted 19th century Malayan sickle shaped sword Parang Ginah, blade 22in., turned hardwood hilt with 10 silver bands, ferrule and pommel button. (Wallis & Wallis) $230

A good mid 17th century rapier, flattened diamond section blade 35in. stamped in the fullers *Geiles Herder Fecit Londini*. Iron hilt, guard pierced and chiselled with flowers and scrolling foliage. Knuckle-bow screwed to fluted pommel, copper wire bound grip. (Wallis & Wallis) $1,155

A 16th century hand and a half sword, late broad straight double edged blade 42½in. with short fullers. Cruciform hilt, crosspiece of swollen octagonal section, tall swollen octagonal pommel, steel wire bound grip. (Wallis & Wallis) $1,680

81

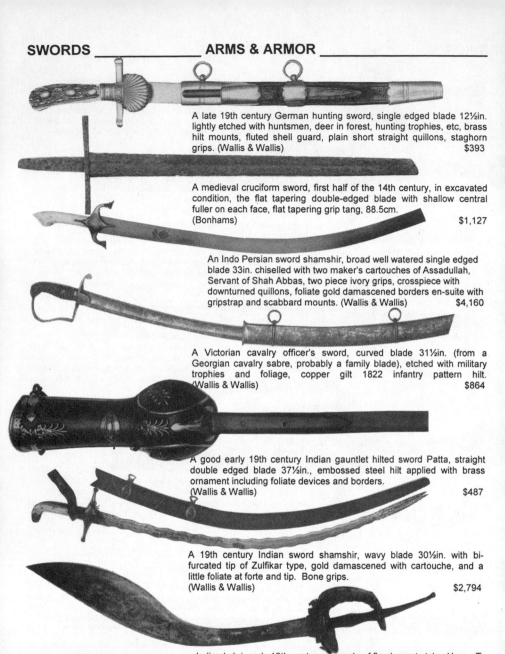

A late 19th century German hunting sword, single edged blade 12½in. lightly etched with huntsmen, deer in forest, hunting trophies, etc, brass hilt mounts, fluted shell guard, plain short straight quillons, staghorn grips. (Wallis & Wallis) $393

A medieval cruciform sword, first half of the 14th century, in excavated condition, the flat tapering double-edged blade with shallow central fuller on each face, flat tapering grip tang, 88.5cm. (Bonhams) $1,127

An Indo Persian sword shamshir, broad well watered single edged blade 33in. chiselled with two maker's cartouches of Assadullah, Servant of Shah Abbas, two piece ivory grips, crosspiece with downturned quillons, foliate gold damascened borders en-suite with gripstrap and scabbard mounts. (Wallis & Wallis) $4,160

A Victorian cavalry officer's sword, curved blade 31½in. (from a Georgian cavalry sabre, probably a family blade), etched with military trophies and foliage, copper gilt 1822 infantry pattern hilt. (Wallis & Wallis) $864

A good early 19th century Indian gauntlet hilted sword Patta, straight double edged blade 37½in., embossed steel hilt applied with brass ornament including foliate devices and borders. (Wallis & Wallis) $487

A 19th century Indian sword shamshir, wavy blade 30½in. with bifurcated tip of Zulfikar type, gold damascened with cartouche, and a little foliate at forte and tip. Bone grips. (Wallis & Wallis) $2,794

Indian kukri, early 19th century example of flamboyant style. Heavy T backed blade, mounted onto a Firangi style hilt, retaining original lining of green velvet, with red edging. Blade length 19in. (Bosley's) $80

An 1854 pattern Grenadier Guards Edward VII officer's sword by Wilkinson, blade 32½in., nicely etched and plated with crowned EVIIR, regimental device, battle honours and owner's initials *F.R.S.* Regulation plated hilt, wire bound sharkskin covered grip. (Wallis & Wallis) $604

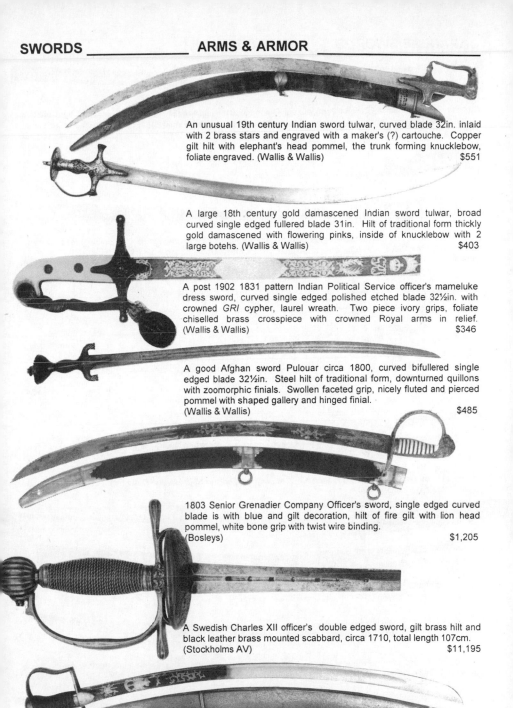

An unusual 19th century Indian sword tulwar, curved blade 32in. inlaid with 2 brass stars and engraved with a maker's (?) cartouche. Copper gilt hilt with elephant's head pommel, the trunk forming knucklebow, foliate engraved. (Wallis & Wallis) $551

A large 18th century gold damascened Indian sword tulwar, broad curved single edged fullered blade 31in. Hilt of traditional form thickly gold damascened with flowering pinks, inside of knucklebow with 2 large botehs. (Wallis & Wallis) $403

A post 1902 1831 pattern Indian Political Service officer's mameluke dress sword, curved single edged polished etched blade 32½in. with crowned *GRI* cypher, laurel wreath. Two piece ivory grips, foliate chiselled brass crosspiece with crowned Royal arms in relief. (Wallis & Wallis) $346

A good Afghan sword Pulouar circa 1800, curved bifullered single edged blade 32½in. Steel hilt of traditional form, downturned quillons with zoomorphic finials. Swollen faceted grip, nicely fluted and pierced pommel with shaped gallery and hinged finial. (Wallis & Wallis) $485

1803 Senior Grenadier Company Officer's sword, single edged curved blade is with blue and gilt decoration, hilt of fire gilt with lion head pommel, white bone grip with twist wire binding. (Bosleys) $1,205

A Swedish Charles XII officer's double edged sword, gilt brass hilt and black leather brass mounted scabbard, circa 1710, total length 107cm. (Stockholms AV) $11,195

1796 Officer's Light Cavalry pattern sword, single edged curved blade with half length blue and gilt decoration, hilt with shield langets and stirrup guard enclosing a black leather wooden grip with twist wire binding. (Bosleys) $1,250

A Japanese sword katana, blade 64.2cm., mumei, O-suriage, 3 mekugi ana (Shinto, late 17th century), tight mokume hada, gunome hamon, shakudo nanako fuchi kashira, tape bound same tsuka, shakudo menuki as flowers. (Wallis & Wallis) $1,160

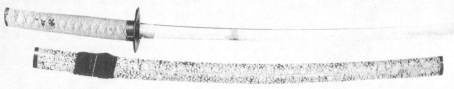

A Japanese sword ito maki no tachi, blade 67.6cm., signed *Kunisuke*, gunome hamon, fair polish, brass koshirae, tape bound same tsuka, Aoi tsuba nashiji lacquered saya with ito maki no tachi binding. (Wallis & Wallis) $1,240

A Japanese sword katana, blade 60.1cm., suriage, mumei, gunome hamon, ito gunome hamon, rebound tsuka, iron mokko tsuba inlaid with soft metal sage beneath tree. (Wallis & Wallis) $840

The blade from a Japanese sword katana, 64.2cm., signed *Echizen Noju Harima Daijo Fuji*, gunome hamon. (Wallis & Wallis) $1,760

A Japanese sword katana, blade 60.8cm. signed *Kanefusa*, gunome hamon, leather bound same tsuka with gilt shakudo menuki as stylized standing figures. (Wallis & Wallis) $1,367

A Japanese sword katana, blade 71.8cm., mumei, 2 mekugi ana, probably Shin-shinto, leather bound same tsuka. (Wallis & Wallis) $2,238

A large Japanese sword katana, blade 71cm., signed *Oshu Shirakawa-Shin Tegarayama Masashige* and dated *Kansei 5th year, 8th month, lucky day (=1803)*, ohu suguha hamon, tight itame hada. (Wallis & Wallis) $6,464

A Shakudo mounted tachi, Mumei, Naminohira School, Muromachi period (late 15th/early16th century), the blade honzukuri, iorimune, chugissaki with torii zori, forging pattern ayasugi. (Christie's) $10,310

An elaborately mounted aikuchi, Kinzogan Mei: Kunihiro, Edo Period (17th Century), the blade hirazukuri, mitsumune, uchizori, koitame-hada with fine ji-nie, 11in. (Christie's) $11,247

A fine daisho, the katana Mumei, style of later Tadayoshi School, Edo Period (19th century); the wakizashi Mei: Mutsu No Kami Shigesane, Edo Period (17th Century). (Christie's) $11,735

A Soshu Tanto in fine mounts, Mumei, Muromachi Period (16th century), the blade hirazukuri, mitsumune with shallow sori, running itame-hada with ji-nie, midare hamon of nie with sunagashi and some tobiyaki, atobori of Fudo and gomabashi, mumei o-suriage nakago, 36.1cm., in a natural karaki wood saya. (Christie's) $22,494

A fine and silver-mounted tachi, Kinzogan Mei: Aoe, Nambokucho Period (14th century), the blade, honzukuri and torii-zori with full length wide grooves, superb itame-mokume hada, medium suguba ko-itame hamon, o-maru boshi, black o-choji utsuri becoming blotched utsuri towards the point, suriage nakago with five mekugi-ana, four plugged, 28in. (Christie's) $32,499

An interesting Japanese shortsword wakizashi, blade 39.5cm signed *Toshitsugu*, one mekugi ana, ubu, hira zukuri. In unusual military mounts, brass mounted cherry wood tsuka. (Wallis & Wallis) $393

A fine Japanese wakizashi, with blade honzukuri and torii-zori, mokume hada, midare hamon, ubu nakago with one mekugi-ana, signed, 17th/18th century, silver-mounted handechi-style kuronuri scabbard decorated in gold and silver hogidoshi with stylised seaweed, 55.6cm. blade. (Bonhams) $4,025

A silver mounted ko-dachi, Katana Mei: Kanemoto, Muromachi Period (late 16th century), the blade honzukuri, iorimune with chugissaki, koshi-zori. (Christie's) $3,353

A Georgian painted wooden truncheon, by Parker of Holborn, painted with 1801-1816 Royal Arms, 18in. (Wallis & Wallis) $240

A Victorian painted wooden truncheon, black background, painted in gold and colours with crown, white rose, and *WRC*, 15½in. . (Wallis & Wallis) $352

A William IV painted wooden truncheon, painted with *WR* Royal Arms, *1836*, and coat of arms with motto. (Wallis & Wallis) $384

A Victorian special constable's painted wooden truncheon, painted in gold and colours, with crown, VR, Hull SC, plain wood grip, 16in. (Wallis & Wallis) $176

A polished wood 19th century life preserver, turned wooden globe head with barrel base, secured to turned wood baluster haft by thick leather cord, 17in. (Wallis & Wallis) $104

A Victorian painted wooden truncheon, black painted background painted in gold and colours. (Wallis & Wallis) $224

A William IV painted wooden truncheon, painted in gold *WR IV*, blue painted body, swelling grip, 14in. (Wallis & Wallis) $192

A Victorian painted wooden truncheon, painted in gold and colours with crown, *VR* in Garter belt and *MS*, turned wood grip, 12in. (Wallis & Wallis) $352

A Victorian painted tipstaff, rounded head, painted in gold and colours with crown, *VR Borough of Stamford 1837*, turned wooden grip, 10in. (Wallis & Wallis) $496

A Victorian painted wood truncheon, black painted, painted in gold and colours with crown, *VR* and in green with numeral *4*. 11½in. (Wallis & Wallis) $400

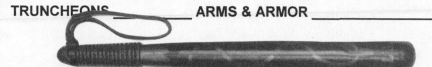

A Victorian painted wooden truncheon, of St Thomas's Hospital, painted with serpent on staff and *St Th* in gold, 15½in. (Wallis & Wallis) $480

A Victorian black painted wooden truncheon painted in gilt and colours with crown *VIR, County of Nottm 570,* 18½in. (Wallis & Wallis) $224

A Victorian painted wooden truncheon of the Naval police, surmounted by carved wood crown, 13in. (Wallis & Wallis)
$560

A George III painted wood truncheon, painted with crown, *GIIIR* and dated *1808* on black background, rounded body, 18in. (Wallis & Wallis) $177

A Victorian painted wooden truncheon, painted in gold and colours with *VR,* Royal Arms, Town arms and *Peterhouse,* 12in. (Wallis & Wallis) $334

A Victorian boxwood painted truncheon, painted in gold with crown, VR and Portcullis device (Westminster), on black background, turned grip, stamped at base *Parker Holborn* 18in. (Wallis & Wallis) $322

A Victorian black painted wooden truncheon, bulbous head painted with crown, VR in gold and colours, 14½in. (Wallis & Wallis) $384

A Victorian turned wood and polychrome decorated truncheon, 17¼in., painted with crowned *VR* and *DPC No 3.* (Wallis & Wallis) $157

A George III black painted wooden truncheon, bulbous head, painted crown, GIIIR, 17in. (Wallis & Wallis)
$496

A Victorian black painted wooden truncheon, painted in gold and colours with crown, VR, turned wood grip, 15in. (Wallis & Wallis) $144

A Victorian polychrome decorated turned wooden truncheon, 17½in., decorated in gilt with crowned *VR Police.* (Wallis & Wallis) $236

A good officer's patrol jacket of Hussar style, astrakhan collar, front and cuffs, mohair braid trim to front, back and sleeves, 5 flat loops with olivets to chest, shoulder straps. (Wallis & Wallis) $2,085

Leinster Regiment post 1881 officer's scarlet tunic, scarlet melton cloth with dark blue facings to the collar and cuffs.(Bosleys) $292

A good early Victorian officer's full dress scarlet jacket of the Queen's Own Worcestershire Yeomanry Cavalry, blue facings, silver lace and braid trim including braided cuff ornaments. (Wallis & Wallis) $486

Battle of Britain Fighter Pilot's service dress tunic and cap, worn by Wing Commander Alexander Rothwell Edge, a service dress cap, tailored by Gieves, Canadian style flying goggles. (Bosleys) $891

WWII Royal Ulster Rifles battledress blouse, 1940 pattern, retaining original insignia. (Bosleys) $306

Uniform of Yeoman of Guard The Tower of London, rare undress example, of dark blue cloth, with scarlet facings. To the chest a large scarlet King's Crown, with EIIR cypher below. (Bosleys) $384

1st Cardiagan Artillery Volunteers Bandsman tunic, pre 1907 example, dark blue cloth, with scarlet facings to the collar. (Bosleys) $426

Beach Signals Combined Operations battledress blouse, scarce 1943 dated example of 1940 pattern, each sleeve bears an embroidered *Beach Signals*. (Bosleys) $556

Royal Devonshire Yeomanry Artillery officer's uniform, Eton style tunic, scarlet melton cloth, with dark blue facings to the collar. (Bosleys) $1,112

A Captain's full dress scarlet tunic of The Norfolk Regiment, yellow facings, gilt shoulder cords, braided lace trim incorporating black lines, good gilt collar badges, name inside *G B Northcote*. (Wallis & Wallis) $308

An officer's pre-1855 full dress scarlet coatee of the 19th (1st York, North Riding) Regiment of Foot, green facings. (Wallis & Wallis) $1,321

Royal Scots Greys officer's 1902 pattern service dress tunic, khaki wool material, with captain rank stars and lace to the cuffs, accompanied by a pigeon message found in the pocket written during a field exercise in 1910. (Bosleys) $994

Lothians and Border Horse Officer's uniform, early post Great War Officer's service dress uniform, the tunic with cornflower blue facings to the shoulder straps which are mounted with Lt rank stars. (Bosleys) $204

2nd Northumberland Artillery Volunteers tunic, dark blue wool, with silver cord decoration to the cuff and edging to the collar and epaulettes. (Bosleys) $441

A Lieutenant's full dress scarlet doublet of The Argyll and Sutherland Highlanders, yellow facings, gilt lace and braid trim, including 3 braided loops with buttons to cuffs and pockets. (Wallis & Wallis) $207

6th Inniskilling Dragoons Officer's mess jacket, Captain's scarlet silk lined example of scarlet melton cloth by Jones, Chalk & Dawson, edged with one inch gold lace. (Bosleys) $156

A Lieutenant's 1857 pattern full dress scarlet tunic of the Coldstream Guards, blue facings, white piping, single crimson shoulder cord on left. (Wallis & Wallis) $580

Lothian & Border Horse Officer's scarlet tunic, scarlet melton cloth with dark blue facings to the collar and cuffs, each decorated with gold bullion lace, mounted with post 1902 rank insignia. (Bosleys) $185

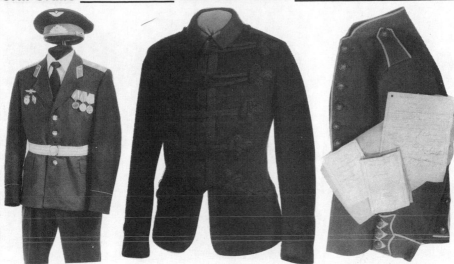

Soviet Russian Airforce Colonel's uniform, of dark blue material retaining gold lace shoulder rank boards and collar insignia. This example retains Russian medals and flying badges to the chest. Complete with trousers. (Bosleys) $98

Victorian Rifle pattern Officer's tunic, unusual Regimental pattern of dark green melton cloth. To each breast five loops of mohair cord, with crows feet, loops and olivettes. (Bosleys) $98

A rare OR's 1857 pattern full dress red tunic of the 24th (2nd, Warwickshire) Regt, with the owner's stamped canvas hold-all containing"Account Book", "Monthly Settlements, Clothing Account and Savings Bank Account" and "Parchment Certificate". (Wallis & Wallis) $609

German Army Infantry Major's tunic, 1942 dated field grey example by C.Louis Weber of Hanover, the tailor's label bearing ink Officer's name *Strasser*. (Bosleys) $518

Victorian Royal Company of Archers uniform, comprising a dark green melton bonnet of Tam-o-shanter style, green tailcoat with three gilt mounted post 1902 pattern buttons to either side. (Bosleys) $176

1868 pattern 2nd Royal Cheshire Militia Officer's tunic, rare scarlet example with dark blue facings to the collar and cuffs, each decorated with silver lace embroidery. (Bosleys) $279

Bengal Lancers officer's mess uniform, of dark blue stable jacket style edged with flat bullion lace. (Bosleys) $526

Royal Naval Air Service officer's tunic, land service tunic conforming to the 1916 Army dress regulations, lightweight khaki cotton material. (Bosleys) $1,092

Royal Horse Guards officer's mess uniform, stable pattern, dark blue cloth with scarlet facings to the cuffs and collar. (Bosleys) $187

Q.O. Cameron Highlanders officer's 1881 pattern scarlet doublet, scarlet melton cloth with dark blue facings to the collar and cuffs. Complete with gilt regimental buttons. (Bosleys) $432

Oxfordshire & Buckinghamshire Light Infantry blouse, of the 1937 pattern style, the label stating 1940 pattern, with cloth Captain rank to shoulder straps. (Bosleys) $200

1st Battalion Gordon Highlanders OR's doublet, 1914 dated example of scarlet cloth with yellow facings. (Bosleys) $145

King's Own Great War issue Other Rank's tunic, 1902 pattern service dress tunic with double pleat to the collar. This example retaining Battalion battle patches, believed indicating 2/5th Battalion of the Regiment. (Bosleys) $967

Black Watch battledress blouse of the 1937 pattern style, label stating 1940 pattern, 51st (Highland) Division printed badge, three red brigade bars and Black Watch badge to sleeve. (Bosleys) $145

RAF aircrew issue Irvin flying jacket, war example with multi piece back. Complete with all original working zips and waist belt. (Bosleys) $161

A Victorian Lieutenant's full dress scarlet tunic of the Grenadier Guards, blue facings, low rounded collar with gilt embroidered loop and grenade badge, 2 pairs of overalls. (Wallis & Wallis) $785

A rare Georgian officer's scarlet coatee of the Duleek Volunteers (Ireland), double breasted, white facings, 2 lines of 12 buttons in pairs to chest. (Wallis & Wallis) $725

A WWI Captain's khaki SD doublet of The Queens Own Cameron Highlanders, rank badges to cuff, medal ribbons WWI named and dated 1916. (Wallis & Wallis) $453

Josephine Baker, signed 4 x 5.5, full-length in elaborate gown, irregularly cut and laid down to album page with another photo to reverse, age toning.
(Vennett Smith) $108

Harry Houdini, a printed admittance card, to Houdini's experiment of attempting to remain submerged one hour in an airtight metal coffin, Hotel Shelton, New York, 5th Aug. 1926, signed by Houdini in pencil.
(Vennett Smith) $1,215

Mahatma Gandhi, a good signed 2.75 x 4.25, full-length seated wearing white loin cloth, dated in his hand *10th September 1931*.
(Vennett Smith) $2,030

Charles Lindbergh, hardback edition of The Spirit Of St. Louis, signed and inscribed to title page *To Richard, Michael Trevethan with best wishes and in memory of pleasant times on HMS Hermes Charles A. Lindbergh 1953*.
(Vennett Smith) $1,323

Astronauts, 20 x 16 photo of the earth from the moon, signed by Alan Bean, Apollo 12 and Charlie Duke, Apollo 16.
(Vennett Smith) $224

Will Hay, signed and inscribed postcard, head and shoulders in oval, together with a typed letter signed, to the same people as the postcard, 11th Dec. 1930, inviting them to a performance.
(Vennett Smith) $277

Oscar Wilde, signed piece, slightly irregularly clipped from the end of a letter, with four additional words in his hand, laid down to an album beneath a photo.
(Vennett Smith) $154

Charles Dickens, autograph signed letter, one and a half pages, no date, to Miss Barry, 3.5 x 4, regretting he was not in when she called. (Vennett Smith) $801

G Marconi, sepia 4 x 6, signed to photographer's mount, *5th Nov. 1909*, 8 x 11 overall, slight fading.
(Vennett Smith) $578

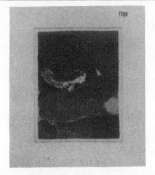

Marc Chagall, signed 8.5 x 11 print of one of his works, entitled Femme Olseau, together with certificate of authenticity and provenance.
(Vennett Smith) $323

Josef Goebbels, signed postcard with German inscription, three quarter length in suit with Nazi armband, 7.9.1938.
(Vennett Smith) $770

Pablo Picasso, an exhibition catalogue for Picasso's paintings at the Demotte Galleries, Dec. 1931, signed by Picasso to front cover.
(Vennett Smith) $6,174

Lloyd Webber & Rice, Andrew Lloyd Webber signed postcard, to lower white border, head and shoulders, photo by Dezo Hoffmann; Tim Rice signed and inscribed 6 x 4, half-length.
(Vennett Smith) $131

Prince Charles & Princess Diana, a signed and inscribed Christmas greetings card by both, featuring a colour photo of the couple seated together on a white settee, with the young Princess William and Harry.
(Vennett Smith) $1,771

Lillie Langtry, signed cabinet card, 4¼ x 7in. sepia, boldly signed along the lower margin, portrait by W. & D. Downey, of London and Newcastle.
(Christie's) $646

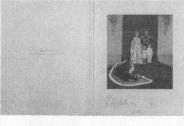

Maria Callas, signed and inscribed 4 x 6, with full married signature, full-length standing in costume from Il Trovatore at La Scala, photo by Piccagliani.
(Vennett Smith) $634

Queen Elizabeth & Prince Philip, signed Christmas greetings card by both individually, beneath image, featuring colour photo of the Queen and Prince Phillip standing in coronation robes alongside the young Prince Charles and Princess Anne, 1953.
(Vennett Smith) $693

Pablo Picasso, signed colour reproduction of one of his prints, Affiches Originales, signed in pencil overmounted in ivory, 14 x 16 overall, certificate of authenticity and statement of provenance.
(Vennett Smith) $1,078

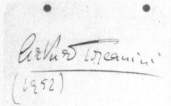

Arturo Toscanini, signed card,
1952, 4½ x 3½in.
(Vennett-Smith) $99

Harry S. Truman, signed card,
3½ x 4½in.
(Vennett-Smith) $107

Jawaharlal Nehru, signed and
inscribed sepia 6 x 9in., August
1952, head and shoulders.
(Vennett-Smith) $132

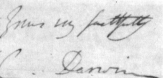

Boris Pasternak, good ink signature
and inscription on card, 10th August
1959, 4.5 x 3.
(T. Vennett-Smith) $352

Ernest Hemingway, signed card, 4
x 3in., rare.
(T. Vennett-Smith) $672

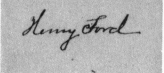

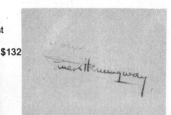

Henry Ford, small signed card, 3 x
1.5.
(T. Vennett-Smith) $428

Princess Diana, a very fine signed
and inscribed 7 x 5½in. photo, to
mount, in original green leather
frame.
(Vennett-Smith) $1,518

Charles Darwin, signed piece, cut
from end of letter, 3 x 1½in.
(Vennett-Smith) $330

Princess Grace of Monaco, and
Prince Rainier, signed postcard,
4 x 6in., seated with children.
(Vennett-Smith) $124

Charles Dickens, autographed
signed note, in third person, 22nd
May 1854, laid down to large
album page with hand-addressed
envelope and unsigned postcard.
(Vennett-Smith) $462

Edward H. White, signed colour
8 x 10in., head and shoulders,
extremely rare, laid down to 8½ x
12in. album page.
(Vennett-Smith) $512

General George Custer, autograph envelope unsigned, addressed in his hand, *Mrs. Genl Custer* in Michigan.
(Vennett-Smith) $842

ANDY WARHOL

Andy Warhol, signed 8 x 10in., head and shoulders.
(Vennett-Smith) $380

Maurice Ravel, signed card with autographed musical quotation signed, one bar, 4¹/₂ x 3¹/₂in.
(Vennett-Smith) $743

Sigmund Freud, printed card, 6 x 4¹/₂in., signed *Freud*, with two additional words in his hand, sending thanks May 1936.
(Vennett-Smith) $1,336

A TIME FOR GREATNESS

U. S. SENATOR JOHN F. KENNEDY FOR PRESIDENT

John F. Kennedy, signed Presidential Campaign Booklet to front cover illustration.
(Vennett-Smith) $1,089

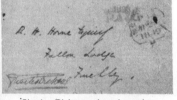

George Orwell, typed signed letter, on one side of a BBC correspondence card, 17th Sept. 1942, to Eugenie Fordham.
(Vennett-Smith) $710

Duke of Wellington, cheque made payable to himself for 650 pounds, dated *4th July 1825*, drawn on Coutts Bank.
(Vennett-Smith) $281

Charles Dickens, signed envelope, hand-addressed to R.H. Horne, 1849.
(Vennett-Smith) $297

Richard Nixon, signed 4 x 5¹/₂in., head and shoulders.
(Vennett-Smith) $165

Igor Stravinsky, signed autograph musical quotation, on album page, inscribed and dated 1955, 4¹/₂ x 3¹/₂in.
(Vennett-Smith) $264

Sarah Bernhardt, signed sepia postcard, head and shoulders.
(Vennett-Smith) $198

Salvador Dali, signed 8½ x 12in. bookweight photo, half-length painting the head of his wife Gala. (Vennett-Smith) $128

Edward VIII, signed sepia 8½ x 11in., as Prince of Wales, three quarter length standing in naval uniform, 1913. (Vennett-Smith) $293

Muhammad Ali, signed 8 x 5½in. bookweight photo, three quarter length in boxing pose, overmounted in ivory. (Vennett-Smith) $209

Josephine Baker, a good signed and inscribed sepia 7 x 9½, with first name only, half-length in French uniform, 1946. (Vennett-Smith) $467

James I, (James VI of Scotland), signed document, one page, folio, 15th March 1600, signed at conclusion, with several counter signatures and good attached red wax seal. (Vennett-Smith) $1,127

George VI, and Queen Elizabeth, a fine signed 8 x 11½in., by both individually to lower mount, 1937, full-length standing in coronation robes with the two princesses. (Vennett-Smith) $684

Enrico Caruso, signed cabinet photo, three quarter length in costume, London, 1907, photo by Alfred Ellis & Walery of Baker Street. (Vennett-Smith) $483

Prince Charles & Princess Diana, signed 4 x 5in., colour photo, by both individually, full-length standing, each holding the infant princes. (Vennett-Smith) $4,025

Maria Callas, an 8 x 10in. black and white photograph signed and dedicated in blue ink by Maria Callas and dated *1957*. (Bonhams) $512

Andy Warhol, signed and inscribed 8 x 10in., head and shoulders. (Vennett-Smith) $130

Princess Margaret, signed 6 x 8in., head and shoulders in tiara, photo by Lord Snowdon. (Vennett-Smith) $211

Roy Lichtenstein, signed postcard of one of his works, girl with ball. (Vennett-Smith) $129

Thomas Edison, small signed piece, cut from end of letter. (Vennett-Smith) £180 $284

Pablo Picasso, signed print of one of his paintings 'Femme III', 7½ x 10½, overmounted in cream, together with a certificate of authenticity from The National Art Guild of America. (Vennett-Smith) $998

Walt Disney, signed album page. (Vennett Smith) $616

Sarah Duchess of York, signed colour 8 x 10in., 1997, full-length posed on motorcycle. (Vennett-Smith) $106

King George V and Queen Mary, pair of 9½ x 13in. photos, each half-length, the King in Army uniform, the Queen in ceremonial dress, each dated by hand 1916. (Vennett-Smith) $342

Prince Charles & Princess Diana, a fine signed colour 5 x 7in. photo, to lower mount, by both individually, dated by Charles 1986, framed and glazed. (Vennett-Smith) $2,898

Charles Dickens, autograph letter, fine early signature, two pages, not dated (Wednesday morning), to Miss Barry. (Vennett-Smith) $798

Cassius Clay, signed 8 x 10in. picture of the boxing great, extremely rare, signed *Cassius Clay*.
(Bonhams) $720

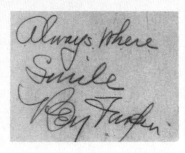

Ben Turpin, signed album page, 4½ x 3½in., in pencil, rare.
(Vennett-Smith) $99

Andy Warhol, signed 6 x 4in. to white border, head and shoulders.
(Vennett-Smith) $198

Francis Bacon, signed 6 x 8½in. full length seated on a stool.
(Vennett Smith) $112

Queen Elizabeth II and Prince Philip, signed 10½ x 9½in., by both individually to lower mount 1958, pictured with the young Prince Charles and Princess Anne.
(Vennett Smith) $600

Nelson Mandela, signed card 4½ x 2½in. overmounted in burgundy beneath colour photo, 11 x 16in overall.
(Vennett Smith) $190

Alphonse Mucha, calendar 'Biscuits Lefevre-Utile', 1897, lithograph, laid on paper, signed in the block with *'F. Champenois-Paris'*, 60.5 x 44cm. (Sotheby's) $5,762

Laurel and Hardy, a good 7 x 5in. signed by both Stan Laurel (inscribed) and Oliver Hardy, head and shoulders in characteristic pose.
(Vennett-Smith) $470

Alfred Hitchcock, signed 8 x 10in., half-length leaning on director's chair.
(Vennett-Smith) $594

A Cecile wooden automaton doll, playing a melody from Beethoven's 5th Piano Concerto on a spinet in a red curtained pavilion, Japanese, circa 1965.
(Auction Team Köln) $352

A three dimensional mechanical picture, 19th century, the painted papier-mâché scene depicting an alpine village with a maiden at a water wheel waving to a sailor, 94 x 80cm. (Christie's) $19,154

Clockwork cobbler, late 19th/early 20th century, composition body, mohair beard and glass eyes, 21in. high. (Skinner) $3,680

A Spanish dancer automaton, probably Lambert, French, circa 1890, with Simon & Halbig 1039 mould head, she turns her head, flicks her tambourine and stamps, 21in. (Sotheby's) $2,646

A monkey violinist automaton, probably Phalibois, French, circa 1865-80, playing two airs, the ape blinks his eyes, opens and closes his mouth, wields his bow and taps his foot, 17¾in.
(Sotheby's) $3,175

A Leopold Lambert 'Marquise' automaton, French, circa 1890, with Simon & Halbig 1039 mould bisque head, she nods and turns her head, blinks her eyes, raises her lorgnette to her face and fans herself, two musical airs, 23½in.
(Sotheby's) $2,646

A Karl Griesbaum singing bird automaton with yellow and black feathered bird, turns its head and moves beak and tail, 1950, 11in. high.
(Auction Team Köln) $838

A rocking ship automaton, the ship in a river-mouth between a windmill and a watermill, with musical movement playing two airs, 19½in. high. (Christie's) $920

A musical timepiece picture diorama, Swiss, circa 1860, enameled dial, glazed gilt wood and composition framed display case, 24in. high.
(Sotheby's) $3,496

A Lambert musical automaton of a lady harpist, French, circa 1890, with blue paperweight eyes, closed mouth, replacement blonde flax wig. (Sotheby's) $3,528

A large and unusual monkey playground automaton, German, circa 1925-35, hand-operated with Strauss waltz, Schuco-style monkeys play instruments, dance and jump on the see-saw and swing on a rope, 13¾in. long. (Sotheby's) $2,646

A Vichy-Triboulet Chinaman tea-drinker, French, circa 1880, with musical and clockwork mechanism housed within the torso, papier-mâché head, 27½in. (Sotheby's) $10,584

A Roullet & Decamps Astronomer & Assistant automaton, French, circa 1890, the teacher nods and turns her head, waves one hand in encouragement at her pupil as he bends to look through the telescope, 21in. (Sotheby's) $5,292

A clown ringmaster automaton German, circa 1900, with smiling composition head, the clockwork mechanism causes him to rotate, the horse to gallop and the rider to tumble in mid air, 17in. (Sotheby's) $3,352

A Lambert musical automaton of a clown on a chair playing the lute, French, circa 1890, the papier-Mâché head with inset brown glass eyes, open mouth with separate tongue, original blue and red checkered clown suit, 22in. (Sotheby's) $5,292

A Phalibois tightrope walker automaton, French circa 1865-80, with good musical mechanism housed within the ebonised base, 27½in. (Sotheby's) $5,292

A singing bird automaton, French, circa 1900, the four animated feathered birds mounted under brass case with gilt wood base, 24½in. high. (Sotheby's) $8,820

A Gustave Vichy 'Incroyable' automaton, French, circa 1890, the dandy taps his long cane, lifts his posy, and nods his head, 54cm., 21in. tall. (Sotheby's) $9,526

Shell, Cars for Hire, a good double sided, wall mounted three color enamel hanging sign, 62 x 38cm. (Bonhams & Brooks) $331

The Rolls-Royce Phantom V. A prestige publication covering the 1961 listed car, beige and blue hard bound cover opening to reveal a fly leaf with text recto. (Bonhams & Brooks) $364

A pair of sided Carl Zeiss electric side lamps, both lamps have their correct etched and ribbed front glasses, reflectors and mounting brackets. (Bonhams) $828

Two Ferrari presentation watches, one set given by Enzo Ferrari to a business associate (one by Breitling, one by Omega). (Christie's) $5,175

A sided pair of Joseph Lucas Ltd., Windtone electric horns, refurbished to a high standard, both have excellent caps and trumpets fitted with the correct fly gauze. (Bonhams & Brooks) $420

A Bowser petrol pump, repainted in Shell livery, with replica Sealed Shell globe, 246cm. high overall. (Bonhams) $759

Brooklands – A B.A.R.C. badge numbered 324 designed by F. Gordon Crosby, the eight-colored enamelled badge shows two racing cars on the banking passing beneath the Members' Bridge. (Bonhams & Brooks) $568

A Drew & Sons of Piccadilly, London, six-person picnic set, in leather case, cooked meat boxes, ceramic based sandwich box, ornate kettle and burner, Thermos ice flask, cups and saucers with matching china plates. (Bonhams) $2,760

A National Roads and Motorist's Association badge of New South Wales, nickel plating on a brass composite, the embellishment wings were a complementary fitting. (Bonhams & Brooks) $140

Nettie Rosenstein, embroidered evening bag, 1950s, champagne pink velvet barrel bag embroidered with metallic goldtone yarns, rhinestones, and gold seed beads, 8¼in. long. (Skinner) $172

Attractive early 20th century bag shaped silver evening purse with panelled engine turned decoration, green satin lined interior, chain handle, 4 x 4in., Birmingham 1918. (G A Key) $136

Hermès taupe alligator shoulder bag, 1970s, rectangular shoulder bag with front flap, circular goldtone clasp, and alligator shoulder strap 10in. long. (Skinner) $1,150

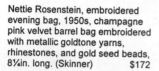

Wilardy, lucite 'Hat Box' handbag, 1950s, caramel-colored hat box shaped bag with mirrored top, 8½in. long. (Skinner) $345

Gucci, camel suede logo print shoulder bag, 1970s, with darker camel overall 'G' print, camel leather trim and piping, stamped *Made in Italy by Gucci 14* on leather lining, 14 x 13in. (Skinner) $575

Hermès, black baby alligator handbag, 1960s, with three inner compartments, gold plated hardware, and black leather lining, lining stamped *Hermes-Paris 24 F. St. Honoré*, 10½ x 8¼in. (Skinner) $1,840

Chanel navy quilted leather handbag, early 1990s, with double 'C' clasp and leather and goldtone chain link strap, burgundy leather lining, 10in. long. (Skinner) $575

A rare Elizabethan drawstring purse, date 16th century/early 17th century, worked in silks, silver and gold threads with floral patterns and applied flowerheads, leaves and tassels, in a later glazed mahogany case. (Bonhams) $5,120

Judith Leiber, python handbag, 1970s, triangular handbag with goldtone frame and bar handle, ivory grosgrain lining and optional shoulder strap, 8½ x 8 x 4in. (Skinner) $518

A mid 19th century banjo shape wheel barometer, mahogany veneered with stringing, 10in. diameter. (Woolley & Wallis) $843

A Victorian Admiral Fitzroy barometer, with glazed oak case, arched top with leafy finial, 46½in. high. (Christie's) $863

A 19th century mahogany cased wheel barometer, by James Kirby, St Neots. 40½in. high overall. (Sworders) $326

An oak Admiral Fitzroy's barometer, English, 1890s, with printed paper back, 103cm. high. (Bonhams) $431

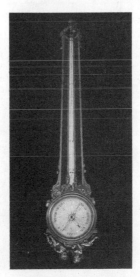

Large English mahogany and inlay wheel barometer, mid 19th century, F. Prandi & Co., Sheffield, 50in. long. (Skinner) $1,725

A George III mahogany and ebony banded stick barometer, circa 1800, with silvered scales, signed *Bate London*, 39in. high. (Christie's) $4,145

An ormolu-mounted and brass-inlaid tortoiseshell barometer, 19th century, of Régence style, the circular dial surmounted by two putti, 43½in. high. (Christie's) $4,526

A Regency rosewood and tulipwood cross-banded wheel barometer, signed *Fasana Furber A, Cheltenham*, 41¾in. high. (Christie's) $2,073

Fine late 19th century ormolu cased carriage clock barometer combination, also featuring a thermómeter and compass, the face inscribed *J & W Mitchell, Glasgow*, overall size 6¾in. tall, with leather travelling case. (G.A. Key) $1,034

Early 20th century barometer clock of rectangular form, applied with a brass carrying handle, the clock below with a circular Roman chapter ring, with adjacent aneroid barometer, 11in. (G.A. Key) $154

A late Victorian nautical clock and combined aneroid barometer, surmounted on a metallic anchor with thermometer and subsidiary 'ship's wheel' day and date dial, 23cm. high. (Bearne's) $1,231

Silver mounted cased table barometer with embossed foliate and 'C' scrolled detail, raised on ogee shaped supports with a strut back, hallmarked for Birmingham 1900, maker's mark W & G. (G.A. Key) $339

An unusual nickel plated and brass drum timepiece with barometer, French, 1880s, enamel dial with outer concentric barometer scale with twin medals awards to Bourdon and Richardson patent 1849, 5in.(Bonhams) $1,104

A holosteric barometer in an ormolu case, English, 1840s-50s, with 7cm. silvered dial and gilt metal bezel in an ormolu case naturalistically modelled as an oyster shell decorated with a limpet and worm, 13cm.(Brooks) $412

A French oval carriage timepiece/aneroid barometer, by Duverdry & Bloquel, with 4.5cm. white enamel circular dials, in a brass oval case with four turned supports, 16cm. with handle raised. (Bristol) $886

A late Victorian black slate and green variegated marble perpetual calendar mantel clock, striking on a single bell, 16½in. high. (Christie's) $1,240

A brass framed clock, thermometer, barometer and compass, in the form of a three-sided lamp on turned supports, 10½in. (Russell Baldwin & Bright) $633

A Raleigh 'Superbe' X-frame bicycle, No. 936217, 1920s gentleman's 26in. frame machine with 28in. Westwood rims, Sturmey K-type 3 speed hub, roller lever brakes, brazed on lugs, bold gear changer, metal chain case and Heron logo lamp bracket. (Bonhams) $304

The Whizzer, a motorised bicycle having a two-stroke power unit with belt-drive assisting chain-drive pedal propulsion, black enamelled frame with red flashes to headstock, circa 1950s. (Christie's) $4,370

Birrell tricycle, a circa 1900, Birrell tricycle manufactured in Markinch, Fife, complete with block type chain and stirrup front brakes, offered for restoration. (Bonhams & Brooks) $579

Mercier racing bicycle, a circa 1946 duraluminium-framed French racing bicycle by Meca Dural with five speed gears. (Bonhams & Brooks) £280 $386

1911 F.N. 2½ h.p. single cylinder motorcycle Reg. No. CL 911, introduced in 1909, the single cylinder lightweight machine was very popular and gained a reputation for reliability and build quality. (Tennants) $9,880

A Higgins racing tricycle, a 1960 lightweight tricycle built to the special order of a former President of The Tricycle Association, complete with 15 speed gears. (Bonhams & Brooks) $414

1912 Indian 1,000 cc motorcycle, Indian Red, 1901 by George Hendee, a bicycling enthusiast, auxiliary pedal starter, leaf spring front suspension, long handle bars and Bosch magneto.(Christie's) $29,900

An H.B. Smith Machine Co. 'The Star' High Bicycle patented by George Pressey in 1880, circa 1884, 51in. driving wheel and 20in. steering wheel, correct lever and ratchet driving gear on either side, but replaced leather straps. (Bonhams) $8,970

A gentleman's tricycle, circa 1896, 21in. frame with a sloping back, top tube, inch pitch dished chain wheel, fixed differential driving two 26in. wheels on a 28in. track, steering wheel 28in. with plunger front brake. (Bonhams) $469

A James Starley Sociable Coventry Lever tricycle, patented in 1877, fully restored sociable with 55in. driving wheels on a 46in. track, 20in. steering wheel, 'V' rims and black rubber tires. The pedal levers operate independently on each driving wheel. (Bonhams) $22,080

A 'Salvo' pattern high wheeled tricycle, circa 1880, 50in. driving wheels, 16in. steering wheel, radial spokes, crescent rims, chain drive to the left wheel with a combination, single balance gear and contracting brake hub installed, rack and pinion steering, three-bar triangular pedals, horizontal frame tube. (Bonhams) $13,800

A rare Sunbeam Tricycle, No. 125588, circa 1913, gentleman's machine with a 24in. frame, Roman rims, 27in. track, two speed chain-wheel gear in oilbath chain case, Abingdon No. 4 differential and brake, Sunbeam aluminium pedals, extended front guard. (Bonhams) $1,242

An English Hobby Horse, after the Johnson pattern with breast support, wrought iron rear axle hanger and direct steering, 26in. wheels apparently modern but the remainder may be late 19th century reproduction or a largely rebuilt machine. (Bonhams) $2,070

The National Arms & Ammunition Co. Ltd. of Birmingham, 'The National' Open Front Tricycle, circa 1885, original patented double-pinion differential axle, driven via a 1:1/8in. pitch chain to the near side wheel, traces of its original nickel plating, rear stabilising wheel, 52in. driving wheels and a 17in. front steering wheel. (Bonhams) $40,020

A Rensch Paris lightweight tricycle, No. 2661/323. 23.5in. Galibier style frame, 27in. Weinmann alloy rims, Mallard hub, double center pull caliper and cantilever brakes and 'GB' steel bars on an alloy stem chain 5 speed Campagnolo Deraileur driving the left hand wheel. (Bonhams) $759

A Humber Light Weight 58in. Ordinary, badged as a Humber, mid 1880s, with a radial spoked wheel with ⅝in. hollow rim, ½in. rear rim, tapered hollow backbone, deeply dropped handle bars with pear handles 6in. slotted cranks and rat-trap pedals. (Bonhams) $4,692

A Hillman Herbert & Cooper, Kangaroo front drive Safety Bicycle, circa 1886, 36in. driving and 22in. rear wheels, double chain drive to the front wheel, crescent rims, radial spokes, tapered round backbone, cranked down handle bars, foot rests and spoon brake, most component parts original. (Bonhams) $1,656

A Straight Tube tricycle, circa 1900 ladies' machine with 22in. frame with tubes closing to pinch bolt bottom bracket, 28 x 1½in. Westwood rims, 27in. track, half inch pitch chain, fixed Abingdon differential and solid fork crown, overpainted on a pitted surface. (Bonhams) $414

A Dursley Pedersen bicycle, No ?36?, circa 1911, Westwood steel 28 x 1½in. rims, Dursley Pedersen 3 speed hub with handlebar control and early extended front guard, green enamel is original, with a DP carrier and tool bag, period green Bluemels narrow pump and double dome bell. (Bonhams) $4,140

A solid tyre safety bicycle, a circa 1891 machine with 21in. diamond frame with curved seat tube, 30 x 1¼in. steering, 28 x 1¼in. driving, 25in. drop bars. (Bonhams) $2,760

Royal Enfield gents tandem, circa 1900, by the Enfield Cycle Co. Ltd. of Redditch, in fair condition. (Bonhams & Brooks) $662

A good 19th century bicycle, oak frame with steel wheels & rubber tires, leather seat, 58in. long. (Jacksons) $575

A recumbent bicycle, having 18in. Westwood rims, aluminum mudguards, cable operated brakes, six speed Deraileur style speed system, two ring chain wheel leading to a three ring sprocket. Also with manual gear change under the saddle but off-road change of drive rings. (Bonhams) $662

A rare 19th century Sterling bicycle, Elgin Bicycle Works serial, 26in. tubeless tires on wood rims, Wood handle bar grips, direct drive, no brakes, guard. Black enamel with gold pinstripes. (Jacksons) $373

A fine Schwinn cycle truck, circa 1960, large basket model, 3 speed with front and rear caliper brakes, red enamel finish, near mint original condition. (Jacksons) $287

A boneshaker bicycle with front drive, forged iron frame and adjustable wooden saddle mounted on a spring, rear brake operational on turning the handlebars, possibly by Pierre Michaux, Paris, circa 1870. (Auction Team Köln) $1,855

A Venetian parcel-gilt polychrome-decorated blackamoor table, in the rococo style, circa 1885, surmounted by a circular platform with egg and dart border, 25½in. diameter. (Christie's) $5,377

A late 20th century glass top table, supported by blackamoor type figures wearing loin cloths, the glass top, 71 x 32½in. (Christie's) $1,240

An Italian polychrome blackamoor torchere, 19th century, of a youth holding a circular cornucopiae and wearing a beret with tunic and culottes with fringes, 42in. high. (Christie's) $2,171

A pair of Venetian parcel-gilt polychrome-decorated blackamoors, in the rococo style, circa 1880, comprising a female and her male companion, each wearing a turban and an elaborate tunic, 69¼in. high. (Christie's) $8,401

A pair of Venetian parcel-gilt, mother of pearl, bone and polychrome-decorated blackamoors, circa 1880, each supporting a giant clam shell on a 'cushion' upon their shoulders, overall 85in. high. (Christie's) $47,840

A pair of Venetian polychrome decorated blackamoor torchères, 19th century, turbanned caryatid half female figures, with pierced foliate trailing stems and tripod scroll supports, tops 13½in. wide. (Christie's) $2,707

A pair of Italian parcel-gilt and polychrome blackamoor torchères, each wearing a foliate decorated jacket tied at the waist, with arms out-stretched supporting a cushion, 19th/early 20th century, 150cm. (Bearne's) $3,500

A pair of polychrome decorated blackamoors, 20th century, each turbanned boy dressed with a breastplate and skirt holding a shell, raised on an Italianate cartouche-centered plinth base, each 67in. high. (Christie's) $12,500

A pair of Venetian parcel-gilt polychrome-decorated blackamoors, in the baroque style, circa 1865, each holding a candlestick to his shoulder, wearing oriental damask costumes, 69in. high. (Christie's) $18,483

Two Vols, 'The Birds Of The British Isles And Their Eggs', by T.A. Coward. (Sworders) $73

A Doctorate diploma from the University of Urbino, handwritten on parchment, 6pp, 220 x 150cm, dated *18 October 1710*, with red wax seal, in metal case. (Stockholms AV) $793

History of the Cunard Steamship Co. extracted from the Illustrated Naval & Military magazine, engraved plates and cabin plans of ships, bound in contemporary gilt embossed morocco, February 1886. (Onslows) $82

Ian Fleming, From Russia With Love, first edition, original cloth with silver and red gun and rose motif on upper cover, dust-jacket, 8vo, Jonathan Cape, 1957. (Bonhams & Brooks) $1,160

R. Aversa a Sanseverino, Philosophia metaphysicam physicamque complectens quaestionibus contexta, Vol. 1, Rome, 1625, 888pp. (Stockholms AV) $498

P.G. Woodhouse, Mike, second impression, 12 plates by T.M.R. Whitwell, 8-page advertisements at end, neat early ownership inscription on front free endpaper, Adam & Charles Black, 1910. (Bonhams & Brooks) $1,015

Laborde (Jean-Benjamin) and others, Voyage Pittoresque de la France, illustrated with circa 472 pages of plates after Moreau, Barbier etc., Paris 1781-89, 10 volumes, folio, tree calf. (Bearne's) $7,865

'Arts Decoratifs & Industriels Modernes', eleven bound volumes, 1925, all with articles and illustrations reporting on the 1925 'L' Exposition Internationale des Artes Décoratifs et Industriels Modernes.(Christie's) $6,385

Gaston Tissandier, Application de l'Eléctricité a la Navigation Aérienne, Paris: Tremblay, 1884, uncut copy, rare offprint from bulletin de la Sociéte d'Encouragement 16pp. (Bonhams) $262

A framed and glazed full color photograph of Ali (Cassius Clay at the time), standing over Liston urging him to get up and fight, signed in gold by Ali, overall size, 28 x 24in.
(Bonhams & Brooks) $490

Williams, Richard Curtis, colored etching, the lower margin with biographical and career details, published by S.W. Fores, Piccadilly, 1820s, 12½ x 19in.
(Sotheby's) $323

Fistiana 1841, The Oracle of The Ring – Results of Prize Battles from 1700-1867, Old and New Rules of the Ring by the Editor of 'Bell's Life in London', 1841, slip case.
(Bonhams & Brooks) $476

Scriven and Gaugain, after Hennet, Robert Gregson, a fine and rare full-length stipple engraving, framed and glazed, slight creases, in good condition, 17¾ x 13¾in.
(Sotheby's) $712

Lennox Lewis shorts, a pair of red and black trim boxing shorts with the boxer's name and *SPX* embroidered to belt and side seams, autographed by the boxer and dated '94.
(Bonhams & Brooks) $336

An extremely rare on-site poster for the 'Rumble in The Jungle' Muhammad Ali v George Foreman, Kinshasa, Zaire, October 30, 1974, thought to be only 1 of 4 in existence, in yellow, green and black.
(Bonhams & Brooks) $8,120

Prominent Pugilists of Today, By J.G.B. Lynch, published Max Goschen, 1914.
(Bonhams & Brooks) $154

Sugar Ray Leonard shorts, a pair of blue and white boxing shorts, signed by Sugar Ray. Mounted in a shadow box frame, 34 x 28in. overall, with a certificate of authenticity.
(Bonhams & Brooks) $364

Geo. Hunt, after J Jackson, R.A. Tom Cribb, Champion of England, a fine full-length colored aquatint of the Champion in the ring with career details in lower margin, 1842. (Sotheby's) $712

An early Lonsdale Belt for the National Sporting Club Light Weight Championship, 1919-30, by Mappin & Webb, in 9ct gold and enamels, hallmarked London 1919. (Sotheby's) $16,200

Sullivan v Papke 1911, a rare single sheet handbill for the Boxing Match Sullivan Papke to be held in the London Palladium June 8, 1911, 10 x 4in.
(Bonhams & Brooks) $147

A silver plated circular dish with pierced rim, the centre inscribed *Welcome to Pakistan – Presented to Mr. Muhammad Ali with compliments from Muhammad Shafi Malik – Chairman – Mumtaz Bakhtawar Memorial – Trust Free Hospital – 1987 – Lahore – Pakistan,* signed on the reverse *To Paddy from Muhammad Ali 5.14.91.*
(Bonhams) $406

An early Lonsdale Belt for the British Boxing Board of Control Welterweight Championship of Great Britain, won outright by Brian Curvis, 1964, by Mappin & Webb. (Sotheby's) $7,560

Muhammad Ali and the Beatles, a black and white photograph of Ali pushing back The Beatles in the ring, Miami Beach, 18th February 1964, signed by *Ali aka Cassius Clay,* 22 x 25in. with certificate of authenticity. (Bonhams & Brooks) $710

A framed display containing an autographed scrap, Best Wishes, Joe Louis, photograph and postcard, list of champions and commemorative plaque, overall 48 x 84cm. (Bonhams) $1,450

A Viewsport fight poster, circa 1972, for Muhammad Ali v. Bob Foster, signed by Muhammad Ali and dated *5.14.92,* with a cartoon in the margin "Ali 3 times King", 30 x 40in. (Bonhams) $348

A French patinated-bronze figure of an elephant entitled 'Eléphant du Sénégal', cast by Ferdinand Barbedienne Fondeur from the model by Antoine-Louis Barye, circa 1875, 25cm. high.
(Christie's) $8,636

Two cold-painted spelter figures, each cast from a model by Lorenzl, signed in the metal and stamped *Austria*, each 27cm. high.
(Christie's) $840

A pair of French gilt- and patinated-bronze five-light candelabra, in the Louis XVI style, circa 1885, each is a scantily clad cherub, holding five vine branches, 16¾in. high.
(Christie's) $5,182

A patinated-bronze bust entitled 'Jeune Abyssinienne', cast from a model by Charles-Henri-Joseph Cordier, circa 1868, wearing a shell-necklace, 23in. high.
(Christie's) $22,050

An Art Deco green painted spelter group depicting Diana chasing a pair of deer, a spear in her hand, on oblong marble base, signed *Carlier*, 37in. wide, 16in. high.
(Andrew Hartley) $257

A bronze Neapolitan figure of Narcissus, after the Antique, the nude youth with grapes in his hair and a buckskin thrown across his shoulder, light brown/green patination, raised on leaf moulded circular base, 14in. high.
(Andrew Hartley) $1,178

A pair of French patinated-bronze figures of Day and Night, cast from the model by Edouard Drouot, circa 1900, each as a scantily clad young lady, Day standing on a fireball, 43¼in. and 35¾in. high.
(Christie's) $13,818

A French bronze-patinated spelter, equestrian group of an Arab hunter, cast from the model by Emile Guillemin, circa 1890, the hunter shown seated on his prancing horse and looking to his right, 31½in. high.
(Christie's) $3,109

A pair of French patinated-bronze figures of Renaissance soldiers, cast after the model by Victor Paillard, circa 1880, one wearing a feathered hat, the other a helmet, *each holding a lance and a sword to the side*, figures: 71¼in. high.
(Christie's) $34,545

A bronze okimono of a standing artisan, wearing waraji, and holding a pipe and kiseru-zutsu, Meiji Period, 20in. high.
(Christie's) $1,177

A P. Hugonnet figure of a javelin thrower, 1930s, brown patinated bronze, stepped rectangular black slate and ochre/white streaked marble base, 15in.
(Sotheby's) $2,347

A French bronze figure entitled 'The Neapolitan Fisherboy', cast from the model by J.B. Carpeaux, late 19th century, 13¾in. high.
(Christie's) $3,763

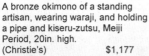

A gilded and cold painted bronze figure cast from a model by Lorenzl, young girl dancer poised on tiptoe with leg extended, 50cm. high.
(Wintertons) $3,882

A pair of bronze Furietti centaurs after the Antique, modern, the pair cast in bronze, one bearded, the other with a satyr face, on shaped bases, inscribed *F De Luca m* 163cm. high.
(Sotheby's) $11,247

A bronze figure of L'Amour after Antoine-Denis Chaudet (1763-1810) French, circa 1860, the winged naked boy is kneeling down and holds a rose in one hand and a butterfly in the other, 59.5cm. high.
(Sotheby's) $9,373

Antoine-Louis Barye, French (1795-1875), Eléphant du Sénégal Chargeant, signed, dark brown patina, 2¾ x 3¾in.
(Sotheby's) $6,198

A J. Lormier figure of a Venetian reveller, 1920s, cold painted, silvered and gilt bronze and ivory, black slate and brown onyx base, 33.5cm. (Sotheby's) $4,333

A leaded bronze cooking pot, 17th century, the tapering slightly bellied body issuing twin angular-shaped handles, with central reeded band, 11in. diameter.
(Christie's) $770

Heinz Mueller gilt bronze of a girl reading, circa 1930, signed, 6in. high. (Skinner) $373

An Edouard Marcel Sandoz figure of a rabbit, executed by Susse Frères, Paris, 1920-30, brown patinated bronze, 2in. (Sotheby's) $1,806

A bronze figural dish by Peter Tereszczuk, of irregular shape surmounted by a maiden and a child, signed and monogrammed, 6in. high. (Andrew Hartley) $157

A very large lacquered bronze figure of a Luohan, Ming Dynasty (1368-1644), the emaciated figure seated stoically on rockwork with one arm resting on his raised left knee, the bronze lacquered a purplish-brown, 33½in. high. (Christie's) $27,600

Raymond Léon Rivoire, cast by Susse Frères, woman and dog, 1930s, modelled as a naked female figure in mid-step walking her dog, 55cm. high. (Sotheby's) $8,570

A bronze trotting stallion, probably Augsburg, early 17th century, inspired by Pietro Tacca, with long tousled mane, the forelock secured with a rosette, the studded horseshoes, light brown patina, 8in. high. (Sotheby's) $51,520

Pierre-Jules Mène, French (1810-1879), Vainqueur du Derby (The Derby Winner), signed, dark brown patina, 16¾ x 17in. (Sotheby's) $8,750

A pair of bronze vases, the first signed *Kyoto no ju Saneyoshi saku,* the other *Miyabe Saneyoshi Koreo Tsukuru,* Meiji Period (late 19th century), 10½in. high. (Christie's) $10,246

Gerdago, exotic dancer, 1920s, cold painted bronze and ivory figure of a dancer wearing a pointed hat and embroidered jacket, 31.5cm. (Sotheby's) $8,073

Rodney Stone, F.M. A bronze figure of a standing bulldog, signed to base, 15cm. high, on black marble plinth. (Bristol) $338

Cast bronze clad hands of Abraham Lincoln, originals by Leonard Wells Volk (American, 1828-1895), document damaged, 6½in. long. (Eldred's) $440

An Art Deco patinated bronze figure group, cast from a model by D.H. Chiparus, incised signature to base, 49cm. high.(Christie's) $700

A pair of bronze figures of maidens and cherubs, late 19th or early 20th century, after Mathurin Moreau (1822-1912), one shown as a huntress, the other dancing, waisted socles and later plinths, 19in. high.(Christie's) $6,948

A French gilt and patinated-bronze paste-inset and enamelled figural reliquary, by Schektel-Soleau, Paris, circa 1890, as two medieval grooms supporting a gothic-style glazed case inset with paste and enamel, with padded interior, 23¼in. high. (Christie's) $17,250

A pair of late 19th century French bronze figures of Bacchanalian putti, each supporting a raised platform and seated upon a circular rouge marble pedestal, 44cm. (Bearne's) $1,884

A French bronze model of a terrier, late 19th century, shown resting on its front legs and with tail swept over the back, 18in. long. (Christie's) $7,360

A pair of 19th century bronze figures of Mercury and Iris after Giambologna, raised on cylindrical plinth, embossed with putti scenes, 33in. high. (Andrew Hartley) $1,694

An Art Deco black patinated bronze elephant, cast from a model by P. Blanc, signed in the bronze No.4, 34cm. high.(Christie's) $1,487

An Art Deco gilt and cold-painted bronze figure cast from a model by Lorenzl, signed in the bronze, 39cm. high.
(Christie's) $5,401

A Japanese bronze figure, of a man seated smoking a pipe, wearing a short coat and knee length trousers, late Meiji, circa 1900, 39.5cm. overall.
(Tennants) $1,570

A patinated bronze clock on a striated brown and black onyx base, 23.5cm. high.
(Christie's) $490

'Vedette', a gilt and patinated bronze figure, cast from a model by Chiparus, incised signature to onyx base, 80cm. high.
(Christie's) $12,255

A Japanese bronze figure of a cock pheasant, modelled standing with silver, enamel and gilded bronze feathers, signed, Meiji period, 10¼in. wide.
(Andrew Hartley) $3,770

'Balancing', a bronze and ivory figure cast from the model by Ferdinand Preiss, 1930s, the female dancer in diamond-patterned leotard and tights, 14¾in. high. (Christie's) $12,558

A bronze imperial gallon measure, for West Riding County Council, Skipton District, inscribed and dated to the base *Grave & Co, London 505, 1904.* (Christie's) $956

An Austrian cold painted bronze model of a rabbit, late 19th or early 20th century, Bergman factory, stamped to the underside with a *B* within an urn and numbered *1215*, 6¼in. long.(Christie's) $4,606

A gilt bronze figure cast from a model by Chiparus, signed in the bronze and stamped marks, 34.5cm. diameter.
(Christie's) $384

A bronze model of a baboon, early 20th century, shown seated, the base inscribed *G.Rigbetti*, 12¼in. high. (Christie's) $5,414

A cold painted bronze model of a retriever, probably Austrian, late 19th century, the dog shown standing, 13in. long. (Christie's) $2,199

A silvered and patinated bronze figure of Puck, late 19th century, shown seated on a toadstool, inscribed *C.Curry Sc. 1883*, 20¾in. high. (Christie's) $6,430

A pair of gilt and patinated bronze candlesticks, parts 19th century, with foliate nozzles above openwork collars hung with graduating faceted glass beads, supported on the heads of storks on naturalistically cast bases, 15in. high. (Christie's) $1,151

A Tokyo School bronze model of Hotei, 19th century, wearing long open robes revealing his large belly, holding a staff over his shoulder, 10¼in. high. (Christie's) $1,809

A pair of Restauration bronze and Siena marble reversible candlesticks, first quarter 19th century, the oviform vase-shaped bodies with twin panther headed handles, 11¼in. high. (Christie's) $4,487

A French gilt bronze model of a seated man, late 19th century, the seated bearded figure in classical dress holding a board and a pair of compasses, 17½in. high. (Christie's) $2,270

A pair of bronze vases, Mieji period, late 19th century, inlaid in silver and gilt, with longtailed birds, among cherry blossoms, the foliate everted necks with arabesques, 15in. high. (Christie's) $2,467

An Austrian cold painted bronze of an Arab on a camel, late 19th or early 20th century, the group mounted on a green variegated marble veneered plinth, 12½in. high overall. (Christie's) $2,961

A French bronze bust of a lady, late 19th century, after Houdon, the figure shown partially draped, the base inscribed *Houdon* 18in. high.
(Christie's) $1,184

A French bronze figure of a cupid, late 19th century, shown recumbent on a naturalistic base and playing with a butterfly, on a stained wood plinth, 17in. wide.
(Christie's) $1,635

A bronze model of a camel, late 19th century, after a model by Antoine Louis Barye, shown standing on a naturalistic base, inscribed *Barye*, 26.3cm. high.
(Christie's) $7,445

An Austrian cold painted bronze figure of a dancing girl, early 20th century, Bergman foundry, the figure shown holding an articulated billowing dress lifting to reveal the nude body underneath, the reverse inscribed *Nam Greb*, 13¾in. high.
(Christie's) $8,290

A pair of parcel silvered and gilt bronze candlesticks, first half 19th century, after a design executed by William Bateman II for Rundell, Bridge & Co., 7¼in. high.
(Christie's) $2,180

A bronze bust of a maiden, late 19th century, the figure shown with crescent moon to her hair, mounted on a waisted rouge griot marble socle and square section plinth, inscribed *P.Gasq*, 24½in. high overall.
(Christie's) $3,046

A pair of French gilt bronze vases and covers, circa 1880, Barbédienne foundry, the covers with berried finials, the ovoid bodies cast in relief with classical figures, 16½in. high.
(Christie's) $5,076

A Continantal bronze bust of a Roman Emperor, 20th century, possibly Hadrian, shown garlanded and semi-cuirassed, on an associated white marble socle, 28½in. high.
(Christie's) $4,113

A pair of French gilt bronze four light candelabra, 20th century, the nozzles and branches cast overall with foliage, emanating from cornucopiae, held aloft by winged cherubs on foliate cast bases, 21in. high. (Christie's) $822

A William IV rosewood and mother of pearl inlaid tea caddy, circa 1835, of sarcophagus form, with twin ring handles and gadrooned feet, 14¾in. wide.
(Christie's) $4,360

Blue and gold painted Tramp Art box, America, circa 1890-1910, the hinged top with cast brass pull opens to a mounted pincushion, on base with two concealed short drawers, 14in. wide.
(Skinner) $805

A Batavian silver metal and tortoiseshell veneered tea caddy, late 18th century, of rectangular form with domed cover, with foliate etched mounts overall, 8¾in. wide.
(Christie's) $5,790

English George III fruitwood apple-form tea caddy, late 18th/early 19th century, hinged lid with ebonized stem, shaped ovoid metal escutcheon, with foil lined interior, 5in. high. (Skinner) $2,530

A George III Scottish satinwood and marquetry inlaid tea caddy, last quarter 18th century, of oval outline, with floral marquetry to the top and front, 6in. wide.
(Christie's) $1,500

Federal walnut and yellow pine inlaid box, Southern states, early 19th century, the hinged top outlined in stringing with ovolo corners, 13¼in. high.
(Skinner) $4,830

Paint decorated doctor's box, Maine, 19th century, the box with copper and brass trim, rope handles, painted green with red and white eagle, flag, and shield motifs, 14in. wide.
(Skinner) $1,092

An Edwardian oak stationery cabinet, the fall front revealing a tooled leather slope, with brass carrying handles, 44cm.
(Bearne's) $640

A mid Victorian tortoiseshell veneered tea caddy, mid 19th century, with stepped front and pagoda style cover, inset with mother-of-pearl escutcheon, 7¼in. wide. (Christie's) $3,257

Mahogany inlaid two-drawer storage box, America, 19th century, dovetailed construction, the lift top lid decorated with exotic wood star inlay at the centre and star points at the corners, 10 x 13 x 20in.
(Skinner) $805

A George III white metal-mounted olivewood tea-caddy, crossbanded overall and inlaid with boxwood lines, the rectangular hinged top with foliate loop handle, 9in. wide.
(Christie's) $1,835

A Victorian brass spice box, of rectangular form, with later engraved decoration to the cover, the interior with divided trays, 11½in. wide. (Christie's) $382

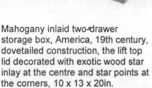

A George III rolled paper tea caddy, circa 1800, of navette outline, decorated overall with gilded rolls in a foliate design, the interior with subsidiary cover, 7½in. wide.
(Christie's) $2,907

Burlwood and brass inlay boxed cordial set, late 19th/ early 20th century, opening to interior fitted for two decanters and ten cordial glasses, together with decanters and thirteen miscellaneous cordials, 10¼in. wide. (Skinner) $115

A Federal inlaid and veneered mahogany tea caddy, Massachusetts, 1790-1800, the rectangular hinged, inlaid and moulded top opening to a conforming case with a diamond-shaped ivory escutcheon and, 10¼in. wide.
(Christie's) $19,550

George III fruitwood apple-form tea caddy, England, late 18th century, with oval metal escutcheon and upright stem, hinged lid, lacking lock, 4¾in. high.
(Skinner) $1,265

A William IV tortoiseshell and mother of pearl tea-caddy, of octagonal shape, with raised hinged top, on ivory bun feet, the interior with ivory-banded borders and a lidded compartment, 4¼in. wide.
(Christie's) $2,502

An early Victorian tortoiseshell veneered tea caddy, of rectangular form with pagoda cover, the top and front panel inlaid with flowers and foliage in mother of pearl, 8in. wide.
(Christie's) $4,724

An early Victorian Tunbridgeware bird's eye maple tea caddy, by Thomas Barton, the cover inlaid with specimen woods in cube pattern, the body with foliate mosaic banding, 7¾in. wide.
(Christie's) $1,316

Late Victorian walnut stationery box, the sloping front with two doors enclosing fitted interior with pen trays, letter rack and perpetual calendar etc, 12½in.
(G.A. Key) $493

Victorian walnut coffer formed caddy box, applied with brass strapwork and hinges, escutcheon etc, void interior, 9½in.
(G.A. Key) $181

Victorian mahogany tea caddy of sarcophagus form, the interior fitted with two lidded compartments, applied on either side with ring handles, mother of pearl escutcheon, 13½in.
(G.A. Key) $181

A Victorian stationery casket, calamander veneered and brass mounted. the domed hinged cover reveals a partitioned interior, 9½iin. wide.(Woolley & Wallis) $294

A 19th century tortoiseshell tea caddy of sarcophagus form with bowed fascia and pewter stringing, hinged lid opening to reveal two compartments, 8in. wide.
(Andrew Hartley) $2,800

An early Victorian sarcophagus shape tea chest, veneered in macassar ebony, the hinged lid with a central tablet and flared sides, inlaid in mother of pearl marquetry, 14in.(Woolley & Wallis) $431

A 19th century coramandel stationery casket of oblong form with domed lid, and with applied green agate studs, and a blotter to match. (Andrew Hartley) $364

A Continental travelling casket, the exterior painted red in Vernis Martin style, with brass fleur de lis design strapwork and side handles, the hinged front and lid with a brass clasp and escutcheon, 15¼in.
(Woolley & Wallis) $1,756

A German beech and wrought iron bound casket, 17th century, the strapwork modelled with lanceolate leaf ornament, (the casket currently locked, with no key), 9½in. wide.
(Christie's) $1,646

A late Regency tortoiseshell veneered mother of pearl inlaid tea caddy, second quarter 19th century, the interior with ivory banding, 12in. wide. (Christie's) $6,580

Carved and sealing wax inlaid trinket box, America, 1850, sliding lid on coffin-shaped box with two carved hearts extending from one end, various inlay decoration, 8in. long. (Skinner) $3,105

An Anglo Indian horn veneered casket, early 19th century, with stepped angled cover and circular raised finial, the sandalwood lined interior formerly fitted, 15in. wide. (Christie's) $2,743

A large inlaid yew tree shoe snuff box or box, 19th century, the toe with carved ivory scroll terminal, the top inlaid with a bird, with hinged cover to the interior recess, 25cm. long. (Christie's) $4,571

A mid Victorian gilt and mother of pearl inlaid papier mâché tea caddy, circa 1860, of bombé sarcophagus form, the rising cover decorated with gilt trailing vines and inlaid with mother of pearl, 13½in. wide. (Bonhams) $647

19th century rosewood large tea caddy of sarcophagus form, the interior fitted with two lidded compartments, (bowl missing); mother of pearl escutcheon, 13½in. (G.A. Key) $229

Vintage wicker cased picnic set, containing original cutlery, enamelled plates and fittings etc, 22in. (G.A. Key) $400

A fine, early Victorian carved ebony casket with scroll carved bracket feet, fitted with a Chubb lock, 14¼in. wide. (David Lay) $659

English bird's-eye maple and inlaid Regency sarcophagus-shaped tea caddy, early 19th century, inlaid with ebonised banding to perimeter and with scrolled banding to front, 12⅛in. long. (Skinner) $690

An Anglo Indian Vizigapatam ivory veneered writing slope, early 19th century, the sandalwood interior with divided compartments about the velvet covered slope, decorated overall with penwork foliate banding, 15¼in. wide. (Christie's) $2,011

A painted and decorated paper-mounted poplar utility box, New England, circa 1810-1830, of oblong octagonal form, the hinged lid decorated with two lions, ribbons and floral motifs in polychrome, 12in. long. (Sotheby's) $1,725

English brass-bound oyster veneered walnut lock box, fitted with Bramah locks, with fitted interior of a well and small drawers, 13in. wide. (Skinner) $863

An early 19th century Colonial stained horn sewing box of sarcophagus form with gadrooned finial on domed lid, fitted interior, ribbed sides and bun feet, 11¾in. wide.(Andrew Hartley) $2,512

A Continental travelling casket, veneered in rosewood with gilt brass strapwork and side handles, the interior with a well above a nest of drawers, 14.5in. (Woolley & Wallis) $1,277

A George III mahogany and marquetry tea-caddy, the rectangular hinged top crossbanded and inlaid with an oval fan medallion, 19cm. wide.
(Christie's) $1,083

A Regency penwork tea-caddy, decorated overall with foliate panels and lines, the stepped rectangular hinged top centred by two dancing figures in a landscape, 7¼in. wide.
(Christie's) $2,502

A George III satinwood and marquetry tea-caddy, crossbanded overall and inlaid with fruitwood lines, the canted rectangular hinged top centred by a vase within an oval, 7½in. wide.
(Christie's) $1,669

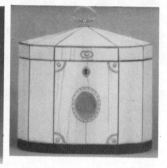

A small needlework casket, the lid worked in coloured silks, chenille and coiled metal thread with a bird perched in a tree on hilly ground, 5in. high, English, 17th century.
(Christie's) $1,208

A George III tortoiseshell and ivory tea-caddy, the canted rectangular domed top with white-metal handle, 4¼in. wide.
(Christie's) $8,009

A George III ivory and tortoiseshell tea-caddy, the ten-sided pointed hinged top, enclosing a tortoiseshell-banded interior with twin divisions with covers, 15cm. wide. (Christie's) $7,508

Bird's-eye maple and inlaid walnut tiered, one drawer, sewing box, America, mid-19th century, 9½in. wide. (Skinner) $373

An unusual tortoiseshell veneered tea caddy, first half 19th century, of hexagonal outline with rising cover, the panels each with impressed foliate decoration about an inlaid silver plated satyr mask, 6¾in. high.
(Christie's) $9,448

An early Victorian mother of pearl tea-caddy, circa 1840, of rectangular form with a pagoda-shaped hinged top, on bun feet, the interior with ivory-banded borders, 18cm. wide.
(Christie's) $3,003

126

Blue painted pine oval two-handled storage box, America, 19th century, 26¾in. wide.
(Skinner) $1,495

Wallpaper covered hat box, America, 19th century, decorated with birds amidst foliage and an architectural view, 16¾in. long.
(Skinner) $488

A good 19th century Tunbridge Ware rectangular tea caddy, probably by Henry Hollamby, the slightly domed lid inlaid with view of Eridge Castle, 14in. wide, circa 1860. (Canterbury) $1,188

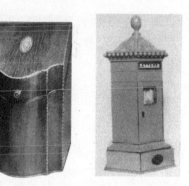

A Victorian oak and brass mounted hall letter box, in the form of a panelled outside door, 13in. high.
(George Kidner) $1,815

Pair of George III inlaid mahogany knife boxes, 19th century, of typical form, inlaid with shells, with fitted interior, 14¾in. high.
(Skinner) $2,645

A Victorian patent oak letter box of hexagonal section, the pagoda top carved with acanthus and with a bud finial, 23in. with associated wall bracket.
(David Lay) $6,240

A George III satinwood tea caddy of oblong from with crossbanding and string inlay, hinged lid revealing fitted interior with two compartments and a glass bowl, 12in. wide.
(Andrew Hartley) $384

An Edwardian walnut writing slope/stationery box, the well-fitted interior with ivory ruler, maroon leather blotter, inset falls, two inkwells, pen rest and stationery racks, 42.5cm. wide.
(Bristol) $656

A German brass Minnekästchen of rectangular form, the cover and sides incised with townscape and portraits, the underside with a hunting scene, 3¾in. wide, the locking mechanism shooting four bolts. (Christie's) $3,565

A William IV tortoiseshell tea-caddy, the top and front inlaid with mother of pearl scrolls and flowerheads, scrolling foliage and birds, 7½in. wide. (Christie's) $5,006

A 19th century walnut stationery box of oblong form with domed lid, pierced gilt metal mounts with opaque glass studs, 8in. wide. (Andrew Hartley) $196

A red cinnabar circular box and cover, carved with a total of nine dragons, divided by key-fret patterns at each rim, Qing Dynasty 11in. diameter. (Christie's) $3,925

A polychrome oak wall-hanging rush-light or candle-box, North European, possibly Icelandic, 18th century, the sliding cover to the front carved in relief with a bird perched on a leafy bough, 15½in. high. (Christie's) $7,130

A pair of Federal inlaid mahogany knife boxes, American or English, 1795-1810, each with a slant lid with an outset serpentine front centered by a shell-within-oval inlaid reserve and banded edges, 9¼in. wide. (Christie's) $12,650

A 19th century artist's box in flame figured mahogany having crossbanded lid enclosing fitted interior and embossed inner lid depicting gothic buildings, J. Newman's Manufactory, 24 Soho Square, 12in. wide. (G.A. Key) $1,670

A George III parquetry tea caddy, early 19th century, of rectangular form with loop handle and on bun feet, the panels with geometric fruitwood inlay, 10½in. wide. (Christie's) $3,864

A Regency rosewood and walnut inlaid tea caddy, first quarter 19th century, of sarcophagus form, with loop handles to the sides, with domed section to the top inlaid with scrolling designs, and within a gadrooned border, 8in. wide. (Christie's) $329

Victorian walnut unusual stationery box, inlaid with boxwood neo-classical designs, with similar stringing, with fitted interiors, 12½in. (G A Key) $566

A 19th century French tea caddy, rectangular with bowed ends, decorated with an off white lacquer, the cover applied cut and polished steel plate and handle, 6.5in. (Woolley & Wallis) $218

An unusual late Regency rosewood and brass inlaid tea caddy, some damage, 17cm. wide. (Bonhams & Brooks) $600

A Near Eastern tortoiseshell and mother of pearl veneered table casket, possibly 18th century, the sloping cover and sides decorated in geometric and stylised foliate patterns, on bracket feet, 14in. wide. (Christie's) $1,961

A 19th century coromandel writing box, hinged lid revealing fitted interior and hinged slope with mother o' pearl and brass marquetry inlay, 10½in. wide. (Andrew Hartley) $240

Italian inlaid lap desk, third quarter 19th century, the front sliding writing surface inlaid with depiction of the prize medal for the 1862 London International Exhibition, 20in. wide. (Skinner) $18,400

Liquor chest, England, late 18th century, the two-handled iron mounted oak chest opens to reveal a compartmented interior, 17⅝in. wide. (Skinner) $460

A George III harewood and marquetry box, of octagonal shape, the hinged lid inlaid with a central oyster veneer within a swagged cartouche with thuya panels, 10¾in. diameter. (Christie's) $4,491

A late George III blonde tortoiseshell rectangular single tea caddy with slight shaped top inlaid with pewter stringings and on turned ivory bun feet, 4¾ x 3¼ x 4¼in. (Canterbury) $1,056

A Victorian mahogany paint box, the fitted interior with a trade label for Reeves & Son 113 Cheapside London, fitted interior, the frieze drawer with sunken brass handle, 9¼in. (Woolley & Wallis) $386

A William IV rosewood portable bookstand, the spindle gallery with side handles above a frieze drawer, 17in.
(Woolley & Wallis) $2,415

Antique tôle-decorated tin box, 5¼in. x 9in.
(Eldred's) $440

A Regency tortoiseshell tea-caddy, the rectangular casket with rounded corners inlaid along the edges with silvered-banding, 7½in. wide.
(Christie's) $3,337

Antique leather-covered brass-studded document box, painted black, with brass label of Washington Bank of Boston, MA., brass handle, 8in. long.
(Eldred's) $242

An early Victorian tortoiseshell veneered and pewter strung tea caddy, circa 1845, of rectangular cavo-convex outline, two division interior, 8in. wide.
(Christie's) $2,760

A Victorian japanned table desk, the lid forming a slope, painted oval floral reserve on gilt strapwork, 12in. (Russell Baldwin & Bright)
                    $478

A Victorian burr walnut tea caddy, of waisted oblong from with brass loop handle and pierced scrolling foliate brass mounts, 10¾ wide.
(Andrew Hartley) $793

A rare and important inlaid mahogany and poplar Bible box with daguerreotype of the maker, probably New York, circa 1850, inlaid with a depiction of a Bible, 13½in. wide.
(Sotheby's) $7,475

A good 19th century Tunbridge Ware writing slope, the split top inlaid with castle and floral panel enclosing two inkwells, pen tray and three other compartments, 33cm. wide. (Bristol) $1,078

An early Victorian tortoiseshell veneered casket, circa 1850, the pagoda shaped top inlaid with a floral panel of mother of pearl ornament, 8½in. wide.
(Christie's) $1,379

A mid-Victorian black, gold, red and green japanned papier mâché tea caddy, decorated overall with foliate patterns, the canted rectangular domed top enclosing two lidded compartments, 9½in. wide. (Christie's) $883

An early Victorian Tunbridge inlaid rosewood writing slope, the hinged fall front with inlaid floral border enclosing central panel of Battle Abbey Cloisters, 14in., circa 1840.
(Dreweatt Neate) $717

A George II mahogany bottle-boxes, with twelve square wells and a ropetwist edge, 23¾in. wide. (Christie's) $4,444

Burled walnut parquetry lap desk on stand. (Remmey) $300

19th century Tunbridgeware writing box, the slope front with a panel of Tonbridge Castle and another of flowers, 15½in. (Ewbank) $1,212

A Victorian japanned blotter, the gilt border and central rose branch inlaid with mother of pearl, 9in. (Russell Baldwin & Bright) $165

An ivory inlaid hardwood table cabinet, Indo-Portuguese, 17th century, with twin iron handles to the sides, with ivory line inlay and floral motifs overall, 14½in. wide. (Christie's) $4,586

Georgian burl walnut and inlaid tea caddy, England, late 18th/early 19th century, of rectangular form with canted corners and boxwood stringing, 7½in. long. (Skinner) $1,092

A Federal style mahogany humidor, 19th/20th century, of inlaid mahogany with two drawers and brass hardware. (Sotheby's) $1,150

A silvered metal mounted burr wood box, possibly Scottish, late 18th century, the cover carved in relief with a figure on horseback attacking a lion or dragon, 3¾in. wide. (Christie's) $695

A George II brass-inlaid and mounted amboyna casket, inlaid overall to each corner with a foliage scroll, the hinged rectangular top with carrying-handle, 10½in. wide. (Christie's) $13,348

Antique English tortoiseshell tea caddy, with mother of pearl inlaid floral decoration, ivory feet, retains two original interior covers, 5in. high. (Eldred's) $1,540

Large Shaker maple and pine oval storage box, America, mid-19th century, nine-lap construction, old surface, 19¾ x 15¼ x 10¾in. (Skinner) $747

A 19th century mahogany sarcophagus shaped tea caddy fitted with two plated cylindrical lidded tea canisters and similar mixing bowl. (G.A. Key) $2,353

Green painted covered circular carrier, possibly Nantucket, Massachusetts, 19th century, 9in. diameter. (Skinner) $431

A French gilt copper-mounted ivory-veneered coffret, early 16th century, the sarcophagus-form lid fitted with secret drawer, 5 x 6¾ x 3⅞in. (Sotheby's) $6,900

Blue painted firkin, C.&A. Wilder, South Hingham, Massachusetts, 19th century, 10in. high. (Skinner) $747

A Georgian mahogany and line inlaid knife box, the hinged sloping lid with oval silver-mounted escutcheon, 12¼in. high. (Christie's) $349

French gilt metal cased travelling tea set, early 20th century, by Maquet, comprising two teapots, four spoons, tongs, burner, tea caddy and two Nymphenburg porcelain teacups and saucers. (Skinner) $518

Matched set of three New England ovoid pantry boxes, 19th century, in ash, unpainted old brown colour, 8½in, 9in. and 9½in. long. (Eldred's) $341

A Nuremberg gilt brass and copper engraved jewellery casket, by Michel Mann, circa 1600, 1¾ x 2⅞ x 2in. (Sotheby's) $7,475

Interesting Continental marquetry tea caddy, circa 1870, with faceted sides and corners, inlaid with scenes of putti at various pursuits, 4¼in. high. (Skinner) $230

An early 19th century 7in. tortoiseshell double compartment tea caddy with fluted front, the hinged cover engraved with initials, on bun feet. (Anderson & Garland) $1,130

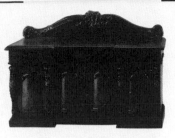

George III chequer strung mahogany knife box, 19th century, now converted to letter box, serpentine form, 13in. high. (Skinner) $431

A rare and unusual Victorian mahogany tea caddy, circa 1840, in the form of a miniature pedestal sideboard, the galleried back above a frieze with a drawer and mock cupboards, 13in. wide. (Christie's) $3,840

A George III serpentine mahogany knife box, with brass carrying handle and lock plate, 13¼in. high. (Andrew Hartley) $439

A Japanese black and gold lacquer table cabinet, fitted with an arrangement of drawers and compartments, Meiji period, 43cm. (Bearne's) $648

A pair of George III mahogany urn shaped cutlery boxes, with string inlay, fitted interior, circa 1780, 26in. high. (Andrew Hartley) $4,082

An Anglo-Indian stag antler workbox of sarcophagus form, the hinged lid opening to reveal a fitted interior, Vizagapatam, circa 1825, 13½in. (Hy. Duke & Son) $1,520

A shagreen covered lap desk, of rectangular form, the slightly domed cover enclosing various covered compartments and glass inkpots, 12¼in. wide.(Christie's) $535

A mid Victorian amboyna writing box, the rectangular lid enclosing a satinwood interior fitted for stationery, 17in. wide. (Bonhams) $827

A rare Charles II stumpwork casket, English, 17th century, the hinged rectangular top opening to a well, 11¾in. wide. (Sotheby's) $2,875

Leica I(a) no. 20621, black, nickel fittings, with a Leitz Elmar f/3.5 50mm. lens and a Fodis (meter) rangefinder, in an ever ready case. (Christie's) $812

Photo-Stereo-Binocle no. 1731, C.P. Goerz, Germany; 45 x 107mm., 75mm. lenses nos. 107688 and 109272, in maker's fitted leather case. (Christie's) $2,708

Leica no. 420821, black, chrome fittings, synchronised, strap-lugs, with a Leitz chrome Elmar 5cm. f/3.5 lens. (Christie's) $181

Micro Technical Camera No. 14366, MPP, England; 5 x 4in. with a Schneider Xenar f/4.5 150mm. lens in a Synchro-Compur shutter, Polaroid back and double darkslides. (Christie's) $658

Stereoscopic Reflex No. M1333, Marion & Co. Ltd., London; 6¾ x 3¼in., internal septum, focusing screen, a pair of Anastigmat f/ 12.5 224mm. lenses, five double darkslides.(Christie's) $2,632

Le Parvo Model G No. 2369, André Debrie, Paris; 35mm., polished-metal body, with a Zeiss/Krauss Tessar f/4.5 15cm. lens no. 132609, in maker's leather case. (Christie's) $658

Field camera, Billcliff, Manchester; half-plate, mahogany and brass, maroon leather bellows, with a Perken, Son & Rayment brass-bound lens, circular lensboard and two mahogany darkslides, in a canvas case. (Christie's) $312

Six-20 Brownie Minor camera, Kodak Ltd., England; 620-rollfilm with plastic lens surround (cracked and repaired) marked Six-20 Brownie-Minor. (Christie's) $164

A 5 x 4in. wet-collodion, mahogany-body, sliding-box camera with brass fittings, removable focusing screen and a Ross, London brass bound focusing lens no. 11823. (Christie's) $1,974

Magnar Camera, Carl Zeiss, Jena; 9 x 12cm., with focal-plane shutter and a Carl Zeiss, Jena Fern-Objectiv f/10 80cm. lens, and six double darkslides, in maker's fitted leather case.
(Christie's) $1,972

An E.B. Koopman Presto camera, American, circa 1896, with rotating front shutter. (Bonhams) $470

Leica M3 no. 777947, chrome, doublewind, with instruction booklet, a Leitz Summicron f/2 5cm. lens no. 1279445, Leica-meter M, in maker's ever ready case.
(Christie's) $1,986

Miragioscope camera obscura, Charles Chevalier, Paris; a collapsable boxform reflex camera obscura, the exterior covered in green paper with gilt cross-hatch decoration.
(Christie's) $11,515

Rolleiflex 3.5F No. 2257815, 120-rollfilm, with meter, a Heidosmat f/2.8 75mm. viewing lens, and a Carl Zeiss Planar f/3.5 75mm. taking lens, in maker's ever ready case. (Christie's) $295

Instantograph 1890 field camera, J. Lancaster & Sons, Birmingham; quarter-plate brass and mahogany, with a Lancaster brass bound lens; a Lancaster Condensor enlarger.
(Christie's) $213

Frena De luxe no. 13233, R. & J. Beck, London; quarter-plate, pigskin-covered body, gilt fittings, with lens. (Christie's) $790

Movikon 16 No. W.94750, Zeiss Ikon AG, Dresden; 16mm., with various Carl Zeiss, Jena Sonnar and Tele-Tessar lenses, lenshoods and instruction booklet, in maker's fitted leather case.
(Christie's) $658

Cinematographic camera, No. 265, Moy & Bastie, England; 35mm. wood-body, brass fittings, (lacks lens) and two wood film magazines.
(Christie's) $1,974

Fag no. 29, bright nickel top and base plates and with a Voomp f/3.5 50mm. lens, the focusing lever numbered 14-6.
(Christie's) $1,144

Hasselblad 1600f no. CH13368 Hasselblad, Sweden; 120-rollfilm, with a Zeiss-Opton Tessar T f/ 2.8 80mm. lens no. 587907.
(Christie's) $1,219

Hansa Canon camera with pop-up viewfinder, the lens mount numbered 263, with a Nippon Kogaku Nikkor f/ 3.5 50mm. lens.
(Christie's) $9,372

A Kodak No. 1 camera by Eastman, with Rapid Rectilinear 1:9/57mm. lens, circa 1890.
(Auction Team Köln) $1,034

Alpa Reflex model 6c no. 46983, Pignons S.A; black, with a Kern Macr-Switar f/ 1.8 50mm. lens no. 1020656, in maker's ever ready case. (Christie's) $4,223

Reid III no. P3109, Reid & Sigrist, England; chrome, with a Taylor-Hobson Anastigmat 2in. f/ 2 lens no.33024. (Christie's) $1,320

A Sanderson Regular camera, leather covered with polished mahogany interior and brass mountings, with Dallmeyer Stigmatic Ser.II No. 2 lens.
(Auction Team Köln) $330

A Wonder Photo Cannon by the Chicago Ferrotype Co., for round 30mm. diameter ferrotypes, with copy of patent, 1908.
(Auction Team Köln) $1,021

Sanderson hand camera no. 16967 Houghtons Ltd., London; half-plate, with red-leather bellows and a Ross Homocentric f/6.3 7inch lens no. 61421. (Christie's) $207

A Kodak Pupille camera with Schneider 1:2,4,5cm. lens and Compur shutter, in original case, 1935.
(Auction Team Köln) $264

A Lizars Challenge Stereo B camera for 7.7 x 16.6cm. prints, by Lizars, Glasgow, in tropical wood case.
(Auction Team Köln) $449

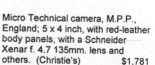

Micro Technical camera, M.P.P., England; 5 x 4 inch, with red-leather body panels, with a Schneider Xenar f. 4.7 135mm. lens and others. (Christie's) $1,781

Leica II Luxus no. 94553, lizard-skin body covering and a Leitz nickel 'push-push' Elmar f/ 3.5 50mm. lens. (Christie's) $13,024

Black Expo camera, Expo Camera Co., New York; with viewfinder. (Christie's) $842

Leica 72 [18 x 24] no. 357167, chrome, swinging viewfinder mask and a Leitz chrome Elmar 3.5cm. f/3.5 lens.
(Christie's) $20,838

Hologon Ultrawide no. VK 10-29, Zeiss Ikon, Germany; with a Carl Zeiss Hologon f/ 8 15mm. lens, specially prepared for use in very cold temperatures.
(Christie's) $7,389

Ergo camera no. 460570, Contessa-Nettel, Germany; 4½ x 6cm., with a Carl Zeiss, Jena Tessar f/4.5 5.5cm. lens no. 542147.
(Christie's) $2,061

Le Photosphère no. 1854, Compagnie Française de Photographie, Paris; 9 x 12cm. metal body, with helically-focusing lens and magazine back.
(Christie's) $1,312

A Premo View mahogany and brass-mounted folding camera by Rochester Optical, for 8 x10 in. prints, 1900.
(Auction Team Köln) $382

A Lancaster aluminium mounted Instantograph Patent mahogany and aluminium camera.
(Auction Team Köln) $528

Compass II no. 1764, Le Coultre et Cie, Switzerland; with a CCL3B Anastigmat f/ 3.5 35mm. lens, in maker's blue-leather slipcase.
(Christie's) $2,624

Hasselblad 2000FC no. UE1511737, 120-rollfilm, with rollfilm magazine back, extension tube, with a Carl Zeiss Planer T* f/2.8 80mm. lens no. 5873695.
(Christie's) $1,264

Vitessa camera, Voigtländer, Germany; with a Voigtländer Ultron f/2 50mm. lens no. 3950246 in a Synchro-Compur shutter, in maker's ever ready case.
(Christie's) $461

Nikon I no. 609419, chrome, 24 x 32mm., the base plate engraved *Made in Occupied Japan* and with a Nippon Kogaku Nikkor-H-C f/ 2.5cm. lens.
(Christie's) $17,480

'Skilady', a silvered spelter car mascot cast for Riley of a young woman skiing down a slope, 5½in. high. (Christie's)　　　$1,083

René Lalique, 'Boar' glass mascot, October 1929, satin and frosted glass. (Bonhams)　　　$690

'Perche', a Lalique post-war clear and frosted car mascot, modelled as a fish, on a circular base, faint molded mark, 10cm. high. (Christie's)　　　$520

French Art Deco car mascot, attributed to Etling, France, circa 1927, stylized figure of a draped woman with outstretched arm in pale topaz glass, threaded disk base, glass 11in. high. (Skinner)　　　$1,150

Lalique crystal car mascot in the form of an eagle's head, engraved signature, early 20th century, 4½in. high. (Eldred's)　　　$440

Lalique, a Faucon clear car mascot, with fitment, after 1925, modelled as a falcon perched on a circular base, molded and wheelcut marks and Breves Galleries retailers mark, 16cm. (Bonhams & Brooks)　　　$1,644

Cristal Lalique, a Coq Nain clear and frosted car mascot, modelled as a cockerel with raised tail plumes, stencil mark, 20.4cm. (Bonhams & Brooks)　　　$480

'Sanglier' No.1157 a clear and frosted car mascot, molded mark *R. Lalique*, 7cm. high. (Christie's)　　　$350

Cristal Lalique, a Chrysis frosted car mascot, of a naked woman kneeling with billowing hair, incised mark, 12.5cm. (Bonhams & Brooks)　　　$356

Carved and painted wood and glass carousel jumper, Charles W. Parker Merry-Go-Round, Leavenworth, Kansas, circa 1915, ornately polychrome decorated with an American flag, 62in. long.
(Skinner) $1,840

Carved and painted carousel figure of a cat, Gustav A. Dentzel Carousel Co., Philadelphia, circa 1905, carved polychromed wood and glass, with bird of prey in its mouth, 77½in.
(Skinner) $63,000

Carved and painted carousel figure of a pig, Gustav A. Dentzel Carousel Co., Philadelphia, circa 1905, carved polychromed wood and glass, with polychrome trappings, 50in. long.
(Skinner) $11,500

Carved and painted wood carousel jumper, Stein and Goldstein Carousel Co., Brooklyn, New York, circa 1907-18, large polychromed wood and glass horse with iron and brass attachments, 75½in. high.
(Skinner) $21,850

A fine carved and painted carousel horse, Charles I.D. Looff, Brooklyn, New York, late 19th century, original vari-colored faceted jewels, original glass eyes, horsehair tail, 62in. long.
(Sotheby's) $20,000

A carved and painted pine carousel horse, Charles I.D. Looff, Brooklyn, New York, third quarter 19th century, an outside row jumper, now mounted on a black base, 56in. long.
(Sotheby's) $7,200

Carved and painted wood carousel figure of a rabbit, Gustav A. Dentzel Carousel Co., Philadelphia, circa 1905, carved polychromed wood and glass, 77½in. high.
(Skinner) $63,000

A carved and painted carousel jumper, late 19th century, white-painted, outfitted in jewel-carved red, green and blue-painted tack and saddle blanket, 50in. wide.
(Christie's) $4,000

A carved and painted carousel horse, American, 20th century, white-painted with articulated head, a black-painted saddle above red, black and gold details, 65in. wide.
(Christie's) $6,325

Kerman carpet, Southeast Persia, third quarter 19th century, large rosette medallion surrounded by floral sprays on the ivory field, 12ft. x 8ft.8in. (Skinner) $4,025

Heriz carpet, Northwest Persia, second quarter 20th century, overall design of paired palmettes, rosettes, and leaf motifs on the terracotta red field, 12ft.6 x 10ft.3in. (Skinner) $8,050

Fereghan-Sarouk carpet, West Persia, late 19th century, indented circular medallion and blossoming vines, on the light red field, 11ft. x 8ft.8in. (Skinner) $17,250

Northwest Persian carpet, early 20th century, overall design of floral sprays, palmettes, and curved leaves on the midnight blue field, 11ft.5 x 8ft.4in. (Skinner) $5,175

Bakhtiari carpet, West Persia, early 20th century, square grid of palmettes, floral sprays, 'cypress trees', and other floral motifs, ivory flowerhead and paired serrated leaf border, 10ft.6 x 9ft.10in. (Skinner) $3,737

Heriz carpet, Northwest Persia, early 20th century, gabled square medallion surrounded by large floral motifs, on the terracotta red field, 13ft.2 x 9ft.4in. (Skinner) $3,737

Senneh carpet, Northwest Persia, late 19th century, dense overall Herati design on the midnight blue field, red 'turtle' variant border, 12ft.10 x 10ft.2in. (Skinner) $5,175

Ushak carpet, West Anatolia, late 19th century, overall Herati variant design, on the ivory field, light green rosette and palmette border, 9ft.7 x 9ft.2in. (Skinner) $5,750

Heriz carpet, Northwest Persia, late 19th/early 20th century, large gabled square medallion surrounded by palmettes, on the light red field, 12ft.10in. x 9ft.7in. (Skinner) $5,750

Heriz carpet, Northwest Persia, early 20th century, large rosette medallion surrounded by palmettes and serrated leaves on the terracotta red field, 12ft.4in. x 9ft.4in. (Skinner) $6,325

Sarouk carpet, West Persia, early 20th century, small rosette medallion, floral sprays, and blossoming vines, on the midnight blue field, 10ft.10in. x 8ft. (Skinner) $4,025

Bidjar carpet, Northwest Persia, last quarter 19th century, stepped diamond medallion, floral 'shield' pendants, and overall Herati design on the ivory field, 12ft. x 7ft.6in. (Skinner) $3,335

Chinese Nichols carpet, second quarter 20th century, vase of flowers and large leaves, butterflies, and delicate floral sprays on the deep wine field, tan border of similar design, 11ft.6in x 9ft. (Skinner) $1,840

Bidjar carpet, Northwest Persia, second quarter 20th century, lobed circular medallion, matching spandrels, and Herati design on the red field, 11ft.2 x 8ft.10in. (Skinner) $8,050

Kashan carpet, West Central Persia, second quarter 20th century, dense overall design of floral and leaf groups separated by sinuous leafy vines on the midnight blue field, 13ft.2 x 9ft.6in. (Skinner) $10,925

Bakshaish carpet, Northwest Persia, second half 19th century, two rows of large blossoming trees with small 'weeping willow' and 'cypress tree' motifs on the camel field, 10ft8in. x 8ft.10in. (Skinner) $3,450

An Amritsar Indian carpet, early 20th century, the centre with a large pink and green medallion, surrounded by ivory floral meanders on a green ground, 463 x 400cm. (Finarte) $21,080

A Donegal carpet, English, circa 1900, olive green central field, decorated with a profusion of palmettes, blooms and foliage in pale tones and terracotta/red, 15ft x 12ft. (Christie's) $11,178

A Northwest Persian serape carpet, early 20th century, the central cusped medallion surrounded by foliate motifs in blue, ochre, red and green on a yellow field, 404 x 295cm. (Finarte) $22,634

A 19th century West Persian mahal carpet, with allover herati motifs in green, blue and red on an ivory field, 19th century, 273 x 267cm. (Finarte) $3,994

A Chinese carpet, late 19th century, open circular medallion in royal blue, ivory and light blue-green on the midnight blue field, 9ft. 7in. x 8ft. (Skinner) $6,325

An Arraiolos double cross stitch carpet, Portugal, circa 1960, the light oatmeal field with a bold open counterposed design of tendrils issuing palmettes, 675 x 387cm. (Christie's) $11,072

A silk Qum carpet, the inner frieze decorated with stylised bird and animal motifs, 308 x 208cm. (Arnold) $1,600

Edouard Bénédictus, floral carpet, circa 1925, wool, woven in polychrome decoration of highly stylised flowers and leaves, against a trellis ground scattered with flowers, 121¼ x 78¾in. (Sotheby's) $24,966

A central Persian Kashan carpet, decorated with horizontal bands of medallions on alternate pink and blue grounds, 19th century, 400 x 324cm. (Finarte) $9,985

A 20th century Chinese carpet, with a central medallion of sparse flowers in blue on an ivory field, blue borders, 295 x 254cm. (Finarte) $11,982

Ersari main carpet, West Turkestan, late 19th century, three columns of octagonal gulli-guls on the rust field, 9ft. x 7ft. 2in. (Skinner) $4,025

Kashan carpet, West Central Persia, second quarter 20th century, lobed diamond medallion, matching spandrels, 11ft. 9in. x 8ft. 6in. (Skinner) $6,325

Karadja carpet, Northwest Persia, late 19th century, three columns of characteristic medallions on the midnight blue field, 11ft. 10in. x 9ft. 9in. (Skinner) $2,415

Sarouk carpet, West Persia, early 20th century, notched diamond medallion, pendants and floral spray on the dark red field, 11ft. 10in. x 8ft. 9in. (Skinner) $4,312

A Louis Philippe Aubusson carpet, the light brown field overlaid with a variety of shaped cartouches with plain ivory and light blue grounds, 376 x 294cm. (Christie's) $8,590

A Kirman carpet, with central diamond medallion issuing foliate sprays, 410 x 290cm. (Arnold) $1,013

Heriz carpet, Northwest Persia, second quarter 20th century, overall design with large curved serrated leaves and blossoming vines, 11ft. 3in. x 8ft. 2in. (Skinner) $8,625

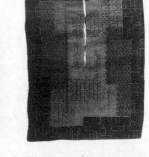

An Empire Aubusson carpet, early 19th century, the chocolate-brown honeycomb lattice containing pale moss-green panels each with a central flowerhead, 15 x 12ft. 6in. (Christie's) $14,231

A Savonnerie carpet, circa 1860, the ivory field with a large lozenge lattice of willow fronds, overlaid by a central panel surmounted by a helmet, 595 x 515cm. (Christie's) $60,922

Da Silva Bruhns, geometric carpet, circa 1930, wool, woven in shades of brown, siena and cream with geometric designs, 148¼ x 105in. (Sotheby's) $18,245

1930 Pierce-Arrow 8 cylinder Sedan, dark green with tan broadcloth interior. Engine: eight cylinder, 366ci., 125bhp at 3,000rpm, Gearbox: manual three speed; Brakes: four wheel Bendix mechanical drums. Left hand drive. (Christie's) $10,925

1938 Buick Special Series 40 Convertible Coupé, maroon with red leather interior and a tan canvas top. Engine: straight-eight, 248ci; Gearbox: three speed manual; Brakes: four wheel hydraulic. Left hand drive. (Christie's) $25,300

1934 Rolls-Royce Phantom II Continental Drophead Sedanca Coupé, coachwork by H.J. Mulliner, gun metal grey with red leather interior. Engine: six cylinder in-line, 7,668cc, Gearbox: four speed manual, Brakes: four wheel drum, mechanical servo. Right hand drive.
(Christie's) $156,500

1912 Ford Model T Torpedo Runabout, blue with black fenders and black leather upholstery. Engine: four cylinder, 176.7ci., 22hp; Gearbox: planetary transmission, two forward, one speed reverse, three pedal one lever; Brakes: contracting band transmission. Right hand drive.
(Christie's) $16,100

1956 Austin FX3 London taxicab, black with black leather interior, Engine: four cylinder B.M.C. 2.2litre diesel, 55hp; Gearbox: manual four speed; Brakes: Girling mechanical, wedge and rollover. Right hand drive.
(Christie's) $4,370

1928 Ford Model A Roadster pickup truck, red with black fenders, yellow wire wheels and black upholstery. Engine: in-line, four cylinder L–head, 200.5ci, Gearbox: three speed manual; Brakes: four wheel drum. Left hand drive. (Christie's) $12,650

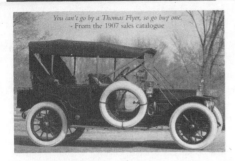

1910 Thomas Flyer Model M6-40 Touring, two-tone Thomas red with black moulding and tan leather interior. Engine: six cylinder, bore and stroke; Gearbox: four speed manual; Brakes: two wheel drum. Right hand drive.
(Christie's) $178,500

1965 Mercedes–Benz 220 SEb Convertible, black with red leather interior. Engine: six cylinder in–line, overhead–cam, Bosch fuel injection, 2,195cc; Gearbox: automatic transmission; Brakes: front disc, rear drums. Left hand drive.
(Christie's) $47,150

Cadillac Fleetwood Sixty Special Sedan, dark blue with tan cloth interior. Engine: L–head V–8, 346ci.; Gearbox: three speed manual; Brakes: hydraulic drums all around.
(Christie's) $9,200

1973 Ferrari 365 GTS/4 Daytona Spyder, coachwork by Pininfarina, built by Scaglietti, fly yellow with black leather interior, Engine: V-12, four-cam, 4,390cc; Gearbox: five speed manual integral with final drive; Brakes: four wheel disc. Left hand drive.
(Christie's) $354,500

1931 Cadillac Series 355-A Roadster, coachwork by Fleetwood, silver and blue with red leather interior, Engine: L–head V–8, 353ci., 95bhp at 3,000rpm; Gearbox: three speed manual; Brakes: four wheel drum. Left hand drive.
(Christie's) $79,500

1929/30 Dupont Model G Speedster, coachwork by Merrimac, yellow body with black leather interior. Engine: straight eight Continental, L–Head, 322ci., Engine: Warner four speed manual; Brakes: four wheel Lockheed hydraulic. Left hand drive.
(Christie's) $332,500

The ex-Motorfair, pre-production prototype 1989 Lotus Elan SE Roadster, originally planned in collaboration with Toyota, Lotus' long-awaited Elan sportscar – code-named project M100 – eventually materialised in 1989 with a front-wheel-drive Isuzu powertrain. (Bonhams & Brooks) $10,695

1961 Mercedes-Benz 190SL Roadster, mounted on a detachable subframe along with the four-speed manual gearbox, front suspension, and steering, the 190's power unit was a 1,897cc overhead-camshaft four, twin Solex downdraft carburettors. (Bonhams & Brooks) $9.798

1930 Austin Seven Tourer, four-seat tourer coachwork, finished in green/black with black interior, hood and sidescreens. (Bonhams & Brooks) $6,348

1966 Volvo 'Amazon' Estate, restored around 1997, this righthand-drive estate once featured in the Yorkshire TV series Heartbeat, finished in light blue with black interior.(Bonhams & Brooks) $1,656

1931 Rolls-Royce Phantom II 40/50hp Six Light Limousine coachwork by Joseph Cockshoot & Co Ltd of Manchester, 7.7 liter, six cylinder, pushrod overhead valve engine, ivory over black livery and the interior features dark blue cloth upholstery to the rear with two occasional seats. (Bonhams & Brooks) $21,390

1912 Unic 10/12hp Drophead Coupé, coachwork by Alford & Alder, London, offset driver and passenger seats with a third, folding side, occasional seat. Driving equipment includes sporting wire wheels, electric starter, delightful brass fittings with acetylene headlamps and oil sidelamps and a running board mounted generator. (Bonhams) $19,320

1930 Bentley 6½ liter Speed Six Drophead Coupé, coachwork by H J Mulliner, restored and presented in excellent condition throughout, with Swansea V5 registration document.(Bonhams) $386,400

1913 Overland Model 69 Tourer, powered by a 4.8 liter engine rated at 25.6hp and producing 30bhp, righthand drive, three-speeds-plus-reverse gearbox. (Bonhams & Brooks) $8,556

1933 Rolls-Royce 20/25hp Sports Saloon, coachwork by Thrupp & Maberly, to original specification in all major respects and is generously furnished and equipped with twin trumpet horns, center driving light, rear mounted spare, a glass panel with blind to the roof, sunblinds to the windscreen and gray leather interior upholstery. (Bonhams) $16,560

1886-1986 Patent-Motorwagen Centenary Replica, a single cylinder engine with vertical crankshaft, driving the twin rear wheels and mounted in a tubular chassis with single speed belt drive and primitive braking by lever actuating a band brake on the countershaft, 984cc engine. (Bonhams) $31,740

The Ex-Equipe National Belge, Paul Frere, Jacques Swaters, Roger Laurent 1955 3 liter V12-engined Ferrari Tipo 750 Monza, coachwork by Carrozzeria Scaglietti, circa 3 liter Ferrari 275GTB-based V12-cylinder engine. (Bonhams) $471,960

1901 Georges Richard Model E 8hp Four Seater Swing-Seat Tonneau, full four-seater, access to the rear seats gained by means of a swinging seat, left hand-drive, tubular chassis frame, the coachwork original, front-mounted engine unusual configuration giving the appearance of two separate single-cylinder vertical water-cooled engines with a common flywheel in between. (Bonhams) $48,300

1928 Willys Overland Crossley Manchester Special 'The Monster', 1928 Manchester chassis, 27-liter Rolls-Royce Meteor B V12 Centurion tank engine dating from the 1950s and the Wilson pre-selector gearbox and fluid flywheel from a 1950s and the Wilson pre-selector gearbox and fluid flywheel from a 1950s Daimler Scout armored car. (Bonhams) $22,080

1908 Lorraine-Dietrich 20hp type CJ Landaulette Coachwork by Pingret, Guion et Breteau, four cylinder, T-head engine and double chain drive to the rear wheels, coachwork reliveried in dark blue with black wings and fine red coachlining. (Bonhams) $44,160

1949 Bentley Mark VI Drophead Coupe, coachwork by Park Ward, midnight blue with blue, grey-piped leather interior. Engine: six cylinder pushrod inlet over exhaust valves, 4257cc; Brakes: servo-assisted. Right hand drive.
(Christie's) $54,360

1965 Rolls-Royce Silver Cloud III Long Wheelbase Saloon, silver and black with red leather interior. Engine: V8, pushrod operated, overhead valve; Gearbox: four speed automatic; Brakes: front, hydraulic and mechanical rear with servo. Left hand drive. (Christie's) $63,000

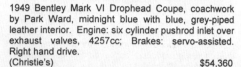

1959 Austin-Healey Sprite Two Seater Sports, leaf green with green interior. Engine: four-cylinder pushrod overhead valves; Gearbox: four-speed manual; Suspension: independent front, rear live axle; Brakes: hydraulically operated drums all round. Right hand drive. (Christie's) $14,996

1941 Plymouth Special De Luxe Business Coupe with Jump Seats, black coachwork. Engine: straight-six, sidevalves, 201.3 cu. in., 87bhp; Gearbox: three speed manual with synchromesh; Brakes: four wheel hydraulically operated drum. Left hand drive. (Christie's) $4,600

1939 American Bantam Model Sixty Coupe, green with tan interior. Engine: four-cylinders in line, 22bhp; Gearbox: manual three speed; Brakes: four wheel mechanical drum. Left hand drive.
(Christie's) $5,175

1939 American Bantam Model Sixty Speedster 'Phaeton', red and black with red interior. Engine: four-cylinder in line, 22bhp; Gearbox: manual three speed; Brakes: four wheel mechanical drum. Left hand drive. (Christie's) $8,625

1908 Renault open drive town car, coachwork by Rothschild et fils, Brewster green with original leather and cloth interior, Engine: four cylinders in line, 4,398cc; Gearbox: manual four-speed; brakes: pedal-operated on transmission. Right hand drive. (Christie's) $33,350

1930 Duesenberg Model J Dual Cowl Phaeton, coachwork by La Grande, black with red wheels and striping and brown leather interior. Engine: straight-eight with twin overhead camshafts; Gearbox: hydraulically operated drums on all wheels. Left hand drive. (Christie's) $618,500

1933 Aston Martin Le Mans Short Chassis Two-Seater Sports, black with black leather interior. Engine: four-cylinder, single overhead camshaft, 1495cc, Gearbox: four-speed close ratio; Brakes: mechanically operated drum all round. Right hand drive. (Christie's) $92,095

1900 Haynes-Apperson Runabout, red with black leather interior. Engine: horizontally-opposed two-cylinder; Gearbox: 3-speed and reverse; Brakes: band type, foot operated, with ratchet. Tiller steered. Left hand drive. (Christie's) $39,100

1897 Panhard-Levassor type M2F Single Phaeton with hood, black with yellow wheels and coachlining. Engine: Panhard-Levassor 'Daimler-Phénix' vertical twin-cylinder, 1.65 litres, Gearbox: 4-speed and reverse; wooden chassis; wooden wheels shod with solid rubber tyres. (Christie's) $235,535

1912 Clément-Bayard Type AC4 Coupé De Ville, dark green and black with yellow coachlines. Engine: 4-cylinder (bi-bloc), 2.6-litre, L-head; Gearbox: 4-speed and reverse; suspension: semi-elliptic front and three-quarter-elliptic rear; Brakes: rear wheels and transmission. Right hand drive. (Christie's) $29,992

1965 Morris Mini Cooper S, jet black with dark red roof and cream leather interior, engine: four cylinder, transverse mounted, 1275cc, gearbox: four speed manual, brakes: front disc, rear drum, right hand drive. (Christie's) $32,200

1953 MG TD Sports Two Seater, red with red interior, engine: four cylinders in-line, pushrod overhead valves, twin SU carburettors, 1250cc, 57bhp, gearbox: manual four-speed, brakes: four wheel hydraulic drum, right hand drive. (Christie's) $13,541

1953 Bentley R Type 4½ litre Two Door Coupé, coachwork by Abbott, two tone blue with blue interior, engine: six cylinder in line, overhead valve, 4,566 cc, gearbox: four speed manual, right hand drive. (Christie's) $30,033

1971 Jaguar E-Type 4.2 Series II Coupé, light metallic blue with black leather interior, engine: six cylinder in-line, double overhead camshaft, 4,235cc, 171bhp at 5,400 rpm, gearbox: four-speed manual, brakes: discs all round, left hand drive. (Christie's) $8,813

1933 Rolls-Royce 20/25hp Limousine, coachwork by Hooper and Co., blue and black, with Bedford cord and black leather interior, engine: straight-six, 3699cc overhead valves, gearbox: four speed manual with side change and synchromesh on top ratios, brakes: four-wheel mechanically operated servo assisted drum, right hand drive. (Christie's) $28,888

1982 Range Rover VIP Ceremonial vehicle, black with black interior and glass viewing platform, engine: Vee-eight, overhead valves, 3528cc, 178bhp at 4750rpm; gearbox with combined transferbox, eight forward and two reverse ratios; brakes: servo assisted discs all round, right hand drive. (Christie's) $17,700

1933 Chrysler series CL Custom Imperial Dual Windshield Phaeton, coachwork by LeBaron, dark red with burgundy fenders and tan leather interior, engine: in-line L-head eight cylinder, 384.84 ci., 125bhp at 3,200rpm, gearbox: four speed manual, brakes: four wheel Lockheed hydraulic drums, left hand drive. (Christie's) $206,000

1908 Panhard-Levassor Type Q 50HP Racing Car, French racing blue with black leather seats, engine: four cylinder, T-head, 145 x 160mm. bore & stroke, 10,568cc (645ci.), gearbox: multi-plate clutch, four-speed with reverse, final drive by side chains, brakes: on rear wheels and transmission, chassis: wood & flitch plate. (Christie's) $138,000

1959 Morris Minor ¼ Ton Pick Up, yellow with black interior, engine: four cylinder, in-line, overhead valve, 1,098cc, 56bhp at 5,500rpm gearbox: four-speed manual, brakes: front discs, rear drums, left hand drive. (Christie's) $8,813

An Austin 10 four door saloon car with green livery, 53,878 recorded miles, circa 1936. (Brightwells) $2,352

1926 Ford Model T Fordor Sedan, red with black wings and grey interior, engine: four cylinder in-line, side valves, 2.9 litres, 22bhp; Gearbox: two-speed epicyclic, Brakes: mechanical drum to rear, right hand drive. (Christie's) $21,252

1929 Buick Series 121 Sport Roadster, red with black fenders and tan top, engine: in-line six cylinder, pushrod operated overhead valves, 310ci., gearbox: three-speed manual, brakes: four wheel mechanical drums, left hand drive. (Christie's) $24,675

1969 Volkswagen "Curved Glass" single cab pick up, Mars red with black vinyl interior, engine: fuel injected, overhead valves, 1,600cc (96.7ci.), 65bhp at 4,600rpm, gearbox: four-speed manual, brakes: front disc with rear drums, left hand drive. (Christie's) $8,225

1963 Alfa Romeo 2600 Spyder Superleggera, coachwork by Touring, red with white vinyl interior and a black convertible top, engine: six cylinder-in-line twin overhead camshafts, 2,582cc, 165bhp at 5,900rpm, gearbox: five-speed manual, brakes: front disc, rear drum, left hand drive. (Christie's) $18,354

1959 Osca Tipo S 750 Sports Racing Two Seater, coachwork by Morelli, Italian racing red with black leather seats and trim, engine; four cylinders in-line, twin overhead camshafts, twin Weber carburettors producing 76bhp at 7,700 rpm, gearbox: four-speed manual, brakes: four-wheel hydraulic drums, left hand drive. (Christie's) $134,887

1960 Buick Lesabre Convertible, silver with red and white interior and a white convertible power top, engine: overhead valve V8, 364ci, 250bhp at 4,400rpm, gearbox: column shift automatic, brakes: four wheel drums, left hand drive. (Christie's) $18,800

1921 Ford Model TT One-Ton Drop-Side Truck, 24hp engine, in green with red coachlining and green upholstery, right-hand drive.
(Bonhams & Brooks) $5,680

1910 Oldsmobile special 40hp Roadster, yellow and black pinstriping and black leather seats, engine: four cylinder, c336ci., 40bhp; gearbox: four-speed manual, brakes: two wheel rear drums. Right hand drive.
(Christie's) $58,750

1915 Pierce-Arrow Model 48 B-3 Five-Passenger Touring Car, Brewster green with black fenders and cream pinstriping with tufted black leather interior and a black Panasote top, engine: T-head, six cylinders cast in pairs, 525ci., gearbox: leather-faced cone clutch, selective transmission. Right hand drive.
(Christie's) $105,000

1922 Ford Model T Roadster, black with black upholstery and black Panasote top, engine: four cylinders, in-line, side valves, 2.9 liters, 22bhp, gearbox: two-speed epicyclic; brakes: mechanical drum to rear. Left hand drive.
(Christie's) $11,163

1935 Bentley 3½ litre Four Seat Drophead Special, six-cylinder overhead valve 3,669cc engine, in yellow with black leather.
(Bonhams & Brooks) $17,750

1986 AC Cobra Replica Two-Seater Roadster, this right hand drive example features Contemporary's massive round-tube chassis, a 302ci 5-liter Ford V8 supplied and built by D. Riley, a '427' four-speed gearbox, glass fiber body, 1962 Jaguar E-type running gear and Hallibrand knock-on alloy wheels.
(Bonhams & Brooks) $10,224

1936 Cord 812 Westchester Supercharged 4.7 litre Four-Door Sedan, in mushroom with burgundy upholstery and burgundy red and cream-piped headlining, Lycoming 4.7 liter V8 engine.
(Bonhams & Brooks) $38,340

1901 Pick 4hp Voiturette forward mounted, vertical, single cylinder engine, believed to be manufactured by Allard, water-cooled, two forward speeds and drives by belt and double chain to the rear axle. (Bonhams) $38,640

1923 itala Tipo 51S Tourer, 18/45hp Model 51 Sport , displacing 2,813cc, the Tipo 51's four-cylinder sidevalve engine has aluminum pistons, forced lubrication, pumped water circulation and electric starting, four-speed gearbox and rear wheel brakes supplemented by a transmission brake. (Bonhams & Brooks) $34,790

1918 Pierce-Arrow model 48 B-5 Seven Passenger Touring car, unpainted, completely new body in primer with blue fenders, engine: T-head, six cylinder, cast in pairs, pressure feed engine lubrication, 525ci. (8,602cc), gearbox: leather-faced cone clutch running in oil, brakes: original two wheel drum on rear wheels with hand brake for rear wheels. Right hand drive. (Christie's) $64,625

1961 Alfa Romeo 2000S Spyder, coachwork by Touring, metallic gray with red leather interior, engine: four cylinders in line, 1975cc, twin overhead camshafts, twin Solex carburettors, 115bhp at 5800rpm, gearbo: five-speed synchromesh, brakes: hydraulic drum. Left hand drive. (Christie's) $11,178

1921 Rolls-Royce 40/50hp 'Silver Ghost' double cabriolet, coachwork by Barker & Co., (Coachbuilders), Ltd, presented in apple green and black livery, opening windscreen, communication porthole for chauffeur in the drop-down division and twin side-mounted spare wheels, a running board toolbox. (Bonhams) $84,180

1941 standard 12hp Light Utility, four cylinder, side valve engine of 1,609cc, driving through a four speed gearbox, in R.A.F. livery with an excellent tilt cover and comes with old log book, Swansea V5 registration document, various handbooks, etc. (Bonhams & Brooks) $4,692

A National Model 400 push button cash register for German currency, bronzed nickel case with drawer and on wooden plinth.
(Auction Team Köln) $442

A good brass National cash register, #442 in ornately molded floral case on oak drawer, original condition, complete with 'Amount Purchased' sign, 28in. high.
(Jacksons) $603

A National No. 78 cash register with four place keyboard, in decorative silvered bronze case with lever action and receipt dispenser, circa 1900.
(Auction Team Köln) $231

A National Model Nr. 14B cash register for German currency, with 25 keys, restored white metal case, 1905.
(Auction Team Köln) $552

An American National Cash Register, the embossed and brass case with brass nameplate, and pounds sterling keys, 44cm. high x 43cm. wide.
(Bonhams) $414

A nickel plated Art Nouveau style National Model 562-X-6C cash register, with till drawers and numbering for six cashiers, for German currency.
(Auction Team Köln) $429

A National Model 400 cash register, with four place keyboard and decorative nickelled bronze case, on wooden base, for Belgian francs, 1910.
(Auction Team Köln) $444

'National' brass and nickel plated cash register, late 19th early 20th century, registers a sale up to $5.95, 17in. high, 16in. deep, 18in. wide. (Eldred's) $275

A National Model 445X push button cash register with four-row keyboard, with silvered bronze casing and on wooden plinth, for Belgian currency, 1915.
(Auction Team Köln) $627

A Louis XVI style gilt metal seventeen light chandelier, the lotus leaf corona supporting the open oval shaped body, enclosing five sconces, 36½in. drop. (Bonhams) $847

A W.A.S. Benson copper and brass ceiling light shade, by William Arthur Smith Benson, circa 1895, the copper petals forming a stylized flower, with brass fittings, 24in. wide. (Christie's) $1,068

A Baroque style brass twelve-light chandelier, in the Dutch Tradition, 19th century, the turned standard issuing two tiers of scrolling candlearms ending in a dished bobêche and candle socket, 34in. high. (Sotheby's) $4,800

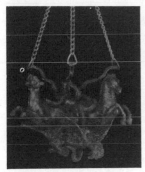

A Neapolitan bronze triform chandelier, late 19th century, attributed to the Chiurazzi foundry, Naples, modelled with chimera, horse's head and griffin above a bird, entwined with snakes, 11in. high. (Christie's) $4,738

A Bohemian pink and clear cut-and molded-glass twelve-light chandelier, circa 1890, surmounted by a trumpet shaped corona, above scrolled arms, 44in. high. (Christie's) $16,803

A Continental gilt bronze and molded glass eighteen light chandelier, first quarter 20th century, the lobed glass drip pans above the nozzles issuing from scrolling branches in six groups of three, 44in. high. (Christie's) $1,562

A twenty-light spelter chandelier, probably French, 19th century, the molded corona supporting five chains and a tapering font issuing two tiers of candlearms, 36in. high. (Sotheby's) $5,700

A chandelier ceiling fitting, with six electric lights, the cast brass ring frieze with horizontal finials and pierced entwined foliage, 15in. diameter. (Woolley & Wallis) $164

A Dutch style brass twelve light chandelier, first half 20th century, the nozzles and dished drip pans issuing in two tiers of six scrolling foliate branches, 27¼in. high. (Christie's) $690

A French glass and gilt bronze eight light chandelier, circa 1840, with glass nozzles and drip pans on foliate capped scroll branches about a pierced circlet, 39in. high. (Christie's) $3,992

A Régence style gilt bronze eight light chandelier, early 20th century, with campana shaped nozzles and drip pans with gadrooned borders on S-scroll branches, 32in. high. (Christie's) $3,266

One of a pair of cut glass five light chandeliers, late 19th or early 20th century, of inverted trumpet shape, hung with chains and tiers of faceted pendants, 46½in. high. (Christie's) (Two) $9,072

A brass and giltwood chandelier, Viennese, early 19th century, the corona with sunken patera suspending a circular bowl with central foliate shaft and pine cone finial, 35in. high. (Christie's) $8,832

A North European brass sixteen light chandelier, possibly late 18th or early 19th century, the scrolling branches radiating in two tiers, intersected by circular convex reflectors, approximately 42in. high. (Christie's) $9,072

A bronze and glass chandelier 'Modèle Chicorée', designed by Louis Majorelle, circa 1905, the chandelier modelled with sinuous whiplash decoration and chicory flowers and leaves, 49in. long. (Christie's) $26,082

A Continental gilt brass and glass twenty-four light chandelier, early 20th century, the nozzles and petal shaped drip pans on twelve scroll branches about the circular well, 48in. high. (Christie's) $2,795

Giltwood eight-light chandelier, early 20th century, the foliate capped scroll branches about the fluted circular well, with gadrooned and tapering wrythen column, 36in. high. (Christie's) $1,592

A gilt-bronze and glass twelve-light chandelier, early 20th century, with drip pans and gadrooned nozzles with wrythen undersides, on two registers of foliate capped part-fluted branches, 53in. high. (Christie's) $6,560

A brass chandelier, Austrian, circa 1905, broad circular band with six brass hanging fitments, the central stem with stylised foliate motifs, 41in. approximate length.
(Christie's) $3,726

A bronze and glass chandelier, designed by Paul Hankar, circa 1895, the four-branch chandelier modelled with stylised whiplash decoration, 33in. high.
(Christie's) $5,589

A French part-patinated gilt bronze four-light hanging light, early 20th century, the lower section in the form of a dark-green patinated torch, 35¾in. high.
(Christie's) $2,005

A large George V ten branch glass chandelier, in two registers of up and downscrolling branches with petal-shaped drip pans suspended overall with strings of faceted beads, 52in. high.
(Christie's) $5,081

A Louis XV style ormolu eighteen-light chandelier, late 19th century, the foliate cast corona above a spirally twisted baluster shaped support cast with stars applied with cupids, 48¼in. high.
(Christie's) $26,450

Style of W.A.S. Benson, chandelier, circa 1890, brass, elaborate openwork frame with formalised motifs, with six opalescent glass shades, 138cm. maximum drop.
(Sotheby's) $4,485

One of a pair of French tôle peinte five light chandeliers, late 19th century, the nozzles with everted foliate drip pans suspended with clear and ruby glass pendants, 25in. high.
(Christie's) (Two) $4,536

René Lalique, lustre 'Fruits', after 1914, composed of panels of clear glass, moulded in high relief or intaglio etched with fruits, 50¾in. approximate drop.
(Sotheby's) $53,820

A French bronze and brass eight light chandelier, second half 19th century, the nozzles as flowerheads, the branches with further foliage issuing from an acanthus clasped terminal, 27in. high. (Christie's) $2,608

A small French gilt-bronze six-light chandelier, late 19th century, the foliate scroll cast branches issuing from a platform mounted with figures of dancing amorini, 18in. high. (Christie's) $1,553

An Italian carved alabaster dish light, early 20th century, with entwined grapevine around the outside edge, with alabaster ceiling attachment, 18in. diameter. (Christie's) $727

A Dutch style brass six light chandelier, 20th century, the moulded nozzles and drip pans issuing from scrolling branches, with knopped stem and spherical terminal, 25in. high. (Christie's) $585

A Daum plafonnier, the glass internally mottled with pink and yellow, engraved *Daum Nancy* with cross of Lorrraine, 38cm. diameter. (Christie's) $1,050

A gilt bronze six light chandelier, early 20th century, the foliate nozzles and drip pans issuing from the heads of Chimaeras on scrolling foliate branches, the waisted body with hemispherical finial and foliate cast terminal, 21in. diamter. (Christie's) $1,280

A Régence style bronze six-light chandelier, 20th century, the scroll branches issuing from a waisted and fluted column with cherub bust mounts, 24in. diameter. (Christie's) $549

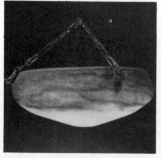

One of a near pair of Muller Frères glass shades, factory marks, 36cm. and 35cm. diameter. (Christie's) (Two) $1,137

French Empire Revival gilt and green patinated metal six-light chandelier, inverted bowl form tier mounted with lion masks, the arms moulded with masks and foliage, 16in. high. (Skinner) $1,955

A Muller Frères wrought-iron and glass plafonnier, factory marks (minor restoration to toprim of one shade), 69cm. diameter at widest point. (Christie's) $1,137

A Continental brass six-light chandelier, 19th century, the scrolling arms issuing from a bulbous baluster knopped column with cruciform finial, 35in. high. (Christie's) $260

An Italian alabaster dish light, 20th century, lobed, with suspension chains, 20in. diameter. (Christie's) $763

A Dutch brass six light chandelier, first half 20th century, the moulded nozzles and drip pans issuing from scrolling foliate branches, 20in. high. (Christie's) $456

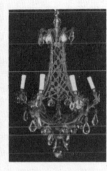

A French gilt bronze and glass eight-light chandelier, early 20th century, the four pairs of reeded branches about the openwork cartouche shaped frame, , suspended overall with glass spheres and pendants, 42in. high. (Christie's) $1,829

A Russian brass fourteen light electrolier, early 20th century, with eight pierced sconces issuing from alternating foliate and winged dragon branches, the quatrefoil frame with cyrillic script to the gallery, 40in. high. (Christie's) $329

A Régence style gilt bronze six light chandelier, early 20th century, the foliate clasped scroll branches issuing from a circular well with satyr masks and bell-flower swags, 34in. high.(Christie's) $3,452

A Dutch brass ten light chandelier, late 19th century, the nozzles and drip pans issuing from scrolling branches in two tiers, with four lights above and six below, 22in. high. (Christie's) $1,188

A novelty wrought-iron and glass plafonnier, factory marks, 61cm. diameter at widest point. (Christie's) $1,137

A North European copper-plated brass six-light chandelier, late 19th/early 20th century, in the Dutch taste, the scrolling branches issuing from a bulbous baluster knopped column, 17in. high. (Christie's) $330

An eight branch gilt metal and glass chandelier, part late 18th century adapted, the branches with glass spire finials, 38in. high.
(Christie's) $2,236

A Dutch brass chandelier, the baluster shaft below fixing ring issuing eight scrolling branches with grotesque beasts, 31in. high.
(Christie's) $6,108

A gilt bronze six light chandelier, early 20th century, the bifurcating naturalistic branches issuing from a conforming foliate column, 28in. high. (Christie's) $4,099

A bronze twenty four light chandelier, early 20th century, of inverted trumpet outline, the lower tiered frame pierced and cast with interlinking scrolls and foliate motifs, 60in. high.
(Christie's) $7,360

Art Deco frosted glass chandelier, 20th century, pod and leaf-form patinated metal ceiling mount and three paperclip chains supporting shade with moulded floral and geometric devices, 25in. drop.
(Skinner) $575

An early Victorian gilt bronze six branch argand chandelier, with branches radiating about the cast circlet with bell flower swags below a conforming openwork tiered cresting, 25in. diameter.
(Christie's) $11,960

A George IV ormolu and cut-glass twelve-light chandelier, with five graduating tiers, each with a fleur-de-lys crown above lozenge-cut rectangular drops, 57in. high.
(Christie's) $28,290

Art Deco moulded frosted glass and bronze chandelier, second quarter 20th century, cast bronze ceiling mount and lower shade mount with border of a stylised bowl of flowers, 26½in. drop.(Skinner) $2,300

A Swedish ormolu and clear and blue cut glass six-light chandelier, the pierced coronet with scrolling ribbon-twist branches suspending swags of droplets, 34in. high.
(Christie's) $8,590

Three Dedham Pottery bread and butter plates, East Dedham, Massachusetts, before 1932, including border with Butterfly and Flower, Swan and Pond Lily, pattern, diameter 6in. (Skinner) $690

Roseville Pottery Carnelian II vase, 1915, Zanesville, Ohio, raised flared rim on bulbous body with angled scrolled handles, mottled matte, mauve drip glaze, 8¼in. high. (Skinner) $546

Grueby Pottery bowl, Boston, circa 1905, swollen spherical form with flared raised rim, repeating raised leaf pattern decorating sides, mustard yellow matte glaze, 7in. high. (Skinner) $4,600

Fulper Art Pottery two-handled vase, Flemington, New Jersey, raised rim on swollen base with two conforming handles, matte purple-blue glaze. (Skinner) $460

Paul Revere pottery three-piece child's breakfast set, Boston, early 20th century, comprised of mug, bowl, and plate decorated with running rabbits in white, green, and blue. (Skinner) $1,380

Paul Revere pottery pitcher, Boston, circa 1926, ovoid pitcher with applied handle in charcoal grey glaze, partial impressed potter's mark, 6¾in. high. (Skinner) $69

A glazed stoneware figure of a dog, Pennsylvania, 19th century, the hollow molded figure in the form of a seated spaniel with articulated head, body and fur, 11in. high. (Christie's) $1,000

Three Saturday Evening Girls pottery lotus blossom plates, Boston, circa 1914, luncheon plates with borders decorated with incised lotus blossoms in white on blue ground with green-blue centre, 7⁵/₈in. (Skinner) $1,092

Owens pottery vase, Zanesville, Ohio, circa 1905, ovoid form in matte green with pierced rectangles on shoulder and panels of stylised swans in relief, 11¾in. high. (Skinner) $1,495

BERLIN _____ CHINA _____

A Berlin (K.P.M.) rectangular plaque, late 19th/early 20th century, finely painted after Bouguereau with Cupid asleep in a woodland glen, 16.1 x 23.3cm., within a carved gesso and giltwood frame.
(Christie's) $7,050

A pair of Berlin large white figures of Venus and Hercules, late 19th century, the scantily clad goddess seated on a conch-shell chariot, a wreath in her left hand, 40.2cm. high. (Christie's) $1,410

19th century Berlin style rectangular porcelain plaque painted with a full length study of a maiden holding an urn in a deserted landscape, titled in pencil verso *Antigone*, 25.5 x 17.5cm. (Wintertons) $882

BESWICK

'Benjamin Bunny' a Beatrix Potter figure, printed gilt mark.
(Christie's) $246

Beswick Beatrix Potter figure 'Tabitha Twitchett and Miss Moppet', brown back stamp, 3½in.
(G.A. Key) $159

'Cheshire Cat' a figure from the Alice Series, printed marks.
(Christie's) $460

BOW

A Bow porcelain sauceboat, of silver shape, with double spurred C shape handle and on three paw feet, 1750–55, 22.5cm.
(Tennants) $1,312

A pair of Bow figures of musicians, circa 1765-70, modelled as a lady and gentleman seated on tree-stumps flanked by flowering foliage, 8¾in. high.(Christie's) $4,259

A rare Bow model of a tawny owl, well coloured and perched high upon a tree stump applied with three coloured fowers, circa 1750-1755, 19.5cm.
(Woolley & Wallis) $13,600

162

A Wiltshaw & Robinson *If He Can Say as You Can Guinness is Good For You,* Toucan bar top model. (Bearne's) $480

A Moorcroft Macintyre sterling silver-mounted Claremont part coffee service, circa 1905, made for Shreve & Co., San Francisco, painted script signature, 3 pieces, 9¾in. high. (Sotheby's) $16,800

A Della Robbia Pottery large two-handled vase, probably by Ruth Bare, 15in. high. (Sotheby's) $1,020

'Finches' a Moorcroft dish, impressed and painted marks, 26cm. diameter. (Christie's) $329

A Crown Devon tall ribbed ovoid jug, shape E20, pattern 5129, decorated with figures in a pagoda landscape on a red ground, 27.2cm. (Woolley & Wallis) $132

A Susie Cooper painted charger, painted marks, 30.5cm. (Bonhams) $735

A Bernard Moore flambé jardinière, circa 1910, painted by Dora M. Billington, painted mark *Bernard Moore,* 11½in. high. (Sotheby's) $3,600

A Pratt type erotic novelty stirrup cup, modelled as a phallus, the bowl moulded with a band of stiff leaves, enriched in a typical palette, circa 1800, 25cm. high. (Christie's) $3,350

A William Moorcroft Spanish small bowl, 1914, (minor restored crack to rim), painted script signature in green, 4¼in. high. (Sotheby's) $1,200

Porcelain teapot with portrait of George Washington, England, 19th century, covered teapot with leaf and vine decoration, 6in. high. (Skinner) $1,150

Brownfields two handled large soup tureen and matching ladle, decorated in flow-blue with sprigs of flowers etc, on a pearl ground, 19th century, 13in.(G.A. Key) $524

Late 19th century Myotts jug and bowl, decorated in flow-blue on a white ground with the 'Denby' pattern. (G A Key) $491

'Camelia' 'Tahiti' an L Allen, Wilkinson Ltd vase, printed factory marks and painted signature, 20.5cm. high. (Christie's) $81

A pair of English porcelain dessert plates, possibly by Samuel Alcock, each finely painted, one with a mountain linnet, the other with a turtle dove, 22.5cm. diameter, mid 19th century. (Bearne's) $354

Royal Lancastrian Pottery luster vase 13½in. tall. (Whitworths) $1,320

Early 19th century slipware two handled cylindrical loving cup, inscribed *Happiness Lies in Imagination Not in Possession*, dated *1800*, 5½in. (Aylsham) $315

Treacle glazed bargee teapot, typically molded and decorated in colors, the cover with finial formed as a small teapot, 13in. (G.A. Key) $290

Large Mocha ware mug, England, 19th century, open chain pattern on pumpkin ground with upper and lower dark brown bands, 5³/₈in. high. (Skinner) $1,955

Unusual Art Deco period majolica style teapot, entitled 'Rooster', modelled as a cockerel, naturalistically decorated in colors, 9in. (G A Key) $65

19th century English pagoda shaped teapot and stand, printed in green with oriental scene of figure amidst woodland with gilded detail on a white ground, 7in. (G.A. Key) $79

Brannam (Barum) small teapot, modelled as a dragon, naturalistically decorated in colors, incised signature mark and dated 1891, 4½in. (G A Key) $240

A Thomas Harley Bonaparte jug titled Johny Bull giving Boney a Pull, printed signature, manufactured by T. Harley, Lane End, 6in. (Academy) $544

Toni Davidson & Alan Smith, a pair of ceramic busts, circa 1965, each with painted features and Edwardian clothing, with painted marks to the underside, each 12in. high. (Christie's) $558

'Peace', a mosaic plaque, designed by Henry George Alexander Holiday, circa 1880, probably manufactured by James Powell and Sons, the painted portrait surrounded by a mosaic of gold and turquoise, 14¼ x 12½in. (Christie's) $10,246

An R.A. Bough milk jug painted to depict crocuses within a patterned border. (T.R. & M) $218

A large blue and white printed meat plate, probably Herculaneum, decorated with a view of the Mausoleum of Sultan Purveiz, near Allahabad, 19½in. (Woolley & Wallis) $668

'Dismal Desmond' dog with maroon painted collar, black ears and spotted coat. (David Lay) $48

An English two-handled hall vase and cover, circa 1840, painted with titled views of Lowther Castle and Alton Abbey bordered in cobalt blue and gilded. (Bonhams) $416

Moorcroft MacIntyre Florian Ware small tapering cylindrical two handled 'Christmas Greetings' cup, decorated in green and blue, with probably 'Violet' design, signed, circa 1904/1913, 1½in.
(G A Key) $2,604

One of a pair of Clews stone china blue and white plates printed with cattle and figures in landscape, 8in. (Brightwells) (Two) $85

A 19th century twin handled mug, transfer printed and overpainted in enamels with various animals, the interior with three yellow frogs, circa 1840. 13cm. high.
(Cheffins) $238

19th century covered character jug modelled as Mr Punch, his hat forming cover, naturalistic face, wearing iron red and black jerkin with gilded detail, 11½in.
(G.A. Key) $208

A Paragon child's mug decorated with an amusing picture of Mickey Mouse and signed *Walter E. Disney*, the base of the mug bearing the legend *Wishing you a Happy Christmas from H.R.H. Duchess of York, Dec 25th 1932.*
(Academy) $816

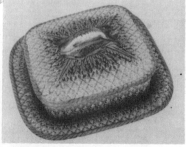

Mocha ware pitcher, England, 19th century, with blue and brown earthworm pattern on celadon green and ocher ground, 8in. high.
(Skinner) $2,530

Majolica covered sardine dish, the handle modelled as fish, molded and decorated in colors with seaweed designs etc., 19th century, 8in. (G A Key) $191

English yellow-ware toby pitcher, 19th century, depicting the face of a man, partial Rockingham glaze, 7½in. high. (Eldred's) $522

A porcelain group of a lavender seller together with her two children, raised, within a shaped reserve *Yardley's Old English Lavender*, 12¼in. high.
(George Kidner) $272

An early 20th century Blakeney ironstone oval foot bath, blue and white transfer printed floral decoration, printed marks, oval length 47cm.
(Wintertons) $638

A Plichta figure of a cat, modelled seated, with pricked ears, inset glass blue eyes, painted with scattered flowering thistles, 27cm.
(Tennants) $912

A Measham or Barge ware brown glazed teapot and cover, of typical baluster form with a small teapot finial and applied with birds and flower heads picked out in blue, green and pink, circa 1890, 34cm.
(Woolley & Wallis) $220

Syd F. Barnes. A commemorative plate transfer printed in color with a portrait and inscribed *Brilliant Bowling by Barnes – Obtained six Wickets for 24 Runs – The English Team in Australia. 1908.*, 20cm. diameter. (Bonhams) $255

A Brown-Westhead and Moore cachepot, with rope twist handles decorated with two oval landscape panels on a rose pompadour ground, registration mark for 1869, 25cm. wide.
(Woolley & Wallis) $441

English banded mocha mug, in blue and green on white with black lines and seaweed decoration, 6½in. high. (Eldred's) $121

An early 20th century English low fired earthenware figure of a seated boy wearing Tyrolean costume and playing a flute, 84cm. high.
(Bearne's) $1,431

19th century English jug, printed en grisaille with scenes: 'Blackburn Riots, May 1878' and 'Colonel Jackson's House on Fire, Blackburn Riots, May 1878', within pale blue borders, 6½in.
(G.A. Key) $272

A Burmantofts faience plaque of circular form depicting fishing boats approaching the coast, in green glazes, impressed mark, 17¾in. wide. (Andrew Hartley) $1,256

A Burmantoft's faience 'Anglo-Persian' vase, late 1880s, painted with three roundels depicting fish amongst waves on a ground decorated with storks, height 14in. (Sotheby's) $4,500

A pair of Burmantofts faience green glaze tiles, relief molded, one depicting a heron, kingfisher and fish in water, the other depicting a rabbit and birds in an undergrowth, 11¾in. wide. (Andrew Hartley) $1,088

CAPODIMONTE

A very rare Capodimonte group of 'Il Cavadenti', circa 1750, modelled by Giuseppe Gricci, the dentist holding pliers in his right hand and his seated patient's mouth open with the left, 19.5cm. (Sotheby's) $58,800

A Capodimonte figural group of 'The Cheats',. (Bonhams & Brooks) $522

A Capodimonte group of a gallant and companion, the porcelain circa 1755, perhaps decorated at Buen Retiro, modelled by Giuseppe Gricci, 8½in. high. (Christie's) $7,297

CHELSEA

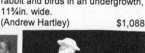

A Chelsea lobed circular botanical dish of Hans Sloane type, circa 1755, Red Anchor mark, painted with a lemon, white bean flowers, leaves, caterpillars and butterflies, 27cm. (Christie's) $3,088

A pair of Chelsea figures of musicians, circa 1758, each modelled seated, the male cellist wearing a gray hat, the female hurdy-gurdy player wearing a puce hat and bodice, 15.5cm. (Sotheby's) $1,676

A Chelsea porcelain octagonal dish, circa 1753, painted in the Kakiemon style with two stylized oriental birds, one in flight, the other seated on the branch of a pine tree, 20.5cm. (Bonhams) $1,205

A very rare Chinese octagonal Hausmaler beaker, the porcelain circa 1700, decorated circa 1720-30, the flared form painted in Schwarzlot with a continuous scene of a dancing couple, 1½in. high. (Sotheby's) $1,680

A famille rose eggshell bowl, painted to the interior with a vase of peony flowers and magnolia beside a bowl of finger citrons and pomegranates, 5½in. diameter, Yongzheng. (Christie's) $731

A Canton famille rose porcelain bowl with ormolu mounts, the pierced scroll rim with bird surmounts and scrolled loop handles, the reserves depicting figures on a terrace, 17½in. wide. (Andrew Hartley) $2,079

A Chinese Export two-handled punch urn and cover, circa 1790, the octagonal vessel painted in brown monochrome on the front and reverse with an oval European landscape panel, 16in. high. (Sotheby's) $64,000

A famille verte dish painted and gilt with a jardinière of peonies, pine and chrysanthemums within a trailing foliate border, 22.5cm. diameter, 18th century. (Christie's) $385

A Chinese blue and white elephant-form kendi, Wanli, 1573-1619, for the South-East Asian market, the stout rectangular body modelled with a short spout formed by his head and with a flared neck upon his back, 20cm. high. (Sotheby's) $14,400

A Chinese blue and white dish painted with a central bouquet of lotus sprays within a border of scrolling peonies and foliage, 11¼in. diameter, Kangxi. (Christie's) $2,310

A Chinese porcelain and gilt-bronze centre bowl, French, circa 1880, decorated in the famille rose palette with two cartouches, 29cm. diameter. (Sotheby's) $2,370

A Ming blue and white dish with everted rim, painted with a kylin among foaming waves within border of chrysanthemum sprays, 36.5cm. diameter. (Christie's) $1,540

Clarice Cliff Newport Fantasque Perth jug, decorated with the 'Orange Lily' pattern, gilt lithograph mark, circa 1928, 5in.
(G A Key) $319

Clarice Cliff Newport 'Celtic Harvest' teapot of baluster form, the cover with fruit molded finial and similar handle, decorated in colors on an off white ground, rubber stamp mark, 9in.
(G A Key) $315

Clarice Cliff Bizarre Newport coffee pot of ribbed cylindrical form, decorated with the 'Bridgewater' pattern, orange colorway, black lithograph mark, 7½in.
(G A Key) $641

'Original Bizarre' a twin-handled Lotus jug, printed mark, 30cm. high.
(Christie's) $822

'Blue Chintz' a pair of 268 vases, in colors, printed marks, 21cm. high.
(Christie's) $2,377

A Clarice Cliff Bizarre candlestick in the form of a water nymph holding aloft a bowl, 17.5cm. high.
(Wintertons) $627

'Rhodanthe' a 'Bizarre' tea for two, printed marks, teapot 14cm. high.
(Christie's) $1,480

A Clarice Cliff toby jug shape 862, 31cm. printed and molded marks.
(Bonhams) $217

'Original Bizarre' a coffee set for six, printed mark, coffee-pot 14cm. high. (Christie's) $1,377

A Clarice Cliff Swan bowl, 25cm.
printed marks.
(Bonhams) $295

A Clarice Cliff conical sugar caster,
painted with the windbells pattern in
orange, yellow, green, blue, black
and violet, early 1930s, 13.5cm.
(Tennants) $1,312

'Tennis' a 'Bizarre' cauldron, printed
mark, 8cm. high.
(Christie's) $789

A Clarice Cliff Farmhouse pattern
biscuit barrel with orange and black
painted cane swing handle,
Newport Pottery, 6½in.
(Michael J. Bowman) $1,394

'Original Bizarre' a Globe tea for
two, in colors, printed marks,
11cm. high.
(Christie's) $1,370

Clarice Cliff Newport 'My Garden'
ewer, baluster form, the reeded
looped handle molded with a floral
terminal, decorated in green, iron
red and brown, on a mushroom
ground, 8½in.
(G A Key) $120

A Clarice Cliff Alton 356 vase,
10.7cm. printed marks (drilled).
(Bonhams) $403

'Sunray' a 'Bizarre' Coronet jug,
printed mark, 17.5cm. high.
(Christie's) $1,562

'Flora' a 'Bizarre' large wall mask, in
colors, printed marks, 35cm. high.
(Christie's) $1,736

A good Coalport teapot, cover and stand, and a similar plate, all molded and painted with flowers on a blue and gilt ground, circa 1820. (Woolley & Wallis) $735

19th century Coalport rectangular dish, the centre painted in colours with spray of flowers within a blue and gilded border, 11in. (G.A. Key) $110

A pair of Coalport two-handled vases and covers, circa 1900, of slender tapering form, painted with titled views 'Ross Castle' and 'Old Weir Bridge Killarney', 13½in. (Skinner) $4,002

COPELAND

Copeland Parian Ware group of three terriers ratting, after P J Mêne, impressed mark, 12½in. (G A Key) $550

A pair of Copeland Spode character jugs, as Churchill and Roosevelt, both seated, printed marks, mid 20th century, 21.5cm. high. (Christie's) $790

A Copeland Parian ware figure Egeria, depicting a standing semi nude maiden flanked by a tree stump, 23½in. high. (Andrew Hartley) $1,309

CREAMWARE

An English creamware cylindrical teapot and cover, probably Leeds, with flower finial and an entwined barley-twist handle with flowerhead and leaf terminals, circa 1775, 13cm. high. (Christie's) $517

A creamware punch-kettle and cover, painted in a famille rose palette with Orientals among furniture, vases and shrubs, probably Leeds, circa 1775, 21cm. high. (Christie's) $1,160

Creamware barrel-form jug, Britain, circa 1820, with alternating slip bands of black and brown decorated with combed blue, black, and white cat's eyes, 7in. high. (Skinner) $8,625

Shakespeare's House, Stratford Upon Avon, Goss nightlight. (Crested China Company) $273

Goss fern wall pocket with bird decoration. (Crested China Company) $350

Goss Parian teapot with embossed decoration. (Crested China Company) $840

Cheshire cat by Grafton China with red mouth, 6½in. high. (Crested China Company) $109

Carlton crested china locomotive, 120mm. long with Castleford crest. (Crested China Co.) $290

Goss china squirrel vase. (Crested China Company) $490

Arcadian China plum pudding bomb. (Crested China Company) $245

Welsh lady, coloured vase, Goss. (Crested China Company) $77

Goss commemorative plate. (Crested China Company) $175

A small Davenport circular basket, decorated in blue, green, gilt and red with an Imari pattern, pattern No. 6065, 1st half 19th century, 8.5cm. (Woolley & Wallis) $118

Davenport platter of canted rectangular form, printed in blue with the 'Fisherman's Advice' pattern, Fisherman Series, circa 1830, impressed mark, 21in. (G A Key) $384

A Davenport rectangular plaque, painted with a portrait of a young man, signed *S. Chester*, and dated *1872*, 25.5 x 21cm. (Woolley & Wallis) $382

DE MORGAN

A good William De Morgan faience charger, 1880s, painted by Charles Passenger, in Persian style with a band of reptiles amongst foliage, 41cm. diameter. (Sotheby's) $18,000

A William De Morgan two-handled small vase, 1890, painted by Miss J. Babb, (one handle restored), 7¾in. high. (Sotheby's) $1,440

A William De Morgan ruby luster charger, painted by Charles Passenger, circa 1890, with a giant stylized fish against a yellow luster foliate ground, 30.8cm. (Bonhams) $2,755

DEDHAM

Dedham Pottery Cherub and Goat Pattern, raised design, blue stamp, diameter 9in. (Skinner) $2,300

Dedham pottery lobster salad plate, East Dedham, Massachusetts, early 20th century, registered blue ink stamp, 7½in. diameter. (Skinner) $287

Six Dedham Pottery rabbit breakfast plates, East Dedham, Massachusetts, early 20th century, marks include blue registered stamp, and 1931 stamp, 8¾in. diameter. (Skinner) $632

A London Delft polychrome Royalist caudle-cup, circa 1690, with a half-length portrait of William III in his coronation robes holding his orb and scepter, 3in. high. (Christie's) $41,454

A Dutch Delft model of a slipper, late 17th century/early 18th century of backless form with high heel and squared off toe, the top and front painted in blue with flowers, 19cm. length. (Bonhams) $647

An English delft blue and white octagonal meat dish, possibly Liverpool, painted with a sampan, a house and a pier, circa 1750, 50cm. wide. (Christie's) $394

Two English Delft powdered-manganese ground plates, circa 1739, probably Bristol, possibly Wincanton, one with a coastal scene in blue, 8¾in. diameter. (Christie's) $1,380

A Lambeth Delft blue and white Royal portrait dish, painted with a half-length portrait of George III, in profile to the left, wearing a sash and the Order of the Garter, circa 1761, 22cm. diameter. (Christie's) $12,337

An English delftware plate, probably Bristol or London, circa 1710, painted in the center with Queen Anne wearing a crown and jeweled pendant flanked by the initials *AR*, 9in. diameter. (Sotheby's) $5,645

DERBY

A Derby botanical dessert dish, circa 1795-1800, attributed to William 'Quaker' Pegg, the shaped square dish finely painted with a flowering stem of China Astor, 9in. (Sotheby's) $5,998

A Derby figure of a warden wearing a blue coat, hatch and leaf-pattern waistcoat and puce breeches, leaning on a cane with his tricorn hat under one arm, circa 1835, 14.5cm. high. (Christie's) $282

A pair of Derby figures with 'Macaroni Dog and Cat', circa 1770, modelled as a young boy and girl, he kneeling upon a rocky mound with his arms encircling a spaniel, incised, 6in. (Sotheby's) $2,470

175

Early Doulton Burslem oval platter, typically printed in blue with the 'Norfolk' pattern, printed marks, 17½in. (G A Key) $587

'Delicia' H.N. 1662 a Royal Doulton figure, printed marks. (Christie's) $410

Royal Doulton Dickens Ware jug of canted rectangular form, molded with Dickens characters, 'Old Curiosity Shop' design, printed marks and No D5584, 7in. (G A Key) $152

A Royal Doulton Dragon 'Chang' vase, signed _Noke_ and by Harry Nixon, modelled with a dragon twisting round the vase, the whole covered with a think 'icing' of running glazes, 20.5cm. (Bonhams) $5,544

Doulton Lambeth, a pair of stoneware vases, decorated by Hannah Barlow and Frank Butler, incised with horses in rural scenes, between floreate and scrolling borders, 40.6cm. (Christie's) $1,960

A Dublin Burslem three handled tyg decorated in the Arts and Crafts style, signed with initials _M.Y.M._, 17cm. high. (T.R. & M) $522

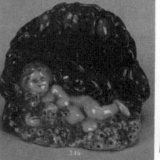

Royal Doulton three handled loving cup, the central panel elaborately molded with Art Nouveau style flowering foliate design, Mark V Marshall & Rosina Brown, impressed marks, 5½in. (G A Key) $660

A Doulton figure 'Under The Gooseberry Bush' H.H.49, designed by Charles Noke, a figure of a nude, painted in colors, printed factory and painted marks. (Christie's) $3,312

A Doulton Lambeth stoneware mantel clock, by John Broad and Mary Thomson, modelled with ostriches and a beaver on a rocky rectangular base, 23.8cm. (Sotheby's) $4,200

A Royal Doulton seriesware chamber stick, D3395, with Crombie golfers, *He Hath A Good Judgement Who Relieth Not Wholly On His Own.* (Phillips) $647

A Royal Doulton Sung figure of an elephant, designed by Charles Noke, covered in a speckled glaze on a flambé ground with off-white tusks, 28cm. high. (Christie's) $5,888

Royal Doulton 'Norfolk' pattern octagonal two handled pedestal bowl, typically printed in blue, printed mark, 9in. (G.A. Key) $708

A Doulton Lambeth silver mounted stoneware lemonade set, by Florence E. Barlow, the tapered jug incised with foliage and two paterae, silver mounts by Henry T Brockwell, London, 1880, the jug 24cm. (Tennants) $973

A Doulton Lambeth stoneware part tea service, 1878, by Hannah Barlow, borders by Lucy Barlow, incised with a band of deer, comprising; teapot and cover, milk jug, sugar bowl and two teacups and saucers, height of teapot 10.5cm. (Sotheby's) $4,200

A large Doulton Lambeth stoneware umbrella stand, circa 1892, by Mark V. Marshall, assisted by Rosina Brown, the shell-form body lavishly carved, modelled and incised with a lion's head, 26in. high. (Sotheby's) $23,750

Doulton Burslem circular plate, printed in blue with 'Oriel' pattern, 10in. (G A Key) $61

An impressive pair of Doulton Lambeth stoneware vases, 1885, by Hannah Barlow, borders by Florence Barlow, incised with a frieze of wolf hounds in a landscape, 15in. high. (Sotheby's) $9,600

Royal Doulton 'Norfolk' pattern octagonal jardinière, typically printed in blue, 8in. (G A Key) $800

A Doulton Lambeth stoneware clockcase, 1883, by John Broad, modelled with two female heads above the circular case, (finial restuck), 27.6cm. high.
(Sotheby's) $1,920

A Royal Doulton stoneware chicken bowl, early 20th century, by Mark V. Marshall, impressed lion, crown and circle mark, 11½in. long.
(Sotheby's) $4,800

A Doulton Lambeth faience large vase, circa 1900, boldly painted with fish swimming amongst swirling waves, (restoration to neck and foot), 21in. high.
(Sotheby's) $4,200

A Doulton Lambeth stoneware silver-mounted lemonade jug and four beakers, 1878, by Hannah B. Barlow, each incised with horses, the silver hallmarked Sheffield 1878, jug 10½in. high.
(Sotheby's) $5,100

A Doulton Lambeth stoneware silver-mounted teaset, 1881, by Hannah B. Barlow, decorated with sheep, comprising: a teapot and hinged cover, a jug and a sugar bowl, the silver hallmarked for Sheffield 1881, teapot 12.4cm high.
(Sotheby's) $3,300

Two Doulton Lambeth stoneware owl form jars and covers, 1880s/90s one with impressed rosette factory mark, the other impressed *Doulton Lambeth England*, 20cm. high.
(Sotheby's) $2,880

A pair of Royal Doulton stoneware vases, by Frank A. Butler, each boldly incised with foliage on a brown ground, 15¼in. high.
(Sotheby's) $2,700

A Doulton Lambeth stoneware clockcase, 1886, by Emily E. Stormer, incised around the dial with foliage, (minor restoration), 11in. high.
(Sotheby's) $1,680

A pair of Royal Doulton stoneware vases, 1903, by Mark V. Marshall, slip-trailed with stylized trees, (one with some restoration to rim), 11in. high. (Sotheby's) $960

A Doulton Lambeth stoneware jug, to commemorate Queen Victoria, inscribed *She wrought her people lasting good*, a silver mounted ring, 16cm. (Woolley & Wallis) $127

Victoria, HN 3125, number 2889 of an edition of 5000, a Royal Doulton figure from the Queens of the Realm Series, 20.3cm., printed marks (with certificate). (Bonhams) $706

A Doulton & Watts brown stoneware relief molded jug, decorated with a stag and a boar hunt, impressed marks, circa 1840, 20cm.(Woolley & Wallis) $106

DRESDEN

A pair of German porcelain vases and covers, possibly Dresden, circa 1890, decorated all over with flowers, fruit and putti, 35¾in. high. (Christie's) $8,065

A Dresden porcelain figure group of a musicale, late 19th century, blue crowned *N* mark, modelled with a gentleman playing the flute, his companion at the piano, a dancing couple and another couple seated, 25½in. wide. (Christie's) $2,760

Dresden porcelain vase, Germany, late 19th century, Thieme factory, alternating panels of figures and yellow ground floral bouquets, 13¼in. (Skinner) $500

ESSEVI

'Nostalgia' an Essevi pottery figure group, painted marks, 28.5cm. high. (Christie's) $1,151

A glazed earthenware figure, circa 1920, modelled as a blushing young girl, her skirts caught by the wind, a cupid at her feet, 13¼in. high, marked *Essevi Made in Italy Torino-Vento di Primavera-Sandro Vacchetti*.(Christie's) $4,000

An Essevi polychrome pottery mask, painted and incised marks, 48cm. high.(Christie's) $1,068

A Czechoslovakian porcelain group depicting a fisherman resting in a boat, with sea nymphs, printed mark, 20in. wide.
(Andrew Hartley) $431

A pair of Continental porcelain figural jardinières modelled as seated boy and girl figures in puce, each leaning against a large wooden tub, 19th century, 9in. wide. (Andrew Hartley) $445

A Swedish terrine with lid and dish, in the form of a melon, in yellow, green, brown and pink, marked *Marieberg*, 1758-66, 29cm. long.
(Stockholms AV) $4,537

A Zürich model of a gardener, circa 1770, blue Z / ..and impressed K··5, wearing a wide-brimmed black hat with pink roses, standing by a tree-stump with a brown watering-can at his feet, 8¼in. high.
(Christie's) $4,259

A pair of large Continental figures, 19th/20th century, after Meissen originals, decorated by Jules Viallate, modelled as a gardener and companion, each with basket of flowers and posies, 43.5cm.
(Bonhams) $575

'The Captured Bird' a polychrome pottery figure, from a model by Lorenzl, incised *Lorenzl,* printed factory marks, 45cm. high.
(Christie's) $2,961

A Katzhutte polychrome pottery figure, printed factory marks, 42.5cm. high.
(Christie's) $493

A Portuguese faience blue and white armorial dish, painted with a shield inscribed *teod/oxa,* reserved on a double-headed eagle below a crown, early 18th century, 36.5cm diameter. (Christie's) $590

A Keramos polychrome pottery figure, printed factory marks, impressed numerals *2001,* 26cm. high. (Christie's) $690

A Brussels (Ferriere La Petite) chicken-tureen, cover and fixed stand, circa 1755, naturally modelled with its head to the left resting on its side, with pink comb and wattle, 14½in. wide.
(Christie's) $34,075

Pablo Picasso, 'Bull and Picador', an earthenware turned pitcher, introduced 1956, limited edition of 500, the white body with oxidised paraffin decoration, impressed Madoura marks, 14cm.
(Christie's) $630

A Continental white model of a recumbent lion, circa 1740-45, perhaps Hewelcke, boldly modelled to the left, his head turned and with incised eyes and muzzle, with shaggy mane, 12½in. wide.
(Christie's) $6,474

A Buen Retiro figure of Bacchus, circa 1760-65, with a garland of grapes and vine leaves about his head, a goat's pelt slung over his right shoulder, 27cm. high overall.
(Christie's) $2,214

A pair of Continental figures of malabars, spurious blue crossed swords marks, in the Meissen style, in fur-lined exotic costumes, on grassy mound bases, the larger 13⁷/₈in. high.
(Christie's) $1,093

A Holics group of the Pietà, circa 1755, grey *HC* mark, modelled with the seated Virgin Mary wearing a long yellow-edged mantle from Her crown and a yellow-edged manganese dress, the crowned dead Christ draped over Her lap, 24.5cm. high.
(Christie's) $1,192

A Continental two handled wine flask and cover, of bulbous form, underglazed decoration, the handles above molded lion masks, 43.5cm.
(Bonhams & Brooks) $362

A Continental faience group, circa 1750, with a scantily clad putto seated astride a barrel, holding a wine-glass and a ewer, a naked putto standing nearby with a wine-glass, 18.7cm. high.
(Christie's) $1,363

A polychrome pottery figure group, by Katzenhutte, 1930s, modelled as two young female dancers in flowing floral dresses on shaped oval base, 26cm. high.
(Christie's) $1,008

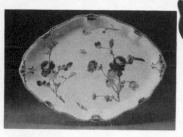

A Marseille faience shaped oval stand, late 18th century, painted with floral sprays and insects within puce and green feather-edged rims, 13½in. (Sotheby's) $2,194

Mosanic model of a cat, decorated in the Gallé manner, with glass eyes, the body decorated with lemon geometric designs, on a green washed ground, 7½in. (G A Key) $272

A porcelain tea for one, designed by Edouard Marcel Sandoz, manufactured by Théodore Haviland at Limoges, circa 1927, a teapot, milk jug and sucrier modelled as stylised birds, teapot 6½in. (Christie's) $1,680

A 'Judgement of Paris' coffee pot and cover, mid 18th century, of lighthouse shape with the continuous scene enamelled in vibrant famille rose colours, 11½in. high. (Christie's) $9,775

A Samson conversation group modelled with figures in 18th century dress drinking coffee at an informal morning gathering, 38cm. wide; and another smaller Samson group, late 19th century. (Christie's) $1,240

A pair of French biscuit porcelain figures of a gentleman and companion, each modelled gazing at a child seated on their shoulder, wearing 18th century dress, late 19th century, 59cm. high. (Christie's) $1,316

GARDNER

A Gardner figure of a cobbler modelled seated repairing a shoe, on rectangular base, printed and impressed iron-red mark, 13cm. high, mid 19th century. (Christie's) $360

Gardner biscuit figure of an old woman, Russia, circa 1860, depicted wearing a shawl and headscarf and carrying a bundle, impressed and printed marks, 8¼in. high. (Skinner) $805

Gardner biscuit figure of an old woman, Russia, mid 19th century, the female figure modelled standing and with a walking stick in one hand, 6½in. high. (Skinner) $748

George Jones rectangular covered tobacco box, the lid moulded with leaves and bud, the border moulded with buds, 7½in. (G A Key) **$666**

A fine George Jones majolica sardine box, cover and stand circa 1874, the oval box and two-handled stand basket-weave-moulded in tones of ochre and brown, 8½in. across. (Sotheby's) **$4,939**

A George Jones majolica dressing table tray, impressed *JC* monogram within a circle and diamond registration mark, 28.9cm. long. (Sotheby's) **$3,000**

GOLDSCHEIDER

A Goldscheider figure of an exotic dancer, full length standing, with head-dress and polychrome painted blue cloak and wrap, 18in. high. (Wintertons) **$1,400**

Goldscheider pottery wall mask modelled as the head of an oriental lady, coiled green hair, naturalistic face with orange lips, 11in. (G.A. Key) **$455**

Goldscheider ceramic bust of a lady wearing a hat, Austria, second quarter 20th century, stylised turquoise hair with mottled orange hat on female with yellow jacket and black 'lace' edges, 15in. high. (Skinner) **$430**

HANS COPER

A stoneware black goblet form by Hans Coper, mounted on a square white base, circa 1961, 6¼in. high. (Bonhams) **$7,865**

Hans Coper, a stoneware spade form vase, the manganese brown body covered in a buff and bluish white slip burnished in areas to reveal brown body, circa 1972, impressed HC seal, 16.6cm. high. (Christie's) **$9,993**

A unique off-white dish by Hans Coper with the powerful design of a swan, open-winged with bent neck and face, circa 1953, 375mm. diameter. (Bonhams) **$15,729**

A Bernard Leach temoku glazed stoneware vase, circa 1950, impressed *BL* monogram and St. Ives Pottery mark, height 12in. (Sotheby's) $3,000

A Bernard Leach slab bottle vase circa 1965, the sides divided into four squares with blue, painted with iron-red motifs, 7½in. (Sotheby's) $1,625

A large Bernard Leach faceted stoneware vase, circa 1950, impressed *BL* monogram and St. Ives Pottery mark, height 14in. (Sotheby's) $4,500

LENCI

A Lenci pottery jug in the form of a fierce rotund man with tall black hat being attacked by children, 30cm. high, 1930. (Bearne's) $1,050

Two polychrome ceramic plaques of the Disney characters Bambi and Orsetto, 1930s, marked *Lenci Made in Italy*, 16 x 14cm. (Finarte) $600

Lenci (Italy) Art Deco period model of lady with her arm resting on circular container applied with an open book, naturalistically decorated in colors, dated *1932*. (G.A. Key) $2,926

LIVERPOOL

A Liverpool globular teapot and cover, polychrome painted with Chinese figures in a garden, circa 1760, 13.5cm. (Woolley & Wallis) $408

Polychrome decorated Liverpool pitcher, England, early 19th century, black transfer decoration depicting a three-masted ship flying an American flag, 9¾in. high. (Skinner) $1,035

A Liverpool globular teapot and cover, with onion finial, painted with a version of the Imari palette with trees beside flowering Oriental shrubs, circa 1780, 18cm. high. (Christie's) $987

LUCIE RIE _____ CHINA _____

Dame Lucie Rie, a deep footed bowl of oval section, covered in a pitted buttercup yellow glaze, circa 1980, impressed *LR* seal, 16.8cm. wide. (Christie's) $6,541

A beautiful yellow stoneware bowl by Dame Lucie Rie, distinguished by a bronze band of sgraffito below the rim, circa 1960, 245mm. diameter.
(Bonhams) $9,437

A Dame Lucie Rie glazed stoneware bowl, circa 1965, with palest blue and pink mottled glaze, impressed *LR* monogram, height 4½in. (Sotheby's) $7,200

LUDWIGSBURG

A white glazed Ludwigsburg model of reclining lovers, perhaps Bacchus and Ariadne, she fills her partner's cup with grapes from a basket at her elbow, 29cm. long. (Woolley & Wallis) $706

A Ludwigsburg rectangular tray, with scroll and shell moulded side handles, painted with scattered Deutsche Blumen, mid 18th century, 33cm.
(Woolley & Wallis) $735

A Ludwigsburg figure of a horn player, circa 1764/1767, modelled by Nees, from the 'Kleine Musiksoli' series, seated on a stool by a round table with a cup, bottle and note sheet, 5in. (Skinner) $1,501

MAJOLICA

An English majolica teapot and cover, circa 1880, formed as a Chinese boy clambering over a large coconut, painter's mark *L*. 14.3cm. high.
(Sotheby's) $1,320

A majolica U-shaped jardinière, moulded with apple blossom on a basket moulded blue ground, circa 1870, 26cm.
(Woolley & Wallis) $366

An English majolica jardinière, circa 1880, moulded with passion flowers, 30.8cm. high.
(Sotheby's) $4,200

A Martin Brothers stoneware grotesque monstrous undersea figure, dated *1898*, inscribed *R.W. Martin & Brothers/London & Southall, 1898*, 7¼in. high. (Sotheby's) $8,400

A Martin Brothers stoneware face jug, incised marks, 4.5 1910, 15cm. high. (Christie's) $3,619

A Martin Brothers stoneware amorphic toast rack, dated *1890*, length 8½in. (Sotheby's) $5,400

A Martin Brothers 'Wally Bird' stoneware jar and cover, dated *1911*, the head slightly turned and titled, with heavy forehead, deep set eyes gazing down and large beak, 30.4cm. (Bonhams) $6,960

Two Martin Brothers stoneware figural wall matcholders, circa 1880, both inscribed *R.W. Martin/Southall*, 13 and 17.1cm. high. (Sotheby's) $3,300

An imposing large Robert Wallace Martin stoneware bird jar, dated 1882, black-painted wood socle, height 25½in. (Sotheby's) $81,250

A large Martin Brothers stoneware jug, dated 1880, incised with swans swimming in lily pad laden waters, with nude maidens along the grassy shores, height 17½in. (Sotheby's) $3,900

A saltglaze stoneware model of a bird with removable head in the Martin Brothers style. (Academy) $624

A good Martin Brothers stoneware vase, dated 1899, well incised with an assortment of undersea creatures, heightened in pale blue and brown slips, height 23.8cm. (Sotheby's) $9,600

An unusual unsigned Martin Brothers stoneware figural group, dated 1880, depicting a grotesque figure riding an iguana, height 10½in. (Sotheby's) $1,680

A Martin Brothers stoneware and carved wood grotesque covered jar of a satyr, dated *1900*, on elaborate carved wood base, inscribed inside and on *flange R.W. Martin and Brothers London & Southall, 10-1900*, 8½in. high. (Sotheby's) $18,000

A rare Martin Brothers stoneware grotesque figural teapot, dated 1896, lid inscribed Martin Bros. London & Southall, 1-1896, height 6¾in. (Sotheby's) $22,600

Martin Brothers, a stoneware vase, dated *1895*, the ovoid body with short everted neck decorated with humming birds amongst orchids in muted tones on a mottled beige and brown ground, 22cm. (Christie's) $2,520

A pair of fine Martin Brothers stoneware incised aquatic vases dated *1897*, both inscribed *R.W. Martin & Bros./ London & Southall, 6-1897*, 16in. high. (Sotheby's) $14,400

A Martin Brothers stoneware 'Wally Bird' stoneware jar and cover, dated *1/1891*, the removable head modelled with deep set eyes, the whole glazed in blues and browns, 31cm. (Bonhams) $21,025

An amusing Martin Brothers stoneware grotesque figure with vase, circa 1890, the brawny figure of an imp holding an amphora, black-painted wood socle, height 23.2cm. (Sotheby's) $3,300

A Martin Brothers stoneware face jug, incised marks, *5/1910*, 14cm. high. (Christie's) $1,809

A very good Martin Brothers stoneware double bird jar, dated 1903, vessel with finely incised feathers, height 10¾in. (Sotheby's) $27,200

A Meissen (outside-decorated) group known as 'The Test of Love', after a model by Michel Victor Acier and Johann Carl Schönheit, modelled as a gallant and companion, seated and standing before a plinth, 74.5cm. high overall. (Christie's) $2,072

A rare Meissen hen tureen and cover, circa 1770, modelled by J.J.Kändler, as a bantam hen protecting her brood, six chicks peer out from beneath her wings and a seventh sits on top of her back, 9½in. across. (Sotheby's) $36,236

A Meissen ormolu-mounted figure of L'Avvocato, circa 1740-50, from the Commedia dell'Arte, modelled by J.J.Kändler, the masked figure with his right hand raised holding a watch and a glove, 7½in. (Sotheby's) $5,645

A Meissen clock-case, circa 1880, after an original 18th century model, the enamelled dial set into a tall rectangular case painted with scattered flower sprigs, 32cm. (Sotheby's) $3,528

Two Meissen 'Cris de Paris' figures of a Peep-show Man and a Poultry-Seller, late 19th century, after the original models by J.J. Kändler and Peter Reinicke, the former wearing a black hat and a lilac jacket, each 14.5cm. (Sotheby's) $2,772

A Meissen 'Cris de Paris' figure of a trinket seller, modelled by J.J. Kändler, holding his black tricorn in his left hand and with an open trinket case balanced on his left arm, 7¼in. (Sotheby's) $5,712

Meissen porcelain figure group, Germany, 19th century, modelled as allegorical female subjects set on an oval base, one holding a ribbon at the wings of Cupid, the other feeding doves, crossed swords mark, 12in. high. (Skinner) $5,175

A large Meissen outside-decorated model of a 'foo dog', late 19th century, modelled after J.G. Kirchner, the large terrier modelled seated snarling, with gilt edged purple buckled collar and russet fur, 17¼in. high. (Christie's) $6,463

A Meissen figure group emblematic of Geography late 19th century, modelled in the round with four putti consulting over a globe, a standing maiden before a palm tree records their findings, 16in. high. (Christie's) $4,935

A Meissen gardening group, circa 1880, after an original model by M.V.Acier and J.C. Schönheit, modelled as young people standing and seated around high rockwork, 29.5cm. (Sotheby's) $2,293

A Meissen figure of a fox, second half 18th century, modelled on all fours in crouching position, its coat and eyes picked out in tones of brown, length 16.3cm. (Sotheby's) $1,764

A Meissen flower-encrusted vase, circa 1740-50, the pierced latticework double-ogee body with flared neck and foot, applied with brightly coloured scattered flowers, 10cm. (Sotheby's) $3,175

A pair of 19th century Meissen porcelain figures of a shepherd and shepherdess, standing in pale blue, lilac and pink floral dress, he with bagpipes, 10in. high. (Andrew Hartley) $1,960

A large Meissen model of a turkey late 18th century, possibly later decorated, modelled by J.J. Kändler, the plumage picked out in shades of brown and the head in blue and red, 22¼in. (Sotheby's) $9,438

A pair of Meissen miniature figures of a hunter and huntress, circa 1750, wearing matching blue-lined yellow tunics and black hats and each holding a rifle, 8cm. (Sotheby's) $4,032

A rare Meissen figure of Harlequin, circa 1775, modelled by J.J. Kändler, in dancing attitude, wearing a puce hat with feather, moustachioed mask, 17.5cm. (Sotheby's) $3,024

A Meissen salt from the Möllendorf service, circa 1761 of preussisch musikalischem Dessin, moulded with panels of musical, astronomical and military trophies and flower bouquets, 2¾in. (Sotheby's) $1,680

A Meissen figure group emblematic of Commerce, mid 19th century, modelled as Mercury seated atop a bundle, holding a book while writing on tablet attached to a column, 10¾in. high. (Christie's) $3,525

A small Meissen partridge tureen and cover, circa 1750, the naturalistically colored game bird modelled seated on an oval nest of shredded grasses and ears of corn, 6in. (Sotheby's) $1,463

A 19th century Meissen porcelain figure of a lady with a basket of flowers, wearing a blue hat and floral dress, 7½in. high. (Andrew Hartley) $872

A Meissen teapot and cover, circa 1730, of ovoid form with faceted spout, painted on one side with a Kauffahrtei scene of a merchant and his family by the bank of an estuary, 3¾in. (Sotheby's) $5,468

A Meissen saucer, circa 1725-30, painted in iron-red with a dramatic European landscape with fortifications within Böttger lustre and gilt arched panels enclosing puce scrollwork, 12.1cm. (Sotheby's) $2,194

Two similar Meissen figures of a boy and a girl flanking pedestals, he with a basket of fruit, she with turquoise and polychrome dress with a dove, 19th century 5in. high. (Andrew Hartley) $675

A Meissen Hausmaler teapot and cover, circa 1720-25, of depressed globular form with a loop handle and slightly curved spout with mask terminal, gilt in Augsburg in the Seuter workshop with chinoiserie figures, 13cm. (Sotheby's) $1,463

A Meissen oval sugar box and cover, circa 1730, each painted in Kakiemon style with two sprigs of indianische Blumen and a phoenix in flight, 4¾in. (Sotheby's) $4,368

A Meissen neo-rococo mantel clock, late 19th century, surmounted by an orb and applied with nymphs and putti emblematic of the Arts, 18½in. high. (Christie's) $11,750

A Meissen porcelain box in the form of a recumbent lion, the base decorated on both sides with flowers, gilt interior, circa 1750, 5.5 x 8.5 x 5cm. (Arnold) $2,642

A Meissen cylindrical chocolate pot with turned wooden handle, and lid with metal handle, brown with foliate decoration on spout, circa 1780, 16.5cm. high.
(Lempertz) $785

A Meissen group of children pressing wine, circa 1880, after an original model by J.C. Schönheit, modelled with seven children in flowered, rustic dress, engaged in various playful pursuits, 12½in.
(Sotheby's) $7,728

A Meissen teapot and cover, the spout modelled as an animal head, one side painted with two dogs frightening a horse, mid 18th century, 4¼in.
(Woolley & Wallis) $1,328

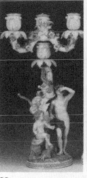

A pair of Meissen models of bustards, each standing before tall turquoise grass and raised on rocky bases, their plumage picked out in brown, 2nd half 19th century, 37cm.
(Woolley & Wallis) $1,716

A pair of Meissen porcelain figures of gardeners, after originals by Michel Victor Acier, she with a basket of flowers, he with flowers in his hat, 17.3cm. high.
(Bearne's) $1,937

A pair of Meissen figural three branch candelabra, late 19th century, emblematic of Autumn and Summer, 35.5cm.
(Christie's) $1,568

A T-form Meissen stick handle, a molded woman's face at one end, wearing a half veil over a hood, the handle decorated with flowers and fruit, mid 18th century, 12.5cm. long. (Lempertz) $1,674

A Meissen Hausmalerei teabowl and saucer, circa 1725, the decoration slightly later, decorated in eisenrot at Augsburg, with wooded landscapes.
(Christie's) $1,180

A Meissen silver-gilt-mounted two-handled bowl and cover, circa 1723-24, circa 1723-24, the bowl painted on both sides with sportsmen at leisure in river-landscapes within shaped gilt cartouches enclosing Böttger luster, 3¼in. (Sotheby's) $7,409

Minton majolica teapot formed as a Japanese dwarf with mask, his head forming the cover and the mask forming the spout, pattern No. 1838, date cipher for 1882, 5½in. high. (G.A. Key) $1,590

A Minton majolica dark-blue-ground two-handled jardinière, molded in relief with a central band adorned with acorns and oak leaves with two ovoid panels of classical goddesses, year cypher for 1876, 32cm. high.
(Christie's) $5,313

A Minton majolica monkey teapot and cover, circa 1875, modelled seated clutching a coconut, a stalk forming the spout, his head forming the cover, 6in.
(Sotheby's) $4,754

'The Three Marys', a Minton Parian figural group, dated 1851, modelled with three female figures standing on an oval base, 35.5cm.
(Bonhams) $471

A Minton majolica oyster-stand modelled with four tapering tiers of oyster shells with white-glazed interiors and brown exteriors, on nests of green seaweed, year cypher for 1864, 26cm. high.
(Christie's) $8,855

A Minton majolica footed jardinière, molded with two panels of female busts divided by the handles, the blue ground with laurel sprigs, Greek key border, 38.5cm.
(Bristol) $2,669

A Minton porcelain plate, the center painted with a melon, grapes, strawberries and mushrooms, signed O.H. Copson, 1879, 25cm.
(Woolley & Wallis) $246

A Minton majolica 'bamboo' cylindrical jardinière and stand, of slightly tapered form and molded with two ribbon bands, year cyphers for 1873, 21cm. high. overall. (Christie's) $886

Mintons terracotta circular plaque, painted in colors with a scene of a putti and butterfly amidst flowers, impressed marks and date cypher for 1873, 9in. (G.A. Key) $80

A majolica spill vase modelled as a cockerel, probably Minton, modelled by John Henk, naturalistically modelled standing by a tub amongst leaves on a rocky oval mound base, 26.5cm. high. (Christie's) $1,594

'The Infant Bacchus', a Minton Parian figure, date code 1874, modelled by John Bell, in vine leaf loin cloth, with wreath in hair, reclining on the back of a leopard, 33cm. long. (Bonhams) $1,694

A Minton's majolica jug, 1874, probably modelled by Paul Comolera, modelled in the form of a cat seated on its haunches its tail forming the handle, with a mouse under its paw, 9¾in. high. (Sotheby's) $12,000

Fine 19th century Minton two handled pot pourri holder and stand, encrusted throughout with flowers and painted in colors with scene of 'Warwick Castle', 10in. (G A Key) $801

A Minton majolica blue-ground 'passion flower' jardinière and stand, with two lion's mask handles, molded in relief with scrolling foliage and passion flowers beneath a latticework frieze, cypher for 1873, 41.5cm. high. (Christie's) $7,084

A Mintons Art Pottery 15¼in. plaque, painted with *Julia*, date code for 1881, anchor mark and *Cottier & Co, London*, 38.9cm. diameter. (Bristol) $724

A pair of Minton turquoise-ground tapering vases, in the Sèvres style, each painted by F.N. Sutton with a winged putto within a shaped rectangular panel, circa 1895, 15cm. high. (Christie's) $2,125

A Minton spittoon decorated with foliate design, impressed and painted marks, 22cm. high. (Christie's) $460

A pair of Minton majolica 'Christmas' mask jugs, with branch-molded handles issuing holly and mistletoe between gadrooned sections, shape 575, impressed marks, year cyphers for 1863 and 1864, 23cm. high. (Christie's) $2,708

A Pearlware 'Flight to Egypt' group, of Sherratt type, with Mary seated on a mule with the Christ Child, Joseph to their side, on hollow mound base moulded with scrolls and painted in colours, circa 1820, 22cm. high. (Christie's) $843

Rare Pearlware baluster-form jug, Britain, circa 1830, with complex looping earthworm decoration in white, rust, blue, and black with black slip-filled rouletted bands, 4⁷/₈in. high.
(Skinner) $5,175

A Pearlware elephant penholder, a caparison formed as a castle with four towers above a red saddle cloth on his back, on rectangular base moulded with a band of stylised shells, circa 1820, 20cm. high. (Christie's) $5,640

A Pearlware 'Tythe Pig' group, of Sherratt type, with the farmer, his wife and baby and the cleric standing before flowering bocage on a hollow mound base, circa 1820, 20.5cm. high.
(Christie's) $1,585

A Pearlware cow creamer, with a milking maid in attendance, on a rectangular base with canted corners, sponged in pink, black and green, circa 1810, 16cm. long.
(Christie's) $705

A Pearlware group of the New Marriage Act, with a parson, clerk and a couple, beneath a plaque inscribed *The New Marreg Act John Frill & Ann Boke.Aged 21 That Is Right.Says The Parson.Amen.Says The.Clark,* circa 1820, 20cm. high. (Christie's) $790

A Pearlware model of a cat, seated on its haunches, sponge-decorated in shades of green, brown and ochre, circa 1820, 19cm. high.
(Christie's) $2,465

A 19th century Pearlware meat plate of rounded oblong form, blue printed with Kirkstall Abbey, Yorkshire, from the Antique Scenery Series, within a floral border, 21in. wide.
(Andrew Hartley) $596

A Pearlware Gretna Green group of a blacksmith and a couple standing either side of an anvil, below a tool box and flowering bocage, circa 1820, 19cm. high.
(Christie's) $1,675

An English pearlware two-handled circular dessert bowl and pierced domed cover, the bowl moulded with interlaced scrolls and wreaths, circa 1790, 23cm. high.
(Christie's) $1,104

A Pearlware circular plaque of Pratt type, with two cows and a female attendant, the border with a band of ovolos, surmounted by a winged putto's head, circa 1800, 17cm. high. (Christie's) $740

A George IV Coronation jug, pearlware, dated *July 19, 1821*, of ovoid form black printed and enamelled with a crown among roses, thistles and foliage, with a rare reference to Queen Caroline, 14cm. (Bonhams) $1,001

A Pearlware figure of a putto wearing loose robes, standing before flowering bocage holding a basket of flowers, on a mound above a square base, circa 1820, 13cm. high.
(Christie's) $195

A Pearlware cottage pastille-burner and cover, the pitched gabled thatched roof with tow chimneys on a Tudor style cottage, the mound base applied with flowers, circa 1830, 12cm. high.
(Christie's) $615

A Pearlware figure of Billy Waters, of Enoch Wood type, standing leaning against a bollard playing a fiddle, his peg-leg resting on the head of the hound beside him, on stepped rectangular base, circa 1825, 18cm. high.
(Christie's) $1,585

A pearlware blue and white dish, printed with figures seated before a tomb, no mark, circa 1820, 31.5cm.
(Woolley & Wallis) $206

Pearlware quart mug, Britain, circa 1830, banded in black, blue, and rust with white trailed four-line slip waves on the black field, 5¾in.
(Skinner) $5,750

A Pearlware model of a pug seated and turned to the onlooker, on a quilted tasselled base, circa 1830, 9cm. high. (Christie's) $1,055

A large Poole Pottery circular dish, decorated with a colourful owl on a moonlit night, marked *Poole England*, 41cm.
(Woolley & Wallis) $177

A CSA large Poole pottery vase by Anne Hatchard, pattern ZB, shape 220, impressed and painted marks, 26.8cm. high.
(Christie's) $1,068

A Carter Stabler Adams, twin-handled vase by Anne Hatchard, pattern BT, shape no. 973, impressed and painted marks, 17.7cm. high.
(Christie's) $1,480

QIANLONG

A large Ming-style blue and white Hu, Qianlong seal mark in underglaze blue and of the Period, shou medallions reserved on a wan fret ground and key pattern on the neck, 44.7cm. high.
(Christie's) $17,250

A famille rose 'Nine-Peach' bottle vase, Qianlong seal mark, 19th century, delicately enamelled mainly in pale pink and green tones, with two entwined gnarled branches bearing clusters of peaches, 13in. high.
(Christie's) $13,330

A copper-red-decorated blue and white moonflask, Qianlong seal mark in underglaze blue and of the Period, each side painted with a five-clawed dragon leaping in pursuit of a flaming pearl, 10¼in. high. (Christie's) $43,700

ROOKWOOD

Rookwood standard glaze iris vase, Cincinnati, 1889, decorated by Amelia Browne Sprague, flared rim over wide neck and bulbous body, yellow iris and dark green leaves, 6½in. high. (Skinner) $575

A Rookwood pottery tea service, circa 1892, decorated by Edward Abel with fuchsia, comprising: teapot and cover, sucrier and cover and milk jug. (Sotheby's) $427

Rookwood standard glaze two-handled vase, Cincinnati, 1891, decorated by Albert Valentien, flared rim on an extended neck over ovoid body, two loop handles at shoulder, 10in. high.
(Skinner) $1,380

Czechoslovakian painted pottery figural group of a nymph on shell, after a Royal Dux model, painted in multicolors, factory marks, 20¼in. high. (Skinner) $863

A pair of Royal Dux standing figures of lady and gentleman holding water vessels, with green flowing robes, tree trunk supports, 20in. high. (Brightwells) $1,078

A Royal Dux figure of a woman with two borzoi, applied pink triangle, stamped *Czechoslovakia*, 37cm. (Christie's) $1,024

RUSKIN

A Ruskin high-fired stoneware baluster vase, shouldered form with collar rim, mottled voilet, purple and mint running glaze, printed factory marks, 1905, 21cm. high. (Christie's) $5,175

A Ruskin Pottery high-fired stoneware bowl and a stand, 1926 and 1933, the steep sided bowl covered with a sponged red and mauve glaze, repeated on the four leg table-form stand, diameter of bowl 25.7cm. (Sotheby's) $1,680

A Ruskin stoneware vase, decorated with lustrous apple green glaze, *Ruskin Pottery, 1910*, impressed, 14.5cm. (Woolley & Wallis) $286

SATSUMA

A Satsuma koro signed *Satsuma-yaki Yukiyama* and sealed, late 19th century, decorated in various coloured enamels and gilt with two panels depicting blossoming cherry trees and a ho-ho bird spreading its wings, 10½in. high. (Christie's) $4,935

A Japanese Satsuma bowl, the exterior decorated with three shaped panels of figures in landscapes on a butterfly strewn ground, Meiji, 1868-1912, 10.75cm. (Woolley & Wallis) $4,158

A 19th century Satsuma vase and cover of ovoid form, with ball finial on flattened lid, truncated branch handles, the body painted with birds in landscapes, 4½in. high. (Andrew Hartley) $1,155

A Sèvres oviform teapot and cover 1771, painter's mark of Micaud, painted with an entwined blue ribbon, berried laurel and a garland of garden flowers continuing up the spout, 12.5cm. high.
(Christie's) $3,748

A Sèvres (hard paste) cylindrical coffee can and saucer (gobelet litron et soucoupe) 1787, painter's mark of Mme. Marie-Anne Gérard.
(Christie's) $7,297

A pair of Sèvres style portrait circular table tops, framed as plaques, painted with half-length portraits of Philippe de France and Louis Dauphin, late 19th century, 45cm. wide.
(Christie's) $2,632

French painted porcelain Sèvres style bronze-mounted lamp base, early 20th century, with *V.F. Limoges* mark, body painted with scene of man playing violin for two ladies, signed *R. Petit*, 23in. high.
(Skinner) $3,105

A Sèvres cup and trembleuse saucer, 1764, painter's marks for *P-A, Méreaud*, the cup painted with garlands of flowers suspended from a border.(Christie's) $3,236

A Sèvres milk-jug pot à lait à trois pieds, circa 1765, the branch handle and three feet enriched with gilding and with foliage terminals, painted by Viellard, 3¾in. high.
(Christie's) $1,533

A French gilt bronze mounted Sèvres porcelain cup and cover, 19th century, the domed cover with spread eagle surmount, the handles as entwined snakes, 12¾in. high.
(Christie's) $1,809

A pair of Sèvres porcelain and gilt metal mounted vases, body painted with a roundel depicting Napoleon and troops, signed *Lancry*, the reverse with a floral spray, early 20th century, vase 20in. high.
(Andrew Hartley) $6,116

A Sèvres two-handled hot-chocolate cup, cover and stand, 1777, the cup with bouquets of pink roses within circular gilt cartouches against vertical bands alternating with trailing branches of blue flowers. (Christie's) $5,111

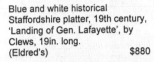

Blue and white historical
Staffordshire platter, 19th century,
'Landing of Gen. Lafayette', by
Clews, 19in. long.
(Eldred's) $880

Staffordshire salt glazed stoneware
sauce boat, England, mid 18th
century, oval form with molded
and enamel decorated leaves and
berries, 7in. long.
(Skinner) $2,645

Antique blue and white historical
Staffordshire platter, 'Gyrn,
Flintshire Wales', by R. Hall., 17 x
13½in. (Eldred's) $550

A pair of figures of Moody and
Sankey, Moody with his right hand
and Sankey with his left hand
resting on a book above a pedestal,
on shaped oval gilt-titled bases,
circa 1873, 44.5cm. high.
(Christie's) $705

An equestrian figure of Garibaldi,
Thomas Parr, Garibaldi wearing
orange shirt and white trousers,
modelled standing before the horse
holding a sword, on titled shaped
oval mound base, circa 1861,
37.5cm. high.
(Christie's) $1,055

A pair of figures of Emily Sandford
and James Rush, she wearing
pale-blue head shawl, blue blouse
and pink skirt, he wearing blue
frockcoat, green waistcoat an pink
trousers, circa 1849, 25cm. and
25.5cm. high.
(Christie's) $1,320

A group of King John and two
pages, King John seated in a tent,
signing the Magna Carta, a page to
either side with a flag behind the,
on shaped oval base, mid 19th
century, 33cm. high.
(Christie's) $616

A model of a horse, standing four
square, painted with brick red
markings with a grey mane and tail,
on a rectangular tree stump base,
late19th century, 30cm. wide.
(Christie's) $1,585

A group of Highland Jessie and a
Soldier, Jessie standing to the right
of a soldier, probably Corporal
Brown, who holds a rifle on a
barrel, on gilt-titled base, circa
1857, 22.5cm. high.
(Christie's) $245

A Joseph Holdcroft majolica teapot, the ovoid body modelled as a Chinese man mounting a coconut, in brown, blue, green and yellow, 14cm. (Bonhams) $1,233

A pair of models of cats, seated on their haunches facing left and right, painted with black and ochre patches, circa 1840, 14.5cm. and 15cm. high. (Christie's) $2,290

A group of Uncle Tom & Eva, Uncle Tom seated holding a book, with Eva standing on a parcel beside him, circa 1852, 28cm. high. (Christie's) $495

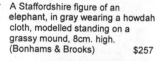

An English earthenware cylindrical mug, blue printed with the 'Piper' pattern, printed mark including the title, circa 1820-40, 12.5cm. (Woolley & Wallis) $172

19th century Staffordshire character jug, modelled as a man seated on a corner chair and wearing a black tricorn hat, naturalistic face, green speckled cravat, iron red waistcoat and puce jacket, 11in. (G.A. Key) $188

A Staffordshire figure of an elephant, in gray wearing a howdah cloth, modelled standing on a grassy mound, 8cm. high. (Bonhams & Brooks) $257

A Walton figure of a shepherd standing before flowering bocage holding a crook in his left hand, a seated hound at his feet, on hollow scroll-moulded base, impressed banner mark, circa 1820, 15cm. high. (Christie's) $440

Two leopard spill vases, standing facing left and right before the tree spill, painted in ochre with black spots, on mounds above scroll-moulded bases, mid 19th century, 17cm. high. (Christie's) $4,230

A group of Napoleon III and Prince Albert, the two figures wearing military uniform, standing before two flags, a wall and a pile of shells between them, on titled shaped rectangular base, circa 1854, 28cm. high. (Christie's) $670

Historic blue and white Staffordshire pearlware coffee pot, England, 19th century, depicting Napoleon in Russia driving a sled with two horses, 12in. high.
(Skinner) $1,092

Two Pratt type 'Peace and Plenty' oviform jugs typically molded in relief with two panels of seated female figures holding attributes and inscribed Peace and Plenty, circa 1802, 18.5cm. high.
(Christie's) $722

A Staffordshire pottery figural spill vase depicting a seated female and a dog flanking a tree trunk, she holding a bird's nest, the dog standing on a kennel, 8in. high.
(Andrew Hartley) $174

19th century Staffordshire clock figure of Wesley, preaching from his pulpit, 10½in.
(G A Key) $188

Pair of Staffordshire 19th century models of iron red spaniels, both with naturalistic faces, gilded collars and black tipped feet, 5½in.
(G.A. Key) $424

Staffordshire group of a young man and his lady, clutching a basket of flowers, painted in colors, minor rim chips, 19th century, 9in.
(G.A. Key) $95

A group representing Ireland and Britannia, Ireland modelled as a woman seated with a harp, shaking hands with a figure representative of Britannia to her side, circa 1882, 32cm. high. (Christie's) $686

A porcelain dog head stirrup cup, naturalistically modelled as the head of a sporting hound, circa 1830, 13cm. high.
(Christie's) $903

A 'Barnstaple' slipware bear jug, naively modelled as a bear scratching his muzzle with his hind legs, *Bruin* on his stomach, 20cm.
(Bonhams & Brooks) $154

A pair of figures of the pugilists Tom Cribb and Tom Molyneux, standing beside a post with their fists raised, on grassy shaped oval bases, 19th century, 23cm. high. (Christie's) $7,050

A group of Samson and the Lion, with Samson wrestling with the lion, on shaped oval gilt line base, second half 19th century, 28cm. high. (Christie's) $423

A pair of Staffordshire models of colourful birds, raised on green and brown rockwork applied with moss, 2nd half 19th century, 24.5cm. (Woolley & Wallis) $712

A group of 'The Victory' with an English sailor seated on a cannon holding a flag, a French soldier to his left holding a flag and a Turkish soldier to his right, on shaped oval gilt-titled base, circa 1856, 35cm. high. (Christie's) $6,000

A figure of the Wounded Soldier, the French soldier and English sailor standing, on titled shaped oval base, circa 1855, 32cm. high. (Christie's) $455

A theatrical group of three figures in a boat, of a Highlander playing the bagpipes, standing between a dancing sailor and female companion, on shaped oval base, mid 19th century, 34.5cm. high. (Christie's) $792

A spill vase group of Smith and Collier, wearing simple dress, a hound leaping on the poacher, before a tree stump on a gilt line base, circa 1866, 34cm. high. (Christie's) $1,938

An equestrian figure of General Sir George Brown and an equestrian figure of General Sir James Simpson, wearing cocked hats and military uniform, 33cm. and 31cm. high. (Christie's) $2,820

A group of the Death Of Nelson, Nelson wearing cocked hat and uniform, between a seated and a standing officer, on titled shaped oval base, circa 1845, 22.5cm. (Christie's) $495

A group of 'Turkey, England, France', with the figures standing on titled shaped rectangular base, circa 1854, 28.5cm. high. (Christie's) $355

A group of Victoria, Albert and Child, Victoria seated holding a baby with Albert standing to her side, on shaped oval mound base, circa 1840, 21cm. high. (Christie's) $195

A duck tureen and cover, the cover naturalistically modelled as a duck, the plain lower section moulded with waves, circa 1870, 23cm. long. (Christie's) $737

A pair of figures of cricketers, wearing caps, flocked shirts, sashes and cravats, the bowler with a bowling ball in his hand, the batsman with a bat in both hands, on shaped oval bases, circa 1865, 34cm. and 36cm. high. (Christie's) $3,525

A Walton figure of a girl seated before a flowering arbour reading a book, a cat on the mound to her side, on shaped base, impressed banner mark, circa 1820, 12cm. high. (Christie's) $1,050

A pair of theatrical figures of Jules Perrot as Albrecht and Carlotta Grisi, wearing theatrical dress, each holding a dance pose before mounds on shaped oval gilt line bases, mid 19th century, 23cm. high. (Christie's) $316

A group of a ram and shepherd of Pratt type, the ram standing with the male attendant to his side, painted in a typical palette, late 18th century, 15.5cm. high. (Christie's) $1,940

A group of Uncle Tom and Eva, Uncle Tom standing in a boat with his arm around Eva who stands on a package to his left, on titled shaped oval gilt base, circa 1852, 33cm. high. (Christie's) $210

A porcelain group of a fox-hunter riding a hound, the hunter wearing a gilt cap, red coat and riding boots, holding a horn, the oversized hound with black markings, circa 1850, 12cm. wide. (Christie's) $565

Stoneware Grotesque face jug, 19th century, brown speckled glaze, no stand, 5½in. high. (Skinner) $14,950

A glazed stoneware overmantel figure of a lion, late 19th century, the regal creature with black painted facial details and ocher glazed mane and tail, 22¾in. long. (Sotheby's) $2,587

A Danesby Ware stoneware swan figure, printed marks, 41cm. wide, and two jugs. (Christie's) $790

A Victorian chinoiserie decorated stoneware jar and cover, 19th century, decorated with oriental figures in river landscapes, 15½in. high. (Christie's) $1,991

A stoneware vase, by Primavera, 1920s, the body decorated in graduating brown glazes with three medallions encompassing naked female figures in various poses, incised *Primavera France*, 11¾in. high. (Christie's) $1,008

Four-gallon cobalt decorated stoneware jug, *S. Hart Fulton*, 1876-78, decorated with a pair of spotted lovebirds, and *4* in script, 15¾in. high. (Skinner) $1,035

Five-gallon cobalt decorated stoneware jug, unmarked, third quarter 19th century, decorated with a bird perched on a cherry branch, 18½in. high. (Skinner) $345

Cobalt decorated stoneware crock, White's Pottery, Utica, New York, 19th century, cylindrical salt glazed crock with lug handles, 12⅜in. high. (Skinner) $2,990

Large cobalt blue decorated stoneware water cooler, 19th century, barrel-form with stylized floral decoration on the front, 21¼in. high. (Skinner) $805

A Sunderland pink luster oviform jug, printed in black and painted in colors with a view of the Iron Bridge beneath a banner titled *Sunderland Coal-Trade*, 17cm. high. (Christie's) $405

S Moore & Co Sunderland luster rectangular plaque, the center bat printed and decorated in colors with the 'Waverley' design, circa early 19th century, 9in. (G.A. Key) $290

A Sunderland pink luster oviform jug, printed in black with a view of the Iron Bridge, the 'Salilor's Farewell' and a panel of verse, circa 1840, 18cm. high. (Christie's) $645

SUSIE COOPER

A Susie Cooper part dinner and coffee set of banded design, printed marks, coffee pot 19cm. (Christie's) (Set) $361

'Skiing' a Susie Cooper Nursery Ware breakfast set, painted in colours, SCP marks (minor nicks), hot-water pot 14cm. (Bonhams) $2,205

A Susie Cooper Grays Pottery leaping gazelle jug printed marks, 19cm. high. (Christie's) $575

SWANSEA

A porcelain plate, probably Swansea, painted with roses an elaborate gilt border, no mark, circa 1810, 23.5cm. (Woolley & Wallis) $116

A Swansea Pearlware teapot and cover, inscribed in brown *Susanna Wing,* 1798 within an underglaze blue foliate cartouche, the reverse painted with a spray of carnations, 24cm. (Bristol) $2,041

A Swansea style plate, painted with colorful flower sprays, a gilt line rim, marked *Swansea* in gilt, 19th century, 20.7cm. (Woolley & Wallis) $71

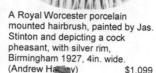

A Royal Worcester porcelain mounted hairbrush, painted by Jas. Stinton and depicting a cock pheasant, with silver rim, Birmingham 1927, 4in. wide. (Andrew Hartley) $1,099

A pair of Royal Worcester flared cylindrical vases, painted with pheasants in a naturalistic setting, by James Stinton, Grainger shape no. 923, date code 1921, 22.5cm. high. (Wintertons) $2,849

A Worcester Parian ware figure, Ariadne on Rock, after a model by W.B. Kirk, unsigned, 16in. high. (Andrew Hartley) $616

A Worcester polychrome teapot and cover, painted with two bouquets of summer flowers and scattered floral sprigs, circa 1775, 17cm. (Tennants) $656

A Worcester blue and white flared fluted coffee-cup, circa 1753, workman's mark of a cross within a circle, painted with a butterfly in flight over bouquets of flowers. (Christie's) $937

A Royal Worcester porcelain bowl of circular form, painted with pheasants to the interior and exterior signed *Jas Stinton*, within gilt banding, 8½in. wide. (Andrew Hartley) $3,542

A pair of Royal Worcester porcelain vases of tapering form, the cream body painted with a floral spray, reserved on a gilded deep blue ground, 9in. high. (Andrew Hartley) $695

A Royal Worcester porcelain trefoil bon-bon dish, with scroll handle, painted with insects, thistles and flowers, 31.5cm. long, signed with the initials *E.R.*, date code for 1895. (Bearne's) $554

A blush Worcester porcelain urn and cover, the body painted with floral sprays by E Raeburn between moulded scrolling strapwork and mask heads, 14½in. high. (Andrew Hartley) $1,207

A Worcester blue and white leaf dish, circa 1758, painted in the 'Picture Scroll Landscape' pattern, the body moulded in low relief with veining within a serrated rim, 18.5cm. long. (Bonhams) $2,329

Arriflex IIC No. 13776, Arnold & Richter, Germany; 35mm., with motor, matte box, instruction book, and 50 years commemorative booklet, in maker's box. (Christie's) $3,619

An important early cinematographic camera, the only known example in private hands, originally from the company collection, Newman & Guardia, London;non-standard perforated 35mm. black-leather covered wood-body. (Christie's) $15,134

B + H 70-DR ciné camera, no.99453, Bell & Howell, U.S.A.; 16mm., with a three-lens turret holding a Taylor-Taylor & Hobson Telekinic 2.8in. f/2.8 lens, Serital 1in. f/1.3 lens and a 0.7in. f/2.5 lens. (Christie's) $263

Arriflex St No. 19646, Arnold & Richter, Germany; 16mm., with angled-viewfinder, lens-turret holding a Schneider Cinegon f/1.8 10mm. no 8720063 and a Schneider Cinegon f/1.4 16mm. no. 1197968. (Christie's) $1,479

Gaumont/Demeny Chrono De Poche no. 396, L. Gaumont, Paris; 16mm., with Demeny movement the lens mount stamped 396 (lacks lens and crank). (Christie's) $493

Kino model A No. 940221, Ernemann-Werke AG., Germany; 35mm. polished-wood body, brass-fittings, with hand-crank, one film magazine and a Carl Zeiss, Jena Tessar f/3.5cm. lens no. 509959. (Christie's) $987

Beaulieu R16 automatic camera, Beaulieu, France; 16mm., with an Angénieux 12-120mm. f/2.2 lens battery holders, two film magazines.(Christie's) $1,151

Cinescopie, Italy; 35mm., the inside stamped controlled under no. 1179.S.I.C. and FABRIQUE EN ITALIE, with sports finder and handcrank. (Christie's) $263

Cameflex Standard No. 192, Caméflex, France; 35mm. with film magazine, motor and lens-turret holding a Cooke Speed Panchro 35mm. f/2. (Christie's) $1,150

A wind-up Kanamo camera by ICA, Dresden, for 35mm. film, with Tessar 1:3.5/4cm. lens and two original cassettes, 1920.
(Auction Team Köln)　　$179

A Bolex H 16mm camera with Leitz Hektor of 11.1.1943, with three lenses, in original leather case, with instructions in German.
(Auction Team Köln)　　$430

A Colorco two-colour film camera for 35mm. film, aluminium body, with Zeiss Jena Tessar 1:2,7/4cm. lens, American, circa 1920.
(Auction Team Köln)　　$1,596

Debrie ciné camera, J. Debrie, Paris; 35mm., polished teak body, with an E. Kraus Tessar f/3.5 50mm. lens no. 118598 lens and hand-crank.
(Christie's)　　$657

A Beaulieu MAR-8 automatic camera for double-8 film, in grey-green case, with rewind and Angenieux 1;1.8/7.5-35mm. lens,
(Auction Team Köln)　　$256

Kinemacolor camera, [?]Williamson, England; 35mm., hand cranked, polished-wood body, rotating two-colour filter holder, inside plate red filter indicator.
(Christie's)　　$1,499

A Pathé cinematographic camera, with Kraus-Tessar 1:3.5/50mm. lens and two 60m. magazines, circa 1914.
(Auction Team Köln)　　$1,659

A Bolex H16 with Pan Cinor ciné camera, for 16mm. film, with Pan Cinor 1:2/17-85mm. lens, by Paillard.
(Auction Team Köln)　　$363

A Kinamo wind-up camera by ICA, Dresden, for 25mm. film on 5m. spools, in original case.
(Auction Team Köln)　　$145

A Beaulieu 5008S ciné camera for Super 8 film, with Schneider Optivaron 1,8/6-66mm. lens.
(Auction Team Köln) $231

An Eumig C 16R for 16mm. film, light grey case with green leather trim, with Eumigar 1,9/25mm. lens with telephoto and wide angle setting.
(Auction Team Köln) $297

A mahogany Ertel ciné camera by Ertel, Munich, for 35mm. film, 1920.
(Auction Team Köln) $430

A Paillard H 16 Reflex camera for 16mm. film, with two Switar and one Yvar lenses, with original leather case, box and accessories.
(Auction Team Köln) $766

An Askania Z ciné camera, by Askania Werke, Berlin, for 35mm. film, with Astro Pan Tachar 1:1 8/35mm. lens, with case, two cables and ten cassettes, 1930.
(Auction Team Köln) $1,981

An Askania shoulder camera by the Askania Werke, Berlin, with three Astro Pan Tachar 1:1,8/28-50-75mm. lenses, for 35mm. film, 1935.
(Auction Team Köln) $1,585

A mahogany and brass-mounted Bioscope Model D by Charles Urban Trading Co., London, with two Voigtländer lenses, 1910.
(Auction Team Köln) $2,425

A 35mm Newman & Sinclair ciné camera, aluminium case and aluminium cassette for 60m film, with Ross Xpress 1:4,5/6 lens, 1942.
(Auction Team Köln) $452

A mahogany, metal mounted Kine Messter cinematographic camera by Oskar Messter, Berlin, for 35mm. film, circa 1900.
(Auction Team Köln) $6,606

A Enigma remote deciphering machine, complete and in working order, for ultra-secret messages, so that not even the operator could read them, circa 1940, one of only three known to exist. (Auction Team Köln) $19,341

A very rare Enigma Schreibmax print-out machine, put on the lamp-holder to print the incoming message directly in clear text, in working order and one of only 3 known.(Auction Team Köln) $31,887

A rare Enigma 'clock' accessory for the Enigma cipher machine, to further increase the number of code options available, 19.5 x 15 x 12cm. (Auction Team Köln) $14,636

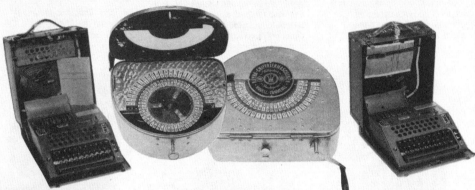

A Swiss Army Nema Type T-D post-war encoding machine, an electric successor to the Enigma, with original manual and documentation, 1947. (Auction Team Köln) $1,242

A rare German Kryha cipher machine, the window showing two circular rows of characters, the outer fixed and the inner rotating, 1926. (Auction Team Köln) $4,077

A Nema Type T-D postwar version of the Enigma encoding machine: only 640 were manufactured, 1947. (Auction Team Köln) $960

A rare 10-row T52a Enigma cipher machine by Siemens & Halske, with manuals and technical descriptions, 1935. (Auction Team Köln) $52,274

A rare American M209 cipher machine by Smith & Corona Typewriters Inc. based on the pre-war Swedish Hagelin-Cryptos system, circa 1953. (Auction Team Köln) $1,149

An Enigma A filament lamp cipher machine, by Heimsoeth & Rinke, Berlin, in original metal case with plug and three spare bulbs, 1944. (Auction Team Köln) $13,068

A Victorian Gothic bracket clock, the gong-striking movement with Roman numeral silvered dial, in a pedimented, oak case,28.5cm. wide. (Bristol) $736

Early 20th century ornate mahogany bracket clock, the raised pediment applied in the center with ormolu finial, the four corners flanked by similar finials, clock 27in. high. (G.A. Key) $5,280

A George III ebonized small striking bracket clock, Coleman, London, fourth quarter 18th century, the gilt-brass-lined case with handle to triple-pad breakarch top, 10in. high. (Christie's) $19,860

A George III mahogany striking bracket clock, George Stuart, Newcastle upon Tyne, circa 1800, the 21cm. painted convex dial with twin fusee striking movement and signed backplate, 46cm. high. (Bonhams) $4,795

A mahogany bracket clock, Finer & Nowland, circa 1815, the twin fusee bell striking and repeating movement with an engraved border and a strike silent lever mounted on the back plate, 22in. (Christie's) $2,352

English George III ebonized bracket clock, second/third quarter 18th century, with two-train movement chiming hourly on single bell, John Prou, London, 19in. high. (Skinner) $2,990

An ebonized chiming bracket clock, German, 1900s, the triple going barrel movement chiming on 8 bells and a coil hour gong, 25in. (Christie's) $1,029

A Dutch gray-painted and parcel-gilt bracket clock, late 18th century, the circular enamelled dial with Roman and Arabic chapters, the movement stamped *RUTGERUS / VANMEURS / AMSTERDAM*, behind a glazed shaped door, (Christie's) $5,658

A Regency style mahogany double fusee bracket clock, 19th century and later, set in a later case with inlaid decoration, 48cm. high. (Bonhams) $493

A George III mahogany striking bracket clock, John Taylor, London, fourth quarter 18th century, the case with flambeau urn finials to the bell top, 25in. high. (Christie's) $12,408

A George III mahogany repeating bracket clock with white painted Roman dial inscribed *John Harper*, 39.5cm. (Bearne's) $3,067

A small mantel clock, the twin fusee movement striking on a bell in a mahogany arched case with a cupola top, 13¼in. (Woolley & Wallis) $2,310

A George III ebonised striking bracket clock, Joseph Stephens London, fourth quarter 18th century, the five pillar twin fusee movement with verge escapement and strike on bell, 17¾in. high. (Christie's) $4,963

A George III mahogany quarter chiming bracket clock, Benjamin Dunkely, Tooting, fourth quarter 18th century, the six pillar fusee triple movement with deadbeat escapement, 24in. high. (Christie's) $6,872

A George III mahogany striking bracket clock, fourth quarter 18th century, dial signed *Jno.Hubbard, Southwark* on silvered signature plaque in the Chinoiserie engraved silvered centre, 18in. (Christie's) $6,872

A George III fruitwood striking small bracket clock, John Pyke, London; fourth quarter 18th century, the case with handle to brass-lined single pad breakarch top, 14¾in. high. (Christie's) $9,545

A George III mahogany striking bracket clock, Leplastrier & Son, London, fourth quarter 18th century, the case with gilt-metal handle and pine cone finials to the bell top, 18¼in. (Christie's) $7,254

A George III ebonised striking bracket clock, Mc.Kensy London, fourth quarter 18th century, the brass-lined case with cast handle to triple-pad top, 17in. high. (Christie's) $6,300

A Victorian gilt-brass carriage timepiece, Dent, London, circa 1848, the foliate engraved case with large bevelled glasses and foliate-cast and engraved handle, 7in. high. (Christie's) $4,514

An English gilt-brass chronometer carriage timepiece, Thomas Mercer, St. Albans, circa 1960, the substantial movement with four double-screwed baluster pillars and chain fusee with maintaining power, 7in. high.(Christie's) $3,611

A French striking giant carriage clock, retailed by The Goldsmiths Company London, the anglaise riche gilt-metal case with reeded composite-capped columns, 9¼in. high. (Christie's) $3,250

A Victorian brass striking large carriage clock, Desbois, last quarter 19th century, the case on bun feet and with cluster columns to the angles surmounted by ball finials to the glazed stepped top, 7in. high. (Christie's) $2,528

A French gilt engraved brass striking small carriage clock, third quarter 19th century, the foliate engraved gorge case with handle and repeat button to top, white enamel Roman chapter disc with blued steel moon hands, 13cm. high. (Christie's) $3,250

An early Victorian ormolu striking carriage clock, Vulliamy, circa 1840, the case with large baluster handle to the top with escapement viewing portal, glazed sides and rear door, 6¼in. high. (Christie's) $3,611

A French engraved gilt-brass striking carriage clock, Drocourt, Paris, foliate engraved cannalée case, the twin barrel movement with strike, repeat and alarm on a gong, 6in. high. (Christie's) $3,611

A French gilt-brass and champlévé enamel striking carriage clock, fourth quarter 19th century, the anglaise riche case richly decorated with multi-coloured champlevé enamel in foliate designs, 7in. high. (Christie's) $6,319

An early Victorian ebonised striking four-glass clock, Dent, 82 Strand, London, No. 477, the case with ripple moulding to the glazed top surmounted by an octagonal section gilt-metal handle, 8¼in. high. (Christie's) $13,541

A French gilt-brass striking and repeating carriage clock with alarm, Le Roy & Fils, circa 1880, the gorge case with white enamel Roman dial, 6in. high. (Christie's) $1,472

A French engraved gilt-brass and lacquer striking and repeating carriage clock with alarm, for the Turkish market, circa 1870, 5½in. high. (Christie's) $3,128

A French engraved brass striking and repeating carriage clock, circa 1885, white enamel Roman chapter disc with Arabic five minutes, 5¼in. high. (Christie's) $2,024

A British engraved silver striking carriage clock, Mappin & Webb, circa 1975, the foliate engraved columnar case on bun feet and with acorn finials, 6in. high. (Christie's) $1,565

A Swiss guilloché enamel and silver plated miniature travel timepiece, early 20th century, the milestone case decorated with blue guilloché enamel, 2¾in. high. (Christie's) $829

A French brass and porcelain-mounted striking and repeating carriage clock with alarm, circa 1890, the bambu case with cream porcelain panels, 6½in. high. (Christie's) $3,312

A French gilt-brass and champlevé enamel mignonnette carriage timepiece, circa 1890, the cannelée case with sky blue enamel panels, 3in. high. (Christie's) $1,472

A Swiss silver-gilt miniature travel timepiece, retailed by Drew & Sons, Piccadilly Circus, circa 1906, the rectangular case with scroll handle. (Christie's) $2,024

A French gilt-brass grande sonnerie striking and repeating carriage clock with alarm, Roblin & Fils Frères à Paris, circa 1880, 5½in. high. (Christie's) $2,024

A strike and repeat on a gong carriage clock by Maurice & Co., decorated with butterflies, 1885, 5½in. high.
(Derek Roberts) $9,200

A very rare full perpetual calendar strike and repeat on a bell carriage clock, by Ellis, circa 1845.
(Derek Roberts) $18,400

A French gilt-brass striking and repeating carriage clock with alarm, retailed by Tiffany & Co., New York, circa 1890, 7¼in. high.
(Christie's) $2,944

A French engraved brass grande sonnerie striking and repeating carriage clock with centre seconds, day of week, alarm and date, Rossel & Fils, Genève, circa 1875, 5¾in. high.
(Christie's) $5,520

A Swiss engraved gilt-brass and Limoges enamel-mounted mignonnette striking and repeating carriage clock, circa 1890, anglaise style case with Limoges enamel panels, 3in. high.
(Christie's) $19,320

A French brass striking and repeating carriage clock, Japy Frères & Cie, circa 1880, the oval case with foliate engraved mask to the white enamel Roman chapter disc, 6in. high. (Christie's)
                    $883

A French gilt-brass mignonnette carriage timepiece, Henry Capt, Genève, circa 1890, the oval case with white enamel Roman dial, 3in. high. (Christie's) $736

A French gilt-brass grande sonnerie striking and repeating carriage clock with alarm, circa 1890, the bambu case with white enamel Roman dial, 6½in. high.
(Christie's) $2,760

A French parcel-silvered brass and polychrome enamel mignonnette carriage timepiece for the eastern market, circa 1885, 3¼in.
(Christie's) $2,208

A 19th century marble clock garniture, 43cm. high.
(Bonhams) $948

A brass and champlevé enamel mantel clock garniture, French, 19th century, 12in., urns 8½in. (Bonhams) $1,106

A French champlevé enamel and gilt bronze mantel clock and garniture, late 19th century, the glazed and panelled case with urn surmount and berried finials, with painted panels of maidens to the angles, 15½in. high, side urns 11½in. high.
(Christie's) $5,890

An Italian gilt-metal, bronzed and marble clock garniture, the striking clock within a lyre-shaped case supported by satyrs, 60cm., with matching six-branch candelabra side ornaments, 20th century.
(Bearne's) $1,570

An ormolu and porcelain mounted mantel clock, French, 19th century, 12½in. (Bonhams) $474

A red and white grained marble clock set, French, circa 1900, 3½in. enamel dial with floral decorated centre, the bell striking movement with a sun burst pendulum, in a drum case suspended between 4 columns, 14in. (Bonhams) $1,078

A gilt ormolu and jewelled porcelain mounted clock garniture, French, circa 1880, 3½in. painted porcelain dial decorated with a cherub in the centre, the bell striking in a drum case surmounted with an urn finial and lower mask heads, together with a pair of matching 3 light candelabra, 12in.
(Bonhams) $2,198

French Egyptian Revival bronze and marble threepiece clock and garniture, late 19th century, height of clock 16½in., garniture 18in. high.
(Skinner) $2,530

A 19th century French jewelled porcelain and gilt metal clock garniture, the drum movement with transfer printed dial depicting a birds nest, and a pair of matching vases with flame finials and domed lids.
(Andrew Hartley) $3,360

A French gilt-metal and black marble mystery pendulum clock garniture, GLT; first quarter 20th century, the truncated column black marble base with foliate ring handles to the sides and surmounted by a gilt-metal mother and child, 23½in. high.
(Christie's) $3,972

A fine cold painted bronze and gilt-bronze clock garniture Paris, circa 1860, the dial signed *Bastien à Paris*, in a drum case surmounted by a Chinese figure with a parasol, clock: 58cm. high.
(Sotheby's) $19,924

A marble and ormolu mounted clock garniture, French, 1900s, 3½in. enamel dial with Arabic numerals, the bell striking movement with a sunburst pendulum, in a gilt drum case surmounted by a crossed torches and quiver finial, together with a pair of matching urn side pieces, 16½in., urns 11in.
(Bonhams) $1,178

A white marble and gilt ormolu clock garniture, French, circa 1880, the bell striking movement in a drum case surmounted by a gilt spread eagle and foliage, together with a pair of matching two light candelabra, 13in. (Bonhams) $1,794

A gilt spelter and porcelain mounted clock garniture French, 19th century, 45cm. garniture, 39cm. (Bonhams) $1,323

A boulle and ormolu mounted mantel clock, Mappin & Webb, last quarter 19th century, the 9cm. convex enamel dial, with a pair of associated garnitures, 37cm. high. (Bonhams) $653

A French clock garniture, painted green with flowers, the 8 day movement striking on a bell, inscribed A. Requier Amiens, in a cartouche shape case with gilt brass mounts, 14in., together with a pair of matching two light candelabra. (Woolley & Wallis) $406

French garniture du cheminée, 8 day striking movement, with a garlanded enamel dial, with an urn surmount to the green onyx gilt brass mounted portico case, and a pair of matching twin light candelabra, 9in. (Woolley & Wallis) $284

A rouge marble and gilt metal clock garniture, French, circa 1880, 3in. dial signed Sauclierers Nice, the bell striking movement in a rectangular case surmounted by a gilt urn, together with a pair of matching 3 light candelabra, 16in. (Bonhams) $359

A green painted clock garniture, French, 1900s, the bell striking movement in a waisted sided case with a foliage finial, applied gilt mounts and a painted scene on the front of a courting couple, together with a pair of three light matching candelabra, 15½in. (Christie's) $882

A brass four glass mantel clock with mercury pendulum, French, 19th century, 9in. (Bonhams) $790

A 19th century French mantel clock garniture, the clock with eight day movement having white enamel dial inscribed *Howell and James*, in leaf chased ormolu oblong case, inset blue jasperware medallions depicting mythological scenes, 13¾in. high, and a pair of matching four light candelabra. (Andrew Hartley) $1,001

An ormolu and porcelain mantel clock together with a pair of spelter side urns, French, circa 1880, 3½in. blue and gilt porcelain dial decorated with putti to the center, signed *Hennessy Swansea*, the bell striking movement in a cast case surmounted by an urn, together with a pair of porcelain and spelter side pieces, 18in. (Christie's) $1,617

A French gilt and patinated bronze and marble mantel clock and garniture, late 19th century, the spherical case amidst stylized clouds and drapery with two cavorting cherubs, the part fluted and stepped rosso lavento base raised on toupie feet, 28¼in. high, and a pair of conforming candlesticks en suite. (Christie's) $7,106

'Sèvres' painted porcelain and ormolu mounted mantel clock and candelabra garniture, early 20th century, comprising a Louis XVI-style clock, with two train half-strike movement, front of case painted with scene of Cupid and Venus, signed *Petit*, 21in. high., together with pair of associated five light candelabra, 21in. high. (Skinner) $2,990

A gold and floral painted clock garniture, French, 1900s, 3in. enamel dial, the bell striking movement in a waisted case decorated with flowers and applied gilt mounts, together with a pair of matching three light candelabra. 14in. (Bonhams) $700

An ormolu and white marble clock garniture, French, circa 1890, 4in. convex enamel dial with floral decorated centre, with a pair of matching two light candelabra held by bronzed putti, 12in. (Bonhams) $1,820

A mottled red marbled and ormolu clock garniture, French, circa 1880, 3in. marble dial signed *Angely Pere a Fils Toulouse*, the bell striking movement in a square case, 17in. (Bonhams & Brooks) $781

French cut and etched glass ormolu and Jasperware mounted three-piece clock garniture, early 20th century, clock with glass columns to each corner, with frosted glass panels to the sides and back, the case topped by glass sphere with scrolled ormolu mounts, with two vasiform glass garnitures, clock 18½in. high. (Skinner) $5,750

A white marble and ormolu clock garniture, French, circa 1880, gilt applied numerals on a black painted globe case with bell striking movement, together with a pair of matching five light candelabra, 51cm. (Bonhams) $2,100

A cast brass clock garniture, French, 1900s, the bell striking movement in a cast gilt case with a stepped pediment surmounted by an urn, together with a matching pair of three light candelabra, 15in. (Bonhams) $560

A green onyx clock garniture, French, 1900s, 3¼in enamel dial with floral decorated centre, the bell striking movement in a rectangular case surmounted by an urn finial, together with a pair of two light candelabra, 13½in. (Bonhams & Brooks) $426

A French ormolu and marble figural clock garniture, circa 1890, in white marble case surmounted by a classical maiden and a cherub, on gilt mounted plinth base with festoon apron, 25cm. wide, and two candelabra, each formed as Pan supporting two foliate cast candle sconces, width 14.8cm. (Bristol) $840

A painted spelter and porcelain timepiece garniture, French, late 19th century, 3in. porcelain dial, drum movement in a silver and gilt painted case surmounted by a rearing horse and rider, together with two warrior side pieces, 16in. (Bonhams & Brooks) $568

A French gilt bronze striking mantel clock and garniture, circa 1880, retailed by Elkington & Co., the case modelled as a swag-hung urn surmounted by a figure of Cupid, supported from the sides by classical maidens, 32in. high, and a pair of seven light candelabra en suite, 31½in. high. (Christie's) $14,262

An ormolu and jewelled blue porcelain clock together with a pair of matched garniture, French, circa 1870, gilt case surmounted by a painted urn decorated with village scenes, with a pair of now electrified five light candelabra, clock 14in. (Bonhams) $2,800

A green onyx champlevé four glass clock garniture, French, 1900s, the gong striking movement stamped with the Japy Freres factory mark, and mercury pendulum, together with a pair of matching urn shaped garnitures, 13½in. (Bonhams) $1,120

A Continental brass and white marble clock garniture, the lyre shaped clock case surmounted by an urn on a plinth base, flanked by a pair of satyrs and matching seven light candelabra on shaped bases and paw feet, 24in. high. (Bonhams) $685

Three-piece gilt bronze boudoir timepiece garniture, early 20th century, the timepiece set into lyre-form body draped by flat leaf swags, topped by fruiting finials, and ending in putto, 11¾in. high with a pair of two-light garnitures. (Skinner) $1,150

An ormolu-mounted Sèvres style pink-ground clock garniture, late 19th/early 20th century, the works stamped *Japy Freres*, the porcelain *Petit*, a cartouche-shaped case, applied with scrolling foliage and painted with a nymph and putto in a garden, five-light candelabra with putti and garden pavilions, 21in. high, candelabra. (Christie's) $9,775

A large French marble striking mantel clock and garniture, last quarter 19th century, the case constructed from rouge griotte, verde antico, bardiglio and broccatello marbles, with fluted arched top and flanked by columns, 23¼in. high, and the pair of ornamental tazze en suite, 13in. high. (Christie's) $353

A Louis XVI-style ormolu-mounted Carrara marble garniture, by Fernand Gervais, Paris, circa 1880, comprising a lyre-shaped clock and a pair of seven-light candelabra: the clock with acanthus finial above a vine-festooned female mask, the clock: 28¾in. high. (Christie's) $27,600

A French Champlevé and porcelain clock garniture, the striking clock with gilded dial above a painted panel depicting a girl and cherub attendant in a garden, signed *Collot*, 31.5cm., with a pair of matching side vases, each signed *Lucot*. (Bearne's) $1,680

Three-piece Empire Revival black slate and rouge marble clock garniture, late 19th/early 20th century, clock with Mougin movement, case topped by round bezel set in round hood, flanked by rouge marble centered roundels, with a pair of similar columnar tazzae, clock 18½in. high, tazzae 9½in. high. (Skinner) $862

A French ormolu three-piece garniture, circa 1880, comprising a clock and pair of associated four-light candelabra, the clock with enamelled dial signed *PREVOST*, with twin train movement, the rocaille case mounted with a pair of putti with vine chain, clock: 15¾in. high. (Christie's) $4,113

A French gilt metal and porcelain clock garniture, late 19th century, the clock with painted panels and surmounted by an urn, together with two matching candle sticks, 13¾in. high. (Bonhams) $493

A late 19th century gilt metal three piece garniture de cheminée, the clock 20in. high. (Dockree's) $1,440

Three-piece slate, marble, and ormolu mounted Louis XV style clock garniture, late 19th century, retailed by Gaudinot, Charleville, clock with Japy Frères two-train movement, together with a pair of four-light candelabra urns, on similar plinth base, clock 22½in. high. (Skinner) $2,000

A 19th century ormolu and porcelain mounted clock garniture, the case surmounted by a porcelain ball with pineapple finial, the porcelain panels painted with figures in a wooded glade, stamped *Japy Freres*, with a pair of matching vases and covers, 35cm. high, all on giltwood stands. (Bearne's) $4,900

A George III oak longcase clock, dials by Richards, Birmingham, 7ft.6in. high. (Russell Baldwin & Bright) $2,887

A heavily carved oak eight-day longcase clock, the square brass dial inscribed *Wm.Cuff*, 207cm. (Bearne's) $2,355

W. Kirton, Newcastle, an early 19th century 8-day mahogany longcase clock, 92in. high.(Dreweatt Neate) $1,416

Federal cherry tall case clock, circa 1800-1810, 94½in. high. (Freeman) $3,360

A heavily carved and stained oak striking longcase clock. Brass dial inscribed *Jos.Greatreau. Old-Swiford,* 215cm. (Bearne's) $879

A Dutch walnut longcase clock, Willem Van Bramer, Amsterdam, second quarter 18th century, 9ft.6in. high. (Christie's) $9,027

An oak eight-day striking longcase clock in the gothic style. Brass dial inscribed *Phillip Polkinghorne. St. Austel,* 231cm. (Bearne's) $2,198

A George II walnut astronomical longcase clock, Alexander Cumming, London, circa 1780, 9ft. high. (Christie's) $22,568

A mahogany tubular chiming longcase clock, English, 1900s, 7ft.6in. (Bonhams) **$5,338**

A Chippendale mahogany tall-case clock, by Benjamin Cleveland, Newark, New Jersey, 1785–1800, 83½in. high. (Christie's) **$12,650**

A good 18th century oak longcase clock by Henry Baker of Malling, 83in. high, 1770. (Canterbury) **$3,726**

A 19th century mahogany and crossbanded longcase clock, eight day movement by Groom of Wellington, 244cm. high. (Wintertons) **$2,666**

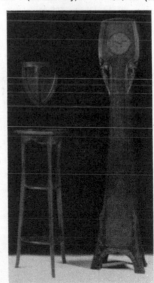

A carved oak 8-day longcase clock with red lacquered face, dated *1781*, striking the half hours on a bell, German, circa 1781, 230cm. high. (Lempertz) **$5,233**

Delaware Chippendale long case clock, circa 1779, works by Duncan Beard, walnut case attributed to John Janvier Sr., 97in. high. (Freeman) **$459,200**

A long case clock, wall bracket and jardinière 'Modèle Chicorée', designed by Louis Majorelle, circa 1905, the clock 80½in. high. (Christie's) **$31,670**

An important marquetry longcase clock with full grande sonnerie striking, Joseph Knibb, Londini Fecit, circa 1680, 6ft. 5in. (Bonhams) **$81,640**

225

A mahogany longcase clock, Thomas Whitford, Smithfield Bars, circa 1820, 7ft.7in. (Bonhams) $6,580

A George III mahogany quarter chiming longcase clock, Henry Bagnall, London, 8ft.1in. high. (Christie's) $11,226

An early longcase movement in a later case, Michael Knight Londini Fecit, circa 1700, 6ft.6in. (Bonhams) $4,760

A black lacquer longcase clock, John Massingham, Fakenham, circa 1770, 7ft. (Bonhams) $980

An oak cased small spring driven chiming longcase clock in a later case, English, 19th/20th century, signed for Kemp Bros Union Street Bristol, 5ft. 11in.(Bonhams & Brooks) $852

A fine Pennsylvania walnut longcase clock with centre seconds, Benjamin Morris, New Britain, 1777, 8ft. 7½in. (Bonhams) $49,000

An oak longcase clock with moonphase, Cuff, Shepton Mallett, circa 1790, 12in. painted dial, 7ft. 2in. (Bonhams & Brooks) $2,840

An 8 day oak longcase with brass dial, chequered inlay to the case Hardwick, Ashwick, 19th century, 214cm. (Bonhams) $2,058

A mahogany longcase clock, German, 1900s, 6ft.6in. (Bonhams) $490

An oak longcase clock, William Kemp, Lewis, circa 1780, 6ft.7in. (Bonhams & Brooks) $3,408

A mahogany longcase clock, W Helliwell, Leeds, circa 1820, 8ft. (Bonhams & Brooks) $1,846

An inlaid mahogany chiming longcase clock, German, 1920s, 6ft. 7in. (Bonhams) $1,764

An oak and mahogany 30 hour longcase clock, S. Noon, Ashby, early 19th century, 7ft. (Bonhams & Brooks) $1,207

An oak Arts & Crafts longcase clock, English, 19th century, 12in. copper dial, marked *In Love Memory and Hope Mary,* 7ft.1in. (Bonhams & Brooks) $639

A 30 hour oak and mahogany longcase clock, W. Wilson, Bellper, early 19th century, 7ft. (Bonhams & Brooks) $1,136

An oak carved longcase clock, Corrie, Langholm, 18th/19th century, 6ft.7in. (Bonhams & Brooks) $710

A mahogany longcase clock, J B Fallows, Manchester, circa 1830, 8ft.3in. (Bonhams) $3,640

A mahogany chiming longcase clock, English, 1900s, 7ft. 9in. (Bonhams & Brooks) $2,272

A black lacquer longcase clock, Richard Eva, Falmouth, circa 1750, 7ft.8in. (Bonhams & Brooks) $3,408

An oak 30 hour longcase clock, William Budgen Reigate, 1st half 18th century, 6ft.5in. (Bonhams & Brooks) $3,976

A George III mahogany and inlaid longcase clock, B.E. Coates & Sons, Wakefield, circa 1810, 91in. high. (Bonhams) $1,932

A late Victorian mahogany and ebonised quarter chiming domestic longcase regulator, Charles Frodsham, London, No. 2008, 6ft.11in. high. (Christie's) $12,091

A mahogany tubular chiming longcase clock, English, circa 1900, signed for R L Knight Plymouth, 7ft. 8in. (Bonhams & Brooks) $6,390

A carved oak chiming longcase regulator, retailed by W & M Dodge, Manchester, 13¾in. engraved round brass dial, 7ft. 2in. (Bonhams & Brooks) $3,692

A mahogany longcase clock with rolling moonphase, Bloor, Newcastle, second half, 18th century, 7ft. 8in. (Bonhams & Brooks) $3,124

A month going black lacquer longcase clock, Daniel Delander, London, circa 1720, 7ft. (Bonhams & Brooks) $6,390

A mahogany drum head longcase clock, G Kistler, Penzance, circa 1850, 6ft7in. (Bonhams) $2,240

A mahogany longcase clock, John Gammon, London, circa 1780, 8ft. 4in.(Bonhams & Brooks) $6,390

 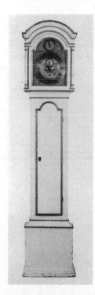  

An inlaid mahogany tubular chiming longcase clock English, circa 1880, Thos Oldroyd Glasgow, 8ft.2in. (Bonhams) $5,320

A white and gilt painted longcase clock, Thomas Hunter Junior London, circa 1750, 12in. dial, 7ft. 6in. (Bonhams & Brooks) $3,408

An Edwardian mahogany longcase clock with eight day movement having Westminster and Whittington chimes, 87½in. high. (Andrew Hartley) $4,928

A walnut longcase clock by Samuel Jackson, London, eight day movement, 100in. high.(Andrew Hartley) $4,930

George III inlaid mahogany tall case clock, the works signed *Wm. Nash, Bridge*, 85in. high.
(Skinner) $6,900

An Essex mahogany eight-day longcase clock, circa 1785, Morris Carter, Bish'p Stortford, 221cm.
(Bristol) $2,233

A Federal mahogany dwarf tall case clock, Joshua Wilder, Massachusetts, circa 1800, 47in. high.
(Christie's) $44,650

A faded mahogany drum head longcase clock, John Todd, Dumfries, circa 1840, 6ft.8in.
(Christie's) $3,528

George III gilt bronze mounted and inlaid mahogany tall case clock, late 18th century, 94in. high.
(Skinner) $7,475

An oak 30 hour longcase clock, W Tanner, Hailsham, 19th century, plinth, 6ft.4in.
(Christie's) $588

A Federal mahogany dwarf clock, Hingham, Massachusetts, circa 1815, 48½in. high.
(Christie's) $36,800

An 8 day mahogany narrow cased clock, English case, French movement, 183cm.
(Bonhams) $441

A mahogany longcase clock with rolling moonphase, W. Smith, early 19th century, 7ft.8in. (Christie's) $956

An oak longcase clock, R Henderson, Scarborough, circa 1740, 6ft.8in. (Christie's) $2,793

A mahogany longcase clock, John Todd, Glasgow, early 19th century, 6ft. 10in. (Christie's) $2,205

A mahogany longcase clock, James Murdoch, Newton Ayr, early 19th century, 7ft. (Christie's) $1,250

George III mahogany and gilt bronze mounted tall case clock, the dial signed *Alexander Farquharson, Edinburgh*, 89in. high. (Skinner) $2,760

A mahogany longcase clock with a rolling moonphase, W.T. Lees, Haslingden, circa 1820, 8ft.3in. (Christie's) $1,617

A mahogany longcase clock, William Vale, London, circa 1785, associated 4 pillar rack and bell striking movement, 8ft. (Christie's) $2,940

English mahogany tall case clock, mid 19th century, with swan's neck cresting, 81in. high. (Skinner) $2,990

231

An ornately carved oak longcase clock, German, circa 1880, 8ft.
(Bonhams) $2,070

An oak longcase clock, John Fielder, Alton, late 18th century, 7ft. 1in.
(Bonhams) $3,036

A light oak longcase clock, James Little, Annan, circa 1820, 7ft. 5in.
(Bonhams) $1,380

A mahogany longcase clock, John Fielder, Alston, Thurson, early 19th century, 7ft. 4in.
(Bonhams) $5,796

A later carved oak longcase with an associated regulator movement and dial, unsigned, 18th century/19th century, 6ft. 8½in.
(Bonhams) $718

A Regency mahogany longcase regulator, John Thwaites, Rosamon Street, Clerkenwell, first quarter 19th century, 6ft.4½in.(Christie's)
$14,993

A green lacquer longcase clock, Windmill & Etkins, Londini Fecit, 18th century, 7ft. 10in.
(Bonhams) $4,830

An Anglo-Dutch stained field maple and ebony quarter chiming longcase clock, Fromanteel & Clarke, 1st quarter 18th century, 8ft. 11in. high.
(Christie's) $15,334

A mahogany longcase clock, J & Mc Nab, Perth, circa 1820, 6ft. 11in. (Bonhams) $2,208

A cream painted longcase, Danish, unsigned, 18th century, 8ft. (Bonhams) $1,380

A black japanned longcase clock, unsigned, 18th century, 7ft 4in. (Bonhams) $1,380

A mahogany longcase clock, Peter Fenwick, Crieff, circa 1800, 7ft. (Bonhams) $2,760

  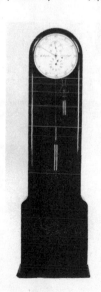 

A mahogany 8 bell chiming longcase clock with a rolling moonphase, Henry Brownbill & Son, Leeds, circa 1785, 8ft. 1in. (Bonhams) $6,900

A Charles II walnut and floral marquetry longcase clock, dial signed *James Hutchin, Southwark*; case basically circa 1680, dial and movement circa 1700, 6ft.7in. (Christie's) $7,666

A mahogany longcase regulator, English, 19th century, 14in. painted dial, signed *M Wherly* Sunderland, 6ft. 5in. (Bonhams) $3,588

A Dutch walnut longcase clock with calendar, Kaspar Friederick Schults, Amsterdam, 3rd quarter 18th century, 8ft.11in. high. (Christie's) $16,185

A Dey Time Register timeclock, in oak case, with separate brass dials for three-shift system, American, circa 1930.
(Auction Team Köln) $1,340

Late Victorian black marble mantel clock, crested with a bronze sphinx over a circular Roman chapter ring, flanked on either side by pilaster, base, by Wassell & Halford, London, 14in.(G.A. Key) $398

A French gilt-bronze striking pendule d'officier, circa 1900, case with waisted pediment surmounted by a conjoined serpent handle, white enamel Arabic dial with retail signature for *Tiffany & Co*, 7¾in. high. (Christie's) $2,576

A French green onyx, gilt-brass and champlevé enamel striking mantel clock, last quarter 19th century, the dial with polychrome enamel bezel and conforming centre, individual painted Arabic chapters, signed below 12 *LE ROY*, 17¾in. high. (Christie's) $1,472

A Louis XVI gilt-bronze mounted white marble portico mantel clock, last quarter 18th century, the white enamel Roman dial with Arabic five minutes signed *Collard A Paris*, 20½in. high.
(Christie's) $1,380

An Empire gilt-bronze striking mantel clock, circa 1815, the white enamel Roman dial signed *L. Ravrio Bronzier à Paris* and *Mesnil P.*, the twin barrel movement with silk suspension and countwheel strike on bell, 19¾in. high. (Christie's) $2,024

A Charles X marble and bronze mantel clock, signed, the movement unsigned, 18in. high.
(Dockree's) $992

A Louis Philippe brass inlaid rosewood striking mantel clock, second quarter 19th century, the stepped rectangular case with ripple-moulded gallery and brass foliate marquetry inlay, on bun feet, 15¼in. high. (Christie's) $736

A fine and rare pewter and brass-mounted inlaid figured mahogany shelf clock, attributed to David Wood, Newburyport, Massachusetts, circa 1800, 34¾in. high. (Sotheby's) $25,300

Sèvres porcelain mantel clock, rectangular body with field of green having fired gold laurel swags and flowers, 13in. high.
(Du Mouchelles) $550

A Jugendstil style brass and wood mantel clock, the circular white enamel dial within arched frame supported by two short tapering cylindrical columns, 27cm. high.
(Christie's) $557

Aesthetic Movement brass and onyx mantel clock, late 19th century, retailed by Camerden & Forster, rectangular case, balustrade cornice and base, 16in. high. (Skinner) $1,092

A Louis Philippe gilt-bronze and white marble striking mantel clock, circa 1840, the case surmounted by the figure of a ship's captain beside nautical trophies, signed *HRY MARC A PARIS*, 22in. high.
(Christie's) $920

A rare gilt-bronze and porcelain 'sector' musical clock by Planchon Paris, circa 1900, the semi-circular dial with Roman numerals ranged from VI to VI, painted with foliage and sun flowers, 65cm. high.
(Sotheby's) $18,745

A French gilt-spelter and alabaster striking mantel clock, late 19th century, the oval case surmounted by a group of a jockey astride his horse, with scroll supports to the sides terminating in lion masks, 14½in. high. (Christie's) $220

A French gilt-bronze and champlevé striking mantel clock, last quarter 19th century, the case with foliate cast finial to the pagoda top, 14¼in. high.
(Christie's) $2,024

A Victorian silver framed circular mantel clock, the dial cast with a hunting scene, the numbers in the form of bits and spurs, London 1890, maker: E.H.S.
(Russell Baldwin & Bright)
                                   $1,155

A Louis XV-style boulle mantel clock, in a waisted case surmounted by a figure of Diana, with gilt metal foliate mounts and feet, 52cm.
(Bearne's) $1,980

A French cartouche shape boudoir timepiece, the lever movement to a circular white enamel dial, the hinged glazed door set with brilliants, 8in. high.
(Woolley & Wallis) $479

Edwardian mahogany large mantel clock of domed form, inlaid with boxwood neo-classical stringing and designs, 13½in.
(G.A. Key) $218

English Regency mahogany veneered and inlaid mantel clock, first half 19th century, with two-train chiming movement, believed to be signed on the works *Wilson*, 28in. high. (Skinner) $5,463

Late Biedermeier marquetry inlaid temple clock, second half 19th century, with two-train quarter-strike movement with pull repeat mechanism, top of case with band of ebonised reeding over fruitwood scroll and fruit inlay, 17in. high. (Skinner) $633

Decorative 19th century gilded spelter mantel clock, crested with a motif of a figure clutching a scroll, shield etc, flanked on either side by two Sévres style panels, 8 day movement, 17in.
(G.A. Key) $841

Decorative brass or gilt metal balloon formed mantel clock applied with foliate scrolls, circular Roman chapter ring and inset with champlevé enamelled panel and raised on splayed feet, circa late 19th century, 16in.
(G.A. Key) $248

19th century bronze cathedral style mantel clock with a battlemented pediment, interspersed with stylised floral mounts, 8 day movement by William Barr of Hamilton, 15½in.
(G.A. Key) $551

Fine early 19th century French ormolu small mantel clock, circular face with Roman chapter ring, elaborately moulded throughout with C scrolls and raised on similar feet, 8 day movement by Savory of Paris, 10in. (G.A. Key) $1,015

Empire-style marble mantel clock, late 19th century, with three-train quarter-striking movement with hour gong and seven bells, 18¹/₈in. high. (Skinner) $575

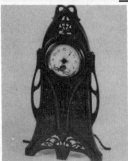

Unusual copper plated mantel clock of Cathedral form, decorated in the Art Nouveau manner with maidens, lion masks and scrolls etc, circular Arabic chapter ring, 13in.
(G.A. Key) $377

Gubelin marble and enamel eight-day clock, Switzerland, 20th century, rectangular, with two front doors with enamel plaques depicting a medieval falconer and lady, 5¹/₈in.(Skinner) $2,875

A 19th century French mantel clock with eight day movement, having white enamel dial, in pierced brass square case with turned finial on domed lid, 15½in. high.
(Andrew Hartley) $770

French figural ormolu and marble mantel clock, late 19th century, with two-train chiming movement incised *L.K. Brevete S.G.D.G.*, enamel face painted with delicate floral swags set into rectangular glass and ormolu mounted case, 17in. high.
(Skinner) $2,645

Unusual ormolu and bronze French mantel clock in the form of a teapot, the cover crested with a pineapple finial, raised on compressed bun feet, 8 day movement, 10½in.
(G.A. Key) $10,875

A 19th century French mantel clock, the eight day movement with white enamel dial, in gilt metal rococo case cast with scrollwork and foliage and centred by a mask, 15½in. high.
(Andrew Hartley) $924

A French red buhl mantel clock, the 8 day drum movement stamped A & N 65396, striking on a gong, with a sunburst bob pendant to a circular brass dial, 13¼in. high, circa 1900.
(Woolley & Wallis) $1,016

A 19th century French oval timepiece standish, the gilt textured cover surmounted by a figure of a bronze dog being ridden by a young boy and carrying in its mouth a basket of grapes, 8¼in. high.
(Woolley & Wallis) $5,748

A 19th century French mantel clock with eight day movement having blue porcelain dial, in gilt metal case with inset jewelled bleu de roi porcelain plaques, stamped *C.A. Richard*, 15¾in. high.
(Andrew Hartley) $1,232

A French gilt-spelter and champlevé enamel desk timepiece, late 19th century, the case flanked by the figures of two standing cherubs, 8¼in. high.
(Christie's) $643

A carved wooden cuckoo clock with acanthus leaf scrolls and pine cone weights, Austria, 1900s, 15cm.
(Bonhams) $462

A 19th century French black slate and malachite inlaid mantel clock, the shaped case with three enamel dials set around a shaped bevelled glass panel, 1ft.8.5in. high.
(Phillips) $1,509

A William IV rosewood and marquetry inlaid mantel clock, with circular dial and swing handle, the eight day movement striking on a bell, 13¾in. high.
(Bonhams) $466

A congreve brass rolling ball escapement clock, with three silvered dials, white and black conforming finials and feet, 16in., perspex cover to the base.
(Woolley & Wallis) $994

Federal mahogany pillar and scroll mantel clock, Eli and Samuel Terry, Plymouth, Connecticut, circa 1825, with large house and lake opening to a white and gilt decorated dial and thirty-hour wooden weight-driven movement, 31½in. high.
(Skinner) $4,600

A Bretby pottery case mantel clock, of Arts and Crafts style set with three ceramic plaques and a copper effect glaze, 39cm. high.
(Wintertons) $647

A small early 20th century Swiss quarter repeating clock in a silver and enamel case, gilt rectangular keywind movement with going barrel, the top, circa 1900, 60mm. high.
(Pieces of Time) $4,071

A red and brass inlaid boulle mantel clock, French, 1890s, the drum gong striking movement in a waisted sided case decorated with brass inlay within a red ground, 12in. (Bonhams) $856

A silvered cased desk alarm timepiece, Longines, 1930s, silvered dial with painted Arabic numerals signed *Longines*, with subsidiaries for seconds and alarm setting, 95mm.
(Bonhams) $440

A novelty ship-strike mantel clock by Allien of New York, constructed in brass with 6in. enamel dial, with Roman numerals, fast/slow regulation above XII, 23½in. high.
(Christie's) $11,811

An ebonised wood and ormolu mounted night clock, the dial painted with a 17th century Bolognese School depiction of the Assumption, late 17th/early 18th century, Rome, 60cm. high.
(Finarte) $17,746

A Viennese architectural mantel clock, of fruitwood with gilt ornamentation and with two rows of alabaster columns, dial with Arabic numerals and automata, circa 1830, 80cm. high.
(Finarte) $3,909

A French ormolu travelling alarm clock for the Japanese market, signed *Thuret AParis*, circa 1690, the circular dial with brass outer chapter ring with Japanese numerals with pierced steel hand, 4¼in. diameter.
(Christie's) $4,333

An Empire silvered brass quarter striking pendule d'officier, Robert Courvoisier, Paris, the case of typical proportions with serpentine handle to the concave-moulded top applied with oak leaves, 7½in. high.
(Christie's) $1,805

A substantial black slate perpetual calendar and moonphase clock, French, circa 1880, 7in. 2 piece enamel dial with a central Brocourt escapement, 23½in.
(Bonhams) $2,198

A wood and paper toy clock, by Bosher of London, late 18th century, the brown wood carved clock with flower decoration, 6¾in. high. (Bonhams) $3,156

A German gilt-metal striking table clock, Martinus Hyllius, Dresden, circa 1665, the square case on foliate paw feet and with D-ended glazed movement viewing panels to the sides, 5in. square.
(Christie's) $27,985

239

A French gilt metal and porcelain mantel clock, the movement stamped *Hry Marc Paris*, 19in. high. (Andrew Hartley) $1,023

A French gilt-spelter and black slate striking mantel clock, last quarter 19th century, the drum-shaped case surmounted by a floral bouquet and flanked by the figure of a classical maiden playing a lyre, 15in. wide. (Christie's) $312

A French black boulle cased mantel clock, the 8 day movement striking a bell, with an outside countwheel, 8½in. wide. (Woolley & Wallis) $644

A French gilt brass mantel clock, the bell-strike movement by J.W.C. Smith, Paris, the 5in. white Roman numeral dial in a drumhead case, 24.5cm. wide. (Bristol) $928

A French gilt-metal striking mantel clock, last quarter 19th century, the case surmounted by a group of a country youth with a horse, on naturalistic base, 14¾in. high. (Christie's) $295

Papier mâché shelf timepiece, labelled *Botsford's improved patent timepiece manufactured by Coe & Co. 52 Dey Street, New York*, 11in. high. (Skinner) $1,265

A French porcelain mantel clock case, with later electric movement, the detachable top of two Turkish dancers, 25.5cm. wide. (Bristol) $360

An Empire gilt-bronze striking mantel clock, first quarter 19th century, the rectangular case incised with simulated brickwork and applied with butterfly mounts, , 14¼in. high. (Christie's) $643

French baroque-style bronze mantel clock, late 19th century, works by Denière, scrolled case and base with foliate and mask mounts, 18in. high. (Skinner) $632

A Victorian sanderswood travelling timepiece with alarm, circa 1835, the dial with narrow silvered Roman chapter ring signed *Vulliamy, London*, 6¾in. high.
(Christie's) $16,597

A silvered, parcel-gilt and lapis lazuli mantel clock by Elkington and Co., Victorian, circa 1880, the dial with a silvered chapter ring in a drum case, 40cm. high.
(Sotheby's) $16,128

A Louis XV style gilt-bronze striking mantel clock, last quarter 19th century, signed *RICHOND*, the twin barrel movement with countwheel strike on bell, 17in. high.
(Christie's) $1,472

Rouen porcelain small mantel clock with circular Arabic chapter ring, moulded with scrolls, painted in colours throughout in the faience manner, late 19th/early20th century, 8½in. high.
(G.A. Key) $224

A white marble and gilt bronze mantel clock, French, late 18th century, movement signed *Louis Musson A Paris*, enamel dial signed *Foucher à Argentan*, contained in a drum with Leda and the Swan on left, fluted marble base,1ft.4in. high.
(Sotheby's) $5,569

Federal mahogany miniature pillar and scroll mantel clock, Eli Terry, Plymouth, Connecticut, circa 1822, the swan's neck cresting above a glazed door, 22½in. high.
(Skinner) $7,475

Georgian-style inlaid mahogany mantel clock, early 20th century, with French works, the stepped case inlaid with stringing and butterfly. (Skinner) $1,380

A 1930s Breguet timepiece, the silvered dial with black Roman numerals and blued hands, in an Art Deco style brass case, 10cm.
(Bearne's) $1,733

Grignon-Meusnier a Paris, a 19th century ormolu and porcelain mantel clock, the bell-striking movement with enamel chapter ring, 38.8cm.
(Bristol) $1,377

A green onyx and champlevé 4 glass mantel clock, French, circa 1880, 3½in. gilt dial signed for Batty & Co Paris, with a champlevé decorated center and surround, 16½in. (Bonhams) $1,258

Late Victorian black marble mantel clock, circular face with Roman chapter ring, supported on two scrolled mounts, with heavy plinth base, 24½in. (G A Key) $606

A mahogany mantel timepiece with a matching bracket, English, 1900s, 5¼in. painted dial signed for Lewns Rye, in arched top case with brass side ring handles, 12in. (Bonhams) $785

Miniature shelf timepiece, Treat and Bishop for George Mitchell, Bristol, Connecticut, circa 1830, the scrolled crest and square plinths above the glazed door with engaged columns and eglomise tablet, 21in. high. (Skinner) $2,530

René Lalique, pendule 'Deux Figurines', after 1926, clear glass, the arched panel molded with two female figures in Grecian dresses holding a flower garland centered by a clock face, 14¾in. (Sotheby's) $12,180

A Restauration gilt bronze mantel clock, second quarter 19th century, the naturalistic case with a figure of Venus seated holding an apple, a snake rising from rushes opposite, the stepped rectangular plinth with floral garlands, 19¼in. high. (Christie's) $2,544

A Louis XV ormolu mantel clock, the case with pierced scrolling foliate asymmetrical surround and with Commedia dell'Arte figures, 19½in. high. (Christie's) $5,030

A gilt ormolu figural mantel clock French, 1880s, 47cm. (Bonhams) $735

An Empire gilt bronze mantel clock, early 19th century, modelled with a seated classical figure, shown seated holding a board inscribed *Les Georgiques L'Eneide* with a lyre to the side, 17¾in. high. (Christie's) $2,171

A Restauration gilt bronze and malachite mounted mantel clock, circa 1830, the case of lyre from with outset columns supporting a classical bust above, 21in. high.
(Christie's) $5,520

A gilt-bronze and porcelain mantel clock, French, circa 1860, the case surmounted by a female figure and flanked by figures of Flora and Pomona, movement stamped *Lerolle Freres à Paris*, 64cm. wide.
(Sotheby's) $7,214

Archibald Knox for Liberty & Co., mantel clock, 1902-05, pewter, the arched top decorated in relief with a stylized honesty motif, set with a circular copper clock face, 20.5cm.
(Sotheby's) $7,308

A Viennese silver and lapis lazuli clock, in the Louis XV style, circa 1865, modelled as an elephant with a raised trunk, supporting a drum-shaped case on its back, surmounted by an oriental man seated on a cushion, 16in. high.
(Christie's) $3,109

A Louis XVI ormolu and white marble mantel clock, set within a naturalistic rocky case flanked by Cupid proffering solace to a classically-draped nymph and emblematic of Love Lost, 17¼in. high. (Christie's) $7,544

A Charles II ebony and gilt-metal mounted early architectural table timepiece, signed *Ahasuerus Fromanteel Londini Fecit*, circa 1665, the case on adjustable gilt-metal ball feet supporting the base with drawer to the front, 26½in. high.(Christie's) $166,420

English George III ebonized mantel clock, late 18th century, with two-train hour-striking movement with anchor escapement, with pull repeater, dial signed *Neville Spencer Liverpool*, 19in. wide.
(Skinner) $2,300

Mahogany shelf clock, Eli Terry, Plymouth, Connecticut, circa 1817-18, the flat cornice above a glazed door enclosing a painted and gilt wooden dial and thirty-hour wooden weight-driven movement.
(Skinner) $4,255

A Regency ebonized mantel clock, the 8 day twin fusee movement striking on bells, the back plate with a lunette engraved border, inscribed *W Nicoll, Gt Portland St.* 11in.
(Woolley & Wallis) $2,160

An ormolu and blue porcelain mantel clock, French, 19th century, 4¼in. thirteen piece enamel dial with a floral decorated centre, 17in. (Bonhams) $3,920

Tiffany & Co., an Art Deco desk timepiece, silvered dial with Breguet numerals,the green and black enamelled case surmounted by a moss agate and rose quartz finial. (Christie's) $2,101

A 19th century French mantel clock with circular white enamel dial inscribed *T. Martin*, 8-day striking movement in white marble case, 21½in. high. (Brightwells) $1,925

A Swiss ormolu grande sonnerie pendule d'officier, 19th century, the arched rectangular case with circular white enamel dial with arabic chapters and signed *Courvoisier & Compe..*, 5¼in. wide. (Christie's) $3,353

A Viennese silvered-metal-mounted and gem-set lazurite and enamel timepiece, circa 1890, surmounted by two doves flanking a nest, the circular dial flanked to each side by a maiden, 5¼in. high. (Christie's) $3,109

An important Austrian ormolu, marble and mahogany perpetual calendar grande sonnerie astronomical skeleton clock, Anton Glückstein, Vienna, 1820, 54½in. high. (Christie's) $138,106

A French gilt- and patinated-bronze clock, in the Louis XV style, circa 1890, of waisted shape, surmounted by a female figure, the gilt dial with enamel numeral plaquettes, 30¼in. high. (Christie's) $1,727

A large mahogany cased striking mantel clock with turned columns, classical gilded mounts and a replaced movement, French, 54cm. (Bonhams) $600

A Meissen figural clock, circa 1880, the domed case framed with heavy floral encrustations and applied with four putti, each one emblematic of the Seasons, 41cm. (Bonhams) $4,082

A George III satinwood striking balloon bracket clock, Barwise, London, the case of typical waisted outline crossbanded and ebony-lined with a marquetry cowrie shell beneath the dial, 19in. high.
(Christie's) $7,254

Cartier, an Art Deco desk timepiece, silvered dial with Breguet numerals and gold moon hands, gilt case on onyx and aventurine quartz support, in fitted case.
(Christie's) $2,101

Napoleon III ormolu-mounted parcel-gilt bleu céléste Sèvres-pattern porcelain and biscuit pot-pourri, circa 1865, surmounted by two cherubs, 17¾in. wide.
(Christie's) $9,761

A Victorian gilt-brass strut timepiece with calendar, Hunt & Roskell, London, the case in the style of Thomas Cole engraved with foliate scrolls and flowers within a hatched ground, 5¼in. high.
(Christie's) $5,329

A Viennese silver-mounted and gem-set pearl-bead and enamel timepiece, circa 1890, surmounted by a cherub playing the drum, the circular dial flanked to each side by a female figure playing an instrument, 7in. high.
(Christie's) $4,836

A French ormolu mantel clock, in the Régence style, circa 1875, surmounted by an octagonal dome, the central circular dial signed *Raingo Fres Paris*, the twin-train movement with countwheel strike on a bell, 28¾in. high.
(Christie's) $6,909

A cast brass Gothic style mantel clock, James Page, Plymouth, 19th century, twin fusee bell striking movement in a mitre shaped case with applied cast gothic mounts, 20in.(Bonhams & Brooks) $540

A French rosewood cased striking mantel clock, 19th century, the 11cm. dial signed *Marr, Paris* the case with brass and mother of pearl inlays, 47cm. high.
(Bonhams) $672

A mahogany mantel clock, Handley & Moore, London, circa 1820, the mitre top case with side lion mask handles and fish scale frets, 20in.
(Bonhams & Brooks) $3,692

A mahogany and brass inlaid chamfered top mantel clock, circa 1820, 8in painted convex dial signed for E R Bailey 51 Bedford St. Strand, the twin fusee bell striking and repeating movement signed on the back plate *Patrick Greenwich*, 17½in.
(Bonhams) $3,312

Jaeger Le Coultre. An Art Deco style mantel timepiece, the perspex case with gilt chinoiserie decoration, 6¼in. high.
(Woolley & Wallis) $522

An early Victorian walnut mantel timepiece, Alex. Guillaume, London, circa 1840, the case with scroll-arched top with carved leafy moldings to the front, 10¹/₃in. high.
(Christie's) $2,045

A French rosewood and boxwood inlaid table clock with echappement à deux roues, Leroy & Fils, Paris, fourth quarter 19th century, the case of plinth form with boxwood border inlay in panels to the four sides and top, 16¼in. high.
(Christie's) $3,430

A very unusual early 19th century eight day quarter repeating Swiss clock in a gold travelling case retailed by Tiffany, nickelled split three quarter plate keyless movement, signed *Tiffany & Co.*, circa 1910, 82 x 90 x 25mm.
(Pieces of Time) $5,382

Miniature pillar and scroll mahogany shelf clock, probably Connecticut, circa 1825, the scrolled cornice joining three plinths with brass urn finials above the glazed door, 13½in. wide.
(Skinner) $1,725

French Empire style gilt bronze mantel clock, with two train half strike movement, urn form body set to center with enamel dial signed *Michelez*, 18¼in. high.
(Skinner) $4,600

Late Victorian black marble and malachite mantel clock, late 19th century, with two train half-strike movement, front inlaid with malachite spandrels, 9⁵/₈in.
(Skinner) $316

A 19th century French revolving chapter ring urn mantel clock, Lepine, Paris, in a gilt bronze Rose Pompadour porcelain case, the time indicated by the tongue issuing from the heads of coiled serpents, 15½in. high.
(Woolley & Wallis) $6,080

A late 19th century steeple mantel timepiece with French eight-day movement, the gilt metal case having extensive gothic decoration, 23in. (Brightwells) $1,316

Late Victorian large marble mantel clock, the circular face with an Arabic chapter ring, raised on a scrolled platform support, by Achille Brocot, 22in. (G A Key) $285

Bretby Pottery Clock, England bronze glaze surmounted by female head with flowing hair, centered by circular clock face, 10in. high. (Skinner) $1,495

A 19th century French ormolu mantel clock with eight day movement by Deniere à Paris, the case of oblong tapering form, surmounted by a figure of a recumbent goat and Bacchanalian cherubs, 18¾in. high. (Andrew Hartley) $847

Late Victorian black and brèche d'Alep marble mantel clock, late 19th century, two train strike on bell movement, 9¾in. wide. (Skinner) $403

English late Regency mantel clock, London, second quarter 19th century, with two-train bell-striking movement, dial signed *Brandreth & Walker*, the mahogany case with cornice inlaid with brass scroll, 19in. high.(Skinner) $1,610

French Louis XVI style enamel and ormolu mantel clock, 19th century, with two train half strike movement, raised on white marble base and ormolu demi-lune legs further accented with blue enamelling, 15³/₈in. (Skinner) $8,050

An Edwardian brass mantel timepiece of chronometer format, Charles Frodsham, circa 1905, the case typical, but with handle and hinged feet, 6¼in. high. (Christie's) $6,035

A 'Hortensia' desk clock, a snake curling round the stem, the base formed as a jardinière, concealing an inkwell and vide-poche, bronze and gilt, Russian, circa 1825. (Galerie Moderne) $4,991

19th century mahogany wall clock, trunk below with canted front covers, also with ebonized stringing, 8 day movement by Benjamin Russell of Norwich, 53in. (G A Key) $2,277

A mahogany wall dial timepiece, English, 1900s, 12in. refinished dial signed for Thos Gammage & Son 60 Queen Victoria St., 15in. (Christie's) $559

A decorative Biedermeier wall clock, striking the half hours, small wooden movement with brass wheels, circa 1890. (Auction Team Köln) $164

Rosewood calendar clock, L..F. and W.W. Carter, Bristol, Connecticut, circa 1865, with brass eight-day weight-driven movement, 32in. (Skinner) $2,070

A mahogany railway wall dial timepiece, English, late 19th century, 12in. painted dial marked *BR (E) 12154*, the single fusee movement with tapered plates in a case with a turned surround and pegged back.(Christie's) $529

A mahogany drop dial wall timepiece, Jno Walker Ltd, London, late 19th century, the single fusee movement with screwed and pinned plates, 31in. (Christie's) $1,103

An Empire mahogany and églomisé wall clock, E. Howard & Company Boston, Massachusetts, circa 1840, the circular molded frame above an arched églomisé panel, 45in. high. (Sotheby's) $4,025

A mahogany wall dial timepiece, English, early 20th century, 12in. painted dial marked *KCC*, the single fusee movement in a case with a turned surround and pegged back, 15in. (Christie's) $412

A Vienna style spring-driven eight-day wall clock, 19th century, the gong-striking movement with two-piece white Roman numeral dial in walnut case surmounted by rearing horse finial to crest, 127cm. approximately. (Bristol) $462

A classic Ansonia office clock, in walnut case with Arabic and Roman numerals, 43 x 63cm., circa 1890. (Auction Team Köln) $422

A French tôle peinte striking wall clock, the octagonal case with brass suspension loop, later gilt decorated against a green ground, with acanthus cast bezel. (Christie's) $885

Ansonia calendar clock, in oak with octagonal head, 17in. across. (Eldred's) $412

A carved oak striking drop dial clock, Piggott, Ross, mid 19th century, the twin fusee bell striking movement in a case with carved acorns and leaves. (Christie's) $1,250

A mahogany drop dial wall timepiece, English, 1920s, 12in. painted dial signed for Harrods Ltd London SW1, the single fusee movement in a case with a turned surround and pegged back, 16in. (Christie's) $470

A Federal eglomisé and giltwood banjo clock, dial signed by Aaron Willard, Boston, 1790-1810, box base with gilded border centering a gilt églomisé panel depicting a female figure in chariot drawn by winged horses, 40in. high, (Christie's) $2,760

A Meissen wall clock, circa 1890, of shaped outline, surmounted by a figure of Chronos, dial flanked by a cherub to each side, the lower part with four hippocampi, a triton and a male figure, 35½in. high. (Christie's) $7,560

Attributed to George Nelson, a ceramic clock, designed circa 1950-55, for Howard Miller, the circular f⌐.ce glazed in colors, with black enamelled metal hands, 14in. diameter. (Christie's) $278

Federal mahogany banjo timepiece, Massachusetts, circa 1815, the case with brass bezel enclosing an iron painted dial and eight-day brass weight-driven movement, 33¼in. high. (Skinner) $1,955

A Viennese mahogany month-going Laterndl-Uhr, unsigned, circa 1820, 63¼in. high. (Christie's) $30,668

Swiss walnut wall regulator, late 19th century, with three-train weighted chiming movement enamelled dial signed *Jos. Stand, Zwittan*, 52in. high. (Skinner) $1,265

A Biedermeier mahogany grande sonnerie Dachl-Uhr, Franz Heckel in Wien, circa 1835, 45in. high. (Christie's) $21,296

A beech Vienna wall regulator, Lenzkirch, 1900s, the movement with a dead beat escapement, maintaining power and striking on a gong, 4ft. 3in. (Bonhams) $828

A fine mahogany wall regulator with original numbered winder, Dent, circa 1860, 12in. silvered dial, with a sweep minute hand and subsidiary second and 1-24 hours, 53in. (Bonhams) $15,400

A Federal eglomisé banjo clock, dial signed by Aaron Willard, Boston, early 19th century, on an eglomisé decorated box base depicting a carriage and horse, 34in. high. (Christie's) $7,475

A Federal inlaid mahogany shelf clock, dial signed by Aaron Willard, Boston, circa 1810, the rectangular top surmounted by pierced fretwork, 36in. high. (Christie's) $14,100

A Victorian mahogany wall regulator with gravity escapement, Dent, 61 Strand & 34 Royal Exchange, London, No. 1344, circa 1852, 57¼in. high. (Christie's) $12,777

A very rare late 16th century oval German quarter striking stackfreed alarm in an octagonal gilt metal case, anonymous German, circa 1590, 84 x 60 x 35mm. (Pieces of Time) $29,813

An unusual Swiss gold quarter repeating keyless chronograph and automata hunter pocketwatch with enamelled jacquemarts, unsigned, 1890s, the frosted gilt movement jewelled to the center, 56mm. diameter. (Christie's) $5,778

An 18ct. gold half hunter keyless center seconds watch, English, 1890, enamel dial signed for W Lockwood, Devonshire Buildings Huddersfield, the ¾ plate movement in a plain polished case, 55mm. (Bonhams) $471

A fine early 19th century quarter repeating ruby cylinder with engine turned silver dial in a gold open face case, anonymous Swiss, circa 1830, 52mm. diameter. (Pieces of Time) $5,088

An 18ct. gold open faced keyless carrousel pocket watch, signed *Sharman D. Neill Ltd, Donegal Place, Belfast, 1907*, movement with spotted plate, lever escapement, diameter 48mm. (Christie's) $3,381

A 20th century Swiss lever deck watch by Rolex in a nickel open face case, nickelled split three quarter plate keyless movement with going barrel, signed *Rolex Cal.548 Rubies*, circa 1930, 52mm. diameter. (Pieces of Time) $952

A good 18ct. gold perpetual calendar minute repeating keyless chronograph hunter pocketwatch with Kew certificate, signed *S. Smith & Son, Strand, London*, 1880s, 59mm. diameter. (Christie's) $14,444

A late 19th century American lever in a gold full hunter case, the front cover with engraved decoration and monogram, signed American *Waltham Watch Co. Safety Pinion 6997102*, circa 1895, 40mm. diameter. (Pieces of Time) $5,984

A large late 19th century Swiss moonphase calendar lever in a silver open face case, keyless gilt bar movement with going barrel, circa 1890, 62mm. diameter. (Pieces of Time) $1,193

A gold and enamel open faced keyless cylinder fob watch, Swiss, circa 1890, pale blue enamel dial with Arabic numerals, stamped *E. Jaccotti, Travers,* 33mm. diameter.
(Christie's) $1,635

An important and rare miniature gold keyless lever watch with hand set facility, signed *Breguet,* 1832, the frosted gilt lever movement constructed on the principles of the garde-temps with five wheel train, 18mm. diameter.
(Christie's) $54,165

A lady's good gold, enamel and seed pearl pendant watch, signed *Romilly à Paris,* 1830s, the back with painted daisy to the centre on burgundy enamel surround, 35mm. diameter.(Christie's) $2,708

A fine gold, painted enamel, and seed pearl set minute repeating keyless hunter pocketwatch for the Chinese market, late 19th century, the gold case with painted enamel scene of a group of minstrels to the front cover, 55mm. diameter.
(Christie's) $5,417

An exceptional gold pre-hairspring pocketwatch with rare raised floral enamel decoration, signed *Charles Bobinet,* third quarter 17th century, the outside of the case centred by a painted portrait of Virtue, 33mm. diameter.
(Christie's) $114,610

A silver gilt, enamel and seed set minute repeating chronograph hunter pocketwatch, unsigned, 1815, the frosted gilt half plate movement, jewelled to the centre with screwed chatons, 52mm. diameter. (Christie's) $2,708

A fine late 19th century Swiss gold and enamel brooch watch in the form of a beetle, oval keywind gilt bar movement with suspended going barrel, circa 1880, 43 x 22 x 14mm.
(Pieces of Time) $7,680

A fine gold keyless minute repeating hunter pocketwatch, signed *A. Lange & Söhne, Glashütte B/Dresden,* 1897-1903, 56mm. diameter, 167gr.
(Christie's) $54,165

A fine and rare gilt metal and rock crystal crucifix watch, in original oval silver fitted box, signed *Jolly Paris Fecit,* circa 1640, chased and engraved gilt brass dial above a crucifixion scene, 65 x 38mm.
(Christie's) $18,170

A 19th century English verge with polychrome dial depicting a train in silver pair cases, full plate fusee movement with round pillars, signed *H Bullingford London 7189*, 58mm. diameter.
(Pieces of Time) $1,840

A late 19th century quarter repeating Swiss lever with an erotic scene in a gold full hunter case, a second lid to the gold cuvette concealing an erotic scene of polychrome enamel figures, circa 1890, 54mm. diameter.
(Pieces of Time) $15,582

An historically important early 17th century gold and enamel verge watch, later movement signed *Jno. Le Roux, Charing Cross, London*, 36mm. diameter.
(Christie's) $16,249

An unusual fine mid 18th century Swiss independent seconds Captain's lever in a gold open face case, keywind gilt bar movement with two going barrels, signed *C Cooper & Sons,* circa 1850, 51mm. diameter.
(Pieces of Time) $3,498

A large skull form watch, the movement signed *J. Miller, London*, the realistically modelled case in the form of a skull with hinged jaw, the cranium opening to reveal the watch, 75 x 45 x 43mm.
(Christie's) $1,817

A gold quarter repeating open faced jaquemart automaton pocket watch, anonymous, Swiss, circa 1830, enamel dial with white centre, Arabic numerals, eccentric winding hole, 54mm. diameter.
(Christie's) $2,544

An early 19th century quarter repeating verge automaton in a gold open face case, flanking the chapter are pierced chased and engraved parcel gilt classical figures, circa 1820, 55mm. diameter.
(Pieces of Time) $6,240

A late 18th century French verge in a gold consular case with a concealed erotic enamel scene, full plate gilt fusee movement, signed *Vacher a Paris,* circa 1780, 37mm. diameter.
(Pieces of Time) $6,678

An 18th century English verge with polychrome enamel dial in gilt metal pair cases, white enamel dial, central polychrome scene of a harbour with a sailing ship, signed *Geo Dickson,* circa 1780, 49mm. diameter.
(Pieces of Time) $1,360

A Turkish market verge watch, by Markwick Markham Borell, in silver pair cases, the outer engraved with a basket of flowers, 1807, 48mm. (Tennants) $640

A gold purse watch with shutters, signed *Vacheron Constantin*, 1920s, contained within gold rectangular outer case engraved with geometric designs, 43 x 41mm. (Christie's) $3,583

A gentleman's gold World Time keyless openface pocketwatch with 24 hour indication, signed *Agassiz Watch Co.*, 1950s, 46mm. diameter. (Christie's) $7,544

An early 18th century English verge with silver champlevé dial in silver pair cases, deep full plate fire gilt movement with Egyptian pillars, signed *Fk Barrett y London*, circa 1710, 56mm. diameter. (Pieces of Time) $4,240

A fine gold, diamond and ruby keyless skeletonised dress watch, signed *Patek Philippe*, 1980s, the finely chased and skeletonised movement jewelled to the centre, 49mm. diameter. (Christie's) $26,726

A gold openface verge pocketwatch, signed *Iac. Kock, Stockholm*, late 18th century, the frosted gilt chain fusee movement with unusual pierced and engraved bridgecock, 57mm. diameter. (Christie's) $1,886

A lady's gold and enamel keyless pendant watch, signed *Tiffany*, 1890s, the chased and engraved covers with enamelled scene of a putto, 25mm. diameter. (Christie's) $1,240

A good 18ct. gold quarter repeating cylinder hunter pocketwatch, signed *Recordon* late Emery, early 1800s, the frosted gilt full plate movement with chain fusee, 54mm. diameter. (Christie's) $2,100

An interesting gilt perfume flask in the form of a keyless openface pocketwatch, signed *Rolex, Perpetually Yours*, 1960s, 54mm. diameter. (Christie's) $2,262

A late 18th century French dumb quarter repeating verge in a gold consular case set with a polychrome enamel portrait, signed *L Chalon a Paris 426.*, circa 1780, 45mm. diameter.
(Pieces of Time) $5,120

A 9 ct. gold purse watch, signed *Rolex Model Sporting Princess,* 1930s, the nickel plated extra prima chronometer movement timed to six positions, 50 x 34mm.
(Christie's) $5,658

A good gold openface keyless pocketwatch, *signed Patek Philippe & Co., Chronometro Gondolo,* 1910s, the frosted gilt bar movement jewelled to the centre, 56mm. diameter.
(Christie's) $3,206

An 18ct. gold half quarter repeating Duplex pocketwatch, signed *Grayhurst, Harvey & Co., Strand, London*, 1820s, in engine turned openface case with ribbed band, hinged back and cuvette, 56mm. diameter. (Christie's) $2,100

A white metal pull quarter repeat and alarm coach watch, signed *Charles Baltazar a Paris*, early 18th century, the frosted gilt chain fusee movement with verge escapement, 117mm. diameter.
(Christie's) $10,373

A gold, enamel and seed pearl openface verge pocketwatch, signed *Roman Melly & Roux, Constance*, 1800s, the back cover with painted scene of a maiden offering fruit to Pegasus, 47mm. diameter. (Christie's) $1,718

A nickel openface keyless deckwatch with power reserve indication, signed *A Lange & Söhne, Glashütte*, 1940s, 59mm. diameter.
(Christie's) $1,886

A most unusual gold and enamel openface cylinder dress watch with enamelled bridges, unsigned, 1820s, the blued steel top plate with floral decoration, 43mm. diameter.
(Christie's) $2,863

An early 19th century English verge, the unusual regulator dial with calendar indications in gilt metal pair cases, circa 1805, signed *Johnson London 876*, 59mm.
(Pieces of Time) $1,592

255

An unsigned verge watch, No. 744, the movement with baluster pillars and enamel dial, in silver pair cases, Birmingham, 1808, 60mm. (Tennants) $512

A keyless lever karrusel, by Thos Russell & Son, Liverpool, No. 107221, in 18ct gold hunter case with inscribed testimonial on the cuvette, Chester, 1902, 56mm. (Tennants) $3,840

A watch, by Samson, the dial depicting a fisherman with boat, church and castle, in plain silver pair cases, 1790, 50mm. (Tennants) $480

A verge watch, by Jas Brickles, London, in gilt metal pair cases, the outer painted with rocks and ferns under translucent horn, circa 1790, 54mm. (Tennants) $576

A rare 9ct gold self winding watch lighter, Dunhill, 1922, the rectangular 15 jewel nickel movement with 3 adjustments, wound via a linkage to the lighter hinged cap, 46mm. (Bonhams & Brooks) $6,300

A verge watch, of Dutch type, by Samson, London, the dial with painted scene depicting a man o' war and pinnace upon a calm sea, 1806, 51mm. (Tennants) $608

A verge watch, by Robert Bowers, Chester, with diamond end stone, the dial painted with a windmill with revolving sails, in silver pair cases, Birmingham, 1803, 53mm. (Tennants) $768

A Turkish market verge watch, by Edward Prior, in silver pair cases, the outer with bright cut bands, 1858, within silver piqué tortoiseshell outer case, 60mm. (Tennants) $880

A verge watch, by W. Ward, Grimsby, the enamel dial painted with a ploughing scene, in silver pair cases, Birmingham, 1865, 57mm. (Tennants) $560

A cylinder watch, by Fras Perigal, London, the later gold dial in gold consular case with pearl and enamel bezels, circa 1790, 45mm.
(Tennants) $576

A silver paircased pocket watch, the painted white enamelled dial depicting a windmill, signed *Langford, London.*
(Bearne's) $330

A cylinder watch, by D & W Morice, London, the enamel dial inscribed in white upon black, in 18ct gold open face case, 1818, 52mm.
(Tennants) $1,760

A verge watch, by D Rutland, London, in gilt metal pair cases, the outer painted with the figure of a huntsman, under translucent horn, circa 1775, 49mm.
(Tennants) $640

A 9ct gold travelling watch, Tavannes for Dunhill, circa 1929, silvered dial with raised gilt Arabic numerals, nickel 15 jewel movement in an engine-turned rectangular case, 37 x 31mm.
(Bonhams & Brooks) $420

A mid 18th century verge watch, by Thos Cope, London, the movement with well pierced cock and slide plate, with later gold dial in gold pair cases, 50mm.
(Tennants) $768

A verge watch, by Markwick Marham Borrell, London, the enamel dial painted with a ploughing scene, '*Speed the Plough*', in silver pair cases, 1826, the outer 1841, 57mm.
(Tennants) $448

An 18ct gold hunter pocket watch, with keywound three-quarter plate lever movement, signed *Johnson Walker & Tolhurst, London.*
(Bearne's) $330

A quarter repeating cylinder watch, by Bautte, à Geneve, the bar movement with engraved silvered dial in gold open face case, circa 1835, 43mm.
(Tennants) $672

A fine and rare enamel and pearl set gold musical and automaton two-train pocket watch in the form of a rose, Swiss, circa 1820, the serpentine pendant set with seed pearls, diameter 48mm.
(Christie's) $244,755

A gold, enamel and diamond set open faced keyless lever fob watch, signed *Tiffany & Co., New York*, 1880s, suspended from a gold and enamelled chain and diamond set bow brooch, diameter 35mm.
(Christie's) $25,358

A vari-coloured gold and diamond set à toc quarter repeating verge pocket watch, Previl A Paris, circa 1770, chased vari-colored case with diamond set bezel, diameter 40mm. (Christie's)
      $3,852

A gold and enamel "Medallion A Tact" watch, signed *Hilaire Bassereau A Paris*, circa 1810, the circular case decorated with dark blue guilloche enamel, the revolving back cover set with à tact arrow, overall diameter 48mm.
(Christie's) $4,733

A rare and important 22ct. gold and enamel hunting cased duplex clockwatch to celebrate the marriage in1863 of HRH Albert Edward, Prince of Wales and HRH Alexandra, Princess of Wales, signed *Jas. Mc.Cabe, Royal Exchange*, London, 1864, diameter 49mm.(Christie's) $37,191

A gold and enamel open faced cylinder pocket watch for the Turkish market, W.F. Dubois, Swiss, 1860, white enamel dial with Turkish numerals, the case with chased decoration and enamel plaque of musical trophies, 42mm.
(Christie's) $2,138

A vari-colored gold and enamel quarter repeating verge watch and chatelaine, Baillon A Paris, late 18th century, chased vari-colored case, the back with an enamel scene of figures in a landscape, diameter 45mm.
(Christie's) $5,602

A Masonic 8-Day keyless lever timepiece, Tempor Watch Co., Swiss, circa 1920, triangular white enamel dial with Masonic symbols, 15-jewel nickel finished movement, 85mm. (Christie's) $1,192

Patek Philippe, a gentleman's 18ct. gold square wristwatch, circa 1960, square silvered dial with gilt baton markers, 18-jewel movement, 28mm. (Christie's) $2,184

Mickey Mouse, an Ingersoll 'de luxe' Mickey Mouse wristwatch, mid-1930s, depicting Mickey Mouse on the rectangular face, the animated hour and minute hands shaped as Mickey's arms with yellow painted hands, 1¼in. long. (Christie's) $484

Rolex, a 9ct. gold rectangular wristwatch, 1926, 15-jewel Rolex Prima movement timed to six positions for all climates, 32 x 24mm. (Christie's) $1,645

A gold world time automatic calendar wristwatch with power reserve and 24-hour dial, Jaeger Le Coultre, Model: Geographique, recent, rotating world time aperture automatically setting the subsidiary meantime dial to the time at the named city, 38mm. (Christie's) $3,947

A stainless steel rectangular cased wristwatch, Reverso, 1930s, silvered dial signed *Reverso Asprey*, the nickel 15 jewel movement with 4 adjustments in a polished case with reeded ends, 37 x 23mm. (Bonhams) $1,397

An 18ct. gold automatic retrograde sector wristwatch, Vacheron & Constantin, Model: Gerard Mercator, 1990's, gilt dial decorated with a map of Europe, Africa and Asia, 35mm. (Christie's) $9,760

Corum, a gold U.S. coin watch, 1960s/70s, the coin case with sprung cover, T-bar lugs, coin edge, opening to reveal the gilt dial signed *Corum*, diameter 30mm. (Christie's) $1,068

Gents stainless steel cased Rolex Oyster Perpetual 'Air King' vintage wrist watch on Rolex stainless steel bracelet, circa 1950s/60s. (G.A. Key) $682

Cartier, an 18ct. gold large rectangular wristwatch, 1975, rectangular painted dial, 17-jewel nickel finished movement with monometallic balance, 35 x 28mm. (Christie's) $2,632

An 18ct. gold quartz chronograph wristwatch, signed *Bulgari*, 1990s, the white dial with raised gilt baton numerals, 35mm. diameter. (Christie's) $3,436

A lady's gold quartz wristwatch, signed *Cartier, Model Tank Chinoise*, 1980s, in typical case with cabochon winder, 27 x 21mm. (Christie's) $2,829

Ladies fine high yellow metal cased Rolex Oyster Perpetual Datejust Chronometer with diamond mounted face. (Aylsham) $4,316

A gold water resistant chronograph wristwatch, signed *Omega, Speedmaster Professional*, 1960s, the pink gilt movement jewelled to the centre with pink gold alloy balance, 40mm. diameter. (Christie's) $5,727

An 18ct. gold self-winding water resistant calendar wristwatch, signed *Vacheron & Constantin*, 1960s, the nickel plated self-winding movement with gold alloy balance, 35mm. diameter. (Christie's) $3,818

A gold self-winding and water resistant calendar wristwatch, signed *Audemars Piguet, Model Royal Oak*, 1980s, in tonneau shaped case, with octagonal bezel and back, 36mm. diameter. (Christie's) $8,018

A gentleman's gold wristwatch, signed *Vacheron & Constantin*, 1950s, the nickel plated movement jewelled to the centre, adjusted to temperatures, 35mm. diameter. (Christie's) $3,395

An 18 carat gold water resistant rectangular wristwatch, signed *Patek Philippe & Cie.*, model Gondolo, recent, with mechanical movement, Calibre 215, 38 x 30mm. (Christie's) $5,727

A gentleman's white gold rectangular wristwatch, signed *Vacheron & Constantin*, 1980s, in tonneau case with snap on back, 35mm. diameter. (Christie's) $1,697

A gentleman's gold wristwatch, , signed *Patek Phillipe,* 1950s, the nickel plated bar movement jewelled to the centre with gold alloy balance, 27 x 35mm. (Christie's) $3,818

A gold reversible quartz wristwatch, signed *Jaeger-LeCoultre, Model Reverso,* 1970s, the two tone silvered dial with Arabic numerals and blued steel hands, 39 x 22mm. (Christie's) $4,149

A lady's gold self-winding water resistant calendar wristwatch, *signed Rolex, Model Oyster Perpetual Datejust Chronometer,* 1990s, 26mm. diameter. (Christie's) $4,526

An interesting gold quartz controlled electronic calendar wristwatch, signed *IWC, DA VINCI,* 1960s, the textured gold dial with raised baton numerals, date aperture, gold hands, 38 x 35mm. (Christie's) $2,850

A gentleman's 18ct. white gold chronograph wristwatch, signed *Daniel Roth,* recent, the silvered and textured dial with blued steel hands and sweep centre seconds, 38 x 35mm. (Christie's) $7,921

A gentleman's 18ct. gold rectangular wristwatch, signed *Patek Philippe, Model Gondolo,* recent, with mechanical movement, the white dial with Arabic numerals, 33 x 25mm. (Christie's) $6,035

A gentleman's gold wristwatch, signed *Patek Philippe,* 1960s, the nickel plated movement jewelled to the centre with gold alloy balance, 33 x 28mm. (Christie's) $3,772

A lady's white gold wristwatch, signed *Piaget,* 1980s, the nickel plated movement jewelled to the centre, adjusted to five positions and temperature, 24mm. diameter. (Christie's) $1,320

A gold single button chronograph wristwatch, *signed Sarda, Besancon,* 1920s, the nickel plated movement jewelled to the centre with bimetallic balance, 32mm. square. (Christie's) $2,075

A gentleman's gold wristwatch with bar lugs, signed *Vacheron & Constantin*, 1980s, the brushed silvered dial with raised baton numerals, 32mm. diameter. (Christie's) $1,886

A silver wristwatch, Rolex, 1914, 32mm. (Bonhams) $471

A gents Longines Flagship automatic, with calendar, in gold case with strap. (Tennants) $624

An 18 carat white gold and diamond set novelty quartz wristwatch, signed *Sarcar, made for Asprey*, recent, the dial consisting of a red and black roulette wheel with a ball bearing running at random, 33mm. diameter. (Christie's) $4,582

A stainless steel military black dial wrist watch by Omega, signed black dial with Ministry of Defence broad arrow, signed *Omega 15 Jewels*, circa 1960, 35mm. diameter. (Pieces of Time) $464

An 18ct. gold self-winding calendar chronograph water resistant wristwatch, signed *Heuer, Carrera*, 1980s, the nickel plated movement, Calibre 11, jewelled to the centre, 38mm. diameter. (Christie's) $3,245

A gentleman's stainless steel split second chronograph wristwatch, signed *Girard Perregaux Chronographe a Rattrapante*, recent, 39mm. diameter. (Christie's) $3,772

A silver wristwatch with enamel dial, Rolex, 1914, 32mm. (Bonhams) $596

A gentleman's 18 ct. yellow gold perpetual calendar moonphase wristwatch, singed *Patek Philippe*, 1980s, in circular case with concave bezel, 36mm. diameter. (Christie's) $26,404

A rare large pink gold self-winding wristwatch, signed *Vacheron & Constantin*, 1950s, 43 x 36mm. (Christie's) $10,373

A stainless steel Oyster wristwatch, Rolex, Royal, 1940s, 29mm. (Bonhams) $392

A stainless steel and gilt triangular Masonic wristwatch, signed *Waltham Watch Co.*, 1930s, the bezel with chain link design, 46 x 39mm. (Christie's) $1,886

A fine gold rectangular wristwatch, signed *Patek Philippe*, 1940s, the nickel plated movement jewelled to the centre with 18 jewels, the gold alloy balance with micrometer regulation, 42 x 24mm. (Christie's) $11,836

Dieter Rams, Dietrich Lubs for Braun, 'DW20' wristwatch, 1977, black metal link strap and housing, digital display with two buttons. (Sotheby's) $1,472

A good 18ct. pink gold triple calendar moonphase water resistant chronograph wristwatch, signed *Ekegren*, *Chronometre, Chronographe,* 1990s, with mechanical movement, 38mm. diameter. (Christie's) $4,963

A gentleman's 18ct. gold automatic bracelet Rolex Oyster Perpetual Day Date watch, black dial with baton numerals, sweep seconds, Model No. 1803/8. (Russell Baldwin & Bright) $4,868

A 9ct gold wristwatch, also a watch movement and a ladies wristwatch, Swiss, various dates. (Bonhams) $439

A lady's Rolex Oyster Perpetual Datejust wristwatch, the blue dial having diamond and sapphire bezel, in 18ct gold case and flexible strap, with leather jewellery box and scarf. (Andrew Hartley) $9,280

Rolex, Genève, Oyster Perpetual Lady's yellow gold, stainless steel, diamond bracelet wristwatch, yellow luminous 'Baton' hands, 28mm. diameter. (Butterfield & Butterfield) $4,887

'Pasha' Gent's heavy yellow gold, diamond chronograph integral bracelet wristwatch, recent, signed *Cartier*, 35mm. diameter. (Butterfield & Butterfield) $19,550

'Baignoire' Lady's yellow gold, leather strap wristwatch, Audemars Piguet movement, signed *Cartier*, on width of bezel 30mm. (Butterfield & Butterfield) $12,000

An early gold wristwatch with hinged lugs and white enamel dial, signed *Patek Philippe & Co.*, 1920s, the frosted gilt movement jewelled to the third with bimetallic balance, 33mm. diameter. (Christie's) $13,444

Waltham USA gold pocket watch with cigar cutter, circa 1912, 14ct yellow gold rectangular hinged case, signed *Black, Starr & Frost* on dial, signed *Waltham* on movement, 56 x 30mm. (Butterfield & Butterfield) $1,265

A gentleman's pink gold wristwatch, signed *Patek Philippe*, 1950s, the nickel plated bar movement jewelled to the centre with bimetallic balance and micrometer regulation, 34mm. diameter. (Christie's) $6,722

A gold chronograph wristwatch, singed *Rolex*, 1940s, the nickel plated movement jewelled to the centre with gold alloy balance, 33mm. diameter. (Christie's) $5,954

Cartier, Paris, Gent's yellow gilt, leather strap wristwatch, recent, yellow gilt case, circular, champagne and white dial, signed *Cartier* on case, dial, movement and clasp, 33mm diameter. (Butterfield & Butterfield) $863

A stainless steel cushion case chronograph wristwatch, signed *Rolex*, 1930s, the nickel plated movement jewelled to the centre with gold alloy balance, 33mm. sq. (Christie's) $9,603

'Vendome' Gent's yellow gold integral bracelet wristwatch, recent, white enamel dial, signed *Cartier*, 32mm. diameter. (Butterfield & Butterfield) $5,175

Zenith Swiss gold hinged leather strap wristwatch, circa 1920, 18ct. yellow gold tonneau case, white dial, 30 x 50mm. (Butterfield & Butterfield) $1,840

A steel and pink gold chronograph wristwatch, singed *Rolex*, anti-magnetic, 1940s, the silvered dial with outer base scale, 37mm. diameter. (Christie's) $6,400

A gentleman's gold self-winding water resistant calendar wristwatch, signed *Patek Philippe*, 1960s, the self-winding movement with gold rotor, gold alloy balance, 37 jewels, adjusted to heat, cold, isochronism and to five positions, 35mm. diameter.(Christie's) $5,762

A white metal and skin covered triple calendar purse watch with moonphase, silvered dial signed *Movado*, circa 1940, Arabic numerals, 50mm x 35mm. (Christie's) $886

Swiss, Gent's rose gold triple calendar, chronograph, moonphase, leather strap wristwatch, circa 1940, signed *Baume & Mercier*, 35mm. diameter. (Butterfield & Butterfield) $2,070

A stainless steel water-resistant chronograph wristwatch, signed *Rolex*, oyster chronograph, 1930s, the matt dial with Arabic numerals, 35mm. diameter. (Christie's) $6,530

Gold, leather strap wristwatch, circa 1929, silvered dial, black luminous Arabic numerals, sunk auxiliary seconds dial, signed *Patek Philippe*, 24mm. wide. (Butterfield & Butterfield) $6,900

A Gentleman's gold wristwatch, signed *Patek Philippe & Co.*, 1950s, the matt silvered dial with raised gold five minute indexes and subsidiary seconds, 33mm. diameter. (Christie's) $2,689

Chased and embossed brass jardinière, ovoid, with beaded rim, neck chased and embossed with florals over swollen reeded body, with grotesque lion mask handles, 19in. long. (Skinner) $632

An Art Nouveau copper wall sconce, 37cm. high. (Christie's) $624

Copper slave tax badge, Charleston, South Carolina, mid-19th century, stamped Charleston 1851 Servant 2376, 1½ x 1½in. (Skinner) $1,840

An English brass novelty umbrella stand, early 20th century, modelled as a partially open umbrella, the embossed sides decorated with figures and foliage and the upright as a handle, 31½in. high. (Christie's) $1,304

A composite set of five Victorian copper haystack measures, from three gallon to quart capacity. (Christie's) $2,317

A Dutch brass and wrought-iron warming pan, 18th century, the cover repoussé decorated with the scene of the two thieves, 49in. long. (Christie's) $696

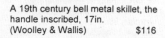

A 19th century bell metal skillet, the handle inscribed, 17in. (Woolley & Wallis) $116

A Flemish brass alms bowl, probably 16th century, the centre repoussé decorated with Adam and Eve, the sides planished and lobed ornament, the rim punched with writhen ornament, 13½in. diameter. (Christie's) $2,674

A copper samovar, urn shape with a square foot on bun feet, brass mouldings, tap and ram's head mask ring side handles, 15¼in. (Woolley & Wallis) $206

One of two floral tapestry cushions, Aubusson, mid 19th century, each with a central floral reserve, 50 x 50cm. and smaller.
(Sotheby's) (Two) $1,823

One of a pair of floral tapestry cushions, Aubusson, circa 1870, woven with trophies of flowers and musical instruments, 52 x 47cm.
(Sotheby's) (Two) $1,823

One of a pair of oblong floral tapestry cushions, Aubusson, 19th century, woven with red poppies on a yellow ground, 50 x 60cm.
(Sotheby's) (Two) $2,734

A Regency silk cushion, celebrating the birth of a baby, ivory satin ground with rosettes to each corner, the cushion decorated with cut steel pins: a leaf in each corner with family initials, 10 x 7in.
(Woolley & Wallis) $352

A set of four Flemish tapestry cushions, the tapestry second half 16th century, woven in wools and silks, depicting game-park motifs with animals, approx. 22 x 17in.
(Christie's) $9,545

One of a pair of oblong floral needlework cushions, 19th century, woven with interlacing grey floral sprays and golden foliage, 44 x 60cm. (Sotheby's)
(Two) $547

One of a pair of floral tapestry chair back cushions, Aubusson, second half 19th century, each woven with groups of musical trophies and flowers, with salmon pink borders, approximately 50 x 48cm.
(Sotheby's) (Two) $2,834

One of a pair of floral tapestry chairback cushions, Aubusson, 19th century, applied with an oval panel on a golden velvet surround, 54cm x 46cm.
(Sotheby's) (Two) $1,823

One of two matching floral tapestry cushions, Aubusson, second half 19th century, each woven with bouquets of roses, other flowers and foliage, one cushion including birds on the wing, approximately 60 x 60cm.
(Sotheby's) (Two) $2,656

A Jumeau bébé with closed mouth, fixed blue eyes, blond mohair wig, jointed composition and wood body, print frock, 18½in. high. (Christie's) $3,290

A painted wood Grodnerthal doll, with yellow comb and original maid's clothes, 5in. high, circa 1830. (Christie's) $568

A Tête Jumeau with fixed brown eyes, open mouth, pierced ears, long brown hair wig and jointed composition body, 15in. high. (Christie's) $739

A Kämmer & Reinhardt 'Hans' bisque character doll, German, circa 1912, with painted blue eyes, pouty closed mouth, original blonde wig, on floating ball jointed composition body, 19¾in. (Sotheby's) $4,939

An Alt, Beck & Gottschalck 1044 shoulder head doll, German, circa 1900, with fixed blue glass eyes, closed mouth and long blonde hair, shoulders leading to cloth body with bisque lower arms and composition lower legs, 12in. tall. (Bonhams & Brooks) $250

A Simon & Halbig for Swaine & Co. child doll, with blue lashed sleeping eyes, fair mohair wig, pierced ears, jointed body and contemporary cream wool frock, 19½in. high. (Christie's) $575

A Jumeau fashionable doll, with swivel head, brown hair wig, closed mouth, fixed blue eyes, pierced ears and gusseted kid body, 12in. high. (Christie's) $1,645

A Jumeau 1907 doll, with sleeping blue eyes, open mouth, pierced ears, blonde mohair wig and jointed composition body, 20in. high, wig replaced. (Christie's) $526

A smiling Bru fashionable doll size D, long blonde curled hair with black velvet ribbon and stuffed cotton body with kid arms, 15in. high. (Christie's) $2,129

A white bakelite teasmade with two lamps and alarm timer, British, circa 1950.
(Auction Team Köln) $102

A very rare wooden Gentleman corkscrew by Syroco Wood, Syracuse, NY. In the form of senator Volstead, unusually large cylinder, circa 1930.
(Auction Team Köln) $267

An 'Automatic Apple Peeler' by Sargent & Fosters, Shelburne Falls NY, with original paper label, circa 1855.
(Auction Team Köln) $152

A Century brass warm air table fan, with pierced urn form column and detachable lid, circa 1910, 20in. high.
(Auction Team Köln) $3,397

A Toastrite Blue Willow ceramic toaster by the Pan Electric Mfg. Co. Cleveland, Ohio, circa 1928.
(Auction Team Köln) $2,195

A Continental corkscrew, with scroll handle and engraved hexagonal sheath, with Dutch control marks, circa 1860.
(Tennants) $596

A Bender mousetrap of unusual form as a suicide water leap! Tempted by the bait the mouse climbs up and falls into the water container, circa 1902.
(Auction Team Köln) $110

Sepp the Bavarian, a German toy tinplate pencil sharpener, circa 1955, 10cm. high.
(Auction Team Köln) $268

An American Vegetable Cutter No.49 by the Enterprise Mfg. Co. Philadelphia, table model with rotating blade, circa 1885.
(Auction Team Köln) $220

A pair of mid-18th century painted outer doors, the upper sections with carved fielded panels and oval glass panes, 212 x 60cm. (Stockholms AV) $2,865

Carved door panel and surround, designed by Jean-Auguste Dampt, circa 1900, the central door panel elaborately carved with a frieze of vine leaves and berries, 73in. wide. (Christie's) $8,383

Grain-painted panelled door, possibly Maine, early 19th century, containing two molded recessed panels, painted to resemble exotic wood, 78½in. high. (Skinner) $920

A carved pine door-surround and a Victorian mahogany door, the surround of George II style, 19th century, the surround surmounted by a scrolled broken pediment centred by a ho-ho bird, the surround 106¼in. high, 54in. wide. (Christie's) $7,728

A pair of Moorish polychrome decorated doors, 19th century, each decorated with floral tendril design, the lower panels fitted with an ogee arched panelled door, 130¼in. high, 27½in. wide. (Christie's) $2,370

Pair of doors from Derry & Toms, later Biba South Kensington, London, circa 1932, clear glass panels in copper banding arranged in zig-zag pattern within wood door frame, 213 x 75.8cm. (Sotheby's) $3,611

Alvar Aalto, a birch plywood door, designed circa 1929-32, for use in a patient's room in the Paimio Sanatorium, rectangular frame with birch-faced plywood panels, 81in. high. (Christie's) $1,083

Painted iron gate, American, late 19th century, composed of eight square spindles with tapering flame tops joined by semi-circular elements, 38in. high, 35in. wide. (Skinner) $632

A carved giltwood and blue painted door and architrave, Italian, circa 1880, in Renaissance style, the panelled door carved in relief and painted with foliage and flowers, 270cm. high. (Sotheby's) $14,059

A rare enamel and gilt snuff box, Battersea/Birmingham, circa 1753-1756, the enamel lid transfer-printed in rust, the exterior with Europa and the Bull, 3in. wide.
(Sotheby's) $7,409

An early 19th century enamelled snuff box of canted oblong form with gilt metal mounts, the domed cover painted with a horse racing scene, 2¼in. wide.
(Andrew Hartley) $270

A rare English enamel snuff box, circa 1765, the lid painted in brilliant colors with the arms and motto of the Worshipful Company of Distillers within raised gilt scrolls, 3¼in. wide.
(Sotheby's) $16,092

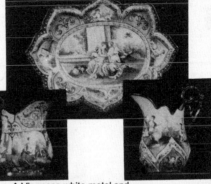

A Viennese copper and enamel tazza, circa 1880, the quatrefoil bowl supported by a faun, on a domed quatrefoil base with rope-twist border, 4½in. high.
(Christie's) $773

A Viennese white metal and enamel dish, with two associated jugs, circa 1880, the dish of elongated star shape, the near pair of jugs each with a cut and shaped spreading rim, dish 15cm. wide, jugs 8.5cm. high.
(Christie's) $1,472

An enamel scent bottle/bonbonnière, Bilston, circa 1765, the stepped hinged lid painted with bright summer flowers, the tapering base with pastoral landscapes, 4in.
(Sotheby's) $1,764

A 19th century Continental porcelain snuff box, the domed cover painted with a coat of arms, the sides with flowers, 1¾in. wide.
(Andrew Hartley) $170

A Swiss enamelled gold zarf for the Turkish market, Geneva, circa 1840, adorned with four oval reserves depicting lakeside landscapes, 48mm. high.
(Christie's) $5,006

A 19th century Continental porcelain snuff box, the cover painted with lovers in a landscape, the sides with landscape vignettes, 1¾in. wide.
(Andrew Hartley) $170

A fan, the leaf painted with the Progress of Love in three vignettes, the borders with vines, the verso with two figures by a tower, 11in., French, circa 1750. (Christie's) $2,302

A fan, the leaf painted with two shaped vignettes of lovers and an elegant couple sitting in a box watching bear baiting, and another vignette of fishermen by a lock, the verso with Bacchus and Ariadne, the guardsticks carved with a gentleman, 10in., circa 1775.
(Christie's) $1,835

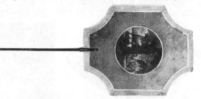

The King of Spain attending a concert in Madrid, a rare printed fan, the leaf a hand-colored etching, the verso with musicians, with ivory sticks, the guardsticks carved with a young man, 10in., French for the Spanish Market, mid-18th century
(Christie's) $3,337

A handscreen with an aquatint transparency, circa 1810. (Christie's) $200

Le Serment Civique, a large printed fan, the leaf a hand-colored etching of Louis XVI, Bailly and Layfayette standing at a flaming altar, on either side the verses of Air: des Dettes, with wooden sticks, 15in. 1789. (Christie's) $3,896

An ivory brise fan, etched recto and verso with monkeys with laburnum branches, signed, Moon or month with personal seal, the guardsticks carved with dragons with mother of pearl eyes, 9in., Japanese, late 19th century. (Christie's) $6,440

A fine Canton topographical fan, painted with a view on the Grand Canal, Canton, the verso with five vignettes of country life, with gilt metal filigree sticks enamelled in blue and green, 13in., circa 1830. (Christie's) $2,760

A handscreen or ventola, of plaited straw with turned wooden handle with bone finial, 17in., probably Venetian, 18th century.
(Christie's) $1,272

An unusual handscreen in the shape of a butterfly, the wings of tortoiseshell carved with four butterflies, the butterflies are loose and only held in place by fronds of plants, the body and handle of ivory, 12in., Chinese, late 19th century.
(Christie's) $25,438

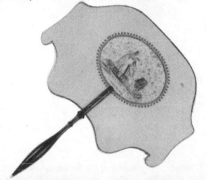

The Fortress at Barra, a Canton cabriolet fan, the leaves painted with a view of the fortress on the Pearl river, the ivory sticks carved and pierced with a frieze of figures, 11in., circa 1840, in lacquer box. (Christie's) $1,840

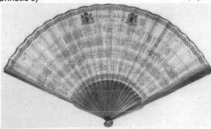

La Mere Adorée, a shaped handscreen applied with an oval stipple engraving, framed with pressed gold paper, with turned ebony handle, with bone finial, 12in., French, circa 1815. (Christie's) $145

The opera fan for 1799, a printed fan with a plan of the boxes and names of the occupants including H.R.H. the Prince of Wales in box 47, Mrs Fitzherbert in box 107 and Lady Lade in box 75, with wooden sticks, 10in. 1799.
(Christie's) $2,362

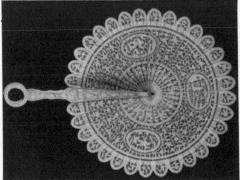

A miniature Canton cockade fan, the ivory brise fan carved and pierced with a pagoda, figures and flowers, 3.5in. radius, 9.5in. high including handle, circa 1810. (Christie's) $6,583

A village dance after Breughel, a painted fan, the verso with a farmhouse interior, the mother of pearl sticks carved and pierced with figures and portraits, gilt and backed with mother of pearl, 9in. circa 1780. (Christie's) $917

David Niven, signed 8 x 10, head and shoulders smiling.
(Vennett-Smith) $77

Bruce Lee, signed 10 x 8in., in English and Chinese, full-length in fighting scene from Enter The Dragon.
(Vennett-Smith) $2,286

Leonardo Di Caprio, signed colour 8 x 10, half-length in dinner jacket from Titanic.
(Vennett-Smith) $112

Tallulah Bankhead, photograph, approximately 6 x 8in., silver print, inscribed and signed to *Warren*. Laid down on archival matte paper and signed on the matte by the photographer, Dorothy Wilding, London, circa 1920ş.
(Christie's) $552

Kid Galahad, Warner Brothers, 1937, title lobby card signed, *Bette Davis*, 11 x 14in.
(Christie's) $1,610

Autograph letter signed *Grace Kelly*, to Greta Garbo, 29 July, n.y. 1 page 8vo, on light blue stationery with accompanying envelope addressed *Miss Garbo*.
(Christie's) $1,035

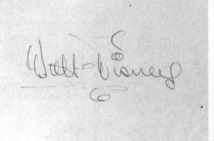

Sepia photograph inscribed and signed *Bela Lugosi*, 5 x 7in., *To my friend / Edward / in remembrance / Bela Lugosi*.
(Christie's) $3,680

Walt Disney, signed album page, 7.25 x 5.25.
(Vennett Smith) $705

Marlene Dietrich, inscribed and signed *With Love / 1955*, vertically on the white, photographic margin, black & white, 14 x 10in.
(Christie's) $1,725

Hedy Lamarr, signed photograph, 11 x 14in., black and white studio portrait. (Christie's) $1,293

Judy Garland, signed programme, to front cover featuring portrait, 'The Judy Garland Show', at the Dominion Theatre, Oct/Nov 1957. (Vennett Smith) $323

Carole Lombard, signed photograph, 4 x 6in. sepia, nicely matted and framed with brass plaque. (Christie's) $447

Charles Chaplin, signed and inscribed, no place or date. 8 x 10in., head and shoulders portrait, *To Brad Orenstein / many thanks / Charles Chaplin.* (Christie's) $1,265

Laurel & Hardy, small signed album page, by both Stan Laurel and Oliver Hardy, overmounted in green beneath 8 x 10 modern reproduction photo of the duo, 12.5 x 17 overall. (Vennett Smith) $308

Harold Lloyd, signed and inscribed sepia 6.5 x 8.5, with first name only, head and shoulders wearing spectacles and white bow-tie, also with facsimile signature. (Vennett Smith) $119

Diana Dors, signed postcard, to lower white border, head and shoulders looking back over one shoulder. (Vennett Smith) $71

Marilyn's Thank You letter from the Chairpersons of the Democratic National Committee, Citizens for Kennedy, for appearing in her most famous performance, singing Happy Birthday Mister President. (Christie's) $19,975

Jean Harlow, photograph signed and inscribed *Betty / Don't forget I adore you first / Jean,* magnificent 11 x 14in. silver print, matted and framed to 19 x 23in. (Christie's) $3,065

Gloria Swanson, signed sepia 7 x 5, half-length.
(Vennett-Smith) $62

Charles Chaplin, signed 8 x 10, three quarter length standing with arms folded, in costume from The Great Dictator.
(Vennett Smith) $1,058

Hedy Lamarr, signed real photograph Picturegoer, 1336.
(Vennett Smith) $106

Jodie Foster, signed 8 x 10, three quarter length in basque, stockings and suspenders, in character from one of her films.
(Vennett Smith) $128

Vivien Leigh, signed 4 x 5 sepia magazine photo, half length embracing, although not signed by Laurence Olivier, mounted to card.
(Vennett Smith) $87

Burt Lancaster, signed and inscribed color 8 x 10.5 bookweight photo, full-length standing holding gun, in barren landscape.
(Vennett Smith) $71

Peter Cushing, signed and inscribed 8 x 10, head and shoulders in profile in costume as Sherlock Holmes, wearing deerstalker hat and smoking a pipe.
(Vennett Smith) $70

John Wayne, a 3 x 4.5 magazine photo, laid down to 4 x 5.75 card, signed by Wayne over both photo and border, full length on horseback.
(Vennett Smith) $464

Errol Flynn, signed and inscribed sepia 5 x 7 head and shoulders smiling holding his hands behind his head, some slight areas of discoloration to image.
(Vennett Smith) $364

A pair of cast iron Indian andirons, American, late 19th century, each molded in the half-round standing with one leg slightly behind and wearing feathered headdress, tunic, fringed pants, moccasins and cape, 19½in. high.
(Christie's) $5,520

A pair of painted cast iron kitten andirons, American, late 19th-early 20th century, each molded in the half-round depicting a seated kitten with articulated ears, facial features, yellow-painted eyes, paws and tail, 10in. high.
(Christie's) $1,495

A pair of cast iron owl andirons, American, late 19th-early 20th century, each molded in the half-round with articulated ears, feathers, and talons grasping a crossed branch base, 21½in. high.
(Christie's) $2,300

A pair of Federal brass lemon-top andirons, American, 1800-1810, each with double lemon-top finial above a circular plinth, 21½in. high.
(Christie's) $1,410

A pair of Continental gilt bronze andirons, late 19th century, with acorn finials of faceted plinths above C scrolls, on square section tapering plinths applied with gargoyle masks to front and sides, 23½in. high. (Christie's) $840

Pair of Chippendale engraved metal and iron bell andirons, possibly Philadelphia, last quarter 18th century, the urn-on-urn finials with engraved tassel bows and swags, 26¾in. high.
(Skinner) $6,900

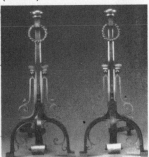

A pair of Louis XVI style gilt and patinated bronze chenets, late 19th century, the winged recumbent sphinx above shaped rectangular platforms with pierced foliate friezes and spiral twist legs, 10in. wide.
(Christie's) $2,362

A pair of bronze chenets, early 20th century, with winged dragons on raised pierced plinths, 10¾in. high.
(Christie's) $1,633

A pair of French steel andirons, late 19th or early 20th century, the standards with cushion finials and writhen rings above openwork scroll bases, 27½in. high.
(Christie's) $1,537

277

A pair of French bronze chenets, late 19th century, in the chinoiserie taste, each modelled with a snarling dragon, seated on their haunches, 12¾in. high.
(Christie's) $7,544

A pair of second Empire bronze chenets, circa 1860, modelled as crossed fruiting cornucopiae, 13½in. wide.
(Christie's) $1,508

A pair of Victorian cast iron and brass andirons, circa 1890, in the manner of Christopher Dresser, the uprights with conical-shaped intersections, 22½in. high.
(Christie's) $1,132

A pair of French wrought iron andirons, 19th century, the square section and part writhen uprights applied with scrolling mounts below bulbous writhen knop surmounts, 32½in. high.
(Christie's) $2,760

A pair of 19th century brass andirons, each with knopped urn finials on a lobed sphere and spreading scrolling plinth, each 73cm. high.
(Phillips) $2,788

A pair of Victorian brass andirons, circa 1880, with twin handled fluted urn surmounts above draped platforms and splayed hairy hoof feet, 17½in. high.
(Christie's) $792

A pair of French Louis XV style ormolu chenets, late 19th century, modelled with berried scrolling acanthus ornament, 15½in. wide.
(Christie's) $7,544

A pair of brass andirons, late 19th century, in the Low Countries 17th century style, the bulbous knopped standards on scrolling bases, 20in. high. (Christie's) $3,128

A pair of brass andirons, possibly New York, circa 1785, each with a spiral-turned finial above a double faceted diamond knob, 24⅛in. high.
(Christie's) $16,100

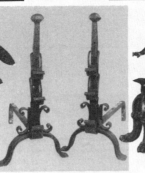

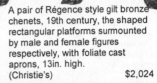

A pair of painted iron running horse andirons, American, early 20th century, the silhouetted textured figures each with head up and tail back, on a footed pedestal, 15¼in. high. (Sotheby's) $1,840

A large pair of wrought iron spit dogs, in the 17th century style, the uprights with mushroom-shaped finials, 35½in. high. (Christie's) $2,935

A pair of Régence style gilt bronze chenets, 19th century, the shaped rectangular platforms surmounted by male and female figures respectively, with foliate cast aprons, 13in. high. (Christie's) $2,024

Pair of brass belted lemon finial andirons, signed *John Molineux Founder Boston*, early 19th century, finials atop tapering columns and square plinths, 18in. high. (Skinner) $1,495

An extremely fine pair of Chippendale brass and wrought iron andirons, Philadelphia or New York, circa 1780, each with a flame finial above a beaded and fluted urn-form support, 28½in. high. (Sotheby's) $54,625

Gaetano Pesce, a pair of wrought iron fire-dogs, executed 1985-86, each of flat wrought iron, with handbeaten finial and chain link, 13in. high. (Christie's) $1,628

A pair of cast iron cat andirons, American, early 20th century, each cast in the half round seated on its haunches on a flaring pedestal, 16in. high. (Sotheby's) $1,495

A pair of French gilt bronze andirons, early 20th century, the knopped standards with outset herms and leaf wrapped berried finials, 25½in. high. (Christie's) $1,633

Pair of brass andirons, New York, early 19th century, signed *Bailey*, urn and belted ball finials above round plinths, spurred legs and ball feet, 22in. high. (Skinner) $1,265

A fine paint decorated pine bucket, Joseph Long Lehn, Elizabeth Township, Lancaster County, 1880–92.
(Sotheby's) $4,600

A French wrought iron firescreen, early 20th century, of rectangular form with curved top, the centre as a flowering urn, 43½in. wide.
(Christie's) $2,024

An Edwardian polished brass coal scuttle, early 20th century, the oval body and cover with urn finial, on four paw feet with circular stretcher, 26½in. high.
(Christie's) $1,840

A French bronze firescreen, 20th century, the mesh ground with putti mount, within a pierced scrolling frame, re-gilt, 28in. wide.
(Christie's) $1,656

A painted leather ceremonial fire bucket, signed *Wm. Caban, Franklin Fire Society*, probably New England, late 18th century, 12in. high. (Sotheby's) $5,750

A French bronze firescreen, 20th century, the rectangular frame with flambeau torchère uprights and floral garland loop handle, 26in. high. (Christie's) $2,760

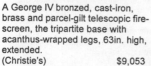

A George IV bronzed, cast-iron, brass and parcel-gilt telescopic fire-screen, the tripartite base with acanthus-wrapped legs, 63in. high, extended.
(Christie's) $9,053

A French bronze and brass fan firescreen, early 20th century, the tapering frame with twin lions flanking a heraldic shield, with further pierced foliage, 30in. high. (Christie's) $1,600

A French bronze firescreen, early 20th century, the frame of chinoiserie style, with winged mythical beast handle and mesh ground, 25in. wide.
(Christie's) $2,208

A George III brass-mounted mahogany plate-bucket, of cylindrical form with pierced vertical sides and lion-mask carrying handles, 14½in. high. (Christie's) $4,100

A brass coal bin, 20th century, of cylindrical form with beaded bands of pierced ovolo decoration and lion's mask ring handles, 30.8cm. diameter. (Christie's) $404

A French bronze firescreen, early 20th century, the pierced foliate border with arabesques, the mesh ground with a suspended urn, 32in. wide. (Christie's) $2,392

An Empire style gilt-brass and bronze folding firescreen, mid 20th century, the rectangular frame with twin lattice work mesh doors with laurel wreath mounts, 43in. high. (Christie's) $1,600

An oval gilt bronze firescreen, late 19th century, the ribbon tied laurel cast border with a floral bouquet to the mesh ground, 19 x 29½in. (Christie's) $2,049

A Napoleon III gilt-bronze and tôle peinte coal basket, circa 1870, of rectangular form, with rounded underside, the ochre ground end panels painted with ribbon-suspended baskets of fruit, 19in. wide. (Christie's) $1,747

A French giltwood and tapestry firescreen, by Charles Bernel, Paris, dated 1914, the feather-carved frame with scroll cartouche crest flanked by floral chains, 47½in. high. (Christie's) $2,760

A mahogany and brass bound coal bin, late 19th/early 20th century, of navette form, the shaped oval top with tin liner above a ring-bound body, 19in. wide. (Christie's) $810

A late Regency or William IV japanned metal and cast iron purdonium, circa 1830, of rectangular form, with rounded underside, the black ground heightened in gilt, 18½in. wide. (Christie's) $1,472

A brown trout attributed to Homer, mounted in a setting of reeds and grasses, with gilt inscription, *Brown Trout, 4lbs. 12ozs. Caught by P.E. Avery at 'Great Belwyn. Wilts.' 1938.* Case 27¾ x 13in. (Bonhams) $947

A stuffed pike mounted in a bow front case with realistic river bed surround, inscribed *Pike. 17lbs. Caught at Crech St. Michael. 21st Oct. 1934.* (Bearne's) $1,272

A stuffed trout in glazed diorama case, *Caught outside the brewery, Tiverton 9th August 1906,* 21in. wide, in case labelled *A.W. Gamage Ltd., Holborn, London.* (Russell Baldwin & Bright) $765

A roach by Homer in a gilt lined bow front case with gilt description, *Roach, 2lbs. 11ozs. Caught by D. Ide at 'Bures' 12.3.54.* Case 22 x 12½in. (Bonhams) $1,263

A common bream by Gunn, mounted in a setting of reeds and grasses against a blue background in a flat front case. Case 21½ x 15½in. with T.E. Gunn trade label to reverse. (Bonhams) $632

Three perch attributed to Cooper, mounted in a setting of reeds and grasses against a blue background in a gilt lined bow front case. Case 35¼ x 20½in. (Bonhams) $1,579

A fine barbel by Cooper, mounted in a setting of reeds and grasses with gilt inscription *Barbel 6¼lbs. Caught at Shiplake. Septr. 15th 1926.* and with J. Cooper & Sons label. Case 31¼ x 13¼in. (Bonhams) $4,263

A fine chub attributed to Cooper, mounted in a setting of ferns and grasses with plaque to interior *Thames Chub, 4lbs. 11ozs. caught by Mr W. Clarke, 15th Nov. 1958.* Case 25 x 13¼in. (Bonhams) $1,105

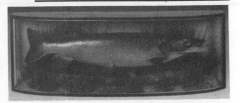

A stuffed pike in bow front case, inscribed *Caught at Ross-on-Wye. Jan. 22nd. 1946. Weight 22lbs.* (Bearne's) $1,399

A stuffed pike in naturalistic river bed setting inscribed *Pike. 22½lbs. Caught near Ross-on-Wye. 21st. Jan. 1935.* (Bearne's) $1,399

A roach by Cooper, mounted in a setting of ferns and grasses with gilt inscription *Roach. 2lbs. 9ozs. Caught by A.R. Bell at Downton, 8th Sept. 1947.* Case 20¹/8 x 12½in. (Bonhams) $979

A Cooper bream, mounted in a setting of reeds and grasses against a blue background in a gilt lined bow front case with J. Cooper & Sons label. Case 26⁷/8 x 16¼in. (Bonhams) $979

A barbel caught by F.W.K. Wallis by Rose of Nottingham, the fish mounted in a setting of reeds, with gilt inscription *Barbel. Weight 8lbs. 13½ozs. Caught at Shadlow by F.W.K. Wallis, July 1911.* Wood case 38¾ x 24¾in. (Bonhams) $1,263

Four rudd by Cooper, mounted in a setting of reeds and grasses against a blue background in a gilt lined bow front case with J. Cooper & Sons label to case interior. Case 31 x 18½in. (Bonhams) $1,579

Four perch by Homer, mounted in a setting of reeds and grasses, with gilt inscription *Caught at Dagenham Augst. 1903 by G. H. Stephens. Wgt's. 2lbs 1¾, 1lb. 8½, 1lb. 7 & 1lb 6½oz.* Case 34 x 17½in. (Bonhams) $1,737

Two stuffed trout in glazed diorama bow fronted case, *Caught at Blagdon Reservoir by M.B. Castle, August 26th 1904, Weights 5.5lbs and 7lbs,* 3ft. 5in. wide, labelled *W.E. Homer, London.* (Russell Baldwin & Bright) $2,148

A carved wooden salmon trophy, finely painted and mounted on a framed oak backboard, inscribed *Caught by H. Peel' 25½lbs, Glanryhd Pool April 28 1934 Danyrallt,* 17¼ x 48½in.
(Bonhams) $1,820

A roach mounted against a setting of reeds and grasses in a gilt lined bow front case, the gilt inscription reads, *Roach 2lbs 01/2oz caught in Club Water by A. W. Jordan V.A. Society "Hayes" September 1914,* bears Cooper label, case 21in.
(Bonhams) $364

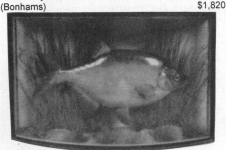

A bream, mounted in a setting of rushes and reeds in a gilt lined bow front case, inscribed label reads, *Taken by J.T. Leighton, at Amberley July 9th 1893 weight 4lbs.* Bears J.Cooper & Son label 28 Radnor Street, St. Luke's, London EC, case 25in.
 (Bonhams) $700

A pike in a gilt lined bow front case, bears gilt, inscribed *Aqualate, March 5th 1940, caught by Major E.H. Tattersall, at the first stakes 11.40am 23lbs.,* case 49in. (Bonhams) $1,470

A trout, mounted against a setting of reeds and grasses in a gilt lined bow front case. Inscribed in gilt *Trout caught by G.T. Goode at Pangbourne Weir, May 17th 1905, weight 8½lbs.* Bears Cooper 28 Radnor Street, St. Luke's London EC label; case 23½in.
(Bonhams) $784

A dace mounted against rushes in a gilt lined bow front case, labelled *Homer, 105 Woodgrange Road, Forest Gate, London E7,* case 17½.in.
(Bonhams) $588

A rudd in reeds and grasses, set in gilt lined bow front case, label *Caught on Torcross Ley by F.W.V.Mitchell, August 18th 1896 weight 2lbs 6oz,* case 21in.
(Bonhams) $960

A rudd, mounted in a setting of reeds and grasses in a gilt lined bow front case, inscribed in gilt *Rudd 2lbs caught at Martham, on the River Thurne Easter Sunday 1926,* case 20in. (Bonhams) $532

An Eaton & Deller, 4¾in. Perty style salmon reel, tapered lignum handle, rim and backplate, reduced brass foot. (Christie's) $812

An Allcocks Match Aerial reel with twin black handles, optional check and adjustable brake. (Bonhams) $143

A rare Percy Wadham Newport I.W brass framed "Cowes" spinning reel, 4½in. perforated ebonite drum, twin white handles. (Bonhams) $630

Hardy Brothers: A 4½in. 'Silex' alloy reel, with solid plates, ivorine handles, tension screw, on/off check button and check lever. (Bearne's) $414

A T. Pape, Newcastle, 3½in. brass reel, with horn handle, plate-wind. (Christie's) $289

A Malloch brass 3¼in. Sidecaster reel, with horn handle, Mallochs Patent oval logo. (Christie's) $342

A G. Little & Co. 4½in. Scottish style salmon reel, the brass faceplate inscribed *G. Little & Co., Makers to H.R.H. Prince of Wales, 63 Haymarket, London*, ebonite handle, rim and backplate. (Christie's) $506

An Abbey and Imbrie, N.Y. 2in. double multiplying compensating reel, with horn handle, crack-winding arm, ebonite back and faceplates, with original back and paper label. (Christie's) $433

A J.J.S. Walker Bampton 'Wallace Watson' No. 3 alloy reel, with twin ivorine handles, ivorine rim handle, brass foot, strapped rim-tension adjuster, line guard. (Christie's) $397

285

A Hardy 'The Perfect' 3¹/₈in. alloy trout fly reel, with 1896 check, brass bearings, brass bridged rim tension regulator.
(Bonhams) $505

A Hardy Uniqua 4in. alloy salmon fly reel with ribbed brass foot ebonite handle and telephone drum latch.
(Bonhams & Brooks) $205

A Hardy 'The Silex Major' 4¼in. alloy bait casting reel, circa 1926, with brass auxiliary rim brake, ivorine rim brake lever with corresponding four position regulator button.
(Bonhams) $308

A scarce 1¹⁵/₁₆in. brass multiplying collar winch, mid 19th century, 1¾in. wide, with brass rim stop lever, offset curved crank with waisted ivory handle.
(Bonhams) $316

A rare Chippindale multiplier, circa 1910, with free swinging line pick-up device on nickel silver support, brass foot and stem.
(Bonhams) $1,184

A very rare 'The Ainsco Reel' alloy threadline casting reel, circa 1930s, reciprocating wire hook bail arm, brass handle and crank.
(Bonham's) $1,060

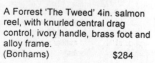

A Forrest 'The Tweed' 4in. salmon reel, with knurled central drag control, ivory handle, brass foot and alloy frame.
(Bonhams) $284

An Edward Vom Hofe Model 550 'Ocean' 2/0 multiplier, black hard rubber with nickel silver fittings, free spool and optional check rim levers. (Bonhams) $474

A scarce Hardy 'The Uniqua' 2⁵/₈in. alloy trout fly reel, with duplicated mark II check, horseshoe latch, ivorine handle and smooth brass foot. (Bonhams) $221

A 4in. Coxon Aerial with 6 spokes, walnut back-plate and ebonite drum.
(Bonhams & Brooks) $725

A scarce Horton The 'Meek No.2' solid nickel-silver multiplying reel, with optional check button, counterweighted offset crank, light horn handle. (Bonham's) $456

A laminated bakelite 'Allcock's Aerial' sea reel with weight regulator, twin xylonite handles and optional check, 4in.
(Bonhams & Brooks) $335

A Hardy all brass 'Perfect' reel with 1896 check unperforated drum, bridged rim tension regulator screw, open ball race and pierced foot, the face plate with domed ivory knob, rod in hand trade mark enclosed oval logo and straight line logo.
(Bonhams & Brooks) $725

A Hardy 'Super Silex' 3½in. bait casting reel with ivorine quadrant casting dial, ivorine mounted rim check lever, twin ebonite handles, smooth brass foot and button drum latch.
(Bonhams & Brooks) $230

A Hardy LRH three-piece dry fly rod with spare tip in green canvas bag (re-whipped) in alloy tube. A three-piece greenheart rod in cloth bag, together with a Hardy Eureka 3½in. reel and a Wheatley six-compartment alloy dry fly box.
(Bonhams & Brooks) $233

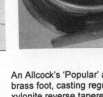

A scarce mahogany and brass Nottingham style wheel back reel with brass lined back plate and optional check, 5in.
(Bonhams & Brooks) $290

A Hardy 'Bougle' alloy raised pillar dry fly reel, ribbed alloy foot, rim tension regulator screw, 3in. ivorine winding knob, duplicated MKII check.
(Bonhams & Brooks) $1,045

An Allcock's 'Popular' aerial with brass foot, casting regulator twin xylonite reverse tapered handles, optional check in maker's box, 3in.
(Bonhams & Brooks) $320

A good Southern French late 17th/early 18th century carved and gilded frame, with ogee sight, scotia, and panels to the cushion-moulded top edge, 80.6 x 67.3 x 8.3cm. (Bonhams) $3,200

An English 19th century gilt composition frame, the raised astragal with imbricated laurel leaves tied at corners and centres, 13³/₈ x 9 x 4¼in. (Christie's) $515

An Italian 17th century gilt reverse profile frame, the reverse ogee moulding with incised scrolling foliage on a punched ground, 47.9 x 38.1 x 13cm. (Christie's) $2,024

A Spanish 16th or 17th century painted and gilded reverse cassetta frame, with various mouldings at outer and raised inner edges, 13 x 8.8 x 8.6cm. (Christie's) $1,011

An Italian late 16th century painted tabernacle frame, the cornice with various mouldings above a frieze with painted scrolling foliage, 17 x 16 x 13in. (Christie's) $5,152

A French Louis XIV carved and gilded top arched drawing frame, the pierced corners of the ovolo with stylised fleur-de-lys, 14½ x 10½ x 2in. (Christie's) $1,011

A pair of French 19th century gilt composition frame, the oval corners of the torus with bead course at sight edge, 27½ x 22¾ x 1½in. (Christie's) $1,288

An Italian 17th century carved and gilded tondo frame, with ogee moulding at outer edge, outer scotia, diameter 79 x 12.3cm. (Christie's) $3,496

A Spanish 17th century ebonised and partly gilded reverse profile frame, with ogee and taenia mouldings at outer edge, 28.2 x 21 x 10.2cm. (Christie's) $736

An Italian 16th century gilded pastiglia frame, with stepped sight, guilloche to the cushion-moulded frieze, 30.5 x 25.8 x 8.9cm.
(Bonhams) $4,704

A Spanish 17th century gilded and polychromed cassetta frame, with pronounced leaf ogee sight, ribbon twist, marbleised panels to the frieze, 61.6 x 49.3 x 15.2cm.
(Bonhams) $2,499

An Italian, possibly Tuscan, 17th century carved and parcel-gilt frame, with leaf sight, double bead-and-reel, repeat flowerhead motif to the hollow, 75.5 x 56.2 x 10.5cm.
(Bonhams) $21,315

A part Louis XV carved, pierced, swept and décapé frame, with foliate oval sight, strapwork and leaf to the crosshatched spandrels, 73.9 x 57.2 x 15.8cm.
(Bonhams) $2,205

A Louis XIV carved and gilded 'Lebrun' frame, with plain panels to the foliate ogee sight, scotia, incised decoration to the cushion-moulded hollow, 127.6 x 96.2 x 12.7cm.
(Bonhams) $4,116

A Spanish 17th century carved and parcel –gilt frame, with leaf ogee sight, reverse hollow with pronounced leaf centres and corners, and leaf back edge, 59.3 x 47.7 x 12.7cm.
(Bonhams) $5,586

An English 18th century carved and stripped frame, with foliate sight, centred husked leaf, leaf and shield top edge, 47.3 x 38.1 x 8.6cm.
(Bonhams) $7,056

An Italian 17th century carved and gilded frame, with cavetto sight, guilloche to the cushion-moulded frieze with cartouche centre bottom, 56.8 x 44.8 x 10.5cm.
(Bonhams) $1,397

An English 19th century carved and gilded Carlo Maratta style frame, with leaf and shield ogee sight, 38½ x 28¾ x 4¼in.
(Bonhams) $21,315

A Louis XIV carved and gilded oak frame, second half 18th century, with dentilled outer edge, the raised corners of the ogee with anthemia in scrolling foliate cartouches, 41.9 x 27 x 6.7cm.
(Christie's) $2,632

A large Continental carved and gilded frame, late 18th or early 19th century, with schematic foliate outer edge, raised course of foliage flowers and acorns in high relief, 60½ x 51 x 7in.
(Christie's) $3,290

A North Italian carved, ebonized and parcel-gilt cassetta frame, 17th century, with raised stylized laurel leaves to the outer edge, the fascia with cauliculi to the centers and corners, 48.7 x 35.6 x 10.4cm.
(Christie's) $3,125

An English carved and gilded frame, early 18th century, with lobed outer edge, the ogee corners with bell-flowers set within scrolling foliage, 34.2 x 68.5 x 10.8cm.
(Christie's) $904

An Italian parcel-gilt and blue painted cassetta frame, 17th century, with raised fillet to the outer edge, descending through further moldings to the fascia with crucifixes to the centers, 41.9 x 28.9 x 5.3cm.
(Christie's) $1,316

An English carved and silvered frame, late 17th century, with stylized foliate outer edge, the ovolo with gadrooned sides and acanthus to the corners, 28¾ x 24 x 4½in. (Christie's) $987

A Florentine parcel-gilt and ebonized cassetta frame, early 17th century, with cavetto and other minor moldings to the outer edge, the fascia with fleurs-de-lys to the corners and foliate sgrafitto to the centers, 41.9 x 37.2 x 12cm.
(Christie's) $2,467

A Spanish carved, gilded and painted frame, early 17th century, with outer ovolo, the raised and pierced corners of the reverse ogee with C-scrolls and stylized foliage, gilded sight edge, 71.4 x 60 x 9.2cm. (Christie's) $2,796

An Italian parcel-gilt and ebonized cassetta frame, early 17th century, with ovolo raised above a cavetto at the outer edge, the fascia with cauliculi to the centers and corners, 132.4 x 91.2 x 14cm.
(Christie's) $4,935

A pair of German Biedermeier walnut armoires, early 19th century, each with stepped rectangular top above two doors, stepped molded plinth and on block feet, 39¾in. wide. (Christie's) $11,316

A Restauration mahogany armoire, the eared, molded, beaded and channelled cornice above two part-glazed and panelled doors, 71¼in. wide. (Christie's) $16,974

A French fruitwood armoire, late 18th/early 19th century, the arched molded cornice above a panelled frieze and a pair of doors with large brass escutcheons, 61in. wide. (Christie's) $1,990

A French ormolu mounted mahogany and reverse-painted mirror armoire, 19th century, the rectangular molded cornice above a frieze with lyre-mounts to the angles, above two triple-panelled doors, 48in. wide. (Christie's) $10,373

A Louis-Philippe acajoué moucheté armoire, of gothic style, the molded rounded rectangular cornice above a pair of doors with blind tracery, enclosing six slides, on bracket feet, with blind tracery, 63in. wide. (Christie's) $5,281

A Normandy carved oak buffet or armoire à deux corps, 19th century, the upper part with pierced projecting wheat sheaf cornucopiae and floral cresting with scale carved cornice, frieze and angles, 58in. wide. (Christie's) $5,451

A French chestnut armoire, late 18th/early 19th century, the rounded channelled stiles with shaped molded panelled doors enclosing hanging space. (Christie's) $1,277

A French chestnut armoire, the doors early 18th century, with molded cornice and channelled frieze, above a pair of triple panelled doors carved with ho-ho birds and foliate scrolls, 55in. wide. (Christie's) $5,067

A Louis XV Breton provincial chestnut Armoire with later glazed panels, circa 1770, 154cm. wide x 50cm. deep x 220cm. high. (Bonhams & Brooks) $1,848

A fruitwood armoire, Louis XV, Provincial, circa 1760, the double arched top above a pair of doors each with two shaped panels, 4ft.3in. wide.
(Sotheby's) $2,689

Louis XV fruitwood armoire, late 18th century, with moulded cresting and a pair of shaped panelled doors opening to a shelved interior, 52in. wide.
(Skinner) $3,000

A French fruitwood and burr-elm armoire, 19th century, the arched molded cornice above a pair of fielded panelled doors enclosing a shelf, 64in. wide.
(Christie's) $4,658

A Flemish oak armoire with a pair of full length panelled doors surmounted by a carved basket of flowers in relief, 53in. wide.
(Anderson & Garland) $845

A Dutch walnut and figured walnut secrétaire armoire, late 18th/early 19th century, decorated with lines, the arched molded cornice centered with a floral carving above a pair of panelled doors, 76in. wide.
(Christie's) $9,747

A French Provincial fruitwood armoire, late 18th/early 19th century, decorated with foliate carvings, on short cabriole legs, 65in. wide.
(Christie's) $2,024

A French Provincial walnut armoire, early 19th century, with a molded cornice above a pair of doors with molded shaped panels.
(Christie's) $2,201

Louis XVI Provincial oak armoire, late 18th/early 19th century, rectangular form, doors with molded detail, raised on plain feet, 44½in. wide.
(Skinner) $4,025

Louis XVI Provincial oak armoire, 19th century, molded cornice over a pair of carved doors, 54in. wide.
(Skinner) $2,415

American Aesthetic Movement ebonised, gilt incised, and marquetry bed, last quarter 19th century, 64½in. wide. (Skinner) $3,162

An oak cradle, Flemish, 19th century, carved overall, the canopy centred with a mask, the panelled sides decorated with rosettes and foliage, on leafy-carved rockers, 35½in. long. (Christie's) $956

Fine and rare Gustav Stickley child's bed, original deep brown finish, Gustav red decal, 35½in. wide. (Skinner) $8,050

A late Federal turned and figured maple bedstead, American, possibly Southern, 1830, the turned, moulded egg-shape finials above ring-turned flaring posts, 4ft. 7in. wide. (Sotheby's) $5,750

An oak and inlaid tester bedstead, English, late 16th/ early 17th century and later, the tester with fifteen panels (three of a later date), eleven inlaid with geometrical motifs and the twelfth inlaid with the Tankred coat of arms, 61in. wide. (Christie's) $14,781

An early Victorian mahogany four poster bed, the front two posts ring-turned and lotus carved terminating in a ceramic castors, 76in. wide. (Christie's) $2,769

George III style paint decorated satinwood full tester bed, late 19th century, 83¼in. wide. (Skinner) $8,625

A Louis Philippe rosewood and boxwood lined lit en bateau, the panelled ends with cylindrical top-rails and panelled, flower and foliate carved stiles, 47in. wide. (Christie's) $920

Federal birch carved red painted tall post tester bed, probably Massachusetts, 1815-20, ring turned head posts and shaped headboard, 73in. long. (Skinner) $13,800

A 19th century painted pine
bedstead, 49in.
(Sworders) $290

American   Sheraton four-post
double bed, in maple with turned
posts, 83in. high.   (Eldred's)
                         $825

A Dutch mahogany and marquetry
inlaid bed, circa 1810, with rails
146cm. wide x 107cm. high.
(Bonhams) $882

A fine 19th century French
mahogany and parcel gilt bedstead,
the floral marquetry inlaid
headboard surmounted by a gilt
gesso dolphin adorned crest-panel,
60in. wide.
(Diamond Mills & Co.) $2,030

An oak tester bedstead, English,
late 17th century, the eight panel
headboard banded with chequer
inlay, the roof with eleven panels
and raised on block and ringturned
baluster columns, 52½in. wide.
(Christie's) $12,121

Federal carved mahogany tall post
bed, possibly New Hampshire, the
ring-turned, reeded, and leaf-
carved footposts continue to
faceted supports with lamb's
tongue corners, 59½in. wide.
(Skinner) $51,750

One of a pair of Aesthetic
Movement carved mahogany beds,
circa 1880, 78in. long.
(Skinner)   (Two) $690

Child's bed, circa 1820, in tiger
maple with acorn finials.
(Eldred's) $357

A Charles X bird's-eye maple lit en
bateau, decorated with lines, with
outswept panelled ends joined by
side rails, 81¼in. long.
(Christie's) $2,030

Gustav Stickley two-door bookcase, gallery top above two doors, eight panes each, medium brown finish, 41¾in. wide.
(Skinner) $9,200

A William IV mahogany bookcase, the molded and tasseled cornice above two sections of six open adjustable shelves, 130in. wide.
(Christie's) $14,996

One of a pair of Louis XVI style kingwood, tulipwood and marble topped bowfront bibliothèques, late 19th century, 27in. wide.
(Christie's)   (Two) $4,077

Pierre Chareau, bibliothèque, circa 1929-30, comprising three elements in palisander and black patinated iron, the left cupboard on two bent metal feet, 288cm. max, width.
(Sotheby's) $278,640

An Edwardian mahogany revolving bookcase, the moulded edged square top with stringing and central marquetry bat wing patera, 20½in. wide.
(Andrew Hartley) $2,106

A George III mahogany breakfront bookcase in the manner of Gillow, with moulded cornice, four doors with gothic style astragal glazing, 126in. wide.
(Andrew Hartley) $14,580

Arts & Crafts oak and leaded glass bookcase, late 19th/early 20th century, two-door bookcase with upper panels of slag and clear glass geometric segments, medium brown finish, 57¾in. high.
(Skinner) $460

A George IV rosewood-veneered open bookcase with shaped arched raised back, 126cm. wide.
(Bearne's) $2,831

Limbert two-door oak bookcase, Grand Rapids, Michigan, early 20th century, the bookcase with two elongated glass panels on each door, three adjustable shelves on each side, 57½in.
(Skinner) $2,760

An early George III mahogany bookcase-on-chest, the upper part with a moulded broken pediment with blind fret-carved ornament, fitted with adjustable shelves and enclosed by a pair of glazed astragal glazed doors, 55in. wide. (Christie's) $10,692

An early Victorian dwarf bookcase, rosewood veneered, the top with replaced green veined marble, the frieze above an inverted front with adjustable open shelves, 5ft.6in. wide.
(Woolley & Wallis) $1,916

A mahogany bookcase in the Sheraton Revival style with stringing and satinwood crossbanding, moulded cornice, two brass trimmed doors with entwined glazing bars, 52in. wide.
(Andrew Hartley) $6,468

A Victorian burr walnut library bookcase, the cavetto cornice above twin arch-top glazed doors, with shaped-front frieze drawer above twin arch panel doors, 109.5cm. wide.
(Bristol) $2,940

An early 19th century mahogany double breakfront library bookcase, the detachable cornice with moulded bellflowers, fluting interspersed wheat sheaves above egg and dart, 18ft. 5½in. wide.
(Woolley & Wallis) $73,444

An oak bookcase, late 19th/ early 20th century in the Gothic style, with a foliate frieze, fitted with adjustable shelves and enclosed by a pair of glazed panelled doors with pierced trefoil and Gothic arched tracery with astragals, 46in. wide.
(Christie's) $2,479

A George III carved mahogany breakfront bookcase, circa 1800, in three parts, the removable paterae-mounted cornice above four mullioned glazed doors, 6ft. 5in. wide. (Sotheby's) $10,350

An early 19th century mahogany open bookcase on stand, the moulded cornice above a reeded frieze and frame to a shelf, 30¼in. wide.
(Woolley & Wallis) $1,680

A William IV mahogany library open bookcase, the rectangular plain breakfront cornice above four open sections, each with three adjustable shelves, 122in. wide.
(Christie's) $21,691

A mahogany and boxwood lined bookcase-on-chest, parts George III, with a dentil-moulded cornice and inlaid frieze above a pair of arched glazed doors, 46in. wide. (Christie's) $1,625

An early Victorian dwarf bookcase, the top with green veined marble, the invented front open central section with adjustable shelves flanked by cupboards, 5ft.7in. wide. (Woolley & Wallis) $4,082

A late 19th century mahogany library bookcase, the detachable cornice with a pierced fretwork, swan neck pediment terminating in scrolls above adjustable shelves, 4ft.½in. wide. (Woolley & Wallis) $3,832

A Regency brass-mounted mahogany bookcase, the rounded rectangular reeded cornice with a plain frieze centred by a panel, above four doors with later brass trelliswork grilles, 108in. wide. (Christie's) $11,200

Edwardian mahogany bookcase/cabinet, W. Walker & Sons, London, circa 1890-1912, upper section with shaped cornice, with open shelving over six cupboard doors enclosing pigeon holes, 68in. long. (Skinner) $2,300

Regency bronze mounted mahogany and mirrored library bookcase, early 19th century, two pairs of glazed doors, the base with two pairs of mirrored doors, flanked by Egyptian Revival caryatids, 90¾in. long. (Skinner) $17,250

Edward William Godwin, probably executed by Reuben Burkitt, bookcase, designed for Dromore Castle, Ireland, 1869, Austrian oak, pierced triangular finials above three stepped shelves, 121.5cm. wide. (Sotheby's) $29,680

A pair of 19th century mahogany bookcases, the upper sections with adjustable shelves the bases fitted with a single drawer above a pair of cupboard doors, 2ft. 11in. wide. (Brightwells) $7,150

A Third Empire library bookcase, mahogany veneered, with gilt bronze mounts, the top with a stepped and cavetto cornice, the oak interior with adjustable shelves enclosed by three glazed doors, 7ft.3in. wide. (Woolley & Wallis) $26,000

An Edwardian mahogany marquetry inlaid and satinwood crossbanded revolving bookcase, fitted with three small drawers, 48cm. wide. x 88cm. (Wintertons) $1,771

A William IV Goncalo Alvez side cabinet, the white marble rectangular top above two frieze cedar lined drawers, flanked by flowerheads and paterae, 55in. wide. (Christie's) $3,125

A Victorian rosewood veneered bookcase, the upper stage with molded cornice and two arched glazed doors, 53in. wide. (Wintertons) $1,656

An early 19th century rosewood floorstanding bookcase, the brass rail gallery above a molded cornice, the shaped rectangular glazed double doors opening to reveal a series of shelves, 4ft. wide. (Wintertons) $1,540

A Victorian oak, ash, marquetry and ebonized dwarf bookcase, in the manner of Bruce Talbert, carved throughout with flowers, foliage and inlaid with quatrefoils, palmettes and dotted lines, 41in. wide. (Christie's) $15,585

A mahogany bookcase, part 18th century, the top and bottom associated, the upper part with a molded cornice enclosed by a pair of glazed astragal doors, 52½in. wide. (Christie's) $5,921

A George III mahogany bookcase with broken dentil pediment and cornice over gothic blind fret frieze, two doors with brass trim each with six astragal glazed panes, 65in. wide. (Andrew Hartley) $9,940

A Regency rosewood open bookcase, with later green marble top, long frieze drawer over two adjustable shelves flanked on either side by leaf carved pilasters, 47½in. wide. (Andrew Hartley) $2,502

An unusual French tulipwood and gilt-metal mounted open bookcase, 19th century, of trefoil design, in the Louis XV taste, the top inset with a veined pale marble panel, within a brass beaded border, the top 24in. wide. (Christie's) $2,180

A large pine open breakfront bookcase, parts late 19th century, with a molded cornice and gilded ribbon-tied floral and foliate-decoration to the frieze centered by a cartouche, 148in. wide.
(Christie's) $9,541

A pair of mahogany and boxwood strung bowfront bookcases, parts 19th century, each with a molded dentil cornice and enclosed by a pair of ogee arched glazed astragal panel doors, 27in. wide.
(Christie's) $11,265

Regency satinwood veneered bookcase with later marble top, rosewood and kingwood crossbanding, 105.5cm. wide.
(Bearne's) $3,303

A Victorian pitch pine library bookcase, with a molded cornice above three pairs of glazed doors, the base with three drawers and panelled cupboards below, 90in. wide. (Christie's) $2,834

A Victorian mahogany breakfront bookcases with molded cornice over four arched glazed doors enclosing shelving, 84in. wide.
(Andrew Hartley) $6,672

A late George III mahogany bookcase, with a shaped tablet centered cornice above a pair of arched astragal glazed doors, two panelled doors below enclosing two drawers, 37in. wide.
(Christie's) $5,757

One of a pair of early 19th century mahogany bookcases with ebony stringing, molded cornice, over two astragal glazed brass trimmed doors, 61in. wide.
(Andrew Hartley)
           (Two) $9,656

A Victorian rosewood open bookcase, the three quarter galleried molded edged protruding top on wrythen turned supports, four molded shelves, on plinth, 57in. wide.
(Andrew Hartley) $1,694

A mahogany two stage bookcase with molded cornice, two brass trimmed glazed doors enclosing shelving, protruding base with two walnut panelled cupboard doors, 19th century, 50¾in. wide.
(Andrew Hartley) $1,112

A walnut, crossbanded and feather-strung bureau cabinet, early 18th century and later, 30¼in. wide. (Christie's) $43,992

An oak bureau cabinet, North West/West Midlands, early 18th century, in three sections, 39½in. wide. (Christie's) $16,560

A Queen Anne carved and figured maple bonnet-top secretary bookcase, Eastern Connecticut, 1740-60, 36in. wide. (Sotheby's) $42,125

A George III mahogany bureau bookcase, crossbanded with stringing, pierced swan neck pediment, 46½in. wide. (Andrew Hartley) $483

A late 18th/early 19th century Colonial padoukwood bureau bookcase, on shaped bracket supports, 122cm. wide. (Bearne's) $2,228

An Italian burr-ash and walnut bureau cabinet, 19th century, crossbanded throughout with a swan neck pediment, 47in. wide. (Christie's) $5,757

A walnut bureau cabinet, 20th century, in the George I style, cross-banded and feather strung, 42in. wide. (Christie's) $7,268

A George I burr-walnut bureau bookcase, the whole with twin reeded moldings, inlaid with herringbone bandings, 37in. wide. (Canterbury) $11,045

A George III mahogany bureau-bookcase, probably North of England, the top and base associated, 49½in. wide. (Christie's) $7,631

George III inlaid mahogany bureau bookcase, third quarter 18th century, with dentil molded cornice, 37in. wide. (Skinner) $4,600

A North Italian bone inlaid walnut and olive wood bureau cabinet, basically 17th/18th century, 50½in. wide. (Bonhams) $18,954

A George III mahogany bureau bookcase with inlaid key banding and stringing, 45in. wide. (Andrew Hartley) $2,085

A George III mahogany bureau, two short and three long drawers flanked by fluted quarter columns, on ogee bracket feet, 46in. wide.
(Andrew Hartley) $1,920

A figured walnut bureau of early 18th century design, slope enclosing shaped interior fitted pigeon holes four small drawers and well, 27 x 34in. (Canterbury) $2,557

A Victorian mahogany cylinder bureau, the top with a molded gallery, the pull out writing surface with three hinged flaps, 4ft. 11.5in.
(Woolley & Wallis) $1,600

Chippendale-style inlaid mahogany slant-lid desk, 19th century, interior with maple drawer fronts and pigeonholes, the case fitted with three long drawers, 41in. wide.
(Skinner) $863

Panelled pine stand-up desk, New England, late 18th/early 19th century, the hinged lid with molded lip opens to fitted interior, a single drawer under and two raised panel doors, 38½in. wide.
(Skinner) $2,070

Chippendale carved wavy birch serpentine slant-lid desk, coastal Essex County, Massachusetts, 1760-1800, the dovetailed case with lid, over an arched top drawer with three long drawers below, 42in. wide.
(Skinner) $7,475

An oak bureau, English, early 18th century, the fall with two short and two long drawers below, on bracket feet, 32½in. wide.
(Bonham's) $2,156

An Edwardian rosewood cylinder bureau, with stringing and foliate marquetry, raised back with inset mirror, fitted interior, 30¾in. wide.
(Andrew Hartley) $1,633

A George III mahogany bureau, the fall front enclosing a fitted interior with drawers and pigeon holes centered by a small cupboard, 42¾in. wide.
(Andrew Hartley) $2,016

A mid-Victorian walnut pier cabinet, the shaped rectangular top above an inlaid frieze and panelled cupboard door, flanked by inlaid turned columns, 36¼in. wide.
(Bonhams) $1,932

A mid Victorian maple and walnut side cabinet, circa 1860, the rectangular top above a mosaic inlaid frieze and two glazed doors with gilt metal applied rosettes, 122cm. wide.
(Bonhams) $2,730

A Japanese export scarlet lacquered cabinet on stand, late 19th/ early 20th century, the cabinet with two doors enclosing two sets of dummy drawers, with niches and trays, English giltwood stand, 41in. wide. (Bonhams) $1,386

A kingwood and gilt-bronze cabinet by François Linke, Paris, circa 1890, marble top, female corner mounts flanking two doors inset with coromandel scenes of figures in a landscape, 140cm. wide.
(Sotheby's) $22,770

A Victorian mahogany artist's material shop display cabinet, the raised back inset with a verre eglomise glass panel inscribed *Winsor and Newton Artist's Materials*, between foliate carved corbels, 60in. wide.
(Christie's) $40,227

A fine mahogany and tulipwood crossbanded lady's bureau cabinet, early 20th century, the slightly domed top and fall front inset with figured oval reserves opening to reveal a comprehensive fitted interior, 31in. wide.
(Bonhams) $16,940

A mid-Victorian walnut, amboyna and marquetry side cabinet, the moulded breakfront top above an inlaid frieze and a pair of cupboard doors inlaid with musical trophies, 58½in. wide.
(Bonhams) $6,624

A lacquer cabinet, Edo period (late 19th century), the two-doored cabinet decorated in gold hiramaki-e on a nashiji ground, with cranes flying amongst maples bordered by geometric designs, 72in. high.
(Christie's) $28,576

A kingwood, parquetry and gilt-bronze side cabinet, Paris, circa 1890, with a shaped moulded fleur de pêcher marble top above a pair of panelled doors applied with swags of flowers, 153cm. wide.
(Sotheby's) $25,802

A mid Victorian walnut cabinet by Gillow and Co, the shaped top above a glazed door, flanked with turned columns and set on a shaped base, 99cm. wide. (Bonhams) $2,310

A Victorian oak folio cabinet, the sliding superstructure with double ratcheted adjustable top with twin elevating hinged ratcheted tooled leather lined surface, with bookrest to the centre and below, 42in. wide. (Christie's) $19,740

A mid Victorian walnut side cabinet, circa 1880, with applied gilt metal mounts and boxwood outline stringing and floral inlays, 80cm. wide. (Bonhams) $672

A Regency mahogany, ebony inlaid and brass mounted side cabinet, with ebony strung rectangular edge top containing a frieze drawer centred by a palm spray between foliate applied ornament, 37½in. wide. (Christie's) $6,909

An early Victorian mahogany serpentine side cabinet, the Carrara marble top surmounted by a mirror glazed back, above a pair of mirror glazed cupboard doors, 48in. wide. (Bonhams) $524

A French rosewood, ormolu and porcelain mounted side cabinet, panel door, with oval porcelain plaque with ribband depicting courting couple, 53¾in. wide. (Christie's) $3,948

A George IV mahogany side cabinet, circa 1825, the later rectangular top above a pair of silk backed wired cupboard doors, flanked by scrolled and acanthus lion's paw monopodia, 52in. wide. (Bonhams) $3,220

A Victorian walnut side cabinet with central glazed door flanked by half round pilasters and bowed glazed ends on plinth base, 3ft.10in. wide. (Brightwells) $3,381

An early 19th century marquetry demi-lune side cabinet with floral and bird marquetry designs to top, 33in. wide. (Brightwells) $1,694

A Napoleon III ebonised, brass and tortoiseshell-inlaid breakfront side cabinet, the shaped rectangular top above an inlaid frieze with gilt-metal mounted moulded edge, 57in. wide. (Christie's) $2,125

A pair of Danish walnut and parcel-gilt bedside cabinets, each with asymmetrical C-scrolled crestings above a serpentine fronted yellow marble top, 17¾in. wide. (Christie's) $1,570

A Victorian mahogany display cabinet, of breakfront outline, with superstructure enclosed by four glazed panel doors with rounded mouldings, the lower part with a moulded projecting edge, 66½in. wide. (Christie's) $2,560

A Victorian ebonised, boulle and gilt metal mounted pier cabinet, circa 1870, the rectangular top above a boullework frieze and a single glazed door with floral gilt metal edge and boulle border, 31½in. wide. (Bonhams) $1,001

A late Victorian walnut and brass mounted music cabinet, in the manner of Jas Shoolbred, the raised superstructure with pierced brass gallery and serpentine shaped shelf, 22in. wide. (Christie's) $2,049

A Victorian walnut side cabinet, with a serpentine top above a pair of beaded panelled cupboards, with similarly panelled sides and flanked by tapering spiral-turned columns, 39in. wide. (Christie's) $886

A late Victorian rosewood and inlaid serpentine and breakfront parlour cabinet, the moulded cornice above a shaped bevelled glass flanked by two further bevelled glass panels, 60in. wide. (T.R. & M) $2,755

A Dutch mahogany and inlaid klap-buffet or sideboard, 19th century, inlaid with chequer lines and satinwood fan inlay, the hinged top with a dentil edge, 44in. wide. (Christie's) $2,392

A Chinese black lacquered, mother of pearl inlaid and hardstone decorated cabinet, 20th century, decorated throughout with birds among flowering and fruiting branches, 32½in. wide. (Christie's) $867

A joined oak chest, English, early 18th century, the hinged plank top above a twin panelled front and with a frieze drawer below, 38½in. wide. (Bonhams) $1,029

A pair of Regency mahogany and specimen-marble side cabinets, each with pierced brass quatrefoil three-quarter gallery and specimen marble top, above a reeded frieze flanked by paterae, 50¼in. and 49¾in. wide.
(Christie's) $122,475

A George III mahogany coin cabinet, late 18th or early 19th century, the rectangular case with twin doors to the interior with fitted trays, 12½in. high.
(Christie's) $2,180

A Dutch walnut and marquetry miniature cabinet-on-later-stand, 19th century, of bombé fronted form and all over interlaced strap-work in purplewood, fitted with three drawers and enclosed by a pair of panel doors, 31in. wide.
(Christie's) $8,177

A partridgewood breakfront side cabinet, 19th century, with a white marble top above a leather-lined slide and six long drawers, flanked on each side by a short drawer and open shelves, 72½in. wide.
(Christie's) $5,106

A Venetian Art Nouveau fruitwood and cream-painted side-cabinet, circa 1900, the upper section surmounted by a female mask above a shield-shaped panel carved with foliage and a gondola, 66¼in. wide.
(Christie's) $47,000

An Edwardian walnut music cabinet, the moulded serpentine top with a low brass gallery above a bevelled glazed door enclosing velvet lined shelves, 19in. wide.
(Christie's) $181

A French mahogany side cabinet, early 19th century, the mottled grey marble top above two gilt-metal mounted frieze drawers and a pair of panelled cupboard doors, 38in. wide. (Christie's) $3,353

A polychrome painted pine armoire, Tyrolean, early 19th century, enclosed by a pair of doors, each with raised panel decorated with a figure and floral decoration, 57in. wide. (Christie's) $2,956

Art Deco vanity, France, 1930, African Bubinga wood with rosewood trim and ebonized handles, 50in. wide.
(Skinner) $1,150

A Victorian walnut and marquetry music cabinet, the raised mirrored back with turned finials and bracket shelf, glazed door with marquetry panel, 21in. wide.
(Andrew Hartley) $924

A Victorian brass inlaid and scarlet-veneered breakfront side cabinet, applied with gilt metal mounts and decorated with panels of meandering foliage, 78in. wide.
(Christie's) $2,812

Napoleon III brass and mother of pearl inlaid, ormolu mounted marble-top side cabinet, circa 1850-70, with serpentine white top and conforming case, 35½in. wide.
(Skinner) $2,645

A French rosewood and brass-inlaid breakfront side cabinet, late 19th century, with a green variegated marble top above a brass lined frieze and a panelled central door, 52in. wide.
(Christie's) $2,467

A mahogany cabinet on chest, the top with a molded dentil cornice, a pierced fretwork swan neck pediment with carved florets and a carved urn on a fluted plinth, 3ft.9½in. wide.
(Woolley & Wallis) $2,041

Art Deco walnut and ash beverage cabinet, France, circa 1930, 37¼in. high, 33¹/₃in., wide.
(Skinner) $1,035

A late Victorian rosewood salon cabinet with string inlay and floral marquetry panels, shelved and mirrored upper section, 52in. wide.
(Andrew Hartley) $1,771

British Provincial oak two-part side cabinet, the upper section with arched panelling and fitted with two doors, 57in. wide.
(Skinner) $1,150

A Victorian mahogany, amboyna and ebony secrétaire cabinet, inlaid overall with ivory lines, the molded rectangular top above a secrétaire drawer, 72in. wide.
(Christie's) $8,280

An ebonized and brass inlaid pier cabinet with gilt metal trim and mounts, waisted frieze, single glazed door enclosing shelving, 19th century, 32in. wide.
(Andrew Hartley) $1,320

A Victorian walnut and burr walnut-veneered side cabinet of D-shaped breakfront outline, applied with gilt-brass mounts, 151cm. wide.
(Bearne's) $4,719

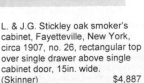

L. & J.G. Stickley oak smoker's cabinet, Fayetteville, New York, circa 1907, no. 26, rectangular top over single drawer above single cabinet door, 15in. wide.
(Skinner) $4,887

A pair of gilt-bronze, porcelain and mahogany side cabinets, Paris, Napoleon III, circa 1860, each with a molded white marble top above a fall front with two panels painted with exotic birds, 80cm. wide.
(Sotheby's) $37,490

An Aesthetic Movement ebonized and amboyna pier cabinet with stringing and gilt embellishment, frieze drawer over two panelled doors depicting birds and flowering branches, 28in. wide, stamped *Gillow & Co.*
(Andrew Hartley) $5,320

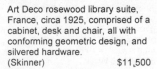

Art Deco rosewood library suite, France, circa 1925, comprised of a cabinet, desk and chair, all with conforming geometric design, and silvered hardware.
(Skinner) $11,500

A William III cabinet on chest, the front veneered in burr walnut with feather banding, the molded cornice above an interior with oak adjustable shelves, 3ft. 7in. wide.
(Woolley & Wallis) $9,296

A Biedermeier walnut and inlaid dwarf cabinet, with a molded top, frieze drawer and a pair of deeply molded shaped cupboards, 35in. wide. (Christie's) $329

A Napoleon III ormolu-mounted Sèvres-pattern porcelain and kingwood étagère, circa 1868, surmounted by a shaped cresting centered by a flying putto, above a shelf supported by two scroll brackets, 33in. high.
(Christie's) $5,520

A Dutch walnut veneered cabinet, 18th century and later, the arched molded cornice with central carved floral finial, above two arched glazed cabinet doors and side panels, with a sloped fall under, 124cm. wide.
(Bonhams) $4,970

A Dutch late 18th century mahogany side cabinet, inlaid with neoclassical urns and ribbon tied tassels, with bands of chequer stringing, 4ft.3in.
(Woolley & Wallis) $2,490

An early Victorian oak and ebonized folio-cabinet, by Johnstone and Jeanes, the molded rectangular top inlaid with geometrical banding above two frieze drawers, and above a pair of panelled doors, 63in. wide.
(Christie's) $19,000

A George III mahogany side cabinet, the moulded rectangular superstructure with paterae to each corner, above a frieze drawer and a panelled crossbanded door enclosing a shelf, 22in. wide.
(Christie's) $2,073

A Regency brass-mounted rosewood breakfront side cabinet, the later purple, green and white veined marble top, above a pair of mirror-backed panelled doors enclosing three shelves, 60¾in. wide.
(Christie's) $4,145

An 18th century oriental black and gold japanned cabinet, decorated with summer palaces, brass side handles, on a later ebonized stand with square tapering legs, 27½in.
(Woolley & Wallis) $621

A Regency brass-mounted and ebony-inlaid, rosewood and marquetry side cabinet, the later gray-veined white rectangular marble top above a frieze with floral and foliate ebony inlay, 48½in. wide. (Christie's) $6,909

An Anglo-Indian carved hardwood side cabinet, enclosed by openwork glazed panelled doors, gadroon plinth molding and pad feet, 4ft.8½in., late 19th century.
(Woolley & Wallis) $304

A mid-Victorian pietra-dura mounted figured-walnut, ebonised and parcel-gilt side cabinet, on a moulded plinth base, 76¼in. wide. (Christie's) $85,444

Eastlake carved mahogany display cabinet, circa 1880, the upper section fitted with a mirror and shelves, the lower section with glazed door enclosing shelves, 44in. wide.
(Skinner) $2,300

A Regency mahogany tea cabinet-on-stand, the hinged rectangular top crossbanded in rosewood, with cushion moulded frieze, 39in. wide. (Christie's) $19,090

A Victorian carved mahogany sideboard, the top with a serpentine frieze, the cupboard enclosed by an oval panel door and panelled canted sides, 4ft.8in.
(Woolley & Wallis) $658

A South German or North Italian marquetry table cabinet, 17th century, the doors to the front, rising top and sides inlaid with panels, fronts later inset with panels of agate glass circa 1700, 21¼in. wide. (Christie's) $3,565

L. & J. G. Stickley Re-Issue two drawer filing cabinet, Manlius, New York, rectangular form, hammered copper hardware, branded *Stickley* and round yellow and red decal in interior drawer, 31in. high. (Skinner) $460

Indo-Portuguese hardwood marquetry and bone inlaid cabinet on chest, probably Goa, 19th century, the top section with twelve drawers, 44in. wide.
(Skinner) $19,550

An oak housekeeper's/display cabinet, North Country, 19th century, the upper section with an alder cornice and tablet inlaid frieze, above a pair of astragal glazed doors and three small drawers below, 43½in. wide.
(Christie's) $4,456

A French ebonised scarlet tortoiseshell and brass-inlaid side cabinet, the sepentine-shaped top above an inlaid frieze between paterae mounted corners, 44½in. wide. (Christie's) $2,392

An Edwardian rosewood, ivorine and marquetry inlaid music cabinet, lacking gallery, 56cm. wide.
(Bonhams) $283

A rosewood bowfront side cabinet, early 19th century, decorated with lines, the later mottled rouge marble top above a frieze fitted with a central drawer, 43in. wide.
(Christie's) $8,570

A black japanned and chinoiserie decorated cabinet on carved wood stand, 105cm. wide.
(Bonhams) $1,669

A late 19th century burr walnut music cabinet, with a pair of boxwood floral inlaid doors enclosing fitted interior and pull out writing slope, on plinth and bracket feet, 24in.
(Dreweatt Neate) $3,218

A mahogany and gilt-bronze side cabinet by Durand, Paris, circa 1880, the bleu turquin marble top with a pierced gallery above twelve small drawers, 124cm. wide.
(Sotheby's) $15,933

W.J. Neatby for Neatby & Evans, writing cabinet, circa 1903, mahogany, the upper section with two fruitwood marquetry roundels, two doors with fitted shelves on inner face, 72cm. wide.
(Sotheby's) $8,073

Ettore Sottsass for Poltronova, 'Nirvana' cabinet, designed in 1965, this example early 1980s, number 3/49, board laminated with white plastic, top with rectangular green box finial, 104cm. square.
(Sotheby's) $5,417

A kingwood and gilt-bronze side cabinet, French, circa 1890, the demi-lune mottled red marble top above the frieze, 112cm. wide.
(Sotheby's) $4,557

A Victorian figured walnut and inlaid cabinet, the D shaped top with a moulded edge over an inlaid frieze, 83cm. (Tennants) $4,082

A George IV rosewood canterbury, after a design by Loudon, with three divisions divided by X-splats, with trefoil finials and belt tied roundel and shield ornament, 21¼in. wide. (Christie's) $3,089

A French walnut canterbury, mid 19th century, pierced and fret-carved throughout, with a shaped molded upper tier, an open shelf and four vertical divisions, 16in. wide. (Christie's) $1,104

A mahogany three division canberbury, early 19th century, with lyre shaped and S-shaped slatted divisions with roundel ornament, containing a drawer below, 25¼in. wide. (Christie's) $3,214

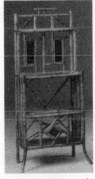

A Victorian bamboo and chinoiserie decorated lacquer canterbury whatnot, the lacquer panels decorated with birds, flowers and foliage, 20in. wide. (Christie's) $658

A Victorian walnut canterbury of shaped oval form with turned finials on leaf banded turned supports, two spindle-supported divisions, 24¼in. wide. (Andrew Hartley) $2,130

A Victorian figured walnut and inlaid music canterbury, the rounded rectangular top inlaid with floral and line decoration, on turned column supports with a lower section below, 27in. wide. (Christie's) $2,242

A Victorian walnut canterbury, parts lacking, 54.5cm. wide. (Bonhams & Brooks) $955

A late 19th century mahogany canterbury in the Islamic style, the revolving top with four vertical dividers, 38cm. wide. (Bonhams) $648

An early Victorian mahogany canterbury, restorations, 50cm. wide. (Bonhams & Brooks) $830

A pair of George III mahogany ladderback open armchairs with pierced serpentine crossbars. (Bearne's) $2,281

Two of a set of twelve mahogany dining chairs, comprising eight George III chairs, including two armchairs, and four of a later date. (Christie's) (Twelve) $22,080

Two of a set of six 19th century mahogany bar back dining chairs, the central horizontal splats carved with stylised flowerheads, on turned legs, stuffed seats. (Ewbank) (Six) $2,472

Gio Ponti, two of a set of eight side chairs, circa 1935, rosewood, with openwork backs extending to form the back legs. (Sotheby's) (Eight) $6,833

A pair of mahogany side chairs, one George II and possibly Irish, the other of a later date, each with shaped toprail with scrolled ends above a pierced strapwork splat. (Christie's) $2,760

Two 17th century Flemish walnut-framed open armchairs, on twist-turned supports and on conforming legs with stretchers. (Bearne's) $2,517

A pair of George III mahogany side chairs, each with a serpentine crested rectangular padded back. (Christie's) $4,600

A pair of George III mahogany dining chairs, each wavy-moulded rounded back with a conforming interlaced splat. (Bearne's) $1,887

Three of a set of ten walnut side chairs, probably Germany, late 19th/early 20th century, each with an armorial back with a crowned cresting and flanked and supported by a lion. (Christie's)   (Ten) $5,814

Two of a set of eight George III mahogany dining chairs, comprising two open armchairs and six side chairs, each channelled overall and with a shield-shaped back. (Christie's)   (Eight) $46,288

Two of a set of four George III mahogany hall chairs, the pierced cartouche shaped backs centred by a carved patera, two matching chairs of a later date. (Tennants)   (Six) $7,222

Two of a composite set of seven mahogany dining chairs including an armchair, each with serpentine top rail, foliate-carved pierced interlaced splat, George III and later. (Bearne's)   (Seven) $4,561

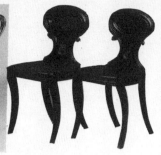

Two of a set of eight painted chairs, late 19th century, probably Scandinavian. (Bonhams & Brooks) (Eight) $1,078

A set of four mid Victorian rosewood side chairs. (Bonhams & Brooks) $462

A pair of Regency mahogany hall chairs, each oval dished back on scrolled supports with a plaque depicting a bird. (Christie's) $2,917

A set of six Victorian style balloon back dining chairs. (Bonhams & Brooks) $296

Two of a set of eight Regency mahogany dining chairs, the backs with rope twist and turned rails, curved veneered crests to molded flame scroll supports.(Woolley & Wallis)   (Eight) $3,795

Queen Anne burl walnut side chair, circa 1720, with shaped backrest and splat, overupholstered seat and shell carved cabriole legs. (Skinner) $2,185

Two of a harlequin set of seven early Victorian mahogany dining chairs, comprising five and two. (Dockrees) (Seven) $640

A Victorian simulated bamboo correction chair, the high back with turned horizontal rails and an oval caned seat. (Christie's) $221

Two of a set of stained beechwood dining chairs, 20th century, comprising a pair of armchairs and a pair of single chairs, in the Georgian style. (Christie's) (Four) $3,722

Two of a set of seven Regency simulated rosewood, rosewood and brass-inlaid dining chairs, including a pair of scroll open armchairs, each back with curved foliate scrolled top-rail and scroll splat. (Christie's) (Seven) $4,724

A French Empire mahogany and ormolu mounted tub shaped single chair, with reeded and foliate scroll curved top-rail applied with griffon neo-classical ornament. (Christie's) $2,194

Two of a set of four Dutch walnut and marquetry chairs, 1st half of the 18th century, inlaid with marquetry of birds, flowers and a vase, marquetry probably 19th century. (Christie's) (Four) $14,536

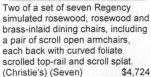

The Templemore chairs. One of a set of twelve Victorian oak dining chairs in Tudor style, made for Sir John Craven Carden of Templemore, County Tipperary, originally a set of 24. (David Lay) (Twelve) $3,140

Three of a set of six Georgian mahogany dining chairs, the square backs with reeded rails, fluted columns and central lattice decoration. (Wintertons) (Six) $8,411

One of a set of four oak ladderback dining chairs by Heal & Co, the backs with three dished ladders between square section uprights. (Andrew Hartley) (Four) $448

Pair of 18th century walnut dining chairs, the solid backs inlaid in the centers with satinwood neo-classical motifs, upholstered drop in seats. (G A Key) $628

An early 18th century oak single chair, the dished top rail on solid vase shaped splat, panel seat, shaped front rail. (Andrew Hartley) $339

Two of a set of six 19th century mahogany side chairs, with brass stringing, the backs with triple horizontal rail and ball splats. (Woolley & Wallis) (Six) $2,560

Two of a set of six Regency mahogany dining chairs, with panelled toprails and carved mid rails.
(George Kidner)   (Six) $2,656

Two of a set of four William IV rosewood side chairs, with scrolled palmette carved open buckle backs.
(Woolley & Wallis)   (Four) $1,909

Two of a set of eight Georgian style ladderback mahogany dining chairs, including two carvers, each with four pierced rails centred by an anthemion.
(Phillips)   (Eight) $3,520

Two of a set of eight Regency simulated rosewood dining chairs, each with scrolling uprights leading into sabre legs, with arched turned and reeded top bar.
(Phillips)   (Eight) $3,360

Two of a set of seven 18th century Portuguese walnut dining chairs, the vase shaped splats carved with foliage, on cabriole front legs.
(Dreweatt Neate)   (Seven) $5,705

Two of a set of six Victorian mahogany buckle back dining chairs.
(Academy Auctioneers) (Six) $2,000

Two of a set of four early 19th century side chairs, in faded rosewood with moulded rails and scroll open backs.
(Woolley & Wallis) (Four) $741

Two of a late 19th century set of twelve mahogany dining chairs, with pierced slat backs.
(Bristol) $4,950

Two of a set of eight oak ladderback chairs, including two armchairs, each with five graduated shaped bars between turned uprights.
(Phillips) (Eight) $1,600

Two of a set of six Regency grained beech side chairs, the open backs with a scrolling ribbed horizontal splat.
(Woolley & Wallis) (Six) $2,324

Two George III style paint-decorated maple side chairs, circa 1930, rectangular back with painted tablet, upholstered seat, 33½in. high.
(Skinner) $690

Two of eight mid Victorian balloon back dining chairs, the moulded top rails above a scroll carved midrail and upholstered seats.
(Phillips) (Eight) $4,000

One of a 19th century set of six ash and elm dining chairs, with arched crest, vase shaped splat. (Andrew Hartley)
(Six) $2,856

Two of a set of eight Regency mahogany dining chairs including two carvers, with ebony stringing, deep curved crest rail. (Andrew Hartley) (Eight) $7,360

One of a set of four Victorian walnut dining chairs, the buckle back with carved splat and turned finials. (Andrew Hartley)
(Four) $1,200

One of a matched pair of William and Mary walnut side chairs, circa 1690, the double 'S' scroll top rail above a conforming splat centred by twin oval caned panels. (Bonhams)   (Two) $1,440

Three of a Harlequin set of ten oak spindle back dining chairs including two carvers. (Academy)   (Ten) $5,610

One of a set of six Victorian rosewood balloon back dining chairs, with leaf carved crest, cabriole legs and peg feet. (Andrew Hartley)
(Six) $2,880

One of a set of nine early Victorian rosewood bar back dining chairs, the top rail with carved C scroll brackets, turned fluted tapering front legs and sabre back legs. (Dreweatt Neate)   (Nine)
$6,270

Two of a set of six early 19th century mahogany dining chairs in the Hepplewhite style, the arched backs with pierced vase splats with foliate ornament. (Phillips) (Six) $2,952

One of a set of six Regency mahogany dining chairs with arched curved rail and cable bar back. (Andrew Hartley)
(Six) $4,000

Two of a set of six George IV mahogany bar back dining chairs, each with reeded top rail, pierced S scroll carved back rest. (Dreweatt Neate) (Six)
$2,640

Crooked-back walnut side chair, probably England or Continental, the pierced crest above an upholstered back and seat. (Skinner)
$748

Two of a set of ten George III mahogany dining chairs including carvers, with arched crest, moulded uprights, pierced waisted splat. (Andrew Hartley)
(Ten) $9,744

A Chippendale mahogany side-chair, the serpentine crestrail with scrolled ears centring a carved shell with volutes above a solid vasiform splat.
(Christie's) $4,600

A pair of George III mahogany open armchairs, each with waved toprail above a pierced Gothic vertical splat and a padded rectangular seat. (Christie's) $8,590

One of a set of four George III mahogany dining chairs with shaped crest rail, pierced and waisted interlacing splat. (Andrew Hartley)
(Four) $2,520

Two of a set of eight 19th century mahogany ladder back dining chairs, in the George III manner, each with four scroll carved and pierced rails.
(Phillips) (Eight) $5,280

Chippendale mahogany carved side chair, Massachusetts, circa 1780, the shaped crest rail with carved terminals above the pierced splat. (Skinner) $1,725

Two of a set of seven Regency mahogany bar back dining chairs, reeded backs with three vertical splats, including one carver. (Wintertons) (Seven) $1,650

319

Two of a set of twelve late 19th century mahogany dining chairs of Chippendale style, each with shaped scroll and leaf carved top rail, pierced vase splat. (Dreweatt Neate) (Twelve) $16,170

A fine and rare pair of Chippendale carved mahogany side chairs, New York, circa 1770, each with a shaped ruffle-, leaf-, and C-scroll-carved crest. (Sotheby's) $68,500

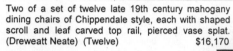

A pair of George III mahogany side chairs, each with pierced circular back with central patera radiating leaves and joined by swags, on scrolling channelled stiles.(Christie's) $5,248

A pair of late Federal carved mahogany side-chairs, New York, 1815—1825, each with carved and inlaid tablet crest above a pierced carved splat centring a roundel. (Christie's) $8,050

Two of a set of eight Regency brass-inlaid grained beech dining-chairs, including two armchairs, each with scrolled cresting and tablet back. (Christie's)　　(Eight)　　$8,997

Two from a set of eight Hepplewhite mahogany dining chairs. (Christopher Matthews) (Eight) $5,280

Two of a set of four George III mahogany dining chairs including one carver, of Sheraton style, the reeded bar and ball back with straight crest. (Andrew Hartley)   (Four) $1,120

Two of a set of six George III mahogany dining-chairs, each with tapering pierced back with cabochon-linked spindles. (Christie's)   (Six) $9,163

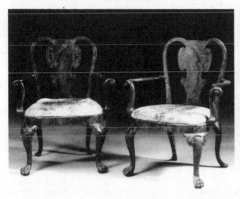

A pair of George II figured walnut open armchairs, each with a solid vase-shaped splat between serpentine uprights, above a padded drop-in seat. (Christie's) $322,040

Two of a set of nine George III mahogany dining-chairs, including one open armchair, each with triple-arched toprail above a pierced tapering rectangular splat. (Christie's)   (Nine) $73,704

A pair of George III mahogany side chairs, on square chamfered beaded legs carved with geometrical blind fretwork. (Christie's) $32,453

Two of a set of twelve Regency mahogany dining chairs, including two carvers, each with reeded swag backs. (Phillips) (Twelve) $11,200

Jacques Adnet, an upholstered lounge chair, designed 1953-55 with the collaboration of Hermès, for Compagnie des Arts Français, the red fabric padded seat with black leather edging.
(Christie's) $3,250

Victorian mahogany spoon back gents chair, the splayed back terminating in scrolled mounts, the two splayed arms joined by foliate scrolled uprights.
(G A Key) $1,472

Gerald Summers, a laminated birch lounge chair, designed circa 1933-34, for Makers of Simple Furniture, the organic undulating form cut and formed from a single sheet of birch.
(Christie's) $21,666

One of a near pair of William IV mahogany and upholstered corner chairs, each with outscrolled back and padded seat.
(Christie's) (Two) $1,276

Tom Dixon, 'S' chair, made by Space, U.K., 1988, bent mild steel frame ending on circular foot, with rush woven 'S' shape seat.
(Bonhams) $2,202

Attributed to Robert Mallet-Stevens, Modernist chair, circa 1930, of strict rectangular construction, with prominent feature screws, ebonised wood seat panel.
(Sotheby's) $10,452

A carved walnut elbow chair, 19th century, the back with a pierced acanthus scroll arched cresting centred by a cherub and upholstered in gros point needlework.
(Christie's) $2,725

Ron Arad for One-Off, 'Rover Chair', 1984, red leather Rover P6 seat on yellow tubular metal frame.
(Sotheby's) $1,288

A carved giltwood bergère, 19th century, the padded back within a channelled frame decorated with rockwork and foliage with flowerhead cresting.
(Christie's) $1,008

Alvar Aalto, a laminated beech and plywood lounge chair, Model No. 41, designed 1931-32, with ebonised scrolling plywood seat on laminated and solid beech frame. (Christie's) $43,332

A pair of William IV mahogany armchairs, each with a padded arched back, scroll arms and seat, on ring-turned tapering legs. (Christie's) $8,722

Emile-Jacques Ruhlmann, pair of armchairs, circa 1925, fully upholstered in brown leather, scrolled back, the side elements with two straight sides forming top front angle. (Sotheby's) $53,820

A Regency mahogany caned bergère, with later removable book-stand. (Christie's) $13,886

A North European white-painted and parcel gilt armchair, late 19th century, with fluted frame, the arms terminating in eagle heads. (Christie's) $7,360

A modern lounge chair and matching ottoman, designed by Charles and Ray Eames and produced by S. Hille & Co. Ltd., Watford, Hertfordshire under licence from Herman Miller. (Canterbury) $3,932

Lady's spindle sided Morris chair, similar to Gustav Stickley no. 367, New York, circa 1907, flat arm with corbel support over twenty square spindles, unsigned.
(Skinner) $5,750

Louis XVI style walnut and parcel gilt chaise longue, late 19th/20th century, arched back, downscrolled arms, raised on circular stop-fluted legs, shaped ottoman.
(Skinner) $1,495

Alvar Aalto, high back chair, version of Armchair 31, early 1930s, laminated cantilever frame, moulded plywood seat.
(Sotheby's) $42,336

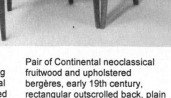

Georgian mahogany cockfighting chair, late 18th century, of typical form, scrolling top rail with carved leaf detail, over rectangular back.
(Skinner) $2,185

Pair of Continental neoclassical fruitwood and upholstered bergères, early 19th century, rectangular outscrolled back, plain arms supported by baluster turned supports. (Skinner) $3,450

Alvar Aalto, manufactured by Metallmestarit Oy and Puusepänliike K.H. Numminen, café chair, designed for the Rautatalo Café interiors, 1954, wooden frame, black leather upholstery.
(Sotheby's) $1,288

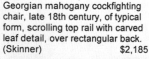

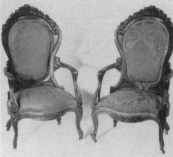

Hoffer for Plan, two 'Plan -O' spider chairs, circa 1958, black tubular metal folding frames, elastic seats, 30½in. diameter.
(Sotheby's) $496

Pair of Rococo Revival laminated rosewood armchairs, mid/late 19th century, shaped crest with rose carving, raised on cabriole legs.
(Skinner) $6,037

Gio Ponti, an aluminium desk chair, designed 1938, for use in the Montecantini building, Milan, the tubular and cast aluminium frame with red vinyl upholstery.
(Christie's) $2,532

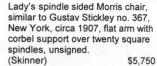

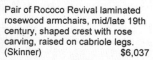

Alvar Aalto, 'Paimio' armchair model No. 41, designed 1931-2 originally for the Paimio Sanatorium, laminated birch seat, painted laminated plywood frame. (Sotheby's) $12,512

Attributed to Gerrit Rietveld, an oak and leather armchair, executed circa 1920 by Cees Uiterwaal, with rectangular panel back and armrests, tan leather seat on ebonised dowels. (Christie's) $18,400

A mid-Victorian mahogany invalid's wheel chair, with the label of John Ward Ltd, with reclining back, hinged arms and drop-in seat, above ratcheted foot-rest. (Christie's) $4,814

Harry Bertoia, a child's wire side chair, designed 1950 for Knoll International, the white plastic-coated wire-rod frame with detachable blue vinyl seat cushion, 24in. high. (Christie's) $325

Pair of Modern Gothic ebonised and parcel gilt corner armchairs, Kimbel & Cabus, New York, circa 1870s, backs with stencilled panels and spindles. (Skinner) $4,485

Alessandro Mendini for Alchimia Zone, 'Non Chair', originally designed in 1974 and destroyed by fire, this example made in 1982, pink laminated wood, 76in. high. (Sotheby's) $15,640

Gustav Stickley bow arm Morris chair, no. 2340, 1902-04, open bow-shaped arm, signed with red decal in a box. (Skinner) $19,550

Two of a set of six American Victorian walnut parlour chairs, mid 19th century, comprising two arm and four side chairs. (Skinner) (Six) $575

Windsor writing armchair, attributed to Ebenezer Tracy, Lisbon, Connecticut, circa 1770-80, comb back crest with six spindles above shaped arm rail. (Skinner) $5,175

One of a pair of French pale blue painted bergères, late 19th century, each with a carved padded back and part-padded arms above a bowed seat.
(Christie's) (Two) $1,288

Martin Eisler for Forma, adjustable chair, 1959, black tubular metal and wire rod frame, brass feet.
(Sotheby's) $4,845

A mahogany library armchair, early 19th century, the tapered caned back with part-upholstered downscrolled arms and close-nailed padded seat.
(Christie's) $1,563

One of a pair of Central European mahogany and upholstered tub armchairs, late 19th century, on bulbous cabriole legs.
(Christie's) (Two) $2,208

An early Victorian mahogany and leather-upholstered library armchair, the waisted buttoned back and outscrolled close-nailed arms above a squab cushion.
(Christie's) $1,656

Alvar Aalto for Finmar, cantilevered armchair, 1938–39, laminated birch, pale red cross woven webbing secured to wooden seat frame with brass tacks.
(Sotheby's) $3,353

One of a pair of French beech and upholstered fauteuils, each with a shaped padded back within a channelled foliate-carved surround.
(Christie's) (Two) $1,011

Ettore Sottsass for Poltronova, 'Harlow' chair, 1971, cast aluminium, orange velvet fabric.
(Sotheby's) $1,080

A Victorian mahogany upholstered open armchair with scrolled padded back, padded open arms with turned supports.
(Christie's) $2,024

A Victorian walnut and upholstered armchair, the padded back with a moulded incised top-rail flanked by fluted and leaf-carved stiles.
(Christie's) $1,472

A pair of French walnut and upholstered bergères, each with an arched chanelled and flowerhead carved back.
(Christie's) $1,472

A George III mahogany open armchair, the arms on reeded downswept supports, on square tapering panelled legs.
(Christie's) $2,811

George J. Sowden for Memphis, 'Mamounia' armchair, designed 1985, no longer in production, lacquered wood, coloured plastic laminate and velvet.
(Sotheby's) $4,844

A fine and rare Federal mahogany barrel-back lolling chair, attributed to Lemuel Church, Massachusetts, circa 1795, the rectangular crest above a concave, tapering, trapezoidal back.
(Sotheby's) $16,100

One of a pair of late Victorian walnut and upholstered armchairs each with a shaped foliate and dolphin carved top-rail and a close-nailed padded back.
(Christie's) (Two) $1,288

A late Victorian easy armchair, with buttoned back and arms, on ring-turned legs with brass castors, stamped *Howard & Sons, Berners St.* (Christie's) $1,656

A pair of hardwood caned bergères, each with a panelled frame, the scrolled backs, arms and seat caned, with buttoned brown leather back and seat cushions.
(Christie's) $20,619

A Napoleon III mahogany and gilt-metal mounted fauteuil, the upholstered back within a gilt-metal mounted frame.
(Christie's) $1,104

Jacques Gruber, pair of armchairs, circa 1903, openwork fruitwood curvilinear frames, carved throughout with stylised flowers, leaves and tendrils. (Sotheby's) $15,249

Gerald Summers for Makers of Simple Furniture, armchair, designed 1933-4, single sheet cut and bent cream tinted French polish finished plywood. (Sotheby's) $23,920

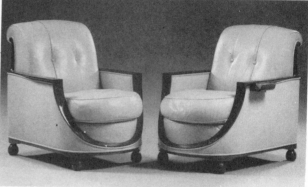

Alvar Aalto for Artek, high back chair, version of Armchair '31', early 1930s, laminated cantilever frame, white painted moulded plywood seat. (Sotheby's) $26,130

Emile-Jacques Ruhlmann, pair of bergères 'Bloch', late 1920s, macassar ebony frame, the shaped arm rests flowing into a U-shaped frame enclosing the seat and cushion. (Sotheby's) $88,140

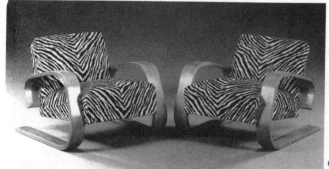

A pair of Alvar Aalto Armchairs 400, model no.37, 1935-6, laminated birch cantilever supports, upholstered seat and back. (Sotheby's) $5,152

Gaetano Pesce made by Bracciodiffero for Cassina, 'Golgotha' chair, 1972-3, moulded fibreglass, cloth and polyester resin. (Sotheby's) $12,880

Alvar Aalto, a lounge chair, Model No. 37, designed 1935-36, the broad upholstered seat flanked by laminated birch cantilever supports. (Christie's) $6,319

A pair of Italian giltwood fauteuils, early 19th century, each with a foliate-carved ribbon tied reeded frame with a cartouche-shaped back. (Christie's) $9,373

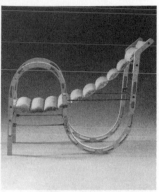

Ludwig Mies van der Rohe, a pair of nickel-plated tubular steel armchairs, MR534G, designed 1927, manufactured by Thonet circa 1931, green caned seat. (Christie's) $25,277

Eileen Gray, the 'S' folding terrace chair, circa 1932-34, made for her home 'Tempe a Pailla' at Castellar, the frame of strips of bent wood separated by rectangular block spacers. (Sotheby's) $140,246

Tom Dixon, two seater throne chair, prototype, 1986, welded metal frame, upholstered red leather seat and back. (Sotheby's) $3,312

A pair of upholstered bergères, French, circa 1920, the fluted legs tapering from the armrests punctuated with carved floral bands. (Christie's) $7,314

One of a pair of Edwardian armchairs.
(Bonhams)   (Two) $502

A William IV mahogany patent reclining leather upholstered armchair, the red leather winged back reclining above padded arms and scrolling mahogany terminals.
(Boardmans)   . $5,177

A Victorian mahogany tub chair.
(Bonhams) $159

A Continental overstuffed armchair,
(Bonhams) $286

A Victorian walnut veneered chair-desk, stamp of Stephen Hedges, New York City, circa 1854, the oval thumbmoulded and flip-top above a conforming case embellished with veneered panels, 33in. wide.
(Christie's) $8,050

An early Victorian mahogany and leather upholstered library chair.
(Bonhams) $1,304

A North Italian carved wood armchair, late 19th century, with silvered shell shaped back and seat. (Christie's) $14,173

Gaetano Pesce, a Dalila side chair, designed 1980 for Cassina, the organic polyurethane form with retextured epoxy coating.
(Christie's) $5,427

An early Victorian mahogany open armchair, with a buttondown padded scroll back, scroll arms and seat, on ring-turned tapering legs.
(Christie's) $2,725

A Regency beechwood open armchair, reeded overall and with rosewood roundels, with scrolled stiles and arms.
(Christie's) $4,784

Verner Panton, Denmark, an early rare heart chair, designed 1958, manufactured by Plus Linje. Tangerine orange cloth fabric, on chromed metal 'X' base.
(Bonhams) $4,404

A George III mahogany library open armchair, possibly by Wright and Elwick, with serpentine toprail and seatrail, serpentine arm-supports with egg-and-dart border.
(Christie's) $32,401

A carved walnut armchair, Italian, circa 1870, in the manner of Brustolon, with a high padded back, the arms in the form of tree branches.
(Sotheby's) $7,292

A George II mahogany wing armchair, attributed to William Hallett, the rectangular padded back, shaped sides and seat covered in close-nailed gros and petit-point associated French early 18th century needlework.
(Christie's) $22,218

A Regency style bergère mahogany framed library armchair with satinwood banding, cane panelled back, seat and sides, on square tapering legs. (Russell Baldwin & Bright) $1,537

A late Victorian mahogany tub shaped armchair, on turned spindle uprights and front finials.
(Christie's) $2,725

A George III mahogany library open armchair, on square legs joined by stretchers.
(Christie's) $4,416

One of a pair of French walnut open armchairs, late 19th/early 20th century, on S-scroll legs joined by undulating stretchers.
(Christie's)   (Two) $1,272

An Italian Empire period rosewood and marquetry tub armchair, early 19th century, with curved bar top-rail inlaid with birds and neo classical foliate scrolls and hounds with standing figures below in the vase splat.(Christie's) $5,451

An oak framed chair, English, late 17th century, with upholstered rectangular back and seat and with tasselled frieze, on ring-turned and block legs. (Christie's) $891

A Louis XV beechwood bergère, by Jean-Baptiste Lelarge, with floral carved seat-rail, on molded cabriole legs with floral carved knees. (Christie's) $3,997

A Directoire later white painted fauteuil en cabriolet, early 19th century, with arched panelled back and padded arm supports, on fluted uprights, having a stuff-over bowed seat, on fluted tapering legs. (Christie's) $1,437

Carlo Mollino, an armchair and stool, designed 1959, for use in the Lutrario Ballroom, Turin, each with red vinyl upholstery on tubular steel frame. (Christie's) $9,687

Charles & Ray Eames, an early Paw armchair, designed 1950, for Zenith Plastics / Herman Miller, the gray fiberglass shell with embedded cord edge and wide diameter shock-mounts, this example circa 1950-55. (Christie's) $3,167

George Nelson, a fiberglass lounge chair, designed 1958, for Herman Miller, with two-part white fiberglass seat, on low angled white enamelled tubular support. (Christie's) $2,980

An early Victorian mahogany bergère, the outscrolled padded back, arms and cushion covered in buttoned red leather, with scrolling acanthus carved arm-supports. (Christie's) $4,724

A Regency mahogany bergère, the reeded frame with a caned back, sides and seat, on saber legs, with later brass attachment for a reading arm. (Christie's) $3,214

A French mahogany and caned bergère, early 20th century, on tapering turned and fluted legs headed by rosette carved and gilded panels.(Christie's) $619

Marcel Breuer, a laminated birch short chair, designed 1935-36, for Isokon, the molded plywood seat within laminated birch frame. (Christie's) $8,383

A Regency simulated rosewood beechwood bergère chair, with scroll-carved top-rail and caned panel back and seat, with scroll arm supports.(Christie's) $4,061

A Victorian walnut gentleman's open armchair, the balloon upholstered panel back with foliate scroll strapwork cresting and padded scroll arm supports. (Christie's) $872

A pair of George IV solid rosewood bergères, by Gillows, each with shaped backs and outscrolling arms carved with acanthus on outscrolling legs, four scrolled feet lacking.(Christie's) $89,270

A Louis XV period walnut bergère, probably German, with curved buttondown upholstered arched back with foliate and floral cresting. (Christie's) $3,271

A Dutch walnut possibly hardwood burgomaster's chair, 18th century, with triple double oval caned back, on splayed baluster-turned uprights and caned seat.
(Christie's) $1,692

Marcel Breuer, a pair of B35 lounge chairs, designed 1928, possibly of early manufacture by Thonet, each with chromed tubular steel frame secured with chromed hexagonal nuts. (Christie's) $4,843

A George III carved mahogany open armchair, in the French taste, with stuff-over cartouche shaped back and padded molded arm supports and stuff-over serpentine seat. (Christie's) $930

One of a pair of German 19th century carved mahogany armchairs.(Bonhams & Brooks) (Two) $277

A mid Victorian walnut lady's chair in the rococo taste. (Bonhams & Brooks) $647

An early Victorian walnut armchair, lacking castors. (Bonhams & Brooks) $847

A William IV mahogany armchair. (Bonhams & Brooks) $847

Pierre Chareau, reclining armchair, Mf219, circa 1923, walnut, the rectangular hinged back panel inset with burr wood, the rectangular open back support with hinged flap offering two alternative seating positions. (Sotheby's) $42,413

A Victorian rosewood nursing chair. (Bonhams & Brooks) $675

Wood and upholstered armchair, designed by Frank Lloyd Wright, circa 1955, manufactured by Heritage Henredon, style no. 1483, raised on geometric design base. (Skinner) $747

A late Victorian walnut office chair, lacking splat and stretcher. (Bonhams & Brooks) $414

Gustav Stickley drop-arm Morris chair, New York, circa 1914, no. 369, reclining back adjusted by removable pegs, drop-arms supported by four corbels above five vertical slats. (Skinner) $9,775

A Victorian mahogany folding campaign chair, with a padded back and part padded overscrolled arms and cushion to the seat, with a removable lower section.
(Christie's) $1,068

A Victorian Howard upholstered armchair, with overscrolled back and downscrolled arms and an upholstered square footstool, 20th century, with squab cushion.
(Christie's) $5,520

A child's mahogany highchair, English 19th century, upholstered with close-nailed and buttoned red leather with a removable tray and pierced cage.
(Christie's) $1,379

A Louis XIV style walnut and parcel-gilt armchair, circa 1890.
(Bonhams & Brooks) $562

A near pair of giltwood upholstered low chairs, late 19th/early 20th century, each with button padded back and arms and seat-rail, on turned legs with brass and horn castors. (Christie's) $624

A late Victorian oak revolving desk chair with a shaped back and solid saddle seat, on cabriole legs joined by a cross stretcher.
(Christie's) $673

A Victorian mahogany and upholstered spoon-back easy chair, on turned tapering legs with brass capped porcelain castors.
(Christie's) $331

A mid Victorian walnut gentleman's armchair, together with the matching lady's chair.
(Bonhams & Brooks) $2,380

English Provincial oak, rush and rattan seat shepherd's chair, 19th century, with domed backrest, the seat above a drawer on block legs.
(Skinner) $1,840

A walnut high back open armchair, Spanish, 18th century, the upholstered back centered with a crest and with lion head finials. (Christie's) $3,011

American steer horn armchair, 20th century, with leather upholstered seat. (Skinner) $575

A carved oak panel back armchair, English, 17th century and later, profusely later carved overall. (Christie's) $3,188

Flemish baroque walnut armchair, with 17th century elements, needlework backrest and seat, foliate carved arms and block and ring turned legs on faceted ball feet. (Skinner) $2,530

A German limewood armchair, 18th century, with scrolling foliate cartouche shaped padded back and arms with acanthus wrapped terminals and seat. (Christie's) $1,646

Italian rococo-style grotto chair, late 19th / early 20th century, with scallop shell seat, dolphin-shaped arms, and rusticated legs. (Skinner) $1,725

A Victorian walnut revolving desk chair, with a shaped cresting above a padded back, open arms and a padded seat. (Christie's) $602

Gustav Stickley oak Morris chair, New York circa 1909, model no. 332, concave crest rail on adjustable back, flat arms with four short corbel supports above five vertical side slats. (Skinner) $6,325

A pair of upholstered X-frame armchairs, early 20th century, each with tasselled back, downswept arms, cushion seat and arched legs with sleigh supports. (Christie's) $6,021

A James II walnut high-back armchair, the back with pierced foliate scroll top-rail and rectangular caned panel splat, with pierced scroll sides and turned uprights with finials. (Christie's) $2,743

A Victorian carved mahogany armchair, in the Chippendale style, with a shaped top-rail and pierced vase splat with trellis and Gothic ornament and trailing blind fret uprights. (Christie's) $2,707

Dark stained sack-back Windsor chair, New England, circa 1780, the bowed crest rail above seven spindles and shaped handholds on a carved saddle seat. (Skinner) $2,645

Maple slat-back high chair, Delaware Valley, 1765-80, the turned finials top the stiles which flank the arched and bent slats above the rush seat. (Skinner) $6,325

A pair of mahogany 'ribband-back' armchairs, 19th century, in the Georgian style, each balloon-shaped back with pierced ribband and foliate scroll splats. (Christie's) $8,122

Turned ash and cherry child's highchair, New York or Connecticut, late 18th century, the vase and ring-turned stiles joining two horizontal turned spindles, 35in. high. (Skinner) $1,035

English Provincial elmwood armchair, with spindle form backrest, shaped arms, and turned legs. (Skinner) $345

A mahogany desk armchair, the bow back with scroll arms on shaped slats, a moulded solid seat (formerly revolving), on four cabriole legs to brass castors. (Woolley & Wallis) $220

Queen Anne maple slat-back armchair, attributed to Solomon Fussell, Philadelphia, 1740s, the six arched slats flanked by turned stiles joined to shaped arms. (Skinner) $20,700

One of a set of ten chairs including two carvers by Robert Thompson of Kilburn, with low panel back, cow hide seat. (Andrew Hartley)
(Ten) $7,056

Two of a set of three Regency black japanned and gilt elbow chairs, with cane seats, the scrolled crest painted with key pattern and vitruvian scroll. (Andrew Hartley)
(Three) $1,560

A Queen Anne style mahogany corner-chair, the yoked crestrail above a pierced and scrolled splat over an outward scrolled arm. (Christie's) $1,840

A Jacobean turned elmwood rush-seat armchair, in part 17th century, the curved back with a shaped crest with tiers of inset spindles. (Sotheby's) $2,300

Pair of Regency beechwood elbow chairs. (Christopher Matthews)
$2,392

An 18th century mahogany elbow chair in the Chippendale style having shaped cresting rail over pierced splat. (Russell Baldwin & Bright) $1,221

A Regency simulated rosewood carver, the curved top rail with incised panel above a pierced and scrolling mid rail. (Phillips) $640

A pair of early George III mahogany open armchairs, each with a waved toprail in a stylised scrolled acanthus leaf, above a pierced Gothic fretwork back. (Christie's) $125,132

A 19th century Anglo-Indian solid ebony armchair in the Regency manner, the back with scroll terminals and with reeded crest rail and matching conforming splat. (Canterbury) $1,680

A Hepplewhite-style painted satinwood open armchair, the shield-shaped back decorated with a dish of fruit and foliage.
(Bearne's) $1,022

Marcel Breuer, a laminated birch long chair, designed 1935-36 for Isokon, the moulded plywood seat within laminated birch frame.
(Christie's) $9,930

A 17th century ash and oak turner's armchair of traditional form with triangular back and solid seat.
(Bearne's) $629

A walnut, cherrywood and elm Windsor armchair, Thames Valley, mid 18th century, label beneath the seat, *John Pitt, Wheelwright and Chairmaker ...*, also with a metal plate stating that *THIS CHAIR WENT WITH CAP. COOK AROUND THE WORLD.*
(Christie's) $23,845

A Regency green painted and parcel-gilt open armchair, the bowed bar top-rail centred with a lion's mask, above a reeded horizontal splat.
(Christie's) $2,236

One of a set of ten dining chairs, designed 1946-47, these examples manufactured late 1940s, laminated oak frames, upholstered in caramel leather with square quilting.
(Sotheby's) (Ten) $9,010

A Gothic Revival oak armchair, late 19th/early 20th century, decorated with tracery panels, the triangular toprail surmounted by a foliate carved finial.
(Christie's) $1,011

Marcel Breuer for Isokon, chaise longue 'BC 1' designed 1935-36, manufactured after 1936, laminated wood and plywood with fitted 'Lionella' cream vinyl cushion, 78cm. long.
(Sotheby's) $6,848

An antique mahogany elbow chair in the Hepplewhite style having arched cresting rail above leafage and rosette carved rail back.
(G.A. Key) $398

An oak armchair, Cheshire, late 17th century, the arched top-rail dated and initialled *A.W. 1680*, above a stylised scrolling foliate panel between uprights. (Christie's) $2,385

Pair of modern wooden armchairs, by W. H. Gunlocke Chair Co., Wayland, New York, late 20th century, arched crest rail sloping to arms, side rails and double cross stretchers. (Skinner) $345

A Morris & Co ebonised and painted Rossetti chair, the lyre-shaped turned back with downswept arms and rush seat, on ring turned legs joined by stretchers. (Christie's) $1,465

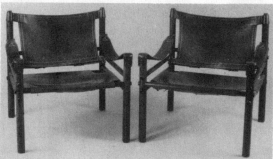

An 18th century ash and elm Windsor chair of traditional design, on baluster turned legs linked by an H stretcher. (Wintertons) $528

Pair of post-war walnut and leather armchairs, Arne Norell, Sweden, square shape, tapered cylindrical posts, leather sling-back arms and seat on through stretchers, 28in. high. (Skinner) $1,265

An Art Nouveau mahogany armchair, the square padded close-nailed back above similar seat. (Christie's) $431

A Regency mahogany bergère armchair, with caning, the reeded frame with arms on front side turned supports. (Woolley & Wallis) $1,380

An American patented original barber's chair by Koken Barber's Supply Co, St. Louis, decorative cast iron with carved wood on the base and seat, leather upholstery. (Auction Team Köln) $468

An elm armchair, probably East Anglia, 18th century, with wavy top-rail and pierced interlaced vase splat, flattened outswept arms. (Christie's) $404

An Edwardian simulated satinwood Adam style floral painted armchair, the shield back with three spars, with outscrolled arms. (Phillips) $800

Queen Anne walnut roundabout commode chair, Pennsylvania, 1740-60, the shaped pillow back joining the out-scrolling arms on three curving supports and two vasiform splats. (Skinner) $3,105

L. & J.G. Stickley armchair, no. 422, circa 1912, V-back over six vertical slats, spring cushion seat, 38in high. (Skinner) $460

An oak X-frame travelling chair, English, late 16th century, the rectangular back with double arcaded guilloche filled back and with a blind centre surround by trailing stylised foliage. (Christie's) $10,902

Bruno Mathsson, Sweden, Pernilla chair, designed circa 1934, manufactured by Karl Mathsson, from 1935. Laminated plywood and solid birch jointed frame with hemp webbing seat. (Bonhams) $708

An unusual George III elm open armchair, the solid back with adjustable iron ratchet above a saddle seat, raised on square tapering legs united by stretchers (one missing). (Cheffins) $2,782

A Chippendale period mahogany elbow chair, the pierced carved splat back with leaf spray decoration. (Woolley & Wallis) $1,159

Painted turned corner chair, New York State, late 18th century, the shaped pillow-back crest joining out-scrolled arms on three vase and ring-turned supports. (Skinner) $4,025

A Regency mahogany framed bergère armchair with reeded crest rail and arm rests, on turned front legs. (Dee Atkinson & Harrison) $5,280

A good Queen Anne carved walnut side chair, Pennsylvania circa 1740, the shell-carved crest above a strapwork splat flanked by outscrolled volute-carved stiles. (Sotheby's) $23,000

Emile-Jacques Ruhlmann, side chair, 1919, macassar ebony, slender tapering slightly everted legs, the front legs with bronze sabots. (Sotheby's) $11,760

The Franklin Family fine Transitional Chippendale carved walnut side chair, Philadelphia, circa 1765, the shaped crest with reverse-scrolling ears centring a ruffle, leaf- and volute-carved device. (Sotheby's) $79,500

One of a pair of mid-Victorian walnut salon chairs by Gillows, the oval button upholstered back above stuffover seats and lobed and fluted legs terminating in brass castors. (Bonhams)   (Two) $1,256

Emile-Jacques Ruhlmann, pair of side chairs, circa 1925, rosewood, the elegantly curved backs supported on shaped triangular tapering sabre legs. (Sotheby's) $21,630

A 17th century oak single chair with moulded rail back, solid seat on bobbin turned and squared supports and square stretchers. (Brightwells) $112

Chippendale walnut carved side chair, Philadelphia, 1755-70, the serpentine crest with beaded edges and raked ears has a central carved shell above the reverse-curved pierced splat. (Skinner) $6,900

A pair of walnut side chairs, of William and Mary style, second quarter 19th century, each with pierced waved toprail covered with foliage above a conforming pierced splat flanked by baluster turned uprights.(Christie's) $5,962

A good Chippendale carved and figured walnut side chair, Boston, Massachusetts, circa 1730, the yoke-form crest above a vasiform splat, the compass seat below on cabriole legs. (Sotheby's) $4,600

An ash and elm Windsor armchair, mid 19th century, the arched back with pierced splat and turned spindles above a saddle seat. (Bonhams) $414

Painted fan-back Windsor armchair, probably Connecticut, circa 1790-1800, the serpentine crest with scroll carved ears above seven spindles continuing through the arm crest. (Skinner) $51,750

A rare black-painted comb-back writing-arm Windsor chair, New England, mid 18th century, the shaped crest above five flaring spindles piercing the concave rail. (Sotheby's) $4,600

An ash elm and fruitwood comb back Windsor armchair, Thames Valley, late 18th century, the waved top rail with scrolled eared corners above a vase solid splat, the saddle seat on cabriole legs. (Bonhams) $1,176

A 19th century vernacular yew and elm stick back open arm chair, the hoop back with pierced splat above dished seat. (Bonhams) $1,016

An ash and fruitwood stickback Windsor armchair, Welsh, early 19th century, the bowed top rail with a surmounted waved crest continuing to turned spindles. (Bonhams) $3,822

An ash and elm highback smoker's Windsor armchair, Yorkshire, mid 19th century, the bowed top rail and pierced splat above bowed arms held by ring turned supports, the solid saddle seat on turned legs. (Bonhams) $1,323

A beech child's Windsor armchair, Thames Valley, early 19th century, the arched bowed top rail above a conforming stretcher, turned arms and caned seat. (Bonhams) $367

A yew and elm low back Windsor armchair, Yorkshire, early 19th century, the bowed back and pierced splat above a solid saddle seat, on turned legs tied by a crinoline stretcher. (Bonhams) $1,617

George III mahogany wing chair, circa 1780, with serpentine cresting, shaped wings and outscrolled arms on square moulded legs joined by stretchers. (Skinner) $1,495

Queen Anne mahogany upholstered wing chair, Massachusetts, circa 1760, the arched crest joining shaped wings continuing to vertically out-scrolled arms above rounded seat. (Skinner) $34,500

Federal mahogany upholstered easy chair, New England, early 19th century, the serpentine crest joining ogival wings and horizontally scrolled arms over shaped supports. (Skinner) $9,775

A George III mahogany wing armchair, the slightly arched brass studded shaped back, sides and outswept scroll arm supports with cushion seat, on molded square legs. (Christie's) $6,332

A George II walnut wingback armchair, with scrolled arms and padded seat on cabriole legs and pad feet, the back reduced in height. (Bonhams) $4,739

A Louis XIV walnut adjustable fauteuil, the arms with cast iron fittings for reclining and with pull-out rods for a later molded rectangular walnut ledge. (Christie's) $8,487

A walnut wing armchair, of small size, with gros point needlework upholstered arched back, sides and stuff-over seat with cushion, on cabriole legs. (Christie's) $3,439

An early Victorian mahogany wing armchair, with a shaped back, out-turned arms and loose cushion to the seat, on turned tapering legs with brass capped castors. (Christie's) $822

A wing armchair, 20th century, with a shaped back, out-turned arms and bowed seat, on square section legs. (Christie's) $715

Paint-decorated pine and poplar chest, Mahatonga Valley, Pennsylvania, early 19th century, the molded lift top painted with the American flag with lattice and banded border, 33in. wide.
(Skinner) $17,250

A good joined oak chest, English, possibly west country, mid 17th century, the four panelled hinged top with molded edge enclosing a candle box, lacking lid, above a lunette carved frieze, 53in. wide.
(Bonham's) $2,156

A small oak boarded chest, English, late 17th century, with molded hinged lid and arcaded front centred with a floral rosette and with an applied molded apron, 20in. wide.(Christie's) $7,487

An oak chest, English or Flemish, circa 1435-1460, the rectangular single panelled lid with morticed iron hinges, decorated with repeated stopped-chamfers to the frame and similarly decorated on the underside, 60in. wide.
(Christie's) $43,608

A George II walnut spice chest, mid 18th century, with panelled cupboard door opening to a compartment fitted with a series of small drawers centered by a single valanced pigeonhole, 21in. wide.
(Christie's) $4,465

A panelled chestnut writing box, English, late 17th century, the hinged domed top with a sliding panel above a drop fall enclosing an arrangement of drawers, restorations, 14½in. wide.
(Bonhams) $2,208

A fine and rare William and Mary green painted pine blanket chest, Long Island, New York, 1720-50, the hinged molded top opening to a panelled well above a long drawer, 42in. wide.
(Sotheby's) $24,150

A cedar and pokerwork decorated box, Italian, 17th century, with a hinged lid and penwork decorated sides and fitted interior, the front with twin panels and friezes in silhouette, 32in. wide.
(Christie's) $7,438

A red-painted chest-over-drawer, New England, 1770-1800, the rectangular lid with hinged batteries under each short end opening to a conforming interior, 37½in. wide.
(Christie's) $3,525

A walnut, mahogany and pine mule chest, 18th century, the fielded panelled top, front and sides above bracket feet, 120cm. wide.
(Bonhams) $504

Serat ebonised coffer, applied with brass studded decoration, enclosing partially fitted interior, base fitted with four drawers, circa late 19th century, 38½in.
(G.A. Key) $550

A 19th century Scandinavian painted pine dower chest, decorated flowers, the lidded compartment with a drawer to the base, on cut out ends, 4ft.8in.
(Woolley & Wallis) $524

English Provincial inlaid oak tack chest, with three-panel fall front above five drawers on slant cabriole feet, 58in. wide.
(Skinner) $1,495

An early oak primitive small chest with rosette carved domed lid, steel lockplate, 2ft.7in. wide.
(Brightwells) $1,085

A North Italian boarded chest, cyprus or cedar, the cleated end hinged lid to a paper lined interior with a lidded candlebox, the front with incised drawer decoration of The Royal Stuart arms, 4ft.6in.
(Woolley & Wallis) $1,463

Painted and decorated six-board chest, New England, early 19th century, the top lifts above a cavity with lidded till, original yellow ground paint with original burnt sienna fanciful graining and inlay simulation, 38in. long.
(Skinner) $10,350

A George III mahogany and inlaid mule chest, with ledge back and hinged top with crossbanded frieze inlaid with lines and with dummy drawer fronts containing five drawers below, 64½in. wide.
(Christie's) $2,632

A late 18th century oak mule chest, of North Country origin, the moulded edge hinged lid above a front with shaped top fielded panels, 4ft.8in.
(Woolley & Wallis) $990

A mahogany domed trunk, 19th century, with iron banding and side handles, set on later shaped peg feet, 88cm. wide.
(Bonhams) $448

An oak clamped-front ark, English, 16th/17century, with a domed lid with moulded edge, on stile feet, part paper lined, 38in. wide.
(Christie's) $3,655

A 17th century oak dower chest with sunken two panel lid above arch carved frieze and rosette carved two panel front, 3ft.10in. wide. (Brightwells) $1,685

Federal walnut inlaid dower chest, Pennsylvania, circa 1800, the rectangular molded top opens to an interior with till, 49in. wide. (Skinner) $1,495

Painted and stencil decorated six-board chest, probably Schoharie County, New York, first quarter 19th century, 39¾in. wide. (Skinner) $2,070

Grain painted and paint decorated poplar six-board chest, Schoharie County, New York, first quarter 19th century, 37³/₄in. wide. (Skinner) $1,265

A fine and very rare blue-green and white-painted pine blanket chest, attributed to Johannes Spitler, Shenandoah County, Virginia, circa 1800, 4ft. wide. (Sotheby's) $74,000

American blanket chest, in pine with old brown finish, moulded upper and lower edges, paneled sides and front, 41¹/₂in. wide. (Eldred's) $1,760

A polychrome-decorated brown-painted pine blanket chest, signed by Johannes Rank or Ranck, Jonestown, Pennsylvania, circa 1795, 4ft. 3¹/₂in. wide. (Sotheby's) $9,775

An English inlaid oak chest in Charles II style, the hinged molded top over two square recessed panels, 47³/₄in. wide. (Sotheby's) $1,380

American lift-top blanket chest, in old brown grain paint with stenciled decoration, 38in. long. (Eldred's) $770

A Charles II oak coffer with triple paneled front and hinged lid, on groove molded block legs, basically late 17th century, 45½in. (Hy. Duke & Son) $672

A red, green and yellow-painted pine blanket chest, Pennsylvania, circa 1790, the hinged rectangular top decorated with two pinwheels, 43in. wide. (Sotheby's) $5,750

A Queen Anne brass-nailed leather trunk, in the manner of Richard Pigge, decorated overall with geometric patterns in nails, 39¼in. wide. (Christie's) $5.345

A fine Italian Renaissance inlaid walnut cassone of sarcophagus form, first half 16th century, 71³/₄in. wide. (Sotheby's) $19,550

An Italian baroque walnut credenza, Bologna, incorporating 17th century elements, with later rectangular top above a tapering well, 51¼in. wide.
(Sotheby's) $2,587

Painted pine and poplar chest over drawer, New England, early 18th century, the molded lift top above a half-round molded case, 36in. wide. (Skinner) $4,600

A carved giltwood and painted cassone, Italian, circa 1860, in High Renaissance style, the hinged top carved above a panel painted with figures beneath an awning within an Italian town scene, 180cm. wide.
(Sotheby's) $13,122

A Victorian simulated mulberry mule chest, last quarter 19th century, the hinged lid above two drawers and set on bracket feet, decorated with a yellow over brown scumble finish, 104cm. wide.
(Bonhams) $568

American lift-top blanket chest, 18th century, in maple with tiger maple top, three drawers with molded fronts and brass escutcheons, 39in. wide.
(Eldred's) $935

A Portuguese Zanzibar hardwood trunk, with brass strapwork, plaques and nailed, the interior with a lidded valuables box, 30¼in.
(Woolley & Wallis) $256

A rare William and Mary green-and brown-painted poplar and pine one-drawer blanket chest, Long Island, New York, 1700–50, 41½in. wide.
(Sotheby's) $8,050

Painted and decorated pine wood box, New England, 1830s, the hinged top lifts above a nailed box with old mustard paint, 29in. wide.
(Skinner) $805

Vinegar putty painted chest over drawers, Southeastern New England, circa 1835, the molded hinged top above a deep well, 40in. wide.
(Skinner) $6,325

Antique American lift-top blanket chest, in pine with moulded top, one false and two real drawers with wooden pulls, scrolled apron, 38½in. wide. (Eldred's) $825

A Continental baroque beechwood chest, probably a North Italian madia, with slanted roof-shaped top with zigzag ends, 42in. wide. (Sotheby's) $1,380

American lift-top blanket chest, in pine with tiger maple, carving done by a man of Annisquam, Massachusetts, top carved with facing griffins, 38in. wide. (Eldred's) $935

An important carved pine blanket chest, New Mexico, 18th century, the rectangular top opening to a well, carved with large rosettes and pomegranates, the front divided into seven panels.
(Sotheby's) $118,000

Queen Anne red painted pine and maple chest over drawer, probably Massachusetts, mid 18th century, the moulded hinged top above a double arch moulded case of single drawer, 35½in. wide.
(Skinner) $54,625

A rare blue-painted pine chest-on-legs, possibly Pueblo, Taos, New Mexico, circa 1800, the hinged rectangular top opening to a well, the panelled sides carved with geometric motifs, 30½in. wide.
(Sotheby's) $26,450

A very fine and rare carved pine chest-on-legs, Velarde area, New Mexico, 18th century, the case sides with raised panels of geometric carving, 37½in. wide.
(Sotheby's) $76,750

A diminutive pine chest-on-legs, Northern New Mexico, possibly Taos area, circa 1840, the rectangular hinged top opening to a well, above a panelled front and sides, 34½in. wide.
(Sotheby's) $12,650

An important brown-painted pine chest, probably Spanish, 17/18th century, the rectangular top with moulded edge opening to a paper lined well, 44½in. wide.
(Sotheby's) $5,175

A Victorian satinwood and tulipwood crossbanded bowfront chest of drawers, circa 1880, with two short and three long graduated drawers, 42¼in. wide.
(Bonhams) $2,072

A 19th century mahogany chest, of two short and four long drawers, with turned wood handles, flanked by protruding wrythen carved and fluted columns, on turned feet, 51in. wide.(Andrew Hartley) $1,727

19th century mahogany serpentined chest of drawers with brushing slide over three graduated drawers, raised on splayed feet, 36in.
(G.A. Key) $1,068

An early 19th century walnut veneered chest, of narrow proportions, crossbanded and inlaid with stringing, two short and three long graduated drawers, 3ft.1in. wide.
(Woolley & Wallis) $3,454

An early 18th century walnut chest of two short and three long drawers with quarter veneered top, feather banding, on bracket feet, 3ft.6in. wide (Brightwells) $3,927

A French mid 19th century chest, flame mahogany veneered, the top with a banded back edge, the top bonnet drawer with a frieze to the outline front above three long drawers.
(Woolley & Wallis) $862

Federal cherry inlaid chest of drawers, possibly Connecticut, circa 1800, the rectangular overhanging top with string inlaid edge above a case of four graduated drawers with mahogany veneer, 39¼in. wide.
(Skinner) $5,750

A walnut and feather-banded chest, early 18th century, with some restoration and later veneering, the quarter-veneered top crossbanded with a moulded edge, 39in. wide.
(Christie's) $7,402

Federal inlaid cherry chest of drawers, attributed to Nathan Lombard, Southern Worcester County, circa 1800, the top with two lines of chevron stringing joining quarter fans at the corners, 42¾in. wide. (Skinner) $365,500

A Regency mahogany chest, the rectangular top above two short and three long graduated drawers, on splayed bracket feet, 42¼in. wide. (Bonhams) $616

A late 17th century oak chest, with plank top and panelled sides, four geometrically moulded drawers, later bun feet, 35½in. wide. (Andrew Hartley) $5,544

Biedermeier elmwood and part-ebonised chest of drawers, with two long drawers, on tapered sabre legs, with ebonised edging and escutcheons, 21⅝in. wide. (Skinner) $3,680

An 18th century bachelor's chest in mahogany fitted with brushing slide above four long graduated drawers, 2ft.7in. wide. (Brightwells) $3,900

An early 19th century mahogany bow front chest, with stringing and satinwood crossbanding, the plum pudding mahogany top with reeded edging, 40½in. wide. (Andrew Hartley) $1,617

An unusual Regency mahogany breakfront chest of drawers, circa 1815, the arched back above four long panelled drawers flanked by locking cupboard doors, 48in. wide. (Bonhams) $2,240

A George IV mahogany veneered chest, in Gillows style, the top with a reeded edge and reeded corner protruding pilasters, 3ft.7in. (Woolley & Wallis) $1,680

A Georgian mahogany serpentine chest of drawers, circa 1790, the shaped top with moulded edge, above three long graduated drawers, with a shaped apron and splayed bracket feet, 44in. wide. (Bonhams) $10,656

A George III mahogany chest, crossbanded with stringing, two short over three long drawers, with brass drop handles, 37in. wide. (Andrew Hartley) $1,155

A Victorian mahogany chest of drawers, 120cm. wide.
(Bonhams & Brooks) $431

A Chippendale mahogany reverse-serpentine front chest-of-drawers, Boston or Salem, 1750-1780, the rectangular top with reverse serpentine front and molded edge above a conforming case, 42in. wide. (Christie's) $17,625

A Victorian Scottish chest of drawers, circa 1860, 122cm. wide.
(Bonhams & Brooks) $1,232

An oak chest with drawers, English, mid-17th century, in two sections, with a molded hinged lid and arcaded frieze above four panels and stiff-leaf carved outer uprights, 47in. wide.
(Christie's) $21,390

A George III oak and fruitwood bookpress, 98cm. wide.
(Bonhams & Brooks) $814

A Federal inlaid mahogany chest-of-drawers, New York, 1800-1820, the rectangular bowed top with inlaid edges above a conforming case with four band-inlaid graduated drawers over a shaped skirt, 41¾in. high.
(Christie's) $9,775

An early 19th century mahogany bowfront chest of drawers, 89cm. wide x 49cm. deep x 88cm. high.
(Bonhams & Brooks) $647

A George III mahogany serpentine chest, the shaped molded rectangular top above four graduated drawers, on bracket feet, the feet probably later, 30in. wide.
(Christie's) $25,438

A George II style walnut serpentine chest of drawers, 92cm. wide.
(Bonhams & Brooks) $1,155

An early Victorian mahogany chest of drawers, 121cm. wide.
(Bonhams & Brooks) $562

A George III mahogany chest, the molded rectangular top, above two short and three long graduated drawers, on shaped later bracket feet, 29¾in. wide.
(Christie's) $9,994

An oak chest of drawers of 17th century form, 96cm. wide.
(Bonhams & Brooks) $825

A Regency mahogany chest, the eared rectangular top with reeded edge, above two short and three long graduated drawers each with cedar-lining, 46¾in. high.
(Christie's) $6,360

A Victorian mahogany Wellington chest, 51cm. wide.
(Bonhams & Brooks) $592

An early Victorian oak chest, by Gillows of Lancaster, after a design by A.W.N. Pugin, circa 1850, the molded rectangular top above three short and three long drawers flanked by chamfered columns, 46½in. wide.
(Christie's) $19,987

A Victorian mahogany bowfronted chest, circa 1860, 121cm. wide.
(Bonhams & Brooks) $600

A George III mahogany chest, the molded rectangular broad crossbanded top, above two short and three graduated long drawers, 37½in. wide.
(Christie's) $8,177

A George IV mahogany cross banded bowfront chest of drawers, 108cm wide.
(Bonhams & Brooks) $847

Cherry stained and inlaid chest of drawers, New England, late 18th century, the dark brown top with inlaid edge overhangs the case of cherry drawers, 36in. wide.
(Skinner) $7,475

A French mahogany dressing chest, mid 19th century, with an oval mirror, on scrolled supports, above a gray fossil marble top with a three quarter gallery, 40in. wide.
(Christie's) $725

An early 18th century walnut chest with cross-banded top above two short and three long drawers having feather banding raised on bracket feet, 3ft. 1in. wide.
(Brightwells) $2,610

A George III mahogany chest, fitted with a slide, with four long drawers below, on bracket feet, 29¾in. wide. (Christie's) $5,814

An Italian walnut, fruitwood and inlaid chest, part 17th century and adapted from a prie-dieu, of concave angular outline, 26in. wide. (Christie's) $3,619

A Regency mahogany bow front chest, with overhung top over four graduated long drawers, 91cm. wide. (Tennants) $2,041

A Regency mahogany bow front chest, the string inlaid panel frieze with roundels, two short and three long drawers, 45in. wide.
(Andrew Hartley) $1,664

Classical mahogany veneer dressing chest, Boston, 1820-30, the veneered mirror flanked by scrolled supports with ormolu mounts above two small drawers, 38in. wide. (Skinner) $977

A Federal grain-painted popular chest of drawers, Pennsylvania, circa 1810, the rectangular top above drawer painted to simulate two graduated long drawers, 40½in. wide. (Sotheby's) $6,900

Federal cherry and birch bow-fronted chest of drawers, New England, circa 1800-1810, the top with string inlaid and swelled front edge, on four flaring French feet, 41½in. wide.
(Skinner) $3,565

A Louis Philippe mahogany and metal-mounted upright chest, early 19th century, with a frieze drawer and five further drawers below, flanked by turned columns, 39in. wide. (Christie's) $1,208

Federal mahogany veneer bow front chest of drawers, Boston area, early 19th century, the figured mahogany top with lunette inlaid edge overhangs a conforming case of cockbeaded veneered graduated drawers, 41⅛in. wide.
(Skinner) $24,150

A mid-Victorian oak chest, inlaid to the front with ebonised lines, the rectangular eared top above a narrow frieze drawer with partitions, 47¼in. wide.
(Christie's) $2,422

A George III mahogany chest, the top with a molded edge above two short and five long drawers, on bracket feet, 44in. wide.
(Christie's) $2,138

A walnut chest, parts 18th century, with a molded rectangular top, two short and three graduated long drawers, on bracket feet, 37½in. wide. (Christie's) $2,303

Federal maple and mahogany veneer bow-front chest of drawers, New Hampshire, circa 1800, the rectangular top with swelled front over a conforming case of four graduated drawers, 40½in. wide.
(Skinner) $3,450

A mother of pearl veneered chest and associated mirror, of recent manufacture, the mirror with a pierced arched cresting, 46½in. wide. (Christie's) $822

Federal cherry inlaid chest of drawers, New England, circa 1800, the rectangular overhanging top with string inlaid edge above a case of four graduated drawers, 42in. wide. (Skinner) $2,990

A Spanish mahogany, rosewood and marquetry chest, early 19th century, decorated with lines and meandering floral borders, 53¼in. wide. (Christie's) $2,024

Chippendale mahogany block-front bureau, Boston 1750–90, the thumb-moulded shaped top above a conforming case of blocked drawers, 33in. wide. (Skinner) $46,000

An early Georgian walnut chest, the banded and quarter veneered top with feather edging, writing slide flanked on either side by a small pen drawer, 36in. wide. (Andrew Hartley) $14,267

A yellow and brown painted pine two-drawer blanket chest, New England, 19th century, the hinged rectangular top above a well, two long drawers, a shaped apron and bracket feet, 40in. wide. (Sotheby's) $2,070

A blue-painted pine apothecary chest, New England, 19th century, the rectangular moulded cornice above an arrangement of twenty-three drawers, 35½in. wide. (Sotheby's) $9,200

A good Chippendale figured walnut chest of drawers, Pennsylvania, circa 1770, the rectangular moulded top above four graduated cockbeaded drawers, 33½in. wide. (Sotheby's) $18,400

An early 19th century bow fronted mahogany chest of four long graduated cock beaded drawers with turned wooden knob handles, 48in. wide. (Peter Francis) $1,379

Unusual English two-part campaign chest, 19th century, in mahogany with moulded top, cockbeaded drawer fronts, top of lower section reads *Major Tudor 40th Regt. her Prince Regent*, 36½in. wide. (Eldred's) $2,860

Antique Pennsylvania walnut six-drawer chest, three small drawers above three graduated drawers, moulded drawer fronts with banded inlay, 36½in. wide. (Eldred's) $1,430

Gio Ponti, an oak chest designed circa 1960-64, the rectangular top with turquoise plastic laminate surface, above three long drawers, 43in. wide.
(Christie's) $7,597

Federal cherry inlaid bow-front chest of drawers, probably Massachusetts, circa 1800, the rectangular top with elliptical front crossbanded and string inlaid edge, 38in. wide.
(Skinner) $6,900

A Chippendale inlaid and figured mahogany blocked serpentine-front chest of drawers, New England, circa 1780, the shaped moulded top above four graduated long drawers, 39¾in. wide.
(Sotheby's) $17,250

Federal mahogany and bird's eye maple veneer bowfront chest, probably New Hampshire, early 19th century, the bowed top with inlaid edge above the case of four cockbeaded drawers, 39¾in. wide.
(Skinner) $9,775

A 19th century Colonial teak campaign chest with brass corner mounts, recessed handles and iron carrying handles, 88.5cm. high x 79cm. wide.
(Bearne's) $3,630

A fine and rare Chippendale carved and figured mahogany reverse-serpentine blocked chest of drawers, Massachusetts, circa 1780, the oblong moulded top above four graduated line-incised long drawers, width of top 38½in.
(Sotheby's) $101,500

A George III mahogany bowfront chest of two short over three long graduated drawers, with banded top, 106cm. wide.
(Bristol) $957

A pair of Edwardian mahogany satinwood and cross-banded tall chests with seven long drawers, on bracket feet, 20½in. wide.
(Dreweatt Neate) $5,508

A George III Chippendale style mahogany chest of four long graduated drawers, on shaped bracket feet, 87cm. wide.
(Wintertons) $3,444

A George III mahogany chest on chest, the moulded cornice above three short and three long drawers between blind fret-carved angles, 42½in. wide.
(Christie's) $2,422

A fine Queen Anne carved maple chest on chest on frame, attributed to Major John Dunlap, New Hampshire 1750–70, in three parts, 38in. wide.
(Sotheby's) $57,500

An early 18th century walnut-veneered tallboy with cavetto cornice, three short and three graduated long drawers flanked by fluted canted corners, 105cm. wide.
(Bearne's) $7,222

A walnut and feather-banded tallboy chest, early 18th century, the quarter veneered crossbanded top centred by an oval and with quartered spandrels, 40½in. wide.
(Christie's) $8,721

A 19th century Continental mahogany tallboy, 108cm. wide.
(Bonhams) $1,896

A mahogany tallboy chest, late 18th century, the dentil-moulded cornice above a blind fret-carved frieze, with two short and three long drawers, 44in. wide.
(Christie's) $4,499

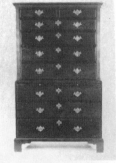

A George III mahogany chest on chest, the upper section with dentil cornice above two short and four long graduated drawers, flanked by quarter stop fluted columns, 110cm. wide. (Wintertons) $4,861

A Chippendale applewood flat-top chest on chest, New England, probably Connecticut, circa 1785, in two parts, the upper section with moulded projecting cornice, upper section 37in. wide.
(Sotheby's) $57,500

Chippendale walnut chest on chest, Pennsylvania, circa 1750-1780, rectangular flat top with moulded cornice, three drawers over seven graduated drawers, 41½in. wide.
(Freeman) $8,960

A fine Queen Anne carved and figured mahogany bonnet-top high chest of drawers, Massachusetts, 1730-50, in two parts; the upper section with broken swan's neck pediment, 37¾in. wide. (Sotheby's) $107,000

An early 18th century walnut-veneered chest on later stand with ovolo carcase mouldings, boxwood and ebony stringing to the three graduated long drawers, 90cm. wide. (Bearne's) $1,887

A George II walnut-veneered collector's cabinet on stand with crossbanded rectangular top, two fielded panel doors with chevron stringing, 80cm. wide. (Bearne's) $5,652

A Queen Anne style chest on stand, English, first half 20th century, the walnut and yew chest with triple arch pediment above six drawers, 6in. tall. (Bonhams) $410

A walnut and marquetry chest in the 16th century German manner fitted with an arrangement of 14 drawers and two doors, 107cm. wide, 16th century and later. (Bearne's) $3,460

An early 18th century walnut chest on stand, the upper section with three short and three long crossbanded drawers, 3ft. 2in. wide. (Russell Baldwin & Bright) $3,169

A small William & Mary laburnum oyster cabinet-upon-stand, the shallow cushion drawer above two doors inlaid in geometric patterns with central eight-point ebony and boxwood stars, 43in. wide. (Boardmans) $35,070

Diminutive Jacobean-style oak high chest, composed of antique elements, the upper section fitted with a bolection moulded frieze drawer above four drawers; the lower section fitted with a drawer, on turned legs, 27in wide. (Skinner) $3,737

An oak and mahogany banded chest-on-stand, North West, early 18th century, with pronounced double moulded cornice and dentil frieze above two short and three long drawers, 44½in. wide. (Christie's) $4,035

Queen Anne chinoiserie decorated tall chest, 18th century, rectangular moulded cornice above a pair of drawers over three graduated drawers, 35½in. wide.
(Skinner) $6,900

A fine Queen Ann carved and figured cherrywood bonnet-top high chest of drawers, attributed to John Brooks, Fairfield, Connecticut, circa 1765, in two parts, 41in. wide.
(Sotheby's) $46,000

An oak and yew-wood crossbanded chest-on-stand, English, early 18th century, the upper section with a moulded top above two short and three long drawers, 42in. wide.
(Christie's) $4,754

A good Queen Anne figured maple flat-top high chest of drawers, New London County, Connecticut, circa 1760, in two parts; the upper section with an overhanging cornice above four graduated long drawers, 39½in. wide.
(Sotheby's) $34,500

Queen Anne maple high chest of drawers, probably Massachusetts, circa 1760-80, the top section with moulded cornice above a case of five thumb moulded graduated drawers above a lower section of two graduated drawers, 37¾in. wide. (Skinner) $9,200

Queen Anne carved, inlaid, and walnut-veneered bonnet-top high chest of drawers, Boston or Ipswich, Massachusetts, circa 1750, in two parts; with swan's neck pediment surmounted by corkscrew finials, 41in. wide.
(Sotheby's) $68,500

BUYER BEWARE

Skillful modern cabinet-making techniques will often lead one to believe that some veneered furniture is older than it appears.
A useful rule-of-thumb is that hand cut veneers were the norm up to the middle of the 19th century, whilst later, machine-cut veneers are of much thinner gauge.

(Amersham Auction Rooms)

A rare Queen Anne carved and figured mahogany bonnet-top high chest of drawers, Philadelphia, circa 1745, the tympanum fitted with a shell- and leaf-carved drawer, 43in. wide.
(Sotheby's) $233,500

Queen Anne figured walnut veneer high chest, Massachusetts, 1730-50, the cornice moulding above a blind frieze drawer, two thumb-moulded short drawers and three graduated long drawers, 34½in. wide. (Skinner) $19,550

Regency period rosewood chiffonier bookcase, arched pediment over two shelves, raised on short ring turned columns over a plain frieze, 41½in. (G.A. Key)　$3,770

A mid Victorian walnut mirror back chiffonier, circa 1880, the marble top above two panelled cupboard doors, restorations, 118cm. wide. (Bonhams)　$1,120

Fine Regency period mahogany chiffonier, the high back with a scroll moulded pediment, over two shelves, supported by ring turned columns, 37½in.
(G.A. Key)　$3,140

A Regency rosewood and gilt-metal mounted chiffonier, with three quarter galleried superstructure, on baluster turned brass columns, above a rectangular top and containing three frieze drawers, 36½in. wide.
(Christie's)　$5,486

An early Victorian walnut veneered chiffonier, mid 19th century, the two tier gallery top with pierced fretwork set on spiral turned pillars, 107cm. wide. (Bonhams)　$2,074

An early Victorian chiffonier, rosewood veneered, the top marble inset, the raised back with a shelf above a mirror flanked by scroll and leaf brackets.
(Woolley & Wallis)　$958

A Regency rosewood veneered chiffonier, with brass marquetry inlay and stringing, the raised back with a shelf above three small drawers, 3ft.
(Woolley & Wallis)　$3,696

A late Victorian rosewood chiffonier, with inlaid decoration, 118cm. wide.
(Bonhams)　$628

A small early 19th century mahogany chiffonier, the top with a gadroon moulded edge, also to the raised back pediment and shelf, on front turned rope twist and rondel block supports, 22in.
(Woolley & Wallis)　$2,826

A parcel-gilt and green painted commode, in the manner of Bonzanigo, the shaped sarancolin moulded top above three drawers, 128cm. wide.
(Sotheby's) $23,431

A pair of late Louis XV tulipwood and parquetry bedside commodes, by Joseph Stocket, each with a slightly bowed and canted rectangular Brocatello marble top and brass three-quarter gallery, 15½in. wide.
(Christie's) $15,272

A pair of Dutch sycamore, satinwood and Chinese lacquer commodes, late 18th century, each inlaid overall with fruitwood and ebonised lines, 33in. wide. (Christie's) $28,635

A George III satinwood, sabicu and mahogany serpentine commode, attributed to Mayhew and Ince, crossbanded to the top and front in rosewood, 41¾in. wide.
(Christie's) $18,860

A Dutch walnut and marquetry bombé commode inlaid throughout with vases of flowers, scrolling foliage, floral sprays and birds, mid-18th century.
(Bearne's) $5,280

A pair of satinwood semi-circular commodes, in George III style, the segmentally veneered tops over ivy painted borders, above frieze drawers and doors, 2ft. 4in. wide.
(Sotheby's) $11,139

A pair of Italian cream-painted and parcel-gilt bedside commodes, first half 19th century, each with a waved and moulded brêche violette marble top above a door, 26¾in. wide. (Christie's) $17,181

A Louis XV Provincial walnut and pine serpentine commode, fitted with two drawers centred with a scroll carved cartouche, 48½in. wide. (Christie's) $4,658

A Venetian green-painted and parcel-gilt bombé commode, mid 18th century, the shaped and moulded top above two shaped long drawers with cartouche-shaped drawer fronts, 62in. wide. (Christie's) $38,180

A pair of Italian walnut bedside commodes, crossbanded overall, each of bombé shape and with a shaped top above a spreading frieze, 27¾in. wide. (Christie's) $15,272

A pair of George II mahogany serpentine commodes, possibly by Wright and Elrick, the tops attributed to Thomas Carter the Younger, each with a Sicilian jasper-veneered white marble serpentine top, 53½in. wide. (Christie's) $191,880

A purpleheart and marquetry serpentine commode, George III, circa 1795, the top inlaid with a lozenge shaped panel of a fruit basket with a bird, 3ft. 11in. wide. (Sotheby's) $14,404

A gilt-metal mounted mahogany and trellis marquetry commode, 20th century, the serpentine mottled white marble top above two long drawers, inlaid à traverse and shaped apron, 69in. wide. (Christie's) $2,961

A Biedermeier walnut commode, 110cm. wide. (Bonhams) $948

A gilt-bronze marquetry and parquetry commode after Riesener, by Victor Raulin Paris, circa 1880, the sarancolin marble top above three drawers cast with foliage and a panelled door centered by a still life, 167cm. wide. (Sotheby's) $29,643

An ormolu mounted, tulipwood and kingwood petit commode, 18th century and adapted, of Louis XV style, surmounted by a serpentine fleur de peche marble top, 25¾in. wide. (Christie's) $5,921

A Louis XV ormolu-mounted tulipwood and floral marquetry commode, by Pierre Roussel, diagonally-banded overall, the molded brèche d'Alep marble top above two drawers inlaid sans traverse with sprays of flowers, 32½in. wide. (Christie's) $50,301

A Dutch carved mahogany and floral marquetry bombé commode, the overhanging serpentine top with a vase of flowers with foliate scrolls, 41in. wide. (Christie's) $6,430

An Italian walnut and ivory (possibly bone) inlaid marquetry bombé commode, 18th century and later, the serpentine top inlaid with figures, birds and trailing floral stems, 42½in. wide. (Christie's) $8,460

A kingwood and metal-mounted commode, late 19th/ early 20th century, in the Louis XV style, with serpentine mottled marble top, above three long drawers, crossbanded and line-inlaid, 50in. wide. (Christie's) $2,834

A Venetian polychrome decorated serpentine commode, 18th century, decorated throughout with cartouches and bouquets of flowers against a pale blue ground, 37in. wide. (Christie's) $736

A baroque style walnut, burr walnut and ormolu mounted bombé commode, with red and white marble top, 136cm. wide.
(Arnold) $840

A French ormolu-mounted lacquer commode, in the Louis XV style, circa 1875, surmounted by a molded serpentine Portasanta marble top, the front bombé-shaped panel depicting figures on a terrace, 59in. wide.
(Christie's) $22,454

A Continental mahogany and gilt-metal mounted commode or meuble d'appui, 20th century, in the Louis XVI style, in the manner of Beneman, 70½in. diameter.
(Christie's) $10,692

A Louis XV/XVI Transitional kingwood, tulipwood inlaid and ormolu mounted commode, surmounted by a gray fossilized marble top, containing three long drawers veneered à quatre faces with purplewood borders, 37¾in. wide. (Christie's) $4,568

A French tulipwood, mahogany, parquetry and ormolu mounted commode, late 19th/early 20th century, with a brocatello marble top above six drawers, 21in. wide.
(Christie's) $658

A French Provincial later decorated commode, 18th century, of undulating arc en arbelète outline with a molded edge, containing three long drawers applied with ormolu rococo pierced cartouche key plates, 52in. wide.
(Christie's) $6,430

Louis XV style marble-top and tulipwood parquetry commode, 20th century, with gray and white veined top above a bombé case fitted with three drawers, 45in. wide.
(Skinner) $3,450

A baroque walnut and inlaid commode, with molded breakfront rounded rectangular top, on bun feet, 108cm. wide, restored.
(Arnold) $2,906

A French kingwood, rosewood marquetry and ormolu mounted serpentine commode, early 20th century, with a variegated gray marble top above two drawers inlaid sans travers, 59½in. wide.
(Christie's) $2,138

A carved oak corner cupboard on stand, 106cm. wide.
(Bonhams & Brooks) $420

18th century mahogany bow front corner cabinet, molded pediment, two doors below enclosing a fitted interior, lower shelf fitted with three drawers, 30in.
(G.A. Key) $2,512

Blue-painted pine panelled cupboard, New England, late 18th century, the cupboard with molded door above two scalloped shelves and a raised panel door, 33¾in. wide. (Skinner) $24,150

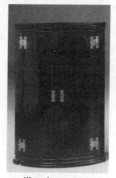

A George III mahogany corner cupboard, the molded cornice fitted with three shelves, enclosed by a pair of panel doors with molding below, 28¼in. wide.
(Christie's) $2,180

A mahogany corner cabinet, designed by Charles Annesley Voysey, 1898, for the dining room of E.R. Hughes Esq., open slatted upper section, twin-doored lower section with shelf-lined interior, 39in. wide.
(Christie's) $129,368

A George III mahogany crossbanded and inlaid bowfront hanging corner cupboard, with molded cornice and enclosed by a pair of panelled doors with arched inlay, 26in. wide.
(Christie's) $1,990

A Victorian mahogany standing corner cupboard with pierced and scrolled foliate surmount, the upper section with mirror back shelving, 28in. wide.
(Andrew Hartley) $1,050

A George III mahogany bow fronted corner cupboard with stringing and parquetry banding, molded cornice, panelled frieze, two brass trimmed doors, 30¼in. wide.
(Andrew Hartley) $2,002

A Victorian mahogany corner cabinet on stand, crossbanded with marquetry, the serpentine fascia with scrolled pediment, single glazed door, protruding base, 30½in. wide.
(Andrew Hartley) $3,542

A Victorian walnut parquetry and marquetry credenza or side cabinet, with gilt-metal mounts, of breakfront and bowed outline, the top with parquetry lozenge inlay, 87in. wide. (Christie's) $19,320

Victorian ebonized and burr walnut gilt metal mounted bow-fronted credenza, elaborately inlaid throughout with boxwood neo-classical designs, 49in. (G A Key) $1,427

A 19th century serpentine credenza, walnut veneered and inlaid floral marquetry with stringing, the top with a molded ebonized edge, 5ft. wide. (Woolley & Wallis) $2,880

A Victorian ebonized and inlaid credenza, the D-shaped top over inlaid frieze, the central door flanked by two glazed bowed compartments, 164cm. wide. (Bristol) $1,288

A late Victrorian ebonized, burr walnut and inlaid credenza, of bowed and breakfront outline, a panel door inset with gilt-metal framed oval Sèvres style panel, 58in. wide. (Christie's) $1,999

A Victorian walnut credenza, crossbanded with stringing and with gilt metal mounts, the serpentine fascia with central marquetry panelled door, 63in. wide. (Andrew Hartley) $4,900

A Victorian credenza cabinet with burr-grain marquetry panels and frieze, the two central doors flanked by pair of pilasters with mirrors behind, 6ft.2in. wide. (Brightwells) $3,602

A Victorian burr-walnut and marquetry credenza or side cabinet, of broken and bowed outline, applied with gilt-metal mounts with an inlaid frieze. (Christie's) $5,451

A Victorian burr walnut credenza of breakfront form with gilt metal mounts and beaded edging, marquetry inlaid frieze over glazed door flanked on either side by a panelled door, with inset porcelain plaques, 92in. wide. (Andrew Hartley) $3,475

An oak press cupboard, Welsh or English, mid 18th century, the upper section with molded cornice and a pair of ogee fielded panelled doors flanking a central arched fielded panel, 67½in. wide. (Christie's) $6,608

An oak press cupboard, Yorkshire, late 17th century and later, the associated upper canopy with panelled sides and arcaded frieze, with double scrolled finials at either end, 60½in. wide. (Christie's) $3,478

An antique oak housekeeper's cupboard, the upper breakfront section fitted with shelves enclosed by triple fielded panel doors, 6ft. 10in. wide. (Russell Baldwin & Bright) $7,938

Antique American (?) stepped-back kitchen cupboard in pine with old red stain, molded cornice, panelled sides, two panelled doors above two small drawers, 50½in.wide. (Eldred's) $4,400

An oak court cup-board, English, mid 17th century, with molded top and arcaded frieze with corner spandrels, the middle tier with a foliate-lunette carved frieze and a further undertier, 50in. wide. (Christie's) $24,530

A Flemish walnut cupboard, the ogee molded edge top set with lion masks above a shelf enclosed by a rectangular fielded panel door, 29in. wide. (Woolley & Wallis) $4,006

Painted pine two-door tall cupboard, probably Rhode Island, late 18th century, the flat molded cornice over a nail constructed scratch-beaded case with two cupboard doors, 41¾in. wide. (Skinner) $6,900

An oak press cupboard, probably Welsh, early 18th century, in two sections with a molded cornice and a pair of arched fielded panelled doors, with two dummy and two true fielded drawers below, 55½in. wide. (Christie's) $2,726

An 18th century panelled oak bacon cupboard, the upper part with molded cornice, now fitted with a hanging rail enclosed by a pair of doors with shaped and molded upper panels, 52in. wide. (Canterbury) $2,754

An oak court cupboard, with lunette carved canopy with turned corner finials, 3ft.9½in. wide.
(Woolley & Wallis) $3,920

An oak tridarn, North Wales, early 18th century, the upper section with later molded and ribbon-twist cornice with drop pendants, 62in. wide. (Christie's) $8,228

Antique American stepped-back cupboard in pine, three shelves with molded edges over a single panelled cupboard door, 38in. wide. (Eldred's) $3,960

Painted pine and glazed step-back cupboard, Pennsylvania, late 18th century, the upper section with flaring molded cornice above two cupboard doors, each with six lights, 52in. wide.
(Skinner) $9,775

Small Federal glazed cherry cupboard, Pennsylvania or Ohio, circa 1830s, the molded top above two beaded small drawers and a similar glazed door, 28in. wide.
(Skinner) $1,840

A yellow-painted pine cupboard, Pennsylvania, circa 1830, in two parts; the overhanging cornice above two glazed cupboard doors opening to shelves, 4ft. 6in. wide.
(Sotheby's) $7,475

Painted recessed panel cupboard, Pennsylvania or Ohio, 1835-45, the flat molded cornice above a case with recessed panelled sides and doors, 36¼in. wide.
(Skinner) $4,600

A large oak press cupboard, North Country, late 17th century, with a later molded cornice and frieze carved with foliage and grotesque type creatures, above a pair of twin panelled doors,18th century base, 76½in. wide.
(Christie's) $5,565

Blue painted pine panelled cupboard, Canada, late 18th century, the two raised panelled doors opening to a shelved interior, 53½in. wide.
(Skinner) $1,725

An oak cupboard, North European, 16th century and later, with later three plank top and plain sides, with a pair of doors centred with large floral rosettes, 58in. wide. (Christie's) $16,043

An oak cupboard, English, late 19th century, with plank top and plain sides, the front with a central door and flanking uprights all with pierced gothic tracery detail, 50in. wide. (Christie's) $2,377

A French Provincial elm sacristy cupboard, with a carved front fitted with a drawer, a fielded panel door pierced with a window, a date *1802* and religious symbols, 26½in. (Woolley & Wallis) $575

A burr-oak press cupboard, Lakes/Lancashire, early 18th century, with a moulded cornice and quadruple panelled sides, the frieze initialled and dated *I.M.B. 1710*, above a pair of twin panelled doors, 53½in. wide. (Christie's) $2,852

An oak press cupboard, Westmorland, late 17th century, with an arcaded overhanging frieze with drop pendants, above a pair of moulded panel doors flanking a single panel, 48½in. wide. (Christie's) $3,922

An oak press cupboard, North Wales, early 18th century, frieze rail initialled and dated *R.R. 1703*, above a pair of twin fielded panelled doors, the base with four fielded panels and a further two later horizontal panels, 61in. wide. (Christie's) $2,317

An oak press cupboard, English, mid 17th century, profusely carved and inlaid overall, with dentil-moulded top and interlaced foliate frieze raised on bulbous carved elm supports, 63in. wide. (Christie's) $26,738

An oak press cupboard, possibly West Country, late 17th century, blind fret-carved overall, the upper section with a foliate lunette front and side frieze and with drop pendants, 58½in. wide. (Christie's) $6,086

An oak press cupboard, North Country, late 18th century, the dentil moulded cornice now with additional upper section, above an arcaded fret frieze and a pair of arched twin panelled doors, 67½in. wide. (Christie's) $7,631

A rare and unusual Regency rosewood brass inlaid and mounted lady's davenport, with pierced spindle brass gallery and crossbanded leather lined fall, enclosing a fitted interior, 19¾in. wide. (Christie's) $6,091

A George IV davenport, veneered in Brazilian rosewood, brass gallery, fitted interior, leather inset easel writing top above drawers, 20in. (Woolley & Wallis) $2,329

A Victorian walnut and burr-walnut davenport, the raised superstructure with a hinged lid enclosing a compartmentalized interior, above a serpentine fronted leather-lined sloping fall, 21¼in. wide. (Christie's) $1,900

A Victorian burr walnut piano-top davenport with pop-up stationery compartment, inset writing surface, 23in. wide. (Russell Baldwin & Bright) $4,480

Fine quality rosewood davenport with sliding top, four graduated drawers to the right hand section, dummy drawers to the left, English, circa 1800, 1ft. 8in. wide. (G.A. Key) $2,862

An early Victorian mahogany davenport, with veneered swivel top fitted a pen and ink drawer above four drawers, 18½in. (Woolley & Wallis) $870

A mid Victorian walnut and walnut grained serpentine davenport 55.5cm. wide. (Bonhams) $1,944

A mahogany davenport, early 19th century, the sliding superstructure with gallery and pigeon holes and compartments above with a pair of sliding doors, 20½in. wide. (Christie's) $3,076

A Victorian walnut and inlaid davenport, 53cm. wide. (Bonhams) $1,185

An Edwardian inlaid mahogany display cabinet of Sheraton influence, the concave sided plinth top above twin astragal glazed doors, 106cm. wide.
(Bristol) $1,047

A late Victorian mahogany glazed display cabinet, 122cm. wide.
(Bonhams) $524

An Edwardian mahogany pier display cabinet of oblong form with stringing and chequer banding, moulded and dentil cornice over trellis inlaid frieze, 29in. wide.
(Andrew Hartley) $1,750

A mahogany breakfront display cabinet, the carved and moulded cornice with pierced fret surmount, astragal glazed centre panel flanked on either side by a similar door, 51¼in. wide, early 20th century.
(Andrew Hartley) $3,234

A Louis XV style giltwood vitrine, circa 1890, the arched acanthus carved top centred by a cabochon crest, above two glazed doors and sides with floral moulded edges, 35in. wide.
(Bonhams) $770

A late Victorian ebonised display case, signed *C. Thorpe, Naturalist 1889*, containing a variety of exotic stuffed birds and a duckbill platypus, arranged around a pond, 73½in. high x 38in. wide.
(Bonhams) $2,512

Italian ivory tortoiseshell, and lapis lazuli mounted ebony display cabinet, Milan, circa 1880, the arched cresting with ivory balustrade above a pair of glazed doors, 48½in. wide.
(Skinner) $3,450

An Edwardian mahogany display cabinet, fitted with a leaded glazed cabinet door inset with three red glass panels, above a tilting sheet music drawer, 61cm. wide.
(Bonhams) $293

A 19th century Dutch walnut and floral marquetry display cabinet, with moulded cornice, single door with glazed canted sides, 46¼in. wide.
(Andrew Hartley) $2,310

A 17th century oak dresser, with moulded edged top, two lunette carved frieze drawers flanked by shaped brackets, 61in. wide.
(Andrew Hartley) $2,590

An 18th century oak enclosed dresser with three central drawers having brass drop handles, flanked on either side by a drawer over a cupboard door, 32in. high.
(Andrew Hartley) $2,100

A Georgian oak dresser base fitted with three drawers with shaped frieze and centre stile, square supports and potboard base.
(Brightwells) $6,909

An oak dresser, the boarded plate rack with moulded cornice, above three moulded edged shelves, the base with three frieze drawers, 65½in. wide, late 18th/early 19th century.
(Andrew Hartley) $5,024

An oak dresser, English, early 19th century, the associated boarded plate rack with moulded cornice and applied split moulding detail above three shelves flanking a central clock, 81in. wide.
(Christie's) $5,851

An oak dresser, English or Welsh, early 19th century, the boarded plate rack with plain overhanging frieze and moulded cornice, above three shelves, with three frieze drawers, 70in. wide.
(Christie's) $10,605

A large oak dresser, West Midlands, 19th century, the later-boarded associated plate rack with moulded cornice and shaped scrolling frieze, above four shelves flanked by cupboard doors, 96½in. wide.
(Christie's) $7,314

A large pine corner dresser, Montgomeryshire, late 18th/early 19th century, the open plate rack with moulded cornice and three shelves, with five frieze drawers and ogee arched aprons, 113in. wide. (Christie's) $4,571

An 18th century oak dresser, the delft rack with moulded cornice over three moulded edges shelves, the pot board base with three frieze drawers, 70½in. wide.
(Andrew Hartley) $6,006

A North Italian yew-wood, possibly pine inlaid kneehole desk, late 18th/early 19th century, in the Neo Classical taste, 42¼in. wide.
(Christie's) $11,763

A Smith Premier mahogany roll-top desk with integral, adjustable height, typewriter table, complete with Royal No. 5 typewriter, American, circa 1895, 122cm. wide.
(Auction Team Köln) $970

A George III mahogany partner's pedestal desk, the rectangular molded top inset with a panel of red tooled leather containing six drawers in the frieze, the lower parts each containing six drawers, 72¼in. wide.
(Christie's) $39,809

A George III mahogany kneehole desk, the rectangular molded top inset with a panel of red tooled leather containing nine drawers about a central recessed cupboard, 44½in. wide.
(Christie's) $3,257

A late Victorian mahogany roll top desk, 89cm. wide.
(Bonhams & Brooks) $1,406

A late George III mahogany pedestal desk, the molded rectangular top with green leather writing surface, above a fitted frieze drawer with central fluted ogee arch, 49¼in. wide.
(Christie's) $5,520

A walnut and brass bound pedestal desk, late 19th century, by Edwards and Roberts, in the French taste, the top of inverted breakfront outline with an inset tooled and green leather lined top, 48in. wide.
(Christie's) $2,896

A Victorian mahogany cylinder pedestal desk, by James Shoolbred & Co, with molded gallery and panelled fall enclosing a fitted interior, having a pull-out slide, 54in. wide.
(Christie's) $8,686

A late 19th century mahogany pedestal desk in the Aesthetic style, the breakfront leathered top surmounted by a gallery rail, above a central frieze drawer, flanked by two sets of three drawers, 107cm wide. (Bonhams) $810

A veneered pedestal desk, designed by Carl Malmsten, circa 1923, the desk decorated overall with floral motifs, central frieze drawer, twin pedestals below, 64½in. wide.
(Christie's) $16,185

A George III mahogany secrétaire kneehole desk, early 19th century, with a molded edge having a frieze drawer with fall inset with later tooled green leather panel, 42in. wide.(Christie's) $5,067

A Victorian walnut four-pedestal desk, with restoration, the crossbanded top inset with a panel of gilt tooled green leather, with a molded edge, the top 60in. wide.
(Christie's) $8,686

A mahogany desk, designed by Henry van de Velde for the Galerie Arnold, Dresden, circa 1905, shaped demi-lune form, central drawer flanked by single cabinet opening to reveal two shelves, 55½in. (Christie's) $17,038

A Victorian mahogany pedestal desk with galleried superstructure and writing slope, 121cm wide x 74cm. deep x 104cm. high.
(Bonhams & Brooks) $2,516

A George III mahogany architect's desk by Gillows, the molded rectangular hinged and ratcheted top above a secrétaire drawer enclosing a leather lined writing-slide, 49½in. wide.
(Christie's) $13,800

A late Victorian ebonised and ivory inlaid kneehole desk, with a red leather-lined top and nine drawers around the kneehole, inlaid with cornucopia and foliate arabesques, 51in. wide.
(Christie's) $1,533

A George I walnut kneehole desk, crossbanded overall, the quarter-veneered top above a frieze drawer and a kneehole, the door flanked on each side by three small drawers, 29in. wide.
(Christie's) $10,902

A George III mahogany kneehole desk, the rounded rectangular top above a fitted frieze drawer with a sliding leather-lined writing surface, 44½in. wide.
(Christie's) $4,940

A George III mahogany linen press with boxwood and ebony stringing, on splayed bracket feet, 131cm. wide. (Bearne's) $4,785

A mahogany linen press with arched molded cornice over two panelled doors with applied florets, two short over three long drawers below, 52in. wide. (Andrew Hartley) $2,464

A George III mahogany linen press, crossbanded and boxwood strung, the upper part with swan neck pediment and later urn finials, with dentil and pear-drop pendant frieze, 52in. wide.(Christie's) $5,088

A George III mahogany tulipwood, crossbanded and inlaid linen press, the upper part with swan-neck pediment, centered by a dentil platform with fluted tablet and frieze with radiating fan medallions, 59¾in. wide. (Christie's) $13,572

A George III mahogany and satinwood-banded linen press, the dentil molded cornice above a pair of flame figured panelled doors and two short and two long drawers below, 50in. wide. (Christie's) $2,467

A George IV mahogany and satinwood-banded linen press, the molded cornice and conch shell inlaid frieze above a pair of panelled cupboard doors with later inlaid ovals, raised on turned tapering feet, 51in. wide. (Christie's) $2,743

A mahogany bowfront linen press, early 19th century, decorated with ebonized lines, the molded cornice above a pair of panelled doors, 55in. wide. (Christie's) $4,124

A George III mahogany linen press, with a molded, line-inlaid cornice and inlaid fluted decoration to the frieze above a pair of panelled doors with inverted corners, 50in. wide. (Christie's) $2,214

George III mahogany linen press, the top with dentil cornice above two glazed doors, the corners of the panels carved with scrolls, 51½in. (Ewbank) $2,523

An early 20th century mahogany bow front linen press with satinwood inlay, 50in. wide. (Jacobs & Hunt) $3,520

A George III mahogany linen press, the upper part with a molded dentil cornice and fitted with trays enclosed by a pair of astragal panel doors, 51in. wide. (Christie's) $4,525

Federal mahogany veneer linen press, Boston, 1820-25, the three-part piece includes a veneered entablature with a central rectangle outlined in stringing, 48in. wide. (Skinner) $6,900

A mahogany and ebony inlaid linen press, early 19th century, the upper part with a molded arched cornice inlaid with tassel ornament, enclosed by a pair of re-entrant panel doors, 49in. wide. (Christie's) $3,108

A George III mahogany linen press, with a dentil molded cornice above a pair of shaped panelled doors enclosing sliding trays, with two short and two long drawers below, 49½in. wide. (Christie's) $2,467

Chippendale mahogany linen press, possibly North Shore, Massachusetts, late 18th century, the cornice molding overhangs the dentil-molded frieze, lower case 48in. wide. (Skinner) $29,900

A George III mahogany linen press, with a molded and brass edged cornice above a feather-banded frieze and a pair of panelled doors, 48in. wide. (Christie's) $4,277

A mahogany linen press, early 19th century, with a molded cornice above a pair of flame figured panelled doors, 53in. wide. (Christie's) $2,418

A late George III mahogany linen press, the molded cornice above a pair of panelled doors with inverted corners, 47¾in. wide. (Christie's) $3,236

A mahogany linen press, Regency, circa 1810, with reeded terminals and a pair of figured panel doors, 4ft.4in. wide.
(Sotheby's) $3,073

A fine Federal figured mahogany linen press, New York, circa 1815, in three parts, the removable reeded cornice above a mid-section with cupboard doors, 4ft. 8in. wide.
(Sotheby's) $7,800

A Regency ebony-inlaid mahogany linen press, inlaid to the front with scrolled lines and foliate motifs, 55in. wide.
(Christie's) $10,309

George III style polychrome decorated linen press, late 19th/early 20th century, rectangular moulded cornice over a pair of blind cabinet doors, 51¼in. wide.
(Skinner) $1,610

A Chippendale figured maple linen press, New York or New Jersey, circa 1780, in two parts; the upper section with stepped rectangular moulding above two arched panelled cupboard doors, width of case 45½in.
(Sotheby's) $9,775

Pennsylvania Chippendale cherry linen press, circa 1770-1800, with overhanging dentil moulded cornice, twin arched panelled doors, 48¾in. wide.
(Freeman) $10,080

A late 19th century inlaid mahogany clothes press in two stages, the upper with moulded cornice above a pair of cock beaded doors inlaid with central oval motifs, 42in. wide.
(Peter Francis) $1,264

An early 19th century Dutch oak linen cabinet with stepped cornice carved with drapery, 156cm. wide.
(Bearne's) $2,359

A George III mahogany linen press with pendant cornice over pair of solid panelled doors enclosing sliding trays, 3ft.8in. wide.
(Russell Baldwin & Bright)
                    $2,772

A late 18th century oak lowboy, one corner of the top with a repair, the drawers with old replaced brass handles, 31½in. wide.
(Woolley & Wallis) $725

An oak lowboy, Welsh, late 18th century, with moulded top and frieze drawer above an ogee arched fret-carved apron with smaller drawers, 34in. wide.
(Christie's) $2,435

A George III oak lowboy, 78.5cm. wide. (Bonhams) $628

Chippendale carved walnut high chest base, Pennsylvania, circa 1760-80, the moulded rectangular top with shaped corners over case of one long and three short thumb-moulded drawers, case 40½in. wide. (Skinner) $4,312

A George II oak lowboy, circa 1750, the rounded rectangular top above three drawers and raised on turned legs, 75cm. wide.
(Bonhams) $476

Queen Anne style carved walnut dressing table, Delaware Valley, 20th century the top with moulded edge and notched corners above a case with thumb-moulded drawers, 34in. wide.(Skinner) $4,025

Chippendale walnut dressing table, Delaware Valley, 18th century, the later moulded and notched top above a case with a scrolled skirt flanked by cabriole legs, case 28in. wide, 17½in. deep.
(Skinner) $5,462

A walnut crossbanded and feather-strung lowboy, early 18th century and later, the rectangular overhanging top quarter-veneered and with molded edge and rounded corners, 29¼in. wide.
(Christie's) $7,728

Queen Anne style oak lowboy, with antique elements, thumb-moulded top with re-entrant corners above three drawers on circular legs ending in pad feet, 34in. wide.
(Skinner) $920

Louis Philippe faux bamboo fall-front secrétaire à abattant, mid 19th century, rectangular case with a frieze drawer, above a fall front simulating drawer fronts.
(Skinner) $4,600

A George III mahogany secrétaire chest, early 19th century, in two sections, the upper part with a molded edge having a dummy drawer front fall, 47¼in. wide.
(Christie's) $4,343

Louis XV/XVI style tulipwood parquetry and marble-top semainière, late 19th century, with canted corners above seven drawers on angular cabriole legs, 28¾in. wide. (Skinner) $1,380

Classical mahogany and tiger maple bureau, Vermont, circa 1820-30, the upper section with three glove drawers over projecting case of one long cockbeaded drawer over three recessed long cockbeaded graduated drawers, 46¼in. wide. (Skinner) $1,150

Export camphorwood two-part campaign chest/desk, the rectangular top above two small drawers over a fold-out writing surface which opens to valanced compartments and small drawers, 41¾in. wide.
(Skinner) $3,335

A classical mahogany veneered secrétaire à abattant, Boston, 1820-1840, the rectangular top above a frieze concealing a drawer over a fall-front lid opening to a compartmented and leather-lined interior, 40½in. wide.
(Christie's) $6,463

A Dutch mahogany and fruitwood inlaid secrétaire à abattant, with fitted interior beneath a frieze drawer, two cupboard doors under, 18th century, 108.5cm. wide.
(Finarte) $7,665

A Victorian hardwood campaign chest, with an arrangement of long and short drawers including a central secrétaire drawer with a fall front, 45in. wide.
(Christie's) $1,682

Louis XVI brass mounted marble-top mahogany secrétaire à abattant, circa 1790, the rectangular top with canted corners above a conforming case fitted with a frieze drawer and a fall front, 34in. wide. (Skinner) $4,312

A George III mahogany crossbanded and inlaid secrétaire chest, with open shelved superstructure with lambrequin frieze and shaped side, possibly of a slightly later date, 31½in. wide. (Christie's) $6,332

A William IV period mahogany secrétaire, 54in. wide. (Dockrees) $960

A small William III walnut veneered fall front secrétaire chest, the molded cornice above a concave frieze drawer, 3ft.wide. (Woolley & Wallis) $6,560

A mahogany and crossbanded secrètaire cabinet-on-chest, 19th century, inlaid with boxwood lines and crossbanded in rosewood, the upper part fitted with by a pair of oval crossbanded and quarter-veneered panelled doors, 31in. wide. (Christie's) $5,451

A George III mahogany secrétaire chest, the fall front revealing a fitted interior of drawers, pigeon holes and cupboards, with two shaped panelled doors below enclosing slides, 42¼in. wide. (Christie's) $2,073

A Queen Anne walnut writing cabinet on stand, circa 1710, the molded cornice and cushion frieze drawer above a fall enclosing a fitted interior of drawers and pigeon holes around a cupboard door, 42in. wide. (Bonhams) $13,300

A North European mahogany secrétaire à abattant, mid 19th century, with a shaped, stepped top and frieze drawer flanked by rosewood corbels, 42in. wide. (Christie's) $1,680

A mahogany secrétaire press cupboard, 19th century, the upper section with a molded and diamond inlaid cornice, above a pair of flame panelled doors enclosing pullout slides, 50½in. wide. (Christie's) $987

A Regency rosewood gilt-metal mounted and parcel-gilt secrétaire on later stand, with frieze drawer above and fall front with laurel wreath motif with anthemion ornament to the corners and flanked by female herm pilasters, 38in. wide.(Christie's) $2,194

An early 19th century mahogany secrétaire cabinet, the top with small splash panel back above shaped panel front secrétaire drawer, 91cm. wide.
(Bristol) $1,008

A Napoleon III mahogany secrétaire à abattant, with a grey fossil marble top above a frieze drawer, the fall front revealing a fitted interior with leather-lined writing surface, 40½in.
(Christie's) $1,999

A secrétaire à abattant, early 19th century, with stepped top flanked by turned finials, with a cushion moulded frieze drawer, 42in. wide.
(Christie's) $2,479

An early 19th century mahogany secrétaire, the veneered top with a moulded edge, the fall flap fitted with a drawer inlaid with stringing, 3ft.7in. wide.
(Woolley & Wallis) $1,916

A Napoleon III ormolu-mounted parquetry and marquetry secrétaire on stand, circa 1870, the oval white marble top surmounted by a pierced three-quarter gallery rail, above a frieze-drawer, 23in. wide.
(Christie's) $25,909

A George III colonial camphorwood campaign secrétaire chest of drawers, late 18th/19th century, in two sections, the fall enclosing a fitted interior of drawers and pigeon holes around a door, 39in. wide.
(Bonhams) $6,512

A Victorian mahogany military secrétaire chest, having brass corners to the two part carcase, the top with a fall front fitted drawer, 3ft.4in.
(Woolley & Wallis) $2,954

A Baltic mahogany secrétaire à abattant, circa 1840, the rectangular cushion top with a demi lune plinth and foliate carved outset corners, 43in. wide.
(Bonhams) $2,926

A Louis XVI brass-inlaid mahogany campaign secrétaire à abattant, by Pierre Garnier, the rectangular fall-front with monogrammed escutcheon enclosing a fitted interior, on a stand with folding rectangular legs, 35¼in. wide.
(Christie's) $34,466

A 19th century mahogany secrétaire bookcase, the moulded cornice over two raised and fielded panel doors enclosing drawers and pigeon holes, 38½in. wide.
(Andrew Hartley) $4,312

A mahogany cabinet on chest, the top with a moulded cornice with satinwood band above shelves enclosed by a pair of glazed tracery doors, 3ft.8in. wide.
(Woolley & Wallis) $3,388

A mahogany and inlaid secrétaire bookcase, early 19th century, with boxwood stringing, the upper part with a moulded cornice and enclosed by a pair of glazed astragal doors, 47½in. wide, 91in. high. (Christie's) $2,743

A Regency inlaid mahogany secrétaire bookcase, with geometric banded frieze above twin astragal glazed doors, the base with twin oval panel inlaid secrétaire drawer, 94.5cm. wide. (Bristol)
$3,062

A Danish painted pine bureau cabinet, late 19th century, the broken arched cornice with a central pediment and applied acanthus carving above a pair of panelled doors with raised moulded cartouches, 45½in. wide.
(Christie's) $2,073

A George III faded mahogany secrétaire bookcase, the top with old alteration and replaced shelves, having a dentil cornice with a swan neck pediment, 3ft.2in. wide.
(Woolley & Wallis) $3,140

A Regency style mahogany secrétaire bookcase, with cavetto cornice above twin astragal glazed doors, on turned tapered squat bun feet, 97cm. wide.
(Bristol) $2,920

A late George III mahogany secrétaire bookcase, the upper section with a dentil moulded cornice and a pair of geometrically astragal glazed doors, 44½in. wide.
(Christie's) $2,764

A George III mahogany secrétaire bookcase, the top with a key dentil moulded frieze and a swan neck pediment terminating in carved chrysanthemum heads, 3ft.9in. wide.
(Woolley & Wallis) $1,232

Stickley Brothers settle, attributed, nine vertical slats, three vertical side slats, 65¼in. (Skinner) £2,070

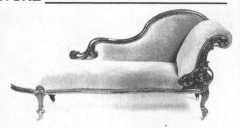

A Victorian mahogany chaise longue, with carved scrolled back and front, on knopped cabriole supports with castors, width 120cm. (Bristol) $1,088

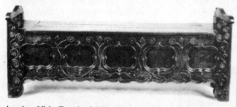

Louis XV Provincial brass mounted bench, late 18th/19th century, with hinged rectangular seat, downscrolled arms with spindle galley, 71in. wide. (Skinner) $1,725

Federal mahogany carved square-back upholstered sofa, probably New Hampshire, circa 1815, the straight crest continuing to shaped sides with carved arms, 78½in. wide. (Skinner) $2,415

Fine Victorian carved walnut double chair back chaise longue, the pierced and buttoned back above an overstuffed seat, shaped frieze and floral carved cabriole supports. (Lawrences) $2,335

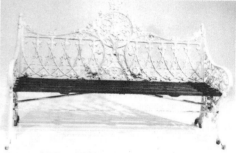

A Coalbrookdale cast iron garden bench of Gothic pattern, the pierced arched tracery back centred with an armorial shield, 60in. wide. (Andrew Hartley) $2,720

An Edwardian mahogany sofa, the buttoned back and sprung seat green damask upholstered, on cabriole supports with leaf carving and brass castors, 142cm. wide. (Bristol) $886

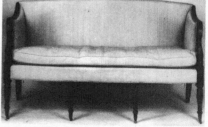

Antique American Sheraton sofa, in mahogany with four ribbed front legs and two rear legs. Cut down from a larger size, 5ft. long. (Eldred's) $990

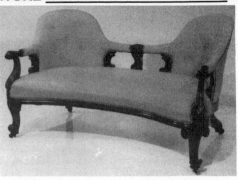

A Victorian carved walnut framed sofa, the oval padded back with arched crest, padded arms on scrolled supports, on cabriole front legs, 16in. wide. (Andrew Hartley) $1,056

A rosewood framed double backed sofa with scroll carved centre splat, scrolled arms on shaped supports, on flower carved front supports. (Andrew Hartley) $1,760

A Knole sofa, early 20th century, upholstered in gilt damask, the rectangular back and sides with acorn shaped finial above a squab cushion, on brass castors, 61½in. wide. (Christie's) $1,288

Cast iron garden settee, John McLean maker, New York, the three-panel pierced back joined to the scrolled arms on the rectangular seat with Gothic valance, painted black, 46in. wide. (Skinner) $862

A George II carved mahogany diminutive camelback sofa, probably 19th century, the shaped back above an overupholstered serpentine-fronted seat flanked by outscrolled arms on shell and leaf-carved knees, 4ft.9in. wide. (Sotheby's) $6,325

A Victorian rosewood framed settee with string and marquetry inlay, the serpentine padded back and incurving arms on pierced foliate splats each centred by a marquetry panel depicting a basket of fruit, 59in. wide. (Andrew Hartley) $2,240

A Regency rosewood scroll end sofa, decorated with scrolling brackets, raised on splay legs and brass paw feet fitted castors, 88in. long.
(Anderson & Garland) $1,485

Italian Renaissance walnut and marquetry cassapanca, rectangular back over hinged seat, scrolled arms, shaped moulded base, 70½in. long.
(Skinner) $1,380

Classical mahogany carved veneer sofa, New England, 1820–40, the veneered cylindrical crest ends in leaf carved volutes above an upholstered seat and rolled veneered seat rail on leaf carved supports ending in carved paw feet, 92in. wide.
(Skinner) $1,610

A William IV style settee with raised camel back and scroll arms, the tapering turned legs mounted with ormolu water leaves upholstered in coral embossed heavy cotton loose weave fabric. (Dee Atkinson & Harrison) $2,970

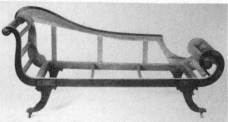

Carved mahogany and bird's-eye maple veneer Grecian sofa, 1805–20, Middle Atlantic States, with scrolled and reeded arm and foot, continuing to a similar reeded seat rail with inlaid dies, 75in. long.
(Skinner) $3,680

Victorian child-size sofa, in walnut with carved grape and leaf design, 58in. long.
(Eldred's) $247

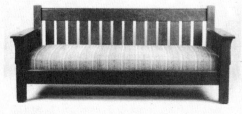

Antique American Mammy's bench, in yellow paint with stencilled decoration, unusual long length of 5ft.
(Eldred's) $770

J.M. Young settle, uneven arm, four side slats, fourteen vertical back slats, paper label, 34½in. high. 81½in. wide, 31½in. (Christie's) $2,185

A French mahogany chaise longue in the Empire taste, the overscrolled back with squab cushion and forward scrolled foot-rest, parts early 19th century, 66in. long. (Christie's) $4,048

A Victorian walnut framed sofa, the padded deep buttoned back with a channelled arched and foliate scroll-carved cresting, curved ends and a serpentine seat, 81in. wide. (Christie's) $1,288

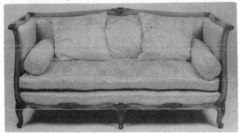

An Edwardian French walnut framed sofa, the rectangular back and sides with upholstered panels enclosed within moulded and flower carved frame, 187cm. across. (Phillips) $3,200

Arts and Crafts settle, uneven arm, fifteen vertical back slats, five side slats, original dark brown finish, 75½in. wide. (Skinner) $2,530

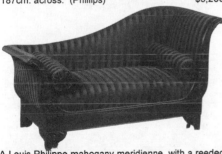

A Louis Philippe mahogany meridienne, with a reeded frame, downswept back between outswept ends with foliate carved terminals, 65in. wide. (Christie's) $3,312

Modern Louis XVI style green painted and upholstered armchair and ottoman, with Neoclassical-style print cotton in greens, blues, and beige, 37in. high. (Skinner) $1,265

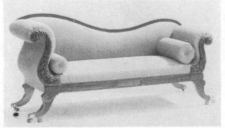

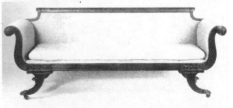

A Regency carved mahogany settee, with damage, 83in. wide. (Dockree's) $1,402

Classical carved mahogany veneer sofa, attributed to the workshop of Duncan Phyfe, New York City, 1815–25, the rolled single panelled crest, above scrolled and reeded arms punctuated with carved rosettes, 85in. long. (Skinner) $4,600

Regency brass inlaid beechwood suede-upholstered récamier, second quarter 19th century, with raised end carved with a shell, reeded sloping backrest inlaid and carved with foliage, 76in. long.
(Skinner) $4,600

A French upholstered beechwood canapé, 19th century, with an undulating floral carved top-rail with part padded arms and channelled downswept supports, with a conforming seat, on flowerhead carved cabriole legs, previously painted, 58in. wide.
(Christie's) $329

A central European mahogany three-seater sofa, mid 19th century, with a tablet line-inlaid top-rail and three urn-shaped and eagle headed decorated vertical splats, 73½in. wide. (Christie's) $1,480

A French mahogany and gilt-metal mounted daybed, late 19th century, in the Empire style, padded swan neck ends, the panelled frieze centered by a medallion of paired winged lions, 67in. long.
(Christie's) $2,961

Batic neo-classical carved mahogany sofa, circa 1825, with panelled cresting, padded arms carved with lion heads and anthemia, above an upholstered seat on shaped feet, 68in. long. (Skinner) $2,185

A small Victorian walnut sofa, with a bowed deep buttoned back and sides and an incurved seat upholstered in floral tapestry effect covers, on carved turned legs with brass capped castors, 74in. wide.
(Christie's) $1,594

A Victorian walnut and upholstered sofa, the shaped deep buttoned back with a central padded oval panel with pierced foliate supports and cresting, 77in. wide.
(Christie's) $604

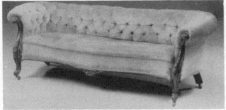

A large mid Victorian Chesterfield type walnut sofa, with button-down back and sides, overswept arm terminals and serpentine seat, 89in. long.
(Christie's) $2,125

Dutch walnut long settee, 19th century, with quintuple chairback, each with cockpen lattice design and outscrolled arms on cabriole legs, 128in. long.
(Skinner) $4,025

Victorian beechwood faux grained chaise longue, circa 1850, of typical form with scrolled end, rounded seat rail, and scrolled feet, on castors, 70in. long.
(Skinner) $2,300

Italian Renaissance Revival walnut settee, late 19th century, with triple chairback and turned legs, carved allover with foliage and cherubs, 51in. long.
(Skinner) $805

A George III mahogany frame scroll-arm sofa, with serpentine stuff-over back and shaped sides and stuff-over seat with cushion, on square tapering legs joined by H-stretchers, 75in. wide. (Christie's) $3,046

A Victorian deep buttoned Chesterfield covered in floral patterned upholstery, the raked back and outscrolled arms above a padded seat, on turned bulbous feet and castors, including a loose cover, 74in. long. (Christie's) $1,280

A giltwood and upholstered sofa, 19th century, in the Régence style, the padded back within a channelled frame with an undulating top-rail decorated with flowers, scrolling foliage and berries, 80in. wide.
(Christie's) $3,291

Early Victorian carved oak chaise longue, circa 1845, one end carved with foliage and gadrooning, on circular gadrooned legs, on casters, 64in. long.
(Skinner) $1,380

Painted and decorated settee, Pennsylvania, 1825-35, the shaped crest above three splats, curving arms, and a rolled plank, original yellow ground paint with fruit and leaf olive-green decoration, 78½in. wide. (Skinner) $3,738

Windsor 'Fancy' settee, New York City, circa 1815, the crest rail divided into four sections over pierced horizontal splats divided by spherules flanked by curving arms above a seat, 85in. long. (Skinner) $3,738

A classical carved mahogany sofa, New York, 1815-1825, the rod-back crest above a rectangular upholstered back flanked by similar rod-shaped arms over column-turned supports, on leaf-carved and tapering lobed feet fitted with castors, 79in. wide. (Christie's) $7,475

A Classical carved mahogany recamier, New York, 1820-1830, the backscrolling slanted crest flanked on one side by an upholstered outward scrolling arm rest and on the other by an inward scrolling footrest, 71in. wide. (Christie's) $7,050

A George III mahogany humpback sofa, with a padded back and seat and overscrolled arms, on square channelled legs, 74¾in. wide. (Christie's) $1,809

A Victorian mahogany sofa with an undulating padded back centered by a floral cresting, overscrolled padded arms, on foliate-decorated scrolled feet, 90in. wide. (Christie's) $493

A classical paint-decorated and gilt-stencilled Grecian couch, possibly the workshop of Duncan Phyfe (1768-1854), New York, circa 1820, the scrolled crestrail decorated with gilt-stencilled flourishes, 81in. wide. (Christie's) $11,750

A pair of Baltic parcel-gilt and white-painted sofas, second quarter 19th century, each with a triple oval panelled toprail with berried laurel flanking paterae, above a padded back, 79½in. wide. (Woolley & Wallis) $6,601

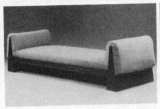

Ernest Boiceau, day bed, 1930s, macassar ebony frame, triangular upright supports, deeply upholstered in gray fabric, 232cm. wide. (Sotheby's) $31,290

Biedermeier fruitwood and ebonized bench, 19th century, outward scrolling sides with curved ebonized slats, on saber legs, 70in. long. (Skinner) $3,335

A black-painted wrought iron garden seat, 19th century, the pierced back and seat with an overscrolled top-rail, 108in. wide. (Christie's) $5,962

A mahogany hump-back sofa, 19th century, with padded overscrolled arms, on square tapering legs joined by a stretcher, restorations, 75in. wide. (Christie's) $839

An 18th century oak curved settle with panelled highback, shaped ends with arm rests, the box seat with hinged lids, 4ft.4in. wide. (Brightwells) $4,576

Archizoom Associati, a Safari seating unit, designed 1968, for Poltronova, comprising two rectangular and two square white fiberglass forms, each with scalloped seating areas, 100 x 84in. (Christie's) $13,024

A Central European painted boxseat settle, 19th century, painted overall with zig-zag and geometrical patterns, the solid panelled back-rail with central baluster gallery, 78in. long. (Christie's) $863

A patented metamorphic oak dining table/settee, circa 1928, the panelled table top supported by reeded and square section end supports, converting to a small settee, including a copy of the patent specification, 53½in. wide. (Christie's) $638

An oak corner settle, North Country, 18th century, the rectangular back with six arched fielded panels, above a drop-in seat, 72in. wide corner to corner. (Christie's) $2,568

Limbert oak daybed, America, early 20th century, two wide over two narrow headboards, curved slanted sideboards, 79in. long. (Skinner) $862

An antique elm and stained wood curved-back settle with shaped sides and scrolled arms, 6ft.8in. wide. (Brightwells) $3,925

A 19th century daybed, upholstered red material, the roll over back with a tassel, a bolster cushion, the seat on turned walnut legs to castors, 6ft. (Woolley & Wallis) $1,054

A mahogany serpentine sideboard, 19th century, with an undulating apron, central frieze drawer flanked by a deep drawer to either side, 73in. wide. (Christie's) $4,705

A George III style mahogany and rosewood banded serpentine fronted sideboard, the central drawer flanked by a deep drawer and a cupboard, all with boxwood stringing, 53½in. wide. (Wintertons) $1,050

A Regency twin pedestal sideboard, with scroll-end back rail above drop center flanked by pedestals, one with fitted cellaret drawer, 166.5cm. wide. (Bristol) $2,924

A Victorian mahogany and ebonized pedestal sideboard, the mirrored superstructure with shelf and floral tiled frieze, above three drawers, 84in. wide. (Christie's) $1,447

A late Victorian oak and ebonized sideboard, with a mirrored gallery back and a shelf supported by turned uprights and panels carved with flowers and rosettes, 75in. wide. (Christie's) $1,480

A George III mahogany small bowfront sideboard, the top above a frieze drawer and a shaped arch, flanked on each side by a deep drawer, 48in. wide. (Christie's) $3,271

An early Victorian mahogany pedestal sideboard, the panelled gallery back with an open shelf and foliate scroll carved brackets above three bolection molded frieze drawers. (Christie's) $2,138

George III style inlaid mahogany diminutive sideboard, late 19th century, with rectangular top and four drawers on reeded circular legs, 38½in.(Skinner) $2,530

A late George III mahogany and inlaid bowfront sideboard, the top with a reeded edge, possibly of a later date, containing a central drawer in the arched apron flanked by a short and a deep drawer, 57in. wide. (Christie's) $7,238

392

A William IV mahogany pedestal sideboard, of reverse breakfront outline, with applied wreaths on a low gallery back above three frieze drawers and an open central section, 84in. wide.
(Christie's) $2,479

Victorian mahogany sideboard, arched back crested with acanthus leaf mount and applied with scrolls, serpentine central drawer, 58in.
(G.A. Key) $1,113

A Sheraton Revival satinwood sideboard of demi lune form with kingwood banding and stringing, the segmented veneered top with harewood ovals centered by a fan, 54in. wide.
(Andrew Hartley) $3,058

A late Victorian Aesthetic walnut sideboard, the mirror back with turned gallery frieze and inset with four hand carved emblematic circular panels, serpent, hare, goose and pineapple, 190cm. wide.
(Wintertons) $1,470

A Victorian mahogany mirror backed sideboard, 132cm. wide.
(Bonhams & Brooks) $1,001

An early 19th century mahogany sideboard, 85in. wide.
(Dockrees) $2,720

Gustav Stickley oak sideboard, New York, circa 1909, no. 817, three section backsplash with plate rail, rectangular top above four graduating center drawers, 70in. long. (Skinner) $12,650

A George III mahogany bowfront sideboard, with a central frieze drawer flanked to the right by a deep cellaret drawer and two drawers to the left, 56½in. wide.
(Christie's) $4,112

British Colonial bone and ebony inlaid padouk wood sideboard, early 19th century, the top with slight concave ends above three drawers and turned pendants, 51in. wide. (Skinner) $9,775

A late Victorian mahogany serving table, the raised back with arched center and carved shell, gadroon edged frieze with two drawers, 72in. long. (Andrew Hartley) $4,448

A Regency mahogany and ebonized pedestal sideboard, with a scrolled roundel decorated gallery back above a sunken bowed potboard with two panelled drawers, 71in. wide. (Christie's) $4,935

A George III mahogany sideboard, with satinwood crossbanding and string inlay, bow fronted central section with napery drawer, flanked on either side by a drawer over a cupboard, 73in. wide. (Andrew Hartley) $2,310

An Irish George IV mahogany sideboard, the gallery with bead-and-reel molding and anthemions to each end, above a shaped, eared top with gadrooned and leaf molding, 97in. wide. (Christie's) $9,085

A heavily carved oak sideboard, 19th century, carved throughout with foliage, fruit, mask-centered cartouches and lion masks and with panels depicting biblical scenes, 106cm. wide.(Christie's) $6,199

A large burr-walnut ships sideboard, early 20th century, with a brass rail gallery, three frieze drawers and panelled cupboards, inscribed to the underside of the top *SS. Montcalm Cabin Dining Saloon*, 110in. wide. (Christie's) $700

A mahogany crossbanded and line-inlaid serpentine sideboard, early 20th century, with two center drawers, a deep cellaret drawer and cupboard, on square tapering legs with spade feet, 60in. wide. (Christie's) $1,480

A Federal inlaid mahogany sideboard, Maryland, 1790-1810, the rectangular top with bowed front with line inlaid edge above a conforming case fitted with one long drawer with line inlay flanked on one side by two short sham drawers revealing a bottle drawer, on the other by two short drawers, 66in. wide.
(Christie's) $56,400

A Victorian oak sideboard, the panelled gallery carved with masks, fruit and foliage with a rope-twist cresting and reeded finials. (Christie's) $4,250

An early Victorian mahogany pedestal sideboard, the panelled ledge back with acanthus and foliate scroll cresting and ornament, containing three drawers in the frieze, 79in. wide. (Christie's) $3,981

A 19th century mahogany sideboard, crossbanded with stringing and checker banding, the shaped front with concave center having drawer over arched apron flanked on one side by a cupboard and on the other by a deep drawer, 16in. wide.
(Andrew Hartley) $2,556

A George IV mahogany sideboard, inlaid overall with ebonized lines, the scrolled gallery with floral patera, above a bowfront rectangular top with two frieze drawers and flanked by a pedestal to each side, 78in. wide. (Christie's) $3,271

A mahogany, satinwood crossbanded and inlaid demi-lune sideboard, 19th century, containing a drawer in the arched apron flanked by a short drawer and deeper drawer below to one side and deep cellaret drawer to the other with liftout compartments between enclosed cupboards, 72¼in. wide.
(Christie's) $8,324

A Scottish figured mahogany and ebony inlaid sideboard, the inverted breakfront top above frieze drawer and inlaid shaped-edge recess flanked by cellaret drawer and cupboard with twist carved shaped corners, 193cm. wide.
(Bristol) $4,116

Federal cherry and bird's-eye maple veneered half sideboard, probably Vermont, circa 1825, the top with ovolo corners above a recessed desk with two cockbeaded sliding doors opening to a fitted interior, 48½in. wide.
(Skinner) $7,475

A substantial late Victorian carved oak mirror back sideboard, with swan neck crest over shield shaped central mirror flanked by two further mirrors above shelves and foliate carved panels, 216cm. wide.
(Bristol) $1,727

A Victorian mahogany mirror backed pedestal sideboard, the arched mirror frame carved with a trailing vine, the base with serpentine fronted white marble top, 84in. wide.
(Andrew Hartley) $3,920

Classical mahogany and mahogany veneer sideboard, Boston or New York, circa 1830, the gallery with beaded edge joining two end plinths with brass inlay and rosewood panels, 42in. wide.
(Skinner) $4,313

An Art Nouveau mahogany sideboard, in the manner of Liberty's, the back with ripple moulded cornice above glass panel twin cupboard doors applied with pierced whiplash curve copper fronts, 138cm. wide.
(Bristol) $1,884

A Classical carved cherrywood and figured maple sideboard, signed *I.M.E.*, Salem, Massachusetts, dated *1836*, the rectangular top surmounted by three short drawers and a backsplash, 4ft.6in. wide.
(Sotheby's) $2,875

An oak sideboard by Robert 'Mouseman' Thompson, the rectangular adzed top above two frieze and three long drawers, flanked by fielded cupboard doors enclosing shelves.
(Christie's) $15,627

A small Sheraton period bowfront sideboard, mahogany veneered with tulipwood banding edged with stringing, 4ft. wide.
(Woolley & Wallis) $6,160

Classical mahogany veneer sideboard, Boston, 1820-30, the centre concave drawer is flanked by end pedestals with lift-top lined moulded storage compartments, 81in. wide.
(Skinner) $43,700

An Arts & Crafts oak sideboard, the low back with inset enamel plaques, the break front with central drawer flanked by open shelves, 170.5cm. wide.
(Bristol) $1,806

A George III mahogany sideboard, crossbanded with stringing, bowed centre section with deep drawer over arched frieze, 70¼in. wide.
(Andrew Hartley) $2,940

An Edwardian mahogany sideboard by Warings, of Georgian design, with satinwood and chequer banding and stringing, 72in. wide.
(Andrew Hartley) $1,680

A George IV mahogany pedestal sideboard, the low raised back fitted with cutlery drawers and sliding compartments, four drawers and two cupboards under, 7ft.8in. wide.
(Brightwells) $4,725

Good quality pollard oak sideboard by Lamb of Manchester, the back elaborately moulded with rosettes in the manner of William Morris, circa late 19th/early 20th century, 8ft. wide. (G.A. Key) $2,826

Regency inlaid mahogany sideboard, early 19th century, rectangular top above drawers and doors on square tapered legs ending in spade feet, 66in. wide.
(Skinner) $1,150

A stripped light oak sideboard, in the style of the Guild of Handicrafts, 140cm. wide.(Bonhams) $169

A demi-lune flame mahogany and ormolu mounted Empire dresser, with black marble top over two drawers and four doors flanked by caryatid supports, late 19th century. (Galerie Moderne) $4,072

A Regency mahogany pedestal sideboard, circa 1820, a long shaped central drawer and napery drawer, restorations, 218cm. wide.
(Bonhams) $2,100

Early 19th century mahogany small bow fronted sideboard, central frieze drawer flanked on either side by cupboards, raised on slender ring turned cylindrical supports, terminating in peg feet, 42½in.
(G.A. Key) $3,234

A Sheraton period serpentine sideboard, mahogany veneered, the crossbanded top inlaid with a central marquetry oval fan and inlaid stringing, 5ft.½in., possibly Irish.
(Woolley & Wallis) $8,008

Gustav Stickley oak sideboard, Syracuse, New York, circa 1902, gallery top over two short drawers and a long drawer, two cupboard doors below, 59¾in. wide.
(Skinner) $32,200

Painted wood ring-toss game on stand, America, probably 20th century, the white painted rectangular board extending nine black point numbered pegs, 56in. high. (Skinner) $460

An Edwardian fiddle back mahogany and satinwood cross banded two tier étagère, 55cm. wide. (Bonhams & Brooks) $888

A Victorian walnut folio stand, the twin rests with interlaced pierced arched slats applied with simulated bamboo half moldings with unusual pull-cord adjustment to the slopes, 30in. wide. (Christie's) $2,715

A Coalbrookdale cast iron walking stick stand, dated *1879*, the openwork rectangular frame with twelve ringed apertures and turned finials, 24½in. long. (Christie's) $3,981

A Federal inlaid walnut stand, North Shore, Massachusetts or New Hampshire, 1790-1810, the rectangular top with serpentine sides above a conforming frame with inlaid birch panels, 15½in. wide. (Christie's) $3,525

A Classical carved mahogany stand, New York, 1815-1830, the shaped oval top above a ring and urn-turned and carved shaft over a circular pedestal, 25¾in. wide. (Christie's) $10,350

A 19th century walnut folio stand, 92cm. wide. (Bonhams & Brooks) $1,155

A 19th century butler's tray on a later folding stand, 70cm. wide. (Bonhams & Brooks) $330

A George III carved beech jardinière stand, circa 1790, the top 42cm. diameter. (Bonhams & Brooks) $1,425

A late 19th century oak hall stand, probably French, the upper part with molded arched cornice with female mask and palm spray with finials, 27½in. wide.
(Christie's) $3,257

A black and gold decorated plant stand, 59cm. wide.
(Bonhams & Brooks) $136

A French carved beech easel, early 20th century, the openwork writhen frame with spiral fluted uprights, the pierced cresting with gothic tracery and crocketed finials, 68in. high.
(Christie's) $2,895

Josef Urban and Berthold Löffler, lectern, 1908, mahogany, the slanted, shaped rectangular top with inset red leather writing surface and nickel-plated metal panel, 84cm. wide.
(Sotheby's) $10,440

A pair of Italian walnut and parcel-gilt pedestals, 19th century, possibly incorporating some earlier elements, each with eared rectangular top above a dentilled frieze, 20½in. wide.
(Christie's) $5,006

A late Victorian or Edwardian mahogany walking stick stand, late 19th or early 20th century, the demi-lune top with forty-nine apertures, on three turned tapering supports, 37½in. high.
(Christie's) $2,715

A Victorian mahogany pedestal, 19th century, the top above a fluted frieze, the front with panelled door and raised molding, the interior with a drawer and division, 37in. high. (Christie's) $3,077

André Arbus, cocktail trolley, 1940s, sycamore, rectangular top on tapering legs, two with wheels, the frieze with two pull-out handles with rectangular metal handle, 24in. wide. (Sotheby's) $13,920

A mid Victorian mahogany and marble hall stand, circa 1870, 125cm. wide.
(Bonhams & Brooks) $930

A William IV rosewood duet stand, the adjustable sheet rest with pierced lyre decoration, triform platform base on turned pad feet. (Dreweatt Neate) $2,888

A pair of Siena marble, bronze and gilt-bronze guéridons, 20th century, each with a circular marble top within a cast border, 62½in. diameter. (Sotheby's) $10,310

Painted and decorated chamberstand, New England, early 19th century, the shaped stencil-decorated splashboard above the wash stand and the medial shelf, 18¼in. wide. (Skinner) $345

Tiger maple, bird's-eye maple and maple chamber stand, probably Pennsylvania, circa 1825, the scrolled gallery above a rectangular top and drawer on four ring-turned legs, 21¾in. wide. (Skinner) $1,150

A Federal red- and black-painted poplar and pine splayed leg one-drawer stand, Pennsylvania, circa 1830, the square top above a frieze drawer on reel-turned tapering legs, 21¼in. wide. (Sotheby's) $1,810

A carved gilt-wood and pietra dura guéridon, Italian, circa 1860, with a circular black marble top centred by a spray of flowers, 71.5cm. high. (Sotheby's) $7,498

A Bavarian carved wood hall-stand, late 19th century, in the form of a bear and a cub seated on a branch, on a naturalistic base fitted with a drip pan, 78in. high. (Christie's) $11,040

Arts & Crafts oak tabouret, America, early 20th century, square top over canted sides with tree and star cut-outs, medium brown finish, 20¼in. high. (Skinner) $201

Classical mahogany veneer chamber stand with dressing glass, New England, 1825-35, the scrolled supports with attached dressing glass, 36½in. wide.
(Skinner) $2,645

A George IV mahogany and parcel gilt bidet stand, attributed to Tatham, Bailey & Saunders, the moulded rectangular removable cover above a frame, 24in. wide.
(Christie's) $6,440

Cherry and maple stand, New England, late 18th century, the square top overhangs the shaped base on four block and turned legs, 17½in. wide. (Skinner) $862

A Victorian walnut folio stand, the adjustable pierced sides on end standards joined by flattened stretcher, on bun feet, 28in. wide.
(Christie's) $4,124

An Edwardian polished brass walking stick stand, the tubular frame with sixteen divisions, the cast iron base with twin retractable trays, 38in. wide.
(Christie's) $1,677

A Victorian burr walnut crossbanded and satinwood strung music stand, the hinged moulded rectangular top with a fretwork three quarter gallery, 64cm. wide.
(Cheffins) $3,180

A Victorian brass-mounted oak hall stand, late 19th century, the backplate divided by balustraded galleries and with platform to the top, 24¼in. wide.
(Christie's) $3,088

A late Regency mahogany three division folio stand, with downcurved dividers, on ring-turned tapering legs, 32½in. wide.
(Christie's) $2,362

A Scottish Victorian walnut boot-stand, the pierced handle toprail with turned finials and pegs above a scalloped tier for boots, 25¾in. wide. (Christie's) $2,944

Arts and Crafts plantstand, original finish, 29½in. high.
(Skinner) $402

Alvar Aalto for Finmar, tea trolley (No.98), designed 1935–36, birch, laminated frame, black rubber tyres, 35½in. long.
(Sotheby's) $3,539

Arts and Crafts drink stand, original finish, 21½in. wide.
(Skinner) $460

A rosewood and marquetry casket on stand, Charles X, circa 1830, the upper part of sarcophagus form, the hinged top with marquetry foliage, 64cm. wide.
(Sotheby's) $5,692

A pair of gilt-bronze and parquetry pedestals, French, circa 1890, in the manner of Riesener, each with a white marble top above a tapering body, 125cm. high.
(Sotheby's) $15,180

A mahogany boot rack, part 19th century, the arched top rail with pegs protruding from either side and brass carrying handle, 27¾in. wide. (Christie's) $920

A bentwood hall stand, the arched top flanked by S-shaped bentwood hooks, above slatted projecting shelf and single frieze drawer, 35½in. wide. (Christie's) $517

A large mahogany cheval linen airer, George IV, circa 1825, the two turned and graduated tiers with tapered rectanguar supports, 6ft. wide. (Sotheby's) $3,073

Federal mahogany reading stand with canterbury, Albany, New York, early 19th century, the stand above a ring-turned tapering post on a rectangular shaped canterbury, 22¼in. wide.
(Skinner) $3,105

Arts and Crafts plantstand, cut-out design, original finish, 30¼in. high. (Skinner) $258

A pair of Colonial padouk tripod torchères, mid-18th century, each with a rosewood hexagonal top with pierced brass gallery, supported by three C-scrolls, 20in. total diameter. (Christie's) $57,270

Gustav Stickley magazine stand, no. 72, three shelves, paper label, original finish, 22in. wide. (Skinner) $3,795

Aesthetic Movement ebonised, polychrome incised, and parcel-gilt pedestal, New York, circa 1878, Kimbel and Cabus, octagonal top, shaped support, stepped plinth base, 37½in. high. (Skinner) $977

A pair of mahogany luggage stands, second quarter 19th century, each with rectangular slatted tops, raised on ringed tapering legs and castors, 2ft. 5in. wide. (Sotheby's) $5,377

A Wardle pottery stickstand, tubeline decorated with stylised flowers and foliage on sinuous stems, in shades of brown and yellow, 56cm. high. (Christie's) $690

An Arts and Crafts oak umbrella stand with close-nailed copper decoration, with original drip-pan, 18in. wide. (Christie's) $189

A brass-bound hardwood jardinière, 19th century, of oval shape, with slatted sides, on rectangular splayed legs, 26in. wide. (Christie's) $662

Grain painted pine stand, New England, early 19th century, the top with shaped corners above a single drawer and square tapering legs, 18in. wide. (Skinner) $1,725

A 19th century rosewood X framed stool, the overstuffed seat in gros point covering, shaped scroll carved supports joined by a turned stretcher, 22in. wide. (Andrew Hartley) $1,330

Two of a set of four oak back stools, of Yorkshire type, the back with scroll finials on square section uprights, two crescent shaped cross splats, carved with scroll work and with turned pendant, 17th century and later. (Andrew Hartley) (Four) $1,668

A beech stool, the saddle shaped seat, with pen work of a knight in armor, on horseback, the four cabriole legs with stretchers. (Woolley & Wallis) $207

A 19th century mahogany piano stool, with overstuffed adjustable circular top raised on four reeded legs with splayed feet, 13¼in. wide. (Andrew Hartley) $336

A pair of mahogany stools, 20th century, of Louis XVI style, each with squab cushion, above a panelled rail with foliate corner-panels, 30½in. wide. (Christie's) $5,658

A 19th century mahogany stool of square form, the overstuffed top with tapestry covering, raised on four reeded tapering legs, 14½in. wide. (Andrew Hartley) $665

A George I mahogany stool of rounded oblong form with drop in upholstered seat, shaped frieze, cabriole front legs and pad feet, 15in. wide. (Andrew Hartley) $556

An ebonized and parcel gilt piano stool, the square padded hinged seat to a chinoiserie decorated frieze with a gadroon edge, on shell carved cabriole legs, 21in. (Woolley & Wallis) $382

A Victorian mahogany X framed stool, the oblong top with gros point covering, scrolled base with roundels joined by a pole stretcher, 19¾in. wide. (Andrew Hartley) $556

An Art Deco three-piece suite, comprising two-seater settee and a pair of armchairs, with contoured shell backs and ribbed sides. (Brightwells) $272

A French carved giltwood and Aubusson, upholstered salon suite, late 19th century, in the Louis XVI style, comprising a canapé and four fauteuils, with floral and pierced ribband cresting to the upholstered oval panelled backs and stuff-over seats. (Christie's) $7,613

A suite of mahogany furniture in the Chinese style, late 19th/early 20th century, probably French, comprising a pair of canapés and four armchairs, each with serpentine back pierced with fret-work and carved with bats, above a floral scene with birds or Chinese lettering, each canapé 50in. wide. (Christie's) $2,520

An Edwardian rosewood three piece suite, inlaid with stringing, with padded backs with marquetry splats, padded arms and sprung seats, the square tapering legs to socket feet on castors. (Woolley & Wallis) $568

A Victorian walnut framed three piece salon suite, comprising a gentleman's spoon back chair, carved top rail, padded arms on scrolled supports, overstuffed seat, cabriole front legs with castors, matching lady's chair and a chaise longue with scrolled back, 68in. wide. (Andrew Hartley) $3,475

A Heal's limed oak bedroom suite comprising: three-door wardrobe, 153cm. wide, cabinet 99cm. wide, dressing table, 121cm. wide, two bedside cabinets, 76cm. and 37cm. wide, two single bedsteads, 107cm. wide, a stool and a pair of associated table lamps. (Bearne's) $2,831

A mid 20th century burr walnut dining suite.   (John Maxwell) $4,000

Fine French giltwood and mother of pearl inlaid three-piece seating suite, circa 1850, probably for the Turkish market, each with elaborate foliate carved frame, the arms inlaid with mother of pearl lunettes, all on cabriole legs. (Skinner) $2,300

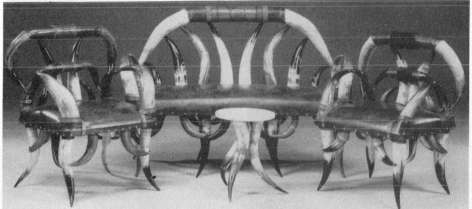

An American steerhorn and leather suite, 20th century, comprising a settee and pair of matching armchairs with curved top-rails covered in pressed leather and straps depicting cows and foliate ornament with arm supports, and a companion circular marble top triple horn occasional table. (Christie's) $9,409

Continental neo-classical marquetry inlaid fruitwood five-piece suite of seating furniture, late 19th century, comprising a low slung settee and four chairs, all inlaid with scrolled foliate vines. (Skinner) $4,312

N.K., Scandinavia, three piece salon, 1930s, comprising sofa, pair of deep armchairs, pale honey oak frames with dark conker brown hide seats and backs, the sofa with three panel back, sofa 64¼in. wide. (Sotheby's) $11,713

A group of four Anglo-Indian parcel-gilt metal-mounted armchairs, circa 1880, each with a fanned top, centered by a roundel crest, inscribed *Nabahstate*, above a padded back and seat, flanked to each side by an armrest with lion terminal. (Christie's) $25,909

An Art Deco period figured walnut dining suite with wide satin birch crossbanding comprising; dining table, length 66in., a set of six dining chairs, serving/cutlery table, length 42in. (John Maxwell) $1,104

A French mahogany salon suite, in the chinoiserie style, circa 1890, comprising two canapés and four armchairs, each with a pierced shaped top centered by playing bats. (Christie's) $4,410

A suite of Louis XV style giltwood seat furniture, late 19th century, comprising four fauteuils and a canapé, each with arched rectangular padded back and seat, within a channelled and foliate-carved frame, on cabriole legs and scroll feet, the canapé 59½in. (Christie's) $34,500

A Victorian rosewood breakfast table, the circular tilt-top on a turned and foliate carved pedestal with a lappeted collar and cabochon and scroll carved legs, 50½in. diameter.
(Christie's) $822

A late Regency mahogany breakfast table, the rectangular tilt top with a reeded edge and rounded corners, 4ft.8in.
(Woolley & Wallis) $1,882

A William IV mahogany breakfast table, the circular top with a beaded edge, on turned, fluted foliate and lotus-leaf carved support and tricorn base, 52¾in. diameter.
(Christie's) $3,948

An early Victorian walnut and parcel-gilt breakfast-table, the octagonal tilt-top with central foliate cartouche with birds and butterflies within a floral and foliate scrolling border and a later giltwood molded edge, 55in. diameter.
(Christie's) $11,226

An early Victorian rosewood breakfast table, the circular tilt top on a turned tapering pedestal with a lapetted collar and a circular base, with an additional later top, in rosewood, 72in. diameter.
(Christie's) $3,948

A mid Victorian inlaid walnut breakfast table, third quarter 19th century, the circular walnut top inlaid with a floral border and central cartouche, set on an octagonal pedestal, 133cm. diameter.(Bonhams) $4,828

A Victorian figured walnut and floral marquetry breakfast table, the circular quarter-veneered inlaid top above a line-inlaid frieze, 54in. diameter. (Christie's) $5,152

A large William IV faded mahogany breakfast table, the rectangular molded edge tilt top on a baluster turned stem to hipped splay legs, 5ft. long.
(Woolley & Wallis) $1,848

A Victorian mahogany breakfast table, the circular top with a molded edge, on a turned, bulbous tripod base with outswept legs, 53½in. diameter.
(Christie's) $1,533

A George III mahogany and oval inlaid breakfast table, the oval snap top flame figured and crossbanded in satinwood, with inlaid lines, the top 70 x 45in.
(Christie's) $16,457

A mahogany breakfast table, the circular tilt top on a vase turned stem, 4ft.4in. diameter.
(Woolley & Wallis) $1,411

A late Regency mahogany breakfast table, the faded well figured rectangular top with a broad band of satinwood, 4ft.11in. long.
(Woolley & Wallis) $6,765

A Regency mahogany ebony and inlaid breakfast table, the circular rosewood crossbanded top with boxwood lines and a reeded edge on ring turned column and molded quadruped splayed legs, 49in. diameter.(Christie's) $14,476

A George III mahogany breakfast table, the oval tilt-top crossbanded in satinwood and rosewood with boxwood and ebonized lines, above a turned shaft, on a tripartite base, 62¼in. wide.
(Christie's) $4,836

A Regency brass-mounted rosewood and simulated rosewood breakfast-table, the rounded rectangular top, crossbanded in kingwood with boxwood and ebony inlay, 53½in. wide.
(Christie's) $7,498

A figured walnut and marquetry circular breakfast table, 20th century, in the Victorian taste, the circular top with foliate inlay and a molded edge, 53½in. diameter.
(Christie's) $1,554

A Regency mahogany breakfast table, first quarter 19th century, the hinged top with rosewood and mahogany banded edge, set on a turned and carved pedestal base, 158cm. long.
(Bonhams) $2,556

A Regency mahogany breakfast table, the rectangular snap top with rounded corners on ring turned, gun barrel column and quadruped reeded splayed legs, 61¼in., wide.
(Christie's) $2,715

A William IV card table, in Brazilian rosewood, the 'D' shape swivel top baize lined, (warped), a mahogany lined well frieze, on an open moulded hoop support, 3ft.
(Woolley & Wallis) $2,079

Classical carved mahogany veneer card table, the rectangular tops with beaded edges above a skirt on acanthus leaf and spiral carved legs on casters, 35in. wide.
(Skinner) $1,380

A 19th century rosewood folding card table, the D shaped swivel top opening to reveal circular baize lining, tapering column with lotus leaf banding, 36in. wide.
(Andrew Hartley) $1,287

A fine late Victorian half round card table, veneered in rosewood on mahogany and inlaid with boxwood and bone stringing, the flap top with further marquetry inlay, 35¼in.
(Woolley & Wallis) $3,640

A late Victorian inlaid rosewood envelope card table, the swivel fold-out baize lined top above single drawer and four square supports with galleried undertier, 54cm. wide.
(Bristol) $602

An early George III mahogany card table, the rectangular top with protruding corners, baize lined with square candlestands, 30in., circa 1760.
(Woolley & Wallis) $2,874

A Victorian figured walnut veneered fold top card table with carved frieze on fluted and carved pedestal with carved quadruple base ending in shell feet.
(David Lay) $1,256

A late Victorian patent card table, circa 1900, the base insert circular top revolving to reveal four small counter trays above square tapered legs joined by a platform stretcher supporting a small cupboard, 24in. diameter. (Bonhams) $1,078

A mid 19th century French serpentine card table, faded walnut veneered, with gilt bronze mounts, the swivel rectangular top with a broad band of floral inlaid marquetry and stringing, 3ft.wide.
(Woolley & Wallis) $1,925

Dutch fruitwood marquetry inlaid walnut games table, 19th century, rounded corners with frieze drawer, on cabriole legs, 34in. wide. (Skinner) $1,725

Federal mahogany veneer carved card table, North Shore, Massachusetts, the serpentine top with ovolo corners above a conforming skirt, 37½in. wide. (Skinner) $1,725

A Queen Anne carved mahogany games table, Philadelphia, circa 1760, the hinged rectangular top above a frieze drawer, 32in. long. (Sotheby's) $6,325

A late Victorian marquetry inlaid envelope card table, the top rosewood veneered and satinwood crossbanded with stringing, 24in. (Woolley & Wallis) $2,244

A Federal mahogany carved card table, carving attributed to Samuel McIntire (1780-1819), Salem, Massachusetts, the rectangular hinged top with serpentine front and sides and gouged edges, 36in. wide. (Christie's) $9,200

A late Victorian marquetry rosewood envelope card table, the square folding top opening to reveal a baize lined interior with counter wells, width 21in. closed. (Michael J. Bowman) $1,558

A Victorian walnut folding card table, the rounded oblong top opening to reveal circular baize, flower and scroll carved frieze, 36in. wide. (Andrew Hartley) $2,061

Federal carved wavy birch card table, Northern New England, 1820–30, the beaded edge of the shaped top above a veneered skirt, 35½in. wide. (Skinner) $690

A early George III mahogany card table with a hinged top enclosing a green baize lining, counter wells and candle stands to each corner, 34½in. wide. (Anderson & Garland) $2,681

A good Federal brass-mounted carved and figured mahogany lyre-base games table, Boston, Massachusetts, circa 1815, 35¼in. wide. (Sotheby's) $12,650

A Dutch walnut, burr-walnut and marquetry card table, 18th century and later, the hinged rounded eared rectangular top inlaid with a central vase issuing scrolling flowers and foliage, 29½in. wide. (Christie's) $3,818

A George III mahogany revolving work/games table, the moulded rectangular double-hinged top enclosing to one side a compartmentalised interior, 27¼in. wide. (Christie's) $6,681

An Edwardian rosewood, marquetry and bone inlaid envelope card table, decorated with meandering floral trails, urns and lines, 23in. wide. (Christie's) $3,128

A pair of brass-inlaid scarlet-veneered and ebonised serpentine card tables, late 19th century, inlaid première and contra-partie, with panels of meandering foliage, 36in. wide. (Christie's) $6,992

A walnut card-table, the eared rectangular folding top inlaid with feather banding enclosing a grey suede-lined interior, 33¼in. wide. (Christie's) $10,499

An early 19th century Sheraton style mahogany and rosewood crossbanded demi-lune card table, plain frieze with satinwood crossbanding and oval inlaid paterae, 92cm. wide. (Wintertons) $2,160

A mahogany card table, 19th century, decorated with lines, the crossbanded rectangular hinged top enclosing a gilt tooled tan leather writing surface, 33¾in. wide. (Christie's) $4,099

A rare Chippendale carved and figured mahogany games table, Philadelphia, circa 1780, the hinged rectangular top above a line-incised frieze drawer, 36in. wide. (Sotheby's) $16,100

A rare Chippendale carved and figured mahogany games table, Massachusetts, circa 1770, the hinged oblong chip-carved top with outset corners, depth open 33in. (Sotheby's) $20,700

A mahogany, kingwood, marquetry and gilt-bronze card table, French, circa 1890, the rectangular shaped folding top within a moulded cast border, 80cm. wide. (Sotheby's) $6,072

A pair of Regency brass-inlaid and brass-mounted rosewood and parcel-gilt scissor-action card tables, each with a rounded rectangular hinged top, 36¼in. wide. (Christie's) $30,544

A George II red walnut envelope table, the moulded triangular three-flap swivel top above a plain frieze, possibly Irish, 29¼in. diameter. (Christie's) $30,544

An Irish George II mahogany card table, the rounded eared rectangular hinged top enclosing four oval counter-wells, four circular candle-stands and a green baize-lined playing surface, 37½in. wide. (Christie's) $15,272

An Edwardian satinwood and polychrome painted envelope card table, decorated with lines, rosewood crossbanding and ribbon-tied floral trails and swags, 25¾in. wide closed. (Christie's) $5,888

A very fine Federal inlaid mahogany bowfront card table, Massachusetts, circa 1805, the shaped hinged line-inlaid top above a conformingly-shaped conch-shell-inlaid frieze. (Sotheby's) $13,800

A George III satinwood card table, with kingwood crossbanding and ebony stringing, folding D shaped top on four square section concave legs and peg feet, 36in. wide. (Andrew Hartley) $6,480

An early 19th century rosewood folding card table, the D shaped top with bead and reel edging and baize lined interior, 36in. wide. (Andrew Hartley) $2,464

A Federal carved and figured mahogany games table, New York, circa 1810, the D-shaped top above a flowerhead-carved frieze on turned tapering legs, 34in. open. (Sotheby's) $4,025

A Classical carved mahogany card table, Boston, 1820-1830, the hinged rectangular top with rounded corners and molding edges swivelling and opening above a conforming veneered frame fitted with a well, 36in. wide. (Christie's) $3,055

A Chippendale mahogany card table, Philadelphia, 1770-1790, the rectangular hinged top above a conforming frame fitted with a cockbeaded long drawer over a shaped apron, 34in. wide. (Christie's) $14,950

Classical carved mahogany veneer card table, Boston Massachusetts, 1825-35, the solid top with mahogany veneer edge over a concave skirt and a leaf-carved lyre base, 34¾in. wide. (Skinner) $2,875

A George IV mahogany card table, the hinged, baize lined rectangular top with a panelled and scrolled frieze, on a panelled, faceted support, 36in. wide. (Christie's) $1,008

A 19th century rosewood folding card table, the D shaped top inlaid with brass stringing and anthemion, canted square section stem with scrolled brackets, 36in. wide. (Andrew Hartley) $2,355

A mahogany grained and ebonized games table, North European, 19th century, of serpentine outline, with a hinged top and a conforming frieze, on a turned beaded and spiral-carved pedestal, 35in. wide. (Christie's) $658

An early Victorian rosewood center table, the top with re-entrant corners above frieze drawer with beaded decoration, 46½in. (Dreweatt Neate) $2,608

An Art Deco rosewood center table, the rectangular top above U-shaped supports, on plinth base, 59½in. wide. (Christie's) $1,690

A George III mahogany center table, the top veneered in a variety of indigenous woods, centered by an oval with two hearts, 57¼in. wide. (Christie's) $29,072

A Victorian rosewood oval center table, with a molded tilt top on a turned trefoil lapetted and foliate-carved pedestal, 54in. wide. (Christie's) $2,303

A fine mahogany center table, the rectangular top later crossbanded and inlaid with stringing, the veneered frieze on reeded hoop and scroll end supports, 22in. x 4ft.7in. (Woolley & Wallis) $2,233

A Victorian rosewood loo table, the shaped and molded top above crossband frieze, supported on four serpentine C-scrolled arms, 147cm. wide. (Phillips) $2,320

A Victorian walnut center table, the shaped top having wide burr-grain border and cross banding to the leather inset, 4ft.9in. (Russell Baldwin & Bright) $4,785

An early Victorian rosewood serpentine center table, the bead and reel decorated frieze with two drawers, on ring-turned and dual splayed scroll end supports, 54in. wide. (Christie's) $2,632

A Victorian ebonized, amboyna-banded, parcel-gilt and ormolu mounted center table, with an oval top on four tapering fluted supports and a shaped cruciform base, 54in. wide. (Christie's) $739

A late Victorian mahogany center table, the circular top edged with a broad band of burr walnut, 137cm. diameter. (Bearne's) $3,218

19th century satin walnut Aesthetic style octagonal center table with gilt tooled leather inset, molded edge over a plain frieze, 50½in. (G.A. Key) $1,280

An early Victorian mahogany center table, the top decorated with rosewood and burr walnut cross-banding, on circular molded base, 52in. diameter. (Anderson & Garland) $5,363

A Continental rococo carved and figured walnut center table, Portuguese, mid-18th century, the rectangular top above three thumb-moulded frieze drawers, top 8ft. 1in. wide. (Sotheby's) $9,200

An Edwardian rosewood octagonal center table, satinwood strung with foliate inlay, on four square section tapering legs, 90cm. wide. (Wintertons) $957

A pair of rosewood center tables, inlaid overall with fruitwood lines, each with a rectangular top crossbanded in satinwood, incorporating early 19th century parts, 28in. wide. (Christie's) $16,031

A George IV rosewood center table, the circular tilt-top banded in burr-elm and with gadrooned edge, above a plain frieze, 28in. diam. (Christie's) $28,290

A pietre dure micromosaic and walnut center table by Orlandi Aristide, Rome, dated 1897, the shaped top inset with a patchwork of sample marbles, 113cm. wide. (Sotheby's) $27,514

A Regency brass-mounted and inlaid rosewood center table, the circular hinged tilt-top with three foliage motifs, above a plain frieze with three ebony-inlaid patera panels, 53½in. diameter. (Christie's) $28,290

A Regency rosewood, simulated-bamboo, red and gilt-japanned and parcel-gilt center table, the octagonal crossbanded top above a plain frieze, 51½in. diameter. (Christie's) $22,632

A German pewter-inlaid rosewood, specimen marble and parcel-gilt center table, second quarter 19th century, inlaid overall with lines, 59¾in. wide. (Christie's) $9,545

A George IV oak, brown-oak and parcel-gilt center table, the circular radiating veneered tilt-top above a plain frieze with beaded edge, 51½in. diameter. (Christie's) $15,088

A giltwood and marble center table French, in Régence style, the verde antico marble top above a frieze with carved rosettes, 182cm. wide.
(Sotheby's) $58,740

A Victorian walnut **center** table, for displaying cold meats, inset rouge fossilised marble.
(Woolley & Wallis) $1,162

A marble and giltwood **center** table, the rectangular green variegated marble top with a moulded giltwood edge supported by four gilt dolphin figures, 80in. wide.
(Christie's) $3,105

A gilt-bronze and porcelain **center** table, Napoleon III, circa 1870, the top with a dished centre painted with a lady at her toilet attended by a gentleman, 80cm. diameter.
(Sotheby's) $43,642

A Tuscan walnut **center** table, late 16th/early 17th century, the hexagonal removeable triple-plank top on a tripartite base, each shaped part with an eagle claw foot, 45in. diameter.
(Christie's) $38,180

A 19th century mahogany **center** table with applied gilt metal mounts, moulded circular black marble top, 32in. wide.
(Andrew Hartley) $9,408

A rare ebonised and gilt-bronze **center** table by Diehl, Paris, circa 1865, the onyx and marble-banded circular top within a moulded border, 124cm. diameter.
(Sotheby's) $28,118

A good Victorian rosewood and marquetry circular **center** table, the walnut and marquetry top with central floral garland, 54in. diameter.
(Canterbury) $11,200

An Irish William IV brass-mounted giltwood **center** table, the rounded rectangular red leather-lined top crossbanded in ebony, 46¼in. wide.
(Christie's) $37,720

A rosewood veneered circular center table, of recent manufacture, the radially veneered top on a faceted column and a trefoil base, 54½in. diameter.
(Christie's) $7,360

A Renaissance style carved oak center table, the rectangular top canted with corners, carved in sections, on paw feet, 3ft.2in.
(Woolley & Wallis) $439

An oak refectory style draw-leaf table, 19th century, the cleated top with brass bound corners, above panelled frieze rails inlaid in ebony and ivory, 107in. extended.
(Christie's) $1,656

A Classical rosewood inlaid carved and figured mahogany center table, probably New York, circa 1825, the circular radiating veneered top above a leaf carved urn form standard, 35in. diameter.
(Sotheby's) $3,450

An Edwardian rosewood and boxwood lined center table, the octagonal top with a moulded edge, on four panelled pierced and fluted supports, 36in. wide.
(Christie's) $643

A mahogany 'elephant' table, designed by Adolf Loos, circa 1903, the scalloped top banded in bronze and inset with mottled marble square panel, above a lower shelf with looping frieze, 33½in. diameter.
(Christie's) $12,109

A 19th century rosewood center table, in the style of Belter, the veneered serpentine moulded top to a heavy foliage carved frieze, 4ft.½in. wide.
(Woolley & Wallis) $913

Antique American Empire center table, in mahogany veneers, three fluted columns on a three-footed base, hexagonal top 34in. across.
(Eldred's) $1,100

An early 19th century mahogany center table with associated rectangular top, two real and two false frieze drawers, 92cm. wide.
(Bearne's) $768

Heavy Victorian oak Gothic style center table, moulded edge and canted corners, the frieze applied all round with lion masks, running animals, putti mounted on horseback etc., full width drawer on one side, 39in.
(G.A. Key) $1,813

Heavy Victorian gothic style oak circular center table, gadroon moulded rim, frieze elaborately moulded with berries and foliage and raised on heavy central lobed and acanthus leaf moulded baluster support, 45in. diameter.
(G.A. Key) $955

A small Portuguese jacaranda center table, circa 1700, the rectangular top with applied ropetwist border above a frieze drawer, 24¼in. wide.
(Bonhams) $2,516

Classical carved mahogany veneer center table, Boston, 1835-45, the Carrara marble top over a veneered apron with two working drawers above a tapered pedestal, 35⅜in. diameter. (Skinner) $4,025

South German walnut and marquetry tilt-top center table, third quarter 19th century, shaped top with hunting scenes and foliage, 29in. wide.
(Skinner) $1,495

Austrian Neoclassical mahogany and parcel-gilt marble-top center table, early 19th century, circular top, plain frieze, supported by figural bird legs, with medial shelf stretcher, shaped feet.
(Skinner) $4,888

Classical mahogany and mahogany veneer marble-top table, Massachusetts, circa 1835, the shaped white marble top with moulded edge on conforming skirt with applied beading, 35in. wide.
(Skinner) $1,840

A Louis XV style gilt metal and 'Sèvres' style porcelain center table, the circular dish top decorated with Watteauesque rustics above gilt metal and porcelain foliate triform base, 20in.
(Bonhams) $3,925

A fine mid Victorian burr walnut center table, the shaped oval top with figured quarter veneers and moulded edge above four foliate carved s-scrolls joined by a substantial lappet carved drum stretcher, 42in. wide.
(Bonhams) $3,234

A Dutch oyster veneered walnut and marquetry table, the rectangular top with panels of seaweed marquetry and geometric designs within checker borders, 47½in. wide.
(Dreweatt Neate) $6,435

A Victorian walnut center table, circa 1860, the serpentine shaped top with moulded edge, 60 x 47in.
(Christie's) $2,509

An Irish George IV burr-yew and marquetry center table, possibly Killarney, the circular crossbanded tilt-top with a border of entwined trailing oak leaves and acorns.
(Christie's) $12,408

A good mahogany piecrust center table, English, mid 18th century, the hinged top on a curved central pillar with three curving legs, 4 x 3½in.
(Bonhams) $2,051

A classical style ormolu-mounted brass inlaid part ebonised and parcel gilt mahogany marble top center table, in the manner of Charles Honoré Lannuier, 32½in. wide. (Sotheby's) $36,800

A late 19th/early 20th century painted satinwood center table decorated with floral sprays, drapery and garlands with circular top, 75cm. diameter.
(Bearne's) $1,573

Renaissance Revival walnut, marquetry, part-ebonised, parcel gilt and porcelain mounted center table, third quarter 19th century, shaped top over a frieze mounted with porcelain roundels, 42½in.
(Skinner) $3,737

Louis XVI style gilt bronze mounted and Sèvres style porcelain inset center table, third quarter 19th century, depicting the king and women of title, 31¾in. diameter.
(Skinner) $13,800

A center table, the rectangular top decorated green and gilt lacquer oriental landscape, gilt gesso backed bellflower pendant frieze, 3ft.6in.
(Woolley & Wallis) $2,475

422

A circular mahogany dining table, parts Victorian, the radially flamed, figured, segmented circular top with a moulded edge and frieze, 60½in. diameter. (Christie's) $1,068

A George III mahogany supper table, the circular moulded tip-up top on a turned baluster column, 81cm. diameter. (Phillips) $1,280

Gustav Stickley Arts & Crafts oak oval dining table, New York, circa 1910, oval top with six leaves above square leg posts with mortise and tenon joinery. (Skinner) $11,500

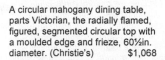

A Continental marquetry games table, 19th century, the hinged circular top profusely inlaid with many veneers, with two chess boards and two backgammon boards about a central starburst, 108cm. diameter. (Bonhams) $3,692

An Arts and Crafts oak extending dining table, attributed to Wylie and Lochhead, the moulded rounded rectangular top set on four quadrant sectioned legs, 195cm. long. (Bonhams) $1,716

A Victorian loo table, mahogany veneered, the circular veneered tilt top with a moulded edge on a tapering hexagonal stem, 4ft. 3½in. diameter. (Woolley & Wallis) $1,096

A Jacobean oak rectangular table having a simple moulded edge, planked top, plain frieze fitted with end drawers with moulded surround, 127 x 68cm. (Locke & England) $2,930

A Dutch decorated and mahogany tea table, 18th century, possibly Anglo Dutch, the oval dished top painted with an Apotheosis or Coronation of a female goddess in the clouds, the top 39 x 22in. (Christie's) $2,199

A mahogany extending dining table, mid 19th century, the rounded rectangular top including three additional leaves, on two rectangular bases with plain frieze and turned tapering legs. (Christie's) $6,486

A Queen Anne carved and figured walnut dressing table, Pennsylvania, circa 1740, the rectangular moulded top with notched corners, top 37½in. wide. (Sotheby's) $28,750

D.I.M. (Décoration Intérieure Moderne), Coiffeuse, 1930s, rosewood, asymmetrical, angular, with a complex configuration of five thick, clear green glass uprights, 41¾in. wide.
(Sotheby's) $7,176

A Chippendale carved walnut dressing table, Pennsylvania or Maryland, 1770-1790, the moulded rectangular top with cusped corners above a conforming case fitted with a thumbmoulded long drawer over three similar short drawers, 36in. wide. (Christie's) $18,400

A George III mahogany enclosed dressing table, decorated with lines and crossbanding, the twin flap hinged top opening to reveal a mirror and compartments, 26¼in. wide. (Christie's) $3,749

An oak dressing table by Gordon Russell from the 'Denbigh' range, and a matching three drawer chest, both 36in. wide.
(Andrew Hartley) $227

A late Georgian mahogany enclosed dressing table with satinwood stringing, the hinged top opening to reveal a mirror, cupboard and drawer beneath, 16in. wide. (Russell Baldwin & Bright) $1,262

A late George III enclosed dressing table, the hinged top enclosing a hinged ratcheted mirror and boxes with sliding lids, 25¼in. wide. (Christie's) $2,362

A Federal mahogany veneered dressing table, possibly New York, 1805-1820, the rectangular case with hinged and banded lids opening to a compartmented well with removable trays, 22in. wide. (Christie's) $3,220

A fine Queen Anne carved and highly figured mahogany dressing table, Salem/Ipswich area, Massachusetts, circa 1750, with rectangular thumbmoulded top above one long and three short drawers, 34½in. wide. (Sotheby's) $101,500

A Queen Anne carved and figured walnut dressing table, Pennsylvania, 1740-60, the rectangular moulded top above four short thumbmoulded drawers, 35½in. wide. (Sotheby's) $9,200

A George III mahogany campaign dressing chest, the rising lid enclosing many fitted compartments, above a writing slide and further drawers, 28in. wide. (Boardmans) $2,589

A late Regency period mahogany dressing table cum wash stand, in disrepair, 30in. wide, 20in. deep. (Dockrees) $1,440

A fine and rare Queen Anne figured cherrywood scallop-top dressing table, Connecticut, 1740-60, the shaped moulded top with outset corners, top 36½in. wide. (Sotheby's) $46,000

An important William and Mary figured walnut and turned maple dressing table, Boston, Massachusetts, 1715-25, the rectangular moulded top with quarter veneered centre section, 82.2.cm. wide. (Sotheby's) $211,500

A fine Queen Anne carved and figured mahogany dressing table, North Shore Massachusetts, 1745-65, the overhanging moulded top with notched corners, 34¼in. wide. (Sotheby's) $55,200

A good Queen Anne carved cherrywood dressing table, Connecticut, circa 1760, the rectangular moulded top above one long and three short moulded drawers, top 34in. wide. (Sotheby's) $48,875

A George III mahogany dressing-table, in the Chinoiserie style, the hinged-rectangular top enclosing a fitted interior and a later mirror, 25½in. wide. (Christie's) $27,773

A Queen Anne carved and figured walnut dressing table, Pennsylvania, circa 1750, the rectangular moulded top with notched corners above one long and three short drawers, 35½in. wide. (Sotheby's) $19,550

Maple butterfly table, New England, 18th century, the half-round leaves on shaped supports above a straight skirt on block, baluster, and ring-turned legs, 38in. wide extended.(Skinner) $19,550

Chippendale mahogany drop-leaf dining table, Massachusetts, 1760-80, the overhanging rectangular top on cabriole legs ending in claw and ball feet above a base with valanced skirt, 46½in. wide. (Skinner) $1,610

Federal tiger maple circular drop leaf table, New England, circa 1800-10, the oval overhanging drop leaf top on four square tapering legs, 41¾in. wide. (Skinner) $2,645

19th century mahogany drop leaf table, satinwood boxwood strung and banded border, raised on tapering square supports and the frieze fitted at one end with a drawer, 32in. (G.A. Key) $522

A George III mahogany spider-leg occasional table, having an ogee arched apron, on ring-turned column gate-leg supports, 30¼in. wide. (Christie's) $3,948

A George II mahogany dropleaf gateleg table, now with oval top, on scroll cabriole supports with ball-and-claw feet, 96.5cm. (Bristol) $534

A Chippendale figured walnut drop-leaf dining table, Pennsylvania, circa 1770, the stationary top flanked by rectangular leaves with notched corners, 4ft.11½in. open. (Sotheby's) $18,400

Federal tiger maple and cherry inlaid drop-leaf table, New England, early 19th century, the rectangular hinged top with ovolo corners falls above square tapering legs outlined in stringing, extension 34½in. (Skinner) $2,645

A Chippendale figured mahogany drop-leaf table, Newport, Rhode Island, circa 1780, the oblong top flanked by rectangular leaves on square stop-fluted legs, 4ft.1in. wide open. (Sotheby's) $7,760

Classical mahogany carved drop-leaf dining table, New York State, 1820s, the rectangular hinged leaves with beaded edges fall over a straight skirt above four acanthus leaf carved and turned legs, extension 61in.(Skinner) **$863**

A Regency mahogany Cumberland action drop-leaf dining table, the hinged top with rounded corners, having a gate-leg action, on ring-turned column and reeded splayed legs, 60in. wide extended. (Christie's) **$2,467**

Tiger maple drop leaf table, New England, 1820s, the rounded hinged leaves flank straight skirts above ring turned legs ending in turned feet, 40¾in. wide extended. (Skinner) **$1,150**

A George III mahogany drop leaf dining table, raised on square section legs, 106cm. wide. (Bonhams) **$277**

A small late 17th century Dutch oak table, the oval drop leaf top on outline vase shape trestle ends and gate supports, 25½ x 35in. (Woolley & Wallis) **$1,005**

Dutch Neoclassical-style fruitwood marquetry inlaid drop-leaf table, 19th century, with D-shaped leaves, frieze drawer and square tapered legs, inlaid with foliage and birds, 46in. long. (Skinner) **$2,415**

A Chippendale carved and figured mahogany drop-leaf dining table, Boston, Massachusetts, circa 1760, the oblong top with bowed ends flanked by D-shaped leaves, the shaped apron below on cabriole legs, 42in. wide open. (Sotheby's) **$3,450**

A George III mahogany double gateleg dining table, circa 1790, the rectangular top above six square chamfered legs, 165cm. long. (Bonhams) **$616**

A mahogany drop-leaf table, 18th century and later, the oval top with a rosette carved edge, on turned tapering legs with claw and ball feet, 56in. wide. (Christie's) **$1,204**

A George IV mahogany drum table, the circular veneered top with recent faded green gilt tooled leather, the frieze with drawers and dummy drawers, 3ft.11½in. diameter.
(Woolley & Wallis) $7680

A mahogany drum table, late 19th century, in the early Georgian style, the segmentally veneered top with an egg-and-dart moulded edge, four true and four false drawers, 46in. wide.(Christie's) $3,064

An early 19th century mahogany library table with crossbanded drum top fitted with four drawers alternating with four dummy fronts, 4ft. diameter. (Russell Baldwin & Bright) $5,920

A George III mahogany drum table with four drawers and four dummy drawers each with brass knob handles, on a turned pedestal, 43in. diameter. (Christie's) $3,069

A George III mahogany and satinwood small drum table, inlaid overall with ebony lines, the circular top with green leather surface, above four short drawers, 18½in. diameter.(Christie's) $4,843

A mahgany drum top library table, 19th century, the circular top inset with a panel of tooled leather and fitted with six drawers inlaid with ebony lettering, on baluster turned column, 48in. diameter. (Christie's) $7,631

A mahogany pedestal library table, the octagonal top with tooled leather insert, the frieze with four fitted drawers and four false drawers, 127cm. diameter, 19th century and later.
(Bearne's) $2,512

A mahogany drum top library table, early 19th century, with alterations, the circular top on turned column and quadruped reeded splayed legs, 39in. diameter.
(Christie's) $5,414

A Regency ebony-inlaid satinwood and ebonized drum table, the circular top with foliate-inlaid border with calamander crossbanding, above four hinged mahogany-lined drawers, 47¼in. wide.
(Christie's) $45,816

A late 17th or early 18th century oak gateleg dining table, the oval top raised on ring and baluster turned supports, 193 x 133 x 78cm.
(Tennants) $7,986

An oak gate-leg table, English, late 17th century, with oval top and frieze drawer with arcaded aprons, on ring-turned legs, 65½in. extended.
(Christie's) $11,006

William and Mary maple gateleg table, Massachusetts, early 18th century, the oval drop leaf top on six block vase and ring-turned legs, 52¼in. deep.
(Skinner) $9,775

A William and Mary turned and figured maple gate-leg table, New England, 1730–50, the oblong moulded top with bowed ends flanked by D-shaped leaves, width open 4ft. 10in.
(Sotheby's) $3,737

A walnut single-flap gateleg table, English, late 17th century, with an associated top and oval drop-leaf with plain moulded friezes and spiral-twist legs, 35in. wide.
(Christie's) $1,783

A William and Mary figured walnut gateleg table, possibly Southern, 1700–30, the oblong moulded top with bowed ends flanked by D-shaped leaves, 44in. wide open.
(Sotheby's) $10,925

A late 17th/early 18th century oak gateleg table with oval top, frieze drawer and on baluster ball-turned legs, 170cm. wide.
(Bearnes) $3,360

A George II mahogany spider-gateleg table, the twin-flap top above two mahogany-lined drawers on turned legs, 35¼in. wide.
(Christie's) $24,070

Walnut gateleg dining table, probably Pennsylvania, late 18th century, with two working drawers above the boldly turned legs, 48¾in. long.
(Skinner) $8,050

Federal mahogany carved and mahogany veneer two-part banquet table, Massachusetts, circa 1825, the D-shaped tops with reeded edges and rectangular drop leaves, 75in. long. (Skinner) $1,725

Federal cherry and bird's-eye maple two-part dining table, New England, 1820–25, the two rectangular ends each with a hinged drop-leaf, 82in. wide. (Skinner) $1,725

An oak refectory table, the cleated end planked top with canted corners an arcaded thumb carved frieze, 7ft.3in. long. (Woolley & Wallis) $3,818

A late Regency mahogany hunting table, the top of demi-lune form with drop flap ends and reeded edge, 183cm. wide. (Phillips) $8,000

A 19th century plain walnut extending dining table, on turned fluted supports with brass castors, with one leaf, overall length 222.5cm. (Bristol) $2,805

A late Victorian oak extending dining table, including five extra leaves, the circular top when closed above a plain frieze, on ring-turned reeded tapering legs, 190in. fully extended. (Christie's) $6,520

Oak and pine table, probably New England, 18th century, the rectangular top on three chamfered cleats and two shaped legs resting on trestle feet and joined by a shaped medial stretcher, 92½in. wide. (Skinner) $8,625

An early 19th century circular mahogany extending dining table, with boxwood and ebony stringing, on a large bulbous reeded baluster and acanthus leaf and reed stage, 248cm. long. (Tennants) $3,200

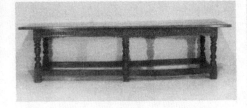

An oak side table with plank top, fluted frieze, six baluster turned legs, 120in. long, 17th century and later. (Andrew Hartley) $5,040

A Victorian mahogany extending dining table, two extra legs added, 72½in. long, 53in. wide. (Dockree's) $1,520

Federal cherry drop-leaf dining table, New England, 1820s, the rectangular leaves and straight skirt above spiral carved tapering legs, 45in. wide. (Skinner) $488

A fine and rare classical carved and figured mahogany two-pedestal dining table, Anthony Quervelle, Philadelphia, circa 1825, in two parts, 8ft. long open. (Sotheby's) $18,400

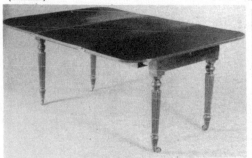

A late George III mahogany extending dining table, the reeded edge top with rounded corners, turned fluted legs on brass caps and castors (two extra leaves), 87in. extended. (Dreweatt Neate) $8,910

A late Victorian mahogany extending dining table, 87in. long, 45in. wide. (Dockree's) $1,680

George III mahogany two-pedestal dining table, early 19th century, top with reeded edge, turned support, moulded tripartite base ending in brass paw feet, 48in. wide. (Skinner) $3,450

A late 19th century mahogany extending dining table, rounded ends, moulded edge, plain frieze, carried on carved cabriole legs, elaborate shoulders, ball and claw feet, 243 x 136cm. (Locke & England) $2,310

A Victorian mahogany extending dining table, with four additional leaves on turned and reeded tapering legs, with brass caps and castors.
(Christie's) $3,125

An early Victorian mahogany extending dining table, having two D ends, raised on turned and reeded legs with brass toes and castors, including two additonal leaves, 103in. long. (Andrew Hartley) $3,408

A Victorian mahogany extending dining table, with four additional leaves, two large and two smaller, the rounded rectangular top with a moulded edge on ring-turned tapering and boldly reeded legs, 114in. fully extended. (Christie's) $3,948

An oak refectory table, probably Welsh, early 18th century, with cleated triple plank top and moulded friezes, on feceted square section legs joined by square section stretchers, 98½in. long. (Christie's)
                                              $10,339

An oak draw-leaf refectory table, English, 19th century, with cleated plank top and arcaded facing frieze, with spandrels, on bulbous gadrooned and block legs headed with stiff leaf and Gothic arched panels, 131in. extended. (Christie's) $3,922

Classical carved mahogany veneer two-part dining table, New York, 1825-35, the rounded ends above the leaf-carved rectangular top with a single drop leaf and front corners flanking the convex veneered skirts on the stepped square pedestal, 89¼in.
(Skinner) $3,220

An oak refectory table, with plank top, the front frieze carved with interlacing strapwork, 86in. long, 17th century and later. (Andrew Hartley) $3,190

A large pine circular table, Swiss, 19th century, with plank top and spreading legs joined by multiple stretchers, 64in. diameter. (Christie's) $3,826

Federal style mahogany dining table, 20th century, with rectangular cross-banded top above two pedestal bases each with foliate carved posts, 72in. long without leaves. (Skinner) $3,220

Large Morris and Company Georgian style mahogany library writing table, late 19th/ early 20th century, with tooled red leather top and gadrooned edge above two end drawers, 90in. long. (Skinner) $3,450

An oak refectory table, the plank top on channel moulded frieze with lunette carving on scrolled brackets, ring turned bulbous legs and block feet, 17th century and later, 108 x 34in. (Andrew Hartley) $5,282

Queen Anne walnut table, Pennsylvania, 18th century, the rectangular top overhangs a conforming skirt with three thumb-moulded drawers over a moulded edge supported on turned cabriole legs ending in pad feet, 66in. wide. (Skinner) $2,415

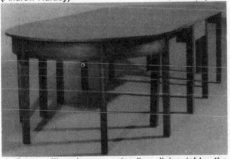

A George III mahogany extending dining table, the rectangular centre drop leaf table with a pair of half round side tables, the veneered friezes on square moulded and chamfered legs, 9ft.3in.long (extended). (Woolley & Wallis) $4,160

A large elm and oak refectory table, English, the top probably 18th century, the slab top with cleated ends and raised on standard end supports with sleigh feet and joined by a central stretcher, 152½in. long. (Christie's) $27,428

Late Regency inlaid mahogany three-part dining table, early 19th century, with D-shaped ends and rectangular centre section all cross-banded in satinwood, 155in. long. (Skinner) $5,175

A mahogany extending dining table, late 19th/early 20th century, with two additional leaves, the rounded rectangular top on ring-turned tapering and part reeded legs, 95in. extended.(Christie's) $2,961

Gustav Stickley hexagonal table, stacking stretcher-form, work to top, original finish on base, 46¾in. wide. (Skinner) $2,300

A Swiss walnut and marquetry occasional table, early 19th century, the shaped top inlaid with an oval medallion depicting mountain goats and an eagle, 25½in. wide. (Christie's) $827

Classical carved mahogany veneer table, Philadelphia, circa 1827, the rectangular top with moulded edge above a cockbeaded frieze with a single central working drawer, 45¼in. wide. (Skinner) $2,530

Painted oval table, New England, 18th century, the pine top overhangs a stretcher base table with splayed vase and ring-turned legs, 30¼in. wide. (Skinner) $4,485

A 19th century rosewood boudoir table, kidney shaped with string and marquetry inlay, 23in. wide. (Andrew Hartley) $2,393

Folding pyrographic decorated table, America, early 20th century, round top hinged at the centre over intersecting shaped legs with Moorish-style cut-outs, 25¼in. high. (Skinner) $517

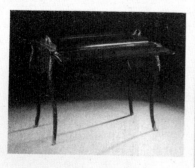

A mahogany and kingwood drinks table, Victorian, circa 1880, opening to reveal a raising glass tray, 96cm. wide. (Sotheby's) $11,385

A George III rectangular mahogany reading table, the gun barrel turned adjustable pillar with screw action stop, 20½in. (Dreweatt Neate) $1,155

A Victorian mahogany 33in. tripod table. (Dockree's) $248

A 19th century rosewood wine table with circular top, faceted tapering stem with scrolled brackets, 18in. wide. (Andrew Hartley) $874

A George III fiddle-back mahogany and mahogany supper-table, the rectangular moulded twin-flap top, above a concave front with a pair of doors and the sides lined with later wire grille, 37¾in. wide, open. (Christie's) $7,772

A good Regency inlaid mahogany reading table, the adjustable top on a ring-turned column, 42cm. wide. (Bristol) $1,353

Paint decorated papier mâché and pine tilt-top stand, attributed to Litchfield Mfg. Co., Litchfield, Connecticut, mid-19th century, 17in. diameter. (Skinner) $2,645

A good William IV rosewood bed reading table, the veneered rectangular top with a lidded compartment and a pair of flaps on easels 35in. (Woolley & Wallis) $1,660

A Regency mahogany reading table with adjustable square top on baluster turned column and reeded tripod base, 15 x 17in. (Russell, Baldwin & Bright) $1,320

A fine George II style occasional table with circular pietra-dura top on tapering moulded and carved pillar support, 15½in. diameter. (Dee Atkinson & Harrison) $3,960

A Victorian campaign mahogany folding table, the central butler's tray with raised sides and pierced carrying handles, on an X framed stand, 83½in. extended. (Dreweatt Neate) $1,793

An early Victorian rosewood occasional table, with moulded edged canted square top on collared and lobed baluster stem. 15½in. wide. (Andrew Hartley) $1,848

Emile Gallé, two-tier table, circa 1900, fruitwood, free-form top and lower tier, inlaid with fruitwoods, the upper tier decorated with a landscape scene, 39¾in. wide.
(Sotheby's) $13,440

A Regency brass-mounted and brass-inlaid rosewood tripod table, the moulded octagonal top inlaid with a central octagon and radiating segments, 20¼in. diameter.
(Christie's) $3,540

Anon, English, low table, circa 1930, inverted U-form, covered in turquoise/green stained galuchat panels, the top edges banded in ivory, 60.2cm. wide.
(Sotheby's) $11,760

A George IV rosewood occasional table, the beaded edged rounded oblong top on turned tapering and fluted stem with carved leaf collar, 22¼in. wide.
(Andrew Hartley) $3,770

A small joined oak cricket table, English, early 18th century, the circular top on turned baluster legs, tied by stretchers, the top 23in. diameter.
(Bonhams) $2,793

A George III satinwood occasional table, circa 1795, the octagonal segmented veneered top centred by a fan patera, above a line inlaid frieze, 20¼in. wide.
(Bonhams) $1,110

A late 19th century mahogany occasional table by Gillows, moulded edged circular top, pierced fretted frieze, raised on four cluster column legs, 24¼in.
(Andrew Hartley) $754

A Spanish walnut altar table, circa 1680, the plank top on twin barleytwist baluster end supports tied by a twin iron shaped stretcher, 49½in. long.
(Bonhams) $4,736

A 19th century rosewood occasional table, with stringing and marquetry flowers and foliage, triangular top with shaped flaps, 27in. wide.
(Andrew Hartley) $708

A 19th century set of mahogany quartetto tables of Georgian design, the beaded oblong top with rosewood crossbanding and radially veneered centres forming a web like pattern, 19½in. wide.
(Andrew Hartley) $3,850

An Edwardian inlaid mahogany occasional table, circa 1905, of heart form, raised on square tapered legs and united by a platform stretcher, 55cm. high.
(Bonhams) $1,540

A set of Edwardian painted satinwood quartetto tables, each beaded top painted with ribbon tied floral festoons with a raised moulding.
(Andrew Hartley) $3,335

An unusual late Regency ash occasional table, circa 1830, the circular segmentally veneered top above a waved frieze applied with pendant bun drops, 20in. diameter.
(Bonhams) $924

An Art Nouveau occasional table, with a triangular beaten copper top, early 20th century, set on three outswept pierced mahogany legs, 50cm. wide.
(Bonhams) $214

A George III mahogany tripod table, possibly American, circa 1760, the dished circular top above a birdcage support and barrel column on three scrolled pierced outswept cabriole legs, 32in. diameter.
(Bonhams) $5,320

A George II mahogany tilt top wine table, circa 1750, the top above a turned column and tripod base, with alterations and restorations, 81cm. diameter. (Bonhams) $644

A 19th century Sheraton style painted satinwood two-tier oval occasional table with cherubs, musical trophy, etc, shaped gallery on square supports, 25in.
(Brightwells) $1,440

Pierre Chareau, table 'Tulipe', 1920s, blondewood, the hexagonal top above six curved vertical supports, the edges of the supports banded with darker wood, 23¼in.
(Sotheby's) $17,605

An elm X-framed table, English, 19th century, the twin-plank figured top on blue painted X-framed chamfered supports joined by a central chamfered stretcher, later painted, 70¼in. long.
(Christie's) $3,565

A Baltic burr ash and ebonized pedestal table stamped *JAC SIOLIN KOPING. No 350*, mid 19th century, 96cm. diameter.
(Bonhams & Brooks) $2,220

'Ducharne', an amaranth and ivory table, designed by Jacques-Emile Ruhlmann, circa 1925, circular top, tripod base, silvered feet, 31½in. diameter.
(Christie's) $32,371

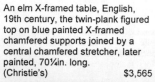

A carved oak occasional table, designed by Mackay Hugh Baillie Scott, circa 1898, the manufacture attributed to the Guild of Handicraft, 40 x 39.5cm.
(Christie's) $7,455

An oak folding table, South Yorkshire, late 17th century, with a canted molded hinged top and triangular base with molded friezes, 38½in. wide.
(Christie's) $34,759

A German ormolu-mounted brass-inlaid walnut and mahogany occasional guéridon, mid 18th century, banded overall, the serpentine tray top above a slide and a frieze-drawer with two divisions, 27in. diameter.
(Christie's) $10,938

A Victorian chinoiserie decorated tripod table, decoration refreshed 35.5cm. wide.
(Bonhams & Brooks) $285

An oak folding table, English, early 17th century, the semi circular hinged top above an angled frieze on baluster turned legs, 39¼in. wide. (Bonham's) $2,926

A George III oak tripod table, 78cm. diameter.
(Bonhams & Brooks) $480

An oak folding table, English, late 17th century, with hinged half-round top and central frieze drawer above arcaded aprons, 47in. wide. (Christie's) $8,021

Cast-iron and oak adjustable artist's work table, 'Designed and Manufactured at The Washburn Shops of the Polytechnic Institute, Worcester, Massachusetts', circa 1872, 31½in. high. (Skinner) $805

An Irish Chippendale style walnut silver table, 80cm. wide. (Bonhams & Brooks) $2,114

A kingwood, crossbanded and ormolu mounted table en chiffonier, 19th century, in the Louis XV style, veneered à quatre faces with three-quarter pierced brass gallery and later black leather lined top, 17¼in. wide. (Christie's) $2,715

An oak counter table, Flemish, early 17th century, the sliding molded plank top opening to reveal a stepped fitted interior with an arrangement of small drawers concealed behind rising flaps, 31¾in. wide. (Christie's) $4,635

A mahogany wine glass table, Georgian base with later top, the detachable revolving superstructure with a brass column with ring carrying handle, on ring turned baluster column and tripod splayed legs with pointed pad feet and brass castors, 55in. diameter. (Christie's) $4,620

A George III mahogany supper table, later carved, 74cm. diameter. (Bonhams & Brooks) $1,386

A 17th century style oak corner table, 93.5cm. wide x 49cm. deep x 76cm. high. (Bonhams & Brooks) $246

A Regency rosewood reading table, 53.5cm. wide x 70cm. high. (Bonhams & Brooks) $1,694

An unusual Regency rosewood bagatelle serving table with ormolu leafage mounts, baize interior to the box top, on fluted turned tapering legs, 5ft. 10in. long. (Russell Baldwin & Bright) $4,705

A George III mahogany tripod table, the cusped circular tip up top on turned barrel stem, raised on cabriole legs and pad feet, 28½in. wide: (Andrew Hartley) $1,463

Arts and Crafts oak trestle table, New York, rectangular top over medial shelf with pegged tenons exposed through shaped sides extending to base, 36¼in. long. (Skinner) $2,300

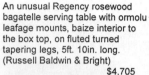

Art Deco typewriter table, America, circa 1930, oval top on table with single drop leaf, the other side with two half-oval open shelves, bird's-eye maple veneer with black lacquered edges, 36in. long. (Skinner) $977

Arts & Crafts oak tabouret, America, circa 1912, octagonal top with corbel supports, the four canted sides with cutouts, 17in. diameter. (Skinner) $977

A late Victorian mahogany and brass mounted coaching games table, on curved X-frame folding supports joined by stretchers, size when open 29¾in. (Christie's) $1,998

A mahogany and green and gilt painted Empire guéridon, the round tray with ormolu band, on waisted painted support on shaped triangular base with paw feet. (Galerie Moderne) $5,237

Brass telephone table, France, circa 1925, rectangular top with radiating rice rain textured panel and skirt with lozenge shaped cut-outs, 31¼in. high. (Skinner) $402

An oak full-size billiard table, early 20th century, the five slate bed covered in green baize, the frieze carved with egg-and-dart and guilloche moldings, 153in. long. (Christie's) $7,268

Red painted pine chair table, New England, 18th century, the scrubbed top tilts above the base on shoe feet.
(Skinner) $1,380

A walnut, oak and pine occasional table, probably French, mid 19th century, with a circular top and octagonal column with socle and a circular platform base applied with roundels, 15½in. diameter.
(Christie's) $434

Charles and Ray Eames, a molded plywood CTW-3 occasional table, designed 1946, for Herman Miller, the circular dished ash top on four tapering uprights, 34in. wide.
(Christie's) $1,083

A George III patience table, veneered in satinwood, the twin flap top with a crossbanded border in harewood, reveals blue baize, the sides with pull out lopers, 20in.
(Woolley & Wallis) $3,045

Painted pine chair table, New England, late 18th century, the scrubbed pine top tilts above the two board plank seat and the square tapering legs joined by square stretchers, 42½in. diameter.
(Skinner) $4,255

A Louis XV style gilt metal mounted and marble topped table ambulante, circa 1880, the circular inset top above a band frieze with applied mounts, 18in. wide.
(Christie's) $2,038

A black lacquered tripod table, late 19th/early 20th century, the circular tilt top with a scrolling foliate-decorated border and inset landscape scene, 31½in. diameter.
(Christie's) $1,151

Classical mahogany and mahogany marble-top table, New York, 1835-45, the rectangular white marble top with rounded corners on conforming ogee-molded skirt and pierced and scrolled supports, 31in. wide. (Skinner) $3,737

A Victorian burr-walnut and rosewood-banded occasional table, with a circular top and revolving galleried undertier, on a turned pedestal, 16in. diameter.
(Christie's) $1,974

Dutch neoclassical style mahogany and floral marquetry Pembroke table, late 19th century, top with D-shaped splats over a frieze drawer, 35½in. wide.
(Skinner) $2,875

A classical carved mahogany Pembroke table, New York, 1810-1820, the rectangular top flanked by hinged elliptical leaves above a conforming frame flanked by inlaid rectangular reserves, 25¼in. wide.
(Christie's) $5,175

A Federal inlaid mahogany Pembroke table, New York, 1795-1810, on square string-inlaid tapering legs headed by bookends over pendant-husk inlay with inlaid cuffs, 49½in. wide (open).
(Christie's) $18,400

Federal mahogany inlaid Pembroke table, New York, circa 1790-1800, the rectangular top with shaped drop leaves bordered by stringing above a crossbanded skirt, 20½in. wide. (Skinner) $2,300

A Federal inlaid mahogany Pembroke table, New York or Connecticut, circa 1800, the oblong line-inlaid top with bowed ends flanked by D-shaped leaves, 36in. wide open.
(Sotheby's) $9,200

Federal cherry inlaid Pembroke table, probably Rhode Island, circa 1800, oval drop-leaf top with incised beaded edges above conforming skirt with drawer, top 36¾ x 32¾in.
(Skinner) $7,475

A George III burr yew Pembroke table in the manner of Mayhew and Ince, the oval drop flap top tulipwood crossbanded, with web shaped boxwood stringing, 28in.
(Dreweatt Neate) $13,370

Federal cherry Pembroke breakfast table, New England, circa 1800, the rectangular drop-leaf top above a straight skirt joining four square tapering legs, 20in. wide, closed.
(Skinner) $920

A satinwood and mahogany-banded Pembroke table, the twin hinged oval crossbanded top with a frieze drawer to one end.
(Christie's) $1,011

An Edwardian satinwood and harewood banded Pembroke table, inlaid with lines, with an oval hinged top and frieze drawer, 38¼in. extended.(Christie's) $3,634

A George III mahogany Pembroke table, inlaid with lines, the banded top with D-shaped hinged leaves, 42¾in. wide extended. (Christie's) $3,088

A George III mahogany oval Pembroke table, the twin-flap top crossbanded in tulipwood and satinwood, above a frieze drawer, 43in. wide, open. (Christie's) $23,144

A George III wavy-wengewood Pembroke table, inlaid overall with boxwood and ebony lines, with concave corners and a central satinwood and harewood marquetry oval, 28in. high. (Christie's) $48,139

A Regency fiddleback mahogany Pembroke table, the moulded rectangular twin-flap top crossbanded in rosewood, 29in. wide, open. (Christie's) $12,512

A George III satinwood Pembroke table, crossbanded overall in tulipwood, the rounded rectangular twin-flap top with central oval panel, 40in. wide. (Christie's) $15,640

George III mahogany oval Pembroke table with satinwood banding and patterned boxwood and ebony line inlay, one drawer, 30 x 41½in. (Ewbank) $924

A 19th century mahogany, inlaid and painted Pembroke table, the rectangular satinwood banded top painted with a central reserve depicting a cherub and goddess, 76cm. (Tennants) $2,355

A Regency mahogany and brass inlaid pedestal Pembroke table, the rectangular twin-flap top with a star border, above a drawer to one end, 37¾in. wide. (Christie's) $5,152

A Federal inlaid mahogany
Pembroke table, New York, 1790-
1810, the rectangular hinged top
with inset curved corners all with
line inlay, 40¾in. wide (open).
(Christie's) $21,150

An Edwardian mahogany
Pembroke table with satinwood
banding and stringing, molded
edged oval top, 19¼ x 33in.
extended.
(Andrew Hartley) $917

A George III mahogany Pembroke
table, with rounded oblong top,
shaped frieze with drawer having
brass drop handle, on molded and
chamfered legs, 36in. wide.
(Andrew Hartley) $806

A George III mahogany,
crossbanded and marquetry oval
Pembroke table, the hinged top
crossbanded in tulipwood and
satinwood inlaid with engraved
composition penwork border, the
top 37½in. extended.
(Christie's) $15,382

A satinwood, crossbanded and
marquetry Pembroke table, late
19th century, in the neo classical
style, the hinged top with rounded
lopers and radiating design with
central flowerhead with garlands,
the top 40in. wide.
(Christie's) $5,076

A Federal inlaid mahogany
Pembroke table, Rhode Island,
1790-1810, the rectangular top with
bowed ends flanked by hinged D-
shaped leaves, all with string-inlaid
edges, 39¼in. wide (open).
(Christie's) $7,638

A Federal inlaid mahogany
Pembroke table, attributed to John
Townsend, Newport, 1790-1800,
the rectangular top with hinged
shaped leaves above a conforming
frame, 35in. wide (open).
(Christie's) $14,100

An Edwardian satinwood Pembroke
table, in the Sheraton Revival style
with crossbanding and stringing,
rounded oblong top with central
marquetry batwing patera, 23in.
wide. (Andrew Hartley)
$3,124

A Federal mahogany Pembroke
table, New York, 1800-1820, the
cloverleaf top with two drop leaves
above a conforming skirt with a
single drawer flanked by fluted
rectangular reserves, 34in. wide.
(Christie's) $2,585

A George III mahogany Pembroke table, 94cm. wide x 102cm. deep x 72cm. high.
(Bonhams & Brooks) $370

A George III mahogany and inlaid oval Pembroke table, the hinged top with a molded edge containing a drawer in the ebony strung frieze, the top 35in. wide.
(Christie's) $1,635

A George III mahogany Pembroke table with ebony stringing, reeded edged rounded oblong top, frieze drawers with turned brass handle, 39in. wide.
(Andrew Hartley) $445

A George III mahogany serpentine top Pembroke table, with a molded edge, containing a drawer, on square tapering legs, 34¼in. wide. (Christie's) $1,269

A Regency mahogany Pembroke table, restorations, 45cm. wide.
(Bonhams & Brooks) $554

A Federal inlaid cherrywood Pembroke table, attributed to William Winchester, Sumner County, Tennessee, circa 1802, the rectangular top with bowed ends, 18¾in. wide.
(Christie's) $16,450

A mahogany Pembroke table, mid 18th century, the twin hinged rectangular top with a drawer to one end, on club legs joined by cross stretcher and pad feet, 47in. wide. (Christie's) $2,713

A George III mahogany Pembroke table, crossbanded with stringing, the molded edged oval top with oval central patera, inlaid panelled frieze, 30½in. wide.
(Andrew Hartley) $2,240

A George III mahogany Pembroke table, with rectangular hinged top and ogee arched frieze containing a drawer above chamfered legs, 34in. wide fully extended.
(Christie's) $1,810

A late Georgian side table with pietra dura top of specimen grained marbles in a trellis design with looped border, the mahogany frame cross-banded and inlaid, 40 x 22in. (Brightwells) **$21,000**

A Queen Anne walnut and elm sidetable, the eared molded rectangular top above a frieze drawer and shaped apron, 84cm. wide. (Cheffins) **$1.300**

18th century oak side table with one drawer with brass ring handles, on cabriole legs with pad feet, 31in. (Ewbank) **$554**

A parquetry, mahogany and gilt-bronze side table by François Linke Paris, circa 1900, the rectangular shaped parquetry-veneered top within a molded border above a frieze drawer with an asymmetric escutcheon, 72cm. wide. (Sotheby's) **$5,998**

A pair of mahogany, rosewood and marquetry semi circular side tables, of recent manufacture, decorated throughout with foliate scrolls and husk swags, with a crossbanded and radially veneered top above, 34½in. wide. (Christie's) **$1,233**

An ebonized carved and inlaid side table, the manufacture attributed to Lamb of Manchester, 1870s, rectangular top inlaid with central burrwood panel, the perpendicular supports carved and gilded with Egyptian motifs, 45in. maximum width. (Christie's) **$8,383**

An oak side table, English, late 17th century, with a single frieze drawer, on ball and fillet turned baluster legs tied by stretchers, 32in. wide. (Bonham's) **$1,386**

An oak and brass side table, designed by Henry van de Velde, 1903, triangular top with brass plate, triangular tripod base, 72cm. high. (Christie's) **$37,483**

An Italian neoclassical giltwood side table, circa 1790, the veneered black marble rectangular top above a molded edge and punched frieze centered by a Bacchante mask, 43in. wide. (Bonhams) **$8,140**

A William and Mary oyster veneered and elm side table, circa 1700, top line inlaid with circular designs above a single frieze drawer, on turned baluster legs, 37½in. wide.
(Bonhams) $18,200

A Spanish walnut and oak side table, parts 18th century, with a rectangular top and a pair of molded drawers to the frieze, on square section and spiral-turned legs. (Christie's) $1,240

A 19th century mahogany side table in the manner of Chippendale, with a rectangular top and blind fret interlaced arcaded frieze, 138cm. wide. (Phillips) $7,544

An ebonized beech side table, designed by Josef Hoffmann, circa 1903, circular section, half-height shelf, cross stretchers, 15¾in. diameter. (Christie's) $3,726

A fine Louis XV style marquetry inlaid kingwood and ormolu mounted side table, by Millet, circa 1890, the shaped serpentine top with floral and ribbon inlay, 26½in. wide. (Christie's) $10,976

A painted and stencilled wood side table, probably Maine, 19th century, the stencilled splash board with yellow ground and green and ocher stripes and scrolled volutes, 31½in. wide. (Christie's) $10,575

An oak side table, English, late 18th century, the rounded rectangular top above three drawers to the arcaded frieze, on turned legs and pad feet, 32½in. wide.
(Bonham's) $893

A late 17th century oak side table, the rectangular top fitted with a single drawer, on barley twist legs and stretchers, 85cm. wide.
(Wintertons) $2,552

A Regency mahogany side table, the rectangular top with reeded edge, above three frieze drawers, on turned reeded legs, 35in. wide.
(Christie's) $8,280

A small George IV faded mahogany sofa table, the rectangular top inlaid ebony stringing and gothic crosses, 31½in.
(Woolley & Wallis) $4,704

A Regency satinbirch and bird's-eye maple sofa table, the rounded rectangular twin-flap top above a pair of frieze drawers flanked by lozenge panels, 59¼in. wide, open.
(Christie's) $14,681

A late Victorian small rosewood sofa or occasional table, the faded veneered oval drop leaf top with marquetry panels and stringing, 34in. open.
(Woolley & Wallis) $856

SUTHERLAND TABLES

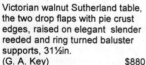

Victorian walnut Sutherland table, the two drop flaps with pie crust edges, raised on elegant slender reeded and ring turned baluster supports, 31½in.
(G. A. Key) $880

A mid Victorian burr walnut Sutherland table, the molded edge drop flap top of undulating outline on four molded and carved cabriole legs, 35½in. wide.
(Dreweatt Neate) $2,557

An Edwardian satinwood Sutherland table, crossbanded with string inlay, molded edged shape oblong top, 24in. wide.
(Andrew Hartley) $1,344

TEA TABLES

A 19th century mahogany folding tea table, with rosewood crossbanding and stringing, D shaped top, plain frieze, 36in. wide.
(Andrew Hartley) $2,059

Chippendale mahogany tilt-top tea table, Delaware Valley, 1760-80, the moulded circular top tilts over a birdcage mechanism on incised vase and ring-turned post, 33in. diameter. (Skinner) $4,600

A Scottish mahogany tea table, early 19th century, with a hinged top above a foliate-carved and crossbanded frieze, on a tapering faceted pedestal, 36in. wide.
(Christie's) $1,240

A mahogany, ebony strung and satinwood inlaid work table, early 19th century, containing a drawer and U-shaped well below with reeded ornament to the sides, 23in. wide. (Christie's) $2,876

William and Mary style seaweed marquetry inlaid walnut games table, with antique elements, the D-shaped top with concave front, the frieze similarly shaped, 32in. wide. (Skinner) $2,875

A Victorian walnut work table, the top marquetry inlaid, a fitted interior to the tapering lidded box top with corner brackets, 20in. (Woolley & Wallis) $932

A late George III mahogany work table, decorated with ebonised lines, the hinged and ratcheted rectangular top above a front with a dummy drawer, 21¼in. wide. (Christie's) $4,471

A 19th century Middle Eastern games table, rectangular fold over top enclosing a removable baize covered board, inlaid with mother of pearl, bone and exotic woods, 61cm. wide. (Wintertons) $3,564

A Regency mahogany drop-leaf work table, the rectangular hinged top with a reeded edge, containing a fitted drawer to one end, 30in. wide extended. (Christie's) $4,724

Federal mahogany and mahogany veneer work table, probably Maryland, circa 1810-15, the rectangular top on case of two graduated drawers flanked by reeded panels, 18¾in. wide. (Skinner) $1,265

Dutch walnut and fruitwood marquetry triple-top games and writing table, late 18th century, the top with marquetry inlaid urns, flanking a central pyrographic wood panel, 28¼in. wide. (Skinner) $5,750

A George III amaranth, mahogany and marquetry work-table, in the manner of Pierre Langlois, inlaid with lines and cross-banded overall in laburnum, the serpentine hinged top with panel of a bird perching on a flower, 19¼in. wide. (Christie's) $6,360

A mid Victorian walnut sewing table, circa 1890, fitted with a frieze drawer and material basket under, 58cm. wide.
(Bonhams) $1,232

An L. Majorelle inlaid work table with shaped rectangular top having wisteria and berry inlay, 29 x 21in., signed.(Brightwells) $2,325

A George IV mahogany sewing table, circa 1825, fitted with two drawers, woolwork basket and slide missing, set on a platform base, 47cm. wide.
(Bonhams) $756

A 19th century Colonial padouk wood sewing table, circa 1890, fitted with a frieze drawer and a basket raised on carved outswept feet, 76cm. wide.
(Bonhams) $742

A 19th century mahogany work table, kidney shaped with stringing and gilt metal mounts, the top with hinged lid revealing fitted satinwood interior, 22½in. wide.
(Andrew Hartley) $1,740

A Federal style mahogany eagle-base games table, in the manner of Duncan Phyfe, 1870-1930, the rectangular top with canted corners swivelling above a well and a conforming frieze, 36in. open.
(Sotheby's) $7,475

A Louis XV style kingwood and parquetry ormolu mounted work table, circa 1860, the serpentine crossbanded top enclosing a well with a tray, above the tapered work basket, 23¾in. wide.
(Bonhams) $966

A matched pair of Regency brass-mounted rosewood games and work-tables, each with a ratcheted brown leather-lined top above a backgammon board, flanked on each side by a semi-circular hinged well, 29in. wide.
(Christie's) $19,562

An early Victorian rosewood sewing basket, circa 1840, the rectangular tray top above two end frieze drawers with basket frame and beaded rim, set on two lyre end supports, 68cm. wide.
(Bonhams) $5,880

A Regency mahogany work table, the rectangular dropleaf top above a single frieze drawer and dummy drawer, 54cm. wide.
(Bonhams) $1,386

A Classical brass-inlaid parcel-gilt and verdigris rosewood games table, attributed to Deming and Bulkeley, New York, circa 1825, the rectangular top with canted corners swivelling above a well, 36in. open.
(Sotheby's) $8,050

A Regency mahogany games-table, the projecting rectangular top with D-shaped ends later inlaid with chessboard with ebony and burr-elm squares, 32¾in. wide.
(Christie's) $3,726

A Regency mahogany work table, circa 1820, the rectangular top above a drawer with a compartmented interior and a sliding basket below, 21½in. wide.
(Bonhams) $3,640

A Federal eagle-inlaid mahogany games table, Massachusetts, circa 1795, the rectangular top with rounded corners above urn-inlaid dies centring a tablet with a spreadwinged eagle, 35½in. wide open.
(Sotheby's) $123,500

An Anglo-Indian amboyna and ebony work-table, early 19th century, the moulded rectangular hinged top enclosing a sandalwood interior with partitions and ivory lids inlaid with ebony, 21in. wide.
(Christie's) $6,707

A Regency rosewood work-table, the rectangular sliding hinged ratcheted reading-slope with inset gilt-tooled leather top above two drawers flanked by implement drawers, 48in. wide open.
(Christie's) $5,962

A George IV mahogany Pembroke work table, the canted rectangular top above two end drawers opposite a lead and marble lined cupboard, lacking work box, 21½in. wide. (Bonhams) $607

A rare Queen Anne carved and figured walnut games table, Philadelphia, circa 1740, the shaped rectangular top with outset corners opening to a fitted playing surface, 32in. open.
(Sotheby's) $68,500

A Federal figured mahogany work table, Boston, Massachusetts, circa 1815, the square top with outset corners, 23¾in. wide. (Sotheby's) $4,025

A Victorian walnut work table, the burr veneered octagonal hinged top revealing a fitted interior, 18in. (Woolley & Wallis) $1,095

A 19th century Milanese ebonised and ivory inlaid workbox, the hinged lid opening onto a satin lined interior. (David Lay) $966

A William IV marquetry circular work table, the hinged top with amboyna stylised foliate marquetry, enclosing a frieze compartment, 58cm. diameter. (Phillips) $3,608

Classical mahogany veneer and grained drop-leaf sewing table, circa 1840, stencil labelled *J. & J. W. Meeks Makers No. 4 Vesey St. New York*, on the inside of the drawer, 26½in. wide. (Skinner) $1,150

An Edwardian satinwood, mahogany, boxwood and harewood-inlaid octagonal work table, the shaped chequer-banded top with raised edge and central hinged section, 22in. wide. (Christie's) $1,656

A Federal figured mahogany two-drawer work table, Massachusetts, circa 1810, the rectangular top with ring-turned outset corners above two cockbeaded drawers, 20½in. wide. (Sotheby's) $2,875

A Victorian rosewood and inlaid work/games table, the serpentine shaped top with chequerboard inlay flanked by floral panels, 21½in. wide. (Christie's) $827

A late 19th century mahogany Continental work table, the crossbanded hinged top with canted corners enclosing central well and lidded compartments, 22in. (Dreweatt Neate) $1,108

A Victorian mahogany pedestal workbox, on turned column with lion paw supports, 42.5cm. wide. (Bristol) $640

Late Empire three-drawer work table, 19th century, in mahogany with mahogany veneers, carved pedestal legs and paw feet, 22½in. wide. (Eldred's) $2,310

A Victorian walnut octagonal sewing table, 16½in. diameter. (Dockree's) $643

Classical mahogany carved and mahogany veneer work table, Massachusetts, circa 1825, the rectangular top with rounded drop leaves above two cockbeaded graduated drawers, 20in. wide. (Skinner) $920

Federal mahogany veneer sewing table, New England, the mahogany top with hinged drop leaves has a reeded edge, 18½in. wide. (Skinner) $1,150

Federal mahogany astragal-end carved and mahogany veneered work table, New York, circa 1815–20, the rectangular top flanked by hinged tops above conforming case, 25¼in. wide. (Skinner) $2,300

Classical tiger maple work table, New England, circa 1820–30, the rectangular drop leaf above two drawers with convex fronts, 16½in. wide. (Skinner) $1,495

A Regency pollard oak and ebony strung drop flap work table, containing a drawer and sliding well below, on a U-shaped stretcher, 73cm. wide. (Phillips) $2,788

A William IV rosewood work table, with a hinged cavetto moulded lid and bowed sides with brass ring carrying handles, 46cm. wide. (Phillips) $2,132

An early 19th century mahogany dropleaf work table, with satinwood crossbanding to the rounded rectangular top, 64cm. wide. (Bearne's) $3,146

Antique Empire two-drawer drop-leaf work table in mahogany with pedestal base and four scroll feet, probably by Vose Co. of Boston, top 20½ x 18½in. plus two 10in. leaves. (Eldred's) $1,430

A Biedermeier walnut work table, second quarter 19th century, decorated with lines, the rectangular hinged top with canted corners, 17¾in. wide. (Christie's) $2,024

A George IV rosewood work table, the rectangular top with a gadrooned border, above a frieze fitted with a drawer, locked, on scrolled supports and downswept legs, 18in. wide. (Christie's) $1,677

Early 19th century pollard oak and rosewood banded sewing table with one fitted drawer and sliding bag, on end supports and splayed legs with brass paw feet, 23in. wide. (Ewbank) $1,078

A Classical mahogany veneered work table, New York City, 1815-1820, the hinged rectangular lid with astragal-ends, opening to a square well flanked by D-shaped wells with removeable trays, 25¼in. (Christie's) $27,600

A 19th century Chinese lacquer and mother of pearl inlaid work box, with allover external and internal decoration of exotic birds and flowers, 18in. wide. (George Kidner) $3,044

An early Victorian amboyna, ebony and rosewood rectangular work table, the whole of serpentine outline, the amboyna top with rosewood crossbanding and ebony mouldings, 26in. (Canterbury) $4,247

A Victorian figured and burr walnut octagonal top sewing table with hinged lid, fitted interior, tapering column and triple carved splay feet, 18in. wide. (John Maxwell) $726

A Regency brass-mounted and rosewood writing-table, attributed to Gillows, the rounded rectangular top inset with brown tooled leather writing-surface, 48in. wide.
(Christie's) $43,378

A George III mahogany writing table, the moulded rectangular brown leather-lined top above three frieze drawers to the front and reverse, 48¼in. wide.
(Christie's) $16,870

A 19th century mahogany writing table with reeded edged oblong top having central ratcheted slope, 42in. wide.
(Andrew Hartley) $3,024

A William IV rosewood pedestal writing table, the rectangular hinged top enclosing a fitted interior, 24½in. wide.
(Christie's) $2,235

A George III mahogany Pembroke writing table, the rectangular twin-flap top with central sliding panel revealing a green baize-lined ratcheted hinged writing-surface, 40in. wide open.
(Christie's) $3,374

A late Victorian mahogany campaign folding writing table, decorated with lines and crossbanding, the hinged top fitted with two drawers, 24in. wide.
(Christie's) $2,944

A George III mahogany, satinwood and marquetry bonheur du jour, in the manner of John Cobb, inlaid overall with floral sprays of roses and pearwood and ebonised lines, 37in. wide.
(Christie's) $8,435

A Chinese Export padouk harlequin table, mid-18th century, the rounded rectangular treble-hinged top, enclosing a plain surface, a games table and a writing table.
(Christie's) $97,442

A Regency brass-mounted partridgewood writing table, in the manner of John McLean, the rounded rectangular green leather-lined top with three-quarter pierced Greek-key gallery, 51½in. wide.
(Christie's) $74,620

A 19th century burr walnut and ebonised bonheur du jour with gilt metal mounts and inset porcelain plaques, the stepped superstructure with pierced gallery, 53¼in. wide. (Andrew Hartley) $5,852

A fine Victorian kingwood and ormolu mounted writing table, by Gillows, circa 1870, the shaped tooled leather inset top with cast edge above three drawers to the shaped frieze, 48¼in. wide. (Bonhams) $20,720

Oriental padouk desk of canted square form, the back elaborately moulded with dragons and smoke clouds and fitted on either side with two drawers and short drawer and cupboard respectively, circa early 20th century, 46in. (G.A. Key) $624

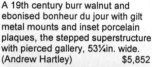

An American mahogany desk, early 19th century, with three short drawers above a hinged sloping baize lined writing surface and with two long drawers below, 36in. wide. (Christie's) $1,570

A North European walnut and ormolu mounted bureau plat, 19th century, of serpentine outline, with a green leather lined top above a conforming frieze with ribbon-tied female mask mounts, 58in. wide. (Christie's) $1,362

A 19th century oak antler and composition writing table, the rectangular top with moulded cornice and re-entrant corners inset with fabric panel, surmounted at the back with interlaced antlers with deer's head, 24in. wide. (Christie's) $3,657

Early 20th century japanned and lacquered kidney shaped desk, rexine inset, frieze inset over two drawers and raised on cabriole supports with claw and ball feet, 42in. (G.A. Key) $725

Edwardian rosewood ladies desk, inlaid throughout with satinwood and boxwood panels of neo classical marquetry, central compartment with lifting lid enclosing a fitted interior, 40in. (G.A. Key) $3,480

A mahogany and line inlaid serpentine outline writing table, late 19th century, the shaped top with back fitted with two secret drawers over shaped central drawer, 137cm. wide. (Bristol) $678

A late Louis XVI brass-mounted mahogany table à écrire, the rectangular bleu turquin marble top, above a panelled frieze with a part cedar-lined drawer with a green leather lined writing surface, 21¾in. wide. (Christie's) $59,454

An early Victorian mahogany pedestal desk of breakfront outline, the top with a moulded edge above a concave frieze drawer, each pedestal with two graduated short drawers, 48in. wide. (Christie's) $1,083

A painted French bonheur du jour, gilt ground, polychrome decorated with floral sprays and birds, the raised superstructure with a bevelled glazed rectangular door, 31½, circa 1900. (Woolley & Wallis) $277

Fine George III cross-banded satinwood roll-top writing desk, circa 1800, with tambour roll-top enclosing an interior fitted with small drawers, pigeonholes and a sliding ratcheted leather-topped writing surface, 36¾in. long. (Skinner) $8,625

A George III satinwood bonheur-du-jour, late 18th/early 19th century, banded and crossbanded overall, the concave-sided superstructure with a shelf above three small drawers and flanked by a door to each side, 36in. wide. (Christie's) $12,513

A Russian ormolu-mounted cedar campaign desk on folding stand, late 18th/early 19th century, inlaid overall with boxwood and green-stained lines, the rectangular top above a sloping and vertical double-hinged fall, 34in. wide. (Christie's) $8,384

A North European walnut bonheur du jour, 19th century, the superstructure with a pierced scroll-carved pediment centred by a carved stag's head, 46in. wide. (Christie's) $1,099

An Italian walnut and burr-veneered bureau plat, 20th century, crossbanded and inlaid with lines, with a roundel centred top fitted with a central frieze drawer, 55in. wide. (Christie's) $2,245

An unusual William IV rosewood and mahogany lady's writing table, the hinged top enclosing a folding hinged writing slope with velvet lined panels, 22½in. wide. (Christie's) $2,138

A French kingwood and ormolu-mounted bureau plat, in the manner of F. Linke, late 19th century, the undulating top inset with a panel of tooled leather, 53½in. wide.
(Christie's) $5,589

A mahogany desk, Dutch, circa 1820, the upper part with a pierced gallery above an arrangement of six small drawers, 125cm. wide.
(Sotheby's) $13,496

A French brass inlaid mahogany writing table, early 20th century, inlaid with lines, the rectangular top centred with a flower-filled urn, 27¾in. wide.
(Christie's) $4,048

A good Regency rosewood and brass inlaid writing table, circa 1810, the pierced brass galleried rectangular top with square central panel flanked by a pair of hinged compartments, 36¼in. wide.
(Christie's) $12,800

A kingwood, marquetry and giltbronze lady's writing table, Paris, circa 1890, the leather-inset top within a moulded cast border, 115cm. wide.
(Sotheby's) $10,436

A Russian Neo-Classical kingwood, marquetry and parquetry inlaid kidney shape writing table, St. Petersburg, circa 1780, the shaped top with a central circular panel inlaid with a basket of flowers, 38½in. wide.
(Christie's) $6,400

A Regency mahogany pedestal writing table, decorated with lines, the square top lacking a ratcheted hinged surface, 31in. wide.
(Christie's) $3,167

A gilt-bronze mounted mahogany small writing table, French, 19th century, in Louis XV style, the tulipwood banded top of serpentine outline, 2ft. wide.
(Sotheby's) $3,841

A Regency mahogany writing-table, in the manner of Gillows, the rectangular green leather-lined top with re-entrant corners, 36¼in. wide.
(Christie's) $12,259

An Empire period mahogany and brass strung tall chest, containing six long drawers between tapered stiles, possibly Dutch, 103cm. wide.
(Phillips) $2,550

Queen Anne maple tall chest of drawers, probably Rhode Island, circa 1750, on bracket feet, 33¾in wide.
(Skinner) $2,645

A crossbanded walnut chest, the rectangular top above five graduated long drawers and a shaped apron, on bracket feet, 23¼in. wide.
(Christie's) $661

A good Chippendale walnut tall chest of drawers, Pennsylvania, circa 1780, the overhanging stepped cornice above three short and five long graduated molded drawers, 45in. wide.
(Sotheby's) $13,800

Cherry and maple tall chest of drawers, New England, circa 1800, the case of six thumbmolded graduated drawers on cut-out bracket base, 36in. wide.
(Skinner) $1,840

Chippendale maple tall chest of drawers, southeastern New England, late 18th century, case of two thumbmolded short drawers and five long drawers on bracket feet, 36in. wide.
(Skinner) $1,725

Chippendale tiger maple tall chest, Rhode Island, late 18th century, the cornice molding over a seven-drawer thumbmolded case, 37in. wide.
(Skinner) $10,350

Chippendale applewood carved tall chest of drawers, probably Concord, Massachusetts, circa 1780, the flat molded cornice above a case of six graduated drawers, 35½in. wide.
(Skinner) $4,025

Chippendale maple tall chest, Rhode Island, late 18th century, the flat molded dentil cornice above the thumbmolded drawers, 36in. wide.
(Skinner) $8,337

A late Regency rosewood teapoy, restorations, 47.5cm. wide.
(Bonhams) $1,088

A William IV bird's-eye maple and rosewood teapoy, with sarcophagus-shaped top, on an octagonal baluster support and circular platform with four scrolled legs with later bun feet, 17½in. wide. (Christie's) $2,907

A Chinese Export lacquer and mother of pearl inlaid teapoy on associated base, circa 1840, 50cm. wide x 90cm. high.
(Bonhams) $435

WARDROBES

An inlaid mahogany neo-gothic wardrobe, attributed to Christopher Pratt & Sons, circa 1860, the mirrored central door opening to reveal drawer-lined interior, 81in. wide. (Christie's) $2,760

Alvar Aalto, wardrobe for patient's room, Paimio Sanatorium, 1929-33, white painted laminated and solid wood, interior with two-tier upper shelf unit, 31½in. wide.
(Sotheby's) $3,312

An oak two-door wardrobe, by Robert 'Mouseman' Thompson, the rectangular top above carved frieze and two fielded cupboard doors, enclosing hanging space and rectangular mirror glass, 48in.wide.
(Christie's) $12,337

WASHSTANDS

A George III mahogany bowfront corner washstand, with a three-quarter gallery and two tiers, with a central frieze drawer to the lower tier, on square outswept legs, 24½in. wide.
(Christie's) $658

A late Georgian rosewood and mahogany kneehole washstand with shallow raised gallery, having a long drawer over, 32½ wide.
(Dee Atkinson & Harrison)
                         $1,980

A George III mahogany washstand, the divided hinged top revealing basin aperture, the fascia with dummy drawer and frieze drawer, 34in. high.
(Andrew Hartley) $691

A Regency rosewood and simulated-rosewood four-tier étagère, the four square tiers with turned columnar supports and four turned finials,19½in. square. (Christie's) $2,249

A late Victorian carved oak buffet, circa 1890, the boar carved back above three tiers and raised on turned legs with castors, 138cm. wide. (Bonhams) $1,178

A Federal mahogany étagère, possibly Philadelphia, 1790-1810, rectangular, with ball finials above ring and baluster-turned supports, 23in. wide. (Christie's) $6,900

A Victorian burr walnut and inlaid canterbury whatnot, the inlaid top on turned supports. (Bristol) $1,680

One of a pair of Victorian carved oak buffets, the tops with mask and foliage crest, open scrolls and carved finials, front putti supports to a galleried undertier, 4ft.4in. (Woolley & Wallis)
(Two) $1,704

A mahogany four tier serpentine whatnot, the two rear supports encrusted with urn finials and joined by a fretwork pierced gallery, 39in. wide. (G A Key) $2,216

A Victorian mahogany whatnot, of four rectangular open tiers and a drawer, the upper tier with a three-quarter gallery, 23½in. wide. (Christie's) $1,417

A Colonial padouk three tier buffet, last quarter 19th century, each rectangular tier held within a carved decorative gallery frieze, supported by profusely foliate carved pier ends, 84cm. wide. (Bonhams) $1,108

A Regency 'bamboo'-painted four-tier étagère, first half 19th century, on supports painted to simulate bamboo, 16¾in. wide. (Sotheby's) $3,162

A George III brass-bound mahogany oval wine-cooler, of slightly tapering form, with vertical slats, and two carrying-handles, 25¾in. wide.
(Christie's) $4,361

A Regency mahogany cellaret, restorations, 44cm. wide.
(Bonhams & Brooks) $539

A Regency mahogany wine-cooler, attributed to Gillows, the rounded rectangular thickly-molded lip around a tapering metal-lined interior, 35in. wide.
(Christie's) $10,902

A George III mahogany and inlaid hexagonal cellaret, the hinged top crossbanded and inlaid with ebony stringing enclosing a once fitted lead inlaid interior on molded square tapered splayed legs, 21¼in. wide.
(Christie's) $2,533

A George III brass-bound mahogany wine-cooler, of oval slatted form with lion-mask ring handles, with later metal liner, 23½in. wide.
(Christie's) $5,451

The Stephen Van Rensselaer III Federal mahogany cellaret, English or American, circa 1790, the rectangular lid with string-inlaid edge and quarter-fan corner inlays opening to a conforming case, 28½in. wide.
(Christie's) $9,775

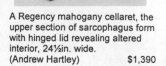

A Regency mahogany cellaret, the upper section of sarcophagus form with hinged lid revealing altered interior, 24½in. wide.
(Andrew Hartley) $1,390

A George III mahogany and brass-bound oval wine cooler on stand, the stand possibly of a slightly later date, with metal liner and lion mask handles, 24in. wide.
(Christie's) $4,229

An unusual George III mahogany cellaret, the hinged top enclosing a fitted interior and containing a drawer and enclosing panel door to the side, 22½in. wide.
(Christie's) $1,991

Patriotic painted folding parcheesi gameboard, New England, late 19th century, 17¾ x 18in. (Skinner) $4,312

Painted double-sided gameboard, 19th century, mustard, red, and green paint, checkers on obverse, backgammon on reverse, 15 x 16in. (Skinner) $3,335

Painted parcheesi gameboard, New England, circa 1870-80, with red, yellow, and green paint, 27½ x 27in. (Skinner) $5,750

Double-sided painted gameboard, New Hampshire, 19th century, six-color parcheesi game scribed and painted in eight colors, checkerboard on the reverse, 20 x 18½in. (Skinner) $21,850

Painted checkerboard, late 19th century, oblong form, green and yellow paint, 10½ x 19½in. (Skinner) $1,955

Painted folding parcheesi gameboard, 19th century, green white, black, and yellow paint with varied geometric designs on game corners, 19½ x 19½in. (Skinner) $2,875

Painted double-sided gameboard, New England, circa 1860, green and yellow paint, 14½ x 14in. (Skinner) $2,530

Painted double-sided gameboard, America, early 19th century, black, white, and green paint, initials *M.B.*, 14 x 11½in.(Skinner) $1,725

Painted checkerboard, New England, 19th century, blue and white with yellowed varnish, 16 x 16in. (Skinner) $3,335

A pair of painted metal recumbent lions, 20th century, stamped *J.W. Fiske Ironworks, New York, Made in U.S.A.*, 4ft. 4in. long. (Sotheby's) $7,475

A pair of composition stone sphinxes, 20th century, each reclining on a rectangular base, 45in. long. (Sotheby's) $4,600

A pair of enamelled stone fruit baskets. 21in. high. (Sotheby's) $5,175

A pair of zinc greyhounds, late 19th century, by J.W.Fiske, New York, oxidised grey-blue patina, 41in. long. (Sotheby's) $10,925

A pair of Neoclassical style cast-iron urns, 19th century, of campana form with an everted rim above a classically decorated frieze, 31in. high. (Sotheby's) $4,600

A pair of terracotta urns on pedestals, each of low bulbous form modelled with ram's masks joined by berried oak leaf swags, 34in. high. (Sotheby's) $5,462

A pair of copper corbels, each voluted bracket cast with foliage, 32in. high. (Sotheby's) $920

A painted stone figure of a lamb, 38in. high. (Sotheby's) $6,325

A lead figure of an eagle on pedestal, circa 1900, overall height 4ft. 4in. (Sotheby's) $3,162

A pair of lead figures of sphinxes, late 19th century, 4ft. 3in. long. (Sotheby's) $25,300

A pair of massive painted cast-iron urns on stands, late 19th century, attributed to J.L. Mott, New York, each waisted vessel with a foliate and floral decorated frieze. (Sotheby's) $37,950

A pair of monumental terracotta urns on pedestals, circa 1910, of campana form, stamped *Galloway*, overall height 7ft. 2¼in. (Sotheby's) $37,375

Polychrome decorated cast-iron giraffe doorstop, early 20th century, ocher painted stylized giraffe figure with dark brown accents, with base, 16½in. high.(Skinner) $2,415

A 19th century alabaster font, with four applied birds, 32cm. diameter. (Bonhams) $176

A Continental polychrome painted terracotta figure of a gnome, 20th century, with forked beard, pointed hood, waistcoat, breeches and slippers, formerly holding a fishing rod, 20in. high. (Christie's) $924

An English lead urn, early 20th century, the knopped acanthus clasped finial and domed cover above body with twin cherubs, floral swags and stiff-leaf decoration, 36in. high.(Christie's) $2,537

A Queen Anne lead demi-lune cistern, the panel moulded front cast with allegorical figures, the initials *T.S.M.*, dated *1707*, 29¼ x 28in. (Bonhams) $3,528

A North European limestone group of St. George and the Dragon, 17th century, Saint George semi-cuirassed astride his steed, damages and restorations, 29in. high. (Christie's) $3,565

A pair of large lead garden urns of baluster form with square bases, 18th/19th century, 89cm. high. (Bearne's) $4,640

An early 19th century painted iron garden seat with reeded scroll-filled back and downswept arms, 168cm. wide. (Bearne's) $3,135

A large pair of Italian terracotta garden urns in the classical style, each molded with ram's heads. 78cm. diameter. (Bearne's) $2,240

An Archimede Seguso macchie ambre verde blown glass basket, designed circa 1952, in clear glass with gold foil inclusions, 9¾in. high. (Sotheby's) $2,875

Amethyst pressed open work glass fruit basket on foot, Boston & Sandwich Glass Company, Sandwich, Massachusetts, 1840-55, sixteen vertical staves and rim of thirty-two even points, 8in. high.(Skinner) $14,100

An opaque white through pale blue cased frill basket with aventurine inclusions, late 19th century, 22cm. high. (Christie's) $375

BEAKERS

A Venetian polychrome enamelled beaker, second half of the 18th century, probably by a member of the Brussa Family, decorated in shades of pink, green, yellow and white with flower-sprays, 4in. high. (Christie's) $1,646

Two ruby flashed Bohemian flared beakers, cut with panels of printies, late 19th/early 20th century, 12.5cm. (Woolley & Wallis) $147

A fine Hessan engraved and gilt armorial beaker, Paderborn, Emde or Altmünder Glashütte, circa 1780, the cylindrical form engraved with two crests accollé, below a coronet and within a leaf and rocaille cartouche, 8cm. (Sotheby's) $5,376

BOTTLES

A sealed wine bottle of cylindrical form, with rounded shoulders and tapering neck, the seal molded in relief *I WATSON Efqr BILTON PARK*, circa 1780, 24cm. high. (Christie's) $365

A Great Western Railway Co. empty whisky spigot bottle, approximately 26in. high. (Academy) $176

A sealed and dated onion wine bottle of olive-green tint with string rim, the seal inscribed *B. Greive* and dated *1727*, 15cm. high. (Christie's) $1,454

A Le Verre Français bowl, etched factory mark, 30.5cm. diameter. (Christie's) $735

A cameo and carved glass bowl, by Daum, circa 1900, etched and wheel-carved with pendant leafy branches above clusters of small berries, 28.5cm. diameter. (Christie's) $3,206

A small Lalique bowl, of Coquilles design, maked R. Lalique France, 13.5cm. wide. (Woolley & Wallis) $225

A Daum bowl, the underside of the gray glass bowl decorated with a series of etched triangular designs, 31cm. diameter. (Christie's) $557

Schlevogt shallow fish bowl, green malachite glass molded in the form of two fish head to tail among waves forming an oblong bowl, 2¾in. high. (Skinner) $373

A cameo glass bowl by Daum, circa 1900, the gray glass internally mottled with yellow and ox-blood, overlaid in mottled yellow, blue and green with leafy branches and fruiting blackberries, 20.5cm. diameter. (Christie's) $2,174

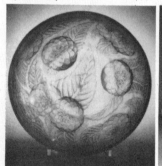

'Dahlias No.1' No.3210 a clear, frosted and blue-stained bowl, molded marks R. Lalique France, 23.6cm. diameter. (Christie's) $624

Two opaque white glass bowls and covers, modelled as a cockerel and hen, 23cm. (Woolley & Wallis) $62

A Lalique glass bowl, of 'Marguerites' design, molded with flowers around the border, traces of green staining, marked R. Lalique, France, 33.5cm. (Woolley & Wallis) $68

'Poissons No.1' No.3262 a clear and opalescent bowl, 30cm. diameter. (Christie's) $1,233

A Lalique clear and opalescent glass bowl, of 'Lys' design, engraved R. Lalique, France, N.382, 24cm. (Woolley & Wallis) $870

'Lys' No.382 a clear, frosted, and gray-stained bowl, wheel-engraved R.Lalique France, 23.5cm. diameter. (Christie's) $904

Two-piece colorless pattern glass punch bowl, Drape pattern bowl and stand, 16in. diameter. (Skinner) $588

A Venetian large standing bowl, circa 1500, the deep bowl with gadrooned lower part and applied with two dark-blue trailed threads with a band of faint granular gilding between, 11½in. diameter. (Christie's) $5,120

Irish cut glass covered fruit bowl, circa 1810, 9in. high. (Eldred's) $330

BOXES

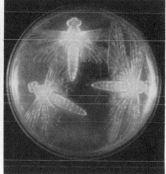

'Quatre Scarabées' No. 15, a blue clear and frosted glass box and cover, molded mark R. Lalique, 8.5cm. diameter. (Christie's) $1,233

'Eglantine' No.94 a clear and frosted box and cover, intaglio, molded R. Lalique, 13.8cm. diameter. (Christie's) $361

'Libellules' No.51 a clear and opalescent box and cover, molded mark R.Lalique, 17cm. diameter. (Christie's) $1,068

Lalique, a Cyprins opalescent large box cover, after 1921, the interior relief moulded with four fish, relief moulded mark, 26cm. (Bonhams & Brooks) $480

Bohemian white overlay cut-to-cranberry glass jewel box, late 19th century, oblong, with gilt-metal hinge mount, cut with roundels and leaves, 5¹/₈in. wide. (Skinner) $1,035

'Trésor de la Mer' a frosted and opalescent hinged box, made for Saks Fifth Avenue, stencil mark R.Lalique France, 14cm. deep. (Christie's) $4,935

A pair of Sowerby turquoise malachite glass candlesticks, the spiral moulded columns with Corinthian capitals, marks for 1877, 19cm.(Woolley & Wallis) $137

Pair of Carder Steuben Amethyst Silverina candleholders, mica flecked light amethyst with controlled bubble pattern, 5in. high. (Skinner) $863

A pair of Baccarat moulded glass candlesticks, with Ionic capitals and spiral columns, marked *Baccarat depose*, 20.5cm. (Woolley & Wallis) $127

T.G. Hawkes cut and engraved crystal bowl and candlesticks, bright cut floral and webbed motif on bowl, 14in. high. (Skinner) $3,105

Two colourless pressed glass dolphin candlesticks, one with petal socket and double-step base (reproduction), and one with petal socket and single-step base. (Skinner) $529

Three colourless free-blown and pressed candlesticks, Boston & Sandwich Glass Company, Sandwich, Massachusetts, 1835-60, with blown sockets and pressed stepped quatrefoil bases, all circa 8½in. high. (Skinner) $588

COUPES

A Gallé maple leaf coupe, circa 1900, hexagonal, gray glass internally decorated with red towards the base and at the rim, 7.3cm. (Sotheby's) $1,444

A Façon de Venise tazza, late 17th or early 18th century, Venice, the flat tray with an upturned rim, the underside applied with turquoise chain ornament, 10¼in. diameter. (Christie's) $2,045

Pink over white cased glass compôte, circa 1880, the gauffered bowl on white base, 7¼in. high. (Skinner) $323

A set of seventeen decanters now in a 19th century mahogany and ebonized decanter-box, of square form with reeded pilasters to the angles, 17¼in. square. (Christie's) $5,839

Bohemian flashed glass and silver plate decanter set, late 19th century, comprising three shouldered decanters flashed blue, green and cranberry respectively and cut with circles and etched with Greek key band, decanter 14in. high. (Skinner) $863

An Edwardian oak three bottle tantalus with electroplated mounts, the glass decanters with circular stoppers and spirit labels, 40cm. (Bearne's) $561

DISHES

Colourless pressed lacy glass footed dish with cover, Boston & Sandwich Glass Company, 1840-45, the cover with Princess Feather medallions with rose and thistle motifs, 9½in., high. (Skinner) $3,525

Pair of Irish cut glass covered sweetmeat dishes, circa 1810, each with a rim chip, 6¼in. high. (Eldred's) $357

Colourless pressed lacy glass dish, Boston & Sandwich Glass Company, Sandwich, Massachusetts, 1835-50, Double Peacock Eye pattern with divided strawberry diamonds, 12¼in., long. (Skinner) $1,293

ÉPERGNES

A cranberry and vaseline épergne, composed of large frilled trumpet flanked by two smaller examples, two clear canes between supporting baskets applied with clear trails, 49cm. (Bonhams) $775

An early 19th century Old Sheffield plated épergne on four supports with paw feet and gadrooned border, circa 1815, 31cm. high x 54cm. (Christie's) $2,115

A sweetmeat tree or.épergne and six baskets, the tree circa 1740, the baskets later repacements, the ribbed bowl with applied flange, set on a vermicular collar above a hollow globe, 10¼in. (Sotheby's) $1,428

Cobalt blue blown quart flask, England or Eastern U.S., 19th century, with white speckle decoration, 10¾in. high. (Skinner) $258

A Spanish green-tinted rectangular bottle flask, 17th/18h century, moulded overall with meshwork terminating in ribbing on the shoulder, 20.7cm. (Sotheby's) $1,176

Blown moulded historical flask, Washington portrait flask, medium green, double collared mouth-iron pontil mark, quart, Lockport Glass Works, Lockport, New York, 1845-60. (Skinner) $4,025

GOBLETS

A baluster goblet, circa 1720, the bell bowl supported on a triple annulated knop above an inverted baluster stem enclosing a tear, 6¾in. (Christie's) $3,748

A façon de venise latticinio goblet, second half of the 16th century, Venice or South Netherlands, in vetro a retorti with fine thread gauze cable decoration, the double-ogee bowl supported on a knop, 11.7cm. high. (Christie's) $7,314

An engraved composite-stemmed goblet, circa 1750, of Jacobite significance and of drawn form, the funnel bowl engraved with a sunflower, 18.8cm. high. (Christie's) $5,111

A large baluster goblet, circa 1710, the generous straight-sided funnel bowl set on an inverted baluster stem enclosing a large tear, on a folded conical foot, 8¼in. high. (Christie's) $3,748

A façon de venise Latticinio goblet, mid 16th century, the tall cylindrical bowl with flared and folded flange at the base and decorated with two horizontal bands in vetro a retorti, 10¼in. high. (Christie's) $23,771

A baluster goblet, circa 1730, the double-ogee bowl supported on a stem with central swelling section set between shoulder and base knobs, 7in. high. (Christie's) $937

472

Colourless pressed lacy glass 'Union' Ship of State octagonal plate, Midwest, 1830-45, the plate with bull's-eye border alternating with triangular points, 6⁵/₈in. diameter. (Skinner) $1,410

A Continental blue glass barrel shaped flask, the body applied with crimped spiralling trails and raised on four scroll feet, 18th/19th century, 18cm. wide. (Woolley & Wallis) $221

Tiffany Studios etched metal and glass letter holder, New York, early 20th century, two-tier gilt-metal holder in the pine needle pattern with striated caramel glass inserts, 10in. long. (Skinner) $575

A pair of Bohemian blue and white overlay lusters, the bowls cut with arched panels painted with portraits of young girls between diamond-cut panels, late 19th century, 33.5cm high. (Christie's) $1,323

Colourless pressed and engraved glass celery, Pittsburgh, circa 1880, with scalloped rim, applied handles on hexagonal standard, fern pattern on reverse, 10in. high. (Skinner) $382

A rare bullet-shaped glass teapot and cover, circa 1740, of spherical form with narrow neck, scroll handle, 5¼in. (Sotheby's) $1,848

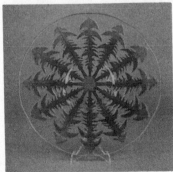

A Lalique Pissenlit clear, frosted and grey stained plate, the underside moulded with dandelion leaves, 31.5cm. (Bonhams) $259

A Venetian vessel in the form of a boot, 16th/17th century, naturally modelled with everted rim, applied with three raspberry prunts with traces of gilding to one side and with an applied footring, 9¼in. high. (Christie's) $6,948

'Ondines' No.3003, a clear, frosted, and opalescent plate, molded mark *R.Lalique*, 28cm. diameter. (Christie's) $2,451

A pâte de verre paperweight by Alméric Walter, after a model by Henri Berge, circa 1920, modelled as a large moth with blue and emerald green spread wings, 4¼in. wide. (Christie's) $2,743

A St. Louis panelled carpet-ground sulphide weight, mid 19th century, the central sulphide profile portrait of a lady to the right set in a large hollow red cane, 2¾in. diameter. (Christie's) $8,176

A pâte de verre paperweight by Alméric Walter, after a model by Henri Berge, circa 1920, modelled as a brown and russet speckled shrimp clinging to a rock with stylised waves, 4½in. wide. (Christie's) $4,571

A Perthshire 'gingham' concentric millefiori weight with predominantly orange, pink and lime-green canes within a white and caramel case, 20th century, 8.5cm. diameter. (Christie's) $875

'Moineau Timide' No.1151 a clear and frosted paperweight, engraved *R.Lalique France*, 13cm. diameter. (Christie's) $361

A Perthshire yellow, white and pink triple overlay faceted flower weight, with stamen formed from a P cane within six purple-edged white petals, 20th century, 7.5cm. diameter. (Christie's) $346

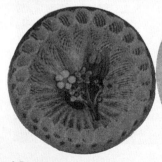

A Paul Ysart bouquet weight with five flowers and a bud above a PY cane on a latticinio basket, 20th century, 7cm. diameter, fitted case and card. (Christie's) $875

A St. Louis pelargonium weight, mid 19th century, the pink flower with five heart-shaped petals about a yellow and black centre, 2½in. diameter. (Christie's) $1,362

A St. Louis fruit weight, mid 19th century, the ripe pear, unripe pear, large apple and four cherries among numerous serrated green leaves, 6.6cm. diameter. (Christie's) $763

A St. Louis small dahlia weight, mid 19th century, the flower with five rows of ribbed mauve petals about a blue-centred orange cane, 2in. diameter. (Christie's) $1,180

A Clichy green-ground sulphide weight, mid 19th century, the bust portrait of the young Queen Victoria in profile to the left, 2½in. diameter. (Christie's) $436

A French green-ground pear weight, mid 19th century, probably Clichy, the large ripe fruit in shades of red, pink, and pale-yellow, 2¾in. diameter. (Christie's) $6,359

A Clichy faceted dark-blue double-overlay concentric millefiori mushroom weight, mid 19th century, the five circles of canes in shades of green, pink, white, purple and dark-blue, 7.3cm. diameter. (Christie's) $3,997

A Clichy millefiori weight, mid 19th century, with alternate spokes of pink staves, white gauze cable and twisted latticinio thread radiating from a large green and white central set-up, 3in. (Christie's) $1,235

A Clichy faceted patterned garlanded millefiori weight, mid 19th century, the central pink rose enclosed within a looped cinquefoil garland of canes in shades of green, pink, dark-blue, white and blue and white, 3in. diameter. (Christie's) $2,544

A Baccarat flat bouquet weight, mid 19th century, the central white and turquoise buttercup with yellow stamen centre flanked by two 'early' pansies, 9.2cm. diameter. (Christie's) $8,176

A Baccarat pink and green snake weight, mid 19th century, the opaque-pink coiled reptile with green mottled spine-markings, 3¼in. diameter. (Christie's) $5,087

A Baccarat faceted garlanded red and white primrose weight, mid 19th century, the flower with five red petals striped in white about a pink and white star centre, 7.3cm. diameter. (Christie's) $817

Thomas Webb cameo glass yellow cologne, white over yellow sphere intricately etched as decumbent fuchsia, total height, 4¾in. (Skinner) $977

René Lalique Epines dresser jar, sepia patine on colourless moulded thorny bramble motif on round bottle, 3½in. high. (Skinner) $460

Webb cameo glass square blue cologne, four panels of etched blossoms on squared amber bottle with screw-on silver cover, total height 5in. (Skinner) $517

An enamelled glass scent bottle and stopper by Daum, circa 1905, etched and enamelled in colours with wild violets and leaves, 9.5cm. high. (Christie's) $2,640

A pair of carved and etched glass scent bottles and stoppers, by Gallé, circa 1880, clear glass etched and carved, with gilt detailing, 14cm. high. (Christie's) $2,263

An Apsley Pellatt sulphide scent bottle and stopper, cut with a rectangular panel containing a profile bust sulphide of the Duke of Wellington, circa 1820, 12cm. high. (Christie's) $1,312

Thomas Webb cameo glass yellow cologne, brilliant red oval bottle layered in white cameo etched on blossoming leafy vines, 5½in. high. (Skinner) $1,495

A pair of large uranium green square section scent bottles and stoppers, moulded in relief *The Crown Perfumery Company London*, late 19th century, 53.5cm. high. (Christie's) $749

René Lalique Le Jade perfume, flattened snuff bottle form with moulded jungle bird decoration, 3¼in. high. (Skinner) $2,185

Carder Steuben gold aurene cologne, eight-lobed bottle with tapered conforming stopper, total height 6½in. (Skinner) $805

Large Lalique Dahlia perfume bottle, France, circular form molded as a dahlia blossom, highlighted with black enamel stamens, 8⅛in. (Skinner) $690

A cut glass scent bottle, the glass with central star motifs surrounded by pierced scroll, flower head and lattice work, 5¾in. high, London 1912. (Andrew Hartley) $693

An enamelled glass scent bottle and stopper, by Gallé, circa 1890, enamelled with two lobed reserves containing a medieval Persian warrior on horseback, 15cm. high. (Christie's) $9,430

René Lalique Bouchon Cassis perfume, vertically ribbed colourless barrel-form bottle with integrated tiara stopper, 4¾in. high. (Skinner) $7,187

An extremely rare Kelsterbach porcelain and gilt-metal mounted scent bottle and stopper, circa 1760–1765, modelled by Vogelmann, 3½in. (Sotheby's) $3,073

An amber tint and cut Apsley Pellatt sulphide scent bottle and silver stopper, cut with a square panel enclosing a sulphide of Princess Charlotte, second quarter 19th century, 7.5cm. high. (Christie's) $244

A pair of late 18th century blue glass scent bottles, probably Bristol, circa 1760, painted in the chinoiserie style with gilt exotic birds, floral decoration and rustic scene, height of box 2⅛in. (Bonhams) $1,120

Lalique for Molinard 'Madrigal', a limited edition, the ovoid body moulded with a frieze of classically draped maidens above a short stem circular foot. (Bonhams) $1,040

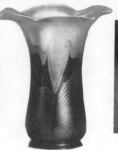

American leaded glass chandelier shade, parasol form with irregular border, designed as a multicoloured flowering vine growing on a trellis of green and olive, 28½in. diameter.
(Skinner) $4,887

Quezal Iridescent pulled feather glass shade, New York, early 20th century, ruffled flared rim on cylindrical shade of iridescent gold, green, and polychromatic glass, signed Quezal, 8in. high.
(Skinner) $3,450

Tiffany flowering water lily chandelier, conical hanging shade composed of favrile glass segments leaded as pastel pink, rose and opalescent white pond lily blossoms, 20in. diameter.
(Skinner) $75,100

An Italian sculpted alabaster ceiling light, early 20th century, incised with a frieze of cavorting children, 15½in. diameter.
(Christie's) $3,322

Arts & Crafts brass and slag glass hanging shade, America, early 20th century, linked metal chain suspending a shade composed of eight panels of green, caramel, and white bent slag glass panels, 20½in. diameter.
(Skinner) $920

A rare wrought iron mounted cameo glass 'bat' chandelier by Daum, circa 1900, the shade mottled with yellow, amber and purple, 15¾in. diameter.
(Christie's) $29,129

Pendant Art Glass ceiling lamp, attributed to Pittsburgh Glass Co., amber glass globe with etched crackle surface and painted blue parrot motif, 10in. diameter.
(Skinner) $1,150

Quezal glass hanging ceiling shade, Brooklyn, New York, early 20th century, radiating iridescent gold and green leaf decorations on domed iridescent ivory glass shade, inscribed Quezal, total drop 21½in.
(Skinner) $6,325

A Netherlandish brass hall lantern, circa 1720, the polygonal glazed frame with domed gadrooned and pierced top with loop suspension, 21¾in. high, overall.
(Christie's) $2,011

Carder Steuben Oriental poppy vase, satin smooth flared oval body of pink colour with sixteen integrated opal stripes, 6in. high. (Skinner) $1,380

Emile Gallé, fuchsias vase, circa 1900, yellow glass overlaid with red and etched with flowering stems, 8¼in. (Sotheby's) $4,225

Emile Gallé, 'Verre de Pekin' waterlilies vase, 1900, pale opaque green glass simulating jade, overlaid with cherry red, 8⅜in. (Sotheby's) $6,722

Schneider, miniature vase 'Aux Grappes de Raisins', 1920s, clear glass cased in speckled yellow, with marqueterie-sur-verre decoration of stems, 3⅝in. (Sotheby's) $3,073

A carved and internally decorated cameo glass vase, by Ernest Leveille, 1890, the watery grey body internally decorated with patches of sandy yellow and orange, 6⅝in. high. (Christie's) $39,364

Attributed to Daum, waterlilies vase, circa 1900, clear glass internally decorated with green, deeply etched and gilded with waterlily pads and flowers amidst rippling water, 10⅜in. (Sotheby's) $1,728

A cameo glass vase, by Gallé, circa 1905, flask-shaped, in grey glass tinted with aqua and coloured blue, 12³⁄₈in. high. (Christie's) $10,872

An enamelled glass vase, by Marcel Goupy, circa 1920, decorated with a frieze of leaping greyhounds against a crazed orange ground, 7¹⁄₈in. high. (Christie's) $4,874

An etched and mould-blown glass vase, by Gallé, circa 1900, grey glass tinted with yellow, overlaid in turquoise and green, 9⅝in. high. (Christie's) $5,623

A pale pink opalescent shouldered vase of flattened form, possibly Moser, the jewelled gilt line rim suspending an enamelled band of lappets, 19th century, 14cm. high.
(Christie's) $1,032

A Lalique baluster glass bottle vase, 'Aras', post 1924, frosted opalescent glass, moulded with exotic birds in branches, 10in.
(Sotheby's) $671

A Gallé vase, the milky white glass overlaid in blue and amethyst, 27.5cm. high.
(Christie's) $4,643

A Fratelli Toso applied blown glass vase, circa 1950s, the flattened teardrop form vessel in emerald green glass overlaid with gold foil, 11½in. high.
(Sotheby's) $1,495

Two fine similar Aureliano Toso oriente glass vases, designed by Dino Martens, circa 1952, the thick walls enclosing coloured ground glass powders, 11¼in. high.
(Sotheby's) $28,750

An Orrefors Ariel glass vase, designed by Edvin Öhrström, circa 1950, the thick ovoid vessel enclosing a pair of reclining odalisques, in deep cobalt blue and aubergine, 6in. high.
(Sotheby's) $17,250

An Archimede Seguso sommerso ribbed glass vase, circa 1960, with thick walls in clear over cranberry and purple, 7¼in. high.
(Christie's) $1,265

A Venini zanfirico fazzeletto vase, designed by Fulvio Bianconi, circa 1949, in clear glass enclosing vertical zanfirico canes, 5½in. high.
(Sotheby's) $2,875

A fine Murano murrhine glass wisteria vase, circa 1920, possibly by Vittorio Zecchin for Artisti Barovier, 6¾in. high.
(Sotheby's) $9,775

Kew-Blas Art Glass vase, cased ambergris oval vessel with gold iridescent feathers on opal body, 7in. high. (Skinner) $977

A pair of Victorian clear glass lustre vases, frieze of painted alternating portrait and floral medallions on gilded leaf ground, 12¾in. high. (Andrew Hartley) $1,023

Ernest-Baptiste Leveille silver mounted carved glass vase, elliptical sang-de-boeuf translucent body intaglio decorated with swirling scrolls, 8in. high. (Skinner) $4,025

Dale Chihuly Navajo Horse Blanket glass cylinder, translucent green glass with intricate surface decoration incorporating Native American weaving techniques, 10¼in. high. (Skinner) $35,560

A pair of cut-glass and gilt-bronze urns in the manner of Baccarat, Paris, circa 1900, each of campana form, with diamond-cut body and stem, 44cm. high. (Sotheby's) $13,282

Daum cameo glass scenic vase, raised rim on mottled blue oval body with etched landscape 'painted' in naturalistic vitrified colouration, 5⅝in. high. (Skinner) $2,760

Schlevogt green malachite glass ingrid vase, heavy walled press moulded oval vessel with four panels depicting partially nude women, 9½in. high. (Skinner) $488

A pair of Continental amber glass vases, one painted with King Charles on horseback, the other with Prince Rupert, 29cm. high. (Bearne's) $429

Schneider Le Verre Art Deco vase, unusual mottled white body colour layered with swirled orange and brown-green glass etched as stylized blossoms, 15½in. high. (Skinner) $1,035

Daum Nancy grapevine cameo glass and applied snail vase, France, early 20th century, flared rim on an ovoid vessel of mottled grey and purple glass rising to yellow, 8¼in. high.
(Skinner) $2,875

'Bresse' No.1073, a peppermint green vase, of footed spherical form, intaglio moulded with stylised design of cockerels, stencil mark *R.Lalique France,* 10.2cm. high.
(Christie's) $1,325

An Aurelio Toso 'Oriente' vase, designed by Dino Martens, circa 1960, with panels of opaque yellow, red, white and blue, copper aventurine, cased in clear glass, 8½in. high.
(Christie's) $5,065

A pair of 19th century Bohemian cranberry glass vases, floral painted panels on gilt ground alternating with white enamelled strawberry cut panels, 11in. high.
(Andrew Hartley) $1,567

'Oran' No.999, a Lalique frosted and opalescent vase, of cylindrical form, moulded in relief with a design of stylised peony blossoms, 25.7cm. high.
(Christie's) $368

A pair of Bohemian double-overlay cut and engraved vases, circa 1865, perhaps Harrach Glasshouse, of oviform, overlaid in blue and white, with flared necks and feet, 30.7cm. high.
(Christie's) $6,359

Mt. Washington Crown Milano 'Albertine' Egyptian scene vase, decorated with enamel scenes of an ethnic costumed man with camel, 12¼in. high.
(Skinner) $6,900

'Sylvia' No.1031, a clear, frosted and sepia stained vase and cover, the plain cylindrical body with two protruding handles moulded in relief as a pair of birds with grapes, *R. Lalique,* 21.5cm. high.
(Christie's) $5,152

A 'Jack in the Pulpit' favrile glass vase by Tiffany Studios, circa 1900, Jack-in-the-pulpit form in gold ground with rose and green lustre, 15¾in. high.
(Christie's) $8,383

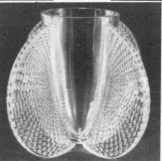

'Formose' No.934, a frosted and green stained vase, moulded in low relief with fan-tailed fish, stencil mark R.Lalique, 17cm. high. (Christie's) $2,024

'Orly' No.10-891, a clear glass vase, of tapering cylindrical form, with four crescent-shaped handles moulded with radiating dots, stencil mark *R.Lalique* France, 16.6cm. high. (Christie's) $2,944

A Lalique clear and blue tinged vase of ovoid form, moulded in relief with stylised berries and branches, moulded mark, 27.5cm. high. (Cheffins) $5,390

Monumental American brilliant-cut glass vase, late 19th century, featuring a border of hobstars within diamonds around scalloped notched rim, 16in. high. (Skinner) $1,725

'Aras' No.919, a clear, frosted and sepia stained vase, moulded in low relief with parrots amongst exotic berried foliage, intaglio moulded mark *R.Lalique*, 23cm. high. (Christie's) $2,392

A fire-polished and enamelled glass vase, by Gallé, circa 1900, the spherical body in shades of burnt sienna, yellow and white, carved and enamelled with apple blossoms, 7¼in. high. (Christie's) $6,520

Emile Gallé, clematis 'Blow-Out' vase, circa 1900, peach glass, overlaid with white and red and mould-blown with flowering clematis stems, 6½in. (Sotheby's) $3,457

A pair of Victorian potichomania vases, of ovoid form with shaped lids, each with polychrome chinoiserie transfers on a white ground, 16¼in. high. (Andrew Harley) $5,966

Tiffany favrile glass Jack-in-the-pulpit vase, circa 1905, lustrous amber gold iridescent glass, the flared and ruffled rim with stretched iridescence to edge, 17½in. high. (Skinner) $14,950

Schneider LeVerre bulbous vase, bright orange frosted bowl-form layered in tortoiseshell brown, 7in. high. (Skinner) $920

'Amiens' No.1023, a clear and frosted two-handled vase, of lozenge section, molded with two handles composed of foliate scrolls, wheel-cut mark *R.Lalique France,* 18cm. high. (Christie's) $827

A Monart whorled pale pink vase, with copper aventurine, 19cm. high. (Christie's) $517

René Lalique electric blue Perruches parrot vase, molded with fourteen pairs of 'love birds' perched on flowering branches, 10in. high. (Skinner) $9,775

Austrian gold papillon glass vase, attributed to Loetz, early 20th century, ruffled trefoil rim on a pinched oval body of colorless glass, 9¹/₈in.high. (Skinner) $632

An Art Nouveau pewter-mounted glass vase, in the style of Palme-Konig, 27.5cm. high. (Christie's) $875

Art Deco glass vase by Marcel Goupy. (G. E. Sworder) $1,280

Carder Steuben gold Aurene vase, New York, early 20th century, flared rim on double-bulbed ribbed form of gold iridescence, polished pontil, 6¹/₈in. high. (Skinner) $632

Gallé enamelled topaz glass vase, France, a double bulbed form of molded spiral ribbed topaz glass, enamel decorated with light blue and mauve trumpet flowers, 9in. high. (Skinner) $1,840

Gallé mold blown glass Rhododendron vase, France, circa 1925, raised rim on a spherical form of yellow amber glass layered in dark amethyst, with flowering rhododendron branches, 10¼in. (Skinner) $9,200

A Continental engraved vase, possibly Baccarat, late 19th century, finely engraved overall with a formal Berainesque pattern of scroll, baskets of flowers and small square panels, 11.5cm. (Sotheby's) $1,147

'Saint-François', by René Lalique, circa 1930, a clear, frosted and opalescent glass vase, molded in relief with chubby birds amongst foliage, 7in. high. (Christie's) $2,184

A Moser enamelled and gilt vase circa 1882, of amber-tint shading to red at the rim, applied with a bird perched on an oak branch, 11¾in. (Sotheby's) $4,586

'Poissons' No. 925 a red, clear and frosted vase, engraved R. Lalique, 24.5cm. high. (Christie's) $11,379

Steuben Rosaline and alabaster acid cut vase, cone-shape acid-etched floral design raised on alabaster base, rough pontil, 12in. high. (Skinner) $1,035

René Lalique Grimpereaux vase, France, design created 1926, slightly flared vessel of pale smoky topaz glass with six feet, decorated with geometric bands of birds on branches, 8¼in. high. (Skinner) $1,495

Steuben Bristol yellow swirl vase, circa 1925, flared rim on cylindrical body raised on circular foot, polished pontil, fleur-de-lis mark, some base wear, 7in. high. (Skinner) $173

Argy Rousseau pâte de verre vase, circa 1915, ovoid body of pâte de verre glass, molded decoration of trailing vines with fruit, in pale aqua, green, gray, and orange-brown, 5³/₈in. high. (Skinner) $575

A Lalique glass vase of tumbler form, moulded with encircling bands of blue tinted daisy like flowers, 14.5cm. high.
(Bearne's) $825

A pair of French opaque trumpet vases, painted in coloured enamels with iris and other flower sprays, gilt line rims, circa 1870, 30cm. high.
(Christie's) $5,623

A Fratelli Toso nerox glass vase, designed by Ermanno Toso, circa 1965, the waisted vessel in clear glass decorated with patches of crimson and orange, 8¹/₈in. high.
(Sotheby's) $460

A rare Orrefors Edvin glass vase, designed by Edvin Öhrström, dated 1944, the cylindrical vessel in turquoise blue glass overlaid in purple, 5½in. high.
(Sotheby's) $20,700

A Barovier & Toso intarsio glass vase, designed by Ercole Barovier, circa 1961-63, composed of triangular inlays in bright red, amber, pale lavender and cobalt blue, 6¾in. high.
(Sotheby's) $7,187

A Cenedese glass aquarium vase, circa 1950s, the flaring cylindrical form with thick walls shading from emerald green to pale green, 11½in. high.
(Sotheby's) $2,760

Loetz vase with applications, circa 1901, golden yellow glass washed with swags of pinky blue-gold iridescence, 5⁵/₈in.
(Sotheby's) $4,225

Iridescent green Art Glass vase, probably Bohemian, 20th century, flared rim on large spherical footed vessel, 12½in. high.
(Skinner) $575

A Daum vase, the cased glass internally decorated with maroon graduating to a mottled design of maroon, tangerine and amber, 25cm. high.
(Christie's) $1,672

Webb Cameo glass tricolour water lily vase, complex oval body composed of transparent ice blue with white layer below etched and carved as pond lilies, 7½in. high. (Skinner) $20,700

Mount Washington Royal Flemish vase, raised rim with applied angular handles on bulbous transparent colourless glass, 4½in. high. (Skinner) $2,645

A Daum Art Deco vase, the grey glass internally mottled with white and overlaid in blue, 22cm. high. (Christie's) $929

Venini Incalmo 'Colletti' vase, design of Ludovico de Santillana, circa 1961, raised crimson red flared rim with medial dark stripe, 10½in. high. (Skinner) $747

Pair of Bohemian mounted Art Glass vases, tall pigeon blood red oval body with purple iridized surface further enhanced by opal-grey random threading, 23in. (Skinner) $3,910

Tiffany heart and vine decorated vase, double bulbed gourd-form amber body with green leaves and amber vines, 5in. high. (Skinner) $1,840

A carved cameo glass vase by Gallé, circa 1900, heavy flattened body internally streaked with inky blue, overlaid in pale clear amber, pink and aubergine, 6¾in. high. (Christie's) $11,137

A Lalique opalescent glass vase, the ovoid body moulded with three bands of running antelope below a slightly everted rim, 17.8cm. high. (Bearne's) $2,160

An enamelled glass vase, by Gallé, circa 1890, in tinted glass, decorated with sprays of stylised flowers and yellow panels, 6¹/₈in. high. (Christie's) $3,561

Moore & Nims (fl.1858-1868), Troy, New York, circa 1860, a 10in. diameter terrestrial table globe made up of twelve delicately and attractively hand-coloured engraved gores. (Christie's) $5,778

Cox, London, 1839, a 12in. diameter terrestrial table globe, four baluster turned legs with turned cross-stretchers, 18in. high. (Christie's) $7,728

Félix Delamarche, Paris, 1863, a decorative 3in. diameter miniature globe made up of twelve hand-coloured engraved gores and two polar calottes, 7¼in. high. (Christie's) $3,069

Alexander & John Donaldson & Son, Edinburgh, 1830, a pair of 12in. diameter library globes, supported by four curved quadrant supports to fluted baluster column, 5¼in. diameter compass with blued-steel needle, 38¼in. high. (Christie's) $12,638

Gabriel Wright / William Bardin, London, 1782, a pair of 12in. diameter terrestrial & celestial table golbes, each made up of twelve delicately hand-coloured engraved gores, 24in. high. (Christie's) $19,860

Charles Smith & Son, London, circa 1835, a handsome pair of 19in. diameter library globes, the mahogany horizon supported by four fluted quadrant supports, 9in. diameter compass with original needle, 40½in. high. (Christie's) $39,721

A 19th century reproduction 30in. diameter terrestrial library globe made up of seventeen hand-coloured paper gores impressionistically fashioned after Willem Jansz. Blaeu, 42in. high. (Christie's) $4,514

Ashworth, England, circa 1880, a 3in. diameter miniature terrestrial globe, the sphere coming apart at the equator to put a reel of cotton inside, the thread emerging at the North Pole through an ivorine ring. (Christie's) $552

Charles Smith & Son, London, circa 1840, a 13in. diameter terrestrial globe made up of twelve hand-coloured engraved gores, on four baluster turned ebonised oak legs united by cross-stretchers, 17½in. high. (Christie's) $5,416

GLOBES

Ginn & Heath / Ellen Eliza Fitz, Boston, USA, circa 1875, a 6in. diameter terrestrial table globe made up of twelve delicately hand-coloured engraved gores and two polar calottes, 9¼in. high.
(Christie's) $4,514

Félix Delamarche, Paris, 1855, a pair of 8½in. diameter terrestrial and celestial table globes, raised on a simple turned ebonised column and plinth base, 18½in. high.
(Christie's) $4,514

Replogle Globes Inc., Chicago, circa 1935, a 10in. diameter terrestrial globe made up of two sets of twelve chromolithographed paper gores joined at the poles, 12in. high. (Christie's) $542

William & Alexander Keith Johnston, London & Edinburgh, circa 1902, a fine 30in. diameter terrestrial library globe made up of two sets of thirty-six colour printed gores and two polar calottes, 45¼in. high.
(Christie's) $57,619

Ekemm, England, a rare 2¾in. diameter miniature terrestrial globe made up to twelve hand-coloured engraved gores, with iron axis pins, in turned mahogany box, the domed lid with flat knop, 4¼in. high.
(Christie's) $4,514

Gilman Joslin, Boston, circa 1850, a 12in. diameter terrestrial table globe made up of twelve hand-coloured engraved gores and two polar calottes, on a cast iron stand, 18¼in. high.
(Christie's) $7,222

A 1930s 12-inch diameter terrestrial lamp globe, unsigned, printed in Great Britain, made up of eighteen chromolithographed gores laid on glass, the Antarctic with metal collar to fit over bulb fitting on black bakelite base, 14¾in. high.
(Christie's) $812

A magnificent pair of 33in. diameter facsimile library globes, signed on the meridian G & T, London, after the celebrated 43in. diameter pair of 1688/1693 by Vincenzo Coronelli, 55in. high.
(Christie's) $50,554

John & William Cary, London, 1818, a 15in. diameter celestial table globe made up of twelve hand coloured engraved gores laid to the ecliptic poles, on four baluster turned mahogany legs united by cross-stretchers, 22in. high.
(Christie's) $7,222

Klinger Kunsthandlung, Nuremburg, a fine 6cm. diameter miniature terrestrial globe made up to twelve hand-coloured engraved gores, the equator and prime meridian graduated in degrees.
(Christie's) $4,048

A rare mid 18th century silver 'Mother and Child' terrestrial/celestial globe pair, unsigned, the two hemispheres threaded to unscrew at the equator to reveal the celestial, 2½ and 2in. diameter.
(Christie's) $32,900

Richard Ebsworth, London, 1825, a miniature orrery, the mechanism turning around a toothed wheel with a brass sunball at the centre, laid into the base of a turned fruitwood case, 4in. diameter.
(Christie's) $1,509

A 14in. diameter terrestrial table globe, of twelve hand-coloured, copied and enlarged facsimile gores and two polar calottes, unsigned, but probably originally by George Woodward, on four baluster turned legs, 21½in. high.
(Christie's) $2,632

George & John Cary, London, 1816/1829, a fine pair of 12in. diameter table globes, on four mahogany quadrant supports to turned central pillar with three cabriole legs, 24½in. high.
(Christie's) $26,320

Early 19th century, an unusual 1¼in. diameter miniature terrestrial globe, possibly originally from an orrery, unsigned, made up of twelve hand-coloured engraved gores with text in English, 2in. high.
(Christie's) $3,290

William & Alexander Keith Johnston, Edinburgh & London, 1907, an extremely fine pair of 18in. diameter library globes, on a fine mahogany stand after the Victorian style, 46½in. high.
(Christie's) $41,125

A New Globe of the Earth by L. Cushee, circa 1760, a fine and rare 2¾in. diameter miniature terrestrial globe made up of twelve partially hand-coloured engraved gores and two polar calottes, the equatorial and equinoctial colure graduated in degrees. (Christie's) $7,402

Six inch Terrestrial globe containing the latest Discoveries. Boston. Gilman Joslin. 1870 Drawn and Engraved by W.B. Annin. A fine 6in. diameter terrestrial globe made up of twelve finely engraved hand-coloured gores and two polar calottes. (Christie's) $6,588

W. and A.K. Johnston 18-Inch terrestrial globe on stand, circa 1900, with black and red painted splay-legged stand, 43in. high. (Skinner) $1,610

Pair of George III 12-inch terrestrial and celestial table globes, circa 1782, by William Bardin, each with turned stand. (Skinner) $13,800

An unusual world timepiece - Maison Delamarche, Paris, (c.1890), an 8in. diameter terrestrial globe, mounted on its axis over the clockwork geared mechanism, 21½in. high. (Christie's) $13,121

John & William Cary, London, 1800, a 12in. diameter terrestrial library globe made up of twelve coloured engraved gores, on four mahogany quadrant supports, 33in. high. (Christie's) $6,909

Johann Baptist Homann, 1664-1724, Nuremberg, an extremely fine and rare 2½in. diameter miniature terrestrial globe, made up of twelve finely engraved hand-coloured paper gores and two polar calottes, most of the text in Latin. (Christie's) $31,293

Columbus-Verlag, Berlin, 1941, a 13in. diameter terrestrial table globe made up of twelve chromolithographed paper gores, raised atop the bronze figure of an eagle with outstretched wings, 32in. high. (Christie's) $1,727

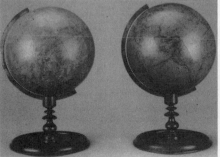

Newton's New & Improved Terrestrial Globe, a 3in. diameter miniature terrestrial globe made up of twelve hand-coloured engraved gores, the equatorial graduated in degrees, 4¼in. high. (Christie's) $4,277

Newton & Son, London, 1850, a fine pair of 10in. diameter table globes, with stamped brass meridian half circle raised on a baluster turned mahogany column, 14¼in. high. (Christie's) $3,948

Heinrich Kiepert, Berlin, 1889, a 13¾in. diameter terrestrial table globe made up of twelve chromolithographed gores and two polar calottes, raised on an elaborate and decorative carved gilt-wood stand, 27in. high. (Christie's) $3,619

A rare George I gold snuff-box set with miniatures, English, circa 1715/1725, the miniature inside by Carl Gustav Klingstedt, signed and dated *1707*, 84mm. wide.
(Christie's) $49,991

A Swiss gold-mounted enamel nécessaire with gold implements, Geneva, circa 1815, funnel-shaped étui with circular top, enamelled in opaque dark and light blue, 124mm. high.
(Christie's) $2,407

A Dutch rococo gold snuff-box, circa 1740/1750, cartouche-shaped box, the cover boldly chased and embossed with Ceres surrounded by rocaille, C-scrolls and foliage on a frosted ground, 55mm. wide.
(Christie's) $4,444

,A Louis XV vari-color gold snuff-box, by German Chayé, the cover, four side panels and base engraved with sunburst motifs and centered by flowersprays, 66mm. wide, 4½oz.
(Christie's) $20,367

A Swiss enamelled and split-pearl set gold cheroot case, Geneva, circa 1820, both sides of the base centered by oval reserves enamelled with scènes champêtres, 90mm. high. (Christie's) $11,109

A very fine German rococo tinted shell, mother of pearl, hardstone and gold snuff-box, Berlin, workshop of Daniel Baudesson, circa 1750/1760, 3¼in. wide.
(Christie's) $99,820

A Louis XVI mother of pearl and gold carnet-de-bal set with a miniature and a hair panel, by Pierre-Denis Chaumont, oval enamel miniature painted with the Death of Lucretia, 85mm. high.
(Christie's) $3,703

An important German rococo jewelled gold snuff-box, Berlin, circa 1750, cartouche-shaped box, the lid boldly chased with the Triumph of Alexander the Great, studded with calibrated and circular-cut rubies, 87mm. wide.
(Christie's) $69,713

A Louis XV enamel and gold snuff-box, Paris, 1755/1756, the hinged cover, sides and base enamelled with cartouches painted with mountainous landscapes in purple and white on a light green ground, 43mm. diameter.
(Christie's) $8,887

A Swiss enamelled gold snuff-box, Geneva, circa 1820, purse-shaped box, the cover panels of reeded engine-turning contrasting with a black enamelled taille d'épargne gold lyre and garland of ivy with butterflies, 3¾in. wide.
(Christie's) $3,148

A Swiss enamelled and split-pearl set gold musical box, Geneva, circa 1840, the slightly domed hinged cover, four sides and four corners enamelled with flowers on a brown ground, 2¼in. wide.
(Christie's) $7,406

A Napoleon III enamel and gold presentation snuff-box, by Louis-François Tronquoy, (fl. 1827-1871), with a chased and engraved gold Imperial eagle seated on a thunderbolt, 81mm. wide.
(Christie's) $7,036

A George II gold snuff-box set with miniatures, English, circa 1756/1760, the larger miniature by Luke Sullivan, signed and dated 1756, 3in. wide.
(Christie's) $48,139

A George II-style gold-mounted hardstone egg bonbonnière, English, 19th century, egg-shaped semi-translucent mottled green moss-agate box, 48mm. high.
(Christie's) $3,148

A Louis XVI-style two-color gold and enamel snuff-box, possibly Swiss, with prestige marks, the enamel miniature by Pierre Pasquier, (1731-1806), 3½in. wide.
(Christie's) $8,327

A Louis XV enamelled gold snuff-box, Paris, 1765/1766, oval box, the cover, four panels and base enamelled en plein with oval reserves depicting playful putti painted in camaïeu on a blue ground, 2½in. wide.
(Christie's) $9,258

A Louis XVI enamelled gold boîte-à-rouge, Paris, 1776/1777, circular box, centered by a rosette of concentric circles and enamelled in transluscent steel-blue/gray, surrounded by matted gold bands, 59mm. diameter.
(Christie's) $4,073

A French agate and enamelled gold snuff-box, by Augustin-Marie-Marcelin-Esprit Mingeaud, (fl. 1809-1822), the cover inset with a slightly domed orange agate panel with brown inclusions mounted à jour, 54mm. wide.
(Christie's) $4,629

493

A Ruskin high fired stoneware inkwell with silver mount and cover by Nelson Dawson, hallmarked London, 1905, the compressed circular body covered in a mint green soufflé glaze, 3½in. diameter. (Christie's) $1,397

A 19th century French brass inkwell modelled as a cockerel's head, hinged to reveal liner on feather cast saucer base, 5½in. wide. (Andrew Hartley) $319

Louis XV style gilt bronze inkstand, late 19th century, with two putti atop a mask mounted base with scrolled candlebranches, 16in. long. (Skinner) $1,380

A gilt-bronze mounted ceramic inkwell, by Pierre Adrien Dalpayrat, circa 1900, of squat circular form with glazed of mottled turquoise and maroon, mounted with curvilinear hinged lid, 4in. high. (Christie's) $6,148

A glazed earthenware and parcel-gilt inkstand, 19th century, decorated overall with gilt scrolls on a brown ground, the sides and canted corners simulating boulle marquetry, 10in. wide. (Christie's) $1,011

A George V tortoiseshell mounted capstan inkwell, the plain sides with hinged cover inset with tortoiseshell panel, 14.5cm. diameter, Birmingham 1912, weighted. (Bearne's) $652

E J & W Barnard, an early Victorian partner's inkstand, the rectangular base with rounded corners centered with a sarcophagus sealing wax box, 10¹/₈in. long, London 1841, 21oz.
(Woolley & Wallis) $1,659

Unusual ink well, modelled as an owl, bronzed cover modelled as an owl's head with glass eyes and enclosing well, the body below constructed from a coconut shell, circa late 19th century, 8in. (G.A. Key) $487

A Powell & Sons glass inkwell and silver cover, probably designed by Harry Powell, the cover hallmarked for 1909, compressed blue glass with silver inclusions, the cover hammered with ball finial, 4in. high. (Christie's) $2,796

A four-case lacquer inro, 19th century, decorated in gold hiramaki-e and gold flakes and aogai inlay with a pine-tree and exotic plants below clouds on a black lacquer ground, gold lacquer interiors, coral ojime, 8.1cm. high. (Christie's) $460

A four-case black lacquer ground inro, decorated in gold, silver and aokin hiramaki-e and takamaki-e and shell with a glowering tiger, 8.6cm., high, signed in gold, 19th century. (Christie's) $8,636

A four-case red lacquer inro, decorated in gold, silver and colored hiramaki-e and takamaki-e and foil with buriburi, with tassels and itomari, 9.2cm. high, signed, late 18/19th century. (Christie's) $2,590

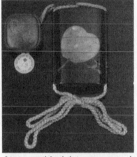

A five-case black lacquer ground elongated inro, decorated in gold, brown and silver takamaki-e with long armed monkeys playing in a flowering plum tree over a stream, 9.8cm., high, signed, 18/19th century. (Christie's) $2,418

A four-case black lacquer ground inro, decorated in gold and colored hiramaki-e and togidash-e with an uchiwa fan, itself decorated with a branch of cherry blossom, 7.3cm. high, signed, late 18/19th century. (Christie's) $6,045

A four-case black lacquer ground inro, decorated in gold, silver and red hiramaki-e and takamaki-e with foil and shell, with Hotei sealed underneath a waterfall, 2¾in. high, late 18/19th century. (Christie's) $2,764

A four-case guri lacquer inro, carved through more layers of black and a red lacquer with a symmetrical scroll design, 3½in. high, unsigned, late 18/19th century. (Christie's) $2,245

A five-case gold lacquer ground inro, decorated in colored togidashi-e with a party of travellers in a boat pulled by two labourers on the shore, 19th century. (Christie's) $6,045

A four-case black lacquer ground inro, decorated in gold, aokin and silver togidashi-e, with gold and silver foil, with a party of travellers in a boat, 3¼in. high, 18th century. (Christie's) $7,772

A magnificent four-case sheath inro signed *Ganshosai Shunsui*, Meiji/Taisho Periods (early 20th century), the outer sheath with a black-lacquer ground decorated in gold, aokin and silver togidashi-e, 3in. high. (Christie's) $8,930

A two-case inro signed *Kyukoku*, Edo Period (19th century), brown lacquer ground; decoration in gold and red takamaki-e, shell and ceramic, 2¼in. high. (Christie's) $2,858

A four-case inro, unsigned, Edo Period (19th century), black lacquer ground, a gourd-vine and tendrils with a basket for gathering fallen leaves, 3¼in. long. (Christie's) $1,410

A four-case inro, signed *Kajikawa* and *Naotsune*, Edo Period (late 18th century), gold lacquer ground, decoration in gold, silver and red hiramaki-e and togidashi-e, tortoiseshell and ivory, 6.7cm. (Christie's) $3,215

A single-case inro or tabacco box signed *Tsuchida Soetsu*, Edo Period (early 18th century), in the form of a leather tobacco-pouch with silver clasps; the decoration of chrysanthemums, birds and willow trees, 6.2cm. (Christie's) $3,215

A four-case inro, signed *Kobayashi Yasuaki,* Edo Period (after 1813), gold lacquer ground, decoration in togidashi sumi-e, compartments and risers gold nashiji, 18th-century ivory netsuke as a sleeping sarumawashi, 8cm. high. (Christie's) $5,000

A three-case inro, unsigned, Edo Period (19th century), black lacquer ground, decoration in gold and silver hiramaki-e with gold flakes and dust, compartments red lacquer, 6.4cm. high. (Christie's) $3,215

A four-case inro, with a seal Shin, Meiji Period (late 19th century), brown-black lacquer ground. A mask for the No-drama role of Kiyohime, 3in. long. (Christie's) $5,640

A four-case inro, unsigned, Edo Period (19th century), black lacquer ground, decoration in gold, silver, black and red hiramaki-e and takamaki-e with inlaid crystal eyes, 7.2cm. high. (Christie's) $4,286

An 18th century brass surveying graphometer, signed on the limb *Pigeon a Lyon*, the protractor scale divided 0°-180°/0°-180°, the compass box attached to the frame by four mounting screws, 11in. wide. (Christie's) $2,585

An Indian brass sundial, bearing inscriptions and hour scales, with compass, plummet and engraved latitude arc 0-55°, 15.5cm. high. (Christie's) $600

A barograph, by Pastorelli and Rapkin Ltd., the lacquered-brass mechanism with 7in. high recording drum, aneroid barometer and centigrade and fahrenheit thermometer, 21in. wide. (Christie's) $2,240

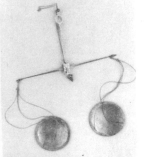

A late 19th century nickel/brass-cased control manometer, by C. Wilh. Stein Sohn Hamburg, the complex barometer mechanism with two sector dials, blued-steel needles, in plush-lined fitted mahogany case, 10½in. long. (Christie's) $450

A rare 17th century Dutch brass compass sundial, signed on the horizontal hour dial *Anthony Sneewins* and dated *1660*, the silvered compass dial with iron needle (possibly later), with jewelled cap, 2¼in. diameter. (Christie's) $6,210

A blue/grey enamelled brass Eltham-pattern transit theodolite, by Stanley, No. 50353, the telescope with fore and aft sights, mounted on an axis incorporating the 5in. vertical circle, in the original fitted mahogany case, 17¾in. wide. (Christie's) $655

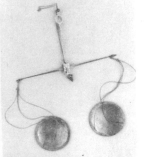

A decorative bronze mortar, the centre panel raised in relief with a marching army of bears depicted as soldiers, the handles formed as two helmeted jesters, 7in. high, with pestle. (Christie's) $2,585

A rare late 17th century brass ring dial, signed in stamped letters *CHA. PROCTO*, the interior engraved with lines of hours with punched numerals, 5.4cm. diameter. (Christie's) $2,760

An early 17th century steel and gilded-brass beam balance, unsigned, the beam with finely modelled ends, brass pans, the beam 9in. long. (Christie's) $1,295

An 18th century brass Butterfield-type dial, signed *Baradelle a Paris*, with folding bird gnomon, compass with blued-iron needle, the underside engraved with the latitudes of twenty-four Continental cities and towns, 3¼in. long.
(Christie's) $550

An 18th century Nuremberg-pattern magnifier, with copper concave section wire frame, in fabric lined wooden case, 5in. long.
(Christie's) $643

An unusual Chinese wood multiple sundial, the octagonal base with four dials hinged from the centre, with inset compass, each dial with ratchet support for degrees of latitude, 6¼in. wide.
(Christie's) $550

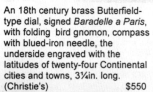

A rare nickel/brass surveyor's folding rule and square, signed on one arm *D. Mauch Cologne*, each arm engraved with scales for various uses and proportions, in original leather carrying case, 7¾in. long. (Christie's) $2,070

A brass range-finder, by Troughton & Simms, the telescope with rack and pinion focusing, lens cap, mounted on twin Y-frames, the upper supports incorporating fore and aft sights, 22in. wide overall.
(Christie's) $1,725

A 19th century gilt-brass specific gravity instrument, by Dring and Fage, London, with signed thermometer and float, with single weight, in plush-lined mahogany case, 12¼in. long.
(Christie's) $172

A 17th century Nuremburg master cup, the lid with handle supported by two figures, seahorse clasp and hinge, the sides decorated with punched geometric motifs, 8¼in. high with handle raised.
(Christie's) $2,070

An 18th century brass Wilson screw-barrel type microscope, unsigned, the screw-barrel focusing with horn stage, sprung slide holder, six objectives, ivory handle, brass slider, 18cm. wide.
(Christie's) $3,105

A fine pair of 18th century watered-steel dividers, damascened in gold, with iron hinge pin, shaped compass points, 7½in. long.
(Christie's) $4,485

An old Argentinian four function disc calculator Calculador Instantaneo, with log entry on reverse.
(Auction Team Köln) $435

A late 16th century ivory and fruitwood diptych dial, possibly by Konrad Karner, the cover with punched calendar scales, decorated in the corners with red-stained neo-classical motifs, 4.8cm. long. (Christie's) $1,120

A brass level by A. Frerk & Sohn, with three level screw, telescope length 33cm., circa 1900.
(Auction Team Köln) $401

A 19th century 4in. astronomical telescope, signed on the back plate *J. Davidson Edinburgh*, with the brass-mounted 60in. rosewood body-tube with rack and pinion focusing, 54in. high.
(Christie's) $12,935

A 19th century lacquered and oxidised-brass reflecting circle, signed *Jecker a Paris No. 578*, with finely divided silvered circle, two verniers, magnifier, tangent-screw fine adjustment and clamp, 12in. wide. (Christie's) $3,450

An 18th century Continental pattern compound monocular microscope, unsigned, the body-tube located on an arm, with lateral adjustment, secured by two clamps, the stage with frog plate and bull's eye condenser, 17in. high.
(Christie's) $2,070

A lacquered-brass compound monocular microscope, signed on the stand *R & J Beck Ltd London No. 20931*, with rack and pinion coarse focusing, fine adjustment, double nose-piece, vulcanite stage, 14¼in. high. (Christie's) $725

A brass horizontal garden sun dial, signed *F. Barker and Son, Scientific Instrument Makers London E.C.*, finely engraved with the latitudes and longitudes and time differences for numerous cities in Asia, Africa, the Americas and Europe, 20in. diameter. (Christie's) $600

A 19th century thermometer, mounted on an ivory plaque stamped *C.W. Dixey Optician To The Queen*, with lacquered-brass mounts in the original plush and silk-lined red morocco case, 6in. long. (Christie's) $295

An Enigma Type M4 (Marine) encoding machine, complete with original box, plugs and lamps, made by Heimsoeth & Rinke, Berlin, 1944.
(Auction Team Köln)
$21,131

A set of six brass weights, of inverted goblet form, indistinctly stamped with the maker's name, the undersides with various proof marks, 7lbs–4oz.
(Christie's)
$331

A brass microscope by C. Reichert, Vienna, on horseshoe base, with height adjustable condenser, with original lenses nos. 2, 4, and 6, circa 1895, 32cm. high.
(Auction Team Köln)
$788

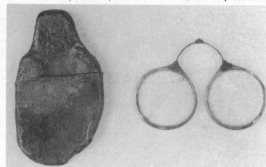

A Contarex and Zeiss phase contrast microscope, comprising a Zeiss Ikon Contarex Professional camera and a Carl Zeiss (Stuttgart) microscope.
(Auction Team Köln)
$1,540

A pair of tortoiseshell framed Nuremberg spectacles, German, 17th century, the tortoiseshell framed 3.5cm. lenses joined by lead rivet bridge with heart shaped mounts, 7.5cm. wide.
(Bonhams)
$1,153

A 'Maurice Stiassnie' brass microscope, on typical claw foot, 4-fold revolver with four original lenses, all in brass cases, 50mm. diameter, circa 1905.
(Auction Team Köln)
$426

A special brass microscope for serial and comparative studies by J. Klönne & G. Müller, Berlin, with revolving plate for 8 slides, 50mm. diameter, circa 1900.
(Auction Team Köln)
$7,873

Rare George III silver encased pocket compass with stem and ringlet mount, 2in. diameter, London 1806.
(G.A. Key)
$620

A brass Culpeper microscope, on wooden base with drawer for equipment, with lenses, mirrors and plates, 40cm. high, 47mm. diameter, circa 1820.
(Auction Team Köln)
$2,233

A brass postal scale by S. Mordan & Co., late 19th century, the brass balance fitted on a rectangular wood base, 8in.
(Sotheby's) $287

A very rare Enigma 'clock', an accessory for the encoding machine, for further extending the 22 billion coding possibilities of the machine, only four models known worldwide. (Auction Team Köln) $12,546

Walnut surveyor's compass, John Dupee, Boston, mid 18th century, with engraved compass rose, with protective cover, 14in. long.
(Skinner) $1,955

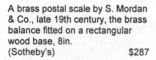

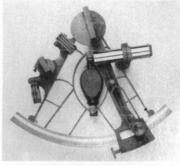

A rare late 17th/early 18th century Chancel sand-clock, signed on the printed paper face of the wall board *Christopher Krem [?***] Sandurmacher in Leipzig,* 29in. high. (Christie's) $14,651

A Spencer Browning & Co. brass sextant, English, mid 19th century, signed *Spencer Browning & Co,* silvered scale from 0-150, two sets of mirrors and coloured filters.
(Bonhams) $791

An Everest brass theodolite by Troughton & Simms with silver scale, fine adjustment and tripod stand, with wooden case, circa 1880.
(Auction Team Köln) $821

An Elektron Wimshurst machine, with gold decoration and two 21cm. diameter hard rubber plates, with original box, circa 1913.
(Auction Team Köln) $394

A brass three drawer refracting telescope signed *Watson and Sons, High Holborn London,* raised on a tapering pillar, tube 38in. long.
(Andrew Hartley) $800

A polished brass theodolite by Cooke, Troughton & Simms, 21 x 30 x 15cm., the base with three levelling screws, circa 1950.
(Auction Team Köln) $590

A 'Thames Tunnel' ladies companion, English, circa 1840, the tooled book-style case titled *Present From The Thames Tunnel*
(Bonhams) $294

A late 19th century mining dial, signed on the silvered compass J.G. Allison, Newcastle Upon Tyne, the dial with edge-bar needle.
(Christie's) $515

An early 19th century lacquered-brass Nairne-pattern chest microscope, signed on the eared stage *Dolland London*.
(Christie's) $5,520

A late 18th century French brass graphometer, signed on the scale *Meurand à Paris*, the silvered scale divided 180°-0°-180°, the frame fret-cut and engraved with scrolls and foliage, the limb mounted with twin slit and wire sights, 14¼in. long.
(Christie's) $950

An 18th century Dutch brass Holland circle, signed on the cruciform limb *H. Sneewins fecit Leydan*, the 5½in. diameter circle finely engraved and divided 0° - 180°/ 180°-0°, the alidade with two fixed sights.
(Christie's) $4,310

An 18th century brass universal equinoctial ring dial, unsigned, engraved on the meridian ring with a quadrant scale on one side, and the latitudes of eight Continental cities and a further eight cities and latitudes on the other side, 2¾in. diameter.(Christie's) $1,550

A 19th century lacquered-brass 'Society-of-Arts'-pattern monocular microscope, unsigned, the tubular limb adjusted by rack and pinion, with stage, swivel mirror, raised on two pillar supports, in mahogany carrying case, 5½in. high.
(Christie's) $190

An 18th century brass universal equinoctial ring dial, unsigned, the equinoctical ring divided I-XII (x2), the meridian ring divided on one side with a quadrant scale (x2), the other side with declination scale, 6in. diameter.
(Christie's) $1,200

A 19th century lacquered-brass student's compound monocular microscope, unsigned with draw-tube focusing, the bull's-eye condenser on articulated mount, complete with accessories in mahogany case, 10¾in. wide.
(Christie's) $200

Cast-Iron flat bull windmill weight, probably Fairbury, Nebraska, early 20th century, 18½ x 25½in. (Skinner) $546

A cast iron fire basket, with brass spire finials, 3ft.1in. (Woolley & Wallis) $411

Cast zinc polychromed stag garden ornament, J.W. Fiske, last quarter 19th century, 47½in. long. (Skinner) $4,140

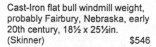

Pair of painted cast-iron architectural posts, America, late 19th century, gadrooned ball finial on baluster-form posts with decorative rosette, scroll, and swirl elements, painted terra-cotta red, 42½in. high. (Skinner) $345

Pair of Classical Revival painted cast-iron garden urns on plinths, America, 1850-75, the footed forms with fluted basins below flaring rims, painted dark green, 40in. high. (Skinner) $2,070

A very rare pair of William and Mary cast brass and wrought-iron andirons, Continental, possibly Dutch, 17th century, each with a faceted finial above with a ball-and-reel beaker-form support, height 25in. (Sotheby's) $7,200

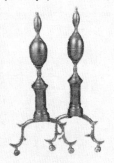

Cast-iron squirrel windmill weight, attributed to Elgin Wind Power and Pump Company, Elgin, Illinois, early 20th century, with traces of black paint on a black painted wood base, 15½ x 13½in. (Skinner) $1,955

A pair of wrought-iron firedogs, by Edgar Brandt, circa 1925, each wrought as a formalised peacock with scrolled wings, one visibly stamped *EBrandt* in the metal, 13¾in. high. (Christie's) $6,385

A pair of Federal cast brass and wrought-iron double-lemon andirons, New York, circa 1800, the hexagonal plinth below on arched spurred legs, height 26in. (Sotheby's) $1,920

Leaded glass table lamp, dome-shaped shade with twelve radiating panels of streaked pink, blue and green, 22in. high.
(Skinner) $690

Jumo, 'Bolide' streamlined desk lamp, 1945, adjustable moulded phenolic shade and base, articulated chrome and copper-plated arm, 5½in. closed.
(Sotheby's) $2,208

Tiffany bronze and favrile glass fluid lamp, gently ribbed opal shade with band of gold iridised, coiled, and pulled feather design, 15½in. high. (Skinner) $5,750

Leaded glass table lamp, attributed to Charles Lamb, circa 1920, drop closed-in apron on domed shade composed of a background of caramel and cream slag glass segments, 22in. high.
(Skinner) $1,725

Suess leaded glass and bronze table lamp, Chicago, circa 1906, a parasol shaped shade with branching striated pink and yellow apple blossoms, 23½in. high.
(Skinner) $9,775

Obverse painted scenic shade table lamp, domed glass shade with textured surface painted on the exterior with a wooded lakeland scene, 19in. high.
(Skinner) $1,265

Bigelow and Kennard bronze and leaded glass table lamp, domical shade composed of radiating panels of marbleised white tiles, 22½in. high.
(Skinner) $4,025

Pierre Chareau, one of a pair of lamps 'La Fleur', circa 1924, nickel-plated metal bases, the shades composed of six removable alabaster panels, each 22cm.
(Sotheby's) (Two) $12,880

Bent panel slag glass table lamp, America, early 20th century, domed shade with six panels in blue, green, purple, white and caramel striated slag glass, 22in. high.
(Skinner) $805

Reverse painted Handel table lamp, Meriden, Connecticut, early 20th century, domical textured glass shade painted on the interior with a continuous band of trees against a shaded pink sky, 24in. high. (Skinner) $6,325

Marcel Louis Baugniet, lamp, circa 1930, thick glass shade in form of a fish with round aperture as eyes, riveted to almost triangular brass 'fin', 11½in. wide. (Sotheby's) $4,865

Leaded glass and bronze table lamp, attributed to Duffner and Kimberly, early 20th century, a conical form shade with radiating pink and caramel glass segments, 25in. high. (Skinner) $3,737

Tiffany Favrile glass and bronze desk lamp, gilt bronze base with 'Zodiac' pattern, supporting a slender standard ending in harp arms, 13in. high. (Skinner) $3,220

Handel bronze and leaded glass lily pad lamp, Meriden, Connecticut, early 20th century, floriform lamp comprised of two lily-form blossoms and two buds in white and striated green slag glass, 10¼in. high. (Skinner) $3,220

Bent panel slag glass table lamp, America, early 20th century, six striated caramel and white bent glass panels mounted in a gilt and enamelled floral decorated framework, 21in. high. (Skinner) $431

Pairpoint puffy boudoir lamp, signed Stratford shade with apple blossoms and roses reverse painted on blue background, 15in. high. (Skinner) $3,335

George Cawardine, an early Anglepoise desk lamp, designed 1932 for Herbert Terry & Sons Ltd., the perforated aluminium shade with bakelite fitting, 36½in. high. (Christie's) $451

Handel obverse painted daffodil lamp, conical glass shade handpainted with green and yellow naturalistic blossoms, 23½in. high. (Skinner) $10,350

Tiffany bronze and leaded glass spreading daffodil lamp, domed shade of yellow, green, amber, and opal white glass segments, 20in. high. (Skinner) $21,850

Leaded glass floral table lamp, shade of caramel amber slag glass segments in brickwork progression, 25in. high. (Skinner) $862

Tiffany Studios bronze desk lamp, dark patina on spun bronze dome shade with silver colour reflective interior, 18in. high. (Skinner) $1,955

Duffner & Kimberly 'Colonial No. 501' table lamp, leaded mosaic dome shade composed of pink, lavender, amber, yellow, and green glass segments, 21½in. high. (Skinner) $4,025

Mount Washington Burmese fluid lamp, late 1890s decorated parlour lamp with fine pink to yellow Burmese glass handpainted and enamelled with Egyptian decoration, 20in. high. (Skinner) $10,350

Handel etched and enamel painted parrot lamp, shade composed of four tapered curved panels, two etched and enamelled with brilliant orange parrots, 28in. high. (Skinner) $4,025

Tiffany bronze and favrile arrowroot lamp, diminutive conical leaded glass shade with twelve repeating green leaf-root elements, 21in. high.
(Skinner) $18,400

Handel overlaid Goldenrod lamp, seven amber slag glass bent panels framed with metal overlay to depict field flowers, 22in. high. (Skinner) $3,335

Etched metal and green slag glass lamp, attributed to Riviere Studios, beaded metal framework in grapevine pattern on shade, 21in. high.   (Skinner) $1,265

Double painted scenic table lamp, painted on exterior in monochromatic winter scene, 23in. high. (Skinner) $1,150

Fine Goldscheider lamp base, finely detailed figure of a woman decorated in colours on a bluish white ground, 18½in. high. (Skinner) $1,610

Overlaid slag glass panel lamp, octagonal metalwork shade with eight bent amber slag panels 20in. high. (Skinner) $575

Important Rookwood Pottery sea green glaze lamp, 1901, decorated by Kataro Shirayamadani, electroplated copper floral sprays over lotus blossoms, shade by Tiffany Studios, overall height 17¾in. (Skinner) $33,350

A Sitzendorf porcelain table lamp, with three scroll feet, applied overall with roses and foliage, 43cm high. (Bearne's) $576

Handel leaded glass harp desk lamp, bronzed metal base with adjustable swivel socket fitted with six sided panelled amber slag glass shade, 19in. high. (Skinner) $1,495

Leaded glass acorn border lamp, domed shade attributed to Tiffany Studios, composed of mottled green, blue opalescent amber rippled glass segments, 25in. high. (Skinner) $7,475

Tiffany bronze and favrile damascene single student lamp, original dark patina on Manhattan single-post model, 24in. high. (Skinner) $4,600

Tiffany bronze and favrile glass 'Harvard' lamp, octagonal leaded glass shade of dichroic and blue-green, amber rectangular segments, 26½in. high. (Skinner) $13,800

Chapelle, peacock lamp, 1920s, wrought iron armature cast as a peacock, the body blown with clear glass internally decorated with pale blue, emerald green, plum, and deep blue, 84cm. wide.
(Sotheby's) $14,059

Roycroft helmet lamp, no. 906, East Aurora, New York, circa 1919, hammered copper, medium patina, 14¼in. high.
(Skinner) $1,840

Pairpoint 'Tapestry' table lamp, with hexagonal 'Directoire' shade featuring frosted, etched panels, 27½in. high.
(Skinner) $2,415

A Muller Frères wrought iron and glass table lamp, factory marks, 34.5cm. high.
(Christie's) $437

A cameo and gilt metal table lamp by Gallé and G. Leleu, circa 1900, the gray glass internally mottled with yellow and overlaid in pinkish red with a large flowerhead and foliage, 43.5cm. high.
(Christie's) $5,073

Emile Gallé, pomegranate and hibiscus lamp, circa 1900, slightly opalescent glass internally decorated with yellow and overlaid with dark red, 55.5cm.
(Sotheby's) $21,528

Miller leaded glass floor lamp, bent panel shoulder in creamy caramel textured slag glass, over wide scalloped slag glass band of light blue and red blossoms, 58½in. high. (Skinner) $1,150

Handel boudoir lamp, domical shade in 'sand-finished' glass, painted on the interior with clusters of roses and flowers in black foliage against a background of yellow vertical segmented lines, 15in. high.
(Skinner) $2,990

Pairpoint puffy boudoir lamp, black border, blue and yellow dogwood blossoms on lavender ground, total height 15in.
(Skinner) $3,450

A WMF glass lamp, height of base 27cm., total height 60.5cm.
(Christie's) $384

Reverse painted table lamp, attributed to Pairpoint, circular textured surface glass shade with dropped flared rim, 23½in. high.
(Skinner) $2,300

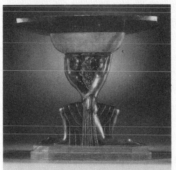

A Daum table lamp, in mottled blue and green glass, engraved *Daum Nancy* with a cross of Lorraine, 62cm. high.
(Christie's) $2,801

'Kneeling Figures' a bronze and onyx figural lamp of two women kneeling supporting the shade, cast and carved from a model by A. Guigner, base engraved *Guigner*, 49cm. high.
(Christie's) $17,522

Emile Gallé, hawthorn lamp, circa 1900, gray glass internally decorated with yellow, overlaid with red and etched with flowering branches, 20¼in.
(Sotheby's) $14,352

An iridescent glass lamp by Loetz, circa 1900, cylindrical opalescent glass stem with four gilt metal columns rising above shaped metal base, 23in. high.
(Christie's) $18,354

An Art Nouveau silvered metal table lamp, the figural stem supporting nautilus shell, 28cm. high. (Christie's) $2,708

A gilt bronze and ivory table lamp, cast from a model by P. Tereszczuk, signed in the bronze, 33cm. high.
(Christie's) $3,151

Tiffany Studios leaded glass table lamp, globe shade decorated with mottled green geometric slag glass segments progressively arranged, 28½in. high.
(Skinner) $19,550

An Empire style gilt bronze and kingwood bouillotte lamp, early 20th century, the flared adjustable shade veneered with kingwood, above a three light fitting, 27½in. high.
(Christie's) $4,099

Handel scenic landscape table lamp, domed shade in 'sand finished' glass, reverse painted as scenic view with mountains, lake, and trees, 21in. high.
(Skinner) $5,635

Pairpoint scenic reverse painted lamp, New Bedford, early 20th century, textured glass Exeter shade, decorated with pastoral scene of trees and grass hillside, 22in. high.
(Skinner) $2,070

Fayral figural Art Deco lamp, France, circa 1920, metal figure of a woman in an architectural setting, backlit by a frosted glass panel, 16½in. high.
(Skinner) $2,300

Leaded glass table lamp, H.A. Best Lamp Company, Chicago, domed shade with repeating panels of floral and geometric slag glass segments in pink, green and blue, 19½in. high.
(Skinner) $1,725

Duffner and Kimberley leaded glass lamp, domical shade with geometric shaped green slag glass segments progressively arranged with tuck-under apron, 23½in. high.
(Skinner) $2,185

Handel table lamp, domed patinated metal framework shade with painted fleur de lys border over caramel slag glass panels, 23¼in. high. (Skinner) $2,070

'Drapery' shade table lamp, attributed to Pittsburgh Lamp, Brass & Glass Co., frosted amber glass shade with shirred drapery look, 23in. high.
(Skinner) $1,092

Pairpoint 'Roses' boudoir lamp, Portsmouth shade, with reverse painted roses on pale yellow and white ground, 14in. high. (Skinner) $2,070

Handel leaded glass table lamp, Meriden, Connecticut, early 20th century, domed shade with multicoloured leaded glass segments depicting baskets of fruit, 23in. high. (Skinner) $1,380

Pairpoint boudoir lamp, surface decorated with autumn-leafed trees amid grass, flowers and butterflies on frosted glass ground, 14½in. high. (Skinner) $1,265

Handel reverse painted table lamp, Meriden, Connecticut, early 20th century, frosted and textured domed shade painted with a wide border of repeating flowers, birds and scrolls, 24½in. high. (Skinner) $4,887

A glazed terracotta table lamp, model No.377, designed by Gudrun Baudisch, manufactured by the Wiener Werkstätte, circa 1926/27, ovoid body applied with loop handles, decorated with abstract geometric motifs, 50cm. high. (Christie's) $4,098

A pair of French onyx and bronze-mounted oil lamps, late 19th century, the tapering columns supporting Corinthian capitals below pink opalescent lustre glass reservoirs, 23in. high. (Christie's) $1,405

Tiffany Studios, wisteria lamp, 1899-1920, the leaded glass shade in the form of a pending wisteria blooms in shades of blue, white and green, 43cm. (Sotheby's) $53,820

A French Art Deco bronze and glass electrolier, circa 1930, the octagonal shade with panels of tubular and frosted glass radiating about a central baluster column, the frame stamped PETITOT, 27in. high. (Christie's) $5,806

Art Nouveau style figural metal lamp, stylised metal figure of a woman in a diaphanous dress, holding two Steuben gold aurene shades, 29in. high. (Skinner) $1,092

Pittsburgh painted scenic table lamp, Pittsburgh Lamp, Brass and Glass Co., circa 1920, domed shade of frosted and textured glass, the exterior painted with pine trees, 27in. high. (Skinner) $1,955

Pair of cobalt blue and white pressed glass lamps, tulip fonts with columnar standards and square bases, 12½in. high. (Skinner) $1,528

Pairpoint scenic reverse-painted table lamp, New Bedford, Massachusetts, early 20th century, frosted and textured Copley shade, painted with a pastoral scene, 21in. high. (Skinner) $1,840

Handel grapevine overlay slag glass table lamp, Meriden, Connecticut, early 20th century, the domed shade composed of geometric tile and grapevine border metal overlay, over eight striated, green bent slag glass panels, 22¾in. (Skinner) $1,955

Bent panel slag glass and metal overlay table lamp, Boston Glass Works, early 20th century, floral and foliate metal overlay shade with bronze patina over six radiating striated caramel and white bent slag glass panels, 22in. high. (Skinner) $747

Handel geometric glass and pottery table lamp, Meriden, Connecticut, early 20th century, broad twelve-panel shade of mottled green progressively arranged geometric slag glass segments with a border band of red glass segments, 25½in. high. (Skinner) $5,750

Bent panel slag glass table lamp, America, early 20th century, six striated caramel and white glass panels and red glass border panels with floral and shield relief decoration, 24½in. high. (Skinner) $805

Handel Teroma glass and patinated metal table lamp, Meriden, Connecticut, early 20th century, conical shade textured glass painted green with light reflective opal white interior, 22¼in. high. (Skinner) $6,325

Handel painted and patinated metal scenic table lamp, Meriden, Connecticut, early 20th century, conical, frosted grey, and textured glass shade, the exterior painted to depict a landscape, 23⅝in. high. (Skinner) $6,325

A gilt-bronze hall lantern, French, circa 1890, of dodecagonal form with glazed panels and male terms, approximately 120cm. high.
(Sotheby's) $14,059

A rare pine lantern, perhaps mid 19th century, possibly Welsh, of rectangular form, with lyre-shaped and broken arched apertures to three sides, fourth with a hinged door, 36cm. high.
(Christie's) $1,652

A gilt bronze hall lantern, 19th century, of cylindrical form with five serpentine glass panels, with a three light fitting, 28in. high.
(Christie's) $4,430

A painted cast-iron hall lantern, 20th century, of hexagonal outline, the terminal in the form of a turret, 33½in. high.
(Christie's) $923

One of a pair of Regency style bronze hall lanterns, 20th century, in the gothic taste, the hexagonal glazed frames with crocketed arches and pierced foliate friezes, 42¹/₈in. high.
(Christie's) (Two) $9,229

Adolf Loos, hanging lamp, circa 1905, brass, inset with panels of bevelled glass, with central hanging ring, chain and ceiling rose, 84⁵/₈in. overall drop.
(Sotheby's) $5,377

A brass and glass hall lantern, 20th century, of tapering cylindrical outline with sectional glass panels, 40in. high.
(Christie's) $2,215

A French bronze hall lantern, early 20th century, of cylindrical outline, with running stiff-leaf mounts to the galleries, below, 27in. high.
(Christie's) $4,061

A glazed bronze hall lantern, late 19th century, of tapering cylindrical form, with flambeau terminal below and scroll cresting, 36in. high.
(Christie's) $2,399

A Neopolitan marble head of Janus, by Chiurazzi, late 19th century, possibly from a doorpost, 9in. high. (Christie's) $2,991

A Victorian carved white marble bust of a gentleman, dated *1871*, sculpted with whiskers, his head to sinister, the reverse signed *H. Weekes R.A. SC. 1871*, on a waisted circular socle, 30½in. high. (Christie's) $1,151

A French white marble figure of a sleeping girl, by Georges Loiseau-Bailly, circa 1895, her head resting on her right arm, supported by an Ionic column, 33½in. high. (Christie's) $4,600

A French white marble bust of a lady, in the manner of Houdon, circa 1875, looking to her left, her hair attached with a bow to her back, 29¾in. high. (Christie's) $8,832

A pair of French gilt bronze mounted variegated marble ornamental urns, late 19th or early 20th century, the ovoid bodies with entwined snake handles and ribbon tied floral swags, 26½in. high. (Christie's) $4,543

French white marble bust of a lady, third / fourth quarter 18th century, depicting a young beauty in powdered wig, with lace-edged bodice, on turned socle, 24½in. high. (Skinner) $3,450

A Continental marble head of a woman, late 19th or early 20th century, modelled wearing a scarf, and inclining to sinister, 13¼in. high. (Christie's) $531

An Italian Breccia marble amphora-shaped vase, 19th century, with integral carved handles below the squat neck, 10½in. high. (Christie's) $4,861

A sculpted white marble bust of a young woman, probably second half 19th century, her head slightly turned to dexter, her hair tied in chignon, 20in. high. (Christie's) $449

U.S. Navy brass clock, by Chelsea, mounted on a wooden shield, 5½in. diameter. (Eldred's) $330

A brass Kelvin & Hughes fluid compass, 24.5cm. diameter, mahogany housing 144cm. high with binnacle and lamp house for spirit lamp, circa 1930. (Auction Team Köln) $660

A carved and painted pine ship's figurehead of a young lady in blue dress, probably New England, circa 1850, with braided red-brown hair and blue dress, 24in. high. (Sotheby's) $7,200

A copper and brass seahorse mast head light, 56cm. high, and a brass porthole, 36cm. diameter. (Onslows) $82

Antique English quadrant, maker's label and eyepiece missing, original pine case. (Eldred's) $412

A ship's figurehead, 19th century, in painted wood carved as a woman's torso, 136cm. (Bristol) $4,185

Cunard Line RMS Lusitania embossed menu card Thursday May 25th 1911, hinged along top to stand on table, reverse with Cunard Line emblem. (Onslows) $548

White Star Line, RMS Baltic ribbon plate, with original red ribbon, printed central color vignette of the ship, 19cm. diameter, in original box. (Onslows) $123

A brass bound wood barrel, 54cm. high, ex ship's Smoking Room. (Onslows) $103

A German Cameraphone wooden portable gramophone, unattributed, unusual celluloid horn, folding deck, circa 1925.
(Auction Team Köln) $678

An incomplete coin-slot Gramophone with coin mechanism, motor and 7-inch turntable, Clark-Johnson soundbox, two Berliner records and rectangular oak case, 26in. long, circa 1899.
(Christie's) $6,564

A Polyphon Nr. 103 coin-operated player for 39.8cm. tin discs, with 78-tone double comb, in walnut case, circa 1900.
(Auction Team Köln) $3,659

A Steck Player Piano, a German version of the American model by the Aeolian Company, New York, inlaid Empire-style case, circa 1910.
(Auction Team Köln) $5,424

An 11in. Polyphon hall clock, German, circa 1900, with two train movement striking on a gong contained within a walnut veneered case with fluted style columns, 66in. high.
(Sotheby's) $3,175

A Harmonipan thirty-three-note portable barrel organ by Frati & Co, Schoenhauser Allee 73, Berlin, late 19th century, the facade with nineteen visible flute pipes screened with interlaced colored ribbons, 22in. wide.
(Christie's) $14,681

A Mignon 32-note organette in japanned case with gilt stencils to front and rear and label of Ph. Hakker Jr., 92 Weste, Wagenstraat, Amsterdam, 23½in. wide, with fourteen rolls.
(Christie's) $827

A twenty-six key barrel organ by G. Bacigalupo, Berlin, playing eight tunes, in walnut case with painted decoration and fifteen visible brass pipes to the front, 19¼in. wide, mid-20th century, with four-wheel rubber-tyred cart.
(Christie's) $8,142

A Pasquali and Co. barrel organ, English, early 20th century, in a wooden case of typical form with moving central panel in a case of typical form, approximately 150cm. high.(Bonhams) $2,002

An 18th century burnished iron framed amputation saw, with blade, with ebony handle and brass butterfly-wing adjusting nut, 18½in. long. (Christie's) $312

An ivory monaural stethoscope, constructed in two parts, the tube arranged to secure to the base for storage purposes, 6½in. long assembled. (Christie's) $550

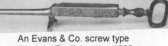

An Evans & Co. screw type lithotrite, English, circa 1865, signed Evans & Co. London, with foliate engraved handle and barrel, 38cm. wide.
(Bonhams) $692

An 18th century mahogany domestic medicine cabinet, arranged in two sections, with compartments for bottles to front and rear, 20¾in. wide open. (Christie's) $883

A rare pair of 17th century dilators, with bistoury cache, the burnished-iron scissor frame with bronze screw adjustment, 9¼in. long. (Christie's) $2,585

A 19th century veterinary enema outfit, by S. Maw Son & Thompson London, with pump, various lignum vitae nozzles, a spray, rubber tube with connections, and other items, contained in a plush-lined mahogany carrying case, 17¾in. wide. (Christie's) $604

A fine mahogany homeopathic domestic medicine case, cross-banded with box and kingwood, the lid decorated with an elongated star in ebony and fruitwood, 21¾in. wide. (Christie's) $2,760

A 19th century mahogany domestic medicine cabinet, the rear with 'poison' compartment containing two (of five) original bottles, the slide secured by secret brass catch, each drawer with ivory pull, 37cm. high. (Christie's) $4,048

A field surgeon's part set of instruments, by Evans & Wormull, containing a bone saw, finger saw, forceps, and other items, in plush-lined mahogany case, 17¾in. wide. (Christie's) $1,840

A pair of deep amethyst globular drug bottles, with gilt and black labels numbered 26 and 27, the necks with folded tops, 28.2cm. high. (Christie's) $1,501

A Weiss mahogany and brass bound cased amputation set, English, circa 1830, all in a velvet lined brass bound air tight case, 37.5cm. (Bonhams) $4,119

A George III carved giltwood oval mirror, early 19th century, in the Chippendale rococo style, surmounted by a floral and foliate spray, with pierced rocaille, C-scroll and cabochon cresting, 56in. high.
(Christie's) $4,606

An Italian giltwood painted wall mirror, circa 1750, the later rectangular plate within a foliate scrolled and rosette and bas relief carved frame 25in. x 19½in.
(Bonhams) $2,516

A George III giltwood wall mirror, the later rectangular plate within a beaded frame and scroll floral carved sides, 45 x 30½in.
(Bonhams) $5,320

Hector Guimard, mirror, circa 1905, gessoed and gilt wood, of shaped rectangular form, modelled with highly stylised organic motifs, 133.5 x 87.5cm.
(Sotheby's) $13,104

A 19th century gilt wood and ebonised overmantel mirror, painted with floral sprays and with black festoon tied urns, flanked on either side by smaller mirrors and shelving, 64in. wide.
(Andrew Hartley) $725

A walnut, crossbanded and gilt gesso wall mirror, elements possibly 18th century and later, in the George II style, with swan neck pediment hung with rosettes of foliate berries, 52¾in. high.
(Christie's) $2,961

A William and Mary walnut and marquetry mirror, the rectangular plate within a scrolling foliate cushion frame, surmounted by a lobed cresting, 24 x 16¼in.
(Christie's) $13,041

Attributed to Edgar Brandt, cheval mirror, circa 1922, black patinated wrought iron, the openwork base elaborately decorated with scrolls and roses, 66¾in.
(Sotheby's) $13,440

A George II giltwood wall mirror, in the manner of William Kent, circa 1735, the associated rectangular bevelled plate within an egg and dart moulded edge of breakfront form, 36½ x 60in.
(Bonhams) $19,240

A George II giltwood wall mirror, circa 1735, the rectangular bevelled plate within a moulded frame with outset corners surmounted by a scallop shell crest, 53 x 34½in. (Bonhams) $14,000

A Dresden oval wall mirror with cherub surmount, floral encrusted border, oval below with scrolled vacant cartouche, blue printed mark, 30in. high. (Brightwells) $862

A George II giltwood wall mirror, circa 1760, the later plate within a moulded frame surmounted by a pierced crest with flowers and scroll decoration, 31 x 54½in. (Bonhams) $4,200

A Regency giltwood and verre eglomisé mirror, the later rectangular plate surmounted by a tablet with fire-grate designs on a white ground flanked on each side by scrolling foliage, 38 x 26in. (Christie's) $10,247

A Regency brown-oak dressing-mirror, the rectangular plate and moulded supports on a shaped base with three mahogany-lined frieze drawers, 23½in. wide. (Christie's) $1,863

A George I giltwood wall mirror, circa 1720, the associated rectangular bevelled plate within a moulded edge and surmounted by a shaped crest carved with scrolls and husks in low relief, 30½ x 46in. (Bonhams) $4,144

Süe et Mare, mirror, circa 1925, gilt and black painted metal, the top of the oval frame moulded with a stylised floral border, 112cm. (Sotheby's) $11,760

A William IV mahogany cheval mirror, the rounded rectangular mirror plate flanked with turned and reeded columns, 116cm. wide. (Bonhams) $4,312

A Georgian wall mirror with scroll arched pediment, shaped frame, with gilt moulded and carved leafage decoration, 4ft. high x 2ft.4in. wide maximum. (Brightwells) $2,940

A walnut mirror, circa 1735, the later oblong plate within a beaded, outstepped frame, 3ft. 2in. high. (Sotheby's) $2,689

A carved wood overmantel, George I, circa 1720, the bell flower cresting and key pattern with the sides of trailing oak leaves, 4ft.9½ x 5ft.5¼in. (Sotheby's) $24,966

A mahogany cheval glass, Edwardian, circa 1910, strung with boxwood, in a trestle frame, 2ft. 4in. wide. (Sotheby's) $3,841

A Regency carved and gilt wood wall mirror of pyramid form with beaded edging and stepped cornice, flanked on either side by a vase of flowers, 30¼in. wide. (Andrew Hartley) $917

A Dutch mahogany and floral swing frame toilet mirror, 19th century, the base with chequer stringing and fitted with a drawer, on later bun feet, 17in. wide. (Christie's $1,099

An early Victorian mahogany cheval mirror, the rectangular swing plate between scrolled supports joined by a flattened arched stretcher, 62½in. high. (Christie's) $2,236

A carved and gilded wall mirror, 19th century, the cartouche shaped frame carved with rococo scroll and rocaille work, 3ft. 3in. high. (Sotheby's) $1,152

A George III giltwood mirror, circa 1760, the oval mirror plate within a conforming rocaille and C-scrolled foliate frame, 27in. wide. (Christie's) $5,750

A Venetian wall mirror, the octagonal bevelled edge upright plate with an edged floral mirrored border, 2ft. 10in. high. (Sotheby's) $423

A grained wall mirror, George II, circa 1740, with a broken scroll swan neck pediment and scallop cresting, 5ft.4in.
(Sotheby's) $36,490

A fine and rare Classical giltwood and part-ebonized overmantel mirror, New York, circa 1825, with a wing-spread eagle finial on a rocky crag, 4ft.8in. wide.
(Sotheby's) $9,200

A marble and giltwood diminutive Bilbao mirror, Spanish or Portuguese, circa 1800, surmounted by an urn issuing a spray of leaves and flowers, 29in. high. (Sotheby's) $5,462

An Italian carved giltwood pierglass Piedmontese, third quarter 18th century, the scrolled and shaped frame surmounted by a laurel wreath cresting supporting trophies, 3ft. 11in. wide.
(Sotheby's) $32,649

A giltwood mirror, in late 17th century style, the arched oblong plate within a frame carved with fruit, shells, putti, birds, masks, 5ft.6½in.
(Sotheby's) $13,443

A parcel-gilt simulated mahogany wall mirror, Italian, circa 1820, with a divided upright plate surmounted by a pediment of military trophies, 7ft.7½in. high.
(Sotheby's) $5,762

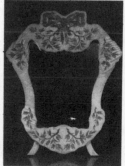

A George III mahogany toilet mirror, circa 1760, the later bevelled oblong plate above a slope fronted base and drawer, 1ft. 7½in. wide.
(Sotheby's) $3,073

A rare pair of Classical giltwood convex two-light mirrors first quarter 19th century, each surmounted by a finial in the form of a sea serpent, 37½in. high.
(Sotheby's) $33,350

A satin birch and marquetry easel dressing mirror, Art Nouveau, circa 1900, the cartouche plate within a shaped frame inlaid with ribbon tied fruit and foliage, 2ft. 4½in. high.
(Sotheby's) $192

An ebonised mirror, Napoleon III, circa 1870, the bevelled plate flanked by columns surmounted by an armorial and cherubs, 66cm. wide. (Sotheby's) $2,062

A George II carved pine and giltwood overmantel mirror, 18th century, the pierced C-scroll and leaf-form cartouche above a tripartite frame, patches to leaf tips, 4ft.9in. wide. (Sotheby's) $3,737

A Regency mahogany cheval mirror, the rectangular plate between ring turned and finialled supports, 79cm. wide. (Tennants) $2,240

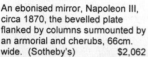

An Edwardian satinwood, mahogany and floral marquetry cheval mirror, decorated with lines, floral borders and bellflower swags, 31in. wide. (Christie's) $3,680

Pair of 19th century French champlevé enamelled frames, the inner borders with flowers on a pale blue ground, 12½in. high. (Ewbank) $792

An 18th century Dutch East Indies rosewood and marquetry dressing table bureau, the whole inlaid into the solid with sprays of flowers, butterflies and boxwood stringings, 22½in. wide. (Canterbury) $1,760

A painted and gilt pier mirror in the manner of William Kent, with broken pediment and frieze with projecting shell and foliate scrolls and vines, 179cm. x 121cm. (Phillips) $9,512

An Art Nouveau wall mirror, the copper frame decorated with a sun motif, flowering plants and a peacock, 56 x 81cm. (Bearne's) $992

A George II giltwood girandole, the later shaped rectangular bevelled plate, within a gadrooned slip, the outer frame with pierced acanthus and foliate scrolls, 51in. x 32in. (Christie's) $16,974

A George IV mahogany cheval mirror, the rounded rectangular plate between rectangular spreading supports, on hipped downswept reeded legs, 23¼in. wide. (Christie's) $2,999

A Swedish giltwood overmantel mirror, second quarter 19th century, the oval plate in a moulded frame with a pierced C-scrolled and acanthus cresting, 36¼in. x 59½in. (Christie's) $2,863

A Queen Anne red lacquer miniature bureau/toilet mirror on stand, part 18th century, the shaped plate within a deep moulded frame held by waved supports, 21¾in. wide. (Christie's) $2,240

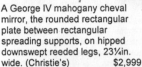

A pair of George III giltwood two-light girandoles, each with two later shaped plates in acanthus and C-scroll frames, with pierced pagoda-shaped acanthus-carved cresting, 42½in. high. (Christie's) $28,290

A pair of Queen Anne giltwood and mirror-bordered pier glasses, each with a shaped arched central plate engraved with a vase of flowers, 75¼ x 36½in. and 71 x 36¾in. (Christie's) $50,922

A Dutch fruitwood mirror, third quarter 17th century, the associated rectangular plate within a frame carved with flowers, acorns, corn and thistles, 48½in. x 37½in. (Christie's) $15,272

A William and Mary raised-work and white-metal thread dressing mirror, the later rectangular plate in a later gilded slip, 24¾ x 21¾in. (Christie's) $7,544

A George II parcel-gilt sand-decorated mirror, of rectangular form with square outset corners centring shells, 27in. wide. (Sotheby's) $2,587

An enamel and gilt-bronze toilet mirror, French, circa 1890, with a shaped bevelled plate flanked by scrolls, 52cm. wide. (Sotheby's) $4,554

A Venetian carved and gilt frame, mounted with a mirror, the inner fascia with rose centered volute carving, the outer with garlands and grapes, 16th century, inner dimensions 72 x 59cm.
(Finarte) $6,622

A Regency gilt convex wall mirror, the circular plate within an ebonized reeded slip and a button-decorated concave molded surround with a spread eagle, 41in. high.
(Christie's) $1,150

A 19th century carved giltwood overmantel mirror, having multiple plates divided by bead and reel moldings beneath a bold leaf-carved cornice, 170 x 178cm.
(Tennants) $3,648

An English beadwork mirror, second half 17th century and later, with raised work, depicting figures, a lion, a leopard, exotic birds, a fish in a pond and buildings, inset with mica, 27¾ x 24¾in.
(Christie's) $7,438

An Italian carved and parcel-gilt Sansovino style mirror frame, late 18th century, the cresting with central mask flanked by scrolling moldings, the sides with stylized capitals and triglyphs above caryatids, 22½ x 20in.
(Christie's) $2,834

A Russian brass-inlaid mahogany and parcel-gilt cheval mirror, early 19th century, with restoration and some redecoration, the associated triangular pediment with central stylized anthemion cresting with coats of arms, 37in. wide.
(Christie's) $2,961

A 19th century carved and gilt wood pier mirror, the arched oblong plate with molded frame, carved with trailing scrolling foliage in low relief, 38in. wide.
(Andrew Hartley) $1,117

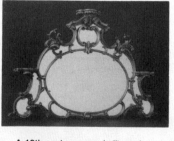

A 19th century carved giltwood overmantel mirror, in the 'Chippendale' style, having an oval central plate within shaped marginal plates divided by C scroll borders, 109cm. wide.
(Tennants) $2,041

A giltwood pier glass of George III style, 20th century, the divided rectangular plate with a mirrored and pierced border, 74 x 36½in.
(Christie's) $4,600

A Victorian gilt composition overmantel mirror with a waterleaf molded cornice above a frieze centered by an urn, 48in. wide. (Christie's) $1,101

An Edwardian inlaid mahogany robing mirror with swan neck pediment, harebell and shell inlay on cheval frame with brass paw toe caps. (Brightwells) $2,131

A giltwood and gesso wall mirror, mid 20th century, the stepped surround with a bead and egg-and-dart cornice and stylised guilloche and fluted frieze with patera, 63in. wide. (Christie's) $12,355

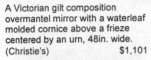

A French Louis XV carved and gilded frame, with chain-link to the outer edge, outer scotia, raised, reeded and tied astragal, 41½ x 29½ x 7in. (Christie's) $4,428

A Dutch walnut and floral marquetry swing frame toilet mirror, 19th century, with arched plate within checker strung border, on shaped uprights with brass finials, 15¼in. wide. (Christie's) $1,860

An 18th century-style giltwood looking glass, the shaped rectangular glass plate within a frame pierced and carved with scrolls and foliage, 168cm. high. (Bearne's) $5,348

A Dutch marquetry rectangular wall or easel mirror, 19th century, inset with a bevelled plate within checker ivory borders and floral foliate surround, 29½in. high. (Christie's) $1,725

A William IV giltwood, gilt-composition and ebonized overmantel mirror, the rectangular plate with a reeded border and an oak-leaf molding 39 x 65in. (Christie's) $6,440

A Venetian octagonal mirror, the projecting frame relief engraved with vases, daisies and flowerheads. (Galerie Moderne) $872

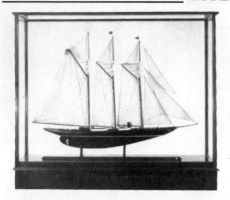

A well detailed and presented display model of the steam auxiliary three-masted schooner yacht Atlantic, the hull finished in red, black and varnish, 42 x 59in. (Christie's) $6,992

An exhibition standard 1:72 scale rigged and partially planked model of the Royal Naval 5th Rate Roebuck, a frigate of 1774 built by W.M. Brown with bound masts, yards with stun's'l booms and foot ropes, 47 x 55in. (Christie's) $14,720

A 20th century bone and horn model of a 91-gun man-of-war, the planked and pinned hull has extensive stern and quarter gallery decoration, 'gun pull' and horn strakes, 16¼ x 17¼in. (Christie's) $3,128

A mid-19th century fully rigged model of a Royal Naval 12-gun sloop with masts, yards with hand holds and foot ropes, standing and running rigging, 43 x 57in. (Christie's) $3,680

A Folk Art Diorama of the clipper ship Tally Ho of New York, anonymous, American 19th century, hull carved from the solid, painted black with a white waist and set in a carved painted sea, 32¾ x 11½ x 20¼in. cased dimensions. (Christie's) $4,370

Cased model of Lord Nelson's Flagship H.M.S. 'Victory', copper-sheathed hull from waterline down, complex rigging with standing and running cords, model height 30in. (Eldred's) $1,760

A detailed builder's model of the S.S. Harpalion and S.S. Harleden, built by R. & W. Hawthorn, Leslie & Co. Ltd., Newcastle-on-Tyne, for J. & C. Harrison Ltd., London, with masts, derricks and rigging, 18¾ x 62½in. (Christie's) $11,960

An extremely fine and detailed exhibition standard builder's style model of 'W' Class Destroyer H.M.S. Walker originally built by William Denny & Co., Dumbarton, 1918, 20 x 76in. (Christie's) $36,800

A well detailed 1:48 scale model of the Steam Dredger Prittlewell, originally built by Simons Lobuitz, Renfrew 1940, and modelled by C.D. Riches, with mast, halyards and rigging, 19½ x 32½in. (Christie's) $1,472

Laid-up pond model hull of an Alden schooner, 19th century, probably never completed, lead keel, 47½in. long. (Eldred's) $1,375

A Southampton Class Cruiser HMS Sheffield, the centre section removable revealing an electric propulsion motor, in oak and glazed case, the model 60 x 22in. high. (Ewbank) $552

A Bing 57cm. Series spirit-fired steam gunboat, fitted with single cylinder oscillating engine and flat bottom boiler, circa 1904. (Christie's) $2,981

A well detailed and presented display model of the steam yacht Corsair IV, with masts and rigging, anchors, winch, anchor winch, fairleads and bollards, 20 x 45in. (Christie's) $11,960

Cased wooden model of a steam/sail ship in dry-dock, case marked W.H. Tyrell, March 1883, height   15in.,   length   33in.,   depth   7in. (Eldred's) $1,870

Trix Trains A4 4-6-2 locomotive and tender 'Merlin', finished in BR green, boxed.
(Andrew Hartley) $82

Trix Trains AH Peppercorn A1 locomotive, finished in LNER green, boxed.
(Andrew Hartley) $91

Bassett-Lowke electric 2-6-0 locomotive and tender: Great Western 'Mogul' No. 4331 painted in lined green with *Great - garter - Western* on tender, circa 1930. (Christie's) $914

Bassett-Lowke electric 'Flying Scotsman': 4-6-2 No. 60103 and eight-wheel tender, lithographed in British Railways dark green with tangerine lining, in original box, circa 1959. (Christie's) $1,553

A finely engineered 5in. gauge model of the BR class 9 4-6-2 locomotive and tender No. 70025 'Western Star' built by R. E. Day, finished in finely lined BR livery and lining, 14½ x 73½in., Dexion trolley, firing shovel, flue brushes. (Christie's) $10,073

A collection of well detailed 5in. gauge freight stock, including two twin bogie three plank open wagons, a twin bogie bolster, a four plank four wheel coal wagon, a four wheel box van with sliding doors and a four wheel guard's van. (Christie's) $3,663

A finely engineered 5in. gauge model of the GWR King Class locomotive and tender No. 6009 'King Charles II' built by W.S. Baker, finished in finely lined GWR livery and lining, firing irons, Dexion trolley, 15 x 72½in. (Christie's) $13,735

A recently completed 5in. gauge 'Speedy' No. 1510 painted B.R. black, designed by L.B.S.C. and modelled on an ex G.W.R. 1500 class 0-6-0 tank locomotive with outside cylinders with piston valves and Walschaerts gear, length 90cm. long. (Bearne's) $3,465

The LMS Duchess class 4-6-2 locomotive and tender No. 6245 'City of London' in LMS red/gold livery, 21⁵/₈in. long. (Christie's) $733

Hornby Dublo Bristol Castle locomotive, finished in BR green, boxed. (Andrew Hartley) $148

Trix Trains 4472 Flying Scotsman locomotive, finished in LNER green with second tender, boxed. (Andrew Hartley) $231

Hornby Dublo Silver King locomotive and tender, finished in BR green, boxed. (Andrew Hartley) $181

Hornby Series electric 'Princess Elizabeth' LMS locomotive No. 6201 and six-wheel tender, painted in lined lake, in original fitted presentation box, circa 1938. (Christie's) $2,011

A Bassett-Lowke electric 4-6-2 A3 Flying Scotsman locomotive, finished in lined BR green, slight paint damage to tender, boxed. (Andrew Hartley) $1,023

A Bassett-Lowke electric 0-6-0 LMS tank locomotive, finished in black with LMS to tank, M8 to cab, boxed. (Andrew Hartley) $412

A Bassett-Lowke clockwork 4-6-2 LNER 'Flying Scotsman' No. 4472 and eight-wheel tender, lithographed in lined green, circa 1939. (Christie's) $695

A 5in. gauge industrial type 0-4-0 saddle tank locomotive 'Ann of Holland', built to the drawings of J.H.E. Rodgers, 1945, with outside cylinders, Walschaerts valve gear, cab operated drain cocks and hand water pump. (Bearne's) $2,228

A 5in. gauge 0-6-0T locomotive 'Twin Sisters', by Austen-Walton, castings by Kennion, painted in L.M.S. livery No. 11665, outside cylinders with Walschaerts valve gear, length of engine 80cm. (Bearne's) $3,300

A Bassett-Lowke Enterprise 4-4-0 live steam locomotive, spirit fired boiler with twin outside cylinder, finished in black, lined red, boxed. (Andrew Hartley) $363

A Märklin O gauge Mitropa restaurant car, four-axle, with celluloid windows, four opening doors and internal lights, 1934, 24.5cm. long. (Auction Team Köln $181

A mandolin musical box by L'Epée, playing four operatic airs, in case with rosewood-veneered front, 23¼in. wide.
(Christie's) $1,747

A Grand Format overture box by Nicole Frères, No. 25791, playing six overtures, with gilt tune-list, 30in. wide.
(Christie's) $8,280

A 22in. inlaid Swiss musical box with '4 bells and drum in sight', the 8in. cylinder playing eight airs, late 19th century.
(Jacobs & Hunt) $1,600

A key-wind musical box by Nicole Frères, No. 37398, playing eight operatic airs, later inside glass cover, 19½in. wide.
(Christie's) $2,208

A Swiss station musical box with interchangeable cylinder sublime harmony nickel-plated movement, two cylinders each playing six airs, 71½in. high, circa 1895.
(Christie's) $11,960

A Lochmann's 'Original' 24³/₈ in. disc musical box, in upright case with coin slot, two combs, two banks of six bar-bells, 90¼in. high, with twenty five discs.
(Christie's) $7,586

A Swiss cylinder musical box by Mermod Frères no. 63070, playing eight airs listed on lithographed tune sheet, trade label for Joseph Riley, Birmingham. (Anderson & Garland) $693

A Swiss cylinder musical box (inlaid rosewood case)

Victorian cylinder musical box in inlaid rosewood case by Mermod.
(Jacobs & Hunt) $924

A coin-operated 'station' musical box, with nickel plated Mermod Frères interchangeable cylinder movement, in walnut case, 38in. wide. (Christie's) $7,586

A 19th century Continental singing bird musical box comprising a tortoiseshell box revealing animated feathered bird, 4in. long.
(Andrew Hartley) $1,512

A Mandoline Piccolo Interchangeable cylinder musical box by Mojon Manger, with 6 cylinders, thuya veneered case with stringing and ebony banding, 47¼in. wide, circa 1885.
(Christie's) $7,728

A musical box with clock, No. 2642, playing eight airs, in burr walnut case, 24in. wide, the cylinder 12¾in.
(Christie's) $4,784

A changeable cylinder musical box on table, with six cylinders playing six airs, thuya-veneered case with ebonised banding, 35¾in. wide.
(Christie's) $9,200

A changeable cylinder musical box, No. 6769, with four mandolin cylinders, rosewood-veneered case with bevelled corners and stringing, 26½in. wide.
(Christie's) $5,416

An orchestral musical box by Greiner, No. 12128, playing twelve popular and operatic airs accompanied by 17- key organ, in burr walnut case with crossbanding, 33½in. wide.
(Christie's) $4,515

A table Regina 15½in. disc musical box, No. 58185, with two combs on long bedplate, in golden oak case with ivorine stringing, 22in. wide, with 25 discs.
(Christie's) $3,612

An Adler 16in. table disc musical box, with two combs on upright pattern bedplate, in walnut case with figured walnut lid panel, 25in. wide, with 9 discs.
(Christie's) $2,392

A 17¾in. Kalliope upright disc musical box, with comb-and-a-third movement, typical walnut case with arched glazed door panel, 35in. high. (Christie's) $2,392

A Fortuna 16-inch disc musical box, with two combs, visible front-wind motor, walnut cross-veneered case, 25in. wide.
(Christie's) $2,890

Taxiphote stereoscope, no. 10527, Richard, Paris; polished mahogany-body, nickel-plated fittings, slide changing mechanism, internal battery-operated light. (Christie's) $493

A classic American magic lantern by McAllister, New York, for 10.5cm. glass strips, with petroleum burner, 54cm. high, circa 1900. (Auction Team Köln) $334

Kaleidoscope, metal viewing barrel with wood banding, mahogany base section, rear ground glass screen and side turning handle. (Christie's) $1,397

Revolving stereoscope, London Stereoscopic & Photographic Co., London; burr walnut body, hinged top with a pair of focusing viewing lenses. (Christie's) $329

Lantern Projector, Gardner & Co, Glasgow; wood-body, lacquered-brass fittings, with chimney, electric illuminant and a 10in. projection lens; a quantity of cinema advertising slides. (Christie's) $181

Photograph viewer, Japanese-lacquer body with decorative bamboo, tree and bird lacquer and gilt design, two painted-glass side panels; two viewing lenses, the viewer holding fifty 3¼ x 2¼in. pairs of albumen prints. (Christie's) $10,692

Praxinoscope theatre, E. Reynaud, Paris; the 21cm. diameter drum on turned wood stand, with candle holder, shade holder etc., five interchangeable paper scenes, and twenty picture strips. (Christie's) $3,290

Mutoscope No. 1039, International Mutoscope Reel Co., N.Y.; grey-painted metal body, with hand-cranked coin-operated mechanism, later electric motor, on matching metal stand, 134cm. high. (Christie's) $2,632

Stereo-Graphoscope, wood-body, with hinged viewing lenses and photograph holder, with base sliding drawer holding a quantity of tissue stereocards and views of Paris. (Christie's) $329

Phenakistiscope set, comprising a handle with retaining screw, 22cm.-diameter slotted viewing disc and nine 16½cm.-diameter coloured picture discs.
(Christie's) $987

A Josef Razin magic lantern, large Czech mahogany projector with metal lamp house and extending bellows, without lighting.
(Auction Team Köln) $282

Child's lantern, red-painted metal-body with gilt line decoration, lens, chimney and star motif.
(Christie's) $164

Kinora viewer, Kinora Ltd., London; hand-cranked, oak frame and lens housing, maker's brass plaque and retailers plaque Henry's, 22 King St., Manchester.
(Christie's) $1,316

Le Diocinescope film viewer, Huet & Daubresse, France; 35mm., wood-body, side winding handle, lever adjustment for film advance and rewind, the front with a pair of focusing viewing lenses.
(Christie's) $8,228

Magic lantern, with metal lamphouse, lacquered-brass lens section, lens chimney, electric illuminant and slide carrier, in a metal case; a quantity of 3¼in. lantern slides.
(Christie's) $164

Zoetrope, 30cm.-diameter metal drum, mounted on a polished mahogany turned stand, with sixteen picture strips, 17¼in. high.
(Christie's) $361

Stereoscope, Brewster-pattern; the black-lacquered body with extensive hand-painted gilt, blue and green floral decoration, ivory fittings. (Christie's) $1,150

Stereoscope, a wood-body, coin-operated stereoscope with advertising board For Men Only. Place Penny In Slot. Machine Does The Rest, holding a quantity of glamour stereocards.
(Christie's) $1,068

Bugatti, a child's pedal car, pressed steel construction with solid wheels and tyres, French, circa 1920s, 50in. long. (Christie's) $1,495

Thunderbird junior electric powered child's car, dusty rose with tan and white leatherette seating, engine: Ford starter motor; brakes: self braking, centre drive steering. (Christie's) $4,935

Ford GT40 "Junior", a half-scale motorised child's car by Mortarini, a superb creation of the 1966 Le Mans 24 Hour Race contender in miniature; built in limited numbers to celebrate Ford's famous victory in this legendary event, this particular example is finished in the livery of the Gulf Racing Team colours of blue and orange, length 78in. (Christie's) $8,575

Caterpillar D4 Bulldozer child's pedal car, as new finish in bright yellow; steering to tracked wheels by lever operation; front shovel lever-operated. (Christie's) $4,600

A child's pedal car model of a Miller-styled race car, well-engineered and detailed with leaf-spring suspension, brake-lever, outside exhaust, fuel-pump, refinished in bright red paintwork with decorative numbers to tail. (Christie's) $8,625

Packard, a good model child's pedal car by American National Co., Toledo, Ohio, steel panels on steel chassis frame, fold-flat windshield, 56in. long. (Christie's) $2,760

Ferrari, a child's pedal car based on the Tipo 500 GP racer, pressed steel construction, white stripes on blue metallic paintwork, circa 1950s, 46in. long. (Christie's) $1,955

Bugatti, a good child's pedal car in the likeness of a "Grand Prix" racing car by Eureka, spring front suspension, adjustable seat and pedals, electric lights and decorative dashboard layout, French, circa 1920s, 53in. long. (Christie's) $2,418

Packard, child's model pedal car by the American National Co., Toledo, Ohio, steel panel construction on steel chassis, superbly presented in pale grey with blue fenders and under-panels, late 1920s period, approximately 80in. long. (Christie's) $13,800

An early child's pedal car, wooden frame with steel axles and fixings, pedal-crank with chain drive to rear-axle, bolster-tank, bolster-tank, radial-spoked wheels, original red paint with blue chassis and race No.5 to front grille, circa 1910. (Christie's) $3,220

Mack, a child's pedal car in the form of a fire truck, steel construction, painted red and white with detailed accessories including dummy headlamps, ladders, warning bell etc, solid tyres on disc wheels. (Christie's) $2,185

A motorised child's car model of the famous Bentley Blower supercharged Le Mans team car by Meynell-Phillips, England, fibre-glass body surmounting steel chassis frame, believed only approximately 150 examples built, English circa 1960s, 68in. long. (Christie's) $13,800

A De La Rue silver 'line and dot' Onoto, the cap crown with silver overlay and with Onoto nib, London, 1913.
(Bonhams) $528

A Waterman's silver 'Barleycorn' (402) eyedropper, with No.2 size nib, London, 1902.
(Bonhams) $495

A Waterman's 0552¹/₂ 'The King', with No.2 nib, American, 1920s.
(Bonhams) $181

A Waterman's gold plated lever filler, with flying V design and No.2 nib, probably Italian, 1920s.
(Bonhams) $495

A Parker red Lucky Curve Duofold Senior, with Duofold pen nib, Canadian, circa 1926.
(Bonhams) $231

A Parker red marble Duofold, with broad, No.30 nib, English, 1941–45.
(Bonhams) $181

A Parker Vermeil 75 Ciselle pen and ballpen, both marked *Sterling*, pen with medium nib, American, circa 1970.
(Bonhams) $528

A Mabie Todd (/61) yellow/black mottled hard rubber Swan SF310 self-filler, with gold plated trim and Mabie Todd New York nib, English, circa 1920.
(Bonhams) $471

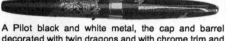

A Pilot black and white metal, the cap and barrel decorated with twin dragons and with chrome trim and 14ct. Pilot nib, Japanese, 1970s.
(Bonhams) $502

A Parker black hard rubber Lucky Curve No.20 jacknife Safety turban cap eyedropper, with No.2 Lucky Curve keyhole nib, barrel engraved, American, circa 1915.
(Bonhams) $363

A Waterman's limited edition Man 'Uno e Venticinque' No.041/500, the white metal body with fluted design, '1963–1993' cap top decal and two-colour 18ct. Waterman's Ideal nib, French, 1993.
(Bonhams) $1,570

A Pelikan limited Asia edition Golden Phoenix No.842/888, barrel marked *925*, the engraved vermeil barrel decorated with a flying phoenix over a scarlet red body and with two-colour 18ct. nib, German, 1996.
(Bonhams) $1,334

An Omas limited edition Collection Bibliothèque Nationale rollerball, the cream celluloid body with gold plated 'Greek key' design cap band and gold plated trim, Italian, 1993.
(Bonhams) $133

An Omas limited edition Tassili No.0804/1500, with dark brown Rams vegetal resin body, and textured, melted bronze cap, with matt 18ct. gold Omas nib, Italian, 1996.
(Bonhams) $353

A Yard-O-Led limited edition Imperial pen No.079/1000, the sterling silver body decorated with twin dragons and with two-colour 18ct. gold nib, English, 1996.
(Bonhams) $942

A Mont Blanc gold plated Pix pencil, with six-sided body decorated with alternating panels of engine turning and stylised floral engraving, German, 1920s.
(Bonhams) $495

A Mont Blanc red and black marbled 2M Safety, with No.2 Mont Blanc nib, German, circa 1920.
(Bonhams) $1,567

A Conway Stewart 22 floral, with Conway No.5 nib, English, 1950s.
(Bonhams) $219

A. S. T. Dupont limited edition Mozart No.0514/1000, the gold plated barrel decorated with round hoops creating a musical stave bearing the first notes of his Requiem, 18ct. Dupont nib, French, 1991.
(Bonhams) $1,099

A Pelikan limited edition 1000 Jahre Osterreich No.0215/1000, marked *925*, the silver barrel with red enamel highlights over a scarlet body with two-colour 18ct. nib, German, 1996.
(Bonhams) $1,099

A Pelikan limited edition silver plated Souveran Jubilee M750, with medium 14ct. nib, German, 1988.
(Bonhams) $314

A Wahl Eversharp pearl and black oversize Gold Seal Equipoise, with Gold Seal flexible nib, American, 1930s.
(Bonhams) $198

A Parker brown TX Falcon No.50, with medium integral nib, American, 1980s.
(Bonhams) $82

A black 'Post' No.1 plunger filling pen, with warranted nib, the barrel engraved *Judd Street, King's Cross*, English, circa 1915.
(Bonhams) $297

Mabie Todd & Co, a black hard rubber Todd's Safety no. 2 non leakable eyedropper, with twin gold plated barrel bands and Edward Todd no. 2 nib, American, circa 1910. (Bonhams) $134

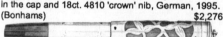

A Mont Blanc limited edition Prince Regent No.2553/4810, filigree marked *925*, the royal blue resin body covered with vermeil filigree incorporating a crown motif in the cap and 18ct. 4810 'crown' nib, German, 1995.
(Bonhams) $2,276

Parker, a white metal filigree no. 14 ring-top button Filler, cap marked *STERLING*, with elegant foliate filigree design and no. 2 Lucky Curve nib, American, circa 1920. (Bonhams) $874

A Parker black 51 Classic, with original marks and with medium oblique nib, English, 1950s.
(Bonhams) $132

A Sheaffer blue PFM Mark IV, with gold plated cap and with fine 14ct. inlaid nib, Australian, circa 1960.
(Bonhams) $188

Mordan, a silver 'Hand' quillholder, marked *S. MORDAN AUGT 3 1842 No. 1390* on the ivory shaft, with ruby set ring, silver-gilt collar, engraved and matted cuff, fingers cut to accept a quill nib, English, 1840s.
(Bonhams) $628

A De La Rue silver fine barley Onoto, with No.3 nib, London, 1922.
(Bonhams) $462

A Sheaffer blue PFM Mark III, with gold plated trim and palladium silver inlaid nib, Australian, circa 1960.
(Bonhams) $188

A Conway Stewart red/green/black/gold marbled Dandy No.720, with Conway Stewart No.3 nib, English, 1920s.
(Bonhams) $78

An Omas limited edition Europa No.2172/3500, with royal blue, twelve-sided body, with two-colour 18ct. Omas nib, Italian, 1992.
(Bonhams) $510

A Waterman's gold plated lever-filler, with alternating panels of low relief floral design and engine turned engraving and No.2 nib, probably Italian, 1920s.
(Bonhams) $495

A Mont Blanc limited edition Imperial Dragon No.2362/5000, clip marked *925*, with black resin body and stylised dragon clip, the eyes set with ruby chips and with two-colour 'dragon' nib, German, 1994.
(Bonhams) $800

Wahl Eversharp, a black chased hard rubber Signature, with roller clip and no 6 size Wahl nib, American, circa 1929.
(Bonhams) $269

A Mont Blanc green Marble 246, with No.6 nib, Danish, late 1940s.
(Bonhams) $231

A Mont Blanc Tiger's Eye 242 G, with Mont Blanc nib, German, late 1950s.
(Bonhams) $693

A MabieTodd Swan filigree chatelaine pen, American, 1907-1911, gold-plated over black hard rubber, bayonet cap with decorated locking ring, over-under fed nib. (Bonhams) $1,323

A W.M.F. silvered metal punch bowl and cover, of footed bulbous form, the gently ribbed body molded in low relief with upper band of stylized fruit and foliage, 34cm. high. (Christie's) $515

A Kayserzinn silvered metal basket, stamped factory mark, 22.5cm. high. (Christie's) $447

A WMF style Art Nouveau pewter dish with central circular panel, stamped and applied with a woman's head facing right, 9¼in. diam. (Christie's) $262

A pewter creamer, attributed to William Will, 1742–98, Philadelphia, with curved and beaded spout, 4½in. high. (Christie's) $6,900

A set of four 19th century Irish haystack pewter measures stamped *Austin Cork*, each with scrolled loop handle, girdled body and moulded base, 4in. to 7½in. high. (Andrew Hartley) $601

A W.M.F. silvered metal centerpiece, the circular clear glass bowl supported on foliate stem cast in relief with a scantily clad maiden, 53.5cm. high. (Christie's) $520

A pewter quart dome-top tankard, attributed to Thomas Danforth II, 1731–82, Middletown, Connecticut, or Thomas Danforth III, 1756–1840, Stepney, Connecticut, 7in. high. (Christie's) $1,495

A pair of WMF pewter syphon stands, on spreading base with Secessionist style pierced sides and reeded tapering feet, 4in. high. (Christie's) $240

A Tudric pewter jug, designed by Archibald Knox, of tapering cylindrical form decorated in relief to the neck with circles and scrolls, the handle covered with interwoven cane work, 12in. high. (Bonhams) $483

LaCroix, photograph of Dali, 1960s, colour photograph of artist Dali with fashion model, numbered *11/50*, signed, image 19 x 24in.
(Skinner) $288

Leonard Misonne, Les Pecheurs, circa 1935, mediobrome, 9³/₈ x 11¾in., inscribed and initialed by the photographer's grandson in pencil on verso, matted.
(Christie's) $1,886

Henri Cartier-Bresson, 'Interlude in Bali - The Dancing Island', 1950, six glossy silver prints, each approx. 6¾ x 9¾in.
(Christie's) $4,526

E.E. Haynes, World record parachute attempt, 1932, ten gelatin silver prints, 6³/₈ x 8¾in. to 6⁷/₈ x 9½in.
(Christie's) $1,809

Thomas Richard Williams (1825-71), portrait of a brother with his sister in formal dress, 1850s, stereoscopic daguerreotype, hand-tinted with gilt highlights, signed on black card surround.
(Christie's) $3,749

David Octavius Hill and Robert Adamson, James Linton, Newhaven, June 1845, calotype, 7⁷/₈. x 5⁵/₈in mounted at top corners on paper.
(Christie's) $3,772

Female Studio Photographer, a gelatin-silver print, heavily retouched, showing a female photographer with camera on stand in her studio, in a decoratively carved wood frame, 31½ x 47in.
(Christie's) $329

Robert Doisneau (1912-1994), 'Le Baiser de l'Hotel de Ville, 1950s', printed later, gelatiin silver print, image size 9½ x 11¾in., signed in ink in margin.
(Christie's) $3,772

Anonymous, 'Manille – Jeune fille Mestiza (métis.)', circa 1870s, albumen print, 10½ x 8¼in., arched corners, mounted on card, titled in ink on mount, matted.
(Christie's) $2,249

Joseph-Philibert Girault de Prangey, 'Abdullah [?Ibn el Kherife] Mecka', early 1840s, daguerreotype, mounted as oval, 4¼ x 3⅝in., titled in pencil on reverse, passe-partout.
(Christie's) $25,333

Anonymous, Sarah Bernhardt, circa 1870s, woodburytype print, trimmed circular approximately 3⅞in. diameter, mounted on grey card with gilt edge, framed.
(Christie's) $658

Julia Margaret Cameron (1815-1879), Mrs. Herbert Duckworth, circa 1867, albumen print, 10¼ x 8³/₈in., mounted on card, signed, titled and inscribed.
(Christie's) $4,112

Alexander Rodchenko, 'Kulaki, 1928' [Kulaks], gelatin silver print on textured paper, 11³/₈ x 9in., titled and dated in pencil and with photographer's ink credit stamp, on reverse.(Christie's) $18,095

Norman Parkinson, Children with Jaguar, 1957, printed later, gelatin silver print, 9 x 11³/₈in., signed in pencil, stamped on the reverse, mounted and framed.
(Christie's) $1,397

Anonymous, Woman with child, late 1840s or early 1850s, half-plate daguerreotype, hand-tinted with gilt highlights, gilt-metal mount, in folding morocco case.
(Christie's) $493

John Jabez Edwin Mayall (1810-1901), Portrait of David Livingstone, 1857, albumen print, 10¹/₈ x 7¾in., mounted on card.
(Christie's) $1,990

Walker Evans (1903-75), South Street, 1932, gelatin silver print, 8 x 9⁷/₈in., notations in pencil and stamped Walker Evans I 104 on reverse.(Christie's) $18,095

Oscar Gustave Rejlander (1813-75), allegorical study, 1850s, albumen print, 7¼ x 4⁷/₈in., arched top, mounted on card, matted.
(Christie's) $6,332

PHOTOGRAPHS

Martin Munkacsi (1896-1963), Count Zichy at the wheel, 1927, gelatin silver print, 9³/8 x 5¾in., stamped *Aufnahme Martin Munkácsy Berlin W. 30, Motzstr. 13 iii* with extended title in German on reverse, inscription. (Christie's) $3,437

Anonymous, 'Le Croisic', 1842, whole-plate daguerreotype, dated on image lower right, 4¹/8 x 8¹/8in., titled and dated in pencil on paper strip, passe-partout. (Christie's) $10,857

Anonymous, 'Nantes. Vue Prise de la Place de la Petite Hollande', early 1840s, whole-plate daguerreotype, the left side masked by a paper strip to 6 x 7¾in., passe-partout, with the corresponding plate from La Loire Inférieure. (Christie's) $19,905

Henri Cartier-Bresson, 1952, Francis Bacon, 1952, printed later, gelatin silver print, 9³/8 x 14¹/8in., signed in margin. (Christie's) $1,810

Anonymous, Tree-lined riverside view, Nantes, with Prefecture building, 1841, whole-plate daguerreotype, dated lower right of image, re-taped, *Pl.13* inscribed in pencil on reverse, with the corresponding plate from La Loire Inférieure. (Christie's) $39,809

Henri Cartier-Bresson (born 1908), Taxi Drivers, Berlin, 1932, printed later, gelatin silver print, 9⁵/8 x 14¹/8in., signed in black ink in the margin, matted. (Christie's) $1,974

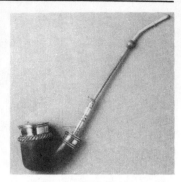

A finely carved meerschaum pipe bowl, 19th century, of a bearded Confederate soldier's head. (Bristol) $175

A German porcelain pipe, 19th century, modelled as a seated grey tabby cat, the head being the cover, with brass mounts and wood and amber stem, 22cm. long. (Bristol) $335

A large bowled leather-covered wood pipe, 19th century, with silver coloured metal mounts and wood stem, 40cm. long. (Bristol) $80

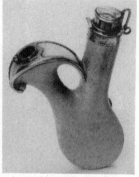

A Prattware pipe, 'The Farmer', of a seated man wearing brown top hat and blue coat smoking a moulded clay pipe, circa 1795, 14cm. (Bristol) $840

A Prattware pipe, 'The Farmer's Wife', of a seated woman wearing a bonnet and blue and ochre spotted dress, circa 1795, 12.3cm. (Bristol) $900

An Austro Hungarian small meerschaum ulmer pipe, 19th century, the silver coloured metal mounts and pierced cover with hallmarks, 12.7cm. high. (Bristol) $220

A German hallmarked meerschaum pipe bowl, second quarter 19th century, 15 x 10cm., silver gilt engraved mounts with pierced lid horn wood stem, 65cm. long. (Bristol) $110

A Nailsea type cranberry and opaque drawn glass decorative pipe, 19th century, bowl 18cm. high, stem 50cm. long. (Bristol) $230

A substantial English meerschaum pipe bowl, 19th century, with fine bas relief carving of the Death of Nelson at the Battle of Trafalgar surrounded by shipmates, 32cm. high. (Bristol) $11,310

A Chinese bone long dry opium pipe, 19th century, with incised figural decoration, glazed polychrome pottery bowl and white metal mount, 35cm.
(Bristol) $465

An English Prattware puzzle pipe, in fine condition, *Tho. Nicholls, 1823* on coil of pipe, 35cm. long.
(Bristol) $2,680

A George IV meerschaum pipe, with foliate carved bowl, silver gilt mounts and cover depicting Frederick II of Prussia within flower and scroll foliate border, full English hallmarks, London 1821.
(Bristol) $305

A Debrecen style meerschaum pipe bowl, 19th century, carved an elaborate 'S' within scroll reserve, the castellated silver lid with Austro Hungarian marks, for 1828, 14cm. long. 13cm. high.
(Bristol) $190

A German fruitwood pipe bowl, 18th century, finely bas relief carved with a scaled fish with pipe shank in mouth, the bowl adorned with figure of Mercury, 13 x 8cm.
(Bristol) $840

An 18th century Continental porcelain pipe bowl, well modelled and painted as an odalisque head, with earrings, turban and three feathers, chipped and lacking metal cover, 11.2cm. long.
(Bristol) $955

An unusual meerschaum pipe, circa 1900: bust of lady in feathered hat, on copper based plinth, slight damage to collar, 13 x 7cm.
(Bristol) $72

An Astro Hungarian meerschaum pipe bowl, 19th century, the silver mounts with maker's mark *E.T.* and engraved *Honi Soit qui Mal y pense*, bowl 10cm. long.
(Bristol) $45

An English Prattware pottery pipe, circa 1805, of a sailor sitting astride a barrel and drinking from a horn, slight damage to stem, 15cm. high.
(Bristol) $1,335

An English double-bowled meerschaum pipe, 19th century, with amber stem, 26cm. long. (Bristol) $65

A fine meerschaum cigar pipe, 19th century, carved in full relief with hawking party, with silver coloured metal bands and amber mouthpiece, 29cm. long. (Bristol) $4,205

An unusual 19th century meerschaum cheroot holder, with an elfin figure in full relief and amber mouthpiece, 12cm. long. (Bristol) $390

A finely carved meerschaum pipe, 19th century, of a Negress carved in full relief, with amber stem, 15cm. long. (Bristol) $465

An unusual meerschaum pipe, 19th century: the bust of an 18th century romantic revolutionary French lady, on a black wood plinth, 13 x 7cm. (Bristol) $160

A 19th century meerschaum pipe, full relief carved as Napoleon, the metal lid as a bicorn hat, with full amber stem, bowl 10cm. high, 22cm. long. (Bristol) $290

A 19th century meerschaum pipe, finely full relief carved as a Cossack wearing a hat, with amber stem, bowl 10cm. high, 15cm. long. (Bristol) $465

A 19th century meerschaum pipe, finely full relief carved as a bearded Arab, with silver coloured metal band and amber stem. (Bristol) $405

An Austro Hungarian meerschaum pipe bowl, early 19th century, bas relief carved as an eagle, with silver coloured metal pierced lid and rim, 12cm. long. (Bristol) $610

A 19th century meerschaum pipe, finely carved in full relief as a boxer dog's head, good colour with amber stem, 16cm. long. (Bristol) $220

A Prattware bear and serpent pipe, circa 1795, modelled as a crouching bear with collar and lead, the looped mouthpiece issuing from mouth, the bowl formed as a coiled serpent, 19.4cm. long. (Bristol) $4,200

An English meerschaum pipe, full relief of a bearded man, with amber stem and silver band with hallmark *B'ham 1907*, maker's mark *AB & Co,* 14cm. long. (Bristol) $100

A North American Indian tomahawk pipe, Hudson Bay Co., 1780-1830, the blade with impressed bird, sun, moon and stars motif. (Bristol) $4,078

A 19th century meerschaum pipe, carved in full relief as a mastiff snarling, with amber stem, 16cm. long. (Bristol) $190

A Staffordshire Prattware puzzle pipe, circa 1800, 30cm. long. (Bristol) $1,420

A meerschaum pipe, 19th century, well-carved as a young lady's head with a straw hat perched on her coiffured hair, wearing a monocle and with bow tie, 8cm. high, 16.8cm. long. (Bristol) $405

A 19th century meerschaum pipe, finely full relief carved as a negro man's head with straw hat, silver coloured metal band and amber stem, bowl 8cm. high, 16cm. long. (Bristol) $565

A meerschaum pipe, 19th century, finely carved as a young lady's head, her coiffured hair with flower ribbon bedecked bonnet perched above her forehead, 8cm. high, 19cm. long. (Bristol) $435

An Austro Hungarian meerschaum pipe bowl, 19th century, with bas relief carving of battle scene, with white metal mounts, maker's mark *JK* and *PA*, 15cm. high. (Bristol) $160

A George IV Ragoczy style meerschaum pipe bowl, the silver mounts once gilt, the flat cover engraved a sword and elbow crest within chased floral circlet, London 1824, 10.5cm. long.(Bristol) $95

An unusual meerschaum cigar holder on stand, 19th century, with two Saxon figures, silver coloured metal mount and lion claw feet to base, 18cm. high. (Bristol) $4,785

A meerschaum pipe, 19th century, finely full relief carved as a cuffed hand holding an egg, with silver coloured metal band on two-piece amber stem, 24cm. long. (Bristol) $320

A well-carved meerschaum pipe, English, 19th century, carved in bas relief with the head of Prince Albert flanked by pair of angels, 55cm. long. (Bristol) $1,100

A meerschaum cheroot pipe, 19th century, carved in full relief as a lightly clad young lady with a scarf around her hair, with wooden stem and amber mouthpiece, 14cm. long. (Bristol) $87

Philip Jean, circa 1790, gentleman, with natural powdered hair, wearing blue coat with gold buttons, oval, 69mm. high.
(Bonhams & Brooks) $3,360

Philip Jean, circa 1795, a fine portrait of a lady, with white ribbon bow in her powdered hair, gold frame, the reverse glazed to reveal lock of hair on blue glass, 67mm. high.
(Bonhams & Brooks) $5,880

John Cox Dillman Engleheart, (1782-/84-1862), a Lady, facing right in lace-bordered black dress with high white collar and fichu, 84mm. high. (Christie's) $3,281

François Ferrière, circa 1795, a gentleman, wearing black coat with gold buttons, white stock and cravat, indistinctly signed, oval, 2½in. high.
(Bonhams & Brooks) $630

Charles G. Dillon, circa 1810, two portraits of a gentleman and a lady, he wears blue coat, wears white lace veil in her hair, reverses glazed to reveal plaited hair, ovals, 2½in. and 2¾in. high.
(Bonhams & Brooks) $910

John Turmeau, circa 1810, a gentleman, said to be John Leigh, with side-whiskers, wearing brown coat, gold frame, the reverse with monogram *JL*, on plaited hair, 66mm. high.
(Bonhams & Brooks) $840

Matthias Finucane, circa 1800, a child, three-quarter length, full-face, wearing white dress with blue sash, gilt-mounted rectangular papier-mâché frame, oval, 2¼in. high.
(Bonhams & Brooks) $1,190

William Douglas, circa 1820, Isabella Gordon, with short curled blonde hair, wearing décolleté white dress, gold frame, oval, 3in. high.
(Bonhams & Brooks) $1,260

Attributed to R. C. Woolnough, circa 1790, a gentleman, with powdered hair en queue, wearing blue coat, gold frame, 60mm. high.
(Bonhams & Brooks) $840

George Chinnery, circa 1800, Hugh Seton, with powdered hair en queue, gold mount with copper reverse, inscribed, oval, 3½in. high.
(Bonhams & Brooks) $12,600

Pierre-Édouard Dagoty (1775-1871), two young Ladies in white dresses, signed and dated *Dagoty, 1837*, 3¼in. diameter.
(Christie's) $4,836

Andrew Plimer, 1787, Mrs David Wedderburne, wearing white bandeau in her long curling hair, oval, 2¾in. high.
(Bonhams & Brooks) $7,000

Johann-Friedrich Ardin, (fl.circa 1700-1720), Cosimo III of Medici, Grand Duke of Tuscany, facing right in gilt-studded armor, ermine-line pink cloak fastened at his left shoulder, enamel on copper, oval, 62mm. high.
(Christie's) $5,184

William Grimaldi, 1810, Mrs. L.M. Hayes, seated in a red upholstered chair, wearing short-sleeved white dress, signed on reverse and dated, 85mm. high.
(Bonhams & Brooks) $350

Italian School, circa 1795, King Louis XVIII (1755-1824) when Comte de Provence, facing left in blue coat with silver-embroidered red facings, 3¼in. diameter.
(Christie's) $3,455

Attributed to Anson Dickinson (1779-1852) a lady in black dress with brown ringlets held in a tortoise comb, watercolor on ivory, 3½ x 2¾in. (Christie's) $805

French School, circa 1800, a young Lady, in profile to the left in lace-bordered white dress, hexagonal, 54mm. high.(Christie's) $1,083

Nanette Rosenzweig, née Windisch, (fl.c. 1790-1820), a young Lady, facing left in low-cut white dress with white lace underdress, signed, rectangular, 58 x 52mm. (Christie's) $5,006

Andrew Plimer, 1786, a fine portrait of a young lady, wearing slate grey dress, white fichu and matching bonnet, oval, 2¼in. high. (Bonhams) $6,594

Attributed to Peter Paul Lens, circa 1740, a lady, wearing black dress with lace collar and red ribbons, oval, 1¾in. high. (Bonhams) $659

School of Isabey, early 19th century, Emperor Napoleon I, in the uniform of the Chasseurs-à-Cheval de la Garde, oval, 3in. high. (Bonhams) $628

Attributed to Karoly Brocky, circa 1820, a lady, wearing décolleté white dress with lace collar and pearl drop earrings, oval, 3¼in. high. (Bonhams) $942

Charles Shirreff, circa 1790, a lady, wearing white dress with yellow waistband and matching turban gold frame, oval, 2¼in. high. (Bonhams) $2,669

Spanish school, circa 1820, an infantry officer, seated beside a table before a green curtain, gold coloured frame, rectangular, 80mm. high. (Bonhams) $863

Attributed to the artist signing V, circa 1780, a young lady, wearing mauve coat, lace trimmed white cap tied beneath her chin, gold bracelet clasp mount, oval, 1½in. high. (Bonhams) $1,335

An oval bust length portrait miniature of Mrs Deane, wearing a white dress and cream hat, attributed to Richard Cosway, 2.8in., in original folding case. (Russell Baldwin & Bright) $1,056

Peter Crosse, circa 1680, a young gentleman, believed to be James Scott, Duke of Monmouth and Buccleuch, K..G., wearing full-bottomed wig, on vellum, oval, 3in. high. (Bonhams) $13,188

English School, circa 1815, an officer of Light Infantry, wearing scarlet uniform with black facings, painted on card, oval, 3in. high. (Bonhams) $251

Possibly Russian School, early 19th century, one of a pair of portraits of a young boy and girl; he, in grey coat, she, in red trimmed green dress, 53mm. high. (Bonhams) (Two) $471

Andrew Plimer, circa 1790, a fine portrait of Sir Guy Johnston, his powdered hair en queue, wearing a blue coat, oval, 3in. high. (Bonhams) $5,966

William Thicke, circa 1780, Nathan Crowe (b. 1721), wearing mole-coloured coat with gold frogging, yellow waistcoat and white stock, oval, 3in. high. (Bonhams) $314

Spanish School, circa 1820, a lady, with dishevelled hair, wearing low-cut grey dress, stamped gilt-mounted wood frame, circular, 2¼in. diameter. (Bonhams) $393

Carl Christian Fiedler, 1820, a pair of portraits of possibly a husband and his wife; he, writing at a desk with a quill, she, seated in red chair, both signed on obverse and dated, ovals, 3in. (Bonhams) $1,020

William Bishop Ford, 1866, after Sir Henry Raeburn, Sir Walter Scott, wearing green coat, yellow waistcoat, black stock and gold chain, enamel, signed on reverse and dated and inscribed, 42mm. high. (Bonhams) $1,099

William Egley, circa 1840, a young officer, wearing scarlet uniform with gold collar, epaulettes and buttons, rectangular, 104mm. high. (Bonhams) $942

English School, early 19th century, a lady wearing Tudor costume, pearl necklace and red and white striped cap, enamel, turned wood frame, oval, 2¼in. high. (Bonhams) $1,256

George Engleheart (1750-1829),
James Sparkes, facing right in
aubergine colored coat, oval
61mm. high.
(Christie's) $5,339

Franciscek Smiadecki (fl. c. 1664),
a Gentleman, facing right in gilt-
studded armor, signed with
monogram and dated, oil on metal,
oval, 3in. high.
(Christie's) $3,947

Rupert Barber (fl. 1736-1772), a
young Gentleman, facing right in
white shirt with high collar, signed
with monogram, enamel on copper,
oval, 1¾in. high.
(Bonhams) $1,835

Alexander Gallaway, 1797, an
officer, wearing red uniform with
gold figured blue facings, gold
epaulette, white sword belt with
gold cross plate, black stock and
white cravat, signed on the
obverse, 2¾in. high.
(Bonhams & Brooks) $2,520

Miss Sarah T. Howard, circa 1845,
the children of Dr. Elliot, seated in a
landscape, in a tooled leather
travelling case, with double doors
and easel reverse, oval, 200mm.
high.
(Bonhams & Brooks) $2,240

George Place, circa 1795, Major
General Sir Barry Close, wearing
scarlet uniform, with blue collar,
gold frogging and epaulettes,
stamped ormolu-mounted
rectangular papier-mâché frame,
oval, 3½in. high.
(Bonhams & Brooks) $6,300

George Engleheart (1750-1829), a
young Lady, facing right in lace-
bordered white dress with blue bow,
oval, 2½in.
(Christie's) $6,674

Pierre-Louis Bouvier (1765-1836), a
young Lady, facing left in white silk
dress, signed and dated, oval,
2½in. high.
(Bonhams) $4,672

Jean-Urbain Guérin (1760-1836), a
young Lady, facing right in muslin
dress with blue bordered sleeves,
signed, 78mm. high.
(Bonhams) $6,674

André Rouquet (1701-1758), a young Lady, facing left in loose lace-bordered white robe, enamel on copper, oval, 2¼in. high. (Christie's) $8,291

Ignazio Pio Vittoriano Campana (1744-1786), a young Lady leaning on a carved gilt-wood table with marble, 3in. diameter. (Christie's) $12,954

J. T. Mitchell, circa 1790, James Grant of Dalvey, wearing brown coat, signed and inscribed, oval, 3½in. high. (Bonhams) $882

John Comerford, circa 1810, Mrs. Tighe, wearing décolleté white dress with gauze collar, a gold ring on a black ribbon about her neck, the reverse with label inscribed with the sitter's name, gilt-metal mount, oval, 72mm. high. (Bonhams & Brooks) $4,200

Reginald Easton, circa 1835, George Olaus Baillie of Leys Castle, as a child, full-length, with blond curls, wearing low-cut blue tartan dress, the reverse with label, 4¼in. high. (Bonhams & Brooks) $1,330

Mrs. Anne Mee, circa 1815, Lady Caroline Lamb, with hair piled high, wearing décolleté white dress with ribbon bow, signed on the reverse, set in a red leather travelling case, 81mm. high. (Bonhams & Brooks) $12,320

Spanish School, circa 1620, a Knight, facing left in slashed black doublet with gold buttons, oil on copper, oval, 62mm. high. (Bonhams) $2,168

N. Freese (fl.1794-1814), a left Eye with brown iris, curling brown lock of hair; sky and cloud surround, oval, 50mm. high, fitted red leather case. (Christie's) $9,176

Jean-Urbain Guérin (1760-1836), a young Lady, facing left in white dress with gauze bodice and triple lace collar, signed, oval, 78mm. high. (Christie's) $6,340

Nathaniel Plimer (1757-1822), a young Lady, facing right in blue riding habit, oval, 3in. high. (Christie's) $11,040

George Engleheart (1750-1829), a young Lady, facing right in lace-bordered white dress, rectangular, 73 x 51mm., gilt metal frame. (Christie's) $3,496

Richard Cosway RA (1742-1821), General Gale, facing right in pale grey coat, oval, 2in. high. (Christie's) $3,496

Nathaniel Plimer (1757-1822), a Gentleman, facing left in blue coat with gold buttons, signed and dated 1787, oval, 2¾in. high. (Christie's) $2,944

John Cox Dillman Engleheart (1782/84-1862), Miss Alison Farrow, facing right in lace-bordered pale pink dress, signed and dated 1814, rectangular, 84 x 65mm. (Christie's) $5,888

George Engleheart (1750-1829), a Gentleman, facing left in scarlet coat, white waistcoat and frilled cravat, oval, 41mm. high. (Christie's) $5,520

Franciszek Smiadecki (fl. circa 1664), a young Gentleman, facing right in black coat with white lawn collar, oil on card, oval, 62mm. high. (Christie's) $6,992

Samuel Collins (1735-1768), Elizabeth Moore as a young girl, facing right in lace-bordered mauve dress, oval, 36mm. high. (Christie's) $3,128

Christian Friedrich Zincke (1683/4-1767), Thomas, 4th Duke of Leeds, facing left in gold bordered brown velvet coat, enamel, oval, 46mm. high. (Christie's) $7,728

John Smart Junior (1776-1809), a Boy, facing left in black coat and waistcoat, signed and dated 1806, oval, 68mm. high. (Christie's) $5,152

Marie-Thérèse de Noireterre (1760-1819), a young Gentleman, facing left in double-breasted dark grey coat, 59mm. diameter. (Christie's) $6,992

Henry Burch (b. 1763), a young Child, facing left in white dress with yellow sash, oval, 2½in. high. (Christie's) $1,472

Johann Heinrich von Hurter (1734-1799), Queen Charlotte, facing left in gold-bordered pale grey dress with fichu, signed and dated 1782, enamel on copper, oval, 52mm. high. (Christie's) $25,760

John Thomas Barber Beaumont (1774-1841), a Child, facing left in blue dress and black bonnet, holding a dove in his arms, signed and dated 1797, oval, 67mm. high. (Christie's) $2,392

Horace Hone ARA (1754/56-1825), Mrs Caulfield of Levitstown, facing left in white dress with ruched neckline, signed and dated 1791, oval, 71mm. high. (Christie's) $15,640

Charles Robertson (circa 1760-1821), a Gentleman, facing left in brown coat, white and red waistcoat, oval, 61mm. high. (Christie's) $1,656

George Engleheart (1750-1829), a young Lady, facing left in low-cut White dress wwith frilled underslip, oval, 53mm. (Christie's) $2,024

Christian Friedrich Zincke (1683/4-1767), a young Gentleman facing left in white shirt, enamel on copper, oval, 46mm. high. (Christie's) $8,400

George Engleheart (1750-1829), Miss Delsel, facing left in white dress with blue buttons, oval, 62mm. (Christie's) $15,850

Henry Pierce Bone (1779-1855), Frederick VI, Landgrave of Hesse-Homburg (1769-1829), signed, inscribed and dated, enamel on copper, oval, 3in. high. (Bonhams) $3,337

John Bogle (1764-1803), a young Gentleman, facing right in green coat with silver buttons, signed with initials and dated, 46mm. high. (Christie's) $4,672

English School, circa 1810, a young Officer, possibly of the Royal Artillery, wearing blue coat with gold figured red facings, oval, 67mm. high. (Bonhams) $1,103

Henri L'Évêque (1769-1832), an Officer, facing right in scarlet coat with blue collar and gold buttons, signed with initials H.L, enamel on copper, octagonal, 62 x 51mm. (Bonhams) $2,670

Antoine Berjon, circa 1790, a Lady, wearing décolleté yellow dress with pink stripes, signed on the obverse, oval, 2¼in. high. (Bonhams) $1,058

Attributed to William Bishops Ford, circa 1865, after Jean-Baptiste Mauzaisse, 1826, a fine portrait of Sir Walter Scott, wearing striped mauve and purple plaid, oval, 1¾in. high. (Bonhams) $1,470

Attributed to Edward Luttrell, 1671, a fine portrait of Catherine of Braganza, wearing gold figured décolleté white dress, rectangular, 9½in. high. (Bonhams) $7.644

French School, circa 1815, Emperor Napoleon I (1769-1821), facing right in red-bordered black coat, with signature and date, oval, 71mm. high. (Christie's) $4,663

Jean-Baptiste Genty (b.circa 1770), a young Lady, facing left in white shirt with high standing lace collar, signed and dated, oval, 72mm. high. (Christie's) $1,501

Nathaniel Plimer, circa 1805, a young Gentleman, with receding hair, wearing brown coat, gold frame with blue glass reverse, oval, 2¾in. high. (Bonhams) $882

S. Moss, circa 1830, an attractive miniature of a young Lady, believed to be Marie Celeste Hora, oil on ivory, signed on the reverse, oval 3in. high. (Bonhams) $1,103

Louis-Marie Autissier (1772-1830), an Equerry to Louis, King of Holland, facing right in blue coat with gold-embroidered border, signed, rectangular, 56 x 47mm. (Christie's) $5,339

Circle of André Lefèvre d'Orgeval, circa 1750, three Ladies; a pilgrim, Santiago de Compostela, a Savoyarde, and a flower girl in pink dress, on parchment, rectangular, 49 x 73mm. (Bonhams) $3,337

Andrew Robertson (1777-1845), the artist's first wife Jenny, in profile to left, in long sleeved white dress, rectangular, 92 x 72mm. (Christie's) $2,670

Naples School, circa 1790, Maria Carolina of Habsburg (1752-1814), Queen of Naples, facing left in lace-bordered russet coloured dress, oval, 2½in. high, gilt-metal mount. (Christie's) $5,839

Andrew Plimer (1763-1837), Louisa Plimer (1801-1864), later Mrs John Scott, rectangular 111 x 83mm. (Christie's) $10,011

Andrew Plimer, circa 1810, Georgina Daniell, with short curled dark hair, wearing décolleté white dress, inscribed on reverse with the sitter's name, oval, 3in. high. (Bonhams) $4,704

Max Schwarzer, (1882-1955), Regina-Bar, lithograph in colours, circa 1927, printed by Kid, München, 49 x 33in. (Christie's) $2,071

Henri de Toulouse-Lautrec, (1864-1901), Les Chansonniers de Montmartre, lithograph in colours, 1893, front cover, backed on linen, 14 x 10½in. (Christie's) $1,806

Radio Lot, lithograph in colours, circa 1930, printed by A. Trüb y Cia, Aarau, 47 x 35in. (Christie's) $867

Jules-Alexandre Grün, (1868-1934), La Cigale, lithograph in colours, 1900, printed by Chaix, Paris, backed on linen, 49 x 35½in. (Christie's) $2,184

Paul Lengelle, Clostermann, Le Grand Cirque, lithograph in colours, circa 1951, printed by M.Dechaux, Paris, backed on linen, 30 x 22½in. (Christie's) $1,083

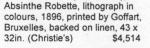

Privat Livemont (1861-1936), Absinthe Robette, lithograph in colours, 1896, printed by Goffart, Bruxelles, backed on linen, 43 x 32in. (Christie's) $4,514

Dudley Hardy, (1867-1922), "A Gaiety Girl", lithograph in colours, 1893, printed by Waterlow & Sons, on two sheets, 90 x 40in. (Christie's) $1,122

Jacques le Tord, Terrot, pub. by Reunies 1939, on linen, 118 x 80cm. (Onslows) $308

H L Roowy, Pneu Vélo Michelin, lithograph in colours, 1912, printed by Chaix, Paris, 39½ x 30in. (Christie's) $1,008

Terence Cuneo, Forging Ahead, British Railways, lithograph in colours, 1950, printed by Waterlow & Sons Limited, London, 40 x 50in. (Christie's) $4,277

Pildoras Ross, offset lithograph in colours, 1950, vertical and horizontal fold marks, backed on linen, 43½ x 29½in. (Christie's) $2,347

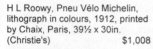

J Georges, Olibet Biscuits, lithograph in colours, circa 1900, printed by Spéciale des Biscuits Olibet, 60 x 43in. (Christie's) $903

Alphonse Mucha, Souvenir de la Belle Jardinière, Paris, lithograph in colours, 1893, printed by F.Champenois, Paris, 3½ x 5½in. (Christie's) $506

Henri de Toulouse-Lautrec, (1864-1901), Aristide Bruant dans son Cabaret, lithograph in colours, 1893, printed by Charles Verneau, Paris, backed on paper, framed, 53 x 38in. (Christie's) $27,636

Philips Radio, London 1948, offset lithograph in colours, 1948, backed on linen, 18 x 12in. and two other 'Philips Radio, London 1948' posters. (Christie's) $1,208

Terence Cuneo, Service To Industry, British Railways, North Eastern Region, lithograph in colours, 1962, printed by Waterlow & Sons Limited, London, 40 x 50in. (Christie's) $1,228

Dépuratif Bleu, lithograph in colours, circa 1920, printed by A.Mulcey, St.Etienne, backed on linen, 23½ x 16in. (Christie's) $325

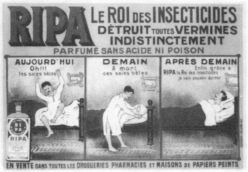

Chales Gesmar, Mistinguett, Moulin Rouge, lithograph in colours, 1926, printed by H. Chachoin, Paris, backed on linen, 47 x 30½in. (Christie's) $1,806

Ripa, lithograph in colours, circa 1900, printed by Em.Wauthy, Verviers, backed on linen, 28 x 40½in. (Christie's) $672

Marc, Pastis Olive, lithograph in colours, printed by Editions Publi-Vente, Paris, backed on linen, 78½ x 51in. (Christie's) $725

Henri de Toulouse-Lautrec, Caudieux, lithograph in colours, 1893, printed by Chaix, Paris, backed on old linen, framed, 49 x 35½in. (Christie's) $36,966

Terence Cuneo, The Royal Albert Bridge, Saltash (Cornwall), British Railways, Western Region, lithograph in colours, 1959, printed by Waterlow & Sons Limited, London, 40 x 50in. (Christie's) $2,632

Spratt's Patent, lithograph in colours, printed by Guèneux Robert R.F., Nantes, 31 x 23in. (Christie's) $796

Walter Schnackenberg, (1880-1961), Odeon Casino, lithograph in colours, 1911, printed by Dr C. Wolf und Sohn, München, 49 x 36in. (Christie's) $12,090

Dick A Dumas, Allons Tous à la consultation, lithograph in colours, circa 1900, printed by Réunies, Lyon, backed on linen, 35 x 49½in. (Christie's) $867

Jean-Gabriel (1889-1962), Gdes. Fêtes De Paris, lithograph in colours, 1934, printed by Alliance Graphique, Paris, backed on linen, 38 x 23½in. (Christie's) $1,295

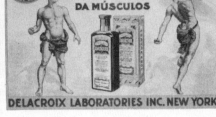

Ludwig Lutz Ehrenberger, Bonbonnière, lithograph in colours, 1909, printed by J.G. Velisch, München, 49 x 37in. (Christie's)   **$4,145**

Guayacerol, lithograph in colours, circa 1910, printed by A. Trüb y Cia., Aarau, 38½ x 54in. (Christie's)   **$2,345**

H. G. Strick, Krone, offset lithograph in colours, printed by Bruckmann, München, 33 x 23½in. (Christie's)   **$436**

Louis John Rhead (1857-1926), Read The Sun, lithograph in colours, 1895, printed by Liebler & Maass, New York, 47 x 30in. (Christie's)   **$3,011**

John Gilroy, My Goodness – My Guinness, lithograph in colours, 1956, printed by Sanders Phillips & Co., Ltd., London, 30 x 40in. (Christie's)   **$650**

Hon. Edward McKnight Kauffer, R.D.I., The Flea, Underground, lithograph in colours, 1926, printed by Vincent Brooks, Day & Son Ltd., London, 40 x 25in. (Christie's)   **$1,645**

Harry Houdini, a rare British poster circa 1912, Houdini – Upside Down In The Water Torture Cell, 30 x 20in., lithograph in colours, printed by The Dangerfield Printing Co., Ltd., London. (Christie's)   **$29,610**

Lewitt-Him (Jan Lewitt, 1907-1991; George Him, 1900-1982), Say It By Cable, GPO, lithograph in colours, circa 1951, condition B; backed on linen, 28½ x 35in. (Christie's)   **$1,260**

Théophile-Alexandre Steinlen, (1859-1923), Lait Pur Stérilisé de la Vingeanne, lithograph in colours, 1894, printed by Charles Verneau, Paris, 55 x 39½in. (Christie's)   **$17,272**

Greig, P&O Cruises, printed by Lamson Agency, 101 x 63cm. (Onslows) $518

Ernest Gabard, (1879-1957), Pau-Aviation, lithograph in colors, circa 1912, printed by Garet & Haristoy, Pau, backed on linen, 31 x 47in. (Christie's) $1,899

Anon, Holland (girl on sailing boat) mounted on linen, 104 x 63cm. (Onslows) $137

Galoches, lithograph in colors, circa 1910, printed by A. Trüb & Cie., Aarau, 39½ x 31½in. (Christie's) $686

J. Matet, "Griffon", lithograph in colors, printed by G. Elleaume, Paris, backed on linen, 46 x 62in. (Christie's) $839

Kodak Poster, chromolithograph, with the legend 'Kodak' Rapide et Súre! Pellicule, 63 x 43cm. (Christie's) $1,233

Loading Ship, A 2 published by Empire Marketing Board, 102 x 63cm. (Onslows) $55

Walter Thor (1870-1929), Automobiles Barré, lithograph in colors, circa 1910, printed by Affiches Kossuth, Paris, backed on linen, 46½ x 62in. (Christie's) $2,708

Walter Till, See Ireland First, Irish Tourist Association, lithograph in colours, printed by Hely's Limited, Dublin, backed on linen, 40 x 25in. (Christie's) $1,646

560

Le Mépris/Contempt, 1963, Interfillm, French, 31½ x 22½in., linen backed, art by Georges Allard. (Christie's) $1,417

Thelma And Louise, 1991, M.G.M., limited edition stone lithograph on art paper, signed by the artist Elins '92, signed in pencil by Ridley Scott, Geena Davis, Susan Sarandon, Mimi Polk and Callie Khouri, 48 x 33½in.
(Christie's) $1,810

La Pièce d'Or, circa 1900, French, 63 x 47in., linen backed, Art by Faria. (Christie's) $1,063

Blow-Up, 1966, M.G.M., French, 63 x 47in., linen backed. Art by Georges Kerfyser.
(Christie's) $1,594

A Social Celebrity/En Sparv I Tranedans, 1926, Paramount, Swedish, 40 x 27½in., linen backed. (Christie's) $4,523

Beauty For Sale/Sköhet Till Salu 1933, M.G.M., Swedish, 39 x 27½in., linen backed, art by Eric Rohman. (Christie's) $1,150

Frankenstein, Universal, 1931, Australian long daybill, 40 x 14in. unfolded, on heavy paper.
(Christie's) $22,325

It's A Wonderful Life, 1946, R.K.O., U.S., one sheet, 41 x 27in., linen backed, framed.
(Christie's) $9,741

Lawrence of Arabia, 1962, Columbia, roadshow style U.S. one-sheet, 41 x 27in., linen-backed. (Christie's) $5,778

The Graduate, 1968, United Artists, British quad, 30 x 40in. (Christie's) $867

Attack of the 50ft. Woman, 1958, Allied Artists, U.S. one-sheet, 41 x 27in., linen-backed. (Christie's) $2,347

E.T. The Extra-Terrestrial, 1982, Universal, U.S. one-sheet, 41 x 27in., withdrawn version, unfolded, photograph by Steven Spielberg. (Christie's) $1,353

Get Carter, 1971, M.G.M., British quad, 30 x 40in. (Christie's) $992

The French Connection, 1972, Twentieth Century Fox, style B, U.S. one-sheet, 41 x 27in. lined with japan paper. (Christie's) $867

Le Sexe Faible, 1933, Nero, French, 63 x 47in., linen-backed, framed, art by Paul Colin (1892-1982). (Christie's) $6,861

Blow Up, 1966, M.G.M., British quad, style B, 30 x 40in., linen-backed. (Christie's) $578

Requiem for a Heavyweight, 1962, Columbia, U.S. three-sheet, 81 x 40in., linen-backed. (Christie's) $144

Raging Bull, 1980, United Artists, advance U.S. one-sheet, 41 x 27in., unfolded.
(Christie's) $433

Help!, 1965, United Artists, British quad, 30 x 40in.
(Christie's) $1,083

The Bat/ Il Mostro che Uccide, 1959, Allied Artists, Italian four-foglio, 79 x 55in., linen-backed, framed. (Christie's) $903

Cat People/La Mujer Pantera, 1942, R.K.O., Spanish, 40 x 27in., linen-backed, art by Chapi (1911-1949). (Christie's) $2,708

Das Cabinett des Dr. Caligari / The Cabinet of Dr. Caligari, 1919, U.F.A., style C, German, 27½ x 37½in., lined with japan paper.
(Christie's) $16,260

The Frozen Ghost, 1944, Universal, U.S. one-sheet, 41 x 27in, linen-backed. (Christie's) $433

Pumping Iron, 1976, White Mountain Films, U.S. 45 x 30in., unfolded.
(Christie's) $108

Frankenstein, 1931, Universal, U.S. lobby card, 11 x 14in.
(Christie's) $3,250

Les Vacances de Mr. Hulot, 1953, Discfilm, French, 63 x 47in., linen-backed, art by René Peron (1904-1972). (Christie's) $5,055

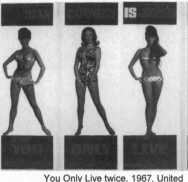

Peeping Tom, 1959, Anglo Amalgamated, British one-sheet, 40 x 27in., linen-backed. (Christie's) $361

You Only Live twice, 1967, United Artists, rare complete set of four U.S. door panels, all 60 x 20in., all linen-backed. (Christie's) $16,250

Saigon, 1948, Paramount, U.S. one-sheet, 41 x 27in., linen-backed. (Christie's) $686

Rembrandt, 1936, London Films, pastel and watercolour on paper, mounted on board, original artwork by Emmerich Weninger for the first German release, 30¾ x 20¼in. (Christie's) $1,173

The Life and Death of Colonel Blimp, 1943, Archers, British quad, 30 x 40in. (Christie's) $922

White Heat/La Furia Umana, 1949, Warner Bros., Italian two-foglio, 55 x 39in., linen-backed, framed, art by Luigi Martinati (1893-1984). (Christie's) $1,534

The Picture of Dorian Gray, 1945, MGM, U.S. one-sheet, 41 x 27in., linen-backed. (Christie's) $451

Dead End, circa 1940s, Samuel Goldwyn/Ealing, British quad, 30 x 40in., paper-backed, art by Clifford Rowe. (Christie's) $1,353

Dark Passage, 1947, Warner Bros., U.S. one-sheet, 41 x 27in., linen-backed. (Christie's) $992

Written on the Wind, 1956,
Universal, U.S. one-sheet, 41 x
27in., linen-backed, art by Bob
Tollen. (Christie's) $542

Goldfinger, 1964, United Artists,
style A, British quad, 30 x 40in., art
by Robert Brown John.
(Christie's) $1,534

Al Capone, 1959, Allied Artists,
French, 63 x 47in., linen-backed,
art by Roger Soubie (b. 1898)
(Christie's) $722

Clouds over Europe/Nubes sobre
Europa, 1939, London Films,
Argentinian, 43 x 29in., linen-
backed (British title is Q Planes), art
by Osvaldo Venturi.
(Christie's) $433

The Ladykillers, 1955, Ealing,
British quad, 30 x 40in. paper-
backed, art by Reginald Mount.
(Christie's) $2,075

Sabrina, 1954, Paramount, style B,
Italian four-foglio, 79 x 55in., linen-
backed, art by Ercole Brini (b.
1907).
(Christie's) $15,347

Panic in the Streets, 1950,
Twentieth Century Fox, U.S. one-
sheet, 41 x 27in., linen-backed.
(Christie's) $217

Caldonia, 1946, Astor Pictures,
U.S. half-sheet, 22 x 28in.
(Christie's) $506

Pickup on South Street, 1953,
Twentieth Century Fox, U.S. one-
sheet, 41 x 27in., linen-backed.
(Christie's) $433

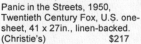

Stanley Pellett, New Zealand Line (Rangitoto), Regular Service via Panama Canal, pub. William Brown, 76 x 51cm. (Onslows) $204

Arthur C. Michael, White Star Line, The Big Ship Route USA & Canada, lithograph in colours, 1931, backed on linen, 36 x 24in. (Christie's) $3,192

Canadian Pacific Tours and Cruises, lithograph in colours, circa 1936, 40 x 25in. (Christie's) $839

Furness Warren Line Serves Canada And United States, lithograph in colours, circa 1950, backed on japan, 39½ x 25in. (Christie's) $433

Cherbourg-New York, "Queen Elizabeth" – "Queen Mary", offset lithograph in colours, circa 1950, backed on linen, 40 x 25in. (Christie's) $863

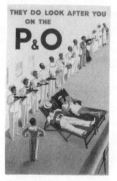

John Gilroy(1898-?), They Do Look After You On The P&O, lithograph in colours, circa 1930, printed by The Benson Group, London, 40 x 25in. (Christie's) $2,889

R Dévignes, Washington-Manhattan, United States Lines, lithograph in colours, printed by L. Delaporte, Paris, 39½ x 25in. (Christie's) $1,091

Cunard Line to all parts of the World, cutaway section of the Mauretania, printed by T Forman, 64 x 102cm. (Onslows) $1,727

W J Aylward, (1875-1958), Majestic, White Star Line, lithograph in colours, circa 1928, printed by O.deRycker, Brussels, 29½ x 19½in. (Christie's) $638

Romana, Lloyd Sabaud, pub. by
Barabino & Grave, 100 x 70cm.,
mounted on board.
(Onslows) $554

W McDowell, Shaw Savill Lines,
England to South Africa, Australia
and New Zealand, 76 x 51cm.
(Onslows) $283

Bernard Gribble, Canadian Pacific
Spans the World, printed by Eyre &
Spottiswoode, mounted on linen,
101 x 63cm. (Onslows)' $1,492

Greig, P&O, Christmas and New
Year Cruises, printed by The
Lamson Agency, 101 x 63cm.
(Onslows) $518

Alo, Red Star Line, Southampton-
New York via Cherbourg
(Belgenland), printed by
Stockmans, mounted on linen, 97 x
62cm. (Onslows) $1,178

Canadian Pacific Tours And
Cruises, lithograph in colours, circa
1936, 40 x 25in.
(Christie's) $839

Harry Hudson Rodmell R.I., (1896-
1984), Sweden, Travel By Swedish
Lloyd, lithograph in colours, printed
by Ronald Massey, London, 40 x
25in. (Christie's) $1,175

Wells, To USA & Canada, White
Star Line, lithograph in colours,
1933, printed by Arthur Upton Ltd.,
London, 40 x 25in.
(Christie's) $1,175

William H Barribal, Canadian
Pacific Cruises, lithograph in
colours, circa 1930, 22 x 13½in.
(Christie's) $839

Roger Broders, Glacier de Bionnassay, PLM, lithograph in colours, circa 1930, 40 x 25in. (Christie's) $2,256

Berta Czegka, St. Anton, Arlberg, offset lithograph in colours, circa 1930, printed by W.U.B., Innsbruck, 27 x 19in. (Christie's) $14,083

After Roger Broders, Villard de Lans, SNCF, lithograph in colours, circa 1937, 39 x 24½in. (Christie's) $992

Anonymous, Davos, offset lithograph in colours, circa 1960, printed by J.C.Müller S.A., Zürich, backed on linen, 40 x 25½in. (Christie's) $722

Herbert Leupin, Sports d'Hiver en Suisse, lithograph in colours, 1939, printed by Säuberlin & Pfeiffer S.A., Vevey, 40 x 25in. (Christie's) $812

Paul Ordner, Combloux Téleski, PLM, lithograph in colours, 1935, printed by Ch. Bahy, Mulhouse, 39½ x 24in. (Christie's) $1,534

Paul Ordner, Combloux, Teleski, PLM, lithograph in colours, circa 1935, printed by M. Dechaux, Paris, 39 x 24½in.(Christie's) $1,534

Viktor Rutz (1913-), Klosters, lithograph in colours, circa 1950, printed by Fretz A.G., Zürich, backed on japan, 40 x 25in. (Christie's) $578

Thio, Morzine, PLM, lithograph in colours, 1935, printed by Monde Publicité, Paris, backed on linen, 39 x 24in. (Christie's) $2,528

Jean Gauyon, St. Lary, lithograph in colours, 1956, printed by Bière, Bordeaux, backed on linen, 38½ x 23½in.
(Christie's) $722

Erich Erler (1870-1946), Winter in Bayern, lithograph in colours, 1905, printed by Klein & Volbert, München, 28½ x 38in.
(Christie's) $2,708

Anonymous, By Swissair to Switzerland, photography and lithography in colours, circa 1950, printed by Brügger A.G., Meiringen, 40 x 25in. (Christie's) $1,083

Ernest Montaut, (1879-1936), L'Alpe Domptée, lithograph in colours, 1913, backed on linen, 34¼ x 17½in.
(Christie's) $8,125

Anonymous, Si Délicieux, Buvez Coca-Cola, lithograph in colours, circa 1950, backed on linen, 20 x 36in. (Christie's) $1,083

Bernard Villemot, (1911-1989), Sports d'Hiver, France, lithograph in colours, 1954, printed by S.A. Courbet, Paris, 39½ x 24½in.
(Christie's) $2,166

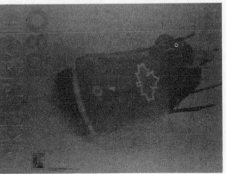

Roger Broders, Le Hohwald, lithograph in colours, circa 1930, printed by Lucien Serre, Paris, backed on linen, 39½ x 34in.
(Christie's) $3,430

Howard E Jennings, Lake Placid 1980, offset lithograph in colours, 1978, 26 x 19½in. and Lake Placid 1980, Bobsleigh.
(Christie's) $306

Paul Ordner (1900-1969), Combloux, lithograph in colours, 1935, printed by Ch.Bahy, Mulhouse, 39½ x 24in.
(Christie's) $2,708

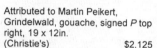

Attributed to Martin Peikert, Grindelwald, gouache, signed *P* top right, 19 x 12in.
(Christie's) $2,125

Georges Slopes (?), Les Sports Alpestres, Le Toboggan dans la Haute-Engadine, offset lithograph in colours, 1906, printed by G de Malherbe, backed on linen, 9½ x 11in. (Christie's) $496

Eric de Coulon, Alpes & Jura, PLM, lithograph in colours, printed by Le Novateur, Paris, 39½ x 24½in.
(Christie's) $2,302

Eric Hermès, Winter In Wallis, lithograph in colours, 1938, printed by Säuberlin & Pfeiffer A.G., Vevey, backed on japan, 40 x 25in.
(Christie's) $708

Otto Baumberger, (1869-1961) Les Plus Belles Vacances en Suisse à Forfait, lithograph in colours, backed on linen, 22 x 25in.
(Christie's) $539

Martin Peikert, Pontresina, offset lithograph in colours, printed by Klausfelder, Vevey, 40 x 25in.
(Christie's) $673

Johannes Handschin (1899-1948), Wintersport Glarnerland, lithograph in colours, printed by A. Trüb & Cie., Aarau, backed on linen, 39½ x 27½in. (Christie's) $6,199

Rossi, winter scene, lithograph in colours, 1914, printed by Champenois, Paris, backed on linen, 22 x 30in.
(Christie's) $744

Louis Tauzin (circa 1845-1914), Les Vosges, lithograph in colours, circa 1913, printed by F. Champenois, Paris, backed on linen, 41 x 30in.
(Christie's) $6,730

Kama, Megève, SNCF, lithograph in colours, printed by H. Truan, Paris, backed on linen, 38½ x 24½in. (Christie's) $3,896

Wintersport – Ausrüstungen, lithograph in colours, circa 1930, backed on linen, 17½ x 23½in. (Christie's) $1,240

Freda Lingström, Norway, For Real Winter Sport, lithograph in colours, circa 1930, 39½ x 25in. (Christie's) $924

Georges Arou, Sports d'Hiver, PLM, offset lithograph in colours, 1931, printed by C. Courtois, Paris, backed on linen, 39 x 24in. (Christie's) $1,948

Carl Kunst (1884-1912), Bilgeri-Sk-Ausrüstung, lithograph in colours, circa 1910, printed by Reichhold & Lang, München, backed on linen, 20 x 30in. (Christie's) $1,240

Roger Soubie, Chamonix Mont-Blanc, Jeux Olympiques 1924, lithograph in colours, 1924, printed by Cornille & Serre, Paris, backed on linen, 39 x 24in. (Christie's) $3,542

Martin Peikert (1901-1975), MOB, lithograph in colours, printed by Säuberlin & Pfeiffer S.A., Vevey, 40 x 25in. (Christie's) $2,479

M Barnard, Winter Cavalcade, lithograph in colours, 1938, printed by Waterlow & Sons Ltd., London, 10 x 12½in. (Christie's) $460

Prof. Kirnig, (Atelier), Autriche, lithograph in colours, printed by Christoph Reisser's Söhne, Vienna, backed on linen, 37½ x 24½in. (Christie's) $1,505

Nathaniel Currier, publisher, 'The Star of the Road,' 1849, lithograph with hand-coloring on paper, sheet size 10 x 14in., matted, unframed. (Skinner) $402

N. Currier (Publisher), The Pursuit, hand colored lithograph, with touches of gum arabic, 1856, after A.F. Tait, on wove paper, 457 x 648mm. (Sotheby's) $5,400

Nathaniel Currier, publisher, Louis Maurer, lithographer, 'Flora Temple and Lancet,' 1856, lithograph with hand-coloring heightened with gum arabic on paper, sheet size 21½ x 28¾in., matted, unframed. (Skinner) $1,610

Nathaniel Currier, publisher, Otto Knirsch, lithographer, 'The Road Winter', 1853, lithograph with hand-coloring heightened with gum arabic on paper, sheet size 21½ x 30in., framed. (Skinner) $52,900

Nathaniel Currier, publisher (American, 1813-1888), Frances Flora (Fanny) Palmer, lithographer (American, circa 1812-1876), 'American Farm Scenes No. Three,' 1853, lithograph with hand-coloring heightened with gum arabic on paper, sheet size 20¾ x 27¾in. (Skinner) $2,415

Currier and Ives (Publishers), The Last Shot, hand colored lithograph, with touches of gum arabic, 1858, after Louis Maurer, on wove paper, framed 442 x 643mm. (Sotheby's) $4,500

Currier and Ives, publishers, John Cameron, lithographer, 'The Champion Trotting Stallion Smuggler, owned by H.S. Russell, Milton, Mass,' 1875, lithograph with hand-coloring heightened with gum arabic on paper, sheet size 21⅝ x 28⅞in. (Skinner) $3,450

Currier and Ives, publishers, after George H. Durrie, 'The Farmyard in Winter,' 1861, lithograph with hand-coloring heightened with gum arabic on paper, sheet size 22 x 28in., framed. (Skinner) $6,900

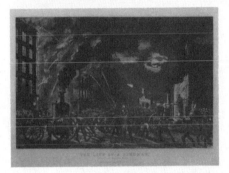

Currier and Ives, publishers, 'The Life of a Fireman. The New Era, Steam and Muscle,' 1861, lithograph with hand-coloring heightened with gum arabic on paper, sheet size 23⅞ x 32½in., matted unframed. (Skinner) $4,887

Nathaniel Currier, publisher, Charles Parsons, lithographer, after Arthur Fitzwilliam Tait, 1819-1905, Endicott and Co., printers, 'American Winter Sports. Trout Fishing 'On Chateaugay Lake' (Franklin Co. NY), 1856, (Conningham, 210). (Skinner) $4,887

Currier & Ives, publishers (American, 1857-1907), Louis Maurer, lithographer, (1832-1932) 'Trotting Cracks on the Snow', lithograph with hand-coloring on paper, sheet size 18¾ x 28¼in. (Skinner) $1,092

Currier and Ives, publishers, Jno. Schutler, delineator, after George Henry Durrie, 'Home to Thanksgiving,' 1867, lithograph with hand-coloring heightened with gum arabic on paper, sheet size 20 x 28in. framed. (Skinner) $11,500

Currier and Ives (Publishers), American Express Train, hand colored lithograph,. with touches of gum arabic, 1864, after Frances F. Palmer, on wove paper, 449 x 705mm. (Sotheby's) $7,800

Currier and Ives (Publishers) Mr. Bonner's Horse, and The Trotting Gelding, two hand-colored lithographs, 1873 and 1884 respectively, after John Cameron and J. McAuliff respectively, on wove paper, images 425 x 672mm. and 480 x 762mm. (Sotheby's) $3,600

The Forbes Lithograph Manufacturing Co., publishers (American, 19th century) E.N. Russell, lithographer (American, 19th century), 'Bark Catalpa of New Bedford', 1876. (Skinner) $517

Joseph Hoover, publisher (American, 19th century), 'American Winter Scene', 1867, lithograph with hand-colouring on paper, image size 18 x 25¾in., framed. (Skinner) $1,035

Currier and Ives, publishers, Charles Parsons, lithographer (American, 1821-1910), after Arthur Fitzwilliam Tait (1819-1905), 'Brook Trout Fishing/An Anxious Moment,' 1862, lithograph with hand-coloring heightened with gum arabic on paper, sheet size 22½in. x 31in., framed. (Skinner) $14,950

Currier & Ives, publishers (American, 1857-1907) and Frances Flora (Fanny) Palmer, lithographer, 'Staten Island and the Narrows from Fort Hamilton, 1861, lithograph with hand-colouring heightened with gum arabic on paper, sheet size 19 x 23⅝in., with walnut frame. (Skinner) $862

Currier & Ives, publishers (American, 1857-1907), 'Frozen Up', 1872, lithograph with hand-colouring heightened with gum arabic on paper, sheet size 8¼ x 10¼in., with tiger maple frame. (Skinner) $948

Nathaniel Currier, publisher, Eliphalet M. Brown Jr., lithographer, 'Clipper Ship Sovereign of the Seas,' 1852, lithograph with hand-coloring heightened with gum arabic on paper, sheet size 19⅞in. x 25⅞in framed. (Skinner) $2,415

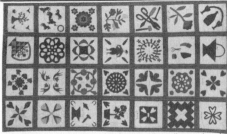

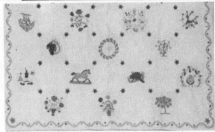

A rare and unusual 'occupational' quilt, variously signed, probably New York, dated 1861-1863, composed of a variety of red, yellow, blue, green and white printed and solid calico patches arranged in a series of forty-two squares, appliquéd and pieced with symbols of a variety of occupations, 80in. x 8ft.3in. (Sotheby's) $7,200

A fine and unusual crewel embroidered cotton quilt, signed *Angeline Nowlen*, American, dated *May 23, 1864*, composed of forty-two blocks of white cotton, twenty-one blocks with crewel embroidery, 68½ x 78in. (Sotheby's) $9,200

Cotton appliquéd quilt, America, mid 19th century, worked in a pattern of red and green rose wreath variant with a meandering vine border on white ground, 79 x 68in. (Skinner) $460

Appliqué quilt, America, mid-19th century, sunburst and rose of Sharon with birds worked in red, green, and terracotta, 83½ x 83½in. (Skinner) $2,415

A rare and unusual pieced calico 'Declaration of Independence' quilt, American, dated 1861-1863, composed of red, white and blue printed and solid calico and cotton patches, at center an English copper printed facsimile of the Declaraton of Independence, 88 x 92in. (Sotheby's) $5,400

A fine pieced and appliquéd 'broderie perse' quilt, Mrs. Freeland, American, circa 1830, composed of pink, yellow, blue and rose printed chintz fabric, at center two sprays of roses and other blossoms set in a diamond point square reserve, 2.51m x 2.90m. (Sotheby's) $5,100

A pieced cotton and appliqued crib quilt, American, circa 1865, composed of red, white and slate blue patches in the form of a stylised American flag, 38 x 28¾in. (Sotheby's) $1,495

An Amish pieced cotton quilted coverlet, Mifflin County, Pennsylvania, 1910-1930, initialled *L..A.Y.*, the rectangular form worked in blue, purple, brown and green cotton in a Nine-Patch pattern, 73¼ x 71in. (Christie's) $5,175

A pieced and appliqued cotton quilt, American, mid 19th century, composed of red, green and orange cotton patches in a grape cluster and flower pattern, the white cotton field heightened with diagonal line and feather quilting, 88 x 88in. (Sotheby's) $1,150

A pieced, appliquéd and embroidered cotton quilted coverlet, American, mid-19th century, the square form worked in red, green, orange and teal cotton centering Rose of Sharon variation blocks separated by red and green striped sashing, 87 x 87in. (Christie's) $4,113

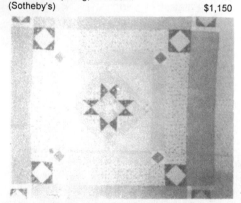

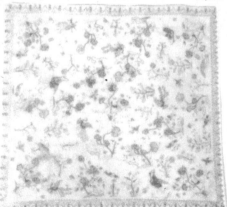

A fresh coloured patchwork quilt pieced from various mainly floral printed cottons, the central frame enclosing an eight pointed star, the field with a red berry print against a white ground, 98 x 88in., possibly Welsh. (Christie's) $818

A 17th century quilt embroidered with all over floral branch and bird designs in natural colours, with a husk pendant and stylised geometric border, signed and dated *MW 1695*, 5ft. 6in. x 6ft. 2in. (Russell Baldwin & Bright) $5,192

Jimi Hendrix's oriental-style jacket, circa 1967. (Sotheby's) $49,000

A rare Apple dartboard, English, 1967 – 1970, black and green with red bullseye *Apple Records* in green script, diameter 45cm. (Bonhams & Brooks) $1,570

A Led Zepplin concert poster, 1971. (Sotheby's) $1,344

Autographs of Elvis Presley and The Jordanaires, 1960s, signed *Elvis Presley* in blue ballpoint, on an album page, together with a colour print of Elvis with his backing singers The Jordanaires signed by all. (Bonhams) $470

John Lennon's and Aunt Mimi's piano stool, purchased circa 1965, the Edwardian stool with ring-turned mahogany legs and upholstered in 1960s bright orange and brown swirly fabric, together with two letters of authenticity, 53.5cm. (Bonhams) $4,704

John Lennon, an autograph page of notes including a fragment of preliminary draft lyrics for Out The Blue, the page of notes written in purple felt pen, circa 1973. (Christie's) $5,534

The Beatles, a rare Japanese album Meet The Beatles, 1964, Odeon Records (OR7041), red translucent vinyl. (Christie's) $590

George Michael's autograph, 1996, signed *George x* in black marker, on the front of the 'Jesus To A Child' C.D. single, 12.5 x 14cm. (Bonhams) $112

A publicity photocard autographed by Elvis Presley, 1960s, signed *To Sandra Thanks from Elvis Presley* in green ballpoint, 23.5 x 18.4cm. (Bonhams) $350

A scarce autographed Bob Marley concert poster, 1980. (Sotheby's) $2,688

Elvis Presley's stage-worn cowboy hat, circa 1974, the extra wide brimmed black cowboy hat with black satin band and 'JB Stetson' and 'lasso' logo. (Bonhams) $2,940

An autographed copy of the album 'Please Please Me', 1963. (Sotheby's) $7,392

The Supremes, an album sleeve The Supremes A' Go Go, 1966, signed and inscribed on the front in blue ballpoint pen *Best Wishes, Supremes, Diana* [Ross], in black ballpoint pen *lots of love, Mary* [Wilson] *and Florence* [Ballard]. (Christie's) $1,383

Rick Parfitt/Status Quo, a Zemaitis Dragon guitar, in red finish, mahogany body with single cutaway, flamed maple top with dragon motif inlaid in mother of pearl, mahogany neck, headstock face. (Christie's) $9,870

Elvis Presley's Radio, circa 1958 - 60, the cream Phillips transistor radio used by Elvis Presley whilst stationed in the Army near Bad Nauheim , 18cm. (Bonhams) $1,050

'The Beatles' (White Album'), Apple, PMC 7067 Mono 1968, number 0000006, record sleeve in good condition, poster, portrait cards of each member and white inner sleeves. (Bonhams) $3,920

Jimi Hendrix Experience, a black and white machine-print promotional photograph possibly taken from a programme, signed and inscribed *Jimi Hendrix EXP, cheers Noel and Mitch*, 11 x 8½in. (Christie's) $2,397

An album Unfinished Music No.1:Two Virgins, 1968, Apple Records, signed *To Christopher Logue, H'll never wear brogue, with love John Lennon*, additionally signed by Yoko Ono. (Christie's) $2,028

Ringo Starr, signed 10 x 8, head and shoulders in profile, from Let it Be, surname signed in darker portion. (Vennett Smith) $70

'The Beatles Book Monthly, No.5, Xmas Edition, Dec 1963'. Signed in ink by each band member and *To Sue love from THE BEATLES.* (Bristol) $471

Elvis Presley, signed colour postcard, overmounted in ivory alongside Heartbreak Hotel single record sleeve, framed and glazed, 16.5 x 12. (Vennett Smith) $420

John Lennon, Yoko Ono and others signed silk necktie, a red and orange print silk tie worn by TV talk show host Dick Cavette on the memorable night when John Lennon, Yoko Ono and Shirley MacLaine appeared on his programme, 21in. (Christie's) $1,998

Jimi Hendrix Sterling silver ring, signed with Celtic/Native American-looking patterns that belonged to Jimi Hendrix, with handwritten letter of provenance from Noel Redding. (Christie's) $5,405

Brian Epstein, a gentleman's 18ct. gold square self-winding, Gubelin, circa 1955, given to Brian Barrett by Epstein's mother, Queenie, in circa 1970, is thought to have originally been given to Brian Epstein as a twenty-first birthday present. (Christie's) $4,427

Paul McCartney, signed and inscribed 5 x 3.5 bookplate photo, three quarter length seated holding guitar. (Vennett Smith) $168

John Lennon, an Aquascutum navy blue cashmere coat, inscribed *John Winston Lennon His Coat* (within spectacles), circa 1964-65, with letter of authenticity. (Bristol) $5,652

Paul and Linda McCartney signatures, a small piece of notebook paper displaying the blue ballpoint ink signatures of the happily married couple, 8 x 5½in. (Christie's) $1,175

Jimi Hendrix's Marshall 4 x 12 speaker, English, 1969, No. 11244, the wooden cabinet covered in black with two recessed handles and four Celestion G12M speakers, 75 x 75 x 35cm.
(Bonhams) $20,580

An Elvis Presley 'Mystery Train' single, Sun #223, 1955, 'I Forgot To Remember To Forget' on side B, framed, 27 x 22cm.
(Bonhams & Brooks) $471

Paul And Linda McCartney, a colour promo. poster, signed and inscribed by McCartney in black felt pen *Cheers from Paul McCartney* and annotated with a self-portrait caricature of himself and Linda, 29½ x 29½in.
(Christie's) $1,845

John Lennon and Paul McCartney, a rare one-sided acetate Bad To Me on Dick James Music Limited Demo Disc printed white label, with typescript track details, 45 r.p.m.
(Christie's) $4,112

The Beatles, a rare Swedish promotional poster The Beatles, 1963, signed in blue ballpoint pen by all four members of the group, 32¼ x 27¼in.
(Christie's) $13,835

Fleetwood Mac, an album sleeve Rumours 1977, signed recently on the front by John McVie, Lindsey Buckingham, Mick Fleetwood, Christine McVie and Stevie Nicks.
(Christie's) $1,014

The Animals, a concert poster Top 10 Stars The Animals "Don't Let Me Be Misunderstood", The Sole Savages featuring Paul Dean, Locarno, Thursday 25th March, 1965, 29½ x 19in.
(Christie's) $369

A 'Kind of Magic' single autographed by Queen, 1980s, signed *Freddie Mercury, Roger Taylor, Brian May* and *John Deacon* in black marker, 18 x 18cm.
(Bonhams) $364

Yomud Ensi, West Turkestan, last quarter 19th century, staggered diamond motifs, on the abrashed aubergine-brown field, 5ft.4in. x 4ft.4in. (Skinner) $1,265

A Tabriz silk Prayer rug, North West Persia, the abrashed ice blue field having a pair of columns and a hanging lamp beneath the ivory stepped mihrab, 5ft.3in. x 4ft. (Phillips) $2,788

A fine Teheran prayer rug, North Persia, the shaded blue field with rows of connecting rosettes around a central ivory panel containing vases issuing floral sprays and delicate flowering vine, 218 x 147cm. (Christie's) $1,562

Northwest Persian rug, second quarter 20th century, overall design with floral groups, circular flowering vines, and paired serrated leaves, on the midnight blue field, 5ft. x 3ft.8in. (Skinner) $1,150

Bessarbian Kelim, Southeast Persia, late 19th/early 20th century, central group of summer blossoms, surrounded by a sky blue lobed circular frame on the black field, 8ft. x 7ft.4in. (Skinner) $920

Kazak rug, Southwest Caucasus, mid 19th century, (rewoven ends and other areas), 4ft.10in. x 3ft.8in. (Skinner) $3,450

Ersari Chuval, West Turkestan, early 20th century, nine chuval guls in midnight and navy blue, red, ivory, gold, and blue-green on the aubergine field, 4ft.2in. x 3ft.2in. (Skinner) $747

Kurd bagface, Northwest Persia, last quarter 19th century, diamond lattice with hooked diamonds in midnight and royal, red, apricot, aubergine, and blue-green, 2ft.6in. x 2ft. (Skinner) $1,035

A Southwest Caucasus Kazak eagle rug, early 20th century, the red field with three eagle medallions linked by polygons, the border with a continuous band of eight-pointed stars, 303 x 158cm. (Finarte) $7,664

South Persian rug, late 19th / early 20th century, flowering tree, six cypress trees and weeping willow motifs, 7ft. 4in. x 5ft. 4in. (Skinner) $5,175

Chinese rug, late 19th century, circular floral medallion and shaped vases in navy and sky blue, rose, ivory and olive, 6ft. 4in. x 4ft. 9in. (Skinner) $1,380

Shirvan rug, East Caucasus, last quarter 19th century, two Lesghi stars in navy blue, red, ivory, gold and green, 3ft. 8in. x 3ft. (Skinner) $2,300

Afshar saddlebags, South Persia, early 20th century, serrated leaves, geometric and floral motifs on the midnight blue field, 3ft. 10in. x 2ft. 8in. (Skinner) $1,380

Fereghan saddle cover, West Persia, last quarter 19th century, vase of flowers and small birds on the midnight blue field, 3ft. 5in. x 3ft. 4in. (Skinner) $1,495

Shirvan rug, East Caucasus, second half 19th century, serrated hexagonal lattice with palmette motifs on the ivory field, 4ft. 7in. x 3ft. 5in. (Skinner) $1,150

Kuba kelim, Northeast Caucasus last quarter 19th century, staggered rows of "race car" medallions on the rust-red field, 10ft. 8in. x 6ft. 8in. (Skinner) $1,150

Soumak bagface, Northwest Persia, early 20th century concentric hooked medallion and 'pinwheel' motifs on the midnight blue field, 1ft. 9in. x 1ft. 9in. (Skinner) $374

Marasali prayer rug, East Caucasus, last quarter 19th century, midnight blue field, ivory boteh variant border, 5ft. 2in. x 3ft. 6in. (Skinner) $4,600

Anatolian kelim, last quarter 19th century, two horizontal bands of stepped hexagons and serrated diamonds, 5ft. x 3ft. 7in. (Skinner) $920

Serapi sampler, Northwest Persia, last quarter 19th century, half serrated hexagonal medallion on the ivory field, 5ft. 10in. x 4ft. 8in. (Skinner) $5,750

Armenian Kazak rug, Southwest Caucasus, early 20th century, large octagonal medallion with pendants and hooks 7ft. 10in. x 5ft 7in. (Skinner) $3,450

Verneh, Southwest Caucasus, second half 19th century, four rows of camels with decorated saddles on the terracotta red field, 8ft. x 5ft. 9in. (Skinner) $19,550

Kurd bagface, Northwest Persia, late 19th century, narrow vertical stripes with double triangle motifs, ivory border of similar design, 2ft. x 1ft. 8in. (Skinner) $1,035

Avar rug, Northeast Caucasus, late 19th century, rust-red field, dark brown geometric border, 4ft. 2in. x 3ft. 2in. (Skinner) $805

Melas prayer rug, Southwest Anatolia, second half 19th century, indented mihrab cartouche and scattered small rosettes , 5ft. x 3ft. 9in. (Skinner) $2,875

Baluch prayer rug, Northeast Persia, last quarter 19th century, elongated rectangular medallion surrounded by flowerheads 3ft. 5in. x 2ft. 10in. (Skinner) $3,738

Yomud Ensi, West Turkestan, last quarter 19th century, staggered stepped diamond motifs in navy and royal blue, red, ivory and apricot, 5ft. 8in. x 4ft. 7in. (Skinner) $633

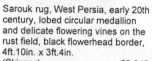

Sarouk rug, West Persia, early 20th century, lobed circular medallion and delicate flowering vines on the rust field, black flowerhead border, 4ft.10in. x 3ft.4in.
(Skinner) $2,645

Shahsavan bagface, Northwest Persia, last quarter 19th century, 2ft.5in. x 2ft.2in.
(Skinner) $3,335

Qashqai kelim, Southwest Persia, late 19th/early 20th century two large stepped diamond medallions flanked by triangles, on the red field, 9ft.8in. x 5ft.3in.
(Skinner) $6,325

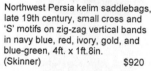

Uzbek flatweave saddlebags, Central Asia, early 20th century, diamond lattice with hooked polygons in navy blue, gold ivory, and dark blue-green on the red field, 5ft.4in. x 2ft.8in.
(Skinner) $488

An American pictorial hooked rug, late 19th/early 20th century, worked in red, yellow, black and blue fabric with the figure of an ocean liner under steam, 30½ x 64in.
(Sotheby's) $5,175

Northwest Persia kelim saddlebags, late 19th century, small cross and 'S' motifs on zig-zag vertical bands in navy blue, red, ivory, gold, and blue-green, 4ft. x 1ft.8in.
(Skinner) $920

Kuba rug, Northwest Caucasus, late 19th century, central 'vase' medallion flanked by two serrated diamond medallions, on the midnight blue field, 6ft. x 4ft.
(Skinner) $1,897

Yarn and cloth hooked rug, New England, first half 19th century, the scrolling vine border centres a reserve of a stylised potted plant, 49 x 48in.
(Skinner) $2,070

A Chinese rug, the deep indigo field regularly interspersed with coral red bats amongst stylised clouds, framed by simple linear borders, 8ft.2in. x 5ft.
(Phillips) $3,444

Konya rug, Central Anatolia, last quarter 19th century, (areas of repiling), 6ft.2in. x 3ft.5in. (Skinner) $2,300

Figural hooked rug, America, late 19th century, depicting a seated black and white dog watching over black and white hens, chicks and ducks, 28 x 43½in. (Skinner) $863

Bordjalou Kazak Prayer rug, Southwest Caucasus, last quarter 19th century, 5ft.7in. x 4ft. (Skinner) $5,175

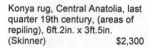

A Marion Dorn handwoven wool rug, rectangular, with geometric design in shades of brown, woven signature Dorn, 168 x 92.5cm. (Bonhams) $435

Whimsical hooked rug, America, 19th century, depicting a flowering tree in a pot flanked by two red leaping stags on a black ground, 41½ x 48in. (Skinner) $5,463

A fine Nain Habibian rug, Central Persia, 20th century, with signature cartouche, silk highlights, 8ft x 5ft.2in. (Sotheby's) $3,808

A Ghom silk rug, possibly Rasti Zadeh, central Persia, 20th century, 216 x 138cm. (Sotheby's) $3,707

Rooster hooked rug, America, late 19th/early 20th century, yarn hooked in red, various shades of brown, with black highlights on an oatmeal-coloured ground with a chequered border, mounted on a frame, 24 x 41in. (Skinner) $1,495

Eagle Karabagh rug, South Caucasus, second half 19th century, (moth damage, rewoven and repiled areas), 7ft.4in. x 4ft.9in. (Skinner) $4,600

A Victorian swing-handled cake basket, of circular form on a shaped circular pedestal foot, with beaded border and engraved and pierced decoration, by Messrs Barnard, 1868, 25.75cm. diameter, 19oz. (Christie's) $442

A modern Scottish basket, R&W Sorley, Glasgow, 1914, the oval basket with slat pierced sides above a reeded border with cut diamond motifs, 12½in., 23.75oz. (Christie's) $1,056

A Chinese silver swing handled basket, maker's mark of Kwan Wo, shaped oval form, pierced and embossed with bamboo, plum blossom and peonies, approximate weight 15oz., 24cm. long. (Bonhams) $470

A George III swing handled sugar basket, London 1790, maker's mark of Robert Hennell, oval bat wing form, reeded swing handle, gilded interior, approximate weight 5oz., 13.9cm. long. (Bonhams) $882

A George III silver basket, London, 1780, maker's mark lacking, the sides pierced and bright-cut engraved with swags, rosettes, urns, latticework and husking, 35.5cm. long, 745gm. (Christie's) $5,790

A George III swing-handled basket, with pierced body and rim of floral garlands intertwined between a reeded band, mark *R.M.* possibly that of Richard Mills, 1772, 33cm. long, 19oz. (Christie's) $2,100

A George III silver cake basket, Samuel Herbert & Co., London, 1760, the body with embossed beading alternating with panels of pierced diaperwork and scrolls, 12½in. long, 21oz. (Christie's) $2,352

An Edward VII fruit basket with pierced and floral embossed sides, scroll embossed handle on four scroll supports, Sheffield 1903. (Brightwells) $631

A George III silver cake-basket, Edward Aldridge and John Stamper, London, 1758, with latticework sides and similar applied border, 12in. long, 10oz. (Christie's) $2,533

An early George IV rectangular cake basket, the moulded waisted foot to a shaped body chased with scrolls and foliage, 10¾in., T & J Settle, Sheffield 1820, 25oz. (Woolley & Wallis) $882

19th century Sheffield plated wirework cake basket with gadrooned rim and swing handle, 11 x 8in. (G.A. Key) $149

A late 19th/early 20th century American metalware swing-handled cake basket, of shaped oval form on cast scroll bracket feet, by Tiffany & Co. (Christie's) $829

A Regency silver-gilt basket, J.W. Story & William Elliott, 1811, the rectangular basket with an openwork grape, vine and leaf motif border with an egg and dart rim, length 34.5cm., 54oz. (Christie's) $6,909

A George III cake basket, William Plummer, 1779, the oval basket with a beaded rim above pierced lattice and foliate scroll motifs, further engraved with swags and a crest, 36.2cm. 36oz. (Christie's) $5,264

A George III silver basket, William Plummer, London, 1772, armorial engraved within crossed branches below chased spiral flutes and side pierced with flowerheads, 14in. long, 989gm. (Sotheby's) $6,794

A silver swing handled sugar basket, London 1916, maker's mark of *MR*, pierced entwined swing handle, the body with pierced scroll and stylised decoration, weight 4oz., diameter 12cm. (Bonhams) $370

A George II silver cake-basket, Benjamin Cartwright, London, 1751, the sides pierced with latticework, with reed-and-tie border, 12¼in. long, 30oz.(Christie's) $4,343

A George III oval sugar basket, Peter Carter, 1790, of plain boat-shaped form with gilt interior, on pedestal foot, the rim and handle with thread mounts, 11oz., 13cm. high excluding swing handle. (Christie's) $822

A fine and rare American silver cake basket, Ezekiel Dodge, New York, circa 1792, flaring octagonal, on an oval foot pierced with alternating pales and foliate scrolls, 13¾in. long, 31oz. 10dwt. (Christie's) $46,000

An American silver cake basket, maker's mark of Ball, Tompkins & Black, New York, circa 1850, oval, on spreading foot, chased with a band of flowers and foliage, 29cm. wide, 26oz. (Christie's) $531

A polylobate silver basket, decorated with garlands of laurel, staves and cartouches, silvered metal liner, French, late 19th/early 20th century, 34cm. high, 600gm. (Finarte) $2,122

A George III silver-gilt bon-bon dish, embossed with beading, floral sprays and pierced with geometric motifs, by Samuel Herbert & Co, 1767, 16cm. long, 6.5oz. (Christie's) $1,264

A swing handled sugar vase, with a cranberry glass liner, on an embossed pedestal foot with openwork sides, Charles Thomas & George Fox, 1857; and a cast parcelgilt sifter spoon 1842, 14oz. weighable silver. (Christie's) $1,299

A George III swing-handled boat shaped sugar basket, with beaded edging, Hester Bateman, London 1787, 17.1cm. 7.2oz. (Bearne's) $1,237

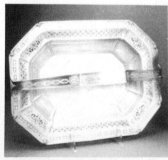

Reed & Barton Sterling cake basket, early 20th century, panelled rectangular form with reticulated rim and handle detail, 5⅜in. high, approximately 20 troy oz. (Skinner) $747

Dr Christopher Dresser: a plain sugar basket, with inturned edge and tubular swing handle, by Hukin & Heath, circa 1880, 16.5cm. (Tennants) $512

An early George III oval bread basket, the reeded interlaced open basketwork flared sides, Thomas Heming, 13¼in., London 1760, 30oz. (Woolley & Wallis) $4,480

A late 17th century Scandinavian beaker of plain tapering form decorated with a matted or sharkskin finish and three oval cartouches, probably Danish, last quarter 17th century, 6cm. high, 2.25oz. (Christie's) $1,682

A tapering beaker, on a moulded circular foot engraved with two trophies of arms and two wreath cartouches, by Samuel Smily 1865, 12cm. high. 7.25oz. (Christie's) $903

An 18th century French beaker with tapered sides and flared reeded rim, 4in. high, Paris 1725, 172gm. (Andrew Hartley) $605

An 18th century French beaker engraved with birds amongst foliage within scrolling cartouches, 4½in. high, Paris 1798, 136gms. (Andrew Hartley) $605

A pair of George III Scottish beakers, flared, with two bands of foliate engraving and initials *A.D* by William Davie, Edinburgh 1781, 10.5oz. (Woolley & Wallis) $1,817

A Swedish parcel-gilt silver beaker Erik Magnus Lundberg, Örebro, circa 1780, the trumpet shaped body wrigglework engraved with foliage, 8in. high, 14oz 3dwt. (Sotheby's) $1,921

An early 18th century Baltic parcel-gilt beaker, later engraved on one side with a knight in armour, by Christofer (II) Mansfeld, Reval, circa 1730, 18.5cm. high, 13.5oz. (Christie's) $1,733

An early 18th century French beaker, engraved with contemporary armorial beneath a coronet and with initials, a moulded rim, 2.5in., Paris circa 1720. (Woolley & Wallis) $1,570

An early 19th century Norwegian parcel-gilt beaker with wrigglework engraving, two applied moulded bands, unascribed, Bergen, 1812/21, 14cm. high, 4.5oz. (Christie's) $1,256

A late Victorian silver rose bowl, London 1891, John Newton Mappin, part fluted and beaded decoration, gilt interior, approximate total weight 30oz., diameter of bowl 25.5cm. (Bonhams) $739

A silver bowl, designed by Josef Hoffmann, manufactured by the Wiener Werkstätte, circa 1925, ribbed and shaped body, gently flared trumpet base, 11¼in. wide. (Christie's) $17,038

A Chinese silver rosebowl, maker's mark of Woshing, embossed with butterflies and peonies, wavy edge border, approximate weight 20oz., diameter 20.8cm. (Bonhams) $808

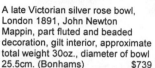

Charles Stuart Harris, an Edwardian rose bowl, the body with an applied girdle, the scalloped rim with moulded scrolls and cherub masks, 7.5in. diameter, London 1903, 19.25oz. (Woolley & Wallis) $387

A Spanish Colonial Holy Water Stoup, stamped *AMAT*, possibly South America, presentation date *1779*, the circular section vessel with robust lobes separated by leaf capped cartouches, 22.4cm., 16oz. (Christie's) $1,974

An early Victorian Irish silver bowl, Dublin 1840, Robert W Smith, of plain circular form, moulded borders, crested, on a spread circular foot, approximate weight 15oz., diameter of bowl 17.5cm. (Bonhams & Brooks) $1,540

An Edwardian bowl, R.H. Halford & Sons, 1907, the oval bowl with a leaf decorated rim, with two applied scroll handles, the body decorated with further leaf motifs, length 46cm., 57oz. (Christie's) $2,467

A Victorian punch bowl by Elkington, the shaped rim embossed with still leaf banding, lion mask handles, on spreading foot, 12in. wide, Sheffield 1895, 48oz 16dwt. (Andrew Hartley) $1,508

A George I silver bowl and cover, Gabriel Sleath, London, circa 1715, stepped domed cover with baluster finial, engraved with a coat-of-arms within a baroque cartouche, 3½in., 9oz. (Christie's) $7,079

Koloman Moser, a Wiener Werkstätte silver and niello box, rectangular with hinged cover, all over checker design, stamped marks, 12cm. (lacks feet).
(Bonhams & Brooks) $5,754

A George III Scottish snuff box, maker's mark *WR*, circa 1790, the elongated octagonal box with an engraved laurel branch cartouche, engraved with initials, with a gilded interior, 8.6cm., 3oz.
(Christie's) $766

A late Victorian cast novelty vesta box, in the form of a two handled wickerwork basket, the top with moulded hamper cloth, 2.5in., E H Stockwell, London, 1892, 3.5oz.
(Woolley & Wallis) $2,499

A Continental silver casket, 19th century, of rectangular form, the domed cover and sides pierced with foliate ornament, on claw and ball feet, 3¾in. wide.
(Christie's) $2,852

An early 19th century Polish spice box, circa 1835, the ovoid body held within a filligree calyx above three scroll supports centred by a wirework basket, 16.5cm. high, 3.75oz.(Bonhams) $1,008

An Edwardian silver mounted and inlaid tortoiseshell jewellery box, by William Comyns, 1908, cover inlaid with floral medallion, swags and festoons terminating in musical trophies, 18 x 19.5 x 7.5cm.
(Bonhams) $2,380

A Victorian trinket box, by George Heath, 1887, the cover finely enamelled with a day at the races, the crowd said to include the Prince of Wales, 9.6 x 6.8 x 2.9cm.
(Bonhams) $2,660

A Victorian coromandel dressing table case with silver mounted fittings, with London hallmark for 1878, of rectangular form with domed cover inset with engraved initials *G.M.W.*, with a leather travelling case, 33.6cm. wide.
(Christie's) $1,594

A 19th century French gilt casket, with allover foliage engraving, applied oval mounts inset with portrait miniatures, plush lined interior, 5¼in. wide.
(Woolley & Wallis) $626

A pair of electroplated candlesticks, unmarked, in the gothic manner, knopped stems, textured columns, on shaped fluted circular bases, 30.5cm. high.
(Bonhams) $314

Italian silver convertible four-socle candelabrum, 18in. high. 46troy oz. (Eldred's) $800

A pair of French table candlesticks with armorial engraved shaped circular bases, 27.5cm high, Joseph Charvet, Paris, 1760, 42.5oz.
(Bearne's) $6,240

A pair of large Charles II style silver candlesticks L A Crichton for Crichton Brothers, London, 1909, the quatrefoil bases moulded as shells, 11in. high, 83oz. 12dwt.
(Sotheby's) $4,973

A pair of Queen Anne cast candlesticks by Jacob Margas, 1706, (traces of gilding), stepped octagonal bases, faceted baluster columns and capitals with octagonal knops, 17.5cm. high, 33.25oz.
(Bonhams) $21,700

A pair of unmarked Continental rococo candlesticks, the spirally fluted baluster columns and capitals on domed circular bases embossed with overlapping waves and scrolls, 20cm. high, 25.25oz.
(Bonhams) $1,540

A pair of George IV silver-gilt candlesticks, John and Thomas Settle, Sheffield, 1824, chased overall with scrolls, shells, flowers and foliage, 10½in. high, 27oz.
(Christie's) $2,497

A rare pair of Queen Anne cast dressing table candlesticks, by David Willaume (I), 1713, faceted capitals and knops and plain circular bases, 9cm. 10.5oz.
(Bonhams) $5,040

A pair of German silver candlesticks, one stem formed as a naked putto astride a dolphin, the other as a putto blowing a conch shell astride a dolphin, 14½in. high, 44oz. (Christie's) $2,713

Fine Edwardian heavy silver sugar caster of baluster octagonal form, chased with panels of flowers and foliage, pierced top, urn finial, 6½in. tall, London 1901 by the Goldsmiths and Silversmiths Co. (G A Key) $624

English Sterling silver pig-form shaker, 20th century, with hallmarks, 4½in. long, 1.8 troy oz. (Eldred's) $330

A Queen Anne silver caster, Christopher Canner, London, 1703, Britannia standard, of small lighthouse form, 4in. high, 2oz 8dwt. (Sotheby's) $4,225

A large late Victorian sugar caster, the vase shape body with part swirl ribbing and a domed gadroon banded foot, 9¾in., 4.5oz. (Woolley & Wallis) $735

A pair of late 19th century Dutch sugar casters, the bodies chased with pastoral and harbour scenes, 21.5cm. high, 18oz. (Christie's) $848

Muffineer, London, 1901, Comyns and Sons, etched at foot *Made in England for Tiffany & Co.*, chased and embossed with stylised wheat motif, 9in., 15 troy oz. approximately. (Skinner) $805

CHAMBERSTICKS

A late Victorian silver chambersticks, Sheffield 1897, Martin, Hall & Co. Ltd., of shaped circular form, gadrooned borders, tapering capital, total weight 8oz., diameter of base 15cm. (Bonhams) $470

A pair of George III chambersticks, Sheffield 1787, maker's mark of Luke, Porctor and Co., oval navette bases, scroll handles, plain thumbpieces, oval urn shaped capital, detachable drip pans, with two conical snuffers, approximate weight 14oz., 15.9cm. long. (Bonhams) $1,386

A Victorian silver leaf shaped chamberstick and snuffer, by Yapp and Woodward, Birmingham 1848, 2oz. (Bonhams) $385

A German cigarette case, circa 1900, enamelled with a nude reclining on a green chaise longue, propped up by pink pillows, 10.2cm. wide. (Bonhams) $1,610

A late 19th century Russian cloisonné enamel and silver cigarette case, by Gustav Klingert, Moscow, circa 1890, rectangular with rounded corners, decorated with a rosette of turquoise coloured beads encircled by a bezel of the same beads, 11cm. long. (Bonhams) $980

An enamelled silver cigarette case, Bernhard Schneider, Vienna, circa 1920, the front painted en plein with groups of ladies enjoying the pleasures of al fresco marbled swimming pool, width 4½in. (Sotheby's) $1,848

CLARET JUGS

An electro-plated mounted clear-glass claret jug, the mounted decorated in relief with Bacchanalian masks, fruiting vines and a heraldic lion and shield finial, by Elkington & Co, 1879, 27.5cm. high. (Christie's) $722

A pair of modern mounted cut-glass claret jugs with angular handles and oviform bodies, by Hukin & Hukin, Birmingham 1913, 19.5cm. high. (Christie's) $1,840

Continental .800 silver mounted cut glass claret jug, Germany, early 20th century, urn form, the domed silver lid with cast bud finial and chased acanthus decoration, 15⁷/₈in. (Skinner) $805

COASTERS

A pair of William IV wine coasters with everting, fruiting vine borders and turned wooden bases, H. Wilkinson & Co, Sheffield, 1835, 19cm. diameter. (Christie's) $3,128

A pair of Victorian coasters of openwork lattice form with vine edging, 23cm. diameter, Hy. Wilkinson & Co., Sheffield 1847, 30.2oz. (Bearne's) $2,997

A pair of late period Old Sheffield plated wine coasters, with turned wooden bases, plain concave sides and broad overhanging rims of fruiting vines, circa 1840, 23cm. diamater. (Christie's) $368

Victorian silver plated coffee pot, melon shaped with rope twist banded decoration, scrolled handle and spout, 9in. tall, circa 1870. (G.A. Key)　　　　　　$45

A Victorian coffee pot decorated in the Indian style with foliate scrolling decoration, 27cm. high, Martin Hall & Co., London, 1880, 26oz. (Bearne's)　　　　　　$652

A George III coffee pot with bright-cut friezes and borders, probably by John Robins, 1799, 30.5cm. high, 27.75oz. (Christie's)　　　$1,728

John Swift, a George II coffee pot, one side of the tapering cylindrical body engraved with a lion rampant reguardant within rococo cartouche, 8½in. high, London 1733, 20oz. all in
(Woolley & Wallis)　　　$3,160

An early 19th century Baltic coffee pot, of shaped circular outline with a straight-sided neck and scroll feet, by William Friedrich Windelbent, Mitau circa 1840, 24cm. high, 38.5oz. (Christie's)　　　$365

George III silver coffee pot, spreading circular foot, ebonised scrolled handle and having a wrythen finial to the hinged lid, 10in. tall, London 1764, 28oz all in. (G A Key)　　　　　$1,872

George III coffeepot, London, 1805, Peter, Ann and William Bateman, on four ball feet, oval trumpet foot, tapered oblong body, 11¾in. high, 30 troy oz. approximately. (Skinner)　　　　　　$1,035

George III coffeepot, London, 1770, W & J Priest, with later foliate repoussé, baluster shaped, on spreading foot, 9¾in., 26 troy oz. approximately. (Skinner)　　　　　　$1,150

American silver coffee pot by Joseph Richardson Jr., classical flattened urn form with fluted urn finial to lid, curved fluted spout, 14½in., 36oz. (Freeman)　　　　　$8,960

Walter & John Barnard, a fine late Victorian coffee-pot, in Regency style, the vase shape body partly ribbed to a skirt foot, 9½in., London, 1895, 27oz. all in.
(Woolley & Wallis) $412

A Victorian coffee pot, Francis David Dexter, 1840, the lobed melon-form coffee pot with a blossom and leaf motif on each lobe, with a blossom capped ivory insulated handle, 21.7cm., 29.5oz.
(Christie's) $1,088

A George III coffee pot of baluster form with urn finial on domed lid, scrolled hardwood handle, swan shaped spout with beaded edging, 12in. high, London 1786, maker's mark *H.B.*, 26oz 1dwt.
(Andrew Hartley) $4,553

A Belgian silver coffee-pot, Mons, 1799, maker's mark *E*, with short covered spout and hinged domed cover chased with acanthus leaves, 13¾in. high, gross 30oz.
(Christie's) $6,520

A pair of silver café au lait pots, Birmingham 1929, maker's mark of Elkington and Co., tapering circular form, scroll handles, domed hinged covers with knop finials, approximate weight 30oz.
(Bonhams & Brooks) $377

A George III coffee biggin on stand, Matthew Boulton Plate Co., Birmingham, 1810, of part-fluted form raised on a spreading foot, the hinged lid with a baluster finial, with a carved wood handle, 28cm. high, 24oz., without stand.
(Christie's) $1,680

A George III Irish silver coffee-jug, William Homer, Dublin, circa 1770, pear-shaped and on a circular gadrooned foot, with wood scroll handle, short spout, and hinged domed cover, 27cm. high, 25oz.
(Christie's) $1,848

A George III coffee pot, Robert Gaze, 1796, of high shouldered circular section, raised on a pedestal foot, the domed hinged cover with a globular finial, height 29cm., 34.5oz.
(Christie's) $822

A French silver coffee-pot, Louis Gantereau, Paris, circa 1860, on three paw and scroll feet terminating in applied acanthus leaves, cover with parrot finial, 13in. high, gross 28oz.
(Christie's) $1,583

A French silver coffee-pot, Emile Puiforcat, Paris, modern, pear-shaped and on circular spreading foot, chased with broad flutes, covered spout, 23cm. high., gross 30oz. (Christie's) $1,863

19th century Sheffield plated coffee pot, melon shaped and supported on scrolled four footed base,10in. tall, circa 1840.
(G.A. Key) $73

A Belgian silver coffee pot, Mons, 1780, maker's mark *P*, overall fluted, covered spout, hinged high-domed cover and bud finial, 13in. high, gross 34oz.
(Christie's) $7,079

A Victorian Irish coffee-pot, of hexagonal form, engraved with flowers and foliate cartouches, handle formed as a branch and a leafy spout, by James Le Bas, Dublin, 1868, 25cm. high, 35oz. (Bonhams) $1,382

A pair of silver café au lait pots, Sheffield 1919 and1921, James Dixon & Sons, of plain tapering form, domed hinged lid with urn shaped finial, approximate weight 35oz., 21cm. high.
(Bonhams) $431

A George II silver coffee-pot, Edward Pocock, London, 1734, plain tapering cylindrical and on moulded foot, with faceted spout and wood scroll handle, 8½in. high, gross 22oz.
(Christie's) $4,135

A Belgian silver coffee-pot, maker's mark *AD*, Mons, 1781, the spirally-fluted pear-shaped body on three scroll feet terminating in shells, 14¾in. high, gross 36oz.
(Christie's) $10,246

Danish coffee pot, late 19th century, Michelsen, body with curved vertical banding offset with chasing and embossing of flowers and rocaille, 7in. high.
(Skinner) $546

A George III coffee pot, Abraham Portal, 1767, of inverted pear form with a carved wood handle, the hinged lid with a fluted spire finial, 27cm., 30oz.
(Christie's) $1,873

An early 19th century Old Sheffield plated coffee percolator, of stepped cylindrical form with gadrooned borders, 10½in. high. (Andrew Hartley) $445

A modern coffee pot with a waisted neck and an oviform ivory handle and finial, by H.G. Murphy, 1930, 21.5cm. high. (Christie's) $384

A Guernsey silver coffee pot, Guernsey, circa 1770, the body cast and chased with flowers and shells, 10½in. high, gross 36oz. (Christie's) $5,377

A George I silver coffee pot, Richard Green, London, 1715, tapering octagonal and on moulded rim foot, with faceted curved spout, 9¾in. high, gross 27oz. (Christie's) $15,748

A Victorian coffee pot, of plain baluster form with a flat base and a domed cover, crested, by Robert Garrard, 1861, 23oz. (Christie's) $583

Dutch coffee-pot and stand, the pot 1876, the stand .833 fine, 1863, the pot lobed pear-shape, on domed foot with shaped edge, approximately 23 troy oz. total. (Skinner) $633

Carrington & Co, a coffee pot, in early George III style, in electro plate German silver, the baluster body with a cast scale and leaf applique swan neck spout. (Woolley & Wallis) $205

A George III plain coffee pot with a case shaped body, navette shaped pedestal foot, by Alexander Field, 1803, 26.5cm. high, 16oz. (Christie's) $1,247

A George III silver coffee biggin, stand and lamp, John and Edward Edwards, London, 1815, partly-fluted pear-shaped and on spreading foot, 10¼in. high, gross 40oz. (Christie's) $3,649

A Victorian oval comport with panelled frieze embossed and chased with masks and vacant cartouches, Glasgow 1900, 35oz., 12.5in. (Russell Baldwin & Bright) $1,505

A pair of silver compôtes, Gorham Mfg. Co., Providence, 1917, martelé, each circular, on shaped domed foot, repoussé and chased with flowers and foliage, 10in. diameter, 53oz. (Christie's) $9,200

An Edwardian silver comport, with a gadrooned rim, fretwork border and set on a knopped stem, Sheffield 1911, John Dixon and Sons, 20cm. diameter, approximately 15oz. (Bonhams) $279

CREAM JUGS

A George II cream pail, with wirework sides and applied foliage, ropework swing handle and blue glass liner, London 1759, 11.5cm. high, including handle, 2oz. (Christie's) $1,417

A George III cream jug and sugar bowl of part fluted circular form with gadrooned borders and angular handles, Daniel Pontifex, 1806, 14cm. diameter, 20oz. (Christie's) $960

A George II 'Sparrow Beak' cream jug, London 1734, maker's mark of Thomas Rush, baluster form, scroll handle, plain spout, the whole on a raised circular foot, approximate weight 3oz., 9cm. high. (Bonhams) $1,470

CRUETS

English silver plated and cut crystal six-bottle cruet set, 8½in. high, 9in. wide, 6in. deep. (Eldred's) $357

A George III silver cruet, Robert and David Hennell, London, 1799. also with mustard-spoon, George Smith, London, 1799 and sugar spoon, London, 1798, 10in. high. (Christie's) $4,705

A George III silver egg-cruet, William Burwash and Richard Sibley, London. 1809, the square stand with cut corners and on four detachable winged sphinx caryatid and lion's paw feet, 11½in. high, 95oz. (Christie's) $4,844

A Victorian claret ewer, in the manner of Dr Christopher Dresser, the glass of angled bellied shape with star cut base, by E. Hutton, 1884, 24cm. to thumbpiece. (Tennants) $1,216

An Italian silver ewer, Naples, late 17th century, with leaf-capped and beaded winged demi-figure handle with grotesque mask terminal, 9in. high, 24oz. (Christie's) $18,630

Portuguese .800 silver ewer, maker's mark *S & P*, late 19th/20th century, bulbous, with molded shaped rim, the body with chased stippled decoration with embossed foliate, scroll, and shell band, approximately 33 troy oz., 11¾in. high. (Skinner) $805

FLATWARE

A William IV fish slice in fiddle pattern with pierced and threaded blade, the haft with engraved crest, 12¼in. wide, London 1831, 4oz 18dwt. (Andrew Hartley) $145

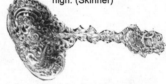

A rare silver-gilt and plique-à-jour bonbon spoon, Tiffany & Co., New York, 1891–1902, the shaped oval bowl elaborately pierced with scrolling foliage and roses, 12¾in. long, gross weight 11oz. (Christie's) $3,450

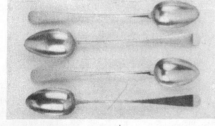

Four George III Scottish Provincial basting spoons, Old English pattern, John Keith, Banff, circa 1795-, 31cm. long, 11.5oz. (Christie's) $4,606

An Edwardian crumb tray, the ivory haft with anthemion banded ferrule, the serpentine pan embossed with flowers and foliage centred by a shell, 14in. wide, Sheffield 1908, 8oz 7dwt. (Andrew Hartley) $189

INKSTANDS

A Victorian crested desk stand by Charles Stuart Harris, with two oval ink bottles having turned finials on hinged lids and clear glass liners, 8¾in. wide, London 1888, 18oz., 13dwt. (Andrew Hartley) $700

Jean Puiforcat, ink pot and cover, circa 1930, the almost cube-shaped base with canted corners in clear and frosted glass etched with geometric motifs, 4⅛in. (Christie's) $5,185

A Spanish silver inkstand, Francisco de Paula Martos, Cordoba, 1831, fitted with three detachable vase-shaped ink and sand holders with bead and scroll borders, one fitted with glass liner, 7½in. long, gross 24oz. (Christie's) $1,677

A George III silver tea urn, John Carter, 1772, the body applied with two ram's mask drop-ring handles hung between rosettes, 20in. high, 115oz gross.
(Christie's) $4,904

A pair of recent cast table ornaments, realistically modelled as a pair of ducks, one standing with head up, the other preening, approximately 15cm. long, 38.5oz.
(Christie's) $1, 119

19th century Indian Army officer's whistle and chains, comprising a heavy circular rope edged boss with portions protruding beyond the edge giving the effect of a circular saw blade. (Bosleys) $209

A martelé silver vase, Gorham Mfg. Co., Providence, circa 1905, the spot-hammered domed lobed base with curled rim and the lobed waisted body repoussé and chased with snowdrops and leaves, 18½in. high; 72oz. 10dwt.
(Christie's) $12,650

A pair of Old Sheffield plated chambersticks, with gadrooned borders, heart-shaped scroll thumbpieces and tall glass shades, circa 1820, 24.5cm. high.
(Christie's) $722

An American silver-gilt coral whistle and bells, Joseph Richardson, Philadelphia, 1740-50, the whistle top engraved with pairs of lines and with a pendant ring, 40gr. gross, 12.4cm. long.
(Sotheby's) $2,300

A 19th century Dutch silver colored metal scallop shape box, the base with an embossed scene of shepherd and shepherdess, 2.25in. (Woolley & Wallis) $88

Madeira, London, 1793, pierced name, a standing ostrich above, 6.5cm. (Christie's) $4,338

A Warwick vase, Sheffield 1916, maker's mark of Walker and Hall, part fluted decoration, reeded handles, beaded borders, approximate weight 67oz., 22.8cm. high. (Bonhams) $2,426

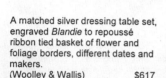

A matched silver dressing table set, engraved *Blandie* to repoussé ribbon tied basket of flower and foliage borders, different dates and makers.
(Woolley & Wallis) $617

A Chinese silver card case, marked 90 and maker's mark of Wang Hing, rectangular form, one side decorated with figural scenes, the other with foliate decoration and Chinese characters, approximate weight 89g. 9.8cm. long.
(Bonhams) $412

Victorian silver plated spoon warmer in the form of a nautilus shell on a rocky base, 6in. wide.
(G.A. Key) $145

A pair of novelty silver cruets, Chester 1906, maker's mark of Cornelius Desormeaux Saunders & James Francis Hollings Shepherd the pepper pot modelled as a chauffeur, the salt modelled as a woman wearing Welsh national dress, 9cm.
(Bonhams) $2,646

A German silver nef, in the Renaissance style, circa 1880, with three masts, each with a flag finial, the central flag above a crow's nest, each with an open sail decorated with Fortune personified, 14cm. high. (Christie's) $2,940

An Edwardian Art Nouveau silver and enamel jam pot and spoon, Birmingham 1905, maker's mark of Liberty and Co., the swing handle set with a turquoise cabochon, pull-off cover with blue / green enamel decoration, height of pot 8.7cm.
(Bonhams) $1,103

A Charles II tumbler, engraved withan armorial (circa 1700) within a baroque foliage cartouche, 2½in. high. Maker probably Francis Singleton, London, 1679, 5.5oz.
(Woolley & Wallis) $9,408

A cigarette lighter in the form of a chromium plated model of an M.G. 1930 Double Twelve.
(Brightwells) $632

A Victorian novelty condiment set by Asprey modelled as a street lamp and three bollards, on triangular base engraved with initials and slate plinth, 7¾in. high, in original case, London 1877.
(Andrew Hartley) $2,748

A Continental silver cistern, unmarked, first half of the 18th century, possibly southern Italian or Maltese, chased all over with bands of vertical leaves, scrolling foliage and tied laurel ornament, 18½in. long, 115oz.
(Christie's) $10,247

An early Victorian silver castle top card case, Birmingham, 1840, maker's mark of Nathaniel Mills, shaped rectangular form, both sides applied with a raised image of Windsor Castle, 69g., 9.5cm. high.
(Bonhams & Brooks) $551

An Edwardian two handled sugar basin, embossed inverted pear shape body, with a gadroon rim, Henry Frazer, Sheffield, 1904, 8.5oz.
(Woolley & Wallis) $147

A French silver-mounted cut-glass travelling dressing-table service, Louis Aucoc Ainé, Paris, circa 1880, all in a fitted wooden case with brass mounts, 13½in. long., 45oz. (Christie's) $1,490

An American silver jardinière, Gorham Mfg. Co., Providence, RI, martelé, .950 standard, 1904, with everted rim and four-footed base, deeply chases with sprays of lilies of-the-valley, 53oz., height 8in.
(Sotheby's) $16,800

A George III silver argyle, London, 1802, maker's mark W? in script, vase-shaped and on circular base, with reeded borders, scroll spout and wood handle, 8¼in. high, gross 17oz. (Christie's) $2,895

Attractive silver nutmeg grater, egg shaped, embossed and chased with bands of foliate decoration and strapwork, steel grater within, 1½in. long, marked with markers mark only in side lid.
(G.A. Key) $691

An Edwardian silver shooter's outdoor lighter, with a number of shots recorder to the side and a vesta compartment, with a gilded interior, H & A, Birmingham 1908.
(Woolley & Wallis) $882

A George III wax jack, Sheffield 1815, maker's mark of S and C. Young, Walker, Kitchen and Co., gadroon border, leaf capped scroll handle, central column with a flame finial, approximate weight 6oz., 14cm. high.
(Bonhams) $1,911

A George II silver mug, Gurney & Cook, London, 1748, baluster body engraved with armorials, 4¾in. high, 13oz 16dwt. (Sotheby's) $1,824

A late Victorian shaving mug, with a scroll handle, the domed cover with a hinged brush holder attached to the interior, crested by Grey & Co., 1899, 10cm. high, 7oz. (Christie's) $744

A China trade silver mug, maker's mark *HC,* late nineteenth century, chased with figures in a mountainous jungle landscape, 4in., 7oz. (Christie's) $342

An 18th century baluster mug, probably American, circa 1770, of plain design with scroll handle and spreading circular foot, 9.9cm. high, 6.25oz. (Bonhams) $700

A George III unusual silver 'hops and barley' ale mug, Benjamin & James Smith, London, 1810, the finely proportioned pear shaped body engraved with a crest below a band of hops and above a band of barley, 6¼in. high, 436gm. (Sotheby's) $8,046

A Victorian chinoiserie mug with a simulated twig handle decorated in low relief with stylised Chinese fighting figures, by Joseph Angell, 1861, 9.5cm. high, 8oz. (Christie's) $883

A George II mug, Thomas Farren, 1735, of slightly tapering circular section with later chased portrait medallion of King William, 14.6cm. 18oz. (Christie's) $1,727

A William IV christening mug, Messrs Barnard, 1836, the circular section mug of lobed form, each lobe decorated with a leaf motif, 11cm., 6oz. (Christie's) $461

A Queen Anne silver mug, John Elston, Exeter, 1704, Britannia Standard, the lower part of the body chased with flutes, 4¼in. high, 7oz. (Christie's) $4,225

A silver pierced mustard pot, London, 1902, 2in. high. (Sworders) $145

Fine Victorian silver mustard pot, drum shaped with foliate pierced sides, plus blue glass liner and spoon, 2½in. diameter, 2in. tall, London 1847. (G A Key) $391

A George III silver mustard pot and matching mustard spoon, London 1780, Hester Bateman, the spoon, London 1788, the body pierced with urns and stylized bands, blue glass liner, weighable 4oz., height 7.5cm. (Bonhams) $1,078

PEPPERS

A pair of Victorian novelty pepperettes, modelled as Middle Eastern rosewater sprinklers with chased lower bodies and gilt interiors, by George Fox, 1875, 9.5cm. high. (Christie's) $506

A 19th century French novelty silver pepper pot, maker's mark of *EE*, modelled as a seated squirrel with a nut, hinged base, the nut pierced, approximate weight 3oz., 7.5cm. high. (Bonhams & Brooks) $420

A pair of George IV silver bun peppers, London 1823, maker's mark WB, the pierced tops and vase shaped bodies joined with reeded decoration, gilt interiors, each 9cm. high. (Bonhams) $580

PIN CUSHIONS

A silver pin cushion in the form of a frog, Birmingham 1909, 5.5cm. long. (Bonhams) $580

A silver pin cushion, Chester 1912, S. Blanckensee and Sons, modelled as a gentleman's shoe, lacking laces, the pin cushion hinged, opening to reveal an interior box, 12.8cm. long. (Bonhams & Brooks) $142

Unusual silver encased pin cusion in the form of a duck, 'jeweled' eyes, 3½in. long, Birmingham 1908, makers C & N. (G.A. Key) $246

Gorham silver medallion water pitcher, 1886, baluster form, three-dimensional stag heads on either side of body, 7¾in., approximately 21 troy oz. (Skinner) $2,875

A silver and mixed-metal pitcher, Tiffany & Co., New York, circa 1880, the spot-hammered surface applied with butterflies amid branches, 8in. high, gross weight 30oz. (Christie's) $25,300

An American silver large water pitcher, R & W. Wilson, Philadelphia, circa 1840, modelled as a tree trunk, applied with grapevine, 68oz., 14in high. (Sotheby's) $5,750

A silver Aesthetic Movement pitcher, Tiffany & Co., New York, circa 1880, the surface repoussé with flowers and leaves against a punched ground, 7¼in. high, 22oz.10dwt. (Christie's) $3,680

A silver Arts and Crafts pitcher, Shreve & Co., San Francisco, circa 1905, the body spot-hammered with angular wooden handle, riveted at joins, 6in. high. gross weight 25oz. (Christie's) $1,955

Verrerie de Sèvres etched, enamelled, and silver mounted pitcher, colourless bottle etched overall and with coloured violet blossoms, 9in. high. (Skinner) $632

A silver Rococo Revival pitcher, Gorham Mfg. Co., Providence, circa 1855, the body, handle and spout chased and repoussé with lotus plants against a punched ground, 10in. high, 36oz. 10dwt. (Christie's) $2,760

Gorham & Co. pitcher, third quarter 19th century, the handle accented with fruiting vines and topped by a finely modelled putto with a cup in his outstretched hand, 11⅝in., approximately 29 troy oz. (Skinner) $1,840

A silver chrysanthemum pitcher, Tiffany & Co., NY, 1902–1907, globular with reeding and raised on four square feet with chrysanthemum joins, 9in. high, 42oz. 10dwt. (Christie's) $5,750

Reed & Barton repoussé Sterling water pitcher, early 20th century, baluster form, chased floral decoration, 9in. high, approximately 20 troy oz. (Skinner) $1,265

Sterling silver water pitcher, by Gorham, hand-hammered finish with chased leaf and butterfly decoration, 8½in. high. (Eldred's) $1,320

Coin silver water pitcher, Fletcher & Gardiner, Philadelphia, 1811–25, baluster form with applied foliate banding, 9¼in. high. 32 troy oz. (Skinner) $1,495

Redlich & Co. Sterling repoussé pitcher, 20th century, baluster form on tapered foot with ruffled edge, ruffled edge spout, monogrammed, 9¼in. high, approximately 36 troy oz. (Skinner) $2,300

A silver and mixed metal japanesque pitcher, Whiting Mfg. Co., New York, circa 1882, spot-hammered body with a frog and insects with copper bodies amid lotus flowers, 9in. high. gross weight 30oz. 10dwt. (Christie's) $17,250

A silver repoussé pitcher, Samuel Kirk & Son Co., Baltimore, circa 1903–1907, the body, neck and handle overall chased and repoussé with flowers and leaves, 7in. high, 18oz. (Christie's) $1,265

Jarvie sterling water pitcher, hand raised hammer textured baluster form, engraved monogram, 8³/₁₆in. high., approx. 29 troy oz. (Skinner) $1,035

A silver classical pitcher, Hugh Wishart, New York, circa 1815, the sides engraved with cartouches within foliage, 10¼in. high. 33oz. (Christie's) $6,325

A silver Art Nouveau pitcher, Gorham Mfg. Co., Providence, 1897, martelé, baluster with undulating circular base, 11¾in high, 52oz. 10dwt. (Christie's) $16,100

A set of twelve American silver service plates, R. Wallace & Sons, Wallingford, Ct, circa 1910, the wide borders applied and chased with foliage, 266oz., 11in. diameter. (Sotheby's) $7,475

A set of eight silver bread-and-butter plates, Tiffany & Co., New York, circa 1917-1947, each circular, the rim with gadrooned and foliate border, 6³/₈in. diameter, 58oz. (Christie's) $1,955

A set of twelve American silver small plates, Gorham Mfg. Co., Providence, RI, 1906, Martelé, .9584 standard, 93oz., 6³/₄in. diameter. (Sotheby's) $7,475

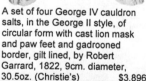

A set of four George III salt cellars on four fluted shell and scroll feet embossed with swirl fluting and beading, by David & Robert Hennell (I), 1765/66, 9cm. wide, 17.75oz. (Christie's) $883

A set of four George IV cauldron salts, in the George II style, of circular form with cast lion mask and paw feet and gadrooned border, gilt lined, by Robert Garrard, 1822, 9cm. diameter, 30.5oz. (Christie's) $3,896

Two of a set of four George III cauldron salts, on three lion mask and paw feet, by S. & C. Young, Walker, Kitchen & Co., Sheffield 1817/18, (with blue glass liners), 10cm. diameter, 22oz weighable silver.(Christie's) (Four) $963

A French late 19th/early 20th century cast silver-gilt salt cellar, supported by two winged beasts on a mask and scroll foot, 14cm. high. (Christie's) $1,063

A matched set of four George I salt cellars, London 1723, possibly John Sanders I, trencher form, on rectangular bases, canted corners, oval bowls, repaired, approximate weight 10oz., 7cm. long.(Bonhams)(Four) $1,617

A pair of George III oval salt cellars with pierced and engraved decoration, on four ball and claw feet, London 1785 and 1786 by Hester Bateman. (Dreweatt Neate) $704

608

A George II Irish sauceboat, on three stepped pad feet with a leaf capped scroll handle, the oval boat-shaped body embossed and chased with floral festoons and a husk cartouche, Dublin, circa 1775, 15.5cm. long, 5.75oz. (Christie's) $722

A George II silver sauce boat, by John Pollock, London 1751, of oval form, leaf capped flying scroll handle, on four shell capped scroll legs with shell feet, crested, approximate weight 8oz., 18cm. long. (Bonhams) $626

Good quality large hallmarked silver sauce boat in Georgian style, having reeded rim, leaf capped flying scrolled handle, supported on four hoof feet, 8in. long. Birmingham 1911, 11½oz. (G.A. Key) $290

A fine pair of American silver sauce boats, circa 1750-60, each on three shell feet headed by stylised trefoils, waved rims, leaf-capped flying double-scroll handles, 7¼in. long. (Sotheby's) $29,500

A George II sauceboat by James Morrison, 1752, on shell and scroll feet with leaf-capped scroll handle, attractively engraved with rococo cartouche, 9oz. (Bonhams) $840

A pair of George II sauceboats of bellied oval form with wavy rims and cast dolphin scroll handles, by John Pollock, 1744, 19cm. long, 28oz. (Christie's) $2,497

Isaac Cookson of Newcastle, a fine pair of cast George II sauceboats, chased raised foliage to the shaped outline rims, the lip with a mask set in a scallop shell, 1744, 30oz. (Woolley & Wallis) $5,586

Hemming & Co., a fine pair of oval sauceboats, in early George II style, the everted fret edge rims with cast capped scroll handles, retailed by Hemming & Co, Conduit Street, London 1932, 22oz. (Woolley & Wallis) $1,341

A pair of American silver sauce boats, Simon Chaudron, Philadelphia, circa 1810, arched serpent handle rising from a collar of palmettes above a shell and anthemion, 1197gr. 8½in. long. (Sotheby's) $21,450

A George II silver tankard, Thomas Mason, London, 1732, plain tapering cylindrical and on molded rim foot, 17.5cm. high, 22oz. (Christie's) $3,108

Victorian silver christening tankard of cup shape with looped hollow handle, circular foot, 3in. tall, Sheffield 1887. (G.A. Key) $101

An American silver tankard, Paul Revere, Jr., Boston, circa 1790, domed cover with flaming urn finial and corkscrew thumbpiece, 29oz., 10in. high. (Sotheby's) $32,200

A German silver tankard, of Daniel Schwestermüller, Augsburg, circa 1690, the sleeve repoussé and chased with figure scenes of Venus and Adonis in landscape, 9¾in. high, 9¾in. high, 35oz. (Christie's) $6,520

An Austrian silver-gilt and verre eglomisé tankard, possibly Salzburg early 17th century, the slightly tapering body with strapwork motifs, centering chased masks and fruit motifs, 10cm., gross weight 8.5oz. (Christie's) $7,772

A German silver-gilt mounted ivory flagon, circa 1875, the hinged slightly domed cover chased with fruit, foliage and satyr masks and with seated bacchic putto finial, 10¼in. high. (Christie's) $6,876

A German large silver tankard, J.D. Schleissner and Sons, Hanau, circa 1900, chased overall with a scene of the fall of Troy, with King Priam in the burning palace, 25in. high, 150oz. (Christie's) $10,246

A fine silver tankard, John Brevoort, New York, circa 1770, on a molded circular base with applied band of leaf-stamped cut-card decoration, 7¼in. high, 40oz. (Christie's) $25,300

A George II silver tankard, Richard Bayley, London 1729, plain tapering cylindrical and on spreading foot, with molded mid-rib, hinged domed cover, 6½in. high, 24oz. (Christie's) $3,726

A Victorian three-piece tea service of compressed circular form, each piece with thread edging, leaf capped double scroll handles and on shell feet, John Lias & Henry Lias, London 1844, 1845, 45oz. (Bearne's) $708

A silver and mixed-metal three-piece tea service, Tiffany & Co., New York, circa 1880, comprising teapot, covered sugar bowl, and cream jug, each shaped square on four bracket feet, the matte-finished body applied with a mokume butterfly, and copper and gold insects, beetles, gourds, and spider amid leaves and vines, the teapot 5¼in. high, gross weight 37oz. 10dwt. (Christie's) $59,700

An American silver three piece tea set, Garret Schanck, New York, 1792-95, comprising teapot, creamer and covered sugar vase, of oval helmet and urn form, 36oz. gross, height of sugar urn 8¼in. (Sotheby's) $9,775

A silver and mixed-metal three-piece tea service, Tiffany & Co., New York, circa 1880, comprising teapot, covered sugar bowl and cream jug, hand-hammered surface applied with mokume butterflies and gold and copper paulownia leaves, dragonfly, and bee amid engraved vines, 4½in. high, gross weight 21oz. 10dwt. (Christie's) $27,600

A rectangular three piece tea service, in Regency style, the curved bodies with a reeded band raised on ball feet to a flared gadroon edge, the teapot with a swan neck spout, Atkin Brothers, Sheffield 1931, 39oz. all in. (Woolley & Wallis) $529

A Victorian four piece tea service, floral engraved with ribbon tied swags, oval cartouches, one with a crest, the pear shape teapot with a beaded swan neck spout, Arthur Sibley, London 1859 (the sugar basin 1857), 50oz. all in. (Woolley & Wallis) $1,352

An American silver six-piece tea and coffee set and matching two-handled tray, Gorham Mfg. Co., Providence, RI, 1928, comprising: kettle on lampstand, coffee pot, teapot, creamer, covered sugar bowl, waste bowl, and oval tray, 304oz., height of kettle 30in. (Sotheby's) $14,375

An American silver four piece tea set, Gale & Stickler, New York, circa 1825, comprising teapot, covered sugar bowl, creamer and waste bowl of lobed and bombé rectangular urn form with die-rolled collars of scrolling roses and other flowers, 2,224gr., height of teapot 10¼in. (Sotheby's) $4,600

A Victorian four piece tea and coffee set, of molded ovoid form with turned finial on domed lid, scroll handle, chased and bright cut with strapwork, central shield with crest, beaded edging and spreading foot, coffee pot 9in. high, Sheffield 1873/74, 69oz. (Andrew Hartley) $1,168

An American silver six-piece tea and coffee set with matching two-handled tray, S. Kirk & Son Co., Baltimore, circa 1918, embossed and chased with romantic landscapes surrounded by foliage, 378 oz. (Sotheby's) $22,600

An Edwardian five piece tea and coffee set including a spirit kettle, eagle finials on domed lids, eagle headed spouts, teapot 10½in. wide, London 1905, stamp for the Goldsmiths and Silversmiths Company, Sheffield 1905, 119oz. 6dwts. (Andrew Hartley) $1,529

An American silver three piece tea set, Alexander Gordon, New York, circa 1800, comprising teapot, creamer and sugar urn with cover, bright-cut with paterae and stemmed flowers, 36oz. gross. (Sotheby's) $5,462

Five-piece English silver tea and coffee service, marks for Goldsmiths and Silversmiths Co., London, 1907, of compressed form with shell and gadroon rim and scrolls and flowers, kettle-on-stand with burner. (Eldred's) $3,520

Seven-piece sterling silver coffee and tea service, made by Sanborns, Mexico, 20th century, includes a coffee pot, teapot, hot water kettle on stand with burner, creamer, covered sugar bowl, waste bowl, and tray, all pieces with lobed sides, handles with scroll decoration, 226 troy oz. Total, 29in. long. (Skinner) $1,725

An American silver 'Japanese style' six-piece tea and coffee set, Dominick & Haff, New York, retailed by William Wilson & Son, Philadelphia, 1881, comprising: Teapot, coffee pot, creamer, covered sugar bowl, waste bowl, and kettle on stand, the spot-hammered frosted bodies finely embossed and chased with aquatic scenes, 134oz. (Sotheby's) $21,450

A Victorian four piece tea and coffee set in the George III style, by John Brashier, 1886, oval with vertical fluted bands, domed fluted covers with ebonized and silver-mounted pineapple finials. (Bonhams) $1,540

A modern four-piece tea service, by Richard Comyns, 1911, the stand and burner, by a different maker, 33in. high, 102oz. (Christie's) $2,125

An American silver five-piece tea and coffee set, Fletcher & Gardner, Philadelphia, circa 1820, comprising: Teapot, coffee pot, creamer, covered sugar bowl, and waste bowl, of plain vase form with die-rolled bands of leaf tips and darts, 166oz. gross, coffee pot 10½in. high. (Sotheby's) $10,200

Eight-piece Art Deco chrome and bakelite beverage set, Manning-Bowman and Co., Meriden, Connecticut, circa 1930, the set comprising a pitcher, six glasses, and a serving tray, made of chromed metal with marbled green and yellow bakelite handles, tray 9 x 18¼in. (Skinner) $575

A George III tea caddy, Daniel Smith & Robert Sharp, 1772, the bombé caddy with a gadroon rim, the body decorated with swag motifs below medallions, height 12.5cm, 9.5oz.
(Christie's) $1,316

A pair of George II tea caddies and a covered mixing bowl en suite, by Samual Taylor, the caddies 1749, the bowl, 1750, contained in original silver-mounted mahogany tea caddy, box 31oz.
(Bonhams) $6,720

An electroplated and ivory tea caddy, 19th century, the hinged oval top above a ribbed body and electroplated base, 14cm. wide.
(Bonhams) $493

TEA KETTLES

A Queen Anne silver teakettle on stand and burner, Richard Green, 1706, burner William Fawdery, 1709, both London, Britannia standard, 26cm. on stand, 1595gm. all in. (Sotheby's) $15,198

Peter Behrens for AEG, Bingwerke, Nürnberg, electric kettle and cover, 1909, nickel and chromium plated metal, ebonized wood and woven cane, 8½in.
(Sotheby's) $1,593

Victorian kettle and stand, Mappin & Webb, London, third quarter 19th century, the vasiform kettle with engraved and chased foliates and scroll and fruit decoration, 19in. high. (Skinner) $517

Early 20th century silver plated spirit kettle, burner and stand, the kettle of compressed oval design, the stand with four curved supports and central burner, 14in. tall.
(G.A. Key) $175

A William IV tea kettle, by James Fray, Dublin 1835, of melon fluted form on a stand with scroll work supports, openwork cast feet and a lift-out burner, 36cm. high, 111oz.
(Bonhams) $4,360

A George II silver teakettle on stand and burner, George Hindmarsh, London, 1743 hinge pin and pin fixture Sebastian Crespell, London, 1854, 12½in. high, 2552gm.
(Sotheby's) $3,576

A George III Scottish teapot, the body and cover with bright-cut engraved borders and laurel wreath cartouches by John McDonald, Edinburgh, 1797, 16cm., 16.25oz gross. (Bonhams) $553

Robert Hennell, a George III oval teapot, bright cut engraved borders, the sides with vacant oval cartouches suspended from ribbon ties, London, 1784, 13oz. all in. (Woolley & Wallis) $911

A Victorian bachelor's teapot, the squat pear shape body engraved with a band of foliage and bellflowers, swan neck spout, Henry Wilkinson, London 1870, 6½oz. all in. (Woolley & Wallis) $512

A Scottish Provincial silver teapot, Robert Luke, Glasgow, 1725-1735, spherical and on spreading circular foot, with tapering straight spout, 6¼in. high, gross 19oz. (Christie's) $4,620

German hallmarked silver teapot, 19th century, panelled rectangular-form, chased exotic and classical decoration, 6¹⁵/₁₆in. high, approx. 25 troy oz. (Skinner) $489

A Dutch silver teapot, Dirk Blom, Amsterdam, 1762, the body with spiral flutes, scoll spout and wood handle, the hinged cover cast with stylized scrolls, 4¼in., gross 12oz. (Christie's) $5,067

TOAST RACKS

Unusual silver plated toast rack of seven hooped bars and having 'horseshoe' shaped ends, 5½ x 3in. (G.A. Key) $34

An early Victorian toast rack, the oval six divisions with an open moulded scroll handle, on a moulded edge frame, Barnard Brothers, London 1843, 9oz. (Woolley & Wallis) $358

George III silver toast rack, marks for London, 1793, maker's mark erased, plain pattern, 6½in. long, 9.8 troy oz. (Eldred's) $600

A Chinese silver salver, maker's mark of Kwong Wa, the centre engraved in the Aesthetic manner, with swallows, bamboo, butterflies and a fan, approximate weight 33oz., diameter 30.8cm. (Bonhams) $1,058

Rare Scottish Provincial circular silver tray, having a plain field and raised half round edge, last quarter 19th century, probably by George Angus, 12½in. diameter, 20oz. (G.A. Key) $2,030

A George II salver, Robert Abercrombie, 1743, the circular salver with a shell heightened pie crust border, flat chased with rocaille, lattice and foliate scroll motifs, 35.2cm. 41oz. (Christie's) $3,619

An 18th century Dutch waiter, Amsterdam 1766, maker's mark of Henddrik Nieuwenhuys, shell and scroll border, the centre with engraved decoration, the whole on three shell bracket feet, approximate weight 5oz., 14.8cm. diameter. (Bonhams) $1,103

A pair of George II silver waiters, William Paradise, London, 1729, shaped square and with incurved corners, each on four hoof feet and with moulded border, 5¾in. square, 13oz. (Christie's) $4,844

A George II salver, London 1750, maker's mark of William Peaston, circular form, shell and scroll border, the centre engraved with a coat of arms, approximate weight 27oz., 30.4cm. high. (Bonhams) $1,617

Attractive Victorian silver wine salver, circular shaped with shell and scrolled edge and engraved centre, supported on three curved feet, 10in. diameter, London 1874 by the Barnards, 16½oz. (G.A. Key) $361

A silver and mixed-metal tray, Tiffany & Co., New York, circa 1881, shaped square on four scroll and ball feet, the spot-hammered body applied and engraved with silver and copper tall grasses and a silver crab, 8½in. long; gross weight 17oz. (Christie's) $8,625

English George II footed salver, London, 1756, maker Frederick Kandler, on three scroll feet, the tray engraved with scrolls and grapes, 13½in. diameter, approximately 38 troy oz. (Skinner) $2,070

A George II Irish Provincial waiter, George Hodder, Cork, circa 1745, also marked for Richard Williams, Dublin, 1778, the shaped circular waiter raised on three hoof feet, 6¾in., 8oz.(Christie's) $1,227

A George II waiter, London 1728, maker's mark of Charles Martin, moulded border, the centre engraved with a coat of arms, approximate weight 6oz., 15.8cm. diameter.(Bonhams) $1,617

A George III silver large salver of American interest, Richard Rugg, London, 1765, the gadroon rim with shells at intervals, 3,126gm, diameter 62.2cm.(Sotheby's) $8,400

English George II small footed salver, London, 1759, by Richard Rugg, raised on three gadrooned feet, the moulded edge with gadrooned rim, engraved to centre with coat of arms in rococo cartouche, 7½in., approximately 10 troy oz. (Skinner) $633

A pair of George I silver waiters, Paul de Lamerie, London, 1720, centre engraved with a coat-of-arms within elaborate cartouche, 5¾in. long, 18oz. (Christie's) $37,260

A silver salver, maker's mark of Philip Syng, Philadelphia, circa 1740, circular, on four scroll legs with hoof feet, moulded and notched everted border, 10in. diameter, 19oz. 10dwt. (Christie's) $23,000

A George IV silver-gilt salver, William Bateman, London, 1820, shaped-circular and on three leaf-capped scroll feet, with gadrooned border, 21in. diameter, 139oz. (Christie's) $21,714

An Edwardian silver salver, with shaped gadrooned rim, each corner embossed with an acanthus leaf, Sheffield 1936, 24cm. wide approximate weight 22½oz. (Bonhams) $368

Good George II period Irish silver waiter with shell and gadrooned edge, engraved centre, on three scrolled feet, 6½in. diameter, by John Wilme, 10oz. (G.A. Key) $725

The Billiard Player, silver, rounded rectangular, the front enamelled with a billiard player readying to pot a ball, George Heath, London 1888, 5cm. (Christie's) $1,379

Diamond set Match, gold, the front applied with a facsimile match, the head set with a diamond, probably American, late nineteenth century, 5.2cm. (Christie's) $759

Tom Cannon, silver, the front enamelled with an oval study of a jockey, Tom Cannon, Birmingham 1881, 3.7cm. (Christie's) $1,138

Hunters Taking a Stream, silver, rectangular, the front with an angled panel enamelled with a scene of two huntsmen jumping a stream, J.M.B., Chester 1902, 5.4cm. (Christie's) $800

An Oarswoman, silver, of rectangular box-type, the front enamelled with a standing lady holding an oar, Sampson Mordan, London 1889, 5.7cm. (Christie's) $1,707

Upstairs, Downstairs, silver, the front enamelled with a scene featuring a gentleman's advances being mildly resisted by a maid, French, late nineteenth century, 4.8cm. (Christie's) $1,518

Girl with Flowers, silver, the cover decorated with an enamelled study of a girl holding flowers, Continental, late nineteenth century, 4.3cm. (Christie's) $1,042

Girl and Owl, silver, the front with an enamelled scene of a girl in a wooded landscape, an owl in flight in the foreground, American, late nineteenth century, 6.2cm. (Christie's) $721

A Cricketer, silver-plated, rectangular, the front enamelled with a cricketer taking a swing, surrounded by engraved foliage, probably English, late nineteenth century, 4.2cm. (Christie's) **$721**

Gold and Agate Horseshoe, the front inset with panels of gold in quartz, unmarked, probably American, late nineteenth century, 5.5cm. (Christie's) **$3,225**

A Concealed Nude, silver, the exterior plain, double hinged to reveal an enamelled study of a standing lady disrobing herself, German, late nineteenth century, 5.7cm. (Christie's) **$1,612**

Nude on Shoreline, silver vesta case, rounded rectangular, the front enamelled with a reclining nude female seated on a shoreline, waves and skyline beyond, London import marks, 5cm. (Christie's) **$1,405**

A Punch and Judy Tent, silver vesta case, rectangular with a pointed dome, the front enamelled with a seaside Punch and Judy tent, featuring Mr. Punch, the Sea Captain, Toby the Dog and a drummer, Sampson Mordan, London 1887, 5.4cm. (Christie's) **$13,120**

Nude by a Lake, silver, rounded rectangular, the front enamelled to one side with a rectangular study of a nude female standing beside a lake amidst extensive foliage, probably German, late 19th century, 4.5cm. (Christie's) **$800**

The Kill, the front enamelled with a scene depicting the conclusion of the Hunt, a huntsman holding aloft a fox, Sampson Mordan, Chester 1903, 5.7cm. (Christie's) **$3,415**

A Female Head and Shoulders, silver, rectangular, the front enamelled with a female head and shoulders study, she in a blue dress, J.M.B., Birmingham 1893, 4.6cm. (Christie's) **$800**

Vintage Car, gold, the front die-stamped with a study of a vintage car, the headlights set with rubies, the radiator set with a diamond, American, 6cm. (Christie's) **$1,518**

A George IV Irish wine funnel, of lobed octagonal form with a shaped rim and detachable inner strainer, by Richard Sawyer, Dublin, 1829, 14.25cm. high, 5oz. (Christie's) $515

A George III Scottish silver wine funnel, W. & P. Cunningham, Edinburgh, circa 1800, plain funnel with three applied ribs and reeded border, the pierced detachable strainer with plain clip, 5¼in. high, 2.5oz. (Christie's) $1,074

A William IV wine funnel, by James Le Bas, Dublin 1831, the detachable strainer section with a circular pattern of drilled holes, 15cm. high, 4.5oz. (Christie's) $817

A George II/III wine funnel, possibly by John Moore, Dublin circa 1760, with a shallow circular bowl and a detachable narrow spout, 11cm. high, 1.75oz. (Bonhams) $909

A George III silver wine funnel, London 1816, Rebecca Emes and Edward Barnard, bellied bowl, detachable inner straining bowl, weight 5oz., 14.5cm. long. (Bonhams & Brooks) $1,008

A George III wine funnel, crowned Harp and Hibernia marks only, Dublin circa 1780, with a squat circular bowl, crested, and a short tapering spout, no strainer, 25cm. high, 2 oz. (Bonhams) $363

WINE TASTERS

A Louis XV silver wine-taster, maker's mark *CIL*, Rouen, 1756-1762, with shaped bracket engraved with a figure of a man with a child on his back, 4½in. long, 4oz. (Christie's) $4,099

A French Provincial silver wine-taster, Jean Hocquet, Wassy, circa 1760, plain circular with kidney-shaped tab handle with ring beneath, 4¼in. long. 2oz. (Christie's) $2,171

A Charles II unascribed Provincial wine taster, circa 1680, flat loop handles, sides punched with small flutes and beading, center stamped with a large rose motif, 4.9cm. diameter. (Bonhams) $1,190

A Beijing four-color overlay glass snuff bottle, carved in pink, yellow, green and blue on a snowstorm ground, 3in. high, 18th/19th century. (Christie's) $942

A Beijing blue overlay glass oviform snuff bottle, carved on a snowstorm ground with cranes wading in a pond, coral stopper, 2¾in. high, 19th century.(Christie's) $1,444

A Beijing four-color overlay glass snuff bottle, carved in green, red, pink and yellow with fish amongst lotus flowers and leaves, 3in. high, 19th century.(Christie's) $631

A rare 'European-subject' famille rose porcelain snuff bottle, indistinct defaced Qianlong mark of the Period (1736-1795), with two shaped cartouches of European ladies and boys with a basket of flowers and bowl of fruit among flowers, 2½in. high. (Christie's) $29,363

A Chinese white jade rounded rectangular snuff bottle, decorated in gilt to one side with two birds perched in a leafy tree, 3in. high, 18th century.(Christie's) $1,083

A rare yellow jade bottle, 1740-1780, possibly Imperial Palace Workshops, carved in the archaic style in low relief with a continuous band of lightly carved circles divided by lion-mask fixed-ring handles to the sides, 6.3cm. high. (Christie's) $34,523

An ivory snuff-bottle and stopper, carved with shaped cartouches of figures carrying lotus and banners among rockwork, 3½in. high, early 19th century. (Christie's) $1,570

A Chinese carnelian agate globular snuff bottle, with white inclusions, carved in high relief with a single flower spray above further trailing flower sprays, ivory, 2in. high, 19th century. (Christie's) $628

A Beijing five-color overlay glass snuff bottle, carved in dark green, lime green, iron-red, yellow and brown on an opaque white ground with a butterfly, 2½in. high, 19/20th century. (Christie's) $1,083

Amber pebble form snuff bottle, 19th century, the honey coloured body semi-translucent and with natural inclusions, 3in. (Butterfield) $632

A Beijing ruby-red overlay glass snuff bottle, carved in high relief on a clear ground with numerous bats in flight, 3¾in. high, 18th/19th century. (Christie's) $1,264

Good carved opal snuff bottle, of baluster form carved to the left with a dragon suspending a flaming jewel on his breath, 2⅜in. (Butterfield & Butterfield) $546

Polychrome enamel decorated glass snuff bottle, early 19th century, painted with a rooster, hen and chicks reversed by cranes of longevity, 2¼in. (Butterfield & Butterfield) $546

Good ruby red glass snuff bottle, 19th century, of tapered ovoid form flaring out from the ring foot to a wide hipped shoulder, 2⅜in. (Butterfield & Butterfield) $1,265

Unusual yellow glass snuff bottle, the globular body fashioned from yellow glass with a pale green cast, green stone, stopper, 2⅛in. (Butterfield & Butterfield) $1,000

An ivory snuff-bottle and stopper, carved with a woman and child among maple and pine branches, the reverse with a fisherman below Immortals among clouds, 3½in. high, early 19th century. (Christie's) $1,173

Fine enamelled bottle depicting European subjects, Qianlong mark, early 19th century, elegantly painted with two foreign ladies in conversation on a terrace, 2in. (Butterfield & Butterfield) $4,025

A Chinese glass snuff bottle simulating amber, modelled as a gourd and carved in shallow relief with trailing fruit sprays, flowers and leaves, coral stopper, 3in. high, 19th century. (Christie's) $3,430

Good ruby glass overlay figural snuff bottle, 19th century, rendered as a harnessed elephant, his saddle blanket decorated in a trigram pattern, 2½in. (Butterfield & Butterfield) $1,265

Good green tourmaline snuff bottle, the baluster body carved to one side with a boy and horse under pines, 2³⁄₈in. (Butterfield & Butterfield) $2,300

Good polychrome painted porcelain snuff bottle, 19th century, elegantly painted with a boatman poling two guests along a lush riverbank, 2¾in. (Butterfield & Butterfield) $1,380

Red overlay portrait snuff bottle, the ovoid body decorated with two portraits of Mao Zedong flanked by paired facsimiles of his signature, 2¹⁄₈in. (Butterfield & Butterfield) $1,035

Peking glass cabinet bottle, simulating jasper, 19th century, one side humorously depicting Liu Hai holding a string of cash, 2⁷⁄₈in. (Butterfield & Butterfield) $2,300

Blue and white snuff bottle, 19th century, rendered in underglaze blue and iron red with a portrait of Li Pu Hou in scholar's robes, 2⁵⁄₈in. (Butterfield & Butterfield) $431

Inside painted glass snuff bottle, signed *Yusan*, elegantly rendered with a bird perched on top of a spider chrysanthemum branch, 2¹⁄₈in. (Butterfield & Butterfield) $920

Good carved amber snuff bottle, 19th century, worked with squirrels climbing on a network of grape vines, 2³⁄₈in. (Butterfield & Butterfield) $1,265

Peachbloom glazed porcelain double gourd form snuff bottle, 18th/19th century, covered with an iron-tone peachbloom glaze, 3⁵⁄₈in. (Butterfield & Butterfield) $2,000

An Aubusson Old Testament tapestry, 17th century, two people on the left emptying a box of jewels and proffering them to an elder man, 2ft.9in. x 6ft.2in. (Sotheby's) $13,800

An Aubusson historical tapestry panel from the series of Alexander the Great, 17th century, Alexander and his attendants to the left before the family of Darius in a tent to the right, 7ft.4in. x 11ft.9in. (Sotheby's) $8,050

A Flemish historical tapestry panel, 17th century, the queen preparing to mount her horse, the scene surrounded by attendants and soldiers, 7ft. 2in. x 7ft. 6in. (Sotheby's) $10,925

An Antwerp historical tapestry, late 17th century, woven in wools and silks, depicting a riding lesson within a garden landscape with a tree and a fountain to the left background,9ft.7in. x 11ft. (Christie's) $23,575

An Aubusson historical tapestry, 17th century, a lady gesturing to two gentlemen to the right, one a soldier supporting a large slab of stone, 9ft. 3in. x 10ft. 4in. (Sotheby's) $10,925

An Aubusson gênre tapestry, 18th century, two ladies conversing with a shepherd in the centre, 7ft.3in. x 9ft.9in. (Sotheby's) $11,500

624

A Flemish verdure tapestry, late 17th century/early 18th century, with birds including a peacock in the central clearing, 8ft. 1in. x 14ft. 5in. (Sotheby's) $33,350

A pastoral tapestry, Aubusson, circa 1870, woven with a young couple dancing to the music of a youth playing a guitar, watched by a girl sitting on a stone bench, 160 x 350cm. wide. (Sotheby's) $12,503

A French or Flemish allegorical tapestry of Justice blindfolded, circa 1600, a man in classical dress seated before Justice and other Virtues, 9ft. 8in. x 9ft. 8in. (Sotheby's) $10,350

A Franco-Flemish allegorical tapestry, first half 16th century, woven in wools and silks, depicting courtly figures playing cards in the foreground, an amorous couple to the right, 9ft.9in. x 9ft.4in. (Christie's) $427,065

A Brussels mythological tapestry of the death of Achilles, from the series of the Story of Achilles, designed after cartoons by Peter Paul Rubens, woven by Ian Raes, circa 1630, 13ft. 5in. x 15ft. (Sotheby's) $44,850

An Aubusson verdure tapestry, 17th century, incorporating a formal garden and a fountain, 9ft. 5in. x 11ft. (Sotheby's) $16,100

A Chiltern musical teddy bear with pale golden mohair, deep amber and black glass eyes, clipped tip of snout, black stitched nose, 17in. tall, circa 1950. (Christie's) $681

A Steiff 50th anniversary Jackie Bear, light blond mohair, articulated, 1953, 17cm. high. (Auction Team Köln) $1,023

'Farnham', a Chad Valley teddy bear, with golden mohair, large amber and black glass eyes, 16in. tall, 1920s. (Christie's) $538

A Chiltern teddy bear, with golden curly mohair, deep amber and black glass eyes, swivel head, jointed shaped limbs, velvet pads and card lined feet, 16in. tall, circa 1930. (Christie's) $395

A musical teddy bear, with long white mohair, clear and black glass eyes painted on reverse, turned-up clipped snout, 12in. tall, 1920s. (Christie's) $753

BUYER BEWARE

With teddy bears fetching the prices they do, many fakes are appearing at fairs and auctions.

Always check that the worn patches are natural. Imagine how a child would hold and hug a bear - does the worn area coincide? Also, how does the bear smell? It should have an old but pleasant smell.

(Clarke Gammon)

A Steiff teddy bear with blond mohair, black boot button eyes, black stitched nose, mouth and claws, swivel head, jointed shaped limbs and button in ear, 13in. tall, circa 1910. (Christie's) $727

A Steiff teddy bear, German, circa 1909, golden mohair with black boot button eyes, jointed straw filled body with hump to back, kid leather paw pads, 18in. tall. (Bonhams) $2,844

A Chad Valley teddy bear with golden mohair, orange and black glass eyes, central facial seam, black stitched 'button' nose and mouth, 32in. tall. (Christie's) $400

An early Farnell dressed teddy bear with remains of white mohair, black shoe button eyes, unjointed cloth body dressed in original highland soldier uniform, 8in. tall, 1912. (Christie's) $344

A Steiff Teddy Baby, golden mohair, fully articulated, with open muzzle, blue collar and brown sewn nose and claws, double press growl, circa 42cm. (Auction Team Köln) $1,452

An early German teddy bear, with cinnamon mohair, black boot button eyes, pronounced snout, black horizontally stitched nose, 14in. tall, circa 1910. (Christie's) $358

A Steiff teddy bear with cinnamon mohair, black boot button eyes, pronounced clipped snout, long jointed shaped limbs, felt pads, hump and button in ear, 13in. tall, circa 1908. (Christie's) $1,725

'Victor', a Dean's teddy bear, with golden mohair, clear and black glass eyes painted on reverse, swivel head, jointed shaped limbs, felt pads and card lined feet, 14in. tall, circa 1930. (Christie's) $717

'Barney', an early German teddy bear, with golden brown mohair, black boot button eyes, pronounced snout, black stitched nose and claws, 22in. tall, circa 1910, possibly Bing. (Christie's) $717

An English green teddy bear with artificial silk plush, clear and black eyes painted on reverse, pronounced clipped snout, swivel head, jointed limbs, cream felt pads and squeaker, 13in. tall, 1930s. (Christie's) $627

A Steiff teddy bear with golden cotton plush, clear and black glass eyes, swivel head, jointed shaped limbs, linen pads and squeaker, 12in. tall, 1940s. (Christie's) $763

A teddy bear with pale blond mohair, black boot button eyes, ears set wide apart, swivel head, jointed shaped limbs, cream felt pads and hump, 18in. tall, circa 1910, probably American. (Christie's) $1,090

A Merrythought cheeky teddy bear, with golden mohair, inset velvet muzzle, black stitched nose, mouth and claws, orange and black plastic eyes, ears with bells, 26in. high, 1960s. (Christie's) $667

A Steiff teddy baby, with brown mohair, pronounced inset short mohair muzzle, brown and black glass eyes, large short mohair feet with cloth pads, 13¾in. high, 1930s. (Christie's) $1,335

A rare Peacock teddy bear, with golden mohair, pronounced cut muzzle, large cupped ears, swivel neck, jointed limbs and beige pads, 26½in. high, 1920s. (Christie's) $1,001

American stick figure golden mohair articulated bear, articulated elongated limbs, swivel head, boot button brown eyes, stitched eyes, nose and mouth, hump back, felt paws, early 20th century, 22in. high. (Christie's) $660

A rare Gebrüder Süssenguth 'Peter' teddy bear, with dark brown tipped mohair, pronounced muzzle, open mouth with composition teeth and tongue, black and white glass moving eyes, in original box with photocopied catalogue, 13in. high, circa 1925.(Christie's) $2,336

A Steiff teddy bear with golden mohair, pronounced clipped muzzle, black stitched nose, mouth and claws, swivel head, jointed elongated limbs and hump, 12¼in. high, circa 1910. (Christie's) $700

'Clifford', a Steiff **center** seam teddy bear, with blond mohair, swivel head, elongated jointed limbs with felt pads and hump, button in ear, 16in., circa 1910. (Christie's) $4,338

A Merrythought cheeky teddy bear, with golden mohair, inset velvet muzzle, ears with bells, swivel head and jointed limbs, white label, 27in. high, late 1960s. (Christie's) $1,251

A Steiff teddy bear with brown mohair, pronounced muzzle, black stitched nose, mouth and claws, brown and black glass eyes, 17½in. high, circa 1930. (Christie's) $2,502

A Steiff teddy bear with white mohair, pronounced clipped muzzle, pale brown stitched nose, mouth and claws, jointed elongated limbs with felt pads and hump, 18in., circa 1908.
(Christie's) $4,338

A rare purse teddy bear with blond mohair, pronounced muzzle, black stitched nose, mouth and claws, metal framed purse opening in back with chain handle, probably British, 8¼in. high, circa 1920.
(Christie's) $1,335

An unusual teddy bear cub, with peach coloured mohair, pronounced inset muzzle and face mask, with original pink bow, probably Merrythought, 12½in. high, 1950s/60s.
(Christie's) $200

A Merrythought cheeky teddy bear, with shaggy gold mohair, inset velvet muzzle, black stitched nose, mouth and claws, large orange and black glass eyes, ears with bells, 26in. high, circa 1960.
(Christie's) $1,167

An unusual Hermann Nachf. bendable dancing bear, with long shaggy grey mohair, pronounced inset short mohair muzzle, ring through nose with chain, swivel head and bendable limbs with airbrushed feet claws, 16in. high, 1950s. (Christie's) $700

A Crämer teddy bear, with brown tipped white mohair, pronounced inset golden mohair muzzle, golden mohair ear lining and tops of feet, swivel head and jointed limbs, 13¾in. high, circa 1925.
(Christie's) $1,001

A Steiff teddy bear with golden mohair, swivel head, jointed elongated limbs with felt pads and hump, button in ear and remains of yellow cloth tag, 17in. high, 1930.
(Christie's) $2,502

A Steiff teddy bear, with blond mohair, swivel head, jointed elongated limbs and hump, button in ear and remains of white tag, 19in. high, circa 1910. $3,169
(Christie's)

A Steiff teddy bear with brown mohair, pronounced cut muzzle, black stitched nose, mouth and claws, brown and black glass eyes, 19½in. high, circa 1930.
(Christie's) $3,169

An extremely rare Strunz polar bear clown, with white mohair head, hand and feet, integral green and pink wool jester's outfit with pointed hat, pom-poms, felt cuffs and collar, 18in. high, circa 1909.
(Christie's) $4,338

A large Steiff white bear, German, circa 1920, with button, brown backed glass eyes, vertically stitched brown nose over red felt, hump, 25½in.
(Sotheby's) $10,584

A Dean's 'Tru-to-Life' teddy bear with black mohair, brown and black glass eyes cut into internal rubber face mask with rubber eye sockets, pink rubber feet pads, paws and claws, 20in. tall, circa 1950.
(Christie's) $1,256

A large Chiltern teddy bear, English, circa 1930, the light brown mohair bear with orange glass eyes, black stitched nose, mouth and claws, swivel head and jointed at shoulders and hips, 24in. tall.
(Bonhams & Brooks) $389

A pair of Eduard Crämer bears, German, circa 1935, of artificial dark golden plush, with brown backed glass eyes, vertically stitched black nose, inset heart shaped face mask and ears of shorter plush, 20½in.
(Sotheby's) $5,998

A musical teddy bear, possibly a Glockenspiel bear by Helvetic, Austrian, circa 1920, the long blonde mohair bear with clear glass eyes, clipped snout and pink stitched nose, swivel head and jointed at shoulders and hips, 12in. tall.(Bonhams & Brooks) $765

An early 20th century golden plush hump-back, plump teddy bear, boot button eyes, clipped muzzle, felt pads, card lined feet, circa 1915, 22in. tall, probably English.
(Woolley & Wallis) $469

A Terry teddy bear, with golden mohair, pronounced cut muzzle, horizontally elliptic stitched nose, black stitched mouth and claws, large ears, 20½in. high, circa 1913.
(Christie's) $2,336

A beige plush slim teddy bear, boot button type eyes, growler, horizontally stitched black nose, mouth and claws, small, set apart ears, first half 20th century, 17in. tall. (Woolley & Wallis) $131

Brass candlestick phone, nickel plate finish, 11in. high. (Jacksons) $69

An SA25 'Cow hoof' desk telephone, with two supplementary keys, produced for Austria Hungary. (Auction Team Köln) $1,407

A British wall telephone, with desk, dial and adjustable mouthpiece. (Auction Team Köln) $185

A Scandinavian wall telephone with desk, battery case and fixed microphone, circa 1895. (Auction Team Köln) $1,138

A German portable telephone with carbon fibre microphone, in wooden case with battery, bell and call button, circa 1895. (Auction Team Köln) $371

A Swedish L.M. Ericsson wall desk telephone, with adjustable microphone, lightning conductor and bell receiver, works missing. (Auction Team Köln) $668

An undocumented Precision telephone with call trumpet and unusual side fixtures, circa 1885. (Auction Team Köln) $3,136

A local battery Ericsson 'skeleton' desk telephone with horn and speech button, decorative receiver cradle, circa 1900. (Auction Team Köln) $510

An Stf 04 wall telephone with desk by Groos & Graf, Berlin, with adjustable mouthpiece and receiver, lacking dial. (Auction Team Köln) $561

A Siemens & Halske desk telephone, with push button line dial, circa 1942. (Auction Team Köln) $97

A first Ericsson domestic telephone with pointer dial, circa 1910. (Auction Team Köln) $711

A Post Office model coin telephone, metal casing, 1965. (Auction Team Köln) $129

Two model K Telegrafverkets Verkstad, Nynäshamn receivers. (Auction Team Köln) $54

An army field telephone, supplementary set to C. Lorenz AG, Berlin field telephone, in wooden case with original receiver. (Auction Team Köln) $149

Two unsigned receivers, with speech keys, bright metal mouthpieces. (Auction Team Köln) $38

A Telegraphie Militaire Model 1927 field telephone, wooden cased, with second receiver, French. (Auction Team Köln) $84

Early Western Electric cradle phone, 9in. long. (Jacksons) $57

A 25-part Siemens & Halske desk telephone, complete with earth key, the handset with wooden handle, circa 1920. (Auction Team Köln) $1,084

An L.M. Ericsson, Stockholm skeleton telephone, the receiver with speech button. (Auction Team Köln) $746

A special edition Ericsson telephone, with dial, ivory color with gold decoration. (Auction Team Köln) $229

A Mix & Genest bakelite wall telephone, made in Belgium in 1942 during the occupation, with earth key. (Auction Team Köln) $96

TELEPHONES

An M 1900 wall extension without desk by R. Stock & Co, , Berlin, with movable speaking tube.
(Auction Team Köln) $1,424

An original mahogany Bell receiver, damage to the earpiece, circa 1880.
(Auction Team Köln) $226

A French desk telephone by the Société Générale des Téléphones, with call button, circa 1900.
(Auction Team Köln) $1,099

Three unsigned receivers, with speaking keys, two with horn-shaped mouthpieces.
(Auction Team Köln) $59

An Ericsson railway telephone with crank, bakelite hand receiver with speech key, with carrying strap.
(Auction Team Köln) $41

Two unsigned receivers, one bakelite, with speaking keys, earphone damaged,
(Auction Team Köln) $49

An L.M. Ericsson, Stockholm skeleton telephone, the receiver with speech key and horn.
(Auction Team Köln) $983

An M89 wall extension by Kehser & Schmidt, Berlin, with Siemens & Halske receiver, circa 1890.
(Auction Team Köln) $4,407

A Bell-Hasler LB desk exchange, 1904.
(Auction Team Köln) $4,204

An OB SDF OO wall telephone, wooden wall desk with moveable receiver, 1900.
(Auction Team Köln) $970

An Elmeg test board in wooden case, with number board, ohmmeter, load indicator and hand receiver with speech key.
(Auction Team Köln) $122

A Seth W. Fuller, Boston, candlestick exchange for 16 lines, brass casing with Bell receiver, circa 1915.
(Auction Team Köln) $611

A gold thimble the wide border chased with a scene of a group of girls sewing, French, circa 1900, 2.5cm. (Christie's) $1,310

A silver-gilt thimble, the body overlaid with a silver sleeve, possibly French, late 18th century, 2.3cm. (Christie's) $3,743

A gold thimble, the border with a blue enamelled Greek Key design, English, circa 1860, 2.2cm. (Christie's) $337

A silver thimble, with three gilt circular cartouches, Birmingham 1896, 2.4cm. (Christie's) $449

A gold thimble, the wide border with applied two-color gold flowers and trailing foliage on a matted ground and with applied vacant shaped cartouche, English, late 19th century, 2.3cm. (Christie's) $686

A gold thimble, cast in the form of the Liberty Bell, probably Simons Bros, late 19th century, 1.8cm. (Christie's) $628

A combination thimble, tape measure and scent bottle holder, the part filigree thimble unscrewing to reveal a recess, English, early 19th century 4.5cm. (Christie's) $898

A gold thimble, the wide border depicting a panoramic architectural study and the legend *Worlds Columbian Exposition, 1492-1892,* Simons Bros, late 19th century. (Christie's) $578

A porcelain thimble, the border painted with gilt flowers and foliage on a white ground, French, early 19th century, 2.1cm. (Christie's) $356

A silver filigree thimble, the sides incorporating a vacant oval cartouche, English, early 19th century, 2.6cm. (Christie's) $412

A wooden thimble, the rim with an applied gilt-metal band chased with stylised foliage, probably French, early 19th century, 2.4cm. (Christie's) $599

A mother of pearl thimble, the border with two applied gilt-metal bands, probably French, early 19th century, 2.5cm. (Christie's) $561

The Largest Vessel and The Largest Floating Crane In The World The White Star Liner Titanic, real photographic 'Book Post' postcard, pub by Hurst, Belfast, post sinking. (Onslow's) $173

A cast name board from a lifeboat on the R.M.S. Titanic, British, CA. 1912, 17¾ x 12½in. (Christie's) $34,500

White Star Line oval meat dish by Elkington on ornate feet, the edge decorated with stars and engraved with company burgee, 42cm. wide. (Onslow's) $816

White Star Line Olympic and Titanic Each 45,000 Tons The Largest Steamers In The World, Cadbury's Bourneville Cocoa trade card, 7 x 4cm. (Onslow's) $659

The arm of a deck chair from R.M.S. Titanic, anonymous (British, 20th century), CA. 1912, from a folding deck chair, carved from white oak, tapered at the end, 18½ x 2¼ x 1¼in. (Christie's) $9,200

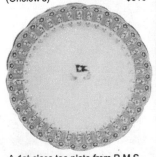

A 1st class tea plate from R.M.S. Titanic, Stonier & Co., Ltd., Liverpool, CA. 1912, decorated along the border with a green and brown floral motif and gold trim along the edge. In the center is the White Star Line burgee, 7½in. diameter. (Christie's) $2,990

Five Minton outside decorated plates from the steam yacht S.Y. Corsair, cyphers circa 1915, one with T. Goode & Co., Ltd. London, mark, gold and blue border with the New York Yacht Club burgee and J.P. Morgan's private signal, 9in. diameter and smaller. (Christie's) $3,220

A railway poster for White Star Line – Titanic, anonymous; British, CA. 1912, one of the few surviving railway warrants issued to passengers to allow them to travel to their port of departure. (Christie's) $2,300

A 1st class passenger ticket for R.M.S. Titanic, White Star Line, British, CA. 1912, printed on a vellum paper with black ink and marked with the White Star Line burgee, 3¾ x 6½in. (Christie's) $8,050

An important oak box crafted from R.M.S. Titanic Driftwood, by William Parker, with dove-tailed joints with a hinged lid and brass hinges, handle and lock, 15 x 10 x 7½in. (Christie's) $18,400

Captain E J Smith, signed certificate of discharge to Samuel Taylor Boatswain on the SS Majestic, date of discharge 31st July 1895, signed by Captain Smith. (Onslow's) $1,256

RMS Titanic, John Gill 2nd Class passenger RMS Titanic postcard sent Southampton April 10th 1912, before he boarded RMS Titanic. (Aldridge) $11,600

RMS Titanic, John Gill 2nd Class passenger RMS Titanic, Mr Gill's pocket comb recovered from his body and sent back to his wife. (Aldridge) $17,400

RMS Titanic onboard letter card. (Aldridge) $25,375

RMS Titanic onboard deck chair. (Aldridge) $49,300

RMS Titanic onboard souvenir. (Aldridge) $25,375

RMS Titanic photograph of Second Class passenger Clear Cameron. (Aldridge) $11,165

RMS Titanic 1st Class dinner menu, April 10th 1912. (Aldridge) $39,150

RMS Titanic, John Gill 2nd Class passenger letter confirming his loss in the disaster. (Aldridge) $16,000

RMS Titanic, John Gill 2nd Class passenger RMS Titanic, pocket watch and chain stopped at 3.21am 15-4-12. (Aldridge) $31,600

A painted wood figural small shop sign, 19th century, of a Highland soldier and Indian snufftakers holding hands, on oval base with iron fixing points to back, 38cm. (Bristol) $6,525

A Georgian brass tavern honesty box by 'Rich Patentee, Bridgwater', rectangular with central handle and two hinged compartments, one with slot for pennies and push releasing the other for tobacco, 24cm. long. (Bristol) $754

An impressive pair of cigar store Indian figures, in painted and gilded wood with leafy crowns and skirts, each with lead lined open sack on their back, on rocky bases and octagonal plinths, 130cm. high and 128cm. (Bristol) $2,600

A musical cheroot holder, Swiss, circa 1900, the octagonal case with eight hinged doors which open to musical movement, 11in. high. (Sotheby's) $353

A Scottish silver-mounted ram's head snuff mull, with glass eyes, the twist horns with clear paste set silver thistle terminals, on wooden base, Edinburgh 1894. (Bristol) $3,915

A carved and stained wood tobacco box, formed as a boxer type dog's head with inset glass eyes, the base carved with leafage, 21cm. high. (Bristol) $625

TÔLEWARE

A pair of French green, black and gold-decorated tôle monteiths, 19th century, each of oval tapering form with a scalloped edge and swan-neck handles, decorated with foliage, on a stepped base, 12½in. wide. (Christie's) $2,829

A pair of English painted tin tea canisters, second quarter 19th century, the sides painted with Oriental townscapes heightened with gilt and embellished with mother-of-pearl, each with label to the reverse, 17¾in. high. (Christie's) $3,972

A paint-decorated tôle tray, American, late 19th century, the everted rim with oak leaves and acorns centring a clipper ship with American flag on stormy seas, on a black ground, 18¼ x 24¼. (Christie's) $1,725

A ripsaw by Hill late Howell.
(Tool Shop Auctions) $84

An 18th century dental chisel with original blackwood handle, 3in. Magnificent.
(Tool Shop Auctions) $560

A brass Victorian confectionery roller.(Tool Shop Auctions) $133

A good Norfolk eel gleave.
(Tool Shop Auctions) $112

A railway platelayer's hammer.
(Tool Shop Auctions) $21

A good beech cooper's brace.
(Tool Shop Auctions) $126

A Marples rosewood and brass 25in. square. Original trade label.
(Tool Shop Auctions) $119

A Norris 20R gunmetal smoothing plane in the original box.
(Tool Shop Auctions) $980

An unused broad axe, 13in. blade, 'The Forest King'.
(Tool Shop Auctions) $91

A 19th century tanner's knife, curved blade 17in. across, marked *DURE.*
(Tool Shop Auctions) $63

A lovely 18th century flared chisel, clearly stamped *John Green*, original handle.
(Tool Shop Auctions) $101

An extremely decorative and early 19th century lead filled brass plumb bob with intricate pineapple finial.
(Tool Shop Auctions) $770

A 30in. 19th century mahogany and brass inclinometer. The teardrop shaped inclinometer folds flat into the body of the level via a wooden knuckle joint. Contained in the glass protected chamber is a tiny lead plumb bob.
(Tool Shop Auctions) $574

A complete set of 'Gentlemens' Tools' by Wm. Marples & Sons, with rosewood handles in a leather roll, contains hammer, cold chisel, firmer chisel, gimlet, bradawl, pincers and screwdriver.
(Tool Shop Auctions) $105

An early European coachmakers' circular plough, early styled ramshorn locking nuts, the front nicely carved, and ornate brass inlay on the body where the fence arm connects.
(Tool Shop Auctions) $701

A rare W.Tates pitchmeter made by J. Robson, Newcastle upon Tyne, 2ft. and twofold with German silver mounts and graduated protractor arm and adjustable spirit level.
(Tool Shop Auctions) $868

A rare Darling patented brace: possibly unique by virtue of it's unquestionably original hardwood head as opposed to the normal iron head.
(Tool Shop Auctions) $560

A super rare, rosewood plated brace with button pad and ebony head with brass disc, almost certainly an early Parker Thompson.
(Tool Shop Auctions) $574

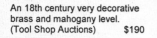

An 18th century very decorative brass and mahogany level.
(Tool Shop Auctions) $190

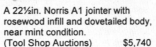

A 22½in. Norris A1 jointer with rosewood infill and dovetailed body, near mint condition.
(Tool Shop Auctions) $5,740

An early Blacksmith made adjustable wrench and hammer, circa 1800, 13in.
(Tool Shop Auctions) $49

An 18th century beheading axe, interesting shape, 10in. blade.
(Tool Shop Auctions) $357

A Stanley 4½H plane, rejapanned, very rare.
(Tool Shop Auctions) $280

An early Dutch carpenters' tool tray, possibly 18th century.
(Tool Shop Auctions) $28

A half ripsaw with beautiful solid ebony handle, a few chips and cracks, but rare.
(Tool Shop Auctions) $189

A 10½in. moulding plane by Robert Wooding, some filled worm, but clear stamp.
(Tool Shop Auctions) $714

An important English 18th century oak carved router with four blades, 12in wide. Important and rare.
(Tool Shop Auctions) $1,302

A rare French cooper's bung hole rasp.(Tool Shop Auctions) $67

Circa 1920s toolkit and airpump.
(Christie's) $207

A beautifully carved boxwood spice grinder, provenance unknown, 19th century.
(Tool Shop Auctions) $70

A steel soled gunmetal Norris 50 G smoothing plane with walnut infill, early 20th century.
(Charles Tomlinson) $600

A steel Lancashire pattern shoulder plane with brass lever and mahogany handle, 9in. long, late 19th century.
(Charles Tomlinson) $120

A 10in. diameter copper oil filler.
(Tool Shop Auctions) $192

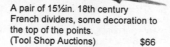

A marvellous pair of 9in. German silver dividers with the face of the moon on both sides of the hinge.
(Tool Shop Auctions) $842

A pair of 15½in. 18th century French dividers, some decoration to the top of the points.
(Tool Shop Auctions) $66

A pair of late 18th century/early 19th century French iron dividers 26in.
(Tool Shop Auctions) $330

An unusual pair of proportional dividers.
(Tool Shop Auctions) $50

A fascinating pair of bentwood dividers, 6in.
(Tool Shop Auctions) $215

An interesting pair of double calipers, all arms move independently, early brass hinge.
(Tool Shop Auctions) $74

A pair of 18th century 9in. iron dividers with tremendous hinge detail.
(Tool Shop Auctions) $264

A pair of 12in. Smith made proportional dividers.
(Tool Shop Auctions) $107

A pair of Dancing Master calipers with folding points.
(Tool Shop Auctions) $446

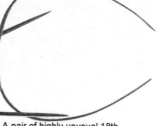

A pair of 22½in. blacksmith made dividers.
(Tool Shop Auctions) $74

A pair of highly unusual 18th century calipers by Dolland, with brass top section, sprung arm providing friction stay and marked *Inland Revenue*.
(Tool Shop Auctions) $281

A fine pair of French coopers' compasses, 'F.Larcchettl Macon'.
(Tool Shop Auctions) $495

An attractive pair of mahogany and brass dividers with pencil holder, heavy brass hinge.
(Tool Shop Auctions) $231

A pair of Dancing Master calipers.
(Tool Shop Auctions) $83

A pair of 18th century French iron compasses with lovely decoration to the legs and hinge, 26in. overall.
(Tool Shop Auctions) $413

An angular boring device by Quimby S. Backus, Mass. patented in 1880. (Tool Shop Auctions) $46

A chairmakers' mahogany brace designed to be used with a breast pad. (Tool Shop Auctions) $41

A quality Cuban mahogany brass and steel archimedian drill. (Tool Shop Auctions) $46

A solid ebony plated brace. (Tool Shop Auctions) $239

A Dutch brace. (Tool Shop Auctions) $66

A rare ebony brass plated brace by Joseph Cooper. (Tool Shop Auctions) $1,386

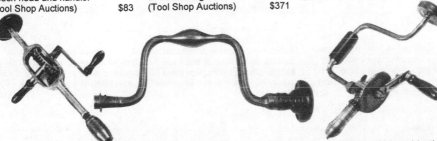

An early European iron brace by Goldenberg with faceted frame and beech head and handle. (Tool Shop Auctions) $83

A most attractive gunmetal and rosewood bowdrill with ivory spool and matching bow. (Tool Shop Auctions) $371

An undertakers' brace, the folding head complete with screwdriver bit. (Tool Shop Auctions) $462

A solid brass breast drill with rosewood handles. (Tool Shop Auctions) $124

A scarce Mathieson Scotch brace with pad variation. (Tool Shop Auctions) $86

A Millers Falls No. 185 combination brace and drill, rosewood handle and lignum head. (Tool Shop Auctions) $32

A stylish beech Continental brace. No pad. (Tool Shop Auctions) $132

A two bar cage head brace, probably 18th century. (Tool Shop Auctions) $99

A beech brass plated brace by Joseph Cooper. (Tool Shop Auctions) $462

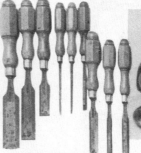

A triptych tool case, of seventy-five turning tools by Holtzapffel & Co., in identified slots, with hardwood handles, in mahogany case with ebony banding, 44in. wide, open. (Christie's) $4,333

A set of nine b/e chisels by Nurse, with London pattern boxwood handles marked *Reg No 429721* from $^1/_8$ to 1½, chip to one blade. (David Stanley) $266

An early 18th century silversmith's repoussé hammer well shaped and chamfered and decorated with foliate chasing, a 6in. turned ebony handle. (David Stanley) $533

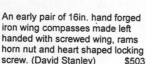

An early pair of 16in. hand forged iron wing compasses made left handed with screwed wing, rams horn nut and heart shaped locking screw. (David Stanley) $503

An American hand sewing machine, the nickel-plated scissor-action mechanism with 1884 patent date, swinging shuttle, separate bobbin-winder, instruction sheet and wood case, the box 9in. wide. (Christie's) $2,348

A rare 18th century French 'Tire Bande', cooper's head vice with brass tipped stag's horn handle well carved with vines and leaves. (David Stanley) $503

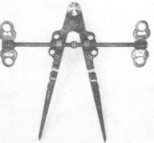

A very rare unrecorded 9in. steel soled gunmetal Norris No 13 smoother with rosewood infill and handle, unusually, front bun is copied from the panel pattern, replaced 2¼in. iron. (David Stanley) $2,368

A superb early pair of 17th century German armorer's 9in. iron compasses with well faceted and molded legs, hand cut cross arms with pierced turning keys working in two reeded brass bushes. (David Stanley) $8,880

A rare ebony and brass mortice gauge with an external adjusting screw. (David Stanley) $207

Edward Hines, Norwich, a Surface Ornamenting Instrument with bronze Automatic Turret Head, six adjustable turrets with wheels of varying serrations, 9/16-inch square shank. (Christie's) $722

An iron Scottish toothing plane, coved front.
(Tool Shop Auctions) $184

A Norris 11 mitre plane, improved pattern, with dovetailed steel case, gunmetal lever, rosewood infill and foregrip with Buck & Ryan stamp and little-used Norris snecked cutter, the sole 10½in. long, circa 1930. (Christie's) $4,333

A 3in. center lathe by Fenn, 9in. between centers on original cast iron treadle base with mahogany top with tool rest and compound slide. (David Stanley) $918

A 22 x 3 x 31in. mahogany tryptich cabinet by Holtzapffel containing a set of 75 matching turning tools with beech handles, most stamped with description of use.
(David Stanley) $1,006

A rare lapping machine by Holtzapffel but unnamed, with mahogany frame, treadle flywheel one lapping plate.
(David Stanley) $363

A rare handled transitional patent plough plane by Silcock & Lowe No 51 original iron by Greaves, pre 1845 partnership.
(David Stanley) $1,406

A fine pair of 11in. brass internal calipers with steel tips, engraved *J.M.Kleman & Zoon, Amsterdam*, reading off hinged vernier scale with molded edges and hinge.
(David Stanley) $370

An attractive 6½in. 19th century Austrian triple screw stem fruitwood croze carved escapement, fence with cupid's bow, large floral carving and dated *1824*.
(David Stanley) $710

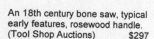 

An 18th century bone saw, typical early features, rosewood handle.
(Tool Shop Auctions) $297

An extremely rare 17th century saw with moulded decoration at the front.
(Tool Shop Auctions) $231

A most unusual French 19th century combination hacksaw and archimedian drill.
(Tool Shop Auctions) $215

An interesting steel backed tenon saw with solid brass handle.
(Tool Shop Auctions) $58

A keyhole saw with decorative handle.
(Tool Shop Auctions) $58

A very rare Disston stairsaw with adjustable fence.
(Tool Shop Auctions) $528

A lovely early miniature hand saw, only 10in. overall.
(Tool Shop Auctions) $74

An 8in. back saw by Moseley & Simpson, Covent Garden.
(Tool Shop Auctions) $132

An 18th century handsaw, original bentwood handle.
(Tool Shop Auctions) $83

An elegant mahogany stair saw.
(Tool Shop Auctions) $63

A medieval stone saw excavated from the basement of a house in Chartres, France.
(Tool Shop Auctions) $198

A 10in. brass backed tenon saw by Hill late Howel, London, cracked handle.
(Tool Shop Auctions) $33

An 8in. tenon saw by Sargent, Reading.
(Tool Shop Auctions) $66

An early stone saw, 16/17th century.
(Tool Shop Auctions) $83

An enormous 25½in. brass backed saw by A.S. Hall, London.
(Tool Shop Auctions) $165

A fine pair of brass and steel right hand tailors' shears stamped *Sycamore Works*.
(Tool Shop Auctions) $248

A pair of brass and steel tailors' right-hand tailors' shears by Wilkinson.
(Tool Shop Auctions) $148

A pair of 16/17th century forged scissors.
(Tool Shop Auctions) $107

A large pair of brass tailors' shears, by Wilkinson.
(Tool Shop Auctions) $297

An interesting pair of bone handled quick return scissors.
(Tool Shop Auctions) $66

An interesting pair of forged 18th century scissors.
(Tool Shop Auctions) $74

TOOLS

An attractive early turnscrew, 21in..
(Tool Shop Auctions) $83

A 29in. mahogany handled
turnscrew.
(Tool Shop Auctions) $66

A 29in. beech handled turnscrew.
(Tool Shop Auctions) $66

A very impressive 36½in. 19th
century turnscrew with rosewood
handle.
(Tool Shop Auctions) $132

An almost unused 26in. beech
handled turnscrew by Mathieson,
original trade label.
(Tool Shop Auctions) $58

A gunstockers' screwdriver by
Holland & Holland, with horn
handle.
(Tool Shop Auctions) $46

A large waggonbuilders' wrench by
William Marples.
(Tool Shop Auctions) $99

A Bonsa 6in. wooden handled
wrench.
(Tool Shop Auctions) $50

An early offset jaw wrench,
'Warranted steel'.
(Tool Shop Auctions) $58

A 19th century coachmans' wrench
and hammer.
(Tool Shop Auctions) $58

A double handled adjustable
wrench.
(Tool Shop Auctions) $173

A No.2 Bullard wrench, pat Oct 27th
'03. (Tool Shop Auctions) $58

The Ewbank cap wrench.
(Tool Shop Auctions) $99

An extremely scarce adjustable
four-way bed wrench by Mathieson.
(Tool Shop Auctions) $43

An extremely interesting and early
adjustable wrench stamped
Matchless Patent.
(Tool Shop Auctions) $83

A Shroeder patented ratchet
spanner.
(Tool Shop Auctions) $80

An interesting wrench by Master
stamped *Patents applied for
Reg.No. 761174*.
(Tool Shop Auctions) $41

The 'Sterling No.1' wrench by Frank
Mossberg Co.
(Tool Shop Auctions) $48

An interesting swivel head ratchet
wrench, maker's stamp unclear.
(Tool Shop Auctions) $66

Parallel jaw pliers, stamped *Parallel
Motion Tool Co., London Patent
Pending*, finely engineered.
(Tool Shop Auctions) $83

An unmarked adjustable hub
wrench.
(Tool Shop Auctions) $50

A pair of farriers' pliers, 10 x 2in., beautifully proportioned and decorated and dated *1706*. (Tony Murland) $5,727

An early pair of wrought iron scissors. (Tony Murland) $26

A wrought iron wrench, Wynn & Co. Patent. (Tony Murland) $75

An 18th century rosewood and brass bevel, dated 1776. (Tony Murland) $647

A 31 x 8in., late 17th century/early 18th century, anvil. (Tony Murland) $631

A pair of primitive 11in. scissors, probably 18th century. (Tony Murland) $60

A 19th century French clogmakers' knife, cleverly carved walnut handle in the form of a booted leg. Small brass pins form eyelets on the boot. Complete with bench vice. (Tony Murland) $531

The Grebe Patented adjustable wrench by Carrington. Wrenches are often named after birds. (Tony Murland) $75

A rare 2ft two-fold mastmakers' boxwood rule with slide by Samson Aston, 1833-1870. There is a scale for the length of gun deck which suggests a date pre 1850. (Tony Murland) $2,160

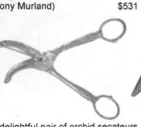

A delightful pair of orchid secateurs with decorated handles and an ingenious device for gently gripping the cut stem to avoid damage. (Tony Murland) $25

A 16th/17th century, 13 x 10in. stake anvil. Classic early form, the hexagonal stake thickens at the bottom to form an elegant buttress. (Tony Murland) $299

An early 19th century, Continental stirrup adze, smith's stamp and initials *PM* on the blade. (Tony Murland) $141

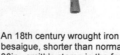

A pair of 18th century scissors. Good for age. (Tony Murland) $3

An 18th century wrought iron besaigue, shorter than normal at 38in., smith's stamp in the form of initials. (Tony Murland) $100

A 31 x 8in. 16/17th century French anvil, early style. Museum quality. (Tony Murland)   £320 $531

A rare type of 17th century felling axe. (Tony Murland) $315

An 18th century French axe, 15 x 5in. (Tony Murland) $141

A No.2 blocking axe by Gilpin. (Tony Murland) $50

A medieval axe head personifying the days of combat and tyranny. (Tony Murland) $91

A bearded side axe, 5½in. blade. (Tony Murland) $100

A coopers' bowl adze, 9¼in. edge and smith's marks. (Tony Murland) $83

A 3½lb. Brades bearded side axe, 5¾in. blade. (Tony Murland) $199

An 18th century decorated axe, 4½in. blade, probably early replaced handle. (Tony Murland) $207

An all purpose Turkish axe with important decoration on the blade. (Tony Murland) $66

A 13in. American broad axe by Yerkes & Plumb, found in a barn in Kansas. (Tony Murland) $174

A fine American side axe by A. Chaney & Co., Ogdensburg, 11in. blade, most unusual scalloped head. (Tony Murland) $249

A French coachbuilders' side axe, some worm to original handle. (Tony Murland) $83

A quality 14in. socketed side axe head. (Tony Murland) $282

An early socketed axe, 6in. blade. (Tony Murland) $149

An 18th century European side axe head. (Tony Murland) $299

A superb 16¾in. dovetailed Mathieson plane.
(Tony Murland) $1,045

A very rare 27½in. beech jointer by I. Sym. Round top iron and wedge.
(Tony Murland) $714

A 4in. beech brass fronted bullnose, Eastwood.
(Tony Murland) $66

An important iron panel plane by Slater, 12½in. long. overstuffed rosewood infill with particularly stylish front bun and rear handle.
(Tony Murland) $764

An early Spiers smoothing plane with screwed sides, tapered iron.
(Tony Murland) $158

A rare and important 6½ x 2¹/₁₆in. block plane by Spiers, the brass lever cap swivels on a pin running through the body of the plane.
(Tony Murland) $2,025

A very rare Preston No. 1355C bullnose, side fenced, rabbet and chamfer plane. The side fence adjusts for ³/₁₆in. to 1in. rabbets and is operated by the milled head screw. (Tony Murland) $805

An important patented block plane by Joseph Fenn, parallel sided beech adjustable smoothing plane, 7 x 2½in., stamped *J. Fenn Registered 12 Nov. 1844.*
(Tony Murland) $1,328

A possibly unique combined plough and fillister by Kimberley, Pat. No. 2848, the body of the plane stamped *Highest Award 3 Gold Medals.* (Tony Murland) $930

A Stanley 196 circular rabbet plane, nickel plating 90% but dull.
(Tony Murland) $830

A pre war Norris A2 dovetailed smoother, rosewood infill, good parallel iron by Marples.
(Tony Murland) $614

A 17½in. Spiers panel plane with original Sorby parallel iron.
(Tony Murland) $342

A Stanley 4½H.
(Tony Murland) $1,062

A Preston beech rebate plane,
3½in. long. (Tony Murland) $42

A fine Stanley No.2C smoothing
plane. (Tony Murland) $400

A Stanley No.10¼in.
carriagemakers' rabbet plane with
tilting handles.
(Tony Murland) $448

A very important iron Vergatthobel,
3¾ x 1¾in., brazed construction
with protruding toe returning to form
a scroll. (Tony Murland) $581

A pre war Norris A6 dovetailed
smoothing plane with rosewood
infill, good parallel iron.
(Tony Murland) $996

An early 19th century gunmetal 2¼
x 1⁵/₈in. flat bottom cellomakers'
plane, German steel sole with the
blade retained by a knurled nut
similar to those examples by Norris
and Preston.
(Tony Murland) $166

A late 16th, early 17th century
European musical Instrument
makers' plane, front tote repaired
with smith-made rivets, with a band
of decoration around the top.
(Tony Murland) $913

A classically shaped 16th/17th
century violinmakers' plane from
Europe, 19th century toothing iron,
brazed construction, 6 x 1⁷/₈in.
(Tony Murland) $747

A ¾in. dovetail rebate by Spiers in
a mahogany box.
(Tony Murland) $116

A Stanley 85 scraper plane, original
blade, remains of trade label.
(Tony Murland) $697

A steel soled gunmetal smoothing
plane, rosewood infill, by Slater.
(Tony Murland) $581

An American flyer tinplate monoplane, American, 1930s, Royal Cord Balloon rubber tyres, with axle connected to clockwork motor with stop/start handle to roof, 21½in. long. (Bonhams) $690

A stationary model locomotive No.311 by Doll & Cie, with oscillating cylinder, on tin base, 34cm. high, circa 1930. (Auction Team Köln) $339

A scarce Dinky elevator loader in blue with yellow chutes and plastic wheel hubs, grey tyres, boxed, with packing. (Wallis & Wallis) $174

A rare pre war Dinky set No 12 postal set, comprising Royal Mail van, telephone box, 2 postmen, Air Mail box and post box. In original display box. (Wallis & Wallis) $1,113

A scarce early 1930s Hornby series modelled miniatures No 4 engineering staff, set of 5, electrician, storekeeper, greaser engine room attendant and 2 fitters. (Wallis & Wallis) $137

A rare pre war Dinky set containing No37c6 Royal Corps of Signals Despatch riders, in an original blue display box, yellow insert with drop down flap to front. Box dated 10-39. (Wallis & Wallis) $1,193

A fine painted wooden Noah's ark and animals, German, late 19th century, the bow bottomed ark with brown painted base, the painted and stencilled sides in pale green with five windows and blue and gold decorative border, 25in. long. (Bonhams & Brooks) $2,085

A Californian doll's pram, white-painted metal frame with black painted handle, brown painted basketweave body and hood, 80cm. long, circa 1920. (Auction Team Köln) $185

Lord Roberts workshop Noah's Ark, painted wood with lifting roof bearing a poem about Noah, containing a quantity of original painted wooden animals and figures, 19½in. long. (Christie's) $402

A tinplate clockwork four door saloon, German, possibly Günthermann circa 1920, finished in green with dark green and cream lining, hinged doors with handles, black tinplate running boards, 9¾in. long. (Bonhams) $1,173

A mid Victorian polychrome wood model of a cottage, embellished with sand to simulate stone, within a shadow box with garden setting, 17 x 24in. (Christie's) $914

A rare pre war Dinky set No 44 AA hut motorcycle patrol and guides, comprising AA phone box with signs to roof, 2 patrolman on foot, and a motorcycle and sidecar. In original display box. (Wallis & Wallis) $954

A Tipp & Co. No. 200 clockwork tank with large rubber caterpillars, start-stop lever, 19cm. long, circa 1936. (Auction Team Köln) $203

A Jouet de Paris Torpedo Delage tinplate clockwork car, with reverse, forward and idle gears, green lithographed body, 34cm. long, 1928. (Auction Team Köln) $2,305

A Tipp & Co. No. 217 lithographed Wehrmacht troop carrier, with eight soldiers, 1938, 22cm. long. (Auction Team Köln) $678

A Tipp & Co. No. 176 anti-aircraft wagon, with five German soldier figures, adjustable AA gun, opening doors, 28cm. long, circa 1938. (Auction Team Köln) $373

Carved and painted wood rocking horse, America, 19th century, painted off white with leather saddle and reins, 27¼in. high. (Skinner) $920

A Schuco Electro Constructions tinplate, battery-powered fire engine No. 6080, with extending adjustable ladder, 29cm. long, post 1956. (Auction Team Köln) $1,356

A Lehmann Oho lithographed tinplate clockwork car and driver, 10.5cm. long, post 1906. (Auction Team Köln) $441

A Steiff elephant on wheels with black boot button eyes, white felt tusks standing on metal wheeled frame, 22in. long, circa 1910. (Christie's) $581

A Lehmann Echo EPL 725 clockwork tinplate motor cyclist, 22.5cm. long, 1920. (Auction Team Köln) $1,830

A Lehmann's tin plate clockwork pig and rider painted chiefly red and white with gilt detail. (Russell, Baldwin & Bright) $518

A rare Motor 219 motorcoach tinplate toy, German, possibly by Lehmann, 11.7cm. long, circa 1935. (Auction Team Köln) $338

A Farnell Lakeland terrier with golden brown and dark brown mohair, wearing original collar, 13in. tall, 1930s. (Christie's) $186

A German Rofa Model IV (straight) typebar machine with straight Universal 3-row keyboard, and upright typebar, 1923.
(Auction Team Köln) $401

An Alexander prototype four-row American front strike machine, which apparently never went into production, only 30 models made, and two complete models now known, 1904. (Auction Team Köln) $991

A rare Lambert flat model by Baker & Hamilton, San Francisco & Sacramento with flat baseplate carriage, 1896.
(Auction Team Köln) $1,115

A Panwriter Japanese typewriter for Japanese characters, by the Nippon Typewriter Co., Tokyo, circa 1950.
(Auction Team Köln) $524

An Imperial Model D British 3-row portable typewriter, with straight Universal keyboard and high type basket, green, 1919.
(Auction Team Köln) $217

The International Electromatic, the first IBM typewriter, with one-piece type shuttle, 1930.
(Auction Team Köln) $119

An American Hall Typewriter index machine, the first really portable typewriter, 1881.
(Auction Team Köln) $1,050

A Sampo typewriter, the first Swedish machine by Ernst Martin, only 1,500 were produced, with original decorative tin cover, 1894.
(Auction Team Köln) $7,924

An Active export model of the German three row type-wheel typewriter, the first with the stationary carriage which led to the golf-ball type in the 1960s, 1913.
(Auction Team Köln) $294

A New American Typewriter No. 5 index typewriter with right angled carriage return for reading type, 1890.
(Auction Team Köln) $1,969

A German Rofa Model IV typebar machine with straight Universal keyboard and lifting typebar, with original wooden cover, 1923.
(Auction Team Köln) $429

A decorative American Odell No.4 pointer typewriter by the Multiplex Mfg. Co., unrestored, 1889.
(Auction Team Köln) $1,048

TYPEWRITERS

A German Edelmann pointer typewriter with type wheel, enamel scale and ribbon printing, 1897. (Auction Team Köln) $459

A very decorative American New Franklin type bar machine with round Ideal keyboard, 1898. (Auction Team Köln) $429

A Hammond No. 2 American type segment typewriter with Ideal keyboard, with wooden case, 1893. (Auction Team Köln) $270

The Hammonia, the first mass produced German typewriter by Guhl & Harbeck, Hamburg, 1882, unrestored and in excellent condition. (Auction Team Köln) $19,810

An early Berlin Graphic pointer typewriter, a successor to the Kneist and with pointer and rubber platen similar to the Hall, unrestored, 1895. (Auction Team Köln) $3,806

A Royal Bar-Lock, British typebar machine with full keyboard in the Columbia Bar-Lock style, 1902. (Auction Team Köln) $426

A Remington Standard Typewriter No. 2, an early American upstrike machine in the style of Sholes & Gidden, lacking wooden platen, 1879. (Auction Team Köln) $1,138

A decorative American Odell No. 4 pointer typewriter by Farquhar and Albrecht, Chicago, 1889. (Auction Team Köln) $958

A North's typewriter, for the French market, with French keyboard, downstroke-from-rear type-bars and japanned cover marked *North's Typewriter*. (Christie's) $5,520

An Imperial Model B British typebar machine with Ideal keyboard and dual shift keys, 1908. (Auction Team Köln) $426

The Keaton Music Typewriter, an American machine for musical notation, with copied instructions and original case, spare typebars and ribbon, 1947. (Auction Team Köln) $3,477

A Remington Scholes typewriter, with 43 keys, basket shift and oxidised copper finished iron frame of architectural form, circa 1898. (Christie's) $1,104

A round Rofa typewriter, with round Ideal keyboard, 1921.
(Auction Team Köln) $142

An early and important Graphic Berlin pointer typewriter, 1895.
(Auction Team Köln) $7,114

A rare Olympia typewriter with Indian typeface, four-row keyboard.
(Auction Team Köln) $129

An unusual Burnett typewriter with protruding type basket and 'streamlined' casing, American,1907.
(Auction Team Köln) $9,700

A Junior toy typewriter, typewheel with colour spools, German, circa 1930.
(Auction Team Köln) $291

An Orzel typewriter, a Polish version of the Adler Model No. 17, with cyrillic and Latin scripts.
(Auction Team Köln) $582

A German Germania No. 5 understrike machine made under licence from the Jewett Typewriter Co, Des Moines, USA, circa 1900.
(Auction Team Köln) $776

A Crandall typewriter, finely inlaid with mother of pearl and with gold decoration, with original tin cover, 1879.
(Auction Team Köln) $4,850

A rare Titania Model 2 of the Berlin front strike machine, the first German machine with ball-bearing type-bar, 1913.
(Auction Team Köln) $646

Kanzler No. 4 German typebar typewriter, with double shift key, 1912.
(Auction Team Köln) $970

A Mignon Model 2 German pointer typewriter, 1905.
(Auction Team Köln) $484

A Rofa Model 1 German type-bar machine with curved three-row Ideal keyboard.
(Auction Team Köln) $582

A Standard Folding Model No. 1 with separate right and left shifts, 1907. (Auction Team Köln) $388

A rare Discret 'secret and world' typewriter by Friedrich Rehmann, Karlsruhe, also used as a cipher machine, with second adjustable scale, 1899. (Auction Team Köln) $10,458

A Picht Steglitz Model 2 braille typewriter, circa 1900. (Auction Team Köln) $156

A Hall Braille typewriter made by Cooper Eng. & Mfg. Co., Chicago, 1892. (Auction Team Köln) $140

A black Oliver No. 9 American cylinder typewriter, 1916. (Auction Team Köln) $390

An Imperial Portable Model D three row English type bar machine with front strike, in decorative case, 1919. (Auction Team Köln) $582

A Hammond No. 12 (Universal) shuttle typewriter with reverse hammer action and wooden case, American, 1893. (Auction Team Köln) $194

A Williams No. 4 4-tier model with shift keys in the style of the American 'grasshopper' type-bar machine, 1900. (Auction Team Köln) $1,293

A Smith Premier No.4 American understrike machine with full keyboard and built-in type cleaning brush, 1895. (Auction Team Köln) $356

A Heady typewriter, French version of the Mignon Model 4, with instructions, 1918. (Auction Team Köln) $291

A North's typewriter, by North Typewriter co. Ltd., with cover. (Christie's) $2,792

An Edelmann German pointer typewriter, with type wheel and enamel dial, 1897. (Auction Team Köln) $905

An ivory mounted malacca walking stick, the handle modelled as the bust of a gentleman in formal attire with sash and decorations, white metal collar, ivory ferrule, 32⁷/₈in.
(Christie's) $1,195

An English carved ivory handled silver mounted cane, modelled as a rabbit, its outstretched ears forming the handle, carved wearing a shirt collar, 86cm. high.
(Bonhams & Brooks) $1,288

A fine and rare carved whale ivory, horn and wood cane, 19th century, having a handle carved in horn in the form of a right whale lying across a whale oil keg, 34½in. long.
(Sotheby's) $4,312

An Edwardian carved ivory handled novelty umbrella, London 1904, maker's mark of Callow, realistically modelled as a rabbit's head, a button operating the ears and opening the mouth, set with glass eyes, 90cm. high.
(Bonhams) $2,618

A late Victorian carved ivory handled walking stick, London 1884, George Francis Preedy, the handle carved as a duck's head, glass eyes, the silver collar with an inscribed cartouche, 89.5cm. high.
(Bonhams & Brooks) $540

A Victorian ivory headed walking stick, late 19th century, the grip carved in the form of a greyhound's head, with open mouth and glass eyes, copper collar, 33½in. high.
(Christie's) $708

A carved ivory parasol handle, in the form of a dog's head, by Kendall.
(Sworders) $261

A silver handled umbrella, modelled as a swan's head, maker Charles William West, London 1914.
(Woolley & Wallis) $206

A malacca walking stick, having a silver colored metal collar embossed with a shooting scene, ivory handle carved as a snarling dog with bead eyes.
(Woolley & Wallis) $552

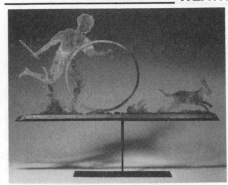

A cut-sheet metal boy with hoop and dog weathervane, American, circa 1930, the silhouetted form of a young boy running with hoop and stick preceded by a running dog, 55½in. long. (Sotheby's) $7,800

A large gilded cast and sheet iron horse weathervane, attributed to Rochester Iron Works, New York, late 19th century, cast in two parts, with molded eyes, nostrils and mouth and protruding forelock, on a modern base, 37in. long.(Christie's) $30,550

A molded copper polo player weathervane, American, 20th century, molded in the form of a polo pony with rider in helmet, full playing gear, and mallet raised, 47in. wide. (Christie's) $25,850

Molded copper polo player weathervane, by an unknown maker, third quarter 19th century, the figure with mallet mounted on a galloping horse, 50in. long. (Skinner) $189,500

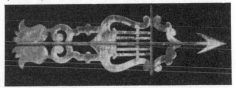

A molded and cut sheet copper bannerette weathervane, American, late 19th century, the cut sheet copper lyre-form body flanked by scrolled strapword terminating in a tulip-form tail, 60½in. wide. (Christie's) $2,233

Molded copper cow weathervane, unknown maker, late 19th century, the figure with all-over verdigris surface, 33¼in. long with stand. (Skinner) $9,200

A painted sheet iron weathervane, American, 19th century, out in the form of a uniformed cannonier, the cannon firing and with balls stacked for loading, 30¼in. long. (Christie's) $11,163

A moulded and painted copper horse and sulky weathervane, A. L. Jewell (active 1852-1865), Waltham, Massachusetts, moulded in two parts and yellow-painted, the rider in helmet and habit seated in a two-wheel sulky, 37in. long. (Christie's) $11,750

A moulded copper Black Hawk weathervane, J.W. Fiske and Company (1870-1893), New York City, the full bodied form with articulated head, mane, and tail open mouth and suggested musculature, 34in. long. (Christie's) $25,850

A gilded sheet copper and cast zinc bannerette weathervane, American, late 19th century, the copper rod centring a scrolled and pierced cut shaft with serrated feather-form tail and cast zinc arrow, 59in. wide. (Christie's) $3,760

Copper merino sheep weather vane, possibly L.W. Cushing and Sons, Waltham, Massachusetts, late 19th century, flattened full body with large and small copper spheres and iron directionals, stand not included, 28½in. long. (Skinner) $9,775

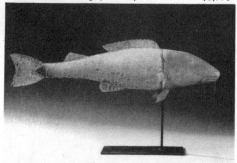

A cast zinc and copper codfish weathervane, J. Howard and Company, West Bridgewater, Massachusetts, moulded in two parts, the zinc head with abstracted round eyes and mouth, the chin with single sheet copper whisker attached to a copper body, 33in. long. (Christie's) $35,250

A moulded copper leaping stag weathervane, Cushing and White, Waltham, Massachusetts, late 19th century, the full bodied form with curved realistic antlers, with forelegs tucked underneath, rear legs extended and tail erect, 30in. long. (Christie's) $30,550

A moulded gilt copper Hackney horse, weathervane, attributed to Cushing and White, Waltham, Massachusetts, late 19th century, the trotting horse with bobbed tail and short mane with applied ears and moulded eyes, 32¼in. wide.
(Christie's) $99,500

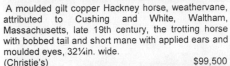

A moulded copper running horse weathervane, A.L. Jewell, Waltham, Massachusetts, moulded in two parts, the abstracted horse with hole-eyes, notched mouth and serrated sheet mane and tail, 37in. long.
(Christie's) $6,463

A moulded copper and cast zinc running horse weathervane, Cushing and White, Waltham, Massachusetts, late 19th century, the cast zinc articulated head and mane above the deeply moulded body with suggested musculature, on a modern base, 45in. long. (Christie's) $17,625

'Jewell' flattened full-bodied copper running horse weather vane, America, late 19th century, stamped *A.L. Jewell Waltham Mass*, on left front shoulder, allover verdigris patina, traces of gilt, 28¼in. long.
(Skinner) $4,025

Moulded copper cow weather vane, America, late 19th century, full-bodied figure with weathered ochre, yellow, and verdigris surface, 33in. wide.
(Skinner) $9,200

A moulded and painted zinc and copper ram weathervane, Cushing and White, Waltham, Massachusetts, late 19th century, the black-painted zinc head with applied black-painted sheet metal ears and curled horns, 29in. long.
(Christie's) $15,275

A Spanish baroque gilt- and painted wood altar, centred by a figure of Christ, 17th century, 35in. high. (Sotheby's) $2,875

A pair of South German gilt and painted three-quarter length wood figures of Saints Barbara and Agnes early 16th century, 10in. and 9⅛in. (Sotheby's) $2,415

An Italian partially gilt wood relief of the Madonna and Child, second half 14th century, 24 x 16¼in. (Sotheby's) $4,887

A pair of South German polychrome and parcel-giltwood figural torchères, 17th century, each modelled as a semi-naked maiden supporting cornucopiae, contro posta, on square bases each inscribed *Francesco di Marcovelt*, 48in. high. (Christie's) $19,608

A pair of German polychrome carved oak relief figure fragments, 16th century, of bearded men, one shown holding a lamb, later mounted on fabric covered plinths, the fragments 9½in. and 9in. high, respectively. (Christie's) $2,317

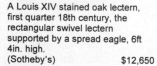

Lacquered wood figure of a seated Oni, Meiji period, the demon finely worked with inlaid glass eyes, 6½in. high. (Butterfield & Butterfield) $1,150

A Louis XIV stained oak lectern, first quarter 18th century, the rectangular swivel lectern supported by a spread eagle, 6ft 4in. high. (Sotheby's) $12,650

A Tirolean silvered and painted wood allegorical figure representing 'Winter', 18th century, the seated figure warming his hands on the flaming cauldron, 17in. high overall. (Sotheby's) $3,105

A Spanish gilt and painted wood armorial relief, second half 16th century, central shield surrounded by a chain, 28¾ x 17¾in. (Sotheby's) $3,450

A pair of George III mahogany candlesticks on spiral twist tapered columns carved with acanthus leaves, 12³/₄in. high. (Anderson & Garland) $298

Lacquered wood figural study, depicting a bald elderly figure wearing an elaborately decorated robe, 2¹/₈in. high. (Butterfield & Butterfield) $805

Sino-Tibetan gilt lacquered wood Marici, 18th century, the eight armed goddess shown with a serene face backed by smaller heads of a pig, lion and demon and seated dhyanasana, 14³/₈in. (Butterfield & Butterfield) $2,300

A South German (probably Ulm) painted wood relief of 'Noli me tangere' circa 1500, the Magdalene on the right kneeling before Christ, 32½ x 22½in. (Sotheby's) $19,550

A Flemish oak relief of the adoration of the Magi, mid-16th century, one king kneeling before the Child kissing His hand, 33⁵/8. x 26¼in. (Sotheby's) $14,950

A carved and painted pine cigar-store Indian, American, late 19th century, the full figured Indian squaw standing on a partial step with one raised hand holding a tin, 77½in. high. (Christie's) $29,900

A carved and painted model of an Indian elephant, 20th century, with two big ears and a long trunk, 54in. long. (Christie's) $3,138

A Norwegian burr birch flagon, 19th century, the bulbous body with loop handle and spout, the hinged cover carved in relief with a lion, on three raised feet modelled as stylised beasts, 9¾in. high.
(Christie's) $5,851

A carved and painted spreadwing courthouse eagle, American, early 20th century, with articulated feathers, beak, eyes and talons, standing on a rocky plinth, 46in. wide. (Christie's) $5,875

A carved salt cellar, Scandinavian, 18th century, modelled as a horse with incised geometric decoration, with a sliding lid to the top and spout to the tail, slight damage, 9in. long. (Bonhams) $235

A pair of Venetian polychrome and parcel-gilt carved pine figures of dwarves, 18th century, one as a lady carrying and a pug dog, emblematic of Smell; the other as a lady biting a sausage, emblematic of Taste, 7½in. high.
(Christie's) $7,825

A Welsh fruitwood love spoon, 19th century, the birdcage handle pierced with heart and keyhole-shaped motifs, with intarsia decorated borders, 10½in. long.
(Christie's) $1,008

A paint-decorated gameboard, American, 19th century, cream-painted ground centring a gameboard of alternating black and cream-painted squares outlined in red line-decoration and each centring a gold painted number, 15⁷/₈ x 16¹/₈in.
(Christie's) $19,975

A Continental limewood applique, 18th century, modelled with cherubim within a nimbus, 14 x 12in. (Christie's) $1,159

A mouse trap, English, first half 19th century, pine ash, of rectangular dead-fall type, 27.5cm. (Christie's) $182

A central European cream-painted and carved wood coat-of-arms, late 17th/early 18th century, 24 x 25in. (Christie's) $2,260

A pine artist's lay figure, late 19th century, with articulated limbs, 12¾in. high.
(Christie's) $1,553

A pair of carved and painted bocages, American or European, late 18th century, each with carved and painted compôte issuing a pyramid of carved and painted fruits, 14in. wide.
(Christie's) $12,925

A treen shoe snuff box, 19th century, with brass tack inlay overall, 3¾in. long.
(Christie's) $417

An oak door, late 19th/early 20th century, constructed from five planks, 36¼in. wide, 66½in. high.
(Christie's) $367

Four German turned wood candlesticks, 19th century, the dished pans with prickets, on waisted knopped stems and domed bases, 11in. high.
(Christie's) $2,194

A pair of Louis XV oak doors, with moulded fielded panels, the upper and centre panels with foliage shell and cartouche ornament with cypher W, each door 34in. wide.
(Christie's) $4,416

Grain painted wooden chequerboard, American, 19th century, square board with allover dark red swirl and sponge decoration on mustard ground, black checks, 16½ x 16½in.
(Skinner) $1,955

A stained carved wood model of a lion, probably Ceylonese, 18th century, of stylised form, shown standing with tail looped over its back, 6¾in. long.
(Christie's) $545

A German polychrome carved wood butcher's or cheese shop counter ornament, second half 19th century, shown modelled as a standing cow with inset glass eyes, 21½in. long.
(Christie's) $2,956

A carved and painted pine cigar store Indian, attributed to Samuel Robb, New York, circa 1880, 66in. high.(Sotheby's) $17,250

Wooden butter churn, 19th century, with four bands, 17in. high. (Eldred's) $176

A Parker Field & Sons tipstaff, English, 1830s, signed *Parker Field & Sons 233 Holburn London*, 18cm. long. (Bonhams) $346

Polychrome carved pine articulated male doll, circa 1930, with green bakelite eyes, with stand, 14in. high. (Skinner) $575

A carved and painted pine cigar store Indian princess, American, third quarter 19th century, wearing a feathered headdress, 62in. overall. (Sotheby's) $12,650

Carved wood bust of a young man, America, early 20th century, the carved head with furrowed brow and inlaid eyes, old dark patina, 13in. high. (Skinner) $575

Carved pine full-form artist's mannequin, 19th century, articulated figure with finely carved facial features, approximately 37½in. high. (Skinner) $9,200

Janus-faced carved rootwood figure, late 19th century, two male faces with bead eyes, on one torso and splayed legs, 13½in. high. (Skinner) $2,875

Carved and turned wood figural stand, America, late 19th/early 20th century, in the form of a telemon, 33in. high. (Skinner) $17,250

Carved and polychrome wooden figure of a haberdashery mannequin, carved head with detailed features, 31½in. high. (Skinner) $10,350

Polychrome carved pine and copper band figure whirligig, possibly Wisconsin, late 19th century, with stand, 20in. (Skinner) $10,925

Carved figure of a man in a bowler hat, Ohio, early 20th century, with blue glass eyes, old dark stain, with stand, 16¾in. high. (Skinner) $7,475

A treen lemon-squeezer, mid 19th century, of acorn-shape, 10in. high, extended.
(Christie's) $749

Polychrome carved wood Indian tobacco princess, America, carved figure with moveable arms, 18½in. high.
(Skinner) $11,500

Carved pine fat cat figure, 20th century, incised signature E. Sweet, 17¼in. high. (Skinner) $431

Carved articulated African /American doll, America, 19th century, hide hair, early textile dress, with stand, 8in. high.
(Skinner) $16,100

A carved and painted pine cigar store figure, American, third quarter 19th century, in the form of the performer 'Rising Star', 57in. high. (Sotheby's) $20,700

Carved and painted root stand, America, painted animal heads radiating from entwined root base, inscribed MAS 1897, 38½in. high.
(Skinner) $1,725

A carved figure of a navigator, American, 19th century, depicted in top hat and tailcoat, holding a telescope, 39½in. high.
(Christie's) $11,500

Spanish polychrome carved wood figure of a saint, late 18th/early 19th century, shown in a gilt cloak with foliate border, 29¼in. high.
(Christie's) $1,646

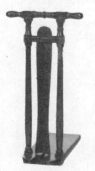

An early 19th century mahogany boot jack, the turned grips on ring turned column supports, on oblong base, 30½in. high.
(Andrew Hartley) $628

Carved and painted wooden figural whirligig, depicting a 'Dandy' advertising figure, Indiana, circa 1910, 33in. high.
(Skinner) $18,400

Primitive carved and painted figure of the boxer Joe Lewis, America, early 20th century, with stand, 9¾in. high.
(Skinner) $517

Painted yellow pine carving of George Washington, possibly South Carolina, circa 1840.
(Skinner) $13,800

A Shaker bentwood box, second half 19th century, the oval with a fitted lid, fastened with three tapered swallow-tail fingers, inscribed *J.W. Adams 1862*, 6in. long.
(Sotheby's) £543 $920

A good fruitwood aubergine shaped tea caddy with finely carved leaf shaped calix lid and stalk finial, 5in. high.
(Woolley & Wallis) £1,000 $1,380

A central European boxwood snuffbox, early 17th century, of bun-shape, the cover in relief with a double headed eagle motif, 2½in. diameter. (Christie's) £633 $981

A Neapolitan polychrome wood creche figure of the Infant Christ, late 18th century, shown standing, with metal thread embroidered robes, on a stepped plinth, the figure 12½in. high.
(Christie's) £863 $1,338

A pair of North European relief carved oak allegorical figures, 17th century, shown standing robed within niches, one holding a sword and scales, the other with a bird and anchor, 8in.high.
(Christie's) £345 $535

A Northern European carved and painted wood stile, possibly 17th century, modelled as a mustachioed gentleman, wearing a cord around his neck with flowerhead pendant, further cord about his waist, 21¾in. high.
(Christie's) £518 $803

A German carved oak relief of the Raising of Drusiana, in the German Renaissance style, 30½in. high, 28in. wide.
(Christie's) £1,380 $2,139

A pair of Italian giltwood altar candlesticks, the lobe-knopped foliate carved stems on trefoil bases, 15in. high.
(Christie's) £288 $446

A Central European carved wood fragment head and shoulders of an angel, 16th century, shown head to dexter, later mounted on an ebonised wood plinth, the fragment, 7½in. high. (Christie's) £805 $1,248

INDEX